The Norton
Introduction to Literature

The Norton
Introduction to Literature

BAIN · BEATY · HUNTER

Drama

EDITED BY

CARL E. BAIN

Emory University

W · W · NORTON & COMPANY · INC.

NEW YORK

COPYRIGHT © 1973 BY W. W. NORTON & COMPANY, INC.

First Edition

Library of Congress Cataloging in Publication Data

Bain, Carl E   comp.
Drama.

(The Norton introduction to literature)
1. Drama—Collections. I. Title. II. Series.
PN6112.B26   808.82   72–14190
ISBN 0–393–09366–2

Ed Bullins, "A Son, Come Home," from *Five Plays by Ed Bullins*, copyright © 1968 by Ed Bullins. Reprinted by permission of the publisher, The Bobbs-Merrill Company, Inc.
Euripides: "The Bacchae," from *The Bacchae and Other Plays*, translated by Philip Vellacott. Copyright © 1954, 1972 by Philip Vellacott. Reprinted by permission of Penguin Books Ltd.
Henrik Ibsen: "The Wild Duck," from *The Wild Duck: A Norton Critical Edition*, translated by Dounia B. Christiani. Copyright © 1968 by W. W. Norton & Company, Inc. Reprinted by permission of the publisher.
Arthur Miller: "A View from the Bridge," copyright 1955, © 1957 by Arthur Miller. All rights reserved. Reprinted by permission of The Viking Press, Inc. This play in its printed form is designed for the reading public only. All dramatic rights in it are fully protected by copyright, and no public or private performance—professional or amateur —may be given without the written permission of the author and the payment of royalty. As the courts have also ruled that the public reading of a play constitutes a public performance, no such reading may be given except under the conditions stated above. Communication should be addressed to the author's representative, International Famous Agency, 1301 Avenue of the Americas, New York, N.Y. 10019.
Molière: "The Misanthrope," translated by Richard Wilbur, copyright © 1954, 1955, by Richard Wilbur. Reprinted by permission of Harcourt Brace Jovanovich, Inc. *Caution:* Professionals and amateurs are hereby warned that this translation being fully protected under the copyright laws of the United States of America, the British Empire, including the Dominion of Canada, and all other countries which are signatories to the Universal Copyright Convention and the International Copyright Union, is subject to royalty. All rights, including professional, amateur, motion picture, recitation, lecturing, public reading, radio broadcasting, and television, are strictly reserved. Particular emphasis is laid on the question of readings, permission for which must be secured from the author's agent in writing. Inquiries on professional rights should be addressed to Mr. Gilbert Parker, Curtis Brown, Ltd., 60 East 55th Street, New York, N.Y. 10022. The amateur acting rights are controlled exclusively by the Dramatists Play Service, Inc., 440 Park Avenue South, New York, N.Y. 10016. No amateur performance of the play may be given without obtaining in advance the written permission of the Dramatists Play Service, Inc. and paying the requisite fee.
Luigi Pirandello: "Six Characters in Search of an Author," from *Naked Masks: Five Plays by Luigi Pirandello*, edited by Eric Bentley, translated by Edward Storer. Dutton Paperback edition. Reprinted by permission of E. P. Dutton & Co., Inc.
William Shakespeare: "Hamlet," from *Hamlet: A Norton Critical Edition*, edited by Cyrus Hoy, copyright © 1963 by W. W. Norton & Company, Inc. Reprinted by permission of the publisher.
Bernard Shaw: "Caesar and Cleopatra," reprinted by permission of The Society of Authors on behalf of the Bernard Shaw Estate. "Major Barbara," copyright 1907, 1913, 1930, 1931 by George Bernard Shaw; copyright 1957 by The Public Trustee as Executor of the Estate of George Bernard Shaw. Reprinted by permission of Dodd, Mead & Company, Inc. and The Society of Authors for the Estate of George Bernard Shaw.
Sophocles: Oedipus Tyrannus," from *Oedipus Tyrannus: A Norton Critical Edition*, translated and edited by Luci Berkowitz and Theodore F. Brunner. Copyright © 1970 by W. W. Norton & Company, Inc. Reprinted by permission of the publisher.
Megan Terry: "The Gloaming, Oh My Darling," from *Viet Rock*, copyright ® 1966, 1967 by Megan Terry. Reprinted by permission of Simon & Schuster, Inc.
Jean-Claude van Itallie: "Interview" from *American Hurrah*, copyright © 1966, 1967 by Jean-Claude van Itallie. Reprinted by permission of Coward-McCann, Inc. *America Hurrah* is the sole property of the author and is fully protected by copyright. It may not be acted either by professionals or amateurs without written consent. Public readings, radio and television broadcasts likewise are forbidden. All inquiries concerning these rights should be addressed to International Famous Agency, 1301 Avenue of the Americas, New York, N.Y. 10019.
"Paper Doll," lyrics by Johnny Black, copyright © Edward B. Marks Music Corporation. Used by permission.

PRINTED IN THE UNITED STATES OF AMERICA

1 2 3 4 5 6 7 8 9 0

Contents

I The Play in Focus: Audience and Action

II The Middle Distance: The Page and the Stage

III The Larger Frame: Contexts of the Play

Foreword

Using This Book

This book is an anthology: a generous collection of what the editors think are, for the most part, enjoyable, stimulating, and significant literary works. With all literature to choose from, the editors had to use additional criteria to limit the selection. Among these criteria are the type of audience, considerations of similarity and variety, and illustrative utility.

We assume an audience of English-speaking, reasonably literate, late-20th-century readers with some experience of literature but not necessarily with specific literary or other background in common. Judging in purely qualitative terms, we have perhaps "over-represented" 20th-century, especially recent-20th-century works, but we feel these are the most readily enjoyable and comprehensible works, requiring intelligence and awareness but not necessarily as much specific information and experience. We have tried to include some works that are familiar to at least some students and to many instructors. We have also tried to include the excellent but unfamiliar, the forgotten, undiscovered, or new, the seldom if ever anthologized, for surely one of the pleasures of reading is the joy of discovery.

We have also tried to include a wide variety of works—in subject matter, in form, in tone, in attitude, in effect. Yet, where offered a choice among equally excellent possibilities, we have chosen works that interact with each other by comparability of subject matter, form, tone, or effect; for reading, like other experiences, is in large measure comparative. Some even say that one can have a pure experience— feeling fur, for example—only once, and that all subsequent fur-feelings are comparisons with the first one. Any alert reader will find multiple instances of comparable works, not only those deliberately juxtaposed by the editors but works from widely separated sections and even from different genres.

Where other considerations—excellence, appropriateness to audience, variety, and comparability—have been satisfied, we have chosen from among works that best illustrate an appropriate and appropriately timed critical or pedagogical point. This is not only an anthology but a textbook; the works are not only selected but arranged or ordered to introduce the reader to the serious study of literature. Any selection of excellent literary works may be read in many meaningful orders, and this anthology is, we trust, no exception, but in a bound book some one order is fixed. We divide literature into genres—fiction, drama, poetry —and within each genre proceed in a pattern as parallel as the nature and exigencies of the genres permit. Each begins with works to be read, or "closely read" discretely and analytically as suggested below, but all or many of them are also grouped by subject matter or theme—

elements readily accessible to all regardless of past reading experience. The early subject matter groupings of stories and plays also introduce and incorporate matters of structure; since the formal elements in poems are more complex, fixed, and defined, these are introduced in groups separate from and subsequent to the subject-matter groups. The second major section of each collection specifically addresses itself to some secondary ways of understanding a literary work in the genre: the relation of a short story to rites and patterns of initiation, the specific elements of language, meter, and forms in a poem, and the relation between a play as a literary work and its actualization upon the stage. The final major section within each genre presents works in biographical or historical contexts: works by a single author, works from a historical period or contiguous periods, and so on.

The arrangement is not meant to classify the works. What it does suggest is a method for introducing students to the serious study of literature. It begins with considerations that assume no specific literary method or experience but assume expectations aroused by certain human situations—subject matter or theme; it builds toward making conscious certain literary expectations, those of form and kind; and finally it introduces contextual expectations—those created by the author's other works, by the norms of a period or a tradition, the historical realities. All these elements and expectations operate simultaneously and interact, of course, and it would be not only possible but desirable to return to works placed early in the selections with the accumulated experience of having read through the entire anthology to discover just what has been gained by heightened awareness of form, kind, and context.

The pattern of arrangement and implied method here described is followed in general within each genre. More specific and detailed description of the order within each genre, with variations and varied emphases necessitated by the inherent differences between genres, appears in sections called "Note on Arrangement" at the end of each separate preface. Since one of our principles—indeed, perhaps, our first principle—is that the study of literature is the reading of literature, we have preferred to fill the pages available to us with literary works, and to let understanding, awareness, and engagement grow out of that reading. At the same time, we recognize the necessity of some assistance. The works are annotated—as is customary in Norton anthologies—in order to free the instructor from spending valuable class time in glossing the texts. Each genre is preceded by a preface, which is designed to raise some general questions about how to expect. Each genre is followed by a section entitled "The Elements of Fiction," "The Elements of Poetry," or "The Elements of Drama," which contain brief essays on such topics as, for example, "Audience," "Tone," or "Metaphor": these essays may be read as introductory chapters to sections of the anthology, as a glossary of literary terms and the necessary technical vocabulary, or ignored. Finally, the teachers' manuals may be drawn on for classroom questions or writing topics.

Studying Literature

Questions of definition and theory are apt to become, over the years, central for a teacher, but for a student the central questions are, at the beginning, practical: how to read literature with enjoyment, interest, and understanding and how to relate it to life beyond the classroom. Of course, no universal how-to formula exists, not only because all individual readers differ from one another but also because different works of literature demand different approaches. Still, there are common grounds among readers and common grounds among works, for although every work is *in a sense* unique, many things about it are not unique at all, and in approaching any work of literature a reader may save himself many difficulties by using some common tools. Ultimately, one's experience with a work is very personal—and at its furthest reaches private—but the experience begins communally. No private insight occurs if the reader does not first participate in a sharing with the writer, and that sharing depends upon uses of language which are agreed on and discoverable. The classroom and the textbook represent places and ways of delineating and articulating what is public and shareable.

But where does one begin? "Read, read, read, read, my unlearned reader" is the advice *Tristram Shandy* offers, and the literal and intense following of that advice is assumed by nearly every college teacher. For almost half a century the *close reading* approach to literature has dominated the college classroom, asking that each student read completely, carefully, analytically each individual literary work, making sure to know exactly the significance of each word, each phrase, each part, each transition. Over the years this approach has undergone many variations and shifts of emphasis and has been known by many names ("the new criticism" and "formalism" are two of the most popular and lasting), but its premises remain fairly constant: that any literary work is a self-existent whole which will reveal its own laws, meanings, and implications if it is approached intensely and sensitively. "Close reading" emphasizes the knowledge of basic tools and the asking of basic questions: What, literally, does each line, or sentence, or unit of dialogue say? What kind of vocabulary (or "diction") does the work use, and how specialized is it? What images does it use, and what are their emotional connotations? How does the setting contribute to the total effect? Who is telling the story, or speaking the dialogue, or addressing us in the poem, and how does knowledge of that speaker color our responses to what he or she says? All such questions mean to get at the work's final effect, helping to explain not only what the work "says" but what responses it evokes, intellectual and emotional, and they articulate both what a reader first feels impressionistically and point toward new areas of feeling and response, extending the range of the work's effect.

A second popular approach to literature is *generic,* and in classroom practice the generic and close-reading approaches often quietly merge. The generic approach assumes that each genre (in the sense that we are using the term to distinguish fiction, poetry, and drama) has some identifying characteristics which may be usefully isolated—that, for example, all plays have some elements in common which differentiate them from stories and poems—and that a reader who knows these characteristics may test an individual work against them to evaluate the work, to clarify it, and to learn at the same time more about the genre as a genre. The generic approach assumes that the writer and reader both approach a work in a certain genre with specific—if not always fully conscious—expectations and that part of the effect depends on whether, and how, those expectations are satisfied. Knowing what to expect, even when one's expectation is not fulfilled—in fact, especially when one's expectation is not fulfilled—puts the reader on a common ground with the author. The writer may, and often does, re-contour that ground quickly, but for a moment at least the commonness of ground allows communication to begin. Writers who choose to write drama rather than fiction commit themselves to the materials and possibilities of the dramatic genre, and this commitment enables the reader to concentrate on terms, problems, and questions that relate especially to drama. The generic approach is primarily an admission that *groups* of works have something in common and that recognizing the *nature* of the grouping provides the basis for further study and consideration.

Some generic critics believe that there are "essential" characteristics of each genre and that the differences between genres are deeply rooted in the ultimate order of the world or of human nature. Others simply find genres a convenient way of describing tendencies. Either group may use the generic approach as a tool for reading individual works, and either may extend the genre distinction to smaller units. Distinctive groups within genres, sometimes called subgenres or types or kinds, often have specific characteristics. Drama is, for example, traditionally divided into comedy and tragedy, each with characteristics which can be described, and many smaller groups are also recognized as having clear group identity: romantic comedy, black comedy, tragicomedy, melodrama, revenge plays, heroic plays, absurd plays are a few of the kinds of drama which provide expectations more specific than those of drama itself. Similarly there are many kinds of fiction (mystery stories, for example, or initiation stories, as well as novels, romances, and novellas) and of poetry (epic, pastoral, satiric, confessional, etc.); writers often choose their kind with great care and precision, to impose specific tasks upon themselves and to guarantee communication with the reader through a well defined common area of expectation. Even when the writer's choice of kind is arbitrary, capricious, or unconscious, the reader can profit from sensible comparisons and contrasts between an individual work and the norm of the group, and when a writer sets out deliberately to make his own unique kind the reader who knows the conventions of the other kinds will see more clearly what is going on.

Other classroom approaches to literature have gone in and out of fashion: the *biographical* approach (which emphasizes the relation of a work to the events and psychological patterns of an author's life), the *historical* approach (which emphasizes the development of forms and strategies and the passing on of techniques from one writer to another), and the *thematic* approach (which groups works by the subjects that they deal with or ideas that they present, rather than by genre, form, or style) have been among the more popular ones. The close-reading and generic approaches—often modified to fit the special interests or needs of a particular moment or a particular instructor—have, however, dominated the literature classroom for many years, and whatever concessions to fashion are made usually occur within the general framework of the close-reading and generic approaches. The selections in Sections I and II of the Norton Introduction to each genre are arranged so as to be especially convenient for these approaches.

In the last few years there has been a growing restlessness about these traditional approaches, and many attempts at experimentation reflect uncertainty about classroom method. The uncertainty is not so much disillusionment with what the close-reading and generic approaches can do, but a worry about what they cannot do; it is not so much a matter of replacing traditional methods as of supplementing them so that literature may seem more integrally related to other things. Students and teachers alike often weary of tool-sharpening, especially if they are not sure what larger tasks the tools are good for; most actors, athletes, and lovers can put up with strenuous discipline if they have a performance in view, but few are enchanted by practice for its own sake.

Seeing the relation of literature to other art and to the larger culture of which it is part is largely a matter of thinking about literature in context, related to a specific time and place—besides having "universal" and "timeless" aspects. Students who insist on knowing how a work relates to political or social or moral questions are, in an important sense, addressing the same issues as scholars trying to "place" a work in its whole cultural setting. (All of the more important critical and scholarly movements of the last few years—phenomenology, structuralism, psychological criticism, contextualism, neo-historicism—share the concern with literature as existing in time and having a specific relationship to the immediate cultural context which it reflects and addresses.) Seeing how one work of an author relates to other works, how specific events shape and control both the theme and the form of a work, how persuasive devices work upon a reader or audience in a specific emotional context, how the ideas of one time may be translated into a world with different assumptions and pressures—all these possibilities represent attempts to expand beyond the self-existent world of an individual work and the galaxy of a particular genre or kind. And such larger concerns often correct and clarify as well as expand, for reading many works by one writer (or knowing more about events to which the author refers) often corrects mistakes or reveals resonances which are not discoverable when one reads the work in isolation. Section III of the Norton Introduction to each genre is arranged to facilitate the investigation of such temporal and cultural matters. As editors, we have tried to arrange this book so that students and teachers can take advantage of classroom procedures already in use and adventure a little beyond what is already familiar or what they already do well.

C. E. B.

J. B.

J. P. H.

A Preface to Drama

A play is written to be performed on a stage before an audience. That audience is a group of people collected together in the same place and at the same time for the purpose of sharing the experience of the theater. Such collective behavior as the theater and similar activities persists in human societies. At different times and places the particular form may vary from the gatherings of primitive tribes to the rock festivals of our own day. Participation in such collective behavior often involves a certain amount of inconvenience and discomfort, yet communal experience persists. In some cases, indeed, the stated object can be attained more perfectly under private conditions, as is true of a rock festival. People do go to a rock festival to hear the music, but they also go to share the experience with others, to become a part of the group. Man needs to mingle his individual experiences with others in which he functions as a part of a larger body, in church, at the stadium, in the theater, or at a rock festival.

Because there are many diverse forms of collective behavior, no audience or group is a random assembly of individuals; rather the audience is a group of people who are like-minded enough to have made the same choice. The average man, however unarticulated his expectation, goes to the theater, the stadium, or the rock festival because he expects the satisfaction of experiencing the performance and the satisfaction of sharing that experience with others. Only drama critics and other masochists do not expect to like what they see. This likeness of intent may express itself in similarities of dress or age, but whatever the differences the individuals gather at the appointed time and place. Traditionally in the theater the new identity as a member of the group is expressed as a seat number, and as the individuals are seated, the house lights are dimmed. Individuality is for a time surrendered.

Among the members of the audience, behavior is largely controlled by the group. Anyone who has laughed at the wrong time in a theater or cheered for the visiting team among the home fans can testify to his own embarrassment and the disapproval of others that attend acting as an individual. When the sense of participation is strong enough, the members of the group will act in ways none of them would act as an individual. This group-controlled behavior also involves certain elements of ritual, the exact repetition of a series of actions. Individual performances occur at different times and places, involve different participants, and include individual variations at optional points, but the pattern of the ritual elements remains the same. The playing of the national anthem and the seventh-inning "stretch" at a baseball game are ritual actions in one kind of collective activity, just as intermissions and curtain calls are ritual actions in the theater. These activities are not so highly ritualized as the Mass, but collective behavior does involve elements of ritual.

The theatrical performance itself is also a ritual. Although no two performances of a play can be precisely the same, exact repetition is an implied goal, the aim of the ser.es of rehearsals which precede the performance. The nature of the play as dramatic ritual is overtly expressed in several modern plays, such as Thornton Wilder's *The Skin of Our Teeth* and Jean Genet's *The Balcony*. At the end of both plays a character dismisses the audience and says that the players must start the dramatic sequence over and repeat it again and again.

The audience also exercises an influence on the content of a performance. Plays are the most public form of literature, and the playwright writes for the group rather than the individual. As Prince Hamlet put it, the drama shows "the very age and body of the time his form and pressure." The subjects treated by a play must have some relevance to its society. The play intended only to entertain will gain its relevance by endorsing the values of its society. Many popular comedies, for example, reflect the attitudes of the society toward marriage. Plays may also reflect historical events as well as values and attitudes. Most of Shakespeare's great tragedies concern the succession to a throne or position of leadership. At the time they are believed to have been written, Elizabeth I was an aging queen without prospect of issue. For two centuries England had been subjected to war and destruction brought on by crises of succession. Stories about succession might well fascinate Shakespeare as well as his audiences. Such contemporary problems are only a part of the relation to society that a classic play has. *The Misanthrope*, for example, deals with the hypocrisy of a particular society, but it speaks to any society where there is hypocrisy.

Another way in which the audience affects the content of the play is that in the theater certain representations are taboo. The exact area of taboo will vary at different periods. The Greeks, for example, eschewed violence on stage. In *The Bacchae* the death of Pentheus must take place offstage and be reported by a messenger. In Shakespeare's time, however, the audience loved violence on stage as can be seen in the final scene of *Hamlet*. In our time the use of racial stereotypes is offensive to audiences. In modern productions of Shakespeare's *The Merchant of Venice* we see therefore a different Shylock from the one that Shakespeare's contemporaries saw. Today another area of taboo, nudity and sexual activity, is losing its forbidden character.

In addition to the contemporary appeal, a play may affect an audience by the use of timeless myth. A myth is a narrative which has a group significance. The first appeal of myth was religious, but the basic narrative sequence of a myth retains an appeal even when the religious significance is lost. The story of Venus and Adonis, a form of the myth of the death and rebirth of the young god, retains an appeal even when we no longer believe that the seasons are caused by that death and rebirth. Certain kinds of drama have strong mythical affinities. Melodrama has a basic narrative pattern in which good and evil are struggling, evil seems about to triumph, and good finally wins out. The popularity of melodrama attests to the appeal of the myth.

The first four plays in this collection illustrate a different way in which the drama uses myth. The scapegoat was originally a victim sacrificed for the redemption of the tribe by being driven into the wilderness. In *The Bacchae* Pentheus is a scapegoat who still has religious significance. He goes out into the wilderness, here Mount Cithaeron, and by his death purges the guilt of Thebes for its failure to recognize the new god Dionysus. In *Hamlet* the myth is used politically. Claudius sends Hamlet to England to die in order to restore the health of his kingdom. Hamlet acquiesces in Claudius' plan to the extent that he leaves without struggle, although he suspects Claudius' intentions, and then he provides substitute victims in Rosencrantz and Guildenstern. In the highly rational world of *The Misanthrope* the religious significance is completely gone, but the language still recalls the myth. Alceste flees from society because of its wickedness, and he offers Célimène the chance to go with him and atone for her treachery. The aura of the scapegoat is about him. In a more personal way, Gregers Werle has gone to the wilderness of Højdal because of his father's guilt, and he encourages Hedvig to sacrifice the duck in his wilderness in the attic to atone for the guilts in her family. She chooses rather to be the scapegoat herself and dies in the attic. The treatment of the scapegoat is vastly different in each of these plays, but the basic mythical pattern is there to lend its appeal.

The theater has emerged twice in Western culture, each time from relatively sophisticated societies and each time in connection with religious rituals in those societies. In Athens the festivals of Dionysus gave birth to the classical drama, and in the later Middle Ages the services of the Christian church produced its own form of drama. These two religious systems share a number of characteristics; an important one is their emphasis on rebirth and on ritual which signifies that the worshipper has become a new creature by virtue of his religious experience.

The literary counterpart of rebirth is peripety (or peripeteia), a sudden reversal of the character of a situation as a result of a particular event. The first play of modern times, the *Quem Quaeritis Trope,* provides an example of peripety, or dramatic event. This play was a dramatization by the participating priests of a part of the liturgy. It occurs in several forms, including the minimal one given here. The scene is the tomb of Jesus on Easter morning as the women approach and find the angel there.

> ANGEL   Whom do you seek in this sepulchre, Christians?
> WOMEN   Jesus of Nazareth, who was crucified, heavenly one.
> ANGEL   He is not here; he is risen as he foretold. Go, announce
> that he is risen from the grave.

The single dramatic event, the angel's announcement that "he is risen," reverses the emotional tone of the situation and the direction of the action.

Conflict is basic to drama, of course, but a conflict without peripety or the possibility of peripety is not truly dramatic. A struggle whose outcome is never in doubt may have other kinds of interest, but it makes a dull play or a dull football game in dramatic terms. If, however, the opposing forces are matched so that neither can control the situation for any considerable period, or the weaker force can mount a credible threat to the stronger, or the apparently weaker can overcome the stronger, then there is drama. In *Hamlet,* for example, the power of the conflict between Hamlet and Claudius depends on their being evenly matched. Claudius has the throne and the Queen, but Hamlet has his relation to the last king and his popularity among the people. Early in the play Claudius has the upper hand, but he realizes that he has underestimated Hamlet and he overreacts. Until he stops the play-within-a-play, the King seems firmly in command, the expected outcome of the action seems to favor him. From that point on Hamlet more and more takes command and ultimately restores the kingdom to the order which Claudius' kingship had disturbed.

The King's outburst is an example of a specific kind of peripety called a climax, the dramatic event about which the typical structure of a play is built. Like the myth of the scapegoat, this typical dramatic structure is realized in many ways in actual practice and with varying degrees of completeness. The structure is useful in interpreting and understanding only if it is used with flexibility and intelligence. This typical dramatic structure consists of five parts: (1) the exposition, the presentation and definition of the established situation from which the play takes rise; (2) the rising action, in which new factors complicate the original situation; (3) the climax or turning point, which reverses the emotional tone and direction of the action; (4) the falling action, in which the various complications begin to find their resolution; and (5) the conclusion, which establishes a new stable situation to end the play. Ibsen's treatment of the exposition in *The Wild Duck* can show us how flexible the parts of the typical structure can be. The play opens with a short scene of pure exposition between Pettersen and the hired waiters, but much of the expository material, including the state of Werle's health and Hedvig's and the circumstances of Hjalmar's marriage to Gina, is presented later in the play. In *The Misanthrope* Molière manipulates three separate plot lines, each with its own dramatic structure.

In addition to the climax or central peripety, a play may include many other instances of sudden, dramatic reverses. The scene at Ophelia's grave can illustrate. When Hamlet enters, he is confident and happy, joking with the First Clown about mortality. Then he learns that the skull he is holding and joking about is the skull of Yorick, and he passes into a mood of nostalgia and reflection. When his reflections reach the use of cosmetics, he falls into a jesting, cynical mood, which is interrupted by the appearance of the cortege. His emotion changes first to curiosity about the identity of the dead lady, then to sorrow when he learns that it is Ophelia. When Laertes jumps into the open grave, Hamlet reacts with violent, impulsive action and rhetoric. Much of the power and tension of the scene comes from this series of reverses of emotional tone.

Peripety renders conflict dramatic, serves as the basis of the typical dramatic structure, and gives power to individual scenes of the play. It is a basic element of drama.

A play is performed on a stage, as mentioned above, and the character of that stage and the conventions which govern it vary from age to age. In Molière's theater the audience was seated on three sides of the playing area, whereas Ibsen worked within a proscenium, with the audience seated on only one side of the action from which they were separated by an invisible fourth wall. This difference has its effect on the convention of place in the two theaters. In *The Misanthrope* the action takes place in and around the house of Célimène and Éliante, but no action depends on a particular location. The whole play can be presented in a single, rather generalized setting. By contrast the action of *The Wild Duck* is closely related to specific places. The first act takes place in a room of the elder Werle's house, which has three entrances, one to the office, one to the dining room, and one to the drawing room and the outside. All of these doors are necessary if the crucial scene in which Hjalmar ignores his father is to work. Doors in Ibsen lead to specific places. If there is not an actual door, then the different entrances must be somehow distinguished. The first act of *The Misanthrope* requires only one door, although more may be used, since nothing in the action depends on the number or positioning of doors.

Both these plays share the convention that the nature of the place represented may be changed by some conventional means, most obviously the lowering and raising of a front curtain. Between acts, if there is a change of place, the objects on stage may be removed and replaced by others more suitable to the new milieu. In cases where there is no curtain, this can be done in full view of spectators who have chosen to remain in their seats during the intermission. They do not "see" the change because the convention requires that they are not "present." Alternatively, the lights may be dimmed during the change, or the change might be accomplished, as in the Chinese theater, by men dressed in black (and therefore invisible).

Greek tragedies were performed in broad daylight without a curtain or other conventional means of changing the place. In consequence almost all the extant Greek tragedies occur in a single place. The action took place in an open semicircular area with a stage building, the **skene,** at the back. In *The Bacchae* the **skene** represented the palace of Pentheus, and the acting area represented a square or public area before the palace which included the tomb of Semele. Shakespeare's plays were also performed in broad daylight, but the acting area was more complex, including a recessed area at the back of the stage and a raised area above. Such areas were easily adapted to serve as the Queen's chamber in *Hamlet,* a cave in *The Tempest,* or a balcony in *Romeo and Juliet.* Because his stage was so flexible, in Shakespeare's plays place becomes a function of character. When the stage is emptied, the characters, in a sense, take the "place" with them, and a new place is established by the appearance of a new character or group of characters.

These differences in the conception of place affect the writing because of the demands that the convention makes. Getting the elder Ekdal on stage in Act 1 of *The Wild Duck* requires an elaborate set of causes, but at the opening of Act 3 of *The Misanthrope* Molière presents Acaste and Clitandre together on stage without any explanation of where they are or how they got there.

Convention governs equally the treatment of time on stage. Only rarely can playing time and elapsed time of the action coincide. The choral odes in *The Bacchae* provide an example of one such convention. Each of them represents a span of time between the two scenes it separates, or joins, since it does both. There is no correlation between the length of the ode and the elapsed time it represents; the elapsed time is determined by the necessities of the action. The earlier odes represent relatively short periods of time, whereas the ode spoken between the departure of Pentheus and Dionysus and the reappearance of the messenger with the report of Pentheus' death represents several hours at the least. Although there is no such formal device, the time difference between scenes in *Hamlet* varies even more greatly. Only a few moments elapse between Hamlet's departure to see his mother at the end of Act 3, Scene 2, and the scene of the King's prayer which follows. By contrast, several weeks must elapse between Scenes 4 and 5 of Act 4 to allow time for the news of Polonius' death to reach Paris and for Laertes' subsequent return to Elsinore. Both *The Misanthrope* and *The Wild Duck,* in comparison with *Hamlet,* have restricted time spans, but, as in the treatment of place, Ibsen is more careful than Molière to define the temporal relation of the acts.

Another area of convention involves the actors. Although early Greek plays were written for a single actor plus a chorus, plays like *The Bacchae* (a relatively late tragedy of the surviving ones) were written for three actors plus a chorus. Individual actors (all men) would of necessity play several roles during the course of such a play, and the actor had to be able, first, to play all kinds of roles without regard to physical suitability and, second, to move quickly from one role to another. On the assumption that a given role was played by a single actor whenever possible, we can see how Euripides used the convention to reinforce the esthetic design in *The Bacchae.* One actor would play Pentheus and Agauë, thus calling attention to the relation between mother and son. A second actor would play the god Dionysus and the seer Teiresias, the two figures who represent the holy in the play. The other parts can be played by the third actor without difficulty.

The conditions of Euripides' theater probably precluded any prior knowledge by the author of the particular actors who would perform his play. Both Shakespeare and Molière, on the other hand, worked with companies of players whose abilities and weaknesses they knew. The role of Polonius suggests that Shakespeare was writing for an actor who was particularly good at portraying sententious old men. The scene with Reynaldo, for example, serves no necessary dramatic function and merely reinforces the characterization established in the earlier scene between Polonius and Laertes. Shakespeare seems to have written the scene to take advantage of the particular abilities of the actor who was to portray Polonius. Shakespeare's acting company was restricted because the female roles were assumed by pre-pubescent boys. Only occasionally, as with Lady Macbeth and Cleopatra, did Shakespeare write complex female parts for his boy actors. Molière's company did include women, and as a rule his female parts are therefore more complex.

By the time of Ibsen, theater had become international. Plays were no longer written for performance at a specific time by a specific group of actors. A play which had a success in London would be performed in Paris, Vienna, or New York. To accommodate this trend, acting companies were composed of specialists in certain "lines," such as leading man, leading lady, juveniles (ingénues) of both sexes, heavies, and character actors. The role of Hedvig is written for an ingénue rather than for a particular actress. In this, as in time and place, the stage convention of the period will exercise an influence on the writing of the play.

Every play has two manifestations: it is a literary work, an order of words on a page to be read, and it is a performance, an order of speeches and visual effects (or gestures) presented on a stage. As a literary work the play is subject to the same canons of literary criticism as other forms, including the canon of internal complexity (or organic unity) which has dominated recent criticism. Many of the same kinds of internal complexity which are found in poems, novels, and short stories can be found in plays.

One kind of internal complexity involving plot structure can be seen in the parallel structures of *The Bacchae*. A series of events in the rising action occurs in the same order as a like series of events in the falling action. When Teiresias and Cadmus appear dressed in Bacchic costumes, they are upbraided for doing so by Pentheus, but later on Pentheus himself, after he has given in to Dionysus, appears dressed as a female worshipper of Bacchus. Shortly after his encounter with Teiresias and Cadmus, Pentheus has a scene with Dionysus in which he cuts Dionysus' hair, takes away his thyrsus, and imprisons him. This sequence gives ironic power to the scene in which Dionysus straightens Pentheus' wig, teaches him to carry his thyrsus properly, and leads him away to his death on the mountain, a more than figurative prisoner. A final set of parallels is provided by the accounts of the mountainside activities of Agauë and her fellow devotees. Each of the messengers describes them first in repose and then in Bacchic frenzy, the first telling how they killed cattle barehanded and the second describing the slaughter of Pentheus.

Another type of complex plotting can be seen in Pirandello's *Six Characters in Search of an Author.* Here two quite different stories are presented in a highly sophisticated blend. The apparent plot of the play, the "outer" story, concerns a group of actors, their director or manager, and others who are needed to present a play. They are interrupted in their rehearsal by a group of six "characters"; these characters are not "real" people, but the persons of a play imagined by an author but not committed to words on a page. The characters try to persuade the manager and the actors to give their story the life its creator refused it, but the attempt is a complete fiasco. The story that the characters tell is the "inner" plot of the play, and by contrast to the outer plot it is a lurid, melodramatic tale of infidelity, suicide, prostitution, and other things. This story is told in fragments and out of chronological order. Parts of it are pieced together from the scenes between the characters on stage, from other scenes they re-enact, and from narration. The method of presentation means that the "inner" story can be used to illustrate ideas rather than merely to titillate the audience.

Another common device in literature to give complexity is allusion, a reference to something which recalls some other work or idea. This can work in the drama, as the use of the number thirteen in *The Wild Duck* will illustrate. A careful reading of the play will reveal several references to thirteen, particularly thirteen at the table. Thus when Gregers says at the end of the play that his destiny is "To be the thirteenth man at the table," the speech is more than obscurantism. One notable example of thirteen people at a meal is the final Passover meal of Jesus and his twelve disciples. This allusion may help us to understand Gregers' enigmatic remark.

A more complex use of allusion can be seen in Arthur Miller's *A View from the Bridge.* The role of Alfieri functions somewhat like the chorus in a Greek tragedy, serving as prologue and epilogue and bridging the scenes with his speeches. Indeed, in the earlier one-act version of this play, Alfieri's speeches were printed as verse. Further the geographical references in his speeches remind us that Alfieri and the other characters of the play are ultimately of Greek descent, for Sicily and Southern Italy were originally Greek colonies. Other bits of information may also help. Count Vittorio Alfieri (1749–1803) was the greatest Italian writer of tragedies. The founder of psychoanalysis, Sigmund Freud, used figures from the Greek tragedies to illustrate his concepts of sexuality, particularly incestuous feelings within the family. Again the knowledge of this information may increase understanding of what is happening in a play.

Another device which lends internal complexity to other forms of literature and which functions in the drama is a recurring pattern of images. Throughout *Hamlet,* for example, images dealing with the body are used as a metaphor of the state as the body politic. Studying the play with this in mind will reveal dozens of such references. To give only one example, when the Ghost tells Hamlet that his death was falsely reported, his choice of words is significant: "So the whole ear of Denmark / Is by a forged process of my death / Rankly abused." This image becomes even more significant when he tells Hamlet the precise manner of his death. He was killed when his brother "in the porches of my ear did pour / The leperous distilment." The knowledge that the king is the "head" of the state and that Hamlet believes the wrong man is king may throw some light on his "madness." The understanding of the play can be greatly increased by watching for such image patterns.

The title of *The Wild Duck* might also suggest that the image of the wild duck is an important one for the reader of the play. Here the image is used symbolically; that means, among other things, that we cannot draw up a simple metaphorical equation between the image and what it represents. The wild duck itself, the method of its capture, the dog that actually captured it, and its life in the attic are used in many ways throughout the play. At one point, for example, Werle tells Gregers that old Ekdal is one of the "people in this world who sink to the bottom the minute they get a couple of slugs in them, and they never come up." Again a careful reading of the play will reveal many other uses of the image of the wild duck.

Yet another kind of internal complexity can result from the use of language. The dialogue of the various plays in this collection illustrates various degrees of attempting to reproduce actual speech. The relatively uneducated characters of *A View from the Bridge* speak substandard English. By contrast, the characters of *The Misanthrope* speak in mannered heroic couplets (alexandrines in the original). The kind of imitation of speech has much to do with the character of a play. Within a given play a writer may choose to give one or more characters individual speech patterns—for example, Hamlet's tendency to repeat the final phrase of a speech, Gina's malapropism, and Madame Pace's peculiar mixture of English and Italian.

Other examples of devices which induce internal complexity might be presented, for as literature the drama has precisely the same kinds of resources as other literary forms. None of these methods is peculiar to the drama.

The play on stage is different from the play as literature, not only because of its transience but also because every performance is a unique expression of the collaborative energies which make up the totality of the performance. In part this is due to the thousands of discrete elements which make up a performance. An actor may forget a line or the technician responsible for the lights may miss the speech which should tell him to change the lighting. Either of these or one of a thousand other possible accidents will make the performance unique. Another factor which makes every performance unique is that no two audiences are quite the same. Some audiences respond with warmth and enthusiasm; others are cold and unresponsive. The character of the audience on a given night invariably affects the performance. A warm, responsive audience brings out the best in the performers, as any actor can testify. No performance can exactly duplicate another.

Among the collaborators in a performance, the actors are the most visible. The actual control of a performance, however, varies in different times and places. In the 19th century performances were often dominated by the star actor-manager who played the lead and controlled the other persons involved. In the American theater in recent years the director has been the person most responsible for the collaborative effort. The stage direction may call for a sofa, but the director and the stage designer must provide a sofa of a particular style and color. In *Six Characters* the Stepdaughter expresses her dismay at their choice thus: "No, no! Green won't do! It was yellow, ornamented with flowers—very large! and most comfortable!"

Before a performance takes place the director and his colleagues must make hundreds of such decisions in such relatively unimportant matters as well as in more substantive ones. The selection of an actor to play Rodolpho in *A View from the Bridge* can serve as an example of a substantive choice. The constant references in the play to Rodolpho's youth, his good looks, his coloring, and the effeminacy which Eddie sees in him suggest a physical appearance different from that which would enable him to earn a living as a longshoreman. Ideally the actor who plays Rodolpho should suggest both facets of his character, but in practice few actors can do both perfectly. Another decision of less substance but of equal importance to the understanding of the play also involves the character of Rodolpho. Some of the dialogue of any play contains clues as to how the play should be realized concretely, however ambiguous. At one point in *A View from the Bridge,* Rodolpho and Catherine have returned from the movie, and Eddie has detained the girl. In order to discredit Rodolpho, Eddie tells her, "What does he do with his first money? A snappy new jacket he buys, records, a pointy pair new shoes and his brother's kids are starvin' over there with tuberculosis? That's a hit-and-run guy, baby." The audience has just seen Rodolpho in his new clothes, and their judgment of Eddie's observation will be affected by what the director has allowed them to see. In other cases the dialogue more explicitly affects the staging. When, for example, in Act 1, Scene 2 of *Hamlet,* the Queen asks Hamlet to "cast thy nighted color off," Hamlet should obviously be dressed in black.

Hamlet's appearance dressed in black in this scene is an example of how an author can imagine or invent a striking stage effect. Hamlet enters at the beginning of the scene with the King, the Queen, and the courtiers. Throughout the scenes with the ambassadors to Norway and then with Laertes, he is on stage but silent and isolated from the other figures by his dress. The stage picture has an effect which can be imagined in reading the scene but which is even more striking in performance. Shaw uses a similar device for the final appearance of Cleopatra in *Caesar and Cleopatra.* Another kind of striking stage effect can be seen in the entrance of Madame Pace in *Six Characters.*

On stage the Father is bustling about, collecting hats and coats from the unwilling actresses and placing the garments on the prop forms provided for them. The audience's attention is forced toward the stage, allowing the actress playing Madame Pace to enter from the back of the seating area without being observed. As he moves about the Father says, "Who knows if, by arranging the stage for her, she does not come here herself, attracted by the very articles of her trade?" At this point the actor playing the Father will turn and point toward her, the spotlight will hit her, and some members of the audience will gasp with surprise.

There are other ways in which a stage-wise playwright can create moments of dramatic power on stage. When Hamlet says of the dead Polonius, "I'll lug the guts into the neighbor room," the ugliness and vulgarity of the language and the sentiments they express must startle the viewer as well as the reader. The entrance of the Mother in the brothel scene in *Six Characters* is carefully prepared for. The audience has been given the information necessary to be powerfully affected by the scene. The violence of the final scene of *Hamlet* is made more graphic by the relatively quiet scene between Hamlet and Horatio, including the comic moments with Osric. The audience has had a chance to relax after the confrontation at Ophelia's grave, and the lull makes the storm which follows more terrible.

The end of Act 1 of *A View from the Bridge* shows how a powerful dramatic effect can be achieved with minimal use of words. Eddie has hit Rodolpho a real blow in the boxing match as a warning to stay away from Catherine. Marco wants to warn Eddie that an injury to Rodolpho will be avenged by his brother. He asks Eddie if he can lift a chair by the bottom of a leg using only one hand. Eddie tries and fails. No more words are needed. Marco silently shows him that it can be done, that his strength is greater than Eddie's. The threat of revenge implicit in this display of strength is brilliantly realized in gestural terms, and the curtain falls at a moment of high dramatic power.

At its best the drama establishes a tension between language and gesture which provides a supreme dramatic event. The great recognition scene in *Six Characters* shows how the two can work together. The Father, as *raisonneur,* propounds several ideas in the play which are presented dramatically in the scene. First, he says that the representation on stage of a scene is limited and impermanent and therefore inferior to the "form" or idea of it. Second, he points out that in art the true (that is, the probable) occurs necessarily. After the exit of Madame Pace in Act 2, the Father and the Stepdaughter begin to play the scene for the Manager and the Actors. Speaking outside the character in the scene, she tells him to make his entrance, but very quickly the reality of the story overcomes both of them and they are trapped in the action. *"The Father does as he is told, looking troubled and perplexed at first. But as soon as he begins to move, the reality of the action affects him, and he begins to smile and be more natural."* The effect makes the Father's second point, using the very means he decries, the interpretive skill of the actor. Once the scene has begun, the Father and the Stepdaughter proceed without noticing the others. The Mother cries, "Oh, my God, my God!" L'Ingénue attempts to interrupt and the Manager scolds her. The Manager tells the Stepdaughter to "Begin again, please!" but the participants in the scene have no choice but to continue. The scene is the reality of art, and it must fulfill itself in that probable world, regardless of distractions. Finally a determined effort by the Manager stops them, although the Stepdaughter pleads to continue: "The best's coming now. Why can't we go on?"

Now the Leading Man and the Leading Lady prepare to play the scene. In spite of the Stepdaughter's objection that the scene will not work because the Leading Lady "isn't dressed in black," the actors begin. *"The rendering of the scene by the Actors from the very first word is seen to be quite a different thing, though it has not in any way the air of parody. . . . The Leading Lady and the Leading Man . . . deliver their words in different tones and with a different psychology."* The effect cannot fail to work, as Pirandello knew, for no two pairs of actors can perform a scene in exactly the same way. Any interpretation is only one of the partial ways of realizing the words, and the difference between the pairs of actors represents the difference between the ideal of the scene contained in the words and any particular realization of it. Before the scene has proceeded very far, the Father interrupts, objecting to the reading of the first line by the Leading Man. The Actors, unlike the Father and the Stepdaughter, can allow themselves to be interrupted and can step out of character, as the Leading Man does to defend his reading. "If I've got to represent an old fellow who's coming into a house of an equivocal character . . . ," he begins. The Manager calms him and tells the Actors to start over. Unlike the characters in the same situation, because they are not "living" it, they can and do begin again. It is acting, not the reality of art, and they are not swept along by the force of probability. The Manager interrupts several times to give them line readings, but they are not disturbed. The Father and the Stepdaughter also interrupt to comment on the "truth" of the performance until it becomes impossible to continue, and the Manager stops the scene. "Well then, let's have no more of it! We'll have the rehearsals by ourselves afterward in the ordinary way." Throughout the scene the visual, gestural resources of the stage reinforce the language and ideas of the play.

So far this introduction has dealt largely with individual plays, but groups of plays have several important relations to one another. One such relation involves plays by a single author, for every art work bears to some extent the imprint of the artist's personality, his education, and his experiences. Where a substantial body of work by a given artist exists, meaningful relations between the separate works can illuminate individual works. In Shakespeare's plays, for example, the issue of orderly succession is examined again and again in the histories and tragedies. Furthermore, the character of Hamlet combines important elements of earlier Shakespearean heroes such as Richard II, Brutus, and Prince Hal.

To illustrate this kind of relation, two plays of George Bernard Shaw are included in this volume; for among playwrights other than Shakespeare who write in English, Shaw is probably the most frequently performed and the one who has more plays which are still viable on stage. Some ten or twelve of his plays are still frequently performed and as many more are played occasionally. Although he was almost forty when he began writing for the theater, Shaw wrote over sixty plays, ranging from vaudeville sketches to his "Metabiological Pentateuch," *Back to Methuselah.* Before he began writing plays, he had been a would-be novelist, a notable reviewer of music and drama for periodicals, and a crowd-pleasing lecturer, particularly on economics. His cogent analyses of the plays and operas performed in London while he was a reviewer and of the performances themselves stood him in good stead as a dramatist. As a lecturer, he learned to please and hold an audience. "I first caught the ear of the British public on a cart in Hyde Park, to the blaring of brass bands, and this not at all as a reluctant sacrifice of instincts of privacy to political necessity, but because, like all dramatists and mimes of genuine vocation, I am a natural-born mountebank." This piece of self-deprecation ignores the other side of Shaw's character, the polemical moralist and social philosopher. He left the platform for the stage, at least in part, because he believed that in his plays and the series of prefaces which he wrote for some of them, he would find a more effective vehicle for propagandizing his ideas about economics and education, about vegetarianism and spelling reform, about "Creative Evolution" and marriage and the legal status of women. His plays would bring their audience to a new and better understanding of themselves and their society.

Shaw's characteristic method in his plays is satiric, for he exhibits the evils of society rather than the way things ought to be. The plays diagnose the ills; the prefaces prescribe the remedies. Shaw consistently deals with the hypocrisies of society, and the central figures of his plays are strong, powerful, and attractive not because they try to reform the world but because they are not deceived by its hypocrisies. They observe what people do, not what they say. The method can be illustrated by the treatment of economics. Shaw was a Fabian socialist, but he does not describe a socialist Utopia in his plays. He concentrates on an analysis of the materialistic, capitalistic society which he sees around him—a society dominated by economic values, whatever people say. An exchange from each of the plays in this collection makes the point. In *Major Barbara* Stephen believes that politicians govern, but his father, the munitions maker Andrew Undershaft, voices Shaw's criticism. "Government of your country! Be off with you, my boy, and play with your caucuses and leading articles and historic parties and great leaders and burning questions and the rest of your toys. *I* am going back to my countinghouse to pay the piper and call the tune." In *Caesar and Cleopatra* Pothinus scoffs at "the conqueror of the world" occupying himself "with such a trifle as our taxes." Caesar reprimands him thus: "My friend: taxes are the chief business of a conqueror of the world." A number of similar passages can be found elsewhere in these two plays as well as in other plays of Shaw.

In structuring his plays, Shaw used a parodistic method, based on his knowledge of the stage gained as a drama critic. He described it thus: "I have always cast my plays in the ordinary practical comedy form in use at all the theatres." The first act of *Major Barbara* and the first part of the third act are in the tradition of the comedy of manners, as exemplified in Shaw's own time by Oscar Wilde's *The Importance of Being Earnest*. Although Wilde moved the setting of his play from the city to the country, he never really left the drawing room, as Shaw did in his visits to the Salvation Army shelter and the munitions factory. Similarly *Caesar and Cleopatra* is based on such historical pageant plays of the period as Bulwer-Lytton's *Richelieu* and Tennyson's *Becket*. The pageantry of the settings and costumes recalls such plays as forcefully as does the rhetoric of Caesar's address to the Sphinx at the beginning of the first act. The speech itself recalls the pseudo-Shakespearean style so popular in the nineteenth century, but Cleopatra's interruption tells the audience exactly what to think of such windy rhetoric. Shaw also parodies the traditional notions of Cleopatra by redefining them in his own terms. For example, when Cleopatra is brought to Caesar swathed in a carpet, the audience expects a declaration of love. Instead Caesar tells her that his soldiers come first. "Cleopatra, when that trumpet sounds, we must take every man his life in his hand, and throw it in the face of Death. And of my soldiers who have trusted me there is not one whose hand I shall not hold more sacred than your head." Thus Shaw uses the tradition of the "Serpent of the Nile" by deflating it.

In his redefinition of the Caesar-Cleopatra relation, Shaw makes Caesar into a consummate pedagogue who teaches by examples as well as by precept and Cleopatra into an apt, if not exactly perfect, pupil. As she tells Pothinus in Act 4, "Now that Caesar has made me wise. . . . If Caesar were gone, I think I could govern the Egyptians." The passion in the relation between Caesar and Cleopatra is still present; Shaw has transformed it from a sexual passion to an intellectual one. In *Major Barbara* although Barbara "loves" Cusins in the conventional way, the passion between Barbara and her father is stronger. Cusins says: "A father's love for a grown-up daughter is the most dangerous of all infatuations. I apologize for mentioning my own pale, coy, mistrustful fancy in the same breath with it." The same pattern of an intellectual passion between an older man and a younger woman can be seen in such plays as *Pygmalion* and *Heartbreak House*.

Shaw's tendency to downgrade sexual relationships often makes the theoretical heroes and heroines of his plays into rather bland figures like Cusins, but he achieves greater success with his strong, aware figures like Caesar and Undershaft, as well as with a series of stereotypes adapted from earlier dramatic forms. Lady Britomart in *Major Barbara*, for example, is Shaw's version of the middle-aged, dominating society matron exemplified by such characters as Lady Wishfort in

Congreve's *The Way of the World* and Lady Bracknell in Wilde's *The Importance of Being Earnest*. Other characters, like Bill Walker and Britannus, are in the comedy of humors tradition, especially as that tradition was used by Dickens. The strongest and most vital characters in the plays, however, are those like Caesar and Undershaft who see the world as clearly as Shaw did and who act on their insights to control and manipulate others.

Because Shaw did not have Pirandello's gift for devising actions to exemplify his ideas, his plays sometimes seem "talky." The scene between Undershaft, Barbara, and Cusins near the end of *Major Barbara* is an example of a scene where the real action is in the play of ideas. However, he was capable of the flashing comic line such as Lady Britomart's assertion that "[I] believe in liberty. Let snobbish people say what they please; Barbara shall marry, not the man they like, but the man *I* like." At other times, the wit lies in the structure of the speeches, using the rhetorical tricks Shaw had learned on the lecture platform. "When you vote, you only change the names of the cabinet. When you shoot, you pull down governments, inaugurate new epochs, abolish old orders and set up new."

In his best work Shaw presented a witty and elegant expression of his unique vision. He saw a society where people lived for money and power but talked of romance and religion, of charity and honor. He attacked the hypocrisies of such a society, many of which are still present in our lives. As long as they are, his plays will be an important part of our dramatic heritage.

Another means of understanding plays in relation to one another is the study of dramatic kinds (or genres). One large group of plays includes comedies, which as a rule end with the marriage of the hero and heroine. *The Misanthrope* is a comedy, but it does not have the traditional ending. Knowledge of this departure should help us understand the play better. *The Misanthrope* is not a "bad" comedy because of its ending, but a unique one worthy of study.

The dramatic kind that has been studied most frequently is tragedy, the subject of Aristotle's *Poetics* and numerous works of later critics. Sophocles' *Oedipus Tyrannus* is close to being the perfect exemplar of Aristotle's definition of tragedy. Tragedy describes the fall from prosperity to adversity of a great individual because he has transgressed against the great moral principles which govern the universe. In his adversity he comes to understand himself and his situation, blessed with enlightenment even though he may be dying. At the beginning of the play Oedipus is prosperous and happy, enjoying the confidence and love of his subjects and the pleasures of warm personal relations. But Oedipus believes that he can save the city, that he can control Fate. He did it once before, when he fled from Corinth to avoid carrying out the destiny assigned him. Oedipus is wrong in his belief, for Fate will carry the day. His attempt to avoid his fate led directly to his carrying it out, to the murder of his own father and the marriage with his mother. At the end of the play, having lost both his kingdom and his eyes, he understands. His final appearance radiates a serene and dignified resignation to his destiny, an enlightenment gained at a terrible price.

Several of the other plays in this collection share some characteristic features of tragedy with *Oedipus Tyrannus,* particularly *Hamlet, The Bacchae,* and *A View from the Bridge.* None of the three is quite like *Oedipus Tyrannus* in every regard, and examining them at the points of dissimilarity can provide one approach to our understanding of them. For example, what kind of Fate or destiny is involved in each of them? What moral principles are at stake in them, and how does the author describe these principles? Although Sophocles and Euripides were closely contemporary, the plays seem to show different attitudes toward the destiny that governs mankind. In *A View from the Bridge,* against what principles does Eddie Carbone transgress? Are they those of some universal truth or of a small, isolated community? What is effect of using a longshoreman as tragic hero, rather than a prince? In an important essay Miller defended the use of the common man as tragic hero, but what are the actual effects in the work itself?

Another opening into the plays can be seen in the characters of their beginnings and endings. Oedipus was prosperous and happy, sure of himself and of his happy future. To what extent is this true of Hamlet, of Pentheus, and of Eddie Carbone? At the end of the play Oedipus, though in terrible circumstances, wins through to enlightenment. Does Eddie Carbone come to understand? What do Hamlet's final speeches tell us about his state of mind as he dies? In *The Bacchae* what are we to make of Pentheus' leaving the stage two-thirds of the way through the play and not returning? We do not witness him in his adversity, and we do not know whether he reached enlightenment. All of these are questions which arise from our knowledge of tragedy.

Most of the serious plays of the contemporary theater have not attempted to be tragedies. One reason for this is that none of the value systems available to the modern dramatist—and here "available" means acceptable to and understandable by his audience—provides a suitable framework for tragedy. Rather than focusing on man's relation to a universal order of some kind, playwrights like Ibsen, Chekhov, and others have turned to depicting man's life on this earth and the ways he finds to deal with it. Transcendent values have tended either to disappear or to become eroded to the point where they cannot be used for dramatic purposes. Only a naive man like Hjalmar Ekdal in *The Wild Duck* can believe that old Werle's loss of eyesight is a punishment; only an old man with a failing mind like Old Ekdal can believe that the forests will have their revenge. The Prozorovs in *The Three Sisters* watch helplessly while the forces of social and economic change destroy the lovely world of the past and replace it with a newer and uglier present. Death without enlightenment is the ending which waits patiently at the end of a road marked by failing powers and compromises with life. Hedvig dies; Tusenbach dies. They are the lucky ones, for the others are compelled to begin another day, to repeat yesterday's routines. Hjalmar will recover from Hedvig's death, just as Irina will recover from Tusenbach's because life goes on. The dramatic event represents only a moment in an otherwise humdrum life. The vivid recognition scene in *Six Characters* is an exceptional experience, but the Actors cannot even recognize that they have been touched by the truth of art. Instead they regret the wasted day and look forward only to returning to the treadmill of their ordinary rehearsals tomorrow. Plays like these are the most typical form of our serious drama, so much a part of our consciousness that we have no name for this dramatic kind.

Here, as in tragedy, the resemblances call our attention to the differences. In Ibsen, for example, the emphasis is on the individual and his fate. For Hjalmar life has been a series of disappointments and compromises which have produced the Hjalmar we see. In Chekhov, by contrast, the emphasis is on the society. The three sisters and their brother personify various ways in which the gleam has been lost; our concern is not with any of them as individuals, but as representatives of a class and a society that is dying.

A third way of studying groups of plays is to examine those written during a certain period of time. The drama is the most social of literary forms, and dramatic styles vary widely even in different decades. The last three plays in this collection are examples of the new dramatic style of the 1960s in America. One obvious characteristic of this style is the use of language. Writers as diverse as Lewis Carroll and Gertrude Stein heralded a breakdown of confidence in the reliability of language, and Pirandello observed that each of us uses words in terms of his own experience and that therefore no two of us use them in the same way. Samuel Beckett, Eugene Ionesco, and other writers of the Theater of the Absurd during the 1950s presented the problems of language in dramatic terms. Real communication between people is impossible because of the dangers of language. Clichés serve a real purpose, for though they mean little (or because they mean little), they are less likely to be misunderstood than more complex utterances. The effect in more recent playwrights is threefold: (1) avoidance of anything that sounds like "literature" or "fine writing," (2) the use of cliché in dialogue, and (3) the use of nonsense and of regular speech treated as nonsense, passages in which words are treated as music or sound effects as in the chorus in the psychoanalysis scene in *Interview*.

Another feature of this style is its concern with the communal and ritual aspects of the theater. Many of the plays begin in theatrical workshops or performing groups in which the playwright is only one of the members of the group. The playwright develops the play in collaboration with the group until a performing script is ready for public presentation. Rewriting parts of a play prior to public performance is a common practice in the commercial theater, but the method and purpose are quite different. The groups from which the new dramatic style springs are more closely knit than had been the case in the recent past, and the members of the group often share a mystique of communality. In some instances this mystique acquires an intense, quasi-religious character (generally with little or no theological content). It is not religious in the traditional sense, but its emotional tone is almost religious. The performances can become theatrical rituals at which the actors are the priests and acolytes and the audience the members of this secular congregation. Accounts of the activities and performances of a group like the Living Theater illustrate this tendency.

A third common feature of this style is the way in which it exposes its theatricality. In the last hundred years the dominant tradition of the drama has been to turn the stage into as perfect a representation of reality as possible. There have been other less illusive styles, but generally a stage living room looks as much as possible like a real living room. In the new style the barriers between the acting area and the auditorium are broken down; movement from one to the other is frequently used. The acting area itself is a part of a total theatrical environment. Sets may imitate by suggesting rather than by copying the real place being represented. The scene in *Interview* where a revolving door is represented by the actor's bodies is an example of the nonillusive, highly theatrical means available and in use in these plays. The treatment of time in all three plays involves little attempt to make stage time imitate real time. Character too makes little attempt to imitate realistically. In *A Son, Come Home,* for example, the Boy and the Girl each play a number of different roles without any attempt to change their appearance and thus increase the illusion. All of the visual means are presented so that the audience is aware that it is watching actors on a stage at all times. Rather than an illusive representation of something outside, the play in performance becomes a theatrical event, governed by its own laws and experience for its own sake. Even plot participates in this theatricality, for a different notion of plot animates the plays; plot as the blueprint for a theatrical performance. Emphasis is on performance, and the plot is not constructed to imitate life but to provide effective means for using the theatrical resources to make the ideal theatrical experience.

The features of this new dramatic style are not really new, for they can be found in earlier plays and traditions of performance. Their combination into a new dramatic style, however, is a significant part of our culture today.

Note on Arrangement

The first four plays in this selection are chosen from different times and places to illustrate the common features of all drama in works of widely diverse styles. Thematically they are similar in that they deal with the conflict between the individual and his society, although the actual conflict in each is different from the others.

The next two plays are chosen to illuminate the relation between the drama as a literary form and as a public performance. Thematically they and the two plays which follow revolve about a relation between a young woman and an older man, though here again the relation is differently defined in each play.

The two plays by Shaw which open the final group illustrate the relation of the individual work to other plays by the same author, the first of the three larger contexts for studying drama examined in this final section. The next two plays are chosen to illustrate generic affinities, *Oedipus Tyrannus* with the tragedy and *Three Sisters* with the serious modern play. The final three are American plays of the 1960s which illustrate the relation of the play to its historic and social contexts.

Acknowledgments

If you are old enough to edit a textbook, you are indebted to literally hundreds of people—family, colleagues, teachers, and students. We are. If you cannot thank them wittily, it is more important anyway to thank them sincerely. We do.

In the preparation of this book we have acquired many new indebtednesses which should be acknowledged. Our colleagues at Emory University, especially in the Department of English and the University Library, continue to be lodes of information, encouragement, and wisdom. Particular information was solicited from and provided by Mr. John Shaw of the Florida State University Library. A place of honor was earned by Mrs. Carolyn Breecher, formerly of the Emory University English Department, for many services and for the engaging wit with which they were performed.

On several occasions during the preparation of this work a retreat from everyday was needed. The Ossabaw Island Project provided it, and we wish to thank the Ossabaw Island Foundation and particularly Mr. and Mrs. Clifford B. West and Mr. and Mrs. Charles B. Wood for the provision and for the grace with which it was offered.

At W. W. Norton & Company, Ann Holler, Carol Paradis, Mill Jonakait, Calvin Towle, and John Benedict have provided assistance and encouragement in many ways and on many occasions.

Arrangements have been made for suitable expressions of gratitude for the assistance and encouragement of our wives at a more appropriate time and place.

The Norton
Introduction to Literature

I

EURIPIDES

The Bacchae*

CHARACTERS

DIONYSUS

CHORUS, *of Oriental women, devotees of Dionysus*

TEIRESIAS, *a blind Seer*

CADMUS, *founder of Thebes, and formerly king*[1]

PENTHEUS, *his grandson, now king of Thebes*

A GUARD, *attending Pentheus*

A HERDSMAN

A MESSENGER

AGAUË, *daughter of Cadmus and mother of Pentheus*

THE SCENE. *Before the palace of Pentheus in Thebes. At one side of the stage is the monument of Semele; above it burns a low flame, and around it are the remains of ruined and blackened masonry.*

DIONYSUS *enters on stage right. He has a crown of ivy, a thyrsus in his hand, and a fawnskin draped over his body.*[2] *He has long flowing hair and a youthful, almost feminine beauty.*

DIONYSUS   I am Dionysus, son of Zeus. My mother was
Semele, Cadmus' daughter. From her womb the fire
Of a lightning-flash delivered me. I have come here
To Thebes and her two rivers, Dirce and Ismenus,
Veiling my godhead in a mortal shape. I see   5
Here near the palace my mother's monument, that records
Her death by lightning. Here her house stood; and its ruins
Smoulder with the still living flame of Zeus's fire—
The immortal cruelty Hera wreaked upon my mother.[3]
Cadmus does well to keep this ground inviolable,   10
A precinct consecrated in his daughter's name;
And I have decked it round with sprays of young vine-leaves.
From the fields of Lydia and Phrygia, fertile in gold,
I traveled first to the sun-smitten Persian plains,
The walled cities of Bactria, the harsh Median country,   15
Wealthy Arabia, and the whole tract of the Asian coast
Where mingled swarms of Greeks and Orientals live
In vast magnificent cities; and before reaching this,
The first city of Hellas I have visited,
I had already, in all those regions of the east,   20

---

* Translated by Philip Vellacott.

1. See the note on Thebes and the House of Cadmus, p. 35.

2. The traditional attributes of Dionysus included a crown of ivy, a fawnskin, and the *thyrsus*, a staff of fennel wrapped with ivy or vine leaves.

3. Hera, as chief goddess of the Greeks and consort of Zeus, the chief god, felt a not unnatural aversion to the mortal girls who were the objects of his frequent adulteries.

Performed my dances and set forth my ritual
To make my godhead manifest to mortal men.[4]

The reason why I have chosen Thebes as the first place
To raise my Bacchic shout, and clothe all who respond
In fawnskin habits, and put my thyrsus in their hands—   25
The weapon wreathed with ivy-shoots—my reason is this:
My mother's sisters said—what they should have been the last
To say—that I, Dionysus, was not Zeus's son;
That Semele, being with child—they said—by some mortal,
Obeyed her father's prompting, and ascribed to Zeus   30
The loss of her virginity; and they loudly claimed
That this lie was the sin for which Zeus took her life.

Therefore I have driven those same sisters mad, turned them
All frantic out of doors; their home now is the mountain;
Their wits are gone. I have made them bear the emblem of   35
My mysteries; the whole female population of Thebes,
To the last woman, I have sent raving from their homes.
Now, side by side with Cadmus' daughters, one and all
Sit roofless on the rocks under the silver pines.
For Thebes, albeit reluctantly, must learn in full   40
This lesson, that my Bacchic worship is a matter
As yet beyond her knowledge and experience;
And I must vindicate my mother Semele
By manifesting myself before the human race
As the divine son whom she bore to immortal Zeus.   45

Now Cadmus has made over his throne and kingly honors
To Pentheus, son of his eldest daughter Agaue. He
Is a fighter against gods, defies me, excludes me from
Libations, never names me in prayers. Therefore I will
Demonstrate to him, and to all Thebes, that I am a god.   50

When I have set all in order here, I will pass on
To another place, and manifest myself. Meanwhile
If Thebes in anger tries to bring the Bacchants home
By force from the mountain, I myself will join that army
Of women possessed and lead them to battle. That is why   55
I have changed my form and taken the likeness of a man.

Come, my band of worshippers, women whom I have brought
From lands of the east, from Tmolus, bastion of Lydia,
To be with me and share my travels! Raise the music
Of your own country, the Phrygian drums invented by   60
Rhea the Great Mother and by me.[5] Fill Pentheus' palace
With a noise to make the city of Cadmus turn and look!
—And I will go to the folds of Mount Cithaeron, where
The Bacchants are, and join them in their holy dance.

---

4. Hellas was another name for Greece,
and the people of Greece were also called
Hellenes. The other places mentioned by
Dionysus are in Asia Minor or Asia proper.

5. Tmolus is a mountain in Asia Minor.
Rhea was a Greek name for the earth goddess responsible for the fertility of the soil,
or the Great Mother.

DIONYSUS *goes out toward the mountain. The* CHORUS *enter where* DIONYSUS *entered, from the road by which they have traveled.*

CHORUS

From far-off lands of Asia, *Strophe 1* 65
From Tmolus the holy mountain,
We run with the god of laughter;
Labor is joy and weariness is sweet,
And our song resounds to Bacchus!

Who stands in our path? *Antistrophe 1* 70
Make way, make way!
Who in the house? Close every lip,
Keep holy silence, while we sing
The appointed hymn to Bacchus!

Blest is the happy man *Strophe 2* 75
Who knows the mysteries the gods ordain,
And sanctifies his life,
Joins soul with soul in mystic unity,
And, by due ritual made pure,
Enters the ecstasy of mountain solitudes; 80
Who observes the mystic rites
Made lawful by Cybele⁶ the Great Mother;
Who crowns his head with ivy,
And shakes aloft his wand in worship of Dionysus.
On, on! Run, dance, delirious, possessed! 85
Dionysus comes to his own;
Bring from the Phrygian hills to the broad streets of Hellas
The god, child of a god,
Spirit of revel and rapture, Dionysus!

Once, on the womb that held him *Antistrophe 2* 90
The fire-bolt flew from the hand of Zeus;
And pains of childbirth bound his mother fast,
And she cast him forth untimely,
And under the lightning's lash relinquished life;
And Zeus the son of Cronos 95
Ensconced him instantly in a secret womb
Chambered within his thigh,
And with golden pins closed him from Hera's sight.
So, when the Fates had made him ripe for birth,
Zeus bore the bull-horned god 100
And wreathed his head with wreaths of writhing snakes;
Which is why the Maenads catch
Wild snakes, nurse them and twine them round their hair.

O Thebes, old nurse that cradled Semele, *Strophe 3*
Be ivy-garlanded, burst into flower 105

6. Cybele was another name for the Great Mother, especially as a goddess of Asia Minor.

With wreaths of lush bright-berried bryony,
Bring sprays of fir, green branches torn from oaks,
Fill soul and flesh with Bacchus' mystic power;
Fringe and bedeck your dappled fawnskin cloaks
With woolly tufts and locks of purest white.   110
There's a brute wildness in the fennel-wands—
Reverence it well. Soon the whole land will dance
  When the god with ecstatic shout
  Leads his companies out
  To the mountain's mounting height   115
  Swarming with riotous bands
  Of Theban women leaving
  Their spinning and their weaving
  Stung with the maddening trance
    Of Dionysus!   120

O secret chamber the Curetes knew!   *Antistrophe 3*
O holy cavern in the Cretan glade
Where Zeus was cradled, where for our delight
The triple-crested Corybantes drew
Tight the round drum-skin, till its wild beat made   125
Rapturous rhythm to the breathing sweetness
Of Phrygian flutes! Then divine Rhea found
The drum could give her Bacchic airs completeness;
  From her, the Mother of all,
  The crazy Satyrs soon,   130
  In their dancing festival
  When the second year comes round,
  Seized on the timbrel's tune
  To play the leading part
  In feasts that delight the heart   135
    Of Dionysus.[7]

O what delight is in the mountains!   *Epode*
There the celebrant, wrapped in his sacred fawnskin,
Flings himself on the ground surrendered,
While the swift-footed company streams on;   140
There he hunts for blood, and rapturously
Eats the raw flesh of the slaughtered goat,
Hurrying on to the Phrygian or Lydian mountain heights.
Possessed, ecstatic, he leads their happy cries;
The earth flows with milk, flows with wine,   145
Flows with nectar of bees;
The air is thick with a scent of Syrian myrrh.
The celebrant runs entranced, whirling the torch
That blazes red from the fennel-wand in his grasp,
And with shouts he rouses the scattered bands,   150
Sets their feet dancing,

7. The Curetes were Cretan spirits who saved the life of the infant Zeus by dancing and shouting so frenziedly that his cries could not be heard. He had been hidden on Crete by his mother Rhea because his father Cronos, or Saturn, had the unpleasant habit of eating his newborn children. The Corybantes were male attendants of Cybele, also known for their frenzied revels. The Satyrs were woodland figures, men from the waist up and goats from the waist down, associated with Pan and Dionysus and known for their exuberance.

As he shakes his delicate locks to the wild wind.
And amidst the frenzy of song he shouts like thunder:
"On, on! Run, dance, delirious, possessed!
You, the beauty and grace of golden Tmolus,   155
Sing to the rattle of thunderous drums,
Sing for joy,
Praise Dionysus, god of joy!
Shout like Phrygians, sing out the tunes you know,
While the sacred pure-toned flute   160
Vibrates the air with holy merriment,
In time with the pulse of the feet that flock
To the mountains, to the mountains!"
And, like a foal with its mother at pasture,
Runs and leaps for joy every daughter of Bacchus.   165

> *Enter* TEIRESIAS. *Though blind, he makes his way unaided to the door, and knocks.*

TEIRESIAS   Who keeps the gate? Call Cadmus out, Agenor's son,
Who came from Sidon here to build these walls of Thebes.
Go, someone, say Teiresias is looking for him.
He knows why; I'm an old man, and he's older still—
But we agreed to equip ourselves with Bacchic wands   170
And fawnskin cloaks, and put on wreaths of ivy-shoots.

> *Enter* CADMUS.

CADMUS   Dear friend, I knew your voice, although I was indoors,
As soon as I heard it—the wise voice of a wise man.
I am ready. See, I have all that the god prescribes.
He is my daughter's son; we must do all we can   175
To exalt and honor him. Where shall we go to dance
And take our stand with others, tossing our grey heads?
You tell me what to do, Teiresias. We're both old,
But you're the expert. [*He stumps about, beating his thyrsus on the ground.*] I could drum the ground all night
And all day too, without being tired. What joy it is   180
To forget one's age!
TEIRESIAS   I feel exactly the same way,
Bursting with youth! I'll try it—I'll dance with the rest.
CADMUS   You don't think we should go to the mountain in a coach?
TEIRESIAS   No, no. That would not show the god the same respect. 185
CADMUS   I'll take you there myself then—old as we both are.
TEIRESIAS   The god will guide us there, and without weariness.
CADMUS   Are we the only Thebans who will dance to him?
TEIRESIAS   We see things clearly; all the others are perverse.
CADMUS   We're wasting time; come, take my hand.   190
TEIRESIAS   Here, then; hold tight.
CADMUS   I don't despise religion. I'm a mortal man.
TEIRESIAS   We have no use for theological subleties.
The beliefs we have inherited, as old as time,
Cannot be overthrown by any argument,   195
Not by the most inventive ingenuity.
It will be said, I lack the dignity of my age,

To wear this ivy-wreath and set off for the dance.
Not so; the god draws no distinction between young
And old, to tell us which should dance and which should not.   200
He desires equal worship from all men; his claim
To glory is universal; no one is exempt.

CADMUS   Teiresias, I shall be your prophet, since you are blind.
Pentheus, to whom I have resigned my rule in Thebes,
Is hurrying here toward the palace. He appears   205
Extremely agitated. What news will he bring?

> Enter PENTHEUS. *He addresses the audience, without at first*
> *noticing* CADMUS *and* TEIRESIAS, *who stand at the opposite side*
> *of the stage.*

PENTHEUS   I happen to have been away from Thebes; reports
Of this astounding scandal have just been brought to me.
Our women, it seems, have left their homes on some pretense
Of Bacchic worship, and now are gadding about   210
On the wooded mountain slopes, dancing in honor of
This upstart god Dionysus, whoever he may be.
Amidst these groups of worshippers, they tell me, stand
Bowls full of wine; and our women go creeping off
This way and that to lonely places and give themselves   215
To lecherous men. They are Maenad priestesses, if you please!
Aphrodite supplants Bacchus in their ritual.[8]
Well, those I've caught, my guards are keeping safe; we've tied
Their hands, and lodged them at state expense. Those still at large
On the mountain I am going to hunt out; and that   220
Includes my own mother Agauë and her sisters
Ino and Autonoe. Once they're fast in iron fetters,
I'll put a stop to this outrageous Bacchism.

They tell me, too, some oriental conjurer
Has come from Lydia, a magician with golden hair   225
Flowing in scented ringlets, his face flushed with wine,
His eyes lit with the charm of Aphrodite; and he
Entices young girls with his Bacchic mysteries,
Spends days and nights consorting with them. Once let me
Get that fellow inside my walls—I'll cut his head   230
From his shoulders; that will stop him drumming with his thyrsus,
Tossing his long hair. *He's* the one—this foreigner—
Who says Dionysus is a god; who says he was
Sewn up in Zeus's thigh. The truth about Dionysus
Is that he's dead, burned to a cinder by lightning   235
Along with his mother, because she said Zeus lay with her.
Whoever the man may be, is not his arrogance
An outrage? Has he not earned a rope around his neck?

> PENTHEUS *turns to go, and sees* CADMUS *and* TEIRESIAS.

Why, look! Another miracle! Here's Teiresias
The prophet—in a fawnskin; and my mother's father—   240

---

8. Aphrodite (Roman name, Venus) was the goddess of love and beauty. Bacchus was
one of the many names used for Dionysus. The women who made up Dionysus' train or
participated in his rites were called "Bacchantes" or "Maenads."

A Bacchant with a fennel-wand! Well, there's a sight
For laughter! [*But he is raging, not laughing.*]

Sir, I am ashamed to see two men
Of your age with so little sense of decency.
Come, you're my grandfather: throw down that ivy-wreath, 245
Get rid of that thyrsus! *You* persuaded him to this,
Teiresias. By introducing a new god, you hope
To advance your augurer's business, to collect more fees
For inspecting sacrifices. Listen: your gray hairs
Are your protection; otherwise you'd be sitting now 250
In prison with all these crazy females, for promoting
Pernicious practices. As for women, I tell you this:
Wherever the sparkle of sweet wine adorns their feasts,
No good will follow from such Bacchic ceremonies.
CHORUS Have you no reverence, Sir, no piety? Do you mock 255
Cadmus, who sowed the dragon-seed of earth-born men?
Do you, Echion's son, dishonor your own race?
TEIRESIAS When a good speaker has a sound case to present,
Then eloquence is no great feat. Your fluent tongue
Promises wisdom; but the content of your speech 260
Is ignorant. Power and eloquence in a headstrong man
Spell folly; such a man is a peril to the state.

This new god, whom you ridicule—no words of mine
Could well express the ascendancy he will achieve
In Hellas. There are two powers, young man, which are supreme 265
In human affairs: first, Demeter[9]—the same goddess
Is also Earth; give her which name you please—and she
Supplies mankind with solid food. After her came
Dionysus, Semele's son; the blessing he procured
And gave to men is counterpart to that of bread: 270
The clear juice of the grape. When mortals drink their fill
Of wine, the sufferings of our unhappy race
Are banished, each day's troubles are forgotten in sleep.
There is no other cure for sorrow. Dionysus,
Himself a god, is thus poured out in offering 275
To the gods, so that through him come blessings on mankind.
And do you scorn this legend, that he was sewn up
In Zeus's thigh? I will explain the truth to you.
When Zeus snatched Dionysus from the lightning-flame
And took the child up to Olympus as a god, 280
Hera resolved to cast him out of heaven. But Zeus
Found such means to prevent her as a god will find.
He took a fragment of the ether that surrounds
The earth, fashioned it like a child, presented it
To Hera as a pledge to soothe her jealousy, 285
And saved Dionysus from her. Thus, in time, because
The ancient words for "pledge" and "thigh" are similar,
People confused them, and the "pledge" Zeus gave to Hera
Became transformed, as time went on, into the tale
That Dionysus was sewn up in Zeus's thigh. 290

9. Demeter (Roman name, Ceres) was a goddess of the harvest and of grain. Here she
and Dionysus are used by metonymy for bread and wine.

And this god is a prophet; the Bacchic ecstasy
And frenzy hold a strong prophetic element.
When he fills irresistibly a human body
He gives those so possessed power to foretell the future.
In Ares' province too Dionysus has his share;   295
Sometimes an army, weaponed and drawn up for battle,
Has fled in wild panic before a spear was raised.
This too is an insanity sent by Dionysus.

Ay, and the day will come when, on the very crags
Of Delphi, you shall see him leaping, amidst the blaze   300
Of torches, over the twin-peaked ridge, waving aloft
And brandishing his Bacchic staff, while all Hellas
Exalts him. Pentheus, pay heed to my words. You rely
On force; but it is not force that governs human affairs.
Do not mistake for wisdom that opinion which   305
May rise from a sick mind. Welcome this god to Thebes,
Offer libations to him, celebrate his rites,
Put on his garland. Dionysus will not compel
Women to be chaste, since in all matters self-control
Resides in our own natures. You should consider this;   310
For in the Bacchic ritual, as elsewhere, a woman
Will be safe from corruption if her mind is chaste.

Think of this too: when crowds stand at the city gates
And Thebes extols the name of Pentheus, you rejoice;
So too, I think, the god is glad to receive honor.   315
Well, I at least, and Cadmus, whom you mock, will wear
The ivy-wreath and join the dancing—we are a pair
Of gray heads, but this is our duty; and no words
Of yours shall lure me into fighting against gods.
For a most cruel insanity has warped your mind;   320
While drugs may well have caused it, they can bring no cure.
CHORUS   What you have said, Teiresias, shows no disrespect
   To Apollo; at the same time you prove your judgment sound
   In honoring Dionysus as a mighty god.[1]
CADMUS   My dear son, Teiresias has given you good advice.   325
   Don't stray beyond pious tradition; live with us.
   Your wits have flown to the winds, your sense is foolishness.
   Even if, as you say, Dionysus is no god,
   Let him have *your* acknowledgement; lie royally,
   That Semele may get honor as having borne a god,   330
   And credit come to us and to all our family.

Remember, too, Actaeon's miserable fate—[2]
Torn and devoured by hounds which he himself had bred,
Because he filled the mountains with the boast that he

1. Apollo was the Greek sun god. He was also associated with such activities as poetry, healing, and divination. As a god of divination and prophecy, his most famous shrine was at Delphi.
2. Actaeon was a cousin of Pentheus. There are several accounts of his tragic end. The one more customary than that used here by Euripides was that one day while hunting, he accidentally saw Artemis, the moon goddess but also a patroness of hunting, bathing in a forest pool. The goddess, renowned for her modesty and chastity, was not amused and caused Actaeon to be turned into a stag and to be killed by his own hounds.

Was a more skilful hunter than Artemis herself.   335
Don't share his fate, my son! Come, let me crown your head
With a wreath of ivy; join us in worshipping this god.
PENTHEUS   Keep your hands off! Go to your Bacchic rites, and don't
Wipe off your crazy folly on me. But I will punish
This man who has been your instructor in lunacy.   340
Go, someone, quickly to his seat of augury,
Smash it with crowbars, topple the walls, throw all his things
In wild confusion, turn the whole place upside down,
Fling out his holy fripperies to the hurricane winds!
This sacrilege will sting him more than anything else.   345
The rest of you—go, comb the country and track down
That effeminate foreigner, who plagues our women with
This new disease, fouls the whole land with lechery;
And once you catch him, tie him up and bring him here
To me; I'll deal with him. He shall be stoned to death.   350
He'll wish he'd never brought his Bacchic rites to Thebes.

Exit PENTHEUS.

TEIRESIAS   Foolhardy man! You do not know what you have said.
Before, you were unbalanced; now you are insane.
Come, Cadmus; let us go and pray both for this man,
Brutish as he is, and for our city, and beg the god   355
To show forbearance. Come, now, take your ivy staff
And let us go. Try to support me; we will help
Each other. It would be scandalous for two old men
To fall; still, we must go, and pay our due service
To Dionysus, son of Zeus. Cadmus, the name   360
Pentheus means *sorrow*. God grant he may not bring sorrow
Upon your house. Do not take that as prophecy;
I judge his acts. Such foolish words bespeak a fool.

Exeunt TEIRESIAS *and* CADMUS.

CHORUS
Holiness, Queen of heaven,   *Strophe 1*
Holiness, golden-winged ranging the earth,   365
Do you hear his blasphemy?
Pentheus dares—do you hear?—to revile the god of joy,
The son of Semele, who when the gay-crowned feast is set
Is named among gods the chief;
Whose gifts are joy and union of soul in dancing,   370
Joy in music of flutes,
Joy when sparkling wine at feasts of the gods
Soothes the sore regret,
Banishes every grief,
When the reveler rests, enfolded deep   375
In the cool shade of ivy-shoots,
On wine's soft pillow of sleep.

The brash, unbridled tongue,   *Antistrophe 1*
The lawless folly of fools, will end in pain.
But the life of wise content   380
Is blest with quietness, escapes the storm
And keeps its house secure.

Though blessed gods dwell in the distant skies,
They watch the ways of men.
To know much is not to be wise.   385
Pride more than mortal hastens life to its end;
And they who in pride pretend
Beyond man's limit, will lose what lay
Close to their hand and sure.
I count it madness, and know no cure can mend   390
The evil man and his evil way.

O to set foot on Aphrodite's island,   *Strophe 2*
On Cyprus, haunted by the Loves, who enchant
Brief life with sweetness; or in that strange land
Whose fertile river carves a hundred channels   395
To enrich her rainless sand;
Or where the sacred pastures of Olympus slant
Down to Pieria, where the Muses dwell—
Take me, O Bromius, take me and inspire
Laughter and worship! There our holy spell   400
And ecstasy are welcome; there the gentle band
Of Graces have their home, and sweet Desire.[3]

Dionysus, son of Zeus, delights in banquets;   *Antistrophe 2*
And his dear love is Peace, giver of wealth,
Savior of young men's lives—a goddess rare!   405
In wine, his gift that charms all griefs away,
Alike both rich and poor may have their part.
His enemy is the man who has no care
To pass his years in happiness and health,
His days in quiet and his nights in joy,   410
Watchful to keep aloof both mind and heart
From men whose pride claims more than mortals may.
The life that wins the poor man's common voice,
His creed, his practice—this shall be my choice.

> *Some of the guards whom* PENTHEUS *sent to arrest* DIONYSUS
> *now enter with their prisoner.* PENTHEUS *enters from the palace.*

GUARD   Pentheus, we've brought the prey you sent us out to catch;   415
We hunted him, and here he is. But, Sir, we found
The beast was gentle; made no attempt to run away,
Just held his hands out to be tied; didn't turn pale,
But kept his florid color, smiling, telling us
To tie him up and run him in; gave us no trouble   420
At all, just waited for us. Naturally I felt
A bit embarrassed. "You'll excuse me, Sir," I said,
"I don't want to arrest you; it's the king's command."

Another thing, Sir—those women you rounded up
And put in fetters in the prison, those Bacchants;   425
Well, they're all gone, turned loose to the glens; and there they are,

---

3. The island of Cyprus was associated with the goddess Aphrodite. Pieria was a region near Mount Olympus associated with the Muses, minor goddesses related to learning and the arts. Loves, Graces, and Desire are figured as minor goddesses attendant on Aphrodite.

Frisking about, calling on Bromius their god.
The fetters simply opened and fell off their feet;
The bolts shot back, untouched by mortal hand; the doors
Flew wide. Master, this man has come here with a load   430
Of miracles. Well, what happens next is your concern.
PENTHEUS   Untie this man's hands. [*The* GUARD *does so.*] He's securely
    in the trap.
He's not so nimble-footed as to escape me now.
Well, friend: your shape is not unhandsome—for the pursuit
Of women, which is the purpose of your presence here.   435
You are no wrestler, I can tell from these long curls
Cascading most seductively over your cheek.
Your skin, too, shows a whiteness carefully preserved;
You keep away from the sun's heat, walk in the shade,
So hunting Aphrodite with your lovely face.   440

Ah, well; first tell me who you are. What is your birth?
DIONYSUS   Your question's easily answered, it is no secret.
Perhaps you have heard of Tmolus, a mountain decked with flowers.
PENTHEUS   A range that curves round Sardis? Yes, I know of it.
DIONYSUS   That is my home. I am a Lydian by birth.   445
PENTHEUS   How comes it that you bring these rituals to Hellas?
DIONYSUS   Dionysus, son of Zeus, himself instructed me.
PENTHEUS   Is there a Lydian Zeus, then, who begets new gods?
DIONYSUS   I speak of Zeus who wedded Semele here in Thebes.
PENTHEUS   Did he possess you in a dream, or visibly?   450
DIONYSUS   Yes, face to face; he gave these mysteries to me.
PENTHEUS   These mysteries you speak of: what form do they take?
DIONYSUS   To the uninitiated that must not be told.
PENTHEUS   And those who worship—what advantage do they gain?
DIONYSUS   It is not for you to learn; yet it is worth knowing.   455
PENTHEUS   You bait your answer well, to arouse my eagerness.
DIONYSUS   His rituals abhor a man of impious life.
PENTHEUS   You say you saw him face to face: what was he like?
DIONYSUS   Such as he chose to be. I had no say in that.
PENTHEUS   Still you sidetrack my question with an empty phrase. 460
DIONYSUS   Just so. A prudent speech sleeps in a foolish ear.
PENTHEUS   Is Thebes the first place where you have introduced this
    God?
DIONYSUS   No; every eastern land dances these mysteries.
PENTHEUS   No doubt. Their moral standards fall far below ours.
DIONYSUS   In this they are superior; but their customs differ.   465
PENTHEUS   Do you perform these mysteries by night or day?
DIONYSUS   Chiefly by night. Darkness promotes religious awe.
PENTHEUS   For women darkness is deceptive and impure.
DIONYSUS   Impurity can be pursued by daylight too.
PENTHEUS   You must be punished for your foul and slippery tongue. 470
DIONYSUS   And you for blindness and impiety to the god.
PENTHEUS   How bold this Bacchant is! A practiced pleader too.
DIONYSUS   Tell me my sentence. What dread pain will you inflict?
PENTHEUS   I'll start by cutting of your delicate long hair.
DIONYSUS   My hair is sacred; I preserve it for the god.   475
PENTHEUS   And next, that thyrsus in your hand—give it to me.
DIONYSUS   Take it from me yourself; it is the god's emblem.

PENTHEUS   I'll lock you up in prison and keep you there.

DIONYSUS   The god
    Himself, whenever I desire, will set me free.

PENTHEUS   Of course—when you, with all your Bacchants, call to him! 480

DIONYSUS   He is close at hand here, and sees what is done to me.

PENTHEUS   Indeed? Where is he, then? Not visible to my eyes.

DIONYSUS   Beside me. You, being a blasphemer, see nothing.

PENTHEUS   [*to the* GUARDS]   Get hold of him; he's mocking me and the
    whole city.

DIONYSUS   [*to the* GUARDS]   Don't bind me, I warn you. [*To* PEN-
    THEUS.] I am sane, and you are mad.   485

PENTHEUS   My word overrules yours. [*To the* GUARDS.] I tell you, bind
    him fast.

DIONYSUS   You know not what you are saying, what you do, nor who
    You are.

PENTHEUS   Who? Pentheus, son of Echion and Agauë.

DIONYSUS   Your name points to calamity. It fits you well.   490

PENTHEUS   Take him away and shut him in my stables, where
    He can stay staring at darkness.—You can dance in there!
    As for these women you've brought as your accomplices,
    I'll either send them to the slave-market to be sold,
    Or keep them in my own household to work the looms;   495
    And that will stop their fingers drumming on tambourines!

DIONYSUS   I'll go. Nothing can touch me that is not ordained.
    But I warn you: Dionysus, who you say is dead,
    Will come in swift pursuit to avenge this sacrilege.
    You are putting *him* in prison when you lay hands on me.   500

        GUARDS *take* DIONYSUS *away to the stables;* PENTHEUS *follows.*

CHORUS
    Dirce sweet and holy maid,[4]   *Strophe*
    Acheloüs' Theban daughter,
    Once the child of Zeus was made
    Welcome in your welling water,
    When the lord of earth and sky   505
    Snatched him from the undying flame,
    Laid him safe within his thigh,
    Calling loud the infant's name:
    "Twice-born Dithyrambus![5] Come,
    Enter here your father's womb;   510
    Bacchic child, I now proclaim
    This in Thebes shall be your name."
    Now, divine Dirce, when my head is crowned
    And my feet dance in Bacchus' revelry—
    Now you reject me from your holy ground.   515
    Why should you fear me? By the purple fruit
    That glows in glory on Dionysus' tree,
    His dread name yet shall haunt your memory!

4. The stream of Dirce in Thebes was associated with a queen of Thebes who was changed into a stream by Dionysus after she had mistreated her husband's niece and been killed by being tied to a bull by that lady's son. According to that legend she had been a worshipper of Dionysus and was changed therefore to a stream as a re- ward. Euripides here seems to be dealing with an earlier myth in which the river nymph Dirce, daughter of the river god Acheloüs, gave sanctuary to the infant Dionysus.

5. Dithyrambus (twice-born) was an- other name for Dionysus.

Oh, what anger lies beneath   *Antistrophe*
Pentheus' voice and sullen face—   520
Offspring of the dragon's teeth,
And Echion's earth-born race,
Brute with bloody jaws agape,
God-defying, gross and grim,
Slander of his human shape!   525
Soon he'll chain us limb to limb—
Bacchus' servants! Yes, and more:
Even now our comrade lies
Deep on his dark prison floor.
Dionysus! do your eyes   530
See us? O son of Zeus, the oppressor's rod
Falls on your worshippers; come, mighty god,
Brandish your golden thyrsus and descend
From great Olympus; touch this murderous man,
And bring his violence to a sudden end!   535

Where are you, Dionysus? Leading your dancing bands   *Epode*
Over the mountain slopes, past many a wild beast's lair,
Or on Corycian crags,[6] with the thyrsus in their hands?
Or in the wooded coverts, maybe, of Olympus, where
Orpheus once gathered the trees and mountain beasts,   540
Gathered them with his lyre, and sang an enchanting air.
Happy vale of Pieria! Bacchus delights in you;
He will cross the flood and foam of the Axius river, and there
He will bring his whirling Maenads, with dancing and with feasts—
Cross the father of waters, Lydias, generous giver   545
Of wealth and luck, they say, to the land he wanders through,
Whose famous horses graze by the rich and lovely river.

> *Suddenly a shout is heard from inside the building—the voice of* DIONYSUS.

DIONYSUS   Io, Io! Do you know my voice, do you hear?
    Worshippers of Bacchus! Io, Io![7]
CHORUS   Who is that? Where is he?   550
    The shout of Dionysus is calling us!
DIONYSUS   Io, Io! hear me again:
    I am the son of Semele, the son of Zeus!
CHORUS   Io, Io, our lord, our lord!
    Come, then, come to our company, lord of joy!   555
DIONYSUS   O dreadful earthquake, shake the floor of the world!
CHORUS   [*with a scream of terror*]   Pentheus' palace is falling, crumbling
     in pieces! [*They continue severally.*]
    —Dionysus stands in the palace; bow before him!
    —We bow before him.—See how the roof and pillars
    Plunge to the ground!—Bromius is with us,   560
    He shouts from prison the shout of victory!

> *The flame on Semele's tomb grows and brightens.*

6. Corycia was a nymph associated with Mt. Parnassus.
7. "Io" was a cry of rather generalized meaning used by worshippers in praise or supplication.

DIONYSUS   Fan to a blaze the flame the lightning lit;
  Kindle the conflagration of Pentheus' palace!
CHORUS   Look, look, look!
  Do you see, do you see the flame of Semele's tomb,   565
  The flame that lived when she died of the lightning-stroke?

  A noise of crashing masonry is heard.

  Down, trembling Maenads! Hurl yourselves to the ground.
  Your god is wrecking the palace, roof to floor;
  He heard our cry—he is coming, the son of Zeus!

  The doors open and DIONYSUS *appears.*

DIONYSUS   Women of Asia, why do you cower thus, prostrate and
      terrified?   570
  Surely you could hear Dionysus shattering Pentheus' palace? Come,
  Lift yourselves up, take good courage, stop this trembling of your
      limbs!
CHORUS   We are saved! Oh, what a joy to hear your Bacchic call ring
      out!
  We were all alone, deserted; you have come, and we rejoice.
DIONYSUS   Were you comfortless, despondent, when I was escorted in, 575
  Helpless, sentenced to be cast in Pentheus' murky prison cell?
CHORUS   Who could help it? What protector had we, once deprived
      of you?
  Tell us now how you escaped the clutches of this wicked man.
DIONYSUS   I alone, at once, unaided, effortlessly freed myself.
CHORUS   How could that be? Did not Pentheus bind your arms with
      knotted ropes?   580
DIONYSUS   There I made a mockery of him. He thought he was bind-
      ing me;
  But he neither held nor touched me, save in his deluded mind.
  Near the mangers where he meant to tie me up, he found a bull;
  And he tied his rope round the bull's knees and hooves, panting with
      rage,
  Dripping sweat, biting his lips, while I sat quietly by and watched. 585
  It was then that Dionysus shook the building, made the flame
  On his mother's tomb flare up. When Pentheus saw this, he supposed
  The whole place was burning. He rushed this way, that way, calling
      out
  To the servants to bring water; every slave about the place
  Was engaged upon this futile task. He left it presently,   590
  Thinking I had escaped; snatched up his murderous sword, darted
      indoors.
  Thereupon Dionysus—as it seemed to me; I merely guess—
  Made a phantom hover in the courtyard. Pentheus flew at it,
  Stabbing at the empty sunlight, thinking he was killing *me*.
  Yet a further humiliation Bacchus next contrived for him: 595
  He destroyed the stable buildings. Pentheus sees my prison now
  Lying there, a heap of rubble; and the picture grieves his heart.
  Now he's dazed and helpless with exhaustion. He has dropped his
      sword.
  He, a man, dared to take arms against a god. I quietly walked
  Out of the palace here to join you, giving Pentheus not a thought.   600
  But I hear his heavy tread inside the palace. Soon, I think,

He'll be out here in the forecourt. After what has happened now,
What will he have to say? For all his rage, he shall not ruffle *me*.
It's a wise man's part to practice a smooth-tempered self-control.

Enter PENTHEUS.

PENTHEUS   This is outrageous. He has escaped—that foreigner.   605
Only just now I had him locked up and in chains.

He sees DIONYSUS *and gives an excited shout.*

He's there! Well, what's going on now? How did you get out?
How dare you show your face here at my very door?
DIONYSUS   Stay where you are. You are angry; now control yourself.
PENTHEUS   You were tied up inside there. How did you escape?   610
DIONYSUS   I said—did you not hear?—that I should be set free—
PENTHEUS   By whom? You're always finding something new to say.
DIONYSUS   By him who plants for mortals the rich-clustered vine.
PENTHEUS   The god who frees his worshippers from every law.
DIONYSUS   Your insult to Dionysus is a compliment.   615
PENTHEUS [*to attendant* GUARDS]   Go round the walls and tell them to
close every gate.
DIONYSUS   And why? Or cannot gods pass even over walls?
PENTHEUS   Oh, you know everything—save what you ought to know.
DIONYSUS   The things most needful to be known, those things I know.   620
But listen first to what this man has to report;
He comes from the mountain, and he has some news for you.
I will stay here; I promise not to run away.

Enter a HERDSMAN.

HERDSMAN   Pentheus, great king of Thebes! I come from Mount
Cithaeron,
Whose slopes are never free from dazzling shafts of snow.
PENTHEUS   And what comes next? What urgent message do you bring?   625
HERDSMAN   I have seen the holy Bacchae, who like a flight of spears
Went streaming bare-limbed, frantic, out of the city gate.
I have come with the intention of telling you, my lord,
And the city, of their strange and terrible doings—things
Beyond all wonder. But first I would learn whether   630
I may speak freely of what is going on there, or
If I should trim my words. I fear your hastiness,
My lord, your anger, your too potent royalty.
PENTHEUS   From me fear nothing. Say all that you have to say;
Anger should not grow hot against the innocent.   635
The more dreadful your story of these Bacchic rites,
The heavier punishment I will inflict upon
This man who enticed our women to their evil ways.
HERDSMAN   At dawn today, when first the sun's rays warmed the earth,
My herd of cattle was slowly climbing up toward   640
The high pastures; and there I saw three separate
Companies of women. The leader of one company
Was Autonoe; your mother Agauë was at the head
Of the second, Ino of the third; and they all lay
Relaxed and quietly sleeping. Some rested on beds   645
Of pine-needles, others had pillows of oak-leaves.
They lay just as they had thrown themselves down on the ground,

But modestly, not—as you told us—drunk with wine
Or flute-music, seeking the solitary woods
For the pursuit of love.   650
When your mother Agauë
Heard the horned cattle bellowing, she stood upright
Among the Bacchae, and called to them to stir themselves
From sleep; and they shook off the strong sleep from their eyes
And leaped to their feet. They were a sight to marvel at   655
For modest comeliness; women both old and young,
Girls still unmarried. First they let their hair fall free
Over their shoulders; some tied up the fastenings
Of fawnskins they had loosened; round the dappled fur
Curled snakes that licked their cheeks. Some would have in their arms 660
A young gazelle, or wild wolf-cubs, to which they gave
Their own white milk—those of them who had left at home
Young children newly born, so that their breasts were full.
And they wore wreathes of ivy-leaves, or oak, or flowers
Of bryony. One would strike her thyrsus on a rock,   665
And from the rock a limpid stream of water sprang.
Another dug her wand into the earth, and there
The god sent up a fountain of wine. Those who desired
Milk had only to scratch the earth with fingertips,
And there was the white stream flowing for them to drink,   670
While from the thyrsus a sweet ooze of honey dripped.
Oh! if you had been there and seen all this, you would
Have offered prayers to this god whom you now condemn.
We herdsmen, then, and shepherds gathered to exchange
Rival reports of these strange and extraordinary   675
Performances; and one, who had knocked about the town,
And had a ready tongue, addressed us: "You who live
On the holy mountain heights," he said, "shall we hunt down
Agauë, Pentheus' mother, and bring her back from these
Rituals, and gratify the king? What do you say?"   680
This seemed a good suggestion; so we hid ourselves
In the leafy bushes, waiting. When the set time came,
The women began brandishing their wands, preparing
To dance, calling in unison on the son of Zeus,
"Iacchus! Bromius!"[8] And with them the whole mountain,   685
And all the creatures there, joined in the mystic rite
Of Dionysus, and with their motion all things moved.

Now, Agauë as she danced passed close to me; and I
At once leaped out from hiding, bent on capturing her.
But she called out, "Oh, my swift-footed hounds, these men   690
Are hunting us. Come, follow me! Each one of you
Arm herself with the holy thyrsus, and follow me!"

So we fled, and escaped being torn in pieces by
Those possessed women. But our cattle were there, cropping
The fresh grass; and the women attacked them, with their bare
hands.   695
You could see one take a full-uddered bellowing young heifer

---

8. "Iacchus" and "Bromius" were names of Dionysus.

And hold it by the legs with her two arms stretched wide;
Others seized on our cows and tore them limb from limb;
You'd see some ribs, or a cleft hoof, tossed high and low;
And rags of flesh hung from pine-branches, dripping blood. 700
Bulls, which one moment felt proud rage hot in their horns,
The next were thrown bodily to the ground, dragged down
By hands of girls in thousands; and they stripped the flesh
From the bodies faster than you could wink your royal eyes.
Then, skimming bird-like over the surface of the ground, 705
They scoured the plain which stretches by Asopus' banks
And yields rich crops for Thebes; and like an enemy force
They fell on Hysiae and Erythrae, two villages
On the low slopes of Cithaeron, and ransacked them both;
Snatched babies out of the houses; any plunder which 710
They carried on their shoulders stayed there without straps—
Nothing fell to the ground, not bronze or iron; they carried
Fire on their heads, and yet their soft hair was not burned.
The villagers, enraged at being so plundered, armed
Themselves to resist; and then, my lord, an amazing sight 715
Was to be seen. The spears those men were throwing drew
No blood; but the women, hurling a thyrsus like a spear,
Dealt wounds; in short, those women turned the men to flight.
There was the power of a god in that. Then they went back
To the place where they had started from, to those fountains 720
The god had caused to flow for them. And they washed off
The blood; and snakes licked clean the stains, till their cheeks shone.

So, master, whoever this divinity may be,
Receive him in this land. His powers are manifold;
But chiefly, as I hear, he gave to men the vine 725
To cure their sorrows, and without wine, neither love
Nor any other pleasure would be left for us.
CHORUS   I shrink from speaking freely before the king; yet I
Will say it: there is no greater god than Dionysus.
PENTHEUS   This Bacchic arrogance advances on us like 730
A spreading fire, disgracing us before all Hellas.
We must act now. [*To the* HERDSMAN.] Go quickly to the Electran
gate;[9]
Tell all my men who carry shields, heavy or light,
All riders on fast horses, all my archers with
Their twanging bows, to meet me there in readiness 735
For an onslaught on these maniacs. This is beyond
All bearing, if we must let women so defy us.
DIONYSUS   You refuse, Pentheus, to give heed to what I say
Or change your ways. Yet still, despite your wrongs to me,
I warn you: stay here quietly; do not take up arms 740
Against a god. Dionysus will not tolerate
Attempts to drive his worshippers from their holy hills.
PENTHEUS   I'll not have you instruct me. You have escaped your
chains;
Now be content—or must I punish you again?
DIONYSUS   I would control my rage and sacrifice to him 745

9. One of the seven gates of Thebes.

If I were you, rather than kick against the goad.
Can you, a mortal, measure your strength with a god's?
PENTHEUS   I'll sacrifice, yes—blood of women, massacred
Wholesale, as they deserve, among Cithaeron's glens.
DIONYSUS   Your army will be put to flight. What a disgrace   750
For bronze shields to be routed by those women's wands!
PENTHEUS   How can I deal with this impossible foreigner?
In prison or out, nothing will make him hold his tongue.
DIONYSUS   My friend, a happy settlement may still be found.
PENTHEUS   How? must I be a slave to my own slave-women?   755
DIONYSUS   I will, using no weapons, bring those women here.
PENTHEUS   Hear that, for the gods' sake! You're playing me some trick.
DIONYSUS   What trick?—if I am ready to save you by my skill.
PENTHEUS   You've planned this with them, so that the rituals can go
on.
DIONYSUS   Indeed I have planned this—not with them, but with the
god.   760
PENTHEUS   Bring out my armor, there!—That is enough from you.
DIONYSUS   [*with an authoritative shout*]   Wait! [*Then quietly.*] Do you
want *to see*
Those women, where they sit together, up in the hills?
PENTHEUS   Why, yes; for that, I'd give a weighty sum of gold.
DIONYSUS   What made you fall into this great desire to see?   765
PENTHEUS   It would cause me distress to see them drunk with wine.
DIONYSUS   Yet you would gladly witness this distressing sight?
PENTHEUS   Of course—if I could quietly sit under the pines.
DIONYSUS   They'll track you down, even if you go there secretly.
PENTHEUS   Openly, then. Yes, what you say is very true.   770
DIONYSUS   Then shall I lead you? You will undertake to go?
PENTHEUS   Yes, lead me there at once; I am impatient.
DIONYSUS   Then,
You must first dress yourself in a fine linen gown.
PENTHEUS   Why in a linen gown? Must I then change my sex?   775
DIONYSUS   In case they kill you, if you are seen there as a man.
PENTHEUS   Again you are quite right. How you think of everything!
DIONYSUS   It was Dionysus who inspired me with that thought.
PENTHEUS   Then how can your suggestion best be carried out?
DIONYSUS   I'll come indoors with you myself and dress you.   780
PENTHEUS   What?
Dress me? In woman's clothes? But I would be ashamed.
DIONYSUS   Do you want to watch the Maenads? Are you less eager
now?
PENTHEUS   What kind of dress did you say you would put on me?
DIONYSUS   First I'll adorn your head with locks of flowing hair.   785
PENTHEUS   And after that? What style of costume shall I have?
DIONYSUS   A full-length robe; and on your head shall be a snood.
PENTHEUS   Besides these, is there anything else you'll put on me?
DIONYSUS   A dappled fawnskin round you, a thyrsus in your hand.
PENTHEUS   I could not bear to dress myself in woman's clothes.   790
DIONYSUS   If you join battle with the Maenads, blood will flow.
PENTHEUS   You are right; I must first go to spy on them.
DIONYSUS   That way
Is better than inviting force by using it.
PENTHEUS   And how shall I get through the town without being seen?   795

DIONYSUS We'll go by empty streets; I will show you the way.
PENTHEUS The Maenads must not mock me; better anything
  Than that. Now I'll go in, and think how best to act.
DIONYSUS You may do so. My preparations are all made.
PENTHEUS I'll go in, then; and either I'll set forth at the head   800
  Of my armed men—or else I'll follow your advice.

Exit PENTHEUS.

DIONYSUS Women, this man is walking into the net. He will
  Visit the Bacchae; and there death shall punish him.

  Dionysus!—for you are not far distant—all is now
  In your hands. Let us be revenged on him! And first   805
  Fill him with wild delusions, drive him out of his mind.
  While sane, he'll not consent to put on woman's clothes;
  Once free from the curb of reason, he will put them on.
  I long to set Thebes laughing at him, as he walks
  In female garb through all the streets; to humble him   810
  From the arrogance he showed when first he threatened me.
  Now I will go, to array Pentheus in the dress
  Which he will take down with him to the house of Death,
  Slaughtered by his own mother's hands. And he shall know
  Dionysus, son of Zeus, in his full nature God,   815
  Most terrible, although most gentle, to mankind.

  DIONYSUS *follows* PENTHEUS *into the palace.*

CHORUS
  O for long nights of worship, gay   *Strophe*
  With the pale gleam of dancing feet,
  With head tossed high to the dewy air—
  Pleasure mysterious and sweet!   820
  O for the joy of a fawn at play
  In the fragrant meadow's green delight,
  Who has leaped out free from the woven snare,
  Away from the terror of chase and flight,
  And the huntsman's shout, and the straining pack,   825
  And skims the sand by the river's brim
  With the speed of wind in each aching limb,
  To the blessed lonely forest where
  The soil's unmarked by a human track,
  And leaves hang thick and the shades are dim.   830

  What prayer should we call wise?   *Refrain*
  What gift of Heaven should man
  Count a more noble prize,
  A prayer more prudent, than
  To stretch a conquering arm   835
  Over the fallen crest
  Of those who wished us harm?
  And what is noble every heart loves best.

  Slow, yet unfailing, move the Powers   *Antistrophe*
  Of Heaven with the moving hours.   840
  When mind runs mad, dishonors God,

And worships self and senseless pride,
Then Law eternal wields the rod.
Still Heaven hunts down the impious man,
Though divine subtlety may hide   845
Time's creeping foot. No mortal ought
To challenge Time—to overbear
Custom in act, or age in thought.
All men, at little cost, may share
The blessing of a pious creed;   850
Truths more than mortal, which began
In the beginning, and belong
To very nature—these indeed
Reign in our world, are fixed and strong.

What prayer should we call wise?   *Refrain* 855
What gift of Heaven should man
Count a more noble prize,
A prayer more prudent, than
To stretch a conquering arm
Over the fallen crest   860
Of those who wished us harm?
And what is noble every heart loves best.

Blest is the man who cheats the stormy sea   *Epode*
And safely moors beside the sheltering quay;
So, blest is he who triumphs over trial.   865
One man, by various means, in wealth or strength
Outdoes his neighbor; hope in a thousand hearts
Colors a thousand different dreams; at length
Some find a dear fulfillment, some denial.
  But this I say,   870
  That he who best
  Enjoys each passing day
  Is truly blest.

> *Enter* DIONYSUS. *He turns to call* PENTHEUS.

DIONYSUS   Come, perverse man, greedy for sights you should not see,
Eager for deeds you should not do—Pentheus! Come out   875
Before the palace and show yourself to me, wearing
The garb of a frenzied Bacchic woman, and prepared
To spy on your mother and all her Bacchic company.

> *Enter* PENTHEUS *dressed as a Bacchic devotee. He is dazed and
> entirely subservient to* DIONYSUS.

You are the very image of one of Cadmus' daughters.
PENTHEUS   Why now! I seem to see two suns; a double Thebes;   880
Our city's wall with seven gates appears double.

> DIONYSUS *takes* PENTHEUS *by the hand and leads him forward.*

You are a bull I see leading me forward now;
A pair of horns seems to have grown upon your head.
Were you a beast before? You have become a bull.

DIONYSUS   The god then did not favor us; he is with us now,   885
 We have made our peace with him; you see as you should see.
PENTHEUS   How do I look? Tell me, is not the way I stand
 Like the way Ino stands, or like my mother Agaüe?
DIONYSUS   Looking at you, I think I see them both. Wait, now;
 Here is a curl has slipped out of its proper place,   890
 Not as I tucked it carefully below your snood.
PENTHEUS   Indoors, as I was tossing my head up and down
 Like a Bacchic dancer, I dislodged it from its place.
DIONYSUS   Come, then; I am the one who should look after you.
 I'll fix it in its place again. There; lift your head.   895
PENTHEUS   You dress me, please; I have put myself in your hands now.
DIONYSUS   Your girdle has come loose; and now your dress does not
 Hang, as it should, in even pleats down to the ankle.
PENTHEUS   That's true, I think—at least by the right leg, on this side;
 But on the other side the gown hangs well to the heel.   900
DIONYSUS   You'll surely count me chief among your friends, when you
 Witness the Maenads' unexpected modesty.
PENTHEUS   Ought I to hold my thyrsus in the right hand—so,
 Or in the left, to look more like a Bacchanal?
DIONYSUS   In the right hand; and raise it at the same time as   905
 Your right foot. I am glad you are so changed in mind.
PENTHEUS   Could I lift up on my own shoulders the whole weight
 Of Mount Cithaeron, and all the women dancing there?
DIONYSUS   You could, if you so wished. The mind you had before
 Was sickly; now your mind is just as it should be.   910
PENTHEUS   Shall we take crowbars? Or shall I put my shoulder under
 The rocks, and heave the mountain up with my two arms?
DIONYSUS   Oh, come, now! Don't destroy the dwellings of the nymphs,
 And the quiet places where Pan sits to play his pipes.
PENTHEUS   You are right. We ought not to use force to overcome   915
 Those women. I will hide myself among the pines.
DIONYSUS   Hide—yes, you'll hide, and find the proper hiding place
 For one who comes by stealth to spy on Bacchic rites.
PENTHEUS   Why, yes! I think they are there now in their hidden nests,
 Like birds, all clasped close in the sweet prison of love.   920
DIONYSUS   What you are going to watch for is this very thing!
 Perhaps you will catch them—if you are not first caught yourself.
PENTHEUS   Now take me through the central streets of Thebes; for I
 Am the one man among them all that dares do this.
DIONYSUS   One man alone, you agonize for Thebes; therefore   925
 It is your destined ordeal that awaits you now.
 Come with me; I will bring you safely to the place;
 Another shall conduct you back.
PENTHEUS   My mother—yes?
DIONYSUS   A sight for all to witness.   930
PENTHEUS   To this end I go.
DIONYSUS   You will return borne high—
PENTHEUS   Royal magnificence!
DIONYSUS   In your own mother's arms.
PENTHEUS   You insist that I be spoiled.   935
DIONYSUS   One kind of spoiling.
PENTHEUS   Yet I win what I deserve.

Exit PENTHEUS.

DIONYSUS   Pentheus, you are a man to make men fear; fearful
        Will be your end—an end that shall lift up your fame
        To the height of heaven.   940
        Agauë, and you her sisters, daughters of Cadmus,
        Stretch out your hands! See, I am bringing this young man
        To his great battle; and I and Bromius shall be
        Victors. What more shall happen, the event will show.

                                                        Exit DIONYSUS.

CHORUS
        Hounds of Madness, fly to the mountain, fly   *Strophe* 945
        Where Cadmus' daughters are dancing in ecstasy!
        Madden them like a frenzied herd stampeding,
        Against the madman hiding in woman's clothes
        To spy on the Maenad's rapture!
        First his mother shall see him craning his neck   950
        Down from a rounded rock or a sharp crag,
        And shout to the Maenads, "Who is the man, you Bacchae,
        Who has come to the mountain, come to the mountain spying
        On the swift wild mountain dances of Cadmus' daughters?
        Which of you is his mother?   955
        No, that lad never lay in a woman's womb;
        A lioness gave him suck, or a Libyan Gorgon!"[1]

        Justice, now be revealed! Now let your sword   *Refrain*
        Thrust—through and through—to sever the throat
        Of the godless, lawless, shameless son of Echion,   960
        Who sprang from the womb of Earth!

        See! With contempt of right, with a reckless rage   *Antistrophe*
        To combat your and your mother's mysteries, Bacchus,
        With maniac fury out he goes, stark mad,
        For a trial of strength against *your* invincible arm!   965
        His proud purposes death shall discipline.
        He who unquestioning gives the gods their due,
        And knows that his days are as dust, shall live untouched.
        I have no wish to grudge the wise their wisdom;
        But the joys *I* seek are greater, outshine all others,   970
        And lead our life to goodness and loveliness:
        The joy of the holy heart
        That night and day is bent to honor the gods
        And disown all custom that breaks the bounds of right.

        Justice, now be revealed! Now let your sword   *Refrain* 975
        Thrust—through and through—to sever the throat
        Of the godless, lawless, shameless son of Echion,
        Who sprang from the womb of Earth!

        *Then with growing excitement, shouting in unison, and dancing
        to the rhythm of their words.*

1. The Gorgons were three monstrous sisters who had live snakes on their heads instead
of hair. Their other features were hardly more beautiful, and they were therefore believed
to be capable of turning to stone anyone who gazed on them. One of them, Medusa, was
slain by the hero Perseus.

Come, Dionysus! *Epode*
Come, and appear to us! 980
Come like a bull or a
Hundred-headed serpent,
Come like a lion snorting
Flame from your nostrils!
Swoop down, Bacchus, on the 985
Hunter of the Bacchae;
Smile at him and snare him;
Then let the stampeding
Herd of the Maenads
Throw him and throttle him, 990
Catch, trip, trample him to death!

Enter a MESSENGER.

MESSENGER   O house that once shone glorious throughout Hellas, home
Of the old Sidonian king who planted in this soil
The dragon's earth-born harvest! How I weep for you!
Slave though I am, I suffer with my master's fate. 995
CHORUS   Are you from the mountain, from the Bacchic rites? What
news?
MESSENGER   Pentheus, son of Echion, is dead.
CHORUS   Bromius, lord! Your divine power is revealed!
MESSENGER   What, woman? What was that you said? Do you exult
When such a cruel fate has overtaken the king? 1000
CHORUS   I am no Greek.
I sing my joy in a foreign tune.
Not any more do I cower in terror of prison!
MESSENGER   Do you think Thebes has no men left who can take com-
mand?
CHORUS   Dionysus commands *me;* 1005
Not Thebes, but Dionysus.
MESSENGER   Allowance must be made for you; yet, to rejoice
At the accomplishment of horrors is not right.
CHORUS   Tell us everything, then: this tyrant king
Bent on cruelty—how did he die? 1010
MESSENGER   When we had left behind the outlying parts of Thebes
And crossed the river Asopus, we began to climb
Toward the uplands of Cithaeron, Pentheus and I—
I went as his attendant—and the foreigner
Who was our guide to the spectacle we were to see. 1015
Well, first we sat down in a grassy glade. We kept
Our footsteps and our talk as quiet as possible,
So as to see without being seen. We found ourselves
In a valley full of streams, with cliffs on either side.
There, under the close shade of branching pines, the Maenads 1020
Were sitting, their hands busy at their happy tasks;
Some of them twining a fresh crown of ivy-leaves
For a stripped thyrsus; others, gay as fillies loosed
From painted yokes, were singing holy Bacchic songs,
Each answering other. But the ill-fated Pentheus saw 1025
None of this; and he said, "My friend, from where we stand
My eyes cannot make out these so-called worshippers;
But if I climbed a towering pine-tree on the cliff

I would have a clear view of their shameful practices."
And then I saw that foreigner do an amazing thing.   1030
He took hold of a pine-tree's soaring, topmost branch,
And dragged it down, down, down to the dark earth. It was bent
In a circle as a bow is bent, as a wheel's curve,
Drawn with a compass, bends the rim to its own shape;
The foreigner took that mountain pine in his two hands   1035
And bent it down—a thing no mortal man could do.
Then seating Pentheus on a high branch, he began
To let the tree spring upright, slipping it through his hands
Steadily, taking care he should not be flung off.
The pine trunk, straightened, soared into the soaring sky,   1040
Bearing my master seated astride, so that he was
More visible to the Maenads than they were to him.
He was just coming into view on his high perch
When out of the sky a voice—Dionysus, I suppose;
That foreigner was nowhere to be seen—pealed forth: 1045
"Women, here is the man who made a mock of you,
And me, and of my holy rites. Now punish him."
And in the very moment the voice spoke, a flash
Of dreadful fire stretched between earth and high heaven.

The air fell still. The wooded glade held every leaf   1050
Still. You could hear no cry of any beast. The women,
Not having caught distinctly what the voice uttered,
Stood up and gazed around. Then came a second word
Of command. As soon as Cadmus' daughters recognized
The clear bidding of Bacchus, with the speed of doves   1055
They darted forward, and all the Bacchae after them.
Through the torrent-filled valley, over the rocks, possessed
By the very breath of Bacchus they went leaping on.
Then, when they saw my master crouched high in the pine,
At first they climbed the cliff which towered opposite,   1060
And violently flung at him pieces of rocks, or boughs
Of pine trees which they hurled as javelins; and some
Aimed with the thyrsus; through the high air all around
Their wretched target missiles flew. Yet every aim
Fell short, the tree's height baffled all their eagerness;   1065
While Pentheus, helpless in this pitiful trap, sat there.
Then, with a force like lightning, they tore down branches
Of oak, and with these tried to prize up the tree's roots.
When all their struggles met with no success, Agauë
Cried out, "Come, Maenads, stand in a circle round the tree   1070
And take hold of it. We must catch this climbing beast,
Or he'll disclose the secret dances of Dionysus."
They came; a thousand hands gripped on the pine and tore it
Out of the ground. Then from his high perch plunging, crashing
To the earth Pentheus fell, with one incessant scream   1075
As he understood what end was near.

His mother first,
As priestess, led the rite of death, and fell upon him.
He tore the headband from his hair, that his wretched mother
Might recognize him and not kill him. "Mother," he cried,   1080

Touching her cheek, "it is I, your own son Pentheus, whom
You bore to Echion. Mother, have mercy; I have sinned,
But I am still your own son. Do not take my life!"

Agauë was foaming at the mouth; her rolling eyes
Were wild, she was not in her right mind, but possessed   1085
By Bacchus, and she paid no heed to him. She grasped
His right arm between wrist and elbow, set her foot
Against his ribs, and tore his arm off by the shoulder.
It was no strength of hers that did it, but the god
Filled her, and made it easy. On the other side   1090
Ino was at him, tearing at his flesh; and now
Autonoe joined them, and the whole maniacal horde.
A single and continuous yell arose—Pentheus
Shrieking as long as life was left in him, the women
Howling in triumph. One of them carried off an arm,   1095
Another a foot, the boot still laced on it. The ribs
Were stripped, clawed clean; and women's hands, thick red with
     blood,
Were tossing, catching, like a plaything, Pentheus' flesh.
His body lies—no easy task to find—scattered
Under hard rocks, or in the green woods. His poor head—   1100
His mother carries it, fixed on her thyrsus-point,
Openly over Cithaeron's pastures, thinking it
The head of a young mountain lion. She has left her sisters
Dancing among the Maenads, and herself comes here
Inside the walls, exulting in her hideous prey,   1105
Shouting to Bacchus, calling him her fellow hunter,
Her partner in the kill, comrade in victory.
But Bacchus gives her bitter tears for her reward.

Now I will go. I must find some place far away
From this horror, before Agauë returns home.   1110
A sound and humble heart that reverences the gods
Is man's noblest possession; and the same virtue
Is wisest too, I think, for those who practice it.

> *Exit the* MESSENGER.

CHORUS
Let us dance a dance to Bacchus, shout and sing
For the fall of Pentheus, heir of the dragon's seed,   1115
Who hid his beard in a woman's gown,
And sealed his death with the holy sign
Of ivy wreathing a fennel reed,
When bull led man to the ritual slaughter ring.
Frenzied daughters of Cadmus, what renown   1120
Your victory wins you—such a song
As groans must stifle, tears must drown!

Emblem of conquest, brave and fine!
A mother's hand, defiled
With blood and dripping red,   1125
Caresses the torn head
Of her own murdered child!

But look! I see her—there, running toward the palace—
Agauë, Pentheus' mother, her eyes wildly rolling.
Come, welcome them—Dionysus' holy company.   1130

> AGAUË *appears, frenzied and panting, with* PENTHEUS' *head held
> in her hand. The rest of her band of devotees, whom the* CHORUS
> *saw approaching with her, do not enter; but a few are seen
> standing by the entrance, where they wait until the end of
> the play.*

AGAUË   Women of Asia! Worshippers of Bacchus!

> AGAUË *tries to show them* PENTHEUS' *head; they shrink from it.*

CHORUS   Why do you urge me? Oh!
AGAUË   I am bringing home from the mountains
A vine branch freshly cut,
For the gods have blessed our hunting.   1135
CHORUS   We see it . . . and welcome you in fellowship.
AGAUË   I caught him without a trap,
A lion cub, young and wild.
Look, you may see him—there!
CHORUS   Where was it?   1140
AGAUË   On Cithaeron;
The wild and empty mountain—
CHORUS   Cithaeron!
AGAUË   . . . spilled his life-blood.
CHORUS   Who shot him?   1145
AGAUË   I was first;
All the women are singing,
"Honor to great Agauë!"
CHORUS   And then—who next?
AGAUË   Why, Cadmus' . . .   1150
CHORUS   What—Cadmus?
AGAUË   Yes, his daughters—
But after me, after me—
Laid their hands to the kill.
Today was a splendid hunt!   1155
Come now, join in the feast!
CHORUS   What, wretched woman? *Feast?*
AGAUË   [*tenderly stroking the head as she holds it*] This calf is young:
how thickly
The new-grown hair goes crisping
Up to his delicate crest!   1160
CHORUS   Indeed, his long hair makes him
Look like some wild creature.
AGAUË   The god is a skilled hunter;
And he poised his hunting women,
And hurled them at the quarry.   1165
CHORUS   True, our god is a hunter.
AGAUË   Do you praise me?
CHORUS   Yes, we praise you.
AGAUË   So will the sons of Cadmus . . .
CHORUS   And Pentheus too, Agauë?   1170
AGAUË   Yes, he will praise his mother
For the lion cub she killed.

CHORUS   Oh, fearful!
AGAUË   Ay, fearful!
CHORUS   You are happy?   1175
AGAUË   I am enraptured;
    Great in the eyes of the world,
    Great are the deeds I've done,
    And the hunt that I hunted there!
CHORUS   Then show it, poor Agauë—this triumphant spoil   1180
    You've brought home; show it to all the citizens of Thebes.
AGAUË   Come, all you Thebans living within these towered walls,
    Come, see the beast we, Cadmus' daughters, caught and killed;
    Caught not with nets or thonged Thessalian[2] javelins,
    But with our own bare arms and fingers. After this   1185
    Should huntsmen glory in their exploits, who must buy
    Their needless tools from armorers? We with our hands
    Hunted and took this beast, then tore it limb from limb.

    Where is my father? Let old Cadmus come. And where
    Is my son Pentheus? Let him climb a strong ladder   1190
    And nail up on the cornice of the palace wall
    This lion's head that I have hunted and brought home.

        Enter CADMUS *with attendants bearing the body of* PENTHEUS.

CADMUS   Come, men, bring your sad burden that was Pentheus. Come,
    Set him at his own door. By weary, endless search
    I found his body's remnants scattered far and wide   1195
    About Cithaeron's glens, or hidden in thick woods.
    I gathered them and brought them here.

    I had already
    Returned with old Teiresias from the Bacchic dance,
    And was inside the walls, when news was brought me of   1200
    My daughters' terrible deed. I turned straight back; and now
    Return, bringing my grandson, whom the Maenads killed.
    I saw Autonoe, who bore Actaeon to Aristaeus,
    And Ino with her, there among the trees, still rapt
    In their unhappy frenzy; but I understood   1205
    That Agauë had come dancing on her way to Thebes—
    And there indeed she is, a sight for misery!
AGAUË   Father! Now you may boast as loudly as you will
    That you have sired the noblest daughters of this age!
    I speak of all three, but myself especially.   1210
    I have left weaving at the loom for greater things,
    For hunting wild beasts with my bare hands. See this prize,
    Here in my arms; I won it, and it shall be hung
    On your palace wall. There, father, take it in your hands.
    Be proud of my hunting; call your friends to a feast; let them   1215
    Bless you and envy you for the splendor of my deed.
CADMUS   Oh, misery unmeasured, sight intolerable!
    Oh, bloody deed enacted by most pitiful hands!
    What noble prize is this you lay at the gods' feet,

---

2. Thessaly is the northeastern section of the Greek peninsula, just south of Macedonia.
It was regarded as less civilized than the other sections of Greece.

Calling the city, and me, to a banquet? Your wretchedness   1220
Demands the bitterest tears; but mine is next to yours.
Dionysus has dealt justly, but pursued justice
Too far; born of my blood, he has destroyed my house.

AGAUË   What an ill-tempered creature an old man is! How full
Of scowls! I wish my son were a great hunter like   1225
His mother, hunting beasts with the young men of Thebes;
But *he* can only fight with gods. Father, you must
Correct him.—Will not someone go and call him here
To see me, and to share in my great happiness?

CADMUS   Alas, my daughters! If you come to understand   1230
What you have done, how terrible your pain will be!
If you remain as you are now, though you could not
Be happy, at least you will not feel your wretchedness.

AGAUË   Why not happy? What cause have I for wretchedness?

CADMUS   Come here. First turn your eyes this way. Look at the sky.   1235

AGAUË   I am looking. Why should you want me to look at it?

CADMUS   Does it appear the same to you, or is it changed?

AGAUË   Yes, it is clearer than before, more luminous.

CADMUS   And this disturbance of your mind—is it still there?

AGAUË   I don't know what you mean; but—yes, I feel a change;   1240
My mind is somehow clearer than it was before.

CADMUS   Could you now listen to me and give a clear reply?

AGAUË   Yes, father. I have forgotten what we said just now.

CADMUS   When you were married, whose house did you go to then?

AGAUË   You gave me to Echion, of the sown race, they said.   1245

CADMUS   Echion had a son born to him. Who was he?

AGAUË   Pentheus. His father lay with me; I bore a son.

CADMUS   Yes; and whose head is that you are holding in your arms?

AGAUË   A lion's—so the women said who hunted it.

CADMUS   Then look straight at it. Come, to look is no great task.   1250

AGAUË *looks; and suddenly screams.*

AGAUË   What am I looking at? What is this in my hands?

CADMUS   Look at it steadily; come closer to the truth.

AGAUË   I see—O gods, what horror! Oh, what misery!

CADMUS   Does this appear to you to be a lion's head?

AGAUË   No! I hold Pentheus' head in my accursed hand.   1255

CADMUS   It is so. Tears have been shed for him, before you knew.

AGAUË   But who killed him? How did he come into my hands?

CADMUS   O cruel hour that brings a bitter truth to light!

AGAUË   Tell me—my heart is bursting, I must know the rest.

CADMUS   It was you, Agauë, and your sisters. You killed him.   1260

AGAUË   Where was it done? Here in the palace? Or where else?

CADMUS   Where, long ago, Actaeon was devoured by hounds.

AGAUË   Cithaeron. But what evil fate took Pentheus there?

CADMUS   He went to mock Dionysus and your Bacchic rites.

AGAUË   Why were we on Cithaeron? What had brought us there?   1265

CADMUS   You were possessed. All Thebes was in a Bacchic trance.

AGAUË   Dionysus has destroyed us. Now I understand.

CADMUS   He was insulted. You refused to call him god.

AGAUË   Father, where is the beloved body of my son?

CADMUS   Here. It was I who brought it, after painful search.   1270

AGAUË   And are his limbs now decently composed?

CADMUS   Not yet.
We came back to the city with all possible haste.
AGAUË   How could I touch his body with these guilty hands?
CADMUS   Your guilt, my daughter, was not heavier than his.   1275
AGAUË   What part did Pentheus have, then, in my insanity?
CADMUS   He sinned like you, refusing reverence to a god.
Therefore the god has joined all in one ruin—you,
Your sisters, Pentheus—to destroy my house and me.
I have no son; and now, my unhappy child, I see   1280
This son of yours dead by a shameful, hideous death.
You were the new hope of our house, its bond of strength,
Dear grandson. And Thebes feared you; no one dared insult
Your old grandfather if he saw you near; you would
Teach him his lesson. But now I shall live exiled,   1285
Dishonored—I, Cadmus the great, who planted here,
And reaped, that glorious harvest of the Theban race.

O dearest son—yes, even in death you shall be held
Most dear—you will never touch my beard again, and call
Me Grandfather, and put your arm round me and say,   1290
"Who has wronged you or insulted you? Who is unkind,
Or vexes or disturbs you? Tell me, Grandfather,
That I may punish him." Never again. For me
All that remains is pain; for you, the pity of death;
For your mother, tears; torment for our whole family.   1295

If any man derides the unseen world, let him
Ponder the death of Pentheus, and believe in gods.

CHORUS   I grieve for your fate, Cadmus; though your grandson's death
Was justly merited, it falls cruelly on you.
AGAUË   Father, you see how one disastrous day has shattered   1300
My whole life . . .

[At this point the two MSS on which the text of this play depends show a lacuna of considerable extent; it covers the end of
this scene, in which Agauë mourns over Pentheus' body, and the
appearance of Dionysus manifested as a god. The MSS resume
in the middle of a speech by Dionysus. A number of quotations
by ancient authors, together with less than 20 lines from *Christus
Patiens* (an anonymous 4th-century A.D. work consisting largely
of lines adapted from Greek tragedies) make it possible to attempt a guess at the content of the missing lines. Since this play
is often performed, it seems worthwhile to provide here a usable
text. In the lines that follow, the words printed in italics are
mere conjecture, and have no value except as a credible com-
pletion of the probable sense; while those in Roman type represent the sources available from *Christus Patiens* and elsewhere.]

. . . my whole life, *turned my pride to shame, my happiness
To horror. Now my only wish is to compose
My son's body for burial, and lament for him;
And then die.* But this is not lawful; for my hands
Are filthy with pollution of their own making.   1305
When I have spilled the blood I bore, and torn the flesh

That grew in my own womb, how can I after this
Enfold him to my breast, or chant his ritual dirge?
And yet, I beg you, pity me, and let me touch
My son, and say farewell to that dear body which   1310
I cherished, and destroyed unknowing. It is right
That you should pity, for your hands are innocent.

CADMUS   *My daughter, you and I and our whole house are crushed*
And broken by the anger of this powerful god.
It is not for me to keep you from your son. Only   1315
Be resolute, and steel your heart against a sight
Which must be fearful to any eyes, but most of all
To a mother's. [To attendants.] *Men, put down your burden on the*
*   ground*
Before Agaue, and remove the covering.
AGAUE   *Dear child, how cruel, how unnatural are these tears,*   1320
Which should have fallen from your eyes on my dead face.
Now I shall die with none to mourn me. This is just;
For in my pride I did not recognize the god,
Nor understand the things I ought to have understood.
You too are punished for the same impiety;   1325
But which is the more terrible, your fate or mine,
I cannot tell. Since you have suffered too, you will
Forgive both what I did, not knowing what I did,
And what I do now, touching you with unholy hands—
At once your cruelest enemy and your dearest friend.   1330

I place your limbs as they should lie; I kiss the flesh
That my own body nourished and my own care reared
To manhood. Help me, father; lay his poor head here.
Make all exact and seemly, with what care we can.
O dearest face, O young fresh cheek! O kingly eyes,   1335
Your light now darkened! O my son! See, with this veil
I now cover your head, your torn and bloodstained limbs.
Take him up, carry him to burial, a king
Lured to a shameful death by the anger of a god.

        Enter DIONYSUS.

CHORUS   *But look! Who is this, rising above the palace door?*   1340
It is he—Dionysus comes himself, no more disguised
As mortal, but in the glory of his divinity!
DIONYSUS   *Behold me, a god great and powerful, Dionysus,*
The son whom Theban Semele bore to immortal Zeus.
I come to the city of seven gates, to famous Thebes,   1345
Whose people slighted me, denied my divinity,
Refused my ritual dances. Now they reap the fruit
Of impious folly. The royal house is overthrown;
The city's streets tremble in guilt, as every Theban
Repents too late his blindness and his blasphemy.   1350
Foremost in sin was Pentheus, who not only scorned
My claims, but put me in fetters and insulted me.
Therefore death came to him in the most shameful way,
At his own mother's hands. This fate he justly earned;
No god can see his worship scorned, and hear his name   1355

Profaned, and not take vengeance to the utmost limit.
Thus men may learn that gods are more powerful than they.

Agauë and her sisters must immediately
Depart from Thebes; their exile will be just penance
For the pollution which this blood has brought on them.   1360
Never again shall they enjoy their native land;
That such defilement ever should appear before
The city's altars, is an offense to piety.

Now, Cadmus, hear what suffering Fate appoints for you.

    [Here the MSS resume.]

You shall transmute your nature and become a serpent.   1365
Your wife Harmonia, whom her father Ares gave
To you, a mortal, likewise shall assume the nature
Of beasts, and live a snake. The oracle of Zeus
Foretells that you, at the head of a barbaric horde,
Shall with your wife drive forth a pair of heifers yoked,   1370
And with your countless army destroy many cities;
But when they plunder Loxias' oracle, they shall find
A miserable homecoming. However, Ares shall
At last deliver both you and Harmonia,
And grant you immortal life among the blessed gods.   1375
I who pronounce these fates am Dionysus, begotten
Not by a mortal father, but by Zeus. If you
Had chosen wisdom, when you would not, you would have lived
In wealth and safety, having the son of Zeus your friend.
CADMUS   Have mercy on us, Dionysus. We have sinned.   1380
DIONYSUS   You know too late. You did not know me when you should.
CADMUS   We acknowledge this; but your revenge is merciless.
DIONYSUS   And rightly; I am a god, and you insulted me.
CADMUS   Gods should not be like mortals in vindictiveness.
DIONYSUS   All this my father Zeus ordained from the beginning.   1385
AGAUË   No hope, father. Our harsh fate is decreed: exile.
DIONYSUS   Then why put off a fate which is inevitable?

                                Exit DIONYSUS.

CADMUS   Dear child, what misery has overtaken us all—
You, and your sisters, and your old unhappy father!
I must set forth from home and live in barbarous lands;   1390
Further than that, it is foretold that I shall lead
A mixed barbarian horde to Hellas. And my wife,
Harmonia, Ares' daughter, and I too, must take
The brutish form of serpents; and I am to lead her thus
At the head of an armed force, to desecrate the tombs   1395
And temples of our native land. I am to reach
No respite from this curse; I may not even cross
The downward stream of Acheron[3] to find peace in death.
AGAUË   And I in exile, father, shall live far from you.
CADMUS   Poor child, why do you cling to me, as the young swan   1400
Clings fondly to the old, helpless and white with age?

---

3. One of the rivers in the classical underworld.

AGAUË   Where can I turn for comfort, homeless and exiled?
CADMUS   I do not know. Your father is little help to you.
AGAUË   Farewell, my home; farewell the land I know.
 Exiled, accursed, and wretched, now I go   1405
 Forth from this door where first I came a bride.
CADMUS   Go, daughter; find some secret place to hide
 Your shame and sorrow.
AGAUË   Father, I weep for you.
CADMUS   I for your suffering, and your sisters' too.   1410
AGAUË   There is strange tyranny in the god who sent
 Against your house this cruel punishment.
CADMUS   Not strange: our citizens despised his claim,
 And you, and they, put him to open shame.
AGAUË   Father, farewell.   1415
CADMUS   Poor child! I cannot tell
 How you can *fare well;* yet I say, Farewell.
AGAUË   I go to lead my sisters by the hand
 To share my wretchedness in a foreign land.

> *She turns to the Theban women who have been waiting at the*
> *edge of the stage.*

Come, see me forth.   1420
Gods, lead me to some place
Where loath'd Cithaeron may not see my face,
Nor I Cithaeron. I have had my fill
Of mountain-ecstasy; now take who will
My holy ivy-wreath, my thyrsus rod,   1425
All that reminds me how I served this god!

> *Exit, followed by* CADMUS.

CHORUS
 Gods manifest themselves in many forms,
 Bring many matters to surprising ends;
 The things we thought would happen do not happen;
 The unexpected God makes possible: 1430
 And that is what has happened here today.

> *Exeunt.*

Thebes and the House of Cadmus

Many of the principal myths of the Greeks centered about royal families who seemed particularly susceptible to sensational crimes and punishments. Few families had more lurid histories than that of Cadmus, the founder of Thebes.

When Cadmus' sister Europa was stolen by Zeus, in the form of a white bull, his father, Agenor of Sidon, sent Cadmus and his brothers forth to search for her. After various adventures, Cadmus, led by Athena, set out to establish a city. Led by a cow chosen by the goddess, he came to a spring where he was to establish the city. When most of his men were killed by a serpent who lived there, Cadmus killed the serpent and, again following the instructions of the goddess, sowed its teeth. From the teeth sprang up armed men who began fighting among themselves until Cadmus stopped them by throwing a stone into their midst. These "Sown Men" and their descendants were the great families of Thebes. Among them were Echion, the father of Pentheus, and an ancestor of Menoeceus, the father of Jocasta and Creon.

The chart below shows the relations of the members of the house of Cadmus who are mentioned in *The Bacchae* and *Oedipus Tyrannus*. A number of their relatives with equally spectacular destinies are omitted to make the chart more useful to readers of these two plays.

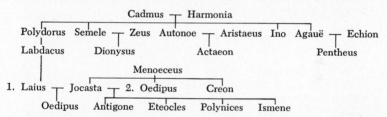

Although *The Bacchae* and *Oedipus Tyrannus* occur in different generations, the figure of Teiresias, the blind prophet, occurs in both. The name may have designated an office rather than an individual.

Thebes was the principal city of Boeotia, a district to the northwest of Attica in which Athens was located. This may help to explain its prominence in the Athenian drama. The two plays here considered make frequent reference to some of the features of the city, including its seven gates (where *The Seven Against Thebes* fought), the great mountain Cithaeron, which was nearby, the streams Ismenus, Dirce, and Asopus, and the neighboring villages of Hysiae and Erythrae.

Hamlet

CHARACTERS

CLAUDIUS, *King of Denmark*
HAMLET, *son of the former and nephew to the present King*
POLONIUS, *Lord Chamberlain*
HORATIO, *friend of Hamlet*
LAERTES, *son of Polonius*
VOLTEMAND
CORNELIUS
ROSENCRANTZ   *courtiers*
GUILDENSTERN
OSRIC
A GENTLEMAN
A PRIEST

MARCELLUS   } *officers*
BERNARDO   }
FRANCISCO, *a soldier*
REYNALDO, *servant to Polonius*
PLAYERS
TWO CLOWNS, *gravediggers*
FORTINBRAS, *Prince of Norway*
A NORWEGIAN CAPTAIN
ENGLISH AMBASSADORS
GERTRUDE, *Queen of Denmark, and mother of Hamlet*
OPHELIA, *daughter of Polonius*
GHOST OF HAMLET'S FATHER

LORDS, LADIES, OFFICERS, SOLDIERS, SAILORS, MESSENGERS, *and* ATTENDANTS

SCENE: *The action takes place in or near the royal castle of Denmark at Elsinore.*

Act 1

SCENE 1: *A guard station atop the castle. Enter* BERNARDO *and* FRANCISCO, *two sentinels.*

BERNARDO   Who's there?
FRANCISCO   Nay, answer me. Stand and unfold yourself.
BERNARDO   Long live the king!
FRANCISCO   Bernardo?
BERNARDO   He.   5
FRANCISCO   You come most carefully upon your hour.
BERNARDO   'Tis now struck twelve. Get thee to bed, Francisco.
FRANCISCO   For this relief much thanks. 'Tis bitter cold,
And I am sick at heart.
BERNARDO   Have you had quiet guard?
FRANCISCO   Not a mouse stirring.   10
BERNARDO   Well, good night.
If you do meet Horatio and Marcellus,
The rivals[1] of my watch, bid them make haste.

Enter HORATIO *and* MARCELLUS.

FRANCISCO   I think I hear them. Stand, ho! Who is there?
HORATIO   Friends to this ground.
MARCELLUS   And liegemen to the Dane.[2] 15

1. companions
2. The "Dane" is the King of Denmark, who is also called "Denmark," as in line 48 of this scene. In line 61 the same figure is used for the King of Norway.

FRANCISCO   Give you good night.
MARCELLUS   O, farewell, honest soldier!
  Who hath relieved you?
FRANCISCO   Bernardo hath my place.
  Give you good night.   *Exit* FRANCISCO.
MARCELLUS   Holla, Bernardo!
BERNARDO   Say—
  What, is Horatio there?
HORATIO   A piece of him.
BERNARDO   Welcome, Horatio. Welcome, good Marcellus.   20
HORATIO   What, has this thing appeared again tonight?
BERNARDO   I have seen nothing.
MARCELLUS   Horatio says 'tis but our fantasy,
  And will not let belief take hold of him
  Touching this dreaded sight twice seen of us.   25
  Therefore I have entreated him along
  With us to watch the minutes of this night,
  That if again this apparition come,
  He may approve[3] our eyes and speak to it.
HORATIO   Tush, tush, 'twill not appear.
BERNARDO   Sit down awhile,   30
  And let us once again assail your ears,
  That are so fortified against our story,
  What we have two nights seen.
HORATIO   Well, sit we down,
  And let us hear Bernardo speak of this.
BERNARDO   Last night of all,   35
  When yond same star that's westward from the pole[4]
  Had made his course t' illume that part of heaven
  Where now it burns, Marcellus and myself,
  The bell then beating one—

        Enter GHOST.

MARCELLUS   Peace, break thee off. Look where it comes again.   40
BERNARDO   In the same figure like the king that's dead.
MARCELLUS   Thou art a scholar; speak to it, Horatio.
BERNARDO   Looks 'a[5] not like the king? Mark it, Horatio.
HORATIO   Most like. It harrows me with fear and wonder.
BERNARDO   It would be spoke to.
MARCELLUS   Speak to it, Horatio.   45
HORATIO   What art thou that usurp'st this time of night
  Together with that fair and warlike form
  In which the majesty of buried Denmark
  Did sometimes march? By heaven I charge thee, speak.
MARCELLUS   It is offended.
BERNARDO   See, it stalks away.   50
HORATIO   Stay. Speak, speak. I charge thee, speak.   *Exit* GHOST.
MARCELLUS   'Tis gone and will not answer.
BERNARDO   How now, Horatio! You tremble and look pale.
  Is not this something more than fantasy?
  What think you on't?   55
HORATIO   Before my God, I might not this believe

3. confirm the testimony of   5. he
4. polestar

Without the sensible[6] and true avouch
Of mine own eyes.

MARCELLUS   Is it not like the king?

HORATIO   As thou art to thyself.
Such was the very armor he had on   60
When he the ambitious Norway combated.
So frowned he once when, in an angry parle,[7]
He smote the sledded Polacks on the ice.
'Tis strange.

MARCELLUS   Thus twice before, and jump[8] at this dead hour,   65
With martial stalk hath he gone by our watch.

HORATIO   In what particular thought to work I know not,
But in the gross and scope of mine opinion,
This bodes some strange eruption to our state.

MARCELLUS   Good now, sit down, and tell me he that knows,   70
Why this same strict and most observant watch
So nightly toils the subject[9] of the land,
And why such daily cast of brazen cannon
And foreign mart for implements of war;
Why such impress of shipwrights, whose sore task   75
Does not divide the Sunday from the week.
What might be toward that this sweaty haste
Doth make the night joint-laborer with the day?
Who is't that can inform me?

HORATIO   That can I.
At least, the whisper goes so. Our last king,   80
Whose image even but now appeared to us,
Was as you know by Fortinbras of Norway,
Thereto pricked on by a most emulate pride,
Dared to the combat; in which our valiant Hamlet
(For so this side of our known world esteemed him)   85
Did slay this Fortinbras; who by a sealed compact
Well ratified by law and heraldry,
Did forfeit, with his life, all those his lands
Which he stood seized of,[1] to the conqueror;
Against the which a moiety competent[2]   90
Was gagéd[3] by our king; which had returned
To the inheritance of Fortinbras,
Had he been vanquisher; as, by the same covenant
And carriage of the article designed,
His fell to Hamlet. Now, sir, young Fortinbras,   95
Of unimprovéd mettle hot and full,
Hath in the skirts of Norway here and there
Sharked up a list of lawless resolutes
For food and diet to some enterprise
That hath a stomach in't; which is no other,   100
As it doth well appear unto our state,
But to recover of us by strong hand
And terms compulsatory, those foresaid lands
So by his father lost; and this, I take it,

6. of the senses   1. possessed
7. parley   2. portion of similar value
8. precisely   3. pledged
9. people

Is the main motive of our preparations,   105
The source of this our watch, and the chief head
Of this post-haste and romage[4] in the land.
BERNARDO   I think it be no other but e'en so.
Well may it sort[5] that this portentous figure
Comes arméd through our watch so like the king   110
That was and is the question of these wars.
HORATIO   A mote[6] it is to trouble the mind's eye.
In the most high and palmy state of Rome,
A little ere the mightiest Julius fell,
The graves stood tenantless, and the sheeted dead   115
Did squeak and gibber in the Roman streets;
As stars with trains of fire, and dews of blood,
Disasters in the sun; and the moist star,
Upon whose influence Neptune's empire stands,[7]
Was sick almost to doomsday with eclipse.   120
And even the like precurse[8] of feared events,
As harbingers preceding still the fates
And prologue to the omen coming on,
Have heaven and earth together demonstrated
Unto our climatures[9] and countrymen.   125

> *Enter* GHOST.

But soft, behold, lo where it comes again!
I'll cross it[1] though it blast me.—Stay, illusion.

> *It spreads [its] arms.*

If thou hast any sound or use of voice,
Speak to me.
If there be any good thing to be done,   130
That may to thee do ease, and grace to me,
Speak to me.
If thou art privy to thy country's fate,
Which happily foreknowing may avoid,
O, speak!   135
Or if thou hast uphoarded in thy life
Extorted treasure in the womb of earth,
For which, they say, you spirits oft walk in death,

> *The cock crows.*

Speak of it. Stay, and speak. Stop it, Marcellus.
MARCELLUS   Shall I strike at it with my partisan[2]?   140
HORATIO   Do, if it will not stand.
BERNARDO   'Tis here.
HORATIO   'Tis here.
MARCELLUS   'Tis gone.   *Exit* GHOST.
We do it wrong, being so majestical,
To offer it the show of violence;
For it is as the air, invulnerable,   145

---

4. stir
5. chance
6. speck of dust
7. Neptune was the Roman sea god; the "moist star" is the moon.
8. precursor
9. regions
1. Horatio means either that he will

move across the Ghost's path in order to stop him or that he will make the sign of the cross to gain power over him. The stage direction which follows is somewhat ambiguous. "It" seems to refer to the Ghost, but the movement would be appropriate to Horatio.
2. halberd

And our vain blows malicious mockery.
BERNARDO   It was about to speak when the cock crew.
HORATIO   And then it started like a guilty thing
   Upon a fearful summons. I have heard
   The cock, that is the trumpet to the morn,   150
   Doth with his lofty and shrill-sounding throat
   Awake the god of day, and at his warning,
   Whether in sea or fire, in earth or air,
   Th' extravagant and erring[3] spirit hies
   To his confine; and of the truth herein   155
   This present object made probation.[4]
MARCELLUS   It faded on the crowing of the cock.
   Some say that ever 'gainst that season comes
   Wherein our Savior's birth is celebrated,
   This bird of dawning singeth all night long,   160
   And then, they say, no spirit dare stir abroad,
   The nights are wholesome, then no planets strike,
   No fairy takes,[5] nor witch hath power to charm,
   So hallowed and so gracious is that time.
HORATIO   So have I heard and do in part believe it.   165
   But look, the morn in russet mantle clad
   Walks o'er the dew of yon high eastward hill.
   Break we our watch up, and by my advice
   Let us impart what we have seen tonight
   Unto young Hamlet, for upon my life   170
   This spirit, dumb to us, will speak to him.
   Do you consent we shall acquaint him with it,
   As needful in our loves, fitting our duty?
MARCELLUS   Let's do't, I pray, and I this morning know
   Where we shall find him most convenient.   *Exeunt.* 175

SCENE 2: *A chamber of state. Enter* KING CLAUDIUS, QUEEN GER-
TRUDE, HAMLET, POLONIUS, LAERTES, OPHELIA, VOLTEMAND, COR-
NELIUS *and other members of the court.*

KING   Though yet of Hamlet our dear brother's death
   The memory be green, and that it us befitted
   To bear our hearts in grief, and our whole kingdom
   To be contracted in one brow of woe,
   Yet so far hath discretion fought with nature   5
   That we with wisest sorrow think on him,
   Together with remembrance of ourselves.
   Therefore our sometime sister, now our queen,
   Th' imperial jointress[6] to this warlike state,
   Have we, as 'twere with a defeated joy,   10
   With an auspicious and a dropping eye,
   With mirth in funeral, and with dirge in marriage,
   In equal scale weighing delight and dole,
   Taken to wife; nor have we herein barred
   Your better wisdoms, which have freely gone   15
   With this affair along. For all, our thanks.

---

3. wandering out of bounds
4. proof
5. enchants

6. A "jointress" is a widow who holds a
jointure or life interest in the estate of her
deceased husband.

Now follows that you know young Fortinbras,
Holding a weak supposal of our worth,
Or thinking by our late dear brother's death
Our state to be disjoint and out of frame,   20
Colleaguéd with this dream of his advantage,
He hath not failed to pester us with message
Importing the surrender of those lands
Lost by his father, with all bands of law,
To our most valiant brother. So much for him.   25
Now for ourself, and for this time of meeting,
Thus much the business is: we have here writ
To Norway, uncle of young Fortinbras—
Who, impotent and bedrid, scarcely hears
Of this his nephew's purpose—to suppress   30
His further gait[7] herein, in that the levies,
The lists, and full proportions are all made
Out of his subject; and we here dispatch
You, good Cornelius, and you, Voltemand,
For bearers of this greeting to old Norway,   35
Giving to you no further personal power
To business with the king, more than the scope
Of these dilated[8] articles allow.
Farewell, and let your haste commend your duty.
CORNELIUS ⎫
VOLTEMAND ⎬ In that, and all things will we show our duty.   40
KING   We doubt it nothing, heartily farewell.

                    Exeunt VOLTEMAND *and* CORNELIUS.

And now, Laertes, what's the news with you?
You told us of some suit. What is't, Laertes?
You cannot speak of reason to the Dane
And lose your voice. What wouldst thou beg, Laertes,   45
That shall not be my offer, not thy asking?
The head is not more native to the heart,
The hand more instrumental[9] to the mouth,
Than is the throne of Denmark to thy father.
What wouldst thou have, Laertes?
LAERTES   My dread lord,   50
Your leave and favor to return to France,
From whence, though willingly, I came to Denmark
To show my duty in your coronation,
Yet now I must confess, that duty done,
My thoughts and wishes bend again toward France,   55
And bow them to your gracious leave and pardon.
KING   Have you your father's leave? What says Polonius?
POLONIUS   He hath, my lord, wrung from me my slow leave
By laborsome petition, and at last
Upon his will I sealed my hard consent.   60
I do beseech you give him leave to go.
KING   Take thy fair hour, Laertes. Time be thine,
And thy best graces spend it at thy will.

---

7. progress   9. serviceable
8. fully expressed

But now, my cousin[1] Hamlet, and my son—
HAMLET [*aside*]   A little more than kin, and less than kind.   65
KING   How is it that the clouds still hang on you?
HAMLET   Not so, my lord. I am too much in the sun.
QUEEN   Good Hamlet, cast thy nighted color off,
    And let thine eye look like a friend on Denmark.
    Do not for ever with thy vailéd lids[2]   70
    Seek for thy noble father in the dust.
    Thou know'st 'tis common—all that lives must die,
    Passing through nature to eternity.
HAMLET   Ay, madam, it is common.
QUEEN   If it be,
    Why seems it so particular with thee?   75
HAMLET   Seems, madam? Nay, it is. I know not "seems."
    'Tis not alone my inky cloak, good mother,
    Nor customary suits of solemn black,
    Nor windy suspiration of forced breath,
    No, nor the fruitful river in the eye,   80
    Nor the dejected havior[3] of the visage,
    Together with all forms, moods, shapes of grief,
    That can denote me truly. These indeed seem,
    For they are actions that a man might play,
    But I have that within which passes show—   85
    These but the trappings and the suits of woe.
KING   'Tis sweet and commendable in your nature, Hamlet,
    To give these mourning duties to your father,
    But you must know your father lost a father,
    That father lost, lost his, and the survivor bound   90
    In filial obligation for some term
    To do obsequious[4] sorrow. But to persever
    In obstinate condolement is a course
    Of impious stubbornness. 'Tis unmanly grief.
    It shows a will most incorrect to[5] heaven,   95
    A heart unfortified, a mind impatient,
    An understanding simple and unschooled.
    For what we know must be, and is as common
    As any the most vulgar thing to sense,
    Why should we in our peevish opposition   100
    Take it to heart? Fie, 'tis a fault to heaven,
    A fault against the dead, a fault to nature,
    To reason most absurd, whose common theme
    Is death of fathers, and who still hath cried,
    From the first corse[6] till he that died today,   105
    "This must be so." We pray you throw to earth
    This unprevailing woe, and think of us
    As of a father, for let the world take note
    You are the most immediate[7] to our throne,
    And with no less nobility of love   110
    Than that which dearest father bears his son
    Do I impart toward you. For your intent

1. "Cousin" is used here as a general term of kinship.
2. lowered eyes
3. appearance
4. suited for funeral obsequies
5. uncorrected toward
6. corpse
7. next in line

In going back to school in Wittenberg,
It is most retrograde[8] to our desire,
And we beseech you, bend you to remain   115
Here in the cheer and comfort of our eye,
Our chiefest courtier, cousin, and our son.
QUEEN   Let not thy mother lose her prayers, Hamlet.
I pray thee stay with us, go not to Wittenberg.
HAMLET   I shall in all my best obey you, madam.   120
KING   Why, 'tis a loving and a fair reply.
Be as ourself in Denmark. Madam, come.
This gentle and unforced accord of Hamlet
Sits smiling to my heart, in grace whereof,
No jocund health that Denmark drinks today   125
But the great cannon to the clouds shall tell,
And the king's rouse[9] the heaven shall bruit[1] again,
Respeaking earthly thunder. Come away.

                    Flourish. Exeunt all but HAMLET.

HAMLET   O, that this too too solid flesh would melt,
Thaw, and resolve itself into a dew,   130
Or that the Everlasting had not fixed
His canon[2] 'gainst self-slaughter. O God, God,
How weary, stale, flat, and unprofitable
Seem to me all the uses of this world!
Fie on't, ah, fie, 'tis an unweeded garden   135
That grows to seed. Things rank and gross in nature
Possess it merely.[3] That it should come to this,
But two months dead, nay, not so much, not two.
So excellent a king, that was to this
Hyperion to a satyr,[4] so loving to my mother,   140
That he might not beteem[5] the winds of heaven
Visit her face too roughly. Heaven and earth,
Must I remember? Why, she would hang on him
As if increase of appetite had grown
By what it fed on, and yet, within a month—   145
Let me not think on't. Frailty, thy name is woman—
A little month, or ere those shoes were old
With which she followed my poor father's body
Like Niobe,[6] all tears, why she, even she—
O God, a beast that wants discourse of reason   150
Would have mourned longer—married with my uncle,
My father's brother, but no more like my father
Than I to Hercules.[7] Within a month,
Ere yet the salt of most unrighteous tears
Had left the flushing in her gallèd eyes,   155
She married. O, most wicked speed, to post
With such dexterity to incestuous sheets!

8. contrary
9. carousal
1. echo
2. law
3. entirely
4. Hyperion, a sun god, stands here for beauty in contrast to the monstrous satyr, a lecherous creature, half man and half goat.

5. permit
6. In Greek mythology Niobe was turned to stone after a tremendous fit of weeping over the death of her fourteen children, a misfortune brought about by her boasting over her fertility.
7. The demigod Hercules was noted for his strength and the series of spectacular labors which it allowed him to accomplish.

It is not, nor it cannot come to good.
But break my heart, for I must hold my tongue.

Enter HORATIO, MARCELLUS, *and* BERNARDO.

HORATIO   Hail to your lordship!
HAMLET   I am glad to see you well.   160
Horatio—or I do forget myself.
HORATIO   The same, my lord, and your poor servant ever.
HAMLET   Sir, my good friend, I'll change[8] that name with you.
And what make you from Wittenberg, Horatio?
Marcellus?   165
MARCELLUS   My good lord!
HAMLET   I am very glad to see you. [*To* BERNARDO.] Good even, sir.—
But what, in faith, make you from Wittenberg?
HORATIO   A truant disposition, good my lord.
HAMLET   I would not hear your enemy say so,   170
Nor shall you do my ear that violence
To make it truster of your own report
Against yourself. I know you are no truant.
But what is your affair in Elsinore?
We'll teach you to drink deep ere you depart.   175
HORATIO   My lord, I came to see your father's funeral.
HAMLET   I prithee do not mock me, fellow-student,
I think it was to see my mother's wedding.
HORATIO   Indeed, my lord, it followed hard upon.
HAMLET   Thrift, thrift, Horatio. The funeral-baked meats   180
Did coldly furnish forth the marriage tables.
Would I had met my dearest[9] foe in heaven
Or ever I had seen that day, Horatio!
My father—methinks I see my father.
HORATIO   Where, my lord?
HAMLET   In my mind's eye, Horatio.   185
HORATIO   I saw him once, 'a was a goodly king.
HAMLET   'A was a man, take him for all in all,
I shall not look upon his like again.
HORATIO   My lord, I think I saw him yesternight.
HAMLET   Saw who?   190
HORATIO   My lord, the king your father.
HAMLET   The king my father?
HORATIO   Season[1] your admiration[2] for a while
With an attent[3] ear till I may deliver[4]
Upon the witness of these gentlemen
This marvel to you.
HAMLET   For God's love, let me hear!   195
HORATIO   Two nights together had these gentlemen,
Marcellus and Bernardo, on their watch
In the dead waste and middle of the night
Been thus encountered. A figure like your father,
Armed at point exactly,[5] cap-a-pe,[6]   200
Appears before them, and with solemn march

8. exchange
9. bitterest
1. moderate
2. wonder

3. attentive
4. relate
5. completely
6. from head to toe

Goes slow and stately by them. Thrice he walked
By their oppressed and fear-surpriséd eyes
Within his truncheon's[7] length, whilst they, distilled
Almost to jelly with the act of fear,   205
Stand dumb and speak not to him. This to me
In dreadful secrecy impart they did,
And I with them the third night kept the watch,
Where, as they had delivered, both in time,
Form of the thing, each word made true and good,   210
The apparition comes. I knew your father.
These hands are not more like.
HAMLET   But where was this?
MARCELLUS   My lord, upon the platform where we watch.
HAMLET   Did you not speak to it?
HORATIO   My lord, I did,
But answer made it none. Yet once methought   215
It lifted up it head and did address
Itself to motion, like as it would speak;
But even then the morning cock crew loud,
And at the sound it shrunk in haste away
And vanished from our sight.
HAMLET   'Tis very strange.   220
HORATIO   As I do live, my honored lord, 'tis true,
And we did think it writ down in our duty
To let you know of it.
HAMLET   Indeed, sirs, but
This troubles me. Hold you the watch tonight?
ALL   We do, my lord.
HAMLET   Armed, say you?
ALL   Armed, my lord.   225
HAMLET   From top to toe?
ALL   My lord, from head to foot.
HAMLET   Then saw you not his face.
HORATIO   O yes, my lord, he wore his beaver[8] up.
HAMLET   What, looked he frowningly?
HORATIO   A countenance more in sorrow than in anger.   230
HAMLET   Pale or red?
HORATIO   Nay, very pale.
HAMLET   And fixed his eyes upon you?
HORATIO   Most constantly.
HAMLET   I would I had been there.
HORATIO   It would have much amazed you.
HAMLET   Very like.
Stayed it long?   235
HORATIO   While one with moderate haste might tell a hundred.
BOTH   Longer, longer.
HORATIO   Not when I saw't.
HAMLET   His beard was grizzled, no?
HORATIO   It was as I have seen it in his life,
A sable silvered.
HAMLET   I will watch tonight.   240
Perchance 'twill walk again.

7. baton of office   8. movable face protector

HORATIO   I warr'nt it will.
HAMLET   If it assume my noble father's person,
    I'll speak to it though hell itself should gape[9]
    And bid me hold my peace. I pray you all,
    If you have hitherto concealed this sight,   245
    Let it be tenable[1] in your silence still,
    And whatsomever else shall hap tonight,
    Give it an understanding but no tongue.
    I will requite your loves. So fare you well.
    Upon the platform 'twixt eleven and twelve   250
    I'll visit you.
ALL   Our duty to your honor.
HAMLET   Your loves, as mine to you. Farewell.

                                   Exeunt all but HAMLET.

    My father's spirit in arms? All is not well.
    I doubt[2] some foul play. Would the night were come!
    Till then sit still, my soul. Foul deeds will rise,   255
    Though all the earth o'erwhelm them, to men's eyes.   *Exit.*

SCENE 3: *The dwelling of* POLONIUS. *Enter* LAERTES *and* OPHELIA.

LAERTES   My necessaries are embarked. Farewell.
    And, sister, as the winds give benefit
    And convoy[3] is assistant,[4] do not sleep,
    But let me hear from you.
OPHELIA   Do you doubt that?
LAERTES   For Hamlet, and the trifling of his favor,   5
    Hold it a fashion and a toy in blood,
    A violet in the youth of primy[5] nature,
    Forward, not permanent, sweet, not lasting,
    The perfume and suppliance of a minute,
    No more.
OPHELIA   No more but so?
LAERTES   Think it no more.   10
    For nature crescent[6] does not grow alone
    In thews and bulk, but as this temple[7] waxes
    The inward service of the mind and soul
    Grows wide withal. Perhaps he loves you now,
    And now no soil nor cautel[8] doth besmirch   15
    The virtue of his will, but you must fear,
    His greatness weighed,[9] his will is not his own,
    For he himself is subject to his birth.
    He may not, as unvalued persons do,
    Carve for himself, for on his choice depends   20
    The safety and health of this whole state,
    And therefore must his choice be circumscribed
    Unto the voice[1] and yielding of that body
    Whereof he is the head. Then if he says he loves you,

9. open (its mouth) wide   6. growing
1. held   7. body
2. suspect   8. deceit
3. means of transport   9. rank considered
4. available   1. assent
5. of the spring

It fits your wisdom so far to believe it   25
As he in his particular act and place
May give his saying deed, which is no further
Than the main voice of Denmark goes withal.
Then weigh what loss your honor may sustain
If with too credent[2] ear you list[3] his songs,   30
Or lose your heart, or your chaste treasure open
To his unmastered importunity.
Fear it, Ophelia, fear it, my dear sister,
And keep you in the rear of your affection,
Out of the shot and danger of desire.   35
The chariest[4] maid is prodigal enough
If she unmask her beauty to the moon.
Virtue itself scapes not calumnious strokes.
The canker[5] galls the infants of the spring
Too oft before their buttons[6] be disclosed,   40
And in the morn and liquid dew of youth
Contagious blastments[7] are most imminent.
Be wary then; best safety lies in fear.
Youth to itself rebels, though none else near.
OPHELIA   I shall the effect of this good lesson keep   45
As watchman to my heart. But, good my brother,
Do not as some ungracious pastors do,
Show me the steep and thorny way to heaven,
Whiles like a puffed and reckless libertine
Himself the primrose path of dalliance treads   50
And recks[8] not his own rede.[9]
LAERTES   O, fear me not.

   Enter POLONIUS.

I stay too long. But here my father comes.
A double blessing is a double grace;
Occasion smiles upon a second leave.
POLONIUS   Yet here, Laertes? Aboard, aboard, for shame!   55
The wind sits in the shoulder of your sail,
And you are stayed for. There—my blessing with thee,
And these few precepts in thy memory
Look thou character.[1] Give thy thoughts no tongue,
Nor any unproportioned thought his act.   60
Be thou familiar, but by no means vulgar.
Those friends thou hast, and their adoption tried,
Grapple them unto thy soul with hoops of steel;
But do not dull[2] thy palm with entertainment
Of each new-hatched, unfledged comrade. Beware   65
Of entrance to a quarrel, but being in,
Bear't[3] that th' opposéd[4] may beware of thee.
Give every man thy ear, but few thy voice;[5]
Take each man's censure, but reserve thy judgment.

2. credulous
3. listen to
4. most circumspect
5. rose caterpillar
6. buds
7. blights
8. heeds

9. advice
1. write
2. make callous
3. conduct it
4. opponent
5. approval

Costly thy habit as thy purse can buy,   70
But not expressed in fancy; rich not gaudy,
For the apparel oft proclaims the man,
And they in France of the best rank and station
Are of a most select and generous chief[6] in that.
Neither a borrower nor a lender be,   75
For loan oft loses both itself and friend,
And borrowing dulls th' edge of husbandry.
This above all, to thine own self be true,
And it must follow as the night the day
Thou canst not then be false to any man.   80
Farewell. My blessing season this in thee!
LAERTES   Most humbly do I take my leave, my lord.
POLONIUS   The time invites you. Go, your servants tend.[7]
LAERTES   Farewell, Ophelia, and remember well
What I have said to you.
OPHELIA   'Tis in my memory locked,   85
And you yourself shall keep the key of it.
LAERTES   Farewell.   *Exit* LAERTES.
POLONIUS   What is't, Ophelia, he hath said to you?
OPHELIA   So please you, something touching the Lord Hamlet.
POLONIUS   Marry, well bethought.   90
'Tis told me he hath very oft of late
Given private time to you, and you yourself
Have of your audience been most free and bounteous.
If it be so—as so 'tis put on me,
And that in way of caution—I must tell you,   95
You do not understand yourself so clearly
As it behooves my daughter and your honor.
What is between you? Give me up the truth.
OPHELIA   He hath, my lord, of late made many tenders
Of his affection to me.   100
POLONIUS   Affection? Pooh! You speak like a green girl,
Unsifted in such perilous circumstance.
Do you believe his tenders, as you call them?
OPHELIA   I do not know, my lord, what I should think.
POLONIUS   Marry, I will teach you. Think yourself a baby   105
That you have ta'en these tenders for true pay
Which are not sterling. Tender yourself more dearly,
Or (not to crack the wind of the poor phrase,
Running it thus) you'll tender me a fool.
OPHELIA   My lord, he hath importuned me with love   110
In honorable fashion.
POLONIUS   Ay, fashion you may call it. Go to, go to.
OPHELIA   And hath given countenance[8] to his speech, my lord,
With almost all the holy vows of heaven.
POLONIUS   Ay, springes[9] to catch woodcocks. I do know,   115
When the blood burns, how prodigal the soul
Lends the tongue vows. These blazes, daughter,
Giving more light than heat, extinct in both
Even in their promise, as it is a-making,
You must not take for fire. From this time   120

6. eminence   8. confirmation
7. await   9. snares

Be something scanter of your maiden presence.
Set your entreatments[1] at a higher rate
Than a command to parle. For Lord Hamlet,
Believe so much in him that he is young,
And with a larger tether may he walk   125
Than may be given you. In few, Ophelia,
Do not believe his vows, for they are brokers,[2]
Not of that dye which their investments[3] show,
But mere implorators[4] of unholy suits,
Breathing like sanctified and pious bawds,   130
The better to beguile. This is for all:
I would not, in plain terms, from this time forth
Have you so slander any moment leisure
As to give words or talk with the Lord Hamlet.
Look to't, I charge you. Come your ways.   135
OPHELIA   I shall obey, my lord.   *Exeunt.*

SCENE 4: *The guard station. Enter* HAMLET, HORATIO *and*
MARCELLUS.

HAMLET   The air bites shrewdly[5]; it is very cold.
HORATIO   It is a nipping and an eager[6] air.
HAMLET   What hour now?
HORATIO   I think it lacks of twelve.
MARCELLUS   No, it is struck.
HORATIO   Indeed? I heard it not. It then draws near the season   5
Wherein the spirit held his wont to walk.
     A flourish of trumpets, and two pieces go off.
What does this mean, my lord?
HAMLET   The king doth wake tonight and takes his rouse,
Keeps wassail, and the swagg'ring up-spring[7] reels,
And as he drains his draughts of Rhenish down,   10
The kettledrum and trumpet thus bray out
The triumph of his pledge.
HORATIO   Is it a custom?
HAMLET   Ay, marry, is't,
But to my mind, though I am native here
And to the manner born, it is a custom
More honored in the breach than the observance.   15
This heavy-headed revel east and west
Makes us traduced and taxed of other nations.
They clepe[8] us drunkards, and with swinish phrase
Soil our addition,[9] and indeed it takes   20
From our achievements, though performed at height,
The pith and marrow of our attribute.[1]
So oft it chances in particular men,
That for some vicious mole of nature in them,
As in their birth, wherein they are not guilty   25
(Since nature cannot choose his origin),

1. negotiations before a surrender
2. panders
3. garments
4. solicitors
5. sharply
6. keen
7. a German dance
8. call
9. reputation
1. honor

By the o'ergrowth of some complexion,
Oft breaking down the pales[2] and forts of reason,
Or by some habit that too much o'er-leavens
The form of plausive[3] manners—that these men,   30
Carrying, I say, the stamp of one defect,
Being nature's livery or fortune's star,
His virtues else, be they as pure as grace,
As infinite as man may undergo,
Shall in the general censure take corruption   35
From that particular fault. The dram of evil
Doth all the noble substance often doubt[4]
To his own scandal.

    Enter GHOST.

HORATIO   Look, my lord, it comes.
HAMLET   Angels and ministers of grace defend us!
  Be thou a spirit of health or goblin damned,   40
  Bring with thee airs from heaven or blasts from hell,
  Be thy intents wicked or charitable,
  Thou com'st in such a questionable[5] shape
  That I will speak to thee. I'll call thee Hamlet,
  King, father, royal Dane. O, answer me!   45
  Let me not burst in ignorance, but tell
  Why thy canonized[6] bones, hearséd in death,
  Have burst their cerements[7]; why the sepulchre
  Wherein we saw thee quietly interred
  Hath oped his ponderous and marble jaws   50
  To cast thee up again. What may this mean
  That thou, dead corse, again in complete steel[8]
  Revisits thus the glimpses of the moon,
  Making night hideous, and we fools of nature
  So horridly to shake our disposition   55
  With thoughts beyond the reaches of our souls?
  Say, why is this? wherefore? What should we do?

    GHOST *beckons.*

HORATIO   It beckons you to go away it,
  As if it some impartment[9] did desire
  To you alone.
MARCELLUS   Look with what courteous action   60
  It waves[1] you to a more removéd[2] ground.
  But do not go with it.
HORATIO   No, by no means.
HAMLET   It will not speak; then I will follow it.
HORATIO   Do not, my lord.
HAMLET   Why, what should be the fear?
  I do not set my life at a pin's fee,[3]   65
  And for my soul, what can it do to that,
  Being a thing immortal as itself?

---

2. barriers
3. pleasing
4. put out
5. prompting question
6. buried in accordance with church canons

7. gravecloths
8. armor
9. communication
1. beckons
2. distant
3. price

It waves me forth again. I'll follow it.

HORATIO   What if it tempt you toward the flood, my lord,
Or to the dreadful summit of the cliff   70
That beetles[4] o'er his base into the sea,
And there assume some other horrible form,
Which might deprive[5] your sovereignty of reason[6]
And draw you into madness? Think of it.
The very place puts toys of desperation,[7]   75
Without more motive, into every brain
That looks so many fathoms to the sea
And hears it roar beneath.

HAMLET   It waves me still.
Go on. I'll follow thee.

MARCELLUS   You shall not go, my lord.

HAMLET   Hold off your hands.   80

HORATIO   Be ruled. You shall not go.

HAMLET   My fate cries out
And makes each petty artere in this body
As hardy as the Nemean lion's nerve.[8]
Still am I called. Unhand me, gentlemen.
By heaven, I'll make a ghost of him that lets[9] me.   85
I say, away! Go on. I'll follow thee.

Exeunt GHOST *and* HAMLET.

HORATIO   He waxes desperate with imagination.

MARCELLUS   Let's follow. 'Tis not fit thus to obey him.

HORATIO   Have after. To what issue will this come?

MARCELLUS   Something is rotten in the state of Denmark.   90

HORATIO   Heaven will direct it.

MARCELLUS   Nay, let's follow him.   *Exeunt.*

SCENE 5: *Near the guard station. Enter* GHOST *and* HAMLET.

HAMLET   Whither wilt thou lead me? Speak. I'll go no further.

GHOST   Mark me.

HAMLET   I will.

GHOST   My hour is almost come,
When I to sulph'rous and tormenting flames
Must render up myself.

HAMLET   Alas, poor ghost!

GHOST   Pity me not, but lend thy serious hearing   5
To what I shall unfold.

HAMLET   Speak. I am bound to hear.

GHOST   So art thou to revenge, when thou shalt hear.

HAMLET   What?

GHOST   I am thy father's spirit,
Doomed for a certain term to walk the night,   10
And for the day confined to fast in fires,
Till the foul crimes done in my days of nature[1]
Are burnt and purged away. But that I am forbid

---

4. juts out
5. take away
6. rational power
7. desperate fancies
8. The Nemean lion was a mythological

monster slain by Hercules as one of his
twelve labors.
9. hinders
1. i.e., while I was alive

To tell the secrets of my prison house,
I could a tale unfold whose lightest word   15
Would harrow up thy soul, freeze thy young blood,
Make thy two eyes like stars start from their spheres,
Thy knotted and combinéd² locks to part,
And each particular hair to stand an end,
Like quills upon the fretful porpentine.³   20
But this eternal blazon⁴ must not be
To ears of flesh and blood. List, list, O, list!
If thou didst ever thy dear father love—

HAMLET   O God!
GHOST   Revenge his foul and most unnatural murder.   25
HAMLET   Murder!
GHOST   Murder most foul, as in the best it is,
But this most foul, strange, and unnatural.
HAMLET   Haste me to know't, that I, with wings as swift
As meditation or the thoughts of love,   30
May sweep to my revenge.
GHOST   I find thee apt,
And duller shouldst thou be than the fat weed
That rots itself in ease on Lethe⁵ wharf,—
Wouldst thou not stir in this. Now, Hamlet, hear.
'Tis given out that, sleeping in my orchard,   35
A serpent stung me. So the whole ear of Denmark
Is by a forgéd process⁶ of my death
Rankly abused. But know, thou noble youth,
The serpent that did sting thy father's life
Now wears his crown.
HAMLET   O my prophetic soul!   40
My uncle!
GHOST   Ay, that incestuous, that adulterate beast,
With witchcraft of his wits, with traitorous gifts—
O wicked wit and gifts that have the power
So to seduce!—won to his shameful lust   45
The will of my most seeming virtuous queen.
O Hamlet, what a falling off was there,
From me, whose love was of that dignity
That it went hand in hand even with the vow
I made to her in marriage, and to decline⁷   50
Upon a wretch whose natural gifts were poor
To those of mine!
But virtue, as it never will be moved,
Though lewdness court it in a shape of heaven,
So lust, though to a radiant angel linked,   55
Will sate itself in a celestial bed
And prey on garbage.
But soft, methinks I scent the morning air.
Brief let me be. Sleeping within my orchard,
My custom always of the afternoon,   60
Upon my secure hour thy uncle stole,

2. tangled
3. porcupine
4. description of eternity
5. The Lethe was one of the rivers of
the classical underworld. Its specific importance was that its waters when drunk
induced forgetfulness. The "fat weed" is
the asphodel which grew there.
6. false report
7. sink

With juice of cursed hebona[8] in a vial,
And in the porches of my ears did pour
The leperous distilment, whose effect
Holds such an enmity with blood of man   65
That swift as quicksilver it courses through
The natural gates and alleys of the body,
And with a sudden vigor it doth posset[9]
And curd,[1] like eager[2] droppings into milk,
The thin and wholesome blood. So did it mine,   70
And a most instant tetter[3] barked about[4]
Most lazar-like[5] with vile and loathsome crust
All my smooth body.
Thus was I sleeping by a brother's hand
Of life, of crown, of queen at once dispatched,   75
Cut off even in the blossoms of my sin,
Unhouseled, disappointed, unaneled,[6]
No reck'ning made, but sent to my account
With all my imperfections on my head.
O, horrible! O, horrible! most horrible!   80
If thou hast nature in thee, bear it not.
Let not the royal bed of Denmark be
A couch for luxury[7] and damnéd incest.
But howsomever thou pursues this act,
Taint not thy mind, nor let thy soul contrive   85
Against thy mother aught. Leave her to heaven,
And to those thorns that in her bosom lodge
To prick and sting her. Fare thee well at once.
The glowworm shows the matin[8] to be near,
And gins to pale his uneffectual fire.   90
Adieu, adieu, adieu. Remember me.   *Exit.*
HAMLET   O all you host of heaven! O earth! What else?
And shall I couple hell? O, fie! Hold, hold, my heart,
And you, my sinews, grow not instant old,
But bear me stiffly up. Remember thee?   95
Ay, thou poor ghost, whiles memory holds a seat
In this distracted globe.[9] Remember thee?
Yea, from the table[1] of my memory
I'll wipe away all trivial fond[2] records,
All saws of books, all forms, all pressures past   100
That youth and observation copied there,
And thy commandment all alone shall live
Within the book and volume of my brain,
Unmixed with baser matter. Yes, by heaven!
O most pernicious woman!   105
O villain, villain, smiling, damnéd villain!
My tables—meet it is I set it down
That one may smile, and smile, and be a villain.
At least I am sure it may be so in Denmark.

8. a poison
9. coagulate
1. curdle
2. acid
3. a skin disease
4. covered like bark
5. leper-like
6. The Ghost means that he died with- out the customary rites of the church, that is, without receiving the sacrament, without confession, and without extreme unction.
7. lust
8. morning
9. skull
1. writing tablet
2. foolish

So, uncle, there you are. Now to my word[3]:   110
It is "Adieu, adieu. Remember me."
I have sworn't.

Enter HORATIO *and* MARCELLUS.

HORATIO   My lord, my lord!
MARCELLUS   Lord Hamlet!
HORATIO   Heavens secure him!
HAMLET   So be it!
MARCELLUS   Illo, ho, ho, my lord!   115
HAMLET   Hillo, ho, ho, boy![4] Come, bird, come.
MARCELLUS   How is't, my noble lord?
HORATIO   What news, my lord?
HAMLET   O, wonderful!
HORATIO   Good my lord, tell it.
HAMLET   No, you will reveal it.
HORATIO   Not I, my lord, by heaven.
MARCELLUS   Nor I, my lord.   120
HAMLET   How say you then, would heart of man once think it?
   But you'll be secret?
BOTH   Ay, by heaven, my lord.
HAMLET   There's never a villain dwelling in all Denmark
   But he's an arrant knave.
HORATIO   There needs no ghost, my lord, come from the grave 125
   To tell us this.
HAMLET   Why, right, you are in the right,
   And so without more circumstance at all
   I hold it fit that we shake hands and part,
   You, as your business and desire shall point you,
   For every man hath business and desire   130
   Such as it is, and for my own poor part,
   I will go pray.
HORATIO   These are but wild and whirling words, my lord.
HAMLET   I am sorry they offend you, heartily;
   Yes, faith, heartily.
HORATIO   There's no offence, my lord.   135
HAMLET   Yes, by Saint Patrick, but there is, Horatio,
   And much offence too. Touching this vision here,
   It is an honest ghost, that let me tell you.
   For your desire to know what is between us,
   O'ermaster't as you may. And now, good friends,   140
   As you are friends, scholars, and soldiers,
   Give me one poor request.
HORATIO   What is't, my lord? We will.
HAMLET   Never make known what you have seen tonight.
BOTH   My lord, we will not.
HAMLET   Nay, but swear't.
HORATIO   In faith,   145
   My lord, not I.
MARCELLUS   Nor I, my lord, in faith.
HAMLET   Upon my sword.
MARCELLUS   We have sworn, my lord, already.

3. for my motto   4. a falconer's cry

HAMLET   Indeed, upon my sword, indeed.

GHOST *cries under the stage.*

GHOST   Swear.
HAMLET   Ha, ha, boy, say'st thou so? Art thou there, truepenny⁵?   150
Come on. You hear this fellow in the cellarage.⁶
Consent to swear.
HORATIO   Propose the oath, my lord.
HAMLET   Never to speak of this that you have seen,
Swear by my sword.
GHOST [*beneath*]   Swear.
HAMLET   Hic et ubique?⁷ Then we'll shift our ground.   155
Come hither, gentlemen,
And lay your hands again upon my sword.
Swear by my sword
Never to speak of this that you have heard.
GHOST [*beneath*]   Swear by his sword.   160
HAMLET   Well said, old mole! Canst work i' th' earth so fast?
A worthy pioneer!⁸ Once more remove, good friends.
HORATIO   O day and night, but this is wondrous strange!
HAMLET   And therefore as a stranger give it welcome.
There are more things in heaven and earth, Horatio,   165
Than are dreamt of in your philosophy.
But come.
Here as before, never, so help you mercy,
How strange or odd some'er I bear myself
(As I perchance hereafter shall think meet   170
To put an antic⁹ disposition on),
That you, at such times, seeing me, never shall,
With arms encumbered¹ thus, or this head-shake,
Or by pronouncing of some doubtful phrase,
As "Well, well, we know," or "We could, and if we would"   175
Or "If we list to speak," or "There be, and if they might"
Or such ambiguous giving out, to note
That you know aught of me—this do swear,
So grace and mercy at your most need help you.
GHOST [*beneath*]   Swear.   *They swear.* 180
HAMLET   Rest, rest, perturbéd spirit! So, gentlemen,
With all my love I do commend me to you,
And what so poor a man as Hamlet is
May do t'express his love and friending² to you,
God willing, shall not lack. Let us go in together,   185
And still your fingers on your lips, I pray.
The time is out of joint. O curséd spite
That ever I was born to set it right!
Nay, come, let's go together.   *Exeunt.*

---

5. old fellow   9. mad
6. below   1. folded
7. here and everywhere   2. friendship
8. soldier who digs trenches

Act 2

SCENE 1: *The dwelling of* POLONIUS. *Enter* POLONIUS
and REYNALDO.

POLONIUS Give him this money and these notes, Reynaldo.
REYNALDO I will, my lord.
POLONIUS You shall do marvellous wisely, good Reynaldo,
Before you visit him, to make inquire[3]
Of his behavior.
REYNALDO   My lord, I did intend it.   5
POLONIUS Marry, well said, very well said. Look you, sir.
Enquire me first what Danskers[4] are in Paris,
And how, and who, what means, and where they keep,[5]
What company, at what expense; and finding
By this encompassment[6] and drift of question   10
That they do know my son, come you more nearer
Than your particular demands[7] will touch it.
Take you as 'twere some distant knowledge of him,
As thus, "I know his father and his friends,
And in part him." Do you mark this, Reynaldo?   15
REYNALDO Ay, very well, my lord.
POLONIUS "And in part him, but," you may say, "not well,
But if't be he I mean, he's very wild,
Addicted so and so." And there put on him
What forgeries[8] you please; marry, none so rank[9]   20
As may dishonor him. Take heed of that.
But, sir, such wanton, wild, and usual slips
As are companions noted and most known
To youth and liberty.
REYNALDO   As gaming, my lord.
POLONIUS Ay, or drinking, fencing, swearing, quarrelling,   25
Drabbing[1]—you may go so far.
REYNALDO My lord, that would dishonor him.
POLONIUS Faith, no, as you may season it in the charge.[2]
You must not put another scandal on him,
That he is open to incontinency.[3]   30
That's not my meaning. But breathe his faults so quaintly[4]
That they may seem the taints of liberty,[5]
The flash and outbreak of a fiery mind,
A savageness in unreclaiméd[6] blood,
Of general assault.[7]
REYNALDO   But, my good lord—   35
POLONIUS Wherefore should you do this?
REYNALDO   Ay, my lord,
I would know that.
POLONIUS   Marry, sir, here's my drift,

---

3. inquiry
4. Danes
5. live
6. indirect means
7. direct questions
8. lies
9. foul

1. whoring
2. soften the accusation
3. sexual excess
4. with delicacy
5. faults of freedom
6. untamed
7. touching everyone

And I believe it is a fetch of warrant.[8]
You laying these slight sullies on my son,
As 'twere a thing a little soiled i' th' working,   40
Mark you,
Your party in converse,[9] him you would sound,
Having ever seen in the prenominate[1] crimes
The youth you breathe[2] of guilty, be assured
He closes with you in this consequence,   45
"Good sir," or so, or "friend," or "gentleman,"
According to the phrase or the addition
Of man and country.
REYNALDO   Very good, my lord.
POLONIUS   And then, sir, does 'a this—'a does—What was I about to
    say?   50
By the mass, I was about to say something.
Where did I leave?
REYNALDO   At "closes in the consequence."
POLONIUS   At "closes in the consequence"—ay, marry,
He closes thus: "I know the gentleman.   55
I saw him yesterday, or th' other day,
Or then, or then, with such, or such, and as you say,
There was 'a gaming, there o'ertook in's rouse,
There falling out at tennis," or perchance
"I saw him enter such a house of sale,"   60
Videlicet,[3] a brothel, or so forth.
See you, now—
Your bait of falsehood takes this carp of truth,
And thus do we of wisdom and of reach,[4]
With windlasses and with assays of bias,[5]   65
By indirections find directions out;
So by my former lecture and advice
Shall you my son. You have me, have you not?
REYNALDO   My lord, I have.
POLONIUS   God b'wi' ye; fare ye well.
REYNALDO   Good my lord.   70
POLONIUS   Observe his inclination in yourself.
REYNALDO   I shall, my lord.
POLONIUS   And let him ply[6] his music.
REYNALDO   Well, my lord.
POLONIUS   Farewell.   *Exit* REYNALDO.

    Enter OPHELIA.

                How now, Ophelia, what's the matter?
OPHELIA   O my lord, my lord, I have been so affrighted!   75
POLONIUS   With what, i' th' name of God?
OPHELIA   My lord, as I was sewing in my closet,[7]
Lord Hamlet with his doublet[8] all unbraced,[9]
No hat upon his head, his stockings fouled,
Ungartered and down-gyvéd[1] to his ankle,   80

8. permissible trick
9. conversation
1. already named
2. speak
3. namely
4. ability

5. indirect tests
6. practice
7. chamber
8. jacket
9. unlaced
1. fallen down like fetters

Pale as his shirt, his knees knocking each other,
And with a look so piteous in purport
As if he had been looséd out of hell
To speak of horrors—he comes before me.
POLONIUS   Mad for thy love?
OPHELIA   My lord, I do not know,   85
But truly I do fear it.
POLONIUS   What said he?
OPHELIA   He took me by the wrist, and held me hard,
Then goes he to the length of all his arm,
And with his other hand thus o'er his brow,
He falls to such perusal of my face   90
As 'a would draw it. Long stayed he so.
At last, a little shaking of mine arm,
And thrice his head thus waving up and down,
He raised a sigh so piteous and profound
As it did seem to shatter all his bulk,[2]   95
And end his being. That done, he lets me go,
And with his head over his shoulder turned
He seemed to find his way without his eyes,
For out adoors he went without their helps,
And to the last bended[3] their light on me.   100
POLONIUS   Come, go with me. I will go seek the king.
This is the very ecstasy of love,
Whose violent property[4] fordoes[5] itself,
And leads the will to desperate undertakings
As oft as any passion under heaven   105
That does afflict our natures. I am sorry.
What, have you given him any hard words of late?
OPHELIA   No, my good lord, but as you did command
I did repel[6] his letters, and denied
His access to me.
POLONIUS   That hath made him mad.   110
I am sorry that with better heed and judgment
I had not quoted[7] him. I feared he did but trifle,
And meant to wrack[8] thee; but beshrew my jealousy.
By heaven, it is as proper to our age
To cast beyond ourselves in our opinions   115
As it is common for the younger sort
To lack discretion. Come, go we to the king.
This must be known, which being kept close, might move
More grief to hide than hate to utter love.
Come.   *Exeunt.* 120

SCENE 2: *A public room. Enter* KING, QUEEN, ROSENCRANTZ
and GUILDENSTERN.

KING   Welcome, dear Rosencrantz and Guildenstern.
Moreover that[9] we much did long to see you,
The need we have to use you did provoke

2. body   6. refuse
3. directed   7. observed
4. character   8. harm
5. destroys   9. in addition to the fact that

Our hasty sending. Something have you heard
Of Hamlet's transformation—so call it,   5
Sith[1] nor th' exterior nor the inward man
Resembles that it was. What it should be,
More than his father's death, that thus hath put him
So much from th' understanding of himself,
I cannot deem of. I entreat you both   10
That, being of so young days[2] brought up with him,
And sith so neighbored[3] to his youth and havior,
That you vouchsafe your rest here in our court
Some little time, so by your companies
To draw him on to pleasures, and to gather   15
So much as from occasion you may glean,
Whether aught to us unknown afflicts him thus,
That opened lies within our remedy.
QUEEN   Good gentlemen, he hath much talked of you,
And sure I am two men there are not living   20
To whom he more adheres. If it will please you
To show us so much gentry[4] and good will
As to expend your time with us awhile
For the supply and profit of our hope,
Your visitation shall receive such thanks   25
As fits a king's remembrance.
ROSENCRANTZ   Both your majesties
Might, by the sovereign power you have of us,
Put your dread pleasures more into command
Than to entreaty.
GUILDENSTERN   But we both obey,
And here give up ourselves in the full bent[5]   30
To lay our service freely at your feet,
To be commanded.
KING   Thanks, Rosencrantz and gentle Guildenstern.
QUEEN   Thanks, Guildenstern and gentle Rosencrantz.
And I beseech you instantly to visit   35
My too much changed son. Go, some of you,
And bring these gentlemen where Hamlet is.
GUILDENSTERN   Heavens make our presence and our practices
Pleasant and helpful to him!
QUEEN   Ay, amen!

                    Exeunt ROSENCRANTZ *and* GUILDENSTERN.

     Enter POLONIUS.

POLONIUS   Th' ambassadors from Norway, my good lord,   40
Are joyfully returned.
KING   Thou still[6] hast been the father of good news.
POLONIUS   Have I, my lord? I assure you, my good liege,
I hold my duty as I hold my soul,
Both to my God and to my gracious king;   45
And I do think—or else this brain of mine
Hunts not the trail of policy[7] so sure

1. since   5. completely
2. from childhood   6. ever
3. closely allied   7. statecraft
4. courtesy

As it hath used to do—that I have found
The very cause of Hamlet's lunacy.
KING   O, speak of that, that do I long to hear.   50
POLONIUS   Give first admittance to th' ambassadors.
My news shall be the fruit[8] to that great feast.
KING   Thyself do grace to them, and bring them in.

Exit POLONIUS.

He tells me, my dear Gertrude, he hath found
The head and source of all your son's distemper.   55
QUEEN   I doubt it is no other but the main,
His father's death and our o'erhasty marriage.
KING   Well, we shall sift[9] him.

Enter Ambassadors (VOLTEMAND *and* CORNELIUS) *with*
POLONIUS.
                            Welcome, my good friends,
Say, Voltemand, what from our brother Norway?
VOLTEMAND   Most fair return of greetings and desires.   60
Upon our first,[1] he sent out to suppress
His nephew's levies, which to him appeared
To be a preparation 'gainst the Polack,
But better looked into, he truly found
It was against your highness, whereat grieved,   65
That so his sickness, age, and impotence
Was falsely borne in hand,[2] sends out arrests[3]
On Fortinbras, which he in brief obeys,
Receives rebuke from Norway, and in fine,
Makes vow before his uncle never more   70
To give th' assay[4] of arms against your majesty.
Whereon old Norway, overcome with joy,
Gives him threescore thousand crowns in annual fee,
And his commission to employ those soldiers,
So levied as before, against the Polack,   75
With an entreaty, herein further shown,   *Gives* CLAUDIUS *a paper.*
That it might please you to give quiet pass[5]
Through your dominions for this enterprise,
On such regards of safety and allowance
As therein are set down.
KING   It likes[6] us well,   80
And at our more considered time[7] we'll read,
Answer, and think upon this business.
Meantime we thank you for your well-took[8] labor.
Go to your rest; at night we'll feast together.
Most welcome home!   *Exeunt* AMBASSADORS.
POLONIUS   This business is well ended.   85
My liege and madam, to expostulate[9]
What majesty should be, what duty is,
Why day is day, night night, and time is time,

8. dessert
9. examine
1. i.e., first appearance
2. deceived
3. orders to stop
4. trial

5. safe conduct
6. pleases
7. time for more consideration
8. successful
9. discuss

Were nothing but to waste night, day, and time.
Therefore, since brevity is the soul of wit, 90
And tediousness the limbs and outward flourishes,[1]
I will be brief. Your noble son is mad.
Mad call I it, for to define true madness,
What is't but to be nothing else but mad?
But let that go.
QUEEN   More matter with less art. 95
POLONIUS   Madam, I swear I use no art at all.
That he is mad, 'tis true: 'tis true 'tis pity,
And pity 'tis 'tis true. A foolish figure,
But farewell it, for I will use no art.
Mad let us grant him, then, and now remains 100
That we find out the cause of this effect,
Or rather say the cause of this defect,
For this effect defective comes by cause.
Thus it remains, and the remainder thus.
Perpend.[2] 105
I have a daughter—have while she is mine—
Who in her duty and obedience, mark,
Hath given me this. Now gather, and surmise.
"To the celestial, and my soul's idol, the most beautified
Ophelia."—That's an ill phrase, a vile phrase, "beautified" is a 110
vile phrase. But you shall hear. Thus:
"In her excellent white bosom, these, etc."
QUEEN   Came this from Hamlet to her?
POLONIUS   Good madam, stay awhile. I will be faithful.

      "Doubt thou the stars are fire, 115
        Doubt that the sun doth move;
      Doubt truth to be a liar;
        But never doubt I love.

  O dear Ophelia, I am ill at these numbers.[3]
I have not art to reckon my groans, but that I love thee best, O 120
most best, believe it. Adieu.
              Thine evermore, most dear lady, whilst
                 this machine[4] is to him, HAMLET."
This in obedience hath my daughter shown me,
And more above, hath his solicitings, 125
As they fell out by time, by means, and place,
All given to mine ear.
KING   But how hath she
Received his love?
POLONIUS   What do you think of me?
KING   As of a man faithful and honorable.
POLONIUS   I would fain prove so. But what might you think, 130
When I had seen this hot love on the wing,
(As I perceived it, I must tell you that,
Before my daughter told me), what might you,
Or my dear majesty your queen here, think,
If I had played the desk or table-book, 135
Or given my heart a winking, mute and dumb,

1. adornments   3. verses
2. consider   4. body

Or looked upon this love with idle sight,[5]
What might you think? No, I went round[6] to work,
And my young mistress thus I did bespeak:
"Lord Hamlet is a prince out of thy star.[7]   140
This must not be." And then I prescripts[8] gave her,
That she should lock herself from his resort,
Admit no messengers, receive no tokens.
Which done, she took[9] the fruits of my advice;
And he repelled, a short tale to make,   145
Fell into a sadness, then into a fast,
Thence to a watch, thence into a weakness,
Thence to a lightness, and by this declension,
Into the madness wherein now he raves,
And all we mourn for.

KING   Do you think 'tis this?   150
QUEEN   It may be, very like.
POLONIUS   Hath there been such a time—I would fain know that—
That I have positively said "'Tis so,"
When it proved otherwise?
KING   Not that I know.
POLONIUS [*pointing to his head and shoulder*]   Take this from this, if
this be otherwise.   155
If circumstances lead me, I will find
Where truth is hid, though it were hid indeed
Within the centre.[1]
KING   How may we try it further?
POLONIUS   You know sometimes he walks four hours together
Here in the lobby.
QUEEN   So he does, indeed.   160
POLONIUS   At such a time I'll loose[2] my daughter to him.
Be you and I behind an arras[3] then.
Mark the encounter. If he love her not,
And be not from his reason fall'n thereon,
Let me be no assistant for a state,   165
But keep a farm and carters.
KING   We will try it.

Enter HAMLET *reading a book.*

QUEEN   But look where sadly the poor wretch comes reading.
POLONIUS   Away, I do beseech you both away,
I'll board[4] him presently.

Exeunt KING *and* QUEEN.

O, give me leave.
How does my good Lord Hamlet?   170
HAMLET   Well, God-a-mercy.
POLONIUS   Do you know me, my lord?
HAMLET   Excellent well, you are a fishmonger.

5. Polonius means that he would have
been at fault if, having seen Hamlet's attention to Ophelia, he had winked at it or
not paid attention, an "idle sight," and if
he had remained silent and kept the information to himself, as if it were written in a
"desk" or "table-book."
   6. directly

7. beyond your sphere
8. orders
9. followed
1. of the earth
2. let loose
3. tapestry
4. accost

POLONIUS   Not I, my lord.
HAMLET   Then I would you were so honest a man.   175
POLONIUS   Honest, my lord?
HAMLET   Ay, sir, to be honest as this world goes, is to be one man
picked out of ten thousand.
POLONIUS   That's very true, my lord.
HAMLET   For if the sun breed maggots in a dead dog, being a god 180
kissing carrion[5]—Have you a daughter?
POLONIUS   I have, my lord.
HAMLET   Let her not walk i' th' sun. Conception is a blessing, but as
your daughter may conceive—friend, look to't.
POLONIUS   How say you by that? [*Aside.*] Still harping on my daughter. 185
Yet he knew me not at first. 'A said I was a fishmonger. 'A is far
gone. And truly in my youth I suffered much extremity for love.
Very near this. I'll speak to him again.—What do you read, my lord?
HAMLET   Words, words, words.
POLONIUS   What is the matter, my lord?   190
HAMLET   Between who?
POLONIUS   I mean the matter that you read, my lord.
HAMLET   Slanders, sir; for the satirical rogue says here that old men
have grey beards, that their faces are wrinkled, their eyes purging
thick amber and plum-tree gum, and that they have a plentiful lack 195
of wit, together with most weak hams[6]—all which, sir, though I
most powerfully and potently believe, yet I hold it not honesty to
have it thus set down, for yourself, sir, shall grow old as I am, if like
a crab you could go backward.
POLONIUS   [*aside*]   Though this be madness, yet there is method in't. 200
—Will you walk out of the air, my lord?
HAMLET   Into my grave?
POLONIUS   [*aside*]   Indeed, that's out of the air. How pregnant sometime his replies are! a happiness that often madness hits on, which
reason and sanity could not so prosperously be delivered of. I will 205
leave him, and suddenly contrive the means of meeting between
him and my daughter.—My lord. I will take my leave of you.
HAMLET   You cannot take from me anything that I will more willingly
part withal—except my life, except my life, except my life.

Enter GUILDENSTERN *and* ROSENCRANTZ.

POLONIUS   Fare you well, my lord.   210
HAMLET   These tedious old fools!
POLONIUS   You go to seek the Lord Hamlet. There he is.
ROSENCRANTZ   [*to* POLONIUS]   God save you, sir!   *Exit* POLONIUS.
GUILDENSTERN   My honored lord!
ROSENCRANTZ   My most dear lord!   215
HAMLET   My excellent good friends! How dost thou, Guildenstern?
Ah, Rosencrantz! Good lads, how do you both?
ROSENCRANTZ   As the indifferent[7] children of the earth.
GUILDENSTERN   Happy in that we are not over-happy;
On Fortune's cap we are not the very button.[8]   220
HAMLET   Nor the soles of her shoe?
ROSENCRANTZ   Neither, my lord.

---

5. A reference to the belief of the period   6. limbs
that maggots were produced spontaneously   7. ordinary
by the action of sunshine on carrion.   8. i.e., on top

HAMLET   Then you live about her waist, or in the middle of her favors.

GUILDENSTERN   Faith, her privates we.

HAMLET   In the secret parts of Fortune? O, most true, she is a [225] strumpet.[9] What news?

ROSENCRANTZ   None, my lord, but that the world's grown honest.

HAMLET   Then is doomsday near. But your news is not true. Let me question more in particular. What have you, my good friends, de-served at the hands of Fortune, that she sends you to prison hither? [230]

GUILDENSTERN   Prison, my lord?

HAMLET   Denmark's a prison.

ROSENCRANTZ   Then is the world one.

HAMLET   A goodly one, in which there are many confines, wards,[1] and dungeons, Denmark being one o' th' worst.   [235]

ROSENCRANTZ   We think not so, my lord.

HAMLET   Why then 'tis none to you; for there is nothing either good or bad, but thinking makes it so. To me it is a prison.

ROSENCRANTZ   Why then your ambition makes it one. 'Tis too narrow for your mind.   [240]

HAMLET   O God, I could be bounded in a nutshell and count myself a king of infinite space, were it not that I have bad dreams.

GUILDENSTERN   Which dreams indeed are ambition; for the very sub-stance of the ambitious is merely the shadow of a dream.

HAMLET   A dream itself is but a shadow.   [245]

ROSENCRANTZ   Truly, and I hold ambition of so airy and light a quality that it is but a shadow's shadow.

HAMLET   Then are our beggars bodies, and our monarchs and out-stretched heroes the beggars' shadows. Shall we to th' court? for, by my fay,[2] I cannot reason.   [250]

BOTH   We'll wait upon you.

HAMLET   No such matter. I will not sort[3] you with the rest of my servants; for to speak to you like an honest man, I am most dread-fully attended. But in the beaten way of friendship, what make you at Elsinore?   [255]

ROSENCRANTZ   To visit you, my lord; no other occasion.

HAMLET   Beggar that I am, I am even poor in thanks, but I thank you; and sure, dear friends, my thanks are too dear a halfpenny.[4] Were you not sent for? Is it your own inclining? Is it a free visita-tion? Come, come, deal justly with me. Come, come, nay speak.   [260]

GUILDENSTERN   What should we say, my lord?

HAMLET   Why anything but to th' purpose. You were sent for, and there is a kind of confession in your looks, which your modesties have not craft enough to color. I know the good king and queen have sent for you.   [265]

ROSENCRANTZ   To what end, my lord?

HAMLET   That you must teach me. But let me conjure you by the rights of our fellowship, by the consonancy of our youth, by the obligation of our ever-preserved love, and by what more dear a better proposer can charge you withal, be even and direct[5] with me [270] whether you were sent for or no.

---

9. Hamlet is indulging in characteristic ribaldry. Guildenstern means that they are "privates" = ordinary citizens, but Hamlet takes him to mean "privates" = sexual or-gans and "middle of her favors" = waist = sexual organs.

1. cells
2. faith
3. include
4. not worth a halfpenny
5. straightforward

ROSENCRANTZ [*aside to* GUILDENSTERN] What say you?

HAMLET [*aside*] Nay, then, I have an eye of you.—If you love me, hold not off.

GUILDENSTERN My lord, we were sent for. 275

HAMLET I will tell you why; so shall my anticipation prevent your discovery,[6] and your secrecy to the king and queen moult no feather. I have of late—but wherefore I know not—lost all my mirth, forgone all custom of exercises; and indeed it goes so heavily with my disposition, that this goodly frame the earth seems to me 280 a sterile promontory, this most excellent canopy the air, look you, this brave o'er-hanging firmament, this majestical roof fretted[7] with golden fire, why it appeareth nothing to me but a foul and pestilent congregation of vapors. What a piece of work is a man, how noble in reason, how infinite in faculties, in form and moving, how express[8] 285 and admirable in action, how like an angel in apprehension, how like a god: the beauty of the world, the paragon of animals. And yet to me, what is this quintessence of dust? Man delights not me, nor woman neither, though by your smiling you seem to say so.

ROSENCRANTZ My lord, there was no such stuff in my thoughts. 290

HAMLET Why did ye laugh, then, when I said "Man delights not me"?

ROSENCRANTZ To think, my lord, if you delight not in man, what lenten[9] entertainment the players shall receive from you. We coted[1] them on the way, and hither are they coming to offer you service.

HAMLET He that plays the king shall be welcome—his majesty shall 295 have tribute on me; the adventurous knight shall use his foil and target[2]; the lover shall not sigh gratis; the humorous[3] man shall end his part in peace; the clown shall make those laugh whose lungs are tickle o' th' sere[4]; and the lady shall say her mind freely, or the blank verse shall halt for't. What players are they? 300

ROSENCRANTZ Even those you were wont to take such delight in, the tragedians of the city.

HAMLET How chances it they travel? Their residence, both in reputation and profit, was better both ways.

ROSENCRANTZ I think their inhibition comes by the means of the late 305 innovation.

HAMLET Do they hold the same estimation they did when I was in the city? Are they so followed?

ROSENCRANTZ No, indeed, are they not.

HAMLET How comes it? Do they grow rusty? 310

ROSENCRANTZ Nay, their endeavor keeps in the wonted pace; but there is, sir, an eyrie of children, little eyases,[5] that cry out on the top of question,[6] and are most tyrannically clapped for't. These are now the fashion, and so berattle the common stages (so they call them) that many wearing rapiers are afraid of goose quills[7] and 315 dare scarce come thither.[8]

HAMLET What, are they children? Who maintains 'em? How are they

6. disclosure
7. ornamented with fretwork
8. well built
9. scanty
1. passed
2. sword and shield
3. eccentric
4. easily set off
5. little hawks
6. with a loud, high delivery
7. pens of satirical writers

8. The passage refers to the emergence at the time of the play of theatrical companies made up of children from London choir schools. Their performances became fashionable and hurt the business of the established companies. Hamlet says that if they continue to act, "pursue the quality," when they are grown, they will find that they have been damaging their own future careers.

escoted[9]? Will they pursue the quality no longer than they can sing? Will they not say afterwards, if they should grow themselves to common players (as it is most like, if their means are no better), 320 their writers do them wrong to make them exclaim against their own succession[1]?

ROSENCRANTZ Faith, there has been much to do on both sides; and the nation holds it no sin to tarre[2] them to controversy. There was for a while no money bid for argument,[3] unless the poet and the 325 player went to cuffs[4] in the question.

HAMLET Is't possible?

GUILDENSTERN O, there has been much throwing about of brains.

HAMLET Do the boys carry it away?

ROSENCRANTZ Ay, that they do, my lord, Hercules and his load too.[5] 330

HAMLET It is not very strange, for my uncle is King of Denmark, and those that would make mouths[6] at him while my father lived give twenty, forty, fifty, a hundred ducats apiece for his picture in little.[7] 'Sblood, there is something in this more than natural, if philosophy could find it out.   *A flourish.* 335

GUILDENSTERN There are the players.

HAMLET Gentlemen, you are welcome to Elsinore. Your hands. Come then. th' appurtenance of welcome is fashion and ceremony. Let me comply with[8] you in this garb, lest my extent[9] to the players, which I tell you must show fairly outwards, should more appear like enter- 340 tainment[1] than yours. You are welcome. But my uncle-father and aunt-mother are deceived.

GUILDENSTERN In what, my dear lord?

HAMLET I am but mad north-north-west; when the wind is southerly I know a hawk from a handsaw.[2]   345

Enter POLONIUS.

POLONIUS Well be with you, gentlemen.

HAMLET Hark you, Guildenstern—and you too—at each ear a hearer. That great baby you see there is not yet out of his swaddling clouts.[3]

ROSENCRANTZ Happily he is the second time come to them, for they say an old man is twice a child.   350

HAMLET I will prophesy he comes to tell me of the players. Mark it. —You say right, sir, a Monday morning, 'twas then indeed.

POLONIUS My lord, I have news to tell you.

HAMLET My lord, I have news to tell you. When Roscius was an actor in Rome—[4]   355

POLONIUS The actors are come hither, my lord.

HAMLET Buzz, buzz.

POLONIUS Upon my honor—

HAMLET Then came each actor on his ass—

POLONIUS The best actors in the world, either for tragedy, comedy, 360

---

9. supported
1. future careers
2. urge
3. paid for a play plot
4. blows
5. During one of his labors Hercules assumed for a time the burden of the Titan Atlas, who supported the heavens on his shoulder. Also a reference to the effect on business at Shakespeare's theater, the Globe.

6. sneer
7. miniature
8. welcome
9. fashion
1. cordiality
2. A "hawk" is a plasterer's tool; Hamlet may also be using "handsaw" = hernshaw = heron.
3. wrappings for an infant
4. Roscius was the most famous actor of classical Rome.

history, pastoral, pastoral-comical, historical-pastoral, tragical-
historical, tragical-comical-historical-pastoral, scene individable, or
poem unlimited. Seneca cannot be too heavy nor Plautus too light.
For the law of writ and the liberty, these are the only men.[5]

HAMLET   O Jephtha, judge of Israel, what a treasure hadst thou![6] 365
POLONIUS   What a treasure had he, my lord?
HAMLET   Why—

> "One fair daughter, and no more,
> The which he loved passing well."

POLONIUS [*aside*]   Still on my daughter.   370
HAMLET   Am I not i' th' right, old Jephtha?
POLONIUS   If you call me Jephtha, my lord, I have a daughter that I
love passing well.
HAMLET   Nay, that follows not.
POLONIUS   What follows then, my lord?   375
HAMLET   Why—

> "As by lot, God wot"

and then, you know,

> "It came to pass, as most like it was."

The first row[7] of the pious chanson[8] will show you more, for look 380
where my abridgement[9] comes.

Enter the PLAYERS.

You are welcome, masters; welcome, all.—I am glad to see thee
well.—Welcome, good friends.—O, old friend! Why thy face is
valanced[1] since I saw thee last. Com'st thou to beard me in Denmark?—What, my young lady and mistress? By'r lady, your ladyship 385
is nearer to heaven than when I saw you last by the altitude of a
chopine.[2] Pray God your voice, like a piece of uncurrent gold, be not
cracked within the ring.—Masters, you are all welcome. We'll e'en
to't like French falconers, fly at anything we see. We'll have a speech
straight. Come give us a taste of your quality,[3] come a passionate 390
speech.
FIRST PLAYER   What speech, my good lord?
HAMLET   I heard thee speak me a speech once, but it was never acted,
or if it was, not above once, for the play, I remember, pleased not
the million; 'twas caviary[4] to the general.[5] But it was—as I received 395

---

5. Seneca and Plautus were Roman writers of tragedy and comedy, respectively.
The "law of writ" refers to plays written
according to such rules as the three unities;
the "liberty" to those written otherwise.
6. To insure victory, Jephtha promised
to sacrifice the first creature to meet him
on his return. Unfortunately, his only
daughter outstripped his dog and was the
victim of his vow. The Biblical story is told
in *Judges* 11.
7. stanza
8. song
9. that which cuts short by interrupting

1. fringed (with a beard)
2. A reference to the contemporary theatrical practice of using boys to play
women's parts. The company's "lady" has
grown in height by the size of a woman's
thick-soled shoe, "chopine," since Hamlet
saw him last. The next sentence refers to
the possibility, suggested by his growth,
that the young actor's voice may soon begin to change.
3. trade
4. caviar
5. masses

it, and others whose judgments in such matters cried in the top of[6] mine—an excellent play, well digested[7] in the scenes, set down with as much modesty as cunning. I remember one said there were no sallets[8] in the lines to make the matter savory, nor no matter in the phrase that might indict the author of affectation, but called it an 400 honest method, as wholesome as sweet, and by very much more handsome than fine. One speech in't I chiefly loved. 'Twas Æneas' tale to Dido, and thereabout of it especially where he speaks of Priam's slaughter.[9] If it live in your memory, begin at this line—let me see, let me see: 405

"The rugged Pyrrhus, like th' Hyrcanian beast"[1]—

'tis not so; it begins with Pyrrhus—

"The rugged Pyrrhus, he whose sable arms,
Black as his purpose, did the night resemble
When he lay couchéd in th' ominous horse,[2]   410
Hath now this dread and black complexion smeared
With heraldry more dismal; head to foot
Now is he total gules,[3] horridly tricked[4]
With blood of fathers, mothers, daughters, sons,
Baked and impasted[5] with the parching[6] streets,   415
That lend a tyrannous and a damnéd light
To their lord's murder. Roasted in wrath and fire,
And thus o'er-sizéd[7] with coagulate[8] gore,
With eyes like carbuncles, the hellish Pyrrhus
Old grandsire Priam seeks."   420

So proceed you.

POLONIUS   Fore God, my lord, well spoken, with good accent and good discretion.

FIRST PLAYER   "Anon he[9] finds him[1]
Striking too short at Greeks. His antique[2] sword,   425
Rebellious[3] to his arm, lies where it falls,
Repugnant to command. Unequal matched,
Pyrrhus at Priam drives, in rage strikes wide.
But with the whiff and wind of his fell sword
Th' unnervéd father falls. Then senseless[4] Ilium,   430
Seeming to feel this blow, with flaming top
Stoops[5] to his base, and with a hideous crash
Takes prisoner Pyrrhus' ear. For, lo! his sword,
Which was declining[6] on the milky head
Of reverend Priam, seemed i' th' air to stick.   435

6. were weightier than
7. arranged
8. spicy passages
9. Aeneas, fleeing with his band from fallen Troy (Ilium), arrives in Carthage, where he tells Dido, the Queen of Carthage, of the fall of Troy. Here he is describing the death of Priam, the aged king of Troy, at the hands of Pyrrhus. the son of the slain Achilles.
  1. tiger
  2. i.e., the Trojan horse
  3. completely red

4. adorned
5. crusted
6. burning
7. glued over
8. clotted,
9. Pyrrhus
1. Priam
2. which he used when young
3. refractory
4. without feeling
5. falls
6. about to fall

So as a painted tyrant Pyrrhus stood,
And like a neutral to his will and matter,[7]
Did nothing.
But as we often see, against some storm,
A silence in the heavens, the rack[8] stand still,   440
The bold winds speechless, and the orb below
As hush as death, anon the dreadful thunder
Doth rend the region; so, after Pyrrhus' pause,
A rouséd vengeance sets him new awork,[9]
And never did the Cyclops' hammers fall   445
On Mars's armor, forged for proof eterne,[1]
With less remorse than Pyrrhus' bleeding sword
Now falls on Priam.
Out, out, thou strumpet, Fortune! All you gods,
In general synod take away her power,   450
Break all the spokes and fellies[2] from her wheel,
And bowl[3] the round nave[4] down the hill of heaven
As low as to the fiends."

POLONIUS   This is too long.

HAMLET   It shall to the barber's with your beard.—Prithee say on. 455
He's for a jig,[5] or a tale of bawdry, or he sleeps. Say on; come to
Hecuba.[6]

FIRST PLAYER   "But who, ah woe! had seen the mobled[7] queen—"

HAMLET   "The mobled queen"?

POLONIUS   That's good. "Mobled queen" is good.   460

FIRST PLAYER   "Run barefoot up and down, threat'ning the flames
With bisson rheum,[8] a clout[9] upon that head
Where late the diadem stood, and for a robe,
About her lank and all o'er-teeméd loins,
A blanket, in the alarm of fear caught up—   465
Who this had seen, with tongue in venom steeped,
'Gainst Fortune's state[1] would treason have pronounced.
But if the gods themselves did see her then,
When she saw Pyrrhus make malicious sport
In mincing[2] with his sword her husband's limbs,   470
The instant burst of clamor that she made,
Unless things mortal move them not at all,
Would have made milch[3] the burning eyes of heaven,
And passion in the gods."

POLONIUS   Look whe'r[4] he has not turned his color, and has tears in's 475
eyes. Prithee no more.

HAMLET   'Tis well. I'll have thee speak out the rest of this soon.—
Good my lord, will you see the players well bestowed?[5] Do you
hear, let them be well used, for they are the abstract[6] and brief

---

7. between his will and the fulfillment of it
8. clouds
9. to work
1. Mars, as befits a Roman war god, had armor made for him by the blacksmith god Vulcan and his assistants, the Cyclops. It was suitably impenetrable, of "proof eterne."
2. parts of the rim
3. roll
4. hub
5. a comic act
6. Hecuba was the wife of Priam and Queen of Troy. Her "loins" are described below as "o'erteemed" because of her unusual fertility. The number of her children varies in different accounts. but twenty is a safe minimum.
7. muffled (in a hood)
8. blinding tears
9. cloth
1. government
2. cutting up
3. tearful (*lit.* milk-giving)
4. whether
5. provided for
6. summary

chronicles of the time; after your death you were better have a bad ⁴⁸⁰
epitaph than their ill report while you live.

POLONIUS   My lord, I will use them according to their desert.

HAMLET   God's bodkin, man, much better. Use every man after his
desert, and who shall 'scape whipping? Use them after your own
honor and dignity. The less they deserve, the more merit is in your ⁴⁸⁵
bounty. Take them in.

POLONIUS   Come, sirs.

HAMLET   Follow him, friends. We'll hear a play tomorrow. [*Aside to*
FIRST PLAYER.] Dost thou hear me, old friend, can you play "The
Murder of Gonzago"?   490

FIRST PLAYER   Ay, my lord.

HAMLET   We'll ha't tomorrow night. You could for a need study a
speech of some dozen or sixteen lines which I would set down and
insert in't, could you not?

FIRST PLAYER   Ay, my lord.   495

HAMLET   Very well. Follow that lord, and look you mock him not.

Exeunt POLONIUS *and* PLAYERS.

My good friends, I'll leave you till night. You are welcome to
Elsinore.

ROSENCRANTZ   Good my lord.

Exeunt ROSENCRANTZ *and* GUILDENSTERN.

HAMLET   Ay, so God b'wi'ye. Now I am alone.   500
O, what a rogue and peasant slave am I!
Is it not monstrous that this player here,
But in a fiction, in a dream of passion,
Could force his soul so to his own conceit⁷
That from her working all his visage wanned;⁸   505
Tears in his eyes, distraction in his aspect,⁹
A broken voice, and his whole function suiting
With forms to his conceit? And all for nothing,
For Hecuba!
What's Hecuba to him or he to Hecuba,   510
That he should weep for her? What would he do
Had he the motive and the cue for passion
That I have? He would drown the stage with tears,
And cleave the general ear with horrid speech,
Make mad the guilty, and appal the free,   515
Confound the ignorant, and amaze indeed
The very faculties of eyes and ears.
Yet I,
A dull and muddy-mettled¹ rascal, peak²
Like John-a-dreams,³ unpregnant⁴ of my cause,   520
And can say nothing; no, not for a king
Upon whose property and most dear life
A damned defeat was made. Am I a coward?
Who calls me villain, breaks my pate across,
Plucks off my beard and blows it in my face,   525

---

7. imagination
8. grew pale
9. face
1. dull-spirited

2. mope
3. a man dreaming
4. not quickened by

Tweaks me by the nose, gives me the lie i' th' throat
As deep as to the lungs? Who does me this?
Ha, 'swounds, I should take it; for it cannot be
But I am pigeon-livered and lack gall[5]
To make oppression bitter, or ere this   530
I should 'a fatted all the region kites[6]
With this slave's offal. Bloody, bawdy villain!
Remorseless, treacherous, lecherous, kindless[7] villain!
Why, what an ass am I! This is most brave,
That I, the son of a dear father murdered,   535
Prompted to my revenge by heaven and hell,
Must like a whore unpack[8] my heart with words,
And fall a-cursing like a very drab,
A scullion![9] Fie upon't! foh!
About, my brains. Hum—I have heard   540
That guilty creatures sitting at a play,
Have by the very cunning of the scene
Been struck so to the soul that presently
They have proclaimed[1] their malefactions;
For murder, though it have no tongue, will speak   545
With most miraculous organ. I'll have these players
Play something like the murder of my father
Before mine uncle. I'll observe his looks.
I'll tent[2] him to the quick. If 'a do blench,[3]
I know my course. The spirit that I have seen   550
May be a devil, and the devil hath power
T' assume a pleasing shape, yea, and perhaps
Out of my weakness and my melancholy,
As he is very potent with such spirits,
Abuses me to damn me. I'll have grounds   555
More relative[4] than this. The play's the thing
Wherein I'll catch the conscience of the king.   *Exit.*

Act 3

SCENE 1: *A room in the castle. Enter* KING, QUEEN, POLONIUS,
OPHELIA, ROSENCRANTZ *and* GUILDENSTERN.

KING   And can you by no drift of conference[5]
Get from him why he puts on this confusion,
Grating so harshly all his days of quiet
With turbulent[6] and dangerous lunacy?
ROSENCRANTZ   He does confess he feels himself distracted,   5
But from what cause 'a will by no means speak.
GUILDENSTERN   Nor do we find him forward[7] to be sounded,[8]
But with a crafty madness keeps aloof

5. bitterness
6. birds of prey of the area
7. unnatural
8. relieve
9. In some versions of the play, the word "stallion," a slang term for a prostitute, appears in place of "scullion."
1. admitted

2. try
3. turn pale
4. conclusive
5. line of conversation
6. disturbing
7. eager
8. questioned

When we would bring him on to some confession
Of his true state.
QUEEN   Did he receive you well?   10
ROSENCRANTZ   Most like a gentleman.
GUILDENSTERN   But with much forcing of his disposition.[9]
ROSENCRANTZ   Niggard of question, but of our demands[1]
Most free in his reply.
QUEEN   Did you assay[2] him
To any pastime?   15
ROSENCRANTZ   Madam, it so fell out that certain players
We o'er-raught[3] on the way. Of these we told him,
And there did seem in him a kind of joy
To hear of it. They are here about the court,
And as I think, they have already order   20
This night to play before him.
POLONIUS   'Tis most true,
And he beseeched me to entreat your majesties
To hear and see the matter.[4]
KING   With all my heart, and it doth much content me
To hear him so inclined.   25
Good gentlemen, give him a further edge,
And drive his purpose[5] into these delights.
ROSENCRANTZ   We shall, my lord.

Exeunt ROSENCRANTZ *and* GUILDENSTERN.

KING   Sweet Gertrude, leave us too,
For we have closely sent for Hamlet hither,
That he, as 'twere by accident, may here   30
Affront[6] Ophelia.
Her father and myself (lawful espials[7])
Will so bestow ourselves that, seeing unseen,
We may of their encounter frankly judge,
And gather by him, as he is behaved,   35
If't be th' affliction of his love or no
That thus he suffers for.
QUEEN   I shall obey you.—
And for your part, Ophelia, I do wish
That your good beauties be the happy cause
Of Hamlet's wildness. So shall I hope your virtues   40
Will bring him to his wonted[8] way again,
To both your honors.
OPHELIA   Madam, I wish it may.   *Exit* QUEEN.
POLONIUS   Ophelia, walk you here.—Gracious,[9] so please you,
We will bestow ourselves.—[*To* OPHELIA.] Read on this book,
That show of such an exercise[1] may color[2]   45
Your loneliness.—We are oft to blame in this,
'Tis too much proved, that with devotion's visage
And pious action we do sugar o'er
The devil himself.

9. conversation   6. confront
1. to our questions   7. justified spies
2. tempt   8. usual
3. passed   9. Majesty
4. performance   1. act of devotion
5. sharpen his intention 2. explain

KING [*aside*]   O, 'tis too true.
How smart a lash that speech doth give my conscience!   50
The harlot's cheek, beautied with plast'ring[3] art,
Is not more ugly to the thing that helps it
Than is my deed to my most painted word.
O heavy burden!
POLONIUS   I hear him coming. Let's withdraw, my lord.   55

Exeunt KING *and* POLONIUS.

Enter HAMLET.

HAMLET   To be, or not to be, that is the question:
Whether 'tis nobler in the mind to suffer
The slings and arrows of outrageous fortune,
Or to take arms against a sea of troubles,
And by opposing end them. To die, to sleep—   60
No more; and by a sleep to say we end
The heartache, and the thousand natural shocks
That flesh is heir to. 'Tis a consummation
Devoutly to be wished—to die, to sleep—
To sleep, perchance to dream, ay there's the rub;   65
For in that sleep of death what dreams may come
When we have shuffled off this mortal coil[4]
Must give us pause—there's the respect[5]
That makes calamity of so long life.
For who would bear the whips and scorns of time,   70
Th' oppressor's wrong, the proud man's contumely,[6]
The pangs of despised love, the law's delay,
The insolence of office, and the spurns[7]
That patient merit of th' unworthy takes,
When he himself might his quietus[8] make   75
With a bare bodkin?[9] Who would fardels[1] bear,
To grunt and sweat under a weary life,
But that the dread of something after death,
The undiscovered country, from whose bourn[2]
No traveller returns, puzzles the will,   80
And makes us rather bear those ills we have
Than fly to others that we know not of?
Thus conscience does make cowards of us all;
And thus the native[3] hue of resolution
Is sicklied o'er with the pale cast of thought,   85
And enterprises of great pitch[4] and moment[5]
With this regard their currents turn awry
And lose the name of action.—Soft you now,
The fair Ophelia.—Nymph, in thy orisons[6]
Be all my sins remembered.
OPHELIA   Good my lord,   90
How does your honor for this many a day?
HAMLET   I humbly thank you, well, well, well.

3. thickly painted
4. turmoil
5. consideration
6. insulting behavior
7. rejections
8. settlement
9. dagger

1. burdens
2. boundary
3. natural
4. height
5. importance
6. prayers

OPHELIA   My lord, I have remembrances of yours
That I have longed long to re-deliver.
I pray you now receive them.
HAMLET   No, not I,   95
I never gave you aught.
OPHELIA   My honored lord, you know right well you did,
And with them words of so sweet breath composed
As made the things more rich. Their perfume lost,
Take these again, for to the noble mind   100
Rich gifts wax[7] poor when givers prove unkind.
There, my lord.
HAMLET   Ha, ha! are you honest?[8]
OPHELIA   My lord?
HAMLET   Are you fair?   105
OPHELIA   What means your lordship?
HAMLET   That if you be honest and fair, your honesty should admit
no discourse to your beauty.
OPHELIA   Could beauty, my lord, have better commerce[9] than with
honesty?   110
HAMLET   Ay, truly, for the power of beauty will sooner transform
honesty from what it is to a bawd than the force of honesty can
translate beauty into his likeness. This was sometime a paradox, but
now the time gives it proof. I did love you once.
OPHELIA   Indeed, my lord, you made me believe so.   115
HAMLET   You should not have believed me, for virtue cannot so in-
oculate[1] our old stock but we shall relish of it. I loved you not.
OPHELIA   I was the more deceived.
HAMLET   Get thee to a nunnery.[2] Why wouldst thou be a breeder of
sinners? I am myself indifferent[3] honest, but yet I could accuse me 120
of such things that it were better my mother had not borne me: I
am very proud, revengeful, ambitious, with more offences at my
beck[4] than I have thoughts to put them in, imagination to give them
shape, or time to act them in. What should such fellows as I do
crawling between earth and heaven? We are arrant[5] knaves all; be- 125
lieve none of us. Go thy ways to a nunnery. Where's your father?
OPHELIA   At home, my lord.
HAMLET   Let the doors be shut upon him, that he may play the fool
nowhere but in's own house. Farewell.
OPHELIA   O, help him, you sweet heavens!   130
HAMLET   If thou dost marry, I'll give thee this plague for thy dowry:
be thou as chaste as ice, as pure as snow, thou shalt not escape
calumny. Get thee to a nunnery, farewell. Or if thou wilt needs
marry, marry a fool, for wise men know well enough what monsters[6]
you make of them. To a nunnery, go, and quickly too. Farewell. 135
OPHELIA   Heavenly powers, restore him!
HAMLET   I have heard of your paintings well enough. God hath given
you one face, and you make yourselves another. You jig, you amble,
and you lisp;[7] you nickname God's creatures, and make your wantonness your ignorance.[8] Go to, I'll no more on't, it hath made me mad. 140

7. become
8. chaste
9. intercourse
1. change by grafting
2. With typical ribaldry Hamlet uses
"nunnery" in two senses, the second as a
slang term for brothel.
3. moderately

4. command
5. thorough
6. horned because cuckolded
7. walk and talk affectedly
8. Hamlet means that women call things
by pet names and then blame the affectation on ignorance.

I say we will have no more marriage. Those that are married already,
all but one, shall live. The rest shall keep as they are. To a nunnery,
go.   *Exit.*

OPHELIA   O, what a noble mind is here o'erthrown!
The courtier's, soldier's, scholar's, eye, tongue, sword,   145
Th' expectancy[9] and rose[1] of the fair state,
The glass[2] of fashion and the mould[3] of form,
Th' observed of all observers, quite quite down!
And I of ladies most deject and wretched,
That sucked the honey of his music[4] vows,   150
Now see that noble and most sovereign reason
Like sweet bells jangled, out of time and harsh;
That unmatched form and feature of blown[5] youth
Blasted with ecstasy. O, woe is me
T' have seen what I have seen, see what I see!   155

    Enter KING *and* POLONIUS.

KING   Love! His affections do not that way tend,
Nor what he spake, though it lacked form a little,
Was not like madness. There's something in his soul
O'er which his melancholy sits on brood,[6]
And I do doubt[7] the hatch and the disclose[8]   160
Will be some danger; which to prevent,
I have in quick determination
Thus set it down: he shall with speed to England
For the demand of our neglected tribute.
Haply the seas and countries different,   165
With variable objects, shall expel
This something-settled matter in his heart
Whereon his brains still beating puts him thus
From fashion of himself. What think you on't?
POLONIUS   It shall do well. But yet do I believe   170
The origin and commencement of his grief
Sprung from neglected love.—How now, Ophelia?
You need not tell us what Lord Hamlet said,
We heard it all.—My lord, do as you please,
But if you hold it fit, after the play   175
Let his queen-mother all alone entreat him
To show his grief. Let her be round[9] with him,
And I'll be placed, so please you, in the ear[1]
Of all their conference. If she find him not,[2]
To England send him; or confine him where   180
Your wisdom best shall think.
KING   It shall be so.
Madness in great ones must not unwatched go.   *Exeunt.*

SCENE 2: *A public room in the castle. Enter* HAMLET *and three of
the* PLAYERS.

HAMLET   Speak the speech, I pray you, as I pronounced it to you, trip-
pingly on the tongue; but if you mouth it as many of our players do,

9. hope	4. musical	8. result
1. ornament	5. full-blown	9. direct
2. mirror	6. i.e., like a hen	1. hearing
3. model	7. fear	2. discover his problem

I had as lief the town-crier spoke my lines. Nor do not saw the air too much with your hand thus, but use all gently, for in the very torrent, tempest, and as I may say, whirlwind of your passion, you must acquire and beget a temperance that may give it smoothness. O, it offends me to the soul to hear a robustious[3] periwig-pated[4] fellow tear a passion to tatters, to very rags, to split the ears of the groundlings,[5] who for the most part are capable of[6] nothing but inexplicable dumb shows and noise. I would have such a fellow whipped for o'erdoing Termagant. It out-herods Herod.[7] Pray you avoid it.

FIRST PLAYER   I warrant your honor.

HAMLET   Be not too tame neither, but let your own discretion be your tutor. Suit the action to the word, the word to the action, with this special observance, that you o'erstep not the modesty of nature; for anything so o'erdone is from[8] the purpose of playing, whose end both at the first, and now, was and is, to hold as 'twere the mirror up to nature, to show virtue her own feature, scorn her own image, and the very age and body of the time his form and pressure.[9] Now this overdone, or come tardy off, though it makes the unskilful[1] laugh, cannot but make the judicious grieve, the censure[2] of the which one must in your allowance o'erweigh a whole theatre of others. O, there be players that I have seen play—and heard others praise, and that highly—not to speak it profanely, that neither having th' accent of Christians, nor the gait of Christian, pagan, nor man, have so strutted and bellowed that I have thought some of nature's journeymen[3] had made men, and not made them well, they imitated humanity so abominably.

FIRST PLAYER   I hope we have reformed that indifferently[4] with us.

HAMLET   O, reform it altogether. And let those that play your clowns speak no more than is set down for them, for there be of them that will themselves laugh, to set on some quantity of barren[5] spectators to laugh too, though in the meantime some necessary question of the play be then to be considered. That's villainous, and shows a most pitiful ambition in the fool that uses it. Go, make you ready.

Exeunt PLAYERS.

Enter POLONIUS, GUILDENSTERN, *and* ROSENCRANTZ.

How now, my lord? Will the king hear this piece of work?

POLONIUS   And the queen too, and that presently.

HAMLET   Bid the players make haste.   *Exit* POLONIUS.
Will you two help to hasten them?

ROSENCRANTZ   Ay, my lord.   *Exeunt they two.*

HAMLET   What, ho, Horatio!
Enter HORATIO.

HORATIO   Here, sweet lord, at your service.

HAMLET   Horatio, thou art e'en as just a man
As e'er my conversation coped[6] withal.

---

3. noisy
4. bewigged
5. the spectators who paid least
6. i.e., capable of understanding
7. Termagant, a "Saracen" deity, and the Biblical Herod were stock characters in popular drama noted for the excesses of sound and fury used by their interpreters.

8. contrary to
9. shape
1. ignorant
2. judgment
3. inferior craftsmen
4. somewhat
5. dull-witted
6. encountered

HORATIO   O my dear lord!
HAMLET   Nay, do not think I flatter,   45
   For what advancement may I hope from thee,
   That no revenue hast but thy good spirits
   To feed and clothe thee? Why should the poor be flattered?
   No, let the candied tongue lick absurd pomp,
   And crook the pregnant[7] hinges of the knee   50
   Where thrift[8] may follow fawning. Dost thou hear?
   Since my dear soul was mistress of her choice
   And could of men distinguish her election,
   S'hath sealed thee for herself, for thou hast been
   As one in suff'ring all that suffers nothing,   55
   A man that Fortune's buffets and rewards
   Hast ta'en with equal thanks; and blest are those
   Whose blood and judgment are so well commingled
   That they are not a pipe[9] for Fortune's finger
   To sound[1] what stop[2] she please. Give me that man   60
   That is not passion's slave, and I will wear him
   In my heart's core, ay, in my heart of heart,
   As I do thee. Something too much of this.
   There is a play tonight before the king.
   One scene of it comes near the circumstance   65
   Which I have told thee of my father's death.
   I prithee, when thou seest that act afoot,
   Even with the very comment[3] of thy soul
   Observe my uncle. If his occulted[4] guilt
   Do not itself unkennel[5] in one speech,   70
   It is a damnéd ghost that we have seen,
   And my imaginations are as foul
   As Vulcan's stithy.[6] Give him heedful note,[7]
   For I mine eyes will rivet to his face,
   And after we will both our judgments join   75
   In censure of his seeming.[8]
HORATIO   Well, my lord.
   If 'a steal aught the whilst this play is playing,
   And 'scape detecting, I will pay[9] the theft.

   Enter Trumpets and Kettledrums, KING, QUEEN, POLONIUS,
   OPHELIA, ROSENCRANTZ, GUILDENSTERN, *and other* LORDS *attendant.*

HAMLET   They are coming to the play. I must be idle.
   Get you a place.   80
KING   How fares our cousin Hamlet?
HAMLET   Excellent, i' faith, of the chameleon's dish.[1] I eat the air,
   promise-crammed. You cannot feed capons so.

---

7. quick to bend	6. smithy
8. profit	7. careful attention
9. musical instrument	8. manner
1. play	9. repay
2. note	1. A reference to a popular belief that
3. keenest observation	the chameleon subsisted on a diet of air.
4. hidden	Hamlet has deliberately misunderstood the
5. break loose	King's question.

KING   I have nothing with this answer, Hamlet. These words are not
mine.   85

HAMLET   No, nor mine now. [*To* POLONIUS.] My lord, you played once
i' th' university, you say?

POLONIUS   That did I, my lord, and was accounted a good actor.

HAMLET   What did you enact?

POLONIUS   I did enact Julius Cæsar. I was killed i' th' Capitol; Brutus   90
killed me.[2]

HAMLET   It was a brute part of him to kill so capital a calf there. Be
the players ready?

ROSENCRANTZ   Ay, my lord, they stay[3] upon your patience.[4]

QUEEN   Come hither, my dear Hamlet, sit by me.   95

HAMLET   No, good mother, here's metal more attractive.

POLONIUS [*to the* KING]   O, ho! do you mark that?

HAMLET   Lady, shall I lie in your lap?

Lying down at OPHELIA's *feet.*

OPHELIA   No, my lord.

HAMLET   I mean, my head upon your lap?   100

OPHELIA   Ay, my lord.

HAMLET   Do you think I meant country matters?[5]

OPHELIA   I think nothing, my lord.

HAMLET   That's a fair thought to lie between maids' legs.

OPHELIA   What is, my lord?   105

HAMLET   Nothing.

OPHELIA   You are merry, my lord.

HAMLET   Who, I?

OPHELIA   Ay, my lord.

HAMLET   O God, your only jig-maker![6] What should a man do but be 110
merry? For look you how cheerfully my mother looks, and my father
died within's two hours.

OPHELIA   Nay, 'tis twice two months, my lord.

HAMLET   So long? Nay then, let the devil wear black, for I'll have a
suit of sables. O heavens! die two months ago, and not forgotten 115
yet? Then there's hope a great man's memory may outlive his life
half a year, but by'r lady 'a must build churches then, or else shall
'a suffer not thinking on, with the hobby-horse, whose epitaph is
"For O, for O, the hobby-horse is forgot!"[7]

The trumpets sound. Dumb Show follows. Enter a KING *and a*
QUEEN *very lovingly; the* QUEEN *embracing him and he her.*
She kneels, and makes show of protestation unto him. He takes
her up, and declines[8] his head upon her neck. He lies him down
upon a bank of flowers; she, seeing him asleep, leaves him.
Anon come in another man, takes off his crown, kisses it, pours
poison in the sleeper's ears, and leaves him. The QUEEN *returns,*
finds the KING *dead, makes passionate action. The* POISONER
with some three or four come in again, seem to condole with
her. The dead body is carried away. The POISONER *woos the*

2. The assassination of Julius Caesar by
Brutus and others is the subject of another
play by Shakespeare.
  3. wait
  4. leisure
  5. Presumably, rustic misbehavior, but
here and elsewhere in this exchange Hamlet treats Ophelia to some ribald double

meanings.
  6. writer of comic scenes
  7. In traditional games and dances one
of the characters was a man represented as
riding a horse. The horse was made of
something like cardboard and was worn
about the "rider's" waist.
  8. lays

QUEEN *with gifts; she seems harsh awhile, but in the end accepts love.* *Exeunt.*

OPHELIA   What means this, my lord? 120
HAMLET   Marry, this is miching mallecho;[9] it means mischief.
OPHELIA   Belike this show imports[1] the argument[2] of the play.

Enter PROLOGUE.

HAMLET   We shall know by this fellow. The players cannot keep counsel; they'll tell all.
OPHELIA   Will 'a tell us what this show meant? 125
HAMLET   Ay, or any show that you will show him. Be not you ashamed to show, he'll not shame to tell you what it means.
OPHELIA   You are naught,[3] you are naught. I'll mark[4] the play.
PROLOGUE   *For us, and for our tragedy,*
Here stooping to your clemency, 130
We beg your hearing patiently. *Exit.*
HAMLET   Is this a prologue, or the posy[5] of a ring?
OPHELIA   'Tis brief, my lord.
HAMLET   As woman's love.

Enter the PLAYER KING *and* QUEEN.

PLAYER KING   *Full thirty times hath Phœbus' cart gone round* 135
Neptune's salt wash and Tellus' orbéd ground,
And thirty dozen moons with borrowed sheen[6]
About the world have times twelve thirties been,
Since love our hearts and Hymen did our hands
Unite comutual[7] in most sacred bands.[8] 140
PLAYER QUEEN   *So many journeys may the sun and moon*
Make us again count o'er ere love be done!
But woe is me, you are so sick of late,
So far from cheer and from your former state,
That I distrust[9] you. Yet though I distrust, 145
Discomfort you, my lord, it nothing must.
For women's fear and love hold quantity,[1]
In neither aught, or in extremity.[2]
Now what my love is proof hath made you know,
And as my love is sized,[3] my fear is so. 150
Where love is great, the littlest doubts are fear;
Where little fears grow great, great love grows there.
PLAYER KING   *Faith, I must leave thee, love, and shortly too;*
My operant powers[4] their functions leave[5] to do.
And thou shalt live in this fair world behind, 155
Honored, beloved, and haply one as kind
For husband shalt thou—

9. sneaking crime
1. explains
2. plot
3. obscene
4. attend to
5. motto engraved inside
6. light
7. mutually
8. The speech contains several mythological references. "Phoebus" was a sun god, and his chariot or "cart" the sun.

The "salt wash" of Neptune is the ocean; "Tellus" was an earth goddess, and her "orbed ground" is the earth, or globe. Hymen was the god of marriage.
9. fear for
1. agree in weight
2. The lady means without regard to too much or too little.
3. in size
4. active forces
5. cease

PLAYER QUEEN   *O, confound the rest!*
Such love must needs be treason in my breast.
In second husband let me be accurst!
None wed the second but who killed the first.[6]   160
HAMLET   That's wormwood.
PLAYER QUEEN   *The instances*[7] *that second marriage move*
Are base respects[8] *of thrift, but none of love.*
A second time I kill my husband dead,
When second husband kisses me in bed.   165
PLAYER KING   *I do believe you think what now you speak,*
But what we do determine oft we break.
Purpose is but the slave to memory,
Of violent birth, but poor validity;
Which now, like fruit unripe, sticks on the tree,   170
But fall unshaken when they mellow be.
Most necessary 'tis that we forget
To pay ourselves what to ourselves is debt.
What to ourselves in passion we propose,
The passion ending, doth the purpose lose.   175
The violence of either grief or joy
Their own enactures[9] *with themselves destroy.*
Where joy most revels, grief doth most lament;
Grief joys, joy grieves, on slender accident.
This world is not for aye,[1] *nor 'tis not strange*   180
That even our loves should with our fortunes change;
For 'tis a question left us yet to prove,
Whether love lead fortune, or else fortune love.
The great man down, you mark his favorite flies;
The poor advanced makes friends of enemies;   185
And hitherto doth love on fortune tend,
For who not needs shall never lack a friend,
And who in want a hollow[2] *friend doth try,*
Directly seasons him[3] *his enemy.*
But orderly to end where I begun,   190
Our wills and fates do so contrary run
That our devices[4] *still are overthrown;*
Our thoughts are ours, their ends none of our own.
So think thou wilt no second husband wed,
But die thy thoughts when thy first lord is dead.   195
PLAYER QUEEN   *Nor earth to me give food, nor heaven light,*
Sport and repose lock from me day and night,
To desperation turn my trust and hope,
An anchor's cheer[5] *in prison be my scope,*
Each opposite that blanks[6] *the face of joy*   200
Meet what I would have well, and it destroy,
Both here and hence[7] *pursue me lasting strife,*
If once a widow, ever I be wife!
HAMLET   If she should break it now!

---

6. Though there is some ambiguity, she
seems to mean that the only kind of woman
who would remarry is one who has killed
or would kill her first husband.
  7. causes
  8. concerns
  9. actions

1. eternal
2. false
3. ripens him into
4. plans
5. anchorite's food
6. blanches
7. in the next world

PLAYER KING *'Tis deeply sworn. Sweet, leave me here awhile.* 205
My spirits grow dull, and fain I would beguile
The tedious day with sleep.   *Sleeps.*
PLAYER QUEEN   *Sleep rock thy brain,*
And never come mischance between us twain!   *Exit.*
HAMLET   Madam, how like you this play?
QUEEN   The lady doth protest too much, methinks.   210
HAMLET   O, but she'll keep her word.
KING   Have you heard the argument? Is there no offence in't?
HAMLET   No, no, they do but jest, poison in jest; no offence i' th'
world.
KING   What do you call the play?   215
HAMLET   "The Mouse-trap." Marry, how? Tropically.[8] This play is the
image of a murder done in Vienna. Gonzago is the duke's name; his
wife, Baptista. You shall see anon. 'Tis a knavish piece of work, but
what of that? Your majesty, and we that have free souls, it touches
us not. Let the galled jade wince, our withers are unwrung.[9]   220
    Enter LUCIANUS.
This is one Lucianus, nephew to the king.
OPHELIA   You are as good as a chorus, my lord.
HAMLET   I could interpret between you and your love, if I could see
the puppets dallying.
OPHELIA   You are keen, my lord, you are keen.   225
HAMLET   It would cost you a groaning to take off mine edge.
OPHELIA   Still better, and worse.
HAMLET   So you mis-take your husbands.—Begin, murderer. Leave
thy damnable faces and begin. Come, the croaking raven doth bel-
low for revenge.   230
LUCIANUS   *Thoughts black, hands apt, drugs fit, and time agreeing,*
Confederate season,[1] else no creature seeing,
Thou mixture rank, of midnight weeds collected,
With Hecate's ban thrice blasted, thrice infected,[2]
Thy natural magic[3] and dire property   235
On wholesome life usurps immediately.
                          Pours the poison in his ears.
HAMLET   'A poisons him i' th' garden for his estate. His name's Gon-
zago. The story is extant, and written in very choice Italian. You
shall see anon how the murderer gets the love of Gonzago's wife.
OPHELIA   The king rises.   240
HAMLET   What, frighted with false fire?
QUEEN   How fares my lord?
POLONIUS   Give o'er the play.
KING   Give me some light. Away!
POLONIUS   Lights, lights, lights!   245
                    Exeunt all but HAMLET *and* HORATIO.
HAMLET   Why, let the strucken deer go weep,
                    The hart ungalléd[4] play.
                    For some must watch while some must sleep;
                    Thus runs the world away.

8. figuratively
9. A "galled jade" is a horse, particularly one of poor quality, with a sore
back. The "withers" are the ridge between
a horse's shoulders; "unwrung withers" are
not chafed by the harness.

1. a helpful time for the crime
2. Hecate was a classical goddess of
witchcraft.
3. native power
4. uninjured

Would not this, sir, and a forest of feathers[5]—if the rest of my for- 250
tunes turn Turk with me—with two Provincial roses on my razed
shoes, get me a fellowship in a cry[6] of players?[7]
HORATIO   Half a share.
HAMLET   A whole one, I.

> For thou dost know, O Damon dear,[8]   255
> This realm dismantled was
> Of Jove himself, and now reigns here
> A very, very—peacock.

HORATIO   You might have rhymed.
HAMLET   O good Horatio, I'll take the ghost's word for a thousand 260
pound. Didst perceive?
HORATIO   Very well, my lord.
HAMLET   Upon the talk of the poisoning.
HORATIO   I did very well note[9] him.
HAMLET   Ah, ha! Come, some music. Come, the recorders.[1]   265
For if the king like not the comedy,
Why then, belike he likes it not, perdy.[2]
Come, some music.

Enter ROSENCRANTZ *and* GUILDENSTERN.

GUILDENSTERN   Good my lord, vouchsafe me a word with you.
HAMLET   Sir, a whole history.   270
GUILDENSTERN   The king, sir—
HAMLET   Ay, sir, what of him?
GUILDENSTERN   Is in his retirement[3] marvellous distempered.[4]
HAMLET   With drink, sir?
GUILDENSTERN   No, my lord, with choler.[5]   275
HAMLET   Your wisdom should show itself more richer to signify this
to the doctor, for for me to put him to his purgation[6] would perhaps
plunge him into more choler.
GUILDENSTERN   Good my lord, put your discourse[7] into some frame,[8]
and start not so wildly from my affair.   280
HAMLET   I am tame, sir. Pronounce.
GUILDENSTERN   The queen your mother, in most great affliction of
spirit, hath sent me to you.
HAMLET   You are welcome.
GUILDENSTERN   Nay, good my lord, this courtesy is not of the right 285
breed. If it shall please you to make me a wholesome[9] answer, I will
do your mother's commandment. If not, your pardon and my return[1]
shall be the end of my business.
HAMLET   Sir, I cannot.
ROSENCRANTZ   What, my lord?   290

---

5. plumes
6. company
7. Hamlet asks Horatio if "this" recitation, accompanied with a player's costume,
including plumes and rosettes on shoes
which have been slashed for decorative effect, might not entitle him to become a
shareholder in a theatrical company in the
event that Fortune goes against him, "turn
Turk."
8. Damon was a common name for a
young man or a shepherd in lyric, especially pastoral poetry. Jove was the chief
god of the Romans. The Reader may sup-

ply for himself the rhyme referred to by
Horatio.
9. observe
1. wooden end-blown flutes
2. *par Dieu* (by God)
3. place to which he has retired
4. vexed
5. bile
6. treatment with a laxative
7. speech
8. order
9. reasonable
1. i.e., to the Queen

HAMLET   Make you a wholesome answer; my wit's diseased. But, sir, such answer as I can make, you shall command, or rather, as you say, my mother. Therefore no more, but to the matter. My mother, you say—

ROSENCRANTZ   Then thus she says: your behavior hath struck her into 295 amazement and admiration.[2]

HAMLET   O wonderful son, that can so stonish a mother! But is there no sequel at the heels of this mother's admiration? Impart.[3]

ROSENCRANTZ   She desires to speak with you in her closet[4] ere you go to bed.   300

HAMLET   We shall obey, were she ten times our mother. Have you any further trade[5] with us?

ROSENCRANTZ   My lord, you once did love me.

HAMLET   And do still, by these pickers and stealers.[6]

ROSENCRANTZ   Good my lord, what is your cause of distemper? You 305 do surely bar the door upon your own liberty, if you deny your griefs to your friend.

HAMLET   Sir, I lack advancement.

ROSENCRANTZ   How can that be, when you have the voice of the king himself for your succession in Denmark?   310

HAMLET   Ay, sir, but "while the grass grows"—the proverb[7] is something musty.

Enter the PLAYERS *with recorders.*

O, the recorders! Let me see one. To withdraw with you[8]—why do you go about to recover the wind of me, as if you would drive me into a toil?[9]   315

GUILDENSTERN   O my lord, if my duty be too bold, my love is too unmannerly.

HAMLET   I do not well understand that. Will you play upon this pipe?[1]

GUILDENSTERN   My lord, I cannot.

HAMLET   I pray you.   320

GUILDENSTERN   Believe me, I cannot.

HAMLET   I do beseech you.

GUILDENSTERN   I know no touch of it,[2] my lord.

HAMLET   It is as easy as lying. Govern[3] these ventages[4] with your fingers and thumb, give it breath with your mouth, and it will 325 discourse most eloquent music. Look you, these are the stops.[5]

GUILDENSTERN   But these cannot I command to any utt'rance of harmony. I have not the skill.

HAMLET   Why, look you now, how unworthy a thing you make of me! You would play upon me, you would seem to know my stops, you 330 would pluck out the heart of my mystery, you would sound[6] me from my lowest note to the top of my compass[7]; and there is much music, excellent voice, in this little organ, yet cannot you make it speak. 'Sblood, do you think I am easier to be played on than a pipe?

2. wonder
3. tell me
4. bedroom
5. business
6. hands
7. The proverb ends "the horse starves."
8. let me step aside
9. The figure is from hunting. "You will approach me with the wind blowing

from me toward you in order to drive me into the net."
1. recorder
2. have no ability
3. cover and uncover
4. holes
5. wind-holes
6. play
7. range

Call me what instrument you will, though you can fret[8] me, you 335
cannot play upon me.

Enter POLONIUS.

God bless you, sir!

POLONIUS   My lord, the queen would speak with you, and presently.[9]

HAMLET   Do you see yonder cloud that's almost in shape of a camel?

POLONIUS   By th' mass, and 'tis like a camel indeed.   340

HAMLET   Methinks it is like a weasel.

POLONIUS   It is backed like a weasel.

HAMLET   Or like a whale.

POLONIUS   Very like a whale.

HAMLET   Then I will come to my mother by and by. [*Aside.*] They 345
fool me to the top of my bent.[1]—I will come by and by.

POLONIUS   I will say so.   *Exit* POLONIUS.

HAMLET   "By and by" is easily said. Leave me, friends.

Exeunt all but HAMLET.

'Tis now the very witching time of night,
When churchyards yawn, and hell itself breathes out   350
Contagion to this world. Now could I drink hot blood,
And do such bitter business as the day
Would quake to look on. Soft, now to my mother.
O heart, lose not thy nature; let not ever
The soul of Nero[2] enter this firm bosom.   355
Let me be cruel, not unnatural;
I will speak daggers to her, but use none.
My tongue and soul in this be hypocrites—
How in my words somever she be shent,[3]
To give them seals[4] never, my soul, consent!   *Exit.* 360

SCENE 3: *A room in the castle. Enter* KING, ROSENCRANTZ
and GUILDENSTERN.

KING   I like him not,[5] nor stands it safe with us
To let his madness range.[6] Therefore prepare you.
I your commission will forthwith dispatch,
And he to England shall along with you.
The terms of our estate[7] may not endure   5
Hazard so near's as doth hourly grow
Out of his brows.

GUILDENSTERN   We will ourselves provide.[8]
Most holy and religious fear it is
To keep those many many bodies safe
That live and feed upon your majesty.   10

ROSENCRANTZ   The single and peculiar[9] life is bound
With all the strength and armor of the mind

---

8. "Fret" is used in a double sense, to
annoy and to play a guitar or similar instrument using the "frets" or small bars on
the neck.
9. at once
1. treat me as an utter fool
2. The Emperor Nero, known for his
excesses, was believed to have been responsible for the death of his mother.
3. shamed
4. fulfillment in action
5. distrust him
6. roam freely
7. condition of the state
8. equip (for the journey)
9. individual

To keep itelf from noyance,[1] but much more
That spirit upon whose weal[2] depends and rests
The lives of many. The cess[3] of majesty   15
Dies not alone, but like a gulf[4] doth draw
What's near it with it. It is a massy[5] wheel
Fixed on the summit of the highest mount,
To whose huge spokes ten thousand lesser things
Are mortised and adjoined,[6] which when it falls,   20
Each small annexment, petty consequence,
Attends[7] the boist'rous ruin. Never alone
Did the king sigh, but with a general groan.
KING   Arm you, I pray you, to this speedy voyage,
For we will fetters put about this fear,   25
Which now goes too free-footed.
ROSENCRANTZ   We will haste us.

> *Exeunt* ROSENCRANTZ *and* GUILDENSTERN.

> *Enter* POLONIUS.

POLONIUS   My lord, he's going to his mother's closet.
Behind the arras I'll convey[8] myself
To hear the process.[9] I'll warrant she'll tax him home,[1]
And as you said, and wisely was it said,   30
'Tis meet that some more audience than a mother,
Since nature makes them partial, should o'erhear
The speech, of vantage.[2] Fare you well, my liege.
I'll call upon you ere you go to bed,
And tell you what I know.
KING   Thanks, dear my lord.   35

> *Exit* POLONIUS.

O, my offence is rank, it smells to heaven;
It hath the primal eldest curse[3] upon't,
A brother's murder. Pray can I not,
Though inclination be as sharp as will.
My stronger guilt defeats my strong intent,   40
And like a man to double business[4] bound,
I stand in pause where I shall first begin,
And both neglect. What if this curséd hand
Were thicker than itself with brothers' blood,
Is there not rain enough in the sweet heavens   45
To wash it white as snow? Whereto serves mercy
But to confront the visage of offence?
And what's in prayer but this twofold force,
To be forestalléd[5] ere we come to fall,
Or pardoned being down[6]? Then I'll look up.   50
My fault is past. But, O, what form of prayer
Can serve my turn? "Forgive me my foul murder"?
That cannot be, since I am still possessed

---

1. harm
2. welfare
3. cessation
4. whirlpool
5. massive
6. attached
7. joins in
8. station

9. proceedings
1. sharply
2. from a position of vantage
3. i.e., of Cain
4. two mutually opposed interests
5. prevented (from sin)
6. having sinned

Of those effects[7] for which I did the murder—
My crown, mine own ambition, and my queen.   55
May one be pardoned and retain th' offence[8]?
In the corrupted currents of this world
Offence's gilded[9] hand may shove by justice,
And oft 'tis seen the wicked prize itself
Buys out the law. But 'tis not so above.   60
There is no shuffling; there the action[1] lies
In his true nature, and we ourselves compelled,
Even to the teeth and forehead of[2] our faults,
To give in evidence. What then? What rests[3]?   65
Try what repentance can. What can it not?
Yet what can it when one can not repent?
O wretched state! O bosom black as death!
O liméd[4] soul, that struggling to be free
Art more engaged! Help, angels! Make assay.   70
Bow, stubborn knees, and heart with strings of steel,
Be soft as sinews of the new-born babe.
All may be well.   *He kneels.*

Enter HAMLET.

HAMLET   Now might I do it pat,[5] now 'a is a-praying,
And now I'll do't—and so 'a goes to heaven,
And so am I revenged. That would be scanned.[6]   75
A villain kills my father, and for that,
I, his sole son, do this same villain send
To heaven.
Why, this is hire and salary, not revenge.
'A took my father grossly, full of bread,[7]   80
With all his crimes broad blown,[8] as flush[9] as May;
And how his audit stands who knows save heaven?
But in our circumstance and course of thought
'Tis heavy with him; and am I then revenged
To take him in the purging of his soul,   85
When he is fit and seasoned[1] for his passage?
No.
Up, sword, and know thou a more horrid hent.[2]
When he is drunk, asleep, or in his rage,
Or in th' incestuous pleasure of his bed,   90
At game a-swearing, or about some act
That has no relish[3] of salvation in't—
Then trip him, that his heels may kick at heaven,
And that his soul may be as damned and black
As hell, whereto it goes. My mother stays.   95
This physic[4] but prolongs thy sickly days.   *Exit.*
KING [*rising*]   My words fly up, my thoughts remain below.
Words without thoughts never to heaven go.   *Exit.*

7. gains
8. i.e., benefits of the offence
9. bearing gold as a bribe
1. case at law
2. face-to-face with
3. remains
4. caught as with bird-lime
5. easily

6. deserves consideration
7. in a state of sin and without fasting
8. full-blown
9. vigorous
1. ready
2. opportunity
3. flavor
4. medicine

SCENE 4: *The Queen's chamber. Enter* QUEEN *and* POLONIUS.

POLONIUS 'A will come straight. Look you lay home to[5] him.
Tell him his pranks have been too broad[6] to bear with,
And that your grace hath screen'd[7] and stood between
Much heat and him. I'll silence me even here.
Pray you be round.
QUEEN   I'll warrant you. Fear[8] me not.   5
Withdraw, I hear him coming.

POLONIUS *goes behind the arras.*

Enter HAMLET.

HAMLET Now, mother, what's the matter?
QUEEN Hamlet, thou hast thy father much offended.
HAMLET Mother, you have my father much offended.
QUEEN Come, come, you answer with an idle tongue.   10
HAMLET Go, go, you question with a wicked tongue.
QUEEN Why, how now, Hamlet?
HAMLET   What's the matter now?
QUEEN Have you forgot me?
HAMLET   No, by the rood,[9] not so.
You are the queen, your husband's brother's wife,
And would it were not so, you are my mother.   15
QUEEN Nay, then I'll set those to you that can speak.
HAMLET Come, come, and sit you down. You shall not budge.
You go not till I set you up a glass[1]
Where you may see the inmost part of you.
QUEEN What wilt thou do? Thou wilt not murder me?   20
Help, ho!
POLONIUS [*behind*] What, ho! help!
HAMLET [*draws*] How now, a rat?
Dead for a ducat, dead!

Kills POLONIUS *with a pass through the arras.*

POLONIUS [*behind*] O, I am slain!   25
QUEEN O me, what hast thou done?
HAMLET   Nay, I know not.
Is it the king?
QUEEN O, what a rash and bloody deed is this!
HAMLET A bloody deed!—almost as bad, good mother,
As kill a king and marry with his brother.   30
QUEEN As kill a king?
HAMLET   Ay, lady, it was my word.

Parting the arras.

Thou wretched, rash, intruding fool, farewell!
I took thee for thy better. Take thy fortune.
Thou find'st to be too busy[2] is some danger.—
Leave wringing of your hands. Peace, sit you down   35
And let me wring your heart, for so I shall
If it be made of penetrable stuff,

5. be sharp with
6. outrageous
7. acted as a fire screen
8. doubt

9. cross
1. mirror
2. officious

If damnéd custom have not brazed it[3] so
That it be proof[4] and bulwark against sense.[5]

QUEEN   What have I done that thou dar'st wag thy tongue   40
In noise so rude against me?

HAMLET   Such an act
That blurs the grace and blush of modesty,
Calls virtue hypocrite, takes off the rose
From the fair forehead of an innocent love,
And sets a blister[6] there, makes marriage-vows   45
As false as dicers' oaths. O, such a deed
As from the body of contraction[7] plucks
The very soul, and sweet religion makes
A rhapsody of words. Heaven's face does glow
And this solidity and compound mass[8]   50
With heated visage, as against the doom[9]—
Is thought-sick at the act.

QUEEN   Ay me, what act,
That roars so loud and thunders in the index[1]?

HAMLET   Look here upon this picture[2] and on this,
The counterfeit presentment of two brothers.   55
See what a grace was seated on this brow:
Hyperion's curls, the front[3] of Jove himself,
An eye like Mars, to threaten and command,
A station[4] like the herald Mercury[5]
New lighted[6] on a heaven-kissing hill—   60
A combination and a form indeed
Where every god did seem to set his seal,[7]
To give the world assurance of a man.
This was your husband. Look you now what follows.
Here is your husband, like a mildewed ear   65
Blasting his wholesome brother. Have you eyes?
Could you on this fair mountain leave to feed,
And batten[8] on this moor? Ha! have you eyes?
You cannot call it love, for at your age
The heyday in the blood is tame, it's humble,   70
And waits upon the judgment, and what judgment
Would step from this to this? Sense sure you have,
Else could you not have motion, but sure that sense
Is apoplexed[9] for madness would not err,
Nor sense to ecstasy was ne'er so thralled   75
But it reserved some quantity[1] of choice
To serve in such a difference. What devil was't
That thus hath cozened[2] you at hoodman-blind[3]?
Eyes without feeling, feeling without sight,
Ears without hands or eyes, smelling sans[4] all,   80
Or but a sickly part of one true sense
Could not so mope.[5] O shame! where is thy blush?

---

3. plated it with brass
4. armor
5. feeling
6. brand
7. the marriage contract
8. meaningless mass (Earth)
9. Judgment Day
1. table of contents
2. portrait
3. forehead
4. bearing

5. Mercury was a Roman god who served as the messenger of the gods.
6. newly alighted
7. mark of approval
8. feed greedily
9. paralyzed
1. power
2. cheated
3. blindman's buff
4. without
5. be stupid

Rebellious hell,
If thou canst mutine[6] in a matron's bones,
To flaming youth let virtue be as wax   85
And melt in her own fire. Proclaim no shame
When the compulsive ardor gives the charge,[7]
Since frost itself as actively doth burn,
And reason panders[8] will.
QUEEN   O Hamlet, speak no more!
Thou turn'st my eyes into my very soul;   90
And there I see such black and grainéd[9] spots
As will not leave their tinct.[1]
HAMLET   Nay, but to live
In the rank sweat of an enseaméd[2] bed,
Stewed in corruption, honeying and making love
Over the nasty sty—
QUEEN   O, speak to me no more!   95
These words like daggers enter in my ears;
No more, sweet Hamlet.
HAMLET   A murderer and a villain,
A slave that is not twentieth part the tithe[3]
Of your precedent lord,[4] a vice of kings,[5]
A cutpurse[6] of the empire and the rule,   100
That from a shelf the precious diadem stole
And put it in his pocket—
QUEEN   No more.

   Enter GHOST.

HAMLET   A king of shreds and patches—
Save me and hover o'er me with your wings,   105
You heavenly guards! What would your gracious figure?
QUEEN   Alas, he's mad.
HAMLET   Do you not come your tardy[7] son to chide,
That lapsed in time and passion lets go by
Th' important acting of your dread command?   110
O, say!
GHOST   Do not forget. This visitation
Is but to whet thy almost blunted purpose.
But look, amazement on thy mother sits.
O, step between her and her fighting soul!   115
Conceit[8] in weakest bodies strongest works.
Speak to her, Hamlet.
HAMLET   How is it with you, lady?
QUEEN   Alas, how is't with you,
That you do bend[9] your eye on vacancy,
And with th' incorporal air do hold discourse?   120
Forth at your eyes your spirits wildly peep,
And as the sleeping soldiers in th' alarm,
Your bedded hairs like life in excrements[1]

6. commit mutiny
7. attacks
8. pimps for
9. ingrained
1. lose their color
2. greasy
3. one-tenth
4. first husband

5. The "Vice," a common figure in the popular drama, was a clown or buffoon.
6. pickpocket
7. slow to act
8. imagination
9. turn
1. nails and hair

Start up and stand an end. O gentle son,
Upon the heat and flame of thy distemper   125
Sprinkle cool patience. Whereon do you look?
HAMLET   On him, on him! Look you how pale he glares.
His form and cause conjoined,[2] preaching to stones,
Would make them capable.[3]—Do not look upon me,
Lest with piteous action you convert   130
My stern effects.[4] Then what I have to do
Will want true color—tears perchance for blood.
QUEEN   To whom do you speak this?
HAMLET   Do you see nothing there?
QUEEN   Nothing at all, yet all that is I see.   135
HAMLET   Nor did you nothing hear?
QUEEN   No, nothing but ourselves.
HAMLET   Why, look you there. Look how it steals away.
My father, in his habit[5] as he lived!
Look where he goes even now out at the portal.   *Exit* GHOST. 140
QUEEN   This is the very coinage[6] of your brain.
This bodiless creation ecstasy[7]
Is very cunning[8] in.
HAMLET   My pulse as yours doth temperately keep time,
And makes as healthful music. It is not madness   145
That I have uttered. Bring me to the test,
And I the matter will re-word, which madness
Would gambol[9] from. Mother, for love of grace,
Lay not that flattering unction[1] to your soul,
That not your trespass but my madness speaks.   150
It will but skin and film the ulcerous place
Whiles rank corruption, mining[2] all within,
Infects unseen. Confess yourself to heaven,
Repent what's past, avoid what is to come,
And do not spread the compost on the weeds,   155
To make them ranker. Forgive me this my virtue,
For in the fatness of these pursy[3] times
Virtue itself of vice must pardon beg,
Yea, curb[4] and woo for leave to do him good.
QUEEN   O Hamlet, thou hast cleft my heart in twain.   160
HAMLET   O, throw away the worser part of it,
And live the purer with the other half.
Good night—but go not to my uncle's bed.
Assume a virtue, if you have it not.
That monster custom[5] who all sense doth eat   165
Of habits evil, is angel yet in this,
That to the use of actions fair and good
He likewise gives a frock or livery
That aptly[6] is put on. Refrain tonight,
And that shall lend a kind of easiness   170
To the next abstinence; the next more easy;
For use almost can change the stamp of nature,

2. working together
3. of responding
4. deeds
5. costume
6. invention
7. madness
8. skilled

9. shy away
1. ointment
2. undermining
3. bloated
4. bow
5. habit
6. easily

And either curb the devil, or throw him out
With wondrous potency. Once more, good night,
And when you are desirous to be blest,   175
I'll blessing beg of you. For this same lord
I do repent; but heaven hath pleased it so,
To punish me with this, and this with me,
That I must be their scourge and minister.
I will bestow[7] him and will answer well   180
The death I gave him. So, again, good night.
I must be cruel only to be kind.
Thus bad begins and worse remains behind.
One word more, good lady.
QUEEN   What shall I do?
HAMLET Not this, by no means, that I bid you do: 185
Let the bloat[8] king tempt you again to bed,
Pinch wanton[9] on your cheek, call you his mouse,
And let him, for a pair of reechy[1] kisses,
Or paddling in your neck with his damned fingers,
Make you to ravel[2] all this matter out,   190
That I essentially am not in madness,
But mad in craft. 'Twere good you let him know,
For who that's but a queen, fair, sober, wise,
Would from a paddock,[3] from a bat, a gib,[4]
Such dear concernings hide? Who would so do?   195
No, in despite of sense and secrecy,
Unpeg the basket on the house's top,
Let the birds fly, and like the famous ape,
To try conclusions, in the basket creep
And break your own neck down.[5]   200
QUEEN Be thou assured, if words be made of breath
And breath of life, I have no life to breathe
What thou hast said to me.
HAMLET I must to England; you know that?
QUEEN   Alack,
I had forgot. 'Tis so concluded on.   205
HAMLET There's letters sealed, and my two school-fellows,
Whom I will trust as I will adders fanged,
They bear the mandate[6]; they must sweep[7] my way
And marshal me to knavery. Let it work,
For 'tis the sport to have the enginer   210
Hoist with his own petar; and't shall go hard
But I will delve[8] one yard below their mines
And blow them at the moon. O, 'tis most sweet
When in one line two crafts directly meet.[9]

7. dispose of
8. bloated
9. lewdly
1. foul
2. reveal
3. toad
4. tomcat
5. Apparently a reference to a now
lost fable in which an ape, finding a basket
containing a cage of birds on a housetop,
opens the cage. The birds fly away. The
ape, thinking that if he were in the basket
he too could fly, enters, jumps out, and
breaks his neck.

6. command
7. prepare
8. dig
9. The "enginer" or engineer is a military man who is here described as being blown up by a bomb of his own construction, "hoist with his own petar." The military figure continues in the succeeding lines where Hamlet describes himself as digging a countermine or tunnel beneath the one Claudius is digging to defeat Hamlet. In line 214 the two tunnels unexpectedly meet.

This man shall set me packing.   215
I'll lug the guts into the neighbor room.
Mother, good night. Indeed, this counsellor
Is now most still, most secret, and most grave,
Who was in life a foolish prating knave.
Come sir, to draw toward an end with you.   220
Good night, mother.

> *Exit the* QUEEN. *Then exit* HAMLET *tugging* POLONIUS.

Act 4

SCENE 1: *A room in the castle. Enter* KING, QUEEN, ROSENCRANTZ
and GUILDENSTERN.

KING   There's matter in these sighs, these profound heaves,
You must translate[1]; 'tis fit we understand them.
Where is your son?
QUEEN   Bestow this place on us a little while.

> *Exeunt* ROSENCRANTZ *and* GUILDENSTERN.

Ah, mine own lord, what have I seen tonight!   5
KING   What, Gertrude? How does Hamlet?
QUEEN   Mad as the sea and wind when both contend
Which is the mightier. In his lawless fit,
Behind the arras hearing something stir,
Whips out his rapier, cries "A rat, a rat!"   10
And in this brainish apprehension[2] kills
The unseen good old man.
KING   O heavy deed!
It had been so with us had we been there.
His liberty is full of threats to all—
To you yourself, to us, to every one.   15
Alas, how shall this bloody deed be answered?
It will be laid to us, whose providence[3]
Should have kept short, restrained, and out of haunt,[4]
This mad young man. But so much was our love,
We would not understand what was most fit;   20
But, like the owner of a foul disease,
To keep it from divulging, let it feed
Even on the pith of life. Where is he gone?
QUEEN   To draw apart the body he hath killed,
O'er whom his very madness, like some ore   25
Among a mineral of metals base,
Shows itself pure: 'a weeps for what is done.
KING   O Gertrude, come away!
The sun no sooner shall the mountains touch
But we will ship him hence, and this vile deed   30
We must with all our majesty and skill
Both countenance and excuse. Ho, Guildenstern!

> *Enter* ROSENCRANTZ *and* GUILDENSTERN.

Friends both, go join you with some further aid.

1. explain   3. prudence
2. insane notion   4. away from court

Hamlet in madness hath Polonius slain,
And from his mother's closet hath he dragged him.   35
Go seek him out; speak fair, and bring the body
Into the chapel. I pray you haste in this.

Exeunt ROSENCRANTZ *and* GUILDENSTERN.

Come, Gertrude, we'll call up our wisest friends
And let them know both what we mean to do
And what's untimely done;   40
Whose whisper o'er the world's diameter,
As level[5] as the cannon to his blank,[6]
Transports his poisoned shot—may miss our name,
And hit the woundless air. O, come away!
My soul is full of discord and dismay.   *Exeunt.* 45

SCENE 2: *A passageway. Enter* HAMLET.

HAMLET   Safely stowed.—But soft, what noise? Who calls on Hamlet?
O, here they come.

Enter ROSENCRANTZ, GUILDENSTERN, *and* OTHERS.

ROSENCRANTZ   What have you done, my lord, with the dead body?
HAMLET   Compounded it with dust, whereto 'tis kin.
ROSENCRANTZ   Tell us where 'tis, that we may take it thence   5
And bear it to the chapel.
HAMLET   Do not believe it.
ROSENCRANTZ   Believe what?
HAMLET   That I can keep your counsel and not mine own. Besides, to
be demanded of[7] a sponge—what replication[8] should be made by   10
the son of a king?
ROSENCRANTZ   Take you me for a sponge, my lord?
HAMLET   Ay, sir, that soaks up the king's countenance,[9] his rewards,
his authorities. But such officers do the king best service in the end.
He keeps them like an apple in the corner of his jaw, first mouthed   15
to be last swallowed. When he needs what you have gleaned, it is
but squeezing you and, sponge, you shall be dry again.
ROSENCRANTZ   I understand you not, my lord.
HAMLET   I am glad of it. A knavish speech sleeps in a foolish ear.
ROSENCRANTZ   My lord, you must tell us where the body is, and go   20
with us to the king.
HAMLET   The body is with the king, but the king is not with the body.
The king is a thing—
GUILDENSTERN   A thing, my lord!
HAMLET   Of nothing. Bring me to him. Hide fox, and all after.[1]   25

Exeunt.

SCENE 3: *A room in the castle. Enter* KING.

KING   I have sent to seek him, and to find the body.
How dangerous is it that this man goes loose!

5. direct
6. mark
7. questioned by
8. answer

9. favor
1. Apparently a reference to a children's
game like hide-and-seek.

Yet must not we put the strong law on him.
He's loved of the distracted[2] multitude,
Who like not in their judgment but their eyes,   5
And where 'tis so, th' offender's scourge[3] is weighed,
But never the offence. To bear all smooth and even,
This sudden sending him away must seem
Deliberate pause.[4] Diseases desperate grown
By desperate appliance are relieved,   10
Or not at all.

    Enter ROSENCRANTZ, GUILDENSTERN, *and all the rest.*

            How now! what hath befall'n?
ROSENCRANTZ   Where the dead body is bestowed, my lord,
  We cannot get from him.
KING   But where is he?
ROSENCRANTZ   Without,[5] my lord; guarded, to know[6] your pleasure.
KING   Bring him before us.
ROSENCRANTZ   Ho! bring in the lord.   15

    They enter with HAMLET.

KING   Now, Hamlet, where's Polonius?
HAMLET   At supper.
KING   At supper? Where?
HAMLET   Not where he eats, but where 'a is eaten. A certain convoca-
  tion[7] of politic[8] worms are e'en at him. Your worm is your only   20
  emperor for diet. We fat all creatures else to fat us, and we fat
  ourselves for maggots. Your fat king and your lean beggar is but
  variable service—two dishes, but to one table. That's the end.
KING   Alas, alas!
HAMLET   A man may fish with the worm that hath eat of a king, and   25
  eat of the fish that hath fed of that worm.
KING   What dost thou mean by this?
HAMLET   Nothing but to show you how a king may go a progress
  through the guts of a beggar.
KING   Where is Polonius?   30
HAMLET   In heaven. Send thither to see. If your messenger find him
  not there, seek him i' th' other place yourself. But if, indeed, you find
  him not within this month, you shall nose[9] him as you go up the
  stairs into the lobby.
KING [*to* ATTENDANTS]   Go seek him there.   35
HAMLET   'A will stay till you come.   *Exeunt* ATTENDANTS.
KING   Hamlet, this deed, for thine especial safety—
  Which we do tender,[1] as we dearly[2] grieve
  For that which thou hast done—must send thee hence
  With fiery quickness. Therefore prepare thyself.   40
  The bark is ready, and the wind at help,
  Th' associates tend, and everything is bent
  For England.
HAMLET   For England?
KING   Ay, Hamlet.

2. confused	7. gathering
3. punishment	8. statesmanlike
4. i.e., not an impulse	9. smell
5. outside	1. consider
6. await	2. deeply

HAMLET   Good.
KING   So it is, if thou knew'st our purposes.
HAMLET   I see a cherub that sees them. But come, for England!   45
Farewell, dear mother.
KING   Thy loving father, Hamlet.
HAMLET   My mother. Father and mother is man and wife, man and
wife is one flesh. So, my mother. Come, for England.   *Exit.*
KING   Follow him at foot[3]; tempt him with speed aboard.   50
Delay it not; I'll have him hence tonight.
Away! for everything is sealed and done
That else leans on th' affair. Pray you make haste.

                                    Exeunt all but the KING.

And, England, if my love thou hold'st at aught—
As my great power thereof may give thee sense,[4]   55
Since yet thy cicatrice[5] looks raw and red
After the Danish sword, and thy free awe
Pays homage to us—thou mayst not coldly set[6]
Our sovereign process,[7] which imports at full
By letters congruing[8] to that effect   60
The present death of Hamlet. Do it, England,
For like the hectic[9] in my blood he rages,
And thou must cure me. Till I know 'tis done,
Howe'er my haps, my joys were ne'er begun.   *Exit.*

   SCENE 4: *Near Elsinore. Enter* FORTINBRAS *with his army.*

FORTINBRAS   Go, captain, from me greet the Danish king.
Tell him that by his license Fortinbras
Craves the conveyance[1] of a promised march
Over his kingdom. You know the rendezvous.
If that his majesty would aught with us,   5
We shall express our duty in his eye,[2]
And let him know so.
CAPTAIN   I will do't, my lord.
FORTINBRAS   Go softly on.   *Exeunt all but the* CAPTAIN.

     Enter HAMLET, ROSENCRANTZ, GUILDENSTERN, *and* OTHERS.

HAMLET   Good sir, whose powers are these?
CAPTAIN   They are of Norway, sir.   10
HAMLET   How purposed, sir, I pray you?
CAPTAIN   Against some part of Poland.
HAMLET   Who commands them, sir?
CAPTAIN   The nephew to old Norway, Fortinbras.
HAMLET   Goes it against the main[3] of Poland, sir,   15
Or for some frontier?
CAPTAIN   Truly to speak, and with no addition,[4]
We go to gain a little patch of ground
That hath in it no profit but the name.

3. closely   9. chronic fever
4. of its value   1. escort
5. wound scar   2. presence
6. set aside   3. central part
7. mandate   4. exaggeration
8. agreeing

To pay five ducats,[5] five, I would not farm it;   20
Nor will it yield to Norway or the Pole
A ranker[6] rate should it be sold in fee.[7]

HAMLET   Why, then the Polack never will defend it.

CAPTAIN   Yes, it is already garrisoned.

HAMLET   Two thousand souls and twenty thousand ducats   25
Will not debate the question of this straw.
This is th' imposthume[8] of much wealth and peace,
That inward breaks, and shows no cause without
Why the man dies. I humbly thank you, sir.

CAPTAIN   God b'wi'ye, sir.   *Exit.*

ROSENCRANTZ   Will't please you go, my lord?   30

HAMLET   I'll be with you straight. Go a little before.

Exeunt all but HAMLET.

How all occasions do inform against me,
And spur my dull revenge! What is a man,
If his chief good and market[9] of his time
Be but to sleep and feed? A beast, no more.   35
Sure he that made us with such large discourse,[1]
Looking before and after, gave us not
That capability and godlike reason
To fust[2] in us unused. Now, whether it be
Bestial oblivion, or some craven scruple   40
Of thinking too precisely on th' event[3]—
A thought which, quartered, hath but one part wisdom
And ever three parts coward—I do not know
Why yet I live to say "This thing's to do,"
Sith[4] I have cause, and will, and strength, and means,   45
To do't. Examples gross as earth exhort me.
Witness this army of such mass and charge,[5]
Led by a delicate and tender prince,
Whose spirit, with divine ambition puffed,
Makes mouths at[6] the invisible event,   50
Exposing what is mortal and unsure
To all that fortune, death, and danger dare,
Even for an eggshell. Rightly to be great
Is not to stir without great argument,
But greatly to find quarrel in a straw   55
When honor's at the stake. How stand I then,
That have a father killed, a mother stained,
Excitements of my reason and my blood,
And let all sleep, while to my shame I see
The imminent death of twenty thousand men   60
That for a fantasy and trick of fame
Go to their graves like beds, fight for a plot
Whereon the numbers cannot try the cause,
Which is not tomb enough and continent

5. i.e., in rent
6. higher
7. outright
8. abscess
9. occupation
1. ample reasoning power

2. grow musty
3. outcome
4. since
5. expense
6. scorns

To hide the slain?[7] O, from this time forth,   65
My thoughts be bloody, or be nothing worth!   *Exit.*

SCENE 5: *A room in the castle. Enter* QUEEN, HORATIO *and a*
GENTLEMAN.

QUEEN   I will not speak with her.
GENTLEMAN   She is importunate, indeed distract.
  Her mood will needs be pitied.
QUEEN   What would she have?
GENTLEMAN   She speaks much of her father, says she hears
  There's tricks i' th' world, and hems, and beats her heart,   5
  Spurns enviously at straws,[8] speaks things in doubt
  That carry but half sense. Her speech is nothing,
  Yet the unshaped use of it doth move
  The hearers to collection[9]; they yawn at it,
  And botch the words up fit to their own thoughts,   10
  Which, as her winks and nods and gestures yield them,
  Indeed would make one think there might be thought,
  Though nothing sure, yet much unhappily.
HORATIO   'Twere good she were spoken with, for she may strew
  Dangerous conjectures in ill-breeding minds.   15
QUEEN   Let her come in.   *Exit* GENTLEMAN.
  [*Aside.*] To my sick soul, as sin's true nature is,
  Each toy[1] seems prologue to some great amiss.[2]
  So full of artless jealousy is guilt,
  It spills itself in fearing to be spilt.   20

        Enter OPHELIA *distracted.*

OPHELIA   Where is the beauteous majesty of Denmark?
QUEEN   How now, Ophelia!
OPHELIA   How should I your true love know   *She sings.*
                From another one?
                By his cockle hat and staff,[3]   25
                And his sandal shoon.[4]
QUEEN   Alas, sweet lady, what imports this song?
OPHELIA   Say you? Nay, pray you mark.

                He is dead and gone, lady,
                He is dead and gone;   30
                At his head a grass-green turf,
                At his heels a stone.

  O, ho!
QUEEN   Nay, but, Ophelia—
OPHELIA   Pray you mark.
                White his shroud as the mountain snow—   35

        Enter KING.

QUEEN   Alas, look here, my lord.

7. The plot of ground involved is so
small that it cannot contain the number of
men involved in fighting nor furnish burial
space for the number of those who will die.
8. takes offense at trifles
9. an attempt to order
1. trifle

2. catastrophe
3. A "cockle hat," one decorated with a
shell, indicated that the wearer had made a
pilgrimage to the shrine of St. James at
Compostela in Spain. The staff also marked
the carrier as a pilgrim.
4. shoes

OPHELIA   Larded all with sweet flowers;
    Which bewept to the grave did not go
    With true-love showers.

KING   How do you, pretty lady?   40

OPHELIA   Well, God dild[5] you! They say the owl was a baker's daughter. Lord, we know what we are, but know not what we may be.
God be at your table!

KING   Conceit[6] upon her father.

OPHELIA   Pray let's have no words of this, but when they ask you   45
what it means, say you this:

    Tomorrow is Saint Valentine's day,
        All in the morning betime,
    And I a maid at your window,
        To be your Valentine.   50
    Then up he rose, and donn'd his clo'es,
        And dupped[7] the chamber-door,
    Let in the maid, that out a maid
        Never departed more.

KING   Pretty Ophelia!   55

OPHELIA   Indeed, without an oath, I'll make an end on't.

    By Gis[8] and by Saint Charity,
        Alack, and fie for shame!
    Young men will do't, if they come to't;
        By Cock,[9] they are to blame.   60
    Quoth she "Before you tumbled me,
        You promised me to wed."

He answers:

    "So would I 'a done, by yonder sun,
        An thou hadst not come to my bed."   65

KING   How long hath she been thus?

OPHELIA   I hope all will be well. We must be patient, but I cannot
choose but weep to think they would lay him i' th' cold ground. My
brother shall know of it, and so I thank you for your good counsel.
Come, my coach! Good night, ladies, good night. Sweet ladies, good 70
night, good night.   *Exit.*

KING   Follow her close; give her good watch, I pray you.

                        Exeunt HORATIO *and* GENTLEMAN.

O, this is the poison of deep grief; it springs
All from her father's death, and now behold!
O Gertrude, Gertrude!   75
When sorrows come, they come not single spies,
But in battalions: first, her father slain;
Next, your son gone, and he most violent author
Of his own just remove; the people muddied,[1]
Thick and unwholesome in their thoughts and whispers   80
For good Polonius' death; and we have done but greenly[2]
In hugger-mugger[3] to inter him; poor Ophelia

---

5. yield   9. God
6. thought   1. disturbed
7. opened   2. without judgment
8. Jesus   3. haste

Divided from herself and her fair judgment,
Without the which we are pictures, or mere beasts;
Last, and as much containing as all these,   85
Her brother is in secret come from France,
Feeds on his wonder, keeps himself in clouds,
And wants not buzzers to infect his ear
With pestilent speeches of his father's death,
Wherein necessity, of matter beggared,[4]   90
Will nothing stick[5] our person to arraign[6]
In ear and ear.[7] O my dear Gertrude, this,
Like to a murd'ring piece,[8] in many places
Gives me superfluous death. Attend,   *A noise within.*

    Enter a MESSENGER.

Where are my Switzers[9]? Let them guard the door.   95
What is the matter?
MESSENGER   Save yourself, my lord.
The ocean, overpeering of his list,[1]
Eats not the flats with more impiteous[2] haste
Than young Laertes, in a riotous head,[3]
O'erbears your officers. The rabble call him lord,   100
And as the world were now but to begin,
Antiquity forgot, custom not known,
The ratifiers and props of every word,
They cry "Choose we, Laertes shall be king."
Caps, hands, and tongues, applaud it to the clouds,   105
"Laertes shall be king, Laertes king."
QUEEN   How cheerfully on the false trail they cry[4]!   *A noise within.*
O, this is counter,[5] you false Danish dogs!
KING   The doors are broke.

    Enter LAERTES, *with* OTHERS.

LAERTES   Where is this king?—Sirs, stand you all without.   110
ALL   No, let's come in.
LAERTES   I pray you give me leave.
ALL   We will, we will.   *Exeunt his followers.*
LAERTES   I thank you. Keep[6] the door.—O thou vile king,
Give me my father!
QUEEN   Calmly, good Laertes.
LAERTES   That drop of blood that's calm proclaims me bastard,   115
Cries cuckold to my father, brands the harlot
Even here between the chaste unsmirchéd brow
Of my true mother.
KING   What is the cause, Laertes,
That thy rebellion looks so giant-like?
Let him go, Gertrude. Do not fear[7] our person.   120
There's such divinity doth hedge a king
That treason can but peep to[8] what it would,
Acts little of his will. Tell me, Laertes,

4. short on facts
5. hesitate
6. accuse
7. from both sides
8. a weapon designed to scatter its shot
9. Swiss guards
1. towering above its limits

2. pitiless
3. with an armed band
4. as if following the scent
5. backward
6. guard
7. fear for
8. look at over or through a barrier

Why thou art thus incensed. Let him go, Gertrude.
Speak, man.
LAERTES   Where is my father?
KING   Dead.   125
QUEEN   But not by him.
KING   Let him demand[9] his fill.
LAERTES   How came he dead? I'll not be juggled with.
To hell allegiance, vows to the blackest devil,
Conscience and grace to the profoundest pit!
I dare damnation. To this point I stand,   130
That both the worlds[1] I give to negligence,[2]
Let come what comes, only I'll be revenged
Most throughly for my father.
KING   Who shall stay you?
LAERTES   My will, not all the world's.
And for my means, I'll husband[3] them so well   135
They shall go far with little.
KING   Good Laertes,
If you desire to know the certainty
Of your dear father, is't writ in your revenge
That, swoopstake,[4] you will draw both friend and foe,
Winner and loser?
LAERTES   None but his enemies.   140
KING   Will you know them, then?
LAERTES   To his good friends thus wide I'll ope my arms,
And like the kind life-rend'ring pelican,[5]
Repast them with my blood.
KING   Why, now you speak
Like a good child and a true gentleman.   145
That I am guiltless of your father's death,
And am most sensibly in grief for it,
It shall as level[6] to your judgment 'pear
As day does to your eye.

    A noise within: "Let her come in."

LAERTES   How now? What noise is that?   150

    Enter OPHELIA.

O, heat dry up my brains! tears seven times salt
Burn out the sense[7] and virtue[8] of mine eye!
By heaven, thy madness shall be paid with weight
Till our scale turn the beam. O rose of May,
Dear maid, kind sister, sweet Ophelia!   155
O heavens! is't possible a young maid's wits
Should be as mortal as an old man's life?
Nature is fine[9] in love, and where 'tis fine
It sends some precious instance of itself
After the thing it loves.[1]   160
OPHELIA   They bore him barefac'd on the bier;

9. question
1. i.e., this and the next
2. disregard
3. manage
4. sweeping the board
5. The pelican was believed to feed her
young with her own blood.

6. plain
7. feeling
8. function
9. refined
1. Laertes means that Ophelia, because
of her love for her father. gave up her
sanity as a token of grief at his death.

Hey non nonny, nonny, hey nonny;
And in his grave rain'd many a tear—

Fare you well, my dove!

LAERTES   Hadst thou thy wits, and didst persuade revenge,   165
It could not move thus.

OPHELIA   You must sing "A-down, a-down, and you call him a-down-a." O, how the wheel becomes it! It is the false steward, that stole his master's daughter.[2]

LAERTES   This nothing's more than matter.   170

OPHELIA   There's rosemary, that's for remembrance. Pray you, love, remember. And there is pansies, that's for thoughts.

LAERTES   A document[3] in madness, thoughts and remembrance fitted.

OPHELIA   There's fennel for you, and columbines. There's rue for you, and here's some for me. We may call it herb of grace a Sundays. O, 175 you must wear your rue with a difference. There's a daisy. I would give you some violets, but they withered all when my father died. They say 'a made a good end.

[*Sings.*]   For bonny sweet Robin is all my joy.

LAERTES   Thought and affliction, passion, hell itself,   180
She turns to favor[4] and to prettiness.

OPHELIA   And will 'a not come again?
            And will 'a not come again?
              No, no, he is dead,
              Go to thy death-bed,   185
            He never will come again.

            His beard was as white as snow,
            All flaxen was his poll[5];
              He is gone, he is gone,
              And we cast away moan: 190
            God-a-mercy on his soul!

And of all Christian souls, I pray God. God b'wi'you.   *Exit.*

LAERTES   Do you see this, O God?

KING   Laertes, I must commune with your grief,
Or you deny me right. Go but apart,   195
Make choice of whom your wisest friends you will,
And they shall hear and judge 'twixt you and me.
If by direct or by collateral[6] hand
They find us touched,[7] we will our kingdom give,
Our crown, our life, and all that we call ours,   200
To you in satisfaction; but if not,
Be you content to lend your patience to us,
And we shall jointly labor with your soul
To give it due content.

LAERTES   Let this be so.

2. The "wheel" refers to the *burden* or refrain of a song, in this case "A-down, a-down, and you call him a-down-a." The ballad to which she refers was about a false steward. Others have suggested that the "wheel" is the Wheel of Fortune, a spinning wheel to whose rhythm such a song might have been sung or a kind of dance movement performed by Ophelia as she sings.
3. lesson
4. beauty
5. head
6. indirect
7. by guilt

His means of death, his obscure funeral— 205
No trophy, sword, nor hatchment,[8] o'er his bones,
No noble rite nor formal ostentation[9]—
Cry to be heard, as 'twere from heaven to earth,
That I must call't in question.
KING   So you shall;
And where th' offence is, let the great axe fall.   210
I pray you go with me.   *Exeunt.*

SCENE 6: *Another room in the castle. Enter* HORATIO *and*
a GENTLEMAN.

HORATIO   What are they that would speak with me?
GENTLEMAN   Sea-faring men, sir. They say they have letters for you.
HORATIO   Let them come in.   *Exit* GENTLEMAN.
I do not know from what part of the world
I should be greeted, if not from Lord Hamlet.   5

    Enter SAILORS.

SAILOR   God bless you, sir.
HORATIO   Let him bless thee too.
SAILOR   'A shall, sir, an't please him. There's a letter for you, sir—it
came from th' ambassador that was bound for England—if your
name be Horatio, as I am let to know[1] it is.   10
HORATIO   [*reads*] "Horatio, when thou shalt have overlooked[2] this,
give these fellows some means[3] to the king. They have letters for
him. Ere we were two days old at sea, a pirate of very warlike ap-
pointment[4] gave us chase. Finding ourselves too slow of sail, we put
on a compelled valor, and in the grapple I boarded them. On the in-   15
stant they got clear of our ship, so I alone became their prisoner.
They have dealt with me like thieves of mercy, but they knew what
they did; I am to do a good turn for them. Let the king have the
letters I have sent, and repair thou to me with as much speed as thou
wouldest fly death. I have words to speak in thine ear will make   20
thee dumb; yet are they much too light for the bore of the matter.[5]
These good fellows will bring thee where I am. Rosencrantz and
Guildenstern hold their course for England. Of them I have much to
tell thee. Farewell.
                He that thou knowest thine, HAMLET."
Come, I will give you way[6] for these your letters,   25
And do't the speedier that you may direct me
To him from whom you brought them.   *Exeunt.*

SCENE 7: *Another room in the castle. Enter* KING *and* LAERTES.

KING   Now must your conscience my acquittance seal,[7]
And you must put me in your heart for friend,
Sith you have heard, and with a knowing ear,
That he which hath your noble father slain

8. coat of arms
9. pomp
1. informed
2. read through
3. access
4. equipment

5. A figure from gunnery, referring to
shot which is too small for the size of the
weapon to be fired.
6. means of delivery
7. grant me innocent

Pursued my life.

LAERTES   It well appears. But tell me   5
Why you proceeded not against these feats,
So criminal and so capital in nature,
As by your safety, greatness, wisdom, all things else,
You mainly were stirred up.

KING   O, for two special reasons,
Which may to you, perhaps, seem much unsinewed,[8]   10
But yet to me th' are strong. The queen his mother
Lives almost by his looks, and for myself—
My virtue or my plague, be it either which—
She is so conjunctive[9] to my life and soul
That, as the star moves not but in his sphere,[1]   15
I could not but by her. The other motive,
Why to a public count[2] I might not go,
Is the great love the general gender[3] bear him,
Who, dipping all his faults in their affection,
Work like the spring that turneth wood to stone,[4]   20
Convert his gyves[5] to graces; so that my arrows,
Too slightly timbered[6] for so loud a wind,
Would have reverted to my bow again,
But not where I have aimed them.

LAERTES   And so have I a noble father lost,   25
A sister driven into desp'rate terms,
Whose worth, if praises may go back again,
Stood challenger on mount of all the age
For her perfections. But my revenge will come.

KING   Break not your sleeps for that. You must not think   30
That we are made of stuff so flat and dull
That we can let our beard be shook with danger,
And think it pastime. You shortly shall hear more.
I loved your father, and we love our self,
And that, I hope, will teach you to imagine—   35

Enter a MESSENGER *with letters.*

MESSENGER   These to your majesty; this to the queen.
KING   From Hamlet! Who brought them?
MESSENGER   Sailors, my lord, they say. I saw them not.
They were given me by Claudio; he received them
Of him that brought them.
KING   Laertes, you shall hear them.—   40
Leave us.   *Exit* MESSENGER.
[*Reads.*] "High and mighty, you shall know I am set naked on
your kingdom. Tomorrow shall I beg leave to see your kingly eyes;
when I shall, first asking your pardon thereunto, recount the occasion
of my sudden and more strange return.   45
                                        HAMLET."
What should this mean? Are all the rest come back?

---

8. weak
9. closely joined
1. A reference to the Ptolemaic cosmology in which planets and stars were believed to revolve about the earth in crystalline spheres concentric with the earth.
2. reckoning

3. common people
4. Certain English springs contain so much lime in the water that a lime covering will be deposited on a log placed in one of them for a length of time.
5. fetters
6. shafted

Or is it some abuse,[7] and no such thing?

LAERTES   Know you the hand?

KING   'Tis Hamlet's character.[8] "Naked"!   50
And in a postscript here, he says "alone."
Can you devise[9] me?

LAERTES   I am lost in it, my lord. But let him come.
It warms the very sickness in my heart
That I shall live and tell him to his teeth   55
"Thus didest thou."

KING   If it be so, Laertes—
As how should it be so, how otherwise?—
Will you be ruled by me?

LAERTES   Ay, my lord,
So you will not o'errule me to a peace.

KING   To thine own peace. If he be now returned,   60
As checking at[1] his voyage, and that he means
No more to undertake it, I will work him
To an exploit now ripe in my device,
Under the which he shall not choose but fall;
And for his death no wind of blame shall breathe   65
But even his mother shall uncharge[2] the practice
And call it accident.

LAERTES   My lord, I will be ruled;
The rather if you could devise it so
That I might be the organ.[3]

KING   It falls right.
You have been talked of since your travel much,   70
And that in Hamlet's hearing, for a quality
Wherein they say you shine. Your sum of parts
Did not together pluck such envy from him
As did that one, and that, in my regard,
Of the unworthiest siege.[4]

LAERTES   What part is that, my lord?   75

KING   A very riband in the cap of youth,
Yet needful too, for youth no less becomes
The light and careless livery that it wears
Than settled age his sables and his weeds,[5]
Importing health and graveness. Two months since   80
Here was a gentleman of Normandy.
I have seen myself, and served against, the French,
And they can[6] well on horseback, but this gallant
Had witchcraft in't. He grew unto his seat,
And to such wondrous doing brought his horse,   85
As had he been incorpsed and demi-natured
With the brave beast. So far he topped my thought
That I, in forgery[7] of shapes and tricks,
Come short of what he did.[8]

---

7. trick
8. handwriting
9. explain it to
1. turning aside from
2. not accuse
3. instrument
4. rank
5. dignified clothing
6. perform

7. imagination
8. The gentleman referred to was so skilled in horsemanship that he seemed to share one body with the horse, "incorpsed." The King further extends the compliment by saying that he appeared like the mythical centaur, a creature who was man from the waist up and horse from the waist down, therefore "demi-natured."

LAERTES   A Norman was't?
KING   A Norman.   90
LAERTES   Upon my life, Lamord.
KING   The very same.
LAERTES   I know him well. He is the brooch indeed
  And gem of all the nation.
KING   He made confession[9] of you,
  And gave you such a masterly report   95
  For art and exercise in your defence,[1]
  And for your rapier most especial,
  That he cried out 'twould be a sight indeed
  If one could match you. The scrimers[2] of their nation
  He swore had neither motion, guard, nor eye,   100
  If you opposed them. Sir, this report of his
  Did Hamlet so envenom with his envy
  That he could nothing do but wish and beg
  Your sudden coming o'er, to play with you.
  Now out of this—
LAERTES   What out of this, my lord?   105
KING   Laertes, was your father dear to you?
  Or are you like the painting of a sorrow,
  A face without a heart?
LAERTES   Why ask you this?
KING   Not that I think you did not love your father,
  But that I know love is begun by time,   110
  And that I see in passages of proof,[3]
  Time qualifies the spark and fire of it.
  There lives within the very flame of love
  A kind of wick or snuff that will abate it,
  And nothing is at a like goodness still,   115
  For goodness, growing to a plurisy,[4]
  Dies in his own too much.[5] That we would do,
  We should do when we would; for this "would" changes,
  And hath abatements and delays as many
  As there are tongues, are hands, are accidents,   120
  And then this "should" is like a spendthrift's sigh
  That hurts by easing. But to the quick of th' ulcer—
  Hamlet comes back; what would you undertake
  To show yourself in deed your father's son
  More than in words?
LAERTES   To cut his throat i' th' church.   125
KING   No place indeed should murder sanctuarize[6];
  Revenge should have no bounds. But, good Laertes,
  Will you do this? Keep close within your chamber.
  Hamlet returned shall know you are come home.
  We'll put on those shall praise your excellence,   130
  And set a double varnish[7] on the fame
  The Frenchman gave you, bring you in fine[8] together,
  And wager on your heads. He, being remiss,[9]
  Most generous, and free from all contriving,

---

9. gave a report
1. skill in fencing
2. fencers
3. tests of experience
4. fullness

5. excess
6. provide sanctuary for murder
7. gloss
8. in short
9. careless

Will not peruse[1] the foils, so that with ease,   135
Or with a little shuffling, you may choose
A sword unbated,[2] and in a pass of practice
Requite him for your father.
LAERTES   I will do't,
And for that purpose I'll anoint my sword.
I bought an unction of a mountebank,   140
So mortal that but dip a knife in it,
Where it draws blood no cataplasm[3] so rare,
Collected from all simples[4] that have virtue
Under the moon, can save the thing from death
That is but scratched withal. I'll touch my point   145
With this contagion, that if I gall[5] him slightly,
It may be death.
KING   Let's further think of this,
Weigh what convenience both of time and means
May fit us to our shape. If this should fail,
And that our drift look[6] through our bad performance,   150
'Twere better not assayed. Therefore this project
Should have a back or second that might hold
If this did blast in proof.[7] Soft, let me see.
We'll make a solemn wager on your cunnings—
I ha't.   155
When in your motion you are hot and dry—
As make your bouts more violent to that end—
And that he calls for drink, I'll have preferred him
A chalice for the nonce, whereon but sipping,
If he by chance escape your venomed stuck,[8]   160
Our purpose may hold there.—But stay, what noise?

              Enter QUEEN.

QUEEN   One woe doth tread upon another's heel,
   So fast they follow. Your sister's drowned, Laertes.
LAERTES   Drowned? O, where?
QUEEN   There is a willow grows aslant the brook   165
   That shows his hoar leaves in the glassy stream.
   Therewith fantastic garlands did she make
   Of crowflowers, nettles, daisies, and long purples
   That liberal[9] shepherds give a grosser[1] name,
   But our cold[2] maids do dead men's fingers call them.   170
   There on the pendent boughs her coronet weeds
   Clamb'ring to hang, an envious[3] sliver broke,
   When down her weedy trophies and herself
   Fell in the weeping brook. Her clothes spread wide,
   And mermaid-like awhile they bore her up,   175
   Which time she chanted snatches of old tunes,
   As one incapable[4] of her own distress,
   Or like a creature native and indued[5]
   Unto that element. But long it could not be

1. examine
2. not blunted
3. poultice
4. herbs
5. scratch
6. intent become obvious
7. fail when tried

8. thrust
9. vulgar
1. coarser
2. chaste
3. malicious
4. unaware
5. habituated

Till that her garments, heavy with their drink,   180
Pulled the poor wretch from her melodious lay
To muddy death.
LAERTES   Alas, then she is drowned?
QUEEN Drowned, drowned.
LAERTES   Too much of water hast thou, poor Ophelia,
And therefore I forbid my tears; but yet   185
It is our trick; nature her custom holds,
Let shame say what it will. When these are gone,
The woman will be out. Adieu, my lord.
I have a speech o' fire that fain would blaze
But that this folly drowns it.   *Exit.*
KING   Let's follow, Gertrude.   190
How much I had to do to calm his rage!
Now fear I this will give it start again;
Therefore let's follow.   *Exeunt.*

Act 5

SCENE 1: *A churchyard. Enter two* CLOWNS.[6]

CLOWN   Is she to be buried in Christian burial when she wilfully
seeks her own salvation?

OTHER   I tell thee she is. Therefore make her grave straight. The
crowner[7] hath sat on her,[8] and finds it Christian burial.

CLOWN   How can that be, unless she drowned herself in her own de- 5
fence?

OTHER   Why, 'tis found so.

CLOWN   It must be "se offendendo";[9] it cannot be else. For here lies
the point: if I drown myself wittingly, it argues an act, and an act
hath three branches—it is to act, to do, to perform; argal,[1] she 10
drowned herself wittingly.

OTHER   Nay, but hear you, Goodman Delver.

CLOWN   Give me leave. Here lies the water; good. Here stands the
man; good. If the man go to this water and drown himself, it is, will
he, nill he, he goes—mark you that. But if the water come to him 15
and drown him, he drowns not himself. Argal, he that is not guilty
of his own death shortens not his own life.

OTHER   But is this law?

CLOWN   Ay, marry, is't; crowner's quest[2] law.

OTHER   Will you ha' the truth on't? If this had not been a gentle- 20
woman, she should have been buried out o' Christian burial.

CLOWN   Why, there thou say'st. And the more pity that great folk
should have count'nance[3] in this world to drown or hang themselves
more than their even-Christen.[4] Come, my spade. There is no ancient
gentlemen but gard'ners, ditchers, and grave-makers. They hold up 25
Adam's profession.

OTHER   Was he a gentleman?

CLOWN   'A was the first that ever bore arms.

6. rustics
7. coroner
8. held an inquest
9. an error for *se defendendo,* in self-
defense

1. therefore
2. inquest
3. approval
4. fellow Christians

OTHER   Why, he had none.

CLOWN   What, art a heathen? How dost thou understand the Scrip- 30
ture? The Scripture says Adam digged. Could he dig without arms?
I'll put another question to thee. If thou answerest me not to the
purpose, confess thyself—

OTHER   Go to.

CLOWN   What is he that builds stronger than either the mason, the 35
shipwright, or the carpenter?

OTHER   The gallows-maker, for that frame outlives a thousand tenants.

CLOWN   I like thy wit well, in good faith. The gallows does well. But
how does it well? It does well to those that do ill. Now thou dost ill
to say the gallows is built stronger than the church. Argal, the gal- 40
lows may do well to thee. To't again,[5] come.

OTHER   Who builds stronger than a mason, a shipwright, or a carpenter?

CLOWN   Ay tell me that, and unyoke.[6]

OTHER   Marry, now I can tell.   45

CLOWN   To't.

OTHER   Mass, I cannot tell.

CLOWN   Cudgel thy brains no more about it, for your dull ass will not
mend his pace with beating. And when you are asked this question
next, say "a grave-maker." The houses he makes lasts till doomsday. 50
Go, get thee in, and fetch me a stoup[7] of liquor. *Exit* OTHER CLOWN.

Enter HAMLET *and* HORATIO *as* CLOWN *digs and sings.*

> In youth, when I did love, did love,
>   Methought it was very sweet,
> To contract[8] the time for-a my behove,[9]
>   O, methought there-a was nothing-a meet.[1]   55

HAMLET   Has this fellow no feeling of his business, that 'a sings in
grave-making?

HORATIO   Custom hath made it in him a property of easiness.

HAMLET   'Tis e'en so. The hand of little employment hath the daintier
sense.   60

CLOWN
> But age, with his stealing steps,
>   Hath clawed me in his clutch,
> And hath shipped me into the land,
>   As if I had never been such.

Throws up a skull.

HAMLET   That skull had a tongue in it, and could sing once. How the 65
knave jowls[2] it to the ground, as if 'twere Cain's jawbone, that did
the first murder! This might be the pate of a politician, which this
ass now o'erreaches[3]; one that would circumvent God, might it not?

HORATIO   It might, my lord.

HAMLET   Or of a courtier, which could say "Good morrow, sweet lord! 70
How dost thou, sweet lord?" This might be my Lord Such-a-one,
that praised my Lord Such-a-one's horse, when 'a meant to beg it,
might it not?

---

5. guess again
6. finish the matter
7. mug
8. shorten
9. advantage

1. The gravedigger's song is a free version of "The aged lover renounceth love"
by Thomas, Lord Vaux, published in *Tot-
tel's Miscellany*, 1557.
2. hurls
3. gets the better of

HORATIO Ay, my lord.

HAMLET Why, e'en so, and now my Lady Worm's, chapless,[4] and 75
knock'd abut the mazzard[5] with a sexton's spade. Here's fine revolution,[6] an we had the trick to see't. Did these bones cost no more the
breeding but to play at loggets with them?[7] Mine ache to think on't.

CLOWN   A pick-axe and a spade, a spade,
                        For and a shrouding sheet: 80
                     O, a pit of clay for to be made
                     For such a guest is meet.

Throws up another skull.

HAMLET There's another. Why may not that be the skull of a lawyer?
Where be his quiddities now, his quillets, his cases, his tenures, and
his tricks? Why does he suffer this mad knave now to knock him 85
about the sconce[8] with a dirty shovel, and will not tell him of his
action of battery? Hum! This fellow might be in's time a great buyer
of land, with his statutes, his recognizances, his fines, his double
vouchers, his recoveries. Is this the fine[9] of his fines, and the recovery
of his recoveries, to have his fine pate full of fine dirt? Will his vouch- 90
ers vouch him no more of his purchases, and double ones too, than
the length and breadth of a pair of indentures[1]? The very convey-
ances of his lands will scarcely lie in this box, and must th' inheritor
himself have no more, ha?[2]

HORATIO Not a jot more, my lord.   95

HAMLET Is not parchment made of sheepskins?

HORATIO Ay, my lord, and of calves' skins too.

HAMLET They are sheep and calves which seek out assurance in that.
I will speak to this fellow. Whose grave's this, sirrah?

CLOWN Mine, sir.   100

          [*Sings.*] O, a pit of clay for to be made—

HAMLET I think it be thine indeed, for thou liest in't.

CLOWN You lie out on't, sir, and therefore 'tis not yours. For my part,
I do not lie in't, yet it is mine.

HAMLET Thou dost lie in't, to be in't and say it is thine. 'Tis for the 105
dead, not for the quick[3]; therefore thou liest.

CLOWN 'Tis a quick lie, sir; 'twill away again from me to you.

HAMLET What man dost thou dig it for?

CLOWN For no man, sir.

HAMLET What woman, then?   110

CLOWN For none neither.

HAMLET Who is to be buried in't?

CLOWN One that was a woman, sir; but, rest her soul, she's dead.

HAMLET How absolute[4] the knave is! We must speak by the card,[5] or
equivocation will undo us. By the Lord, Horatio, this three years I 115
have took note of it, the age is grown so picked[6] that the toe of the
peasant comes so near the heel of the courtier, he galls his kibe.[7]
How long hast thou been a grave-maker?

4. lacking a lower jaw
5. head
6. skull
7. "Loggets" were small pieces of wood
thrown as part of a game.
8. head
9. end
1. contracts

2. In this speech Hamlet reels off a list
of legal terms relating to property trans-
actions.
3. living
4. precise
5. exactly
6. refined
7. rubs a blister on his heel

CLOWN   Of all the days i' th' year, I came to't that day that our last
King Hamlet overcame Fortinbras.   120
HAMLET   How long is that since?
CLOWN   Cannot you tell that? Every fool can tell that. It was that
very day that young Hamlet was born—he that is mad, and sent
into England.
HAMLET   Ay, marry, why was he sent into England?   125
CLOWN   Why, because 'a was mad. 'A shall recover his wits there; or,
if 'a do not, 'tis no great matter there.
HAMLET   Why?
CLOWN   'Twill not be seen in him there. There the men are as mad
as he.   130
HAMLET   How came he mad?
CLOWN   Very strangely, they say.
HAMLET   How strangely?
CLOWN   Faith, e'en with losing his wits.
HAMLET   Upon what ground?   135
CLOWN   Why, here in Denmark. I have been sexton here, man and
boy, thirty years.
HAMLET   How long will a man lie i' th' earth ere he rot?
CLOWN   Faith, if 'a be not rotten before 'a die—as we have many
pocky[8] corses now-a-days that will scarce hold the laying in—'a will 140
last you some eight year or nine year. A tanner will last you nine
year.
HAMLET   Why he more than another?
CLOWN   Why, sir, his hide is so tanned with his trade that 'a will keep
out water a great while; and your water is a sore decayer of your 145
whoreson[9] dead body. Here's a skull now hath lien[1] you i' th' earth
three and twenty years.
HAMLET   Whose was it?
CLOWN   A whoreson mad fellow's it was. Whose do you think it was?
HAMLET   Nay, I know not.   150
CLOWN   A pestilence on him for a mad rogue! 'A poured a flagon of
Rhenish on my head once. This same skull, sir, was, sir, Yorick's
skull, the king's jester.
HAMLET   [*takes the skull*]   This?
CLOWN   E'en that.   155
HAMLET   Alas, poor Yorick! I knew him, Horatio—a fellow of infinite
jest, of most excellent fancy. He hath bore me on his back a thousand
times, and now how abhorred in my imagination it is! My gorge[2]
rises at it. Here hung those lips that I have kissed I know not how
oft. Where be your gibes now, your gambols, your songs, your flashes 160
of merriment that were wont to set the table on a roar? Not one now
to mock your own grinning? Quite chap-fall'n[3]? Now get you to my
lady's chamber, and tell her, let her paint an inch thick, to this favor[4]
she must come. Make her laugh at that. Prithee, Horatio, tell me one
thing.   165
HORATIO   What's that, my lord?
HAMLET   Dost thou think Alexander looked o' this fashion i' th' earth?
HORATIO   E'en so.
HAMLET   And smelt so? Pah!   *Throws down the skull.*

---

8. corrupted by syphilis   2. throat
9. bastard (not literally)   3. lacking a lower jaw
1. lain   4. appearance

HORATIO   E'en so, my lord.   170

HAMLET   To what base uses we may return, Horatio! Why may not
imagination trace the noble dust of Alexander till 'a find it stopping
a bung-hole?

HORATIO   'Twere to consider too curiously[5] to consider so.

HAMLET   No, faith, not a jot, but to follow him thither with modesty[6] 175
enough, and likelihood to lead it. Alexander died, Alexander was
buried, Alexander returneth to dust; the dust is earth; of earth we
make loam; and why of that loam whereto he was converted might
they not stop a beer-barrel?

> Imperious Cæsar, dead and turned to clay,   180
> Might stop a hole to keep the wind away.
> O, that that earth which kept the world in awe
> Should patch a wall t'expel the winter's flaw![7]

But soft, but soft awhile! Here comes the king,
The queen, the courtiers.

> *Enter* KING, QUEEN, LAERTES, *and the Corse with a* PRIEST *and*
> LORDS *attendant.*

                              Who is this they follow?   185
And with such maiméd[8] rites? This doth betoken
The corse they follow did with desperate hand
Fordo[9] it own life. 'Twas of some estate.[1]
Couch[2] we awhile and mark.   *Retires with* HORATIO.

LAERTES   What ceremony else[3]?   190

HAMLET   That is Laertes, a very noble youth. Mark.

LAERTES   What ceremony else?

PRIEST   Her obsequies have been as far enlarged[4]
As we have warranty. Her death was doubtful,
And but that great command o'ersways the order,[5]   195
She should in ground unsanctified been lodged
Till the last trumpet. For charitable prayers,
Shards, flints, and pebbles, should be thrown on her.
Yet here she is allowed her virgin crants,[6]
Her maiden strewments,[7] and the bringing home   200
Of bell and burial.

LAERTES   Must there no more be done?

PRIEST   No more be done.
We should profane the service of the dead
To sing a requiem and such rest to her
As to peace-parted souls.

LAERTES   Lay her i' th' earth,   205
And from her fair and unpolluted flesh
May violets spring! I tell thee, churlish priest,
A minist'ring angel shall my sister be
When thou liest howling.[8]

HAMLET   What, the fair Ophelia!

QUEEN   Sweets to the sweet. Farewell!   *Scatters flowers.* 210

---

5. precisely
6. moderation
7. gusty wind
8. cut short
9. destroy
1. rank
2. conceal ourselves

3. more
4. extended
5. usual rules
6. wreaths
7. flowers strewn on the grave
8. in Hell

I hoped thou shouldst have been my Hamlet's wife.
I thought thy bride-bed to have decked, sweet maid,
And not have strewed thy grave.

LAERTES   O, treble woe
Fall ten times treble on that curséd head
Whose wicked deed thy most ingenious sense[9]   215
Deprived thee of! Hold off the earth awhile,
Till I have caught her once more in mine arms.

Leaps into the grave.

Now pile your dust upon the quick and dead,
Till of this flat a mountain you have made
T' o'er-top old Pelion or the skyish head   220
Of blue Olympus.[1]

HAMLET [*coming forward*]   What is he whose grief
Bears such an emphasis, whose phrase of sorrow
Conjures[2] the wand'ring stars, and makes them stand
Like wonder-wounded hearers? This is I,
Hamlet the Dane.   225

    HAMLET *leaps into the grave and they grapple.*

LAERTES   The devil take thy soul!
HAMLET   Thou pray'st not well.
I prithee take thy fingers from my throat,
For though I am not splenitive[3] and rash,
Yet have I in me something dangerous,
Which let thy wisdom fear. Hold off thy hand.   230
KING   Pluck them asunder.
QUEEN   Hamlet! Hamlet!
ALL   Gentlemen!
HORATIO   Good my lord, be quiet.

    The ATTENDANTS *part them, and they come out of the grave.*

HAMLET   Why, I will fight with him upon this theme   235
Until my eyelids will no longer wag.[4]
QUEEN   O my son, what theme?
HAMLET   I loved Ophelia. Forty thousand brothers
Could not with all their quantity of love
Make up my sum. What wilt thou do for her?   240
KING   O, he is mad, Laertes.
QUEEN   For love of God, forbear[5] him.
HAMLET   'Swounds, show me what th'owt do.
Woo't[6] weep, woo't fight, woo't fast, woo't tear thyself,
Woo't drink up eisel,[7] eat a crocodile?   245
I'll do't. Dost come here to whine?
To outface[8] me with leaping in her grave?
Be buried quick with her, and so will I.
And if thou prate of mountains, let them throw

9. lively mind
1. The rivalry between Laertes and Hamlet in this scene extends even to their rhetoric. Pelion and Olympus, mentioned here by Laertes, and Ossa, mentioned below by Hamlet, were Greek mountains noted in mythology for their height. Olympus was the reputed home of the gods, and the other two were piled one on top of the other by the Giants in an attempt to reach the top of Olympus and overthrow the gods.
2. casts a spell on
3. hot-tempered
4. move
5. bear with
6. will you
7. vinegar
8. get the best of

Millions of acres on us, till our ground,   250
Singeing his pate against the burning zone,[9]
Make Ossa like a wart! Nay, an thou'lt mouth,
I'll rant as well as thou.
QUEEN   This is mere madness;
And thus awhile the fit will work on him.
Anon, as patient as the female dove   255
When that her golden couplets[1] are disclosed,
His silence will sit drooping.
HAMLET   Hear you, sir.
What is the reason that you use me thus?
I loved you ever. But it is no matter.
Let Hercules himself do what he may,   260
The cat will mew, and dog will have his day.
KING   I pray thee, good Horatio, wait upon[2] him.
                              Exeunt HAMLET *and* HORATIO.
[*To* LAERTES.] Strengthen your patience in our last night's speech.
We'll put the matter to the present push.[3]—
Good Gertrude, set some watch over your son.—   265
This grave shall have a living monument.
An hour of quiet shortly shall we see;
Till then in patience our proceeding be.   *Exeunt.*

SCENE 2: *A hall or public room. Enter* HAMLET *and* HORATIO.

HAMLET   So much for this, sir; now shall you see the other.
You do remember all the circumstance?
HORATIO   Remember it, my lord!
HAMLET   Sir, in my heart there was a kind of fighting
That would not let me sleep. Methought I lay   5
Worse than the mutines[4] in the bilboes.[5] Rashly,
And praised be rashness for it—let us know,
Our indiscretion sometime serves us well,
When our deep plots do pall; and that should learn[6] us
There's a divinity that shapes our ends,   10
Rough-hew them how we will—
HORATIO   That is most certain.
HAMLET   Up from my cabin,
My sea-gown scarfed[7] about me, in the dark
Groped I to find out them, had my desire,
Fingered[8] their packet, and in fine[9] withdrew   15
To mine own room again, making so bold,
My fears forgetting manners, to unseal
Their grand commission; where I found, Horatio—
Ah, royal knavery!—an exact[1] command,
Larded[2] with many several sorts of reasons,   20
Importing Denmark's health, and England's too,
With, ho! such bugs and goblins in my life,[3]
That on the supervise,[4] no leisure bated,

9. sky in the torrid zone
1. pair of eggs
2. attend
3. immediate trial
4. mutineers
5. stocks
6. teach

7. wrapped
8. stole
9. quickly
1. precisely stated
2. garnished
3. such dangers if I remained alive
4. as soon as the commission was read

No, not to stay the grinding of the axe,
My head should be struck off.
HORATIO   Is't possible?   25
HAMLET   Here's the commission; read it at more leisure.
But wilt thou hear now how I did proceed?
HORATIO   I beseech you.
HAMLET   Being thus benetted[5] round with villainies,
Or I could make a prologue to my brains,   30
They had begun the play. I sat me down,
Devised[6] a new commission, wrote it fair.[7]
I once did hold it, as our statists[8] do,
A baseness to write fair, and labored much
How to forget that learning; but sir, now   35
It did me yeoman's service. Wilt thou know
Th' effect[9] of what I wrote?
HORATIO   Ay, good my lord.
HAMLET   An earnest conjuration from the king,
As England was his faithful tributary,[1]
As love between them like the palm might flourish,   40
As peace should still her wheaten garland wear
And stand a comma 'tween their amities,[2]
And many such like as's of great charge,[3]
That on the view and knowing of these contents,
Without debatement[4] further more or less,   45
He should those bearers put to sudden death,
Not shriving-time allowed.[5]
HORATIO   How was this sealed?
HAMLET   Why, even in that was heaven ordinant,[6]
I had my father's signet in my purse,
Which was the model of that Danish seal,   50
Folded the writ up in the form of th' other,
Subscribed it, gave't th' impression,[7] placed it safely,
The changeling[8] never known. Now, the next day
Was our sea-fight, and what to this was sequent[9]
Thou knowest already.   55
HORATIO   So Guildenstern and Rosencrantz go to't.
HAMLET   Why, man, they did make love to this employment.
They are not near[1] my conscience; their defeat[2]
Does by their own insinuation grow.
'Tis dangerous when the baser nature comes   60
Between the pass[3] and fell[4] incensèd points
Of mighty opposites.
HORATIO   Why, what a king is this!
HAMLET   Does it not, think thee, stand me now upon—
He that hath killed my king and whored my mother,
Popped in between th' election and my hopes,   65
Thrown out his angle[5] for my proper life,

---

5. caught in a net   6. operative
6. made   7. of the seal
7. legibly   8. alteration
8. politicians   9. followed
9. contents   1. do not touch
1. vassal   2. death
2. link friendships   3. thrust
3. import   4. cruel
4. consideration   5. fishhook
5. without time for confession

And with such coz'nage[6]—is't not perfect conscience
To quit[7] him with this arm? And is't not to be damned
To let this canker of our nature come
In further evil?   70
HORATIO   It must be shortly known to him from England
What is the issue[8] of the business there.
HAMLET   It will be short[9]; the interim is mine.
And a man's life's no more than to say "one."
But I am very sorry, good Horatio,   75
That to Laertes I forgot myself;
For by the image of my cause I see
The portraiture of his. I'll court his favors.
But sure the bravery[1] of his grief did put me
Into a tow'ring passion.
HORATIO   Peace; who comes here?   80

Enter OSRIC.

OSRIC   Your lordship is right welcome back to Denmark.
HAMLET   I humbly thank you, sir. [*Aside to* HORATIO.] Dost know
this water-fly?
HORATIO [*aside to* HAMLET]   No, my good lord.
HAMLET [*aside to* HORATIO]   Thy state is the more gracious, for 'tis a   85
vice to know him. He hath much land, and fertile. Let a beast be
lord of beasts, and his crib shall stand at the king's mess. 'Tis a
chough,[2] but as I say, spacious in the possession of dirt.
OSRIC   Sweet lord, if your lordship were at leisure, I should impart a
thing to you from his majesty.   90
HAMLET   I will receive it, sir, with all diligence of spirit. Put your
bonnet to his right use. 'Tis for the head.
OSRIC   I thank your lordship, it is very hot.
HAMLET   No, believe me, 'tis very cold; the wind is northerly.
OSRIC   It is indifferent[3] cold, my lord, indeed.   95
HAMLET   But yet methinks it is very sultry and hot for my com-
plexion.[4]
OSRIC   Exceedingly, my lord; it is very sultry, as 'twere—I cannot tell
how. My lord, his majesty bade me signify to you that 'a has laid
a great wager on your head. Sir, this is the matter—   100
HAMLET   I beseech you, remember.

HAMLET *moves him to put on his hat.*

OSRIC   Nay, good my lord; for my ease, in good faith. Sir, here is
newly come to court Laertes; believe me, an absolute[5] gentleman,
full of most excellent differences,[6] of very soft society and great
showing.[7] Indeed, to speak feelingly of him, he is the card or cal-   105
endar[8] of gentry, for you shall find in him the continent[9] of what
part a gentleman would see.
HAMLET   Sir, his definement[1] suffers no perdition in you, though I
know to divide him inventorially[2] would dozy[3] th' arithmetic of

6. trickery
7. repay
8. outcome
9. soon
1. exaggerated display
2. jackdaw
3. moderately
4. temperament

5. perfect
6. qualities
7. good manners
8. measure
9. sum total
1. description
2. examine bit by bit
3. daze

memory, and yet but yaw[4] neither in respect of his quick sail. But [110]
in the verity of extolment, I take him to be a soul of great article,[5]
and his infusion[6] of such dearth and rareness as, to make true
diction[7] of him, his semblage[8] is his mirror, and who else would
trace[9] him, his umbrage,[1] nothing more.

OSRIC   Your lordship speaks most infallibly of him. [115]

HAMLET   The concernancy,[2] sir? Why do we wrap the gentleman in
our more rawer breath?[3]

OSRIC   Sir?

HORATIO   Is't not possible to understand in another tongue? You will
to't, sir, really. [120]

HAMLET   What imports the nomination[4] of this gentleman?

OSRIC   Of Laertes?

HORATIO [*aside*]   His purse is empty already. All's golden words are
spent.

HAMLET   Of him, sir. [125]

OSRIC   I know you are not ignorant—

HAMLET   I would you did, sir; yet, in faith, if you did, it would not
much approve me. Well, sir.

OSRIC   You are not ignorant of what excellence Laertes is—

HAMLET   I dare not confess that, lest I should compare[5] with him in [130]
excellence; but to know a man well were to know himself.

OSRIC   I mean, sir, for his weapon; but in the imputation[6] laid on him
by them, in his meed he's unfellowed.[7]

HAMLET   What's his weapon?

OSRIC   Rapier and dagger. [135]

HAMLET   That's two of his weapons—but well.

OSRIC   The king, sir, hath wagered with him six Barbary horses,
against the which he has impawned,[8] as I take it, six French rapiers
and poniards, with their assigns,[9] as girdle, hangers, and so. Three
of the carriages, in faith, are very dear to fancy,[1] very responsive to [140]
the hilts, most delicate[2] carriages, and of very liberal conceit.[3]

HAMLET   What call you the carriages?

HORATIO [*aside to* HAMLET]   I knew you must be edified by the
margent[4] ere you had done.

OSRIC   The carriages, sir, are the hangers. [145]

HAMLET   The phrase would be more germane to the matter if we
could carry a cannon by our sides. I would it might be hangers till
then. But on! Six Barbary horses against six French swords, their
assigns, and three liberal conceited carriages; that's the French bet
against the Danish. Why is this all impawned, as you call it? [150]

OSRIC   The king, sir, hath laid, sir, that in a dozen passes between
yourself and him he shall not exceed you three hits; he hath laid on
twelve for nine, and it would come to immediate trial if your lordship would vouchsafe the answer.

HAMLET   How if I answer no? [155]

OSRIC   I mean, my lord, the opposition of your person in trial.

4. steer wildly
5. scope
6. nature
7. telling
8. rival
9. keep pace with
1. shadow
2. meaning
3. cruder words
4. naming

5. i.e., compare myself
6. reputation
7. unequaled in his excellence
8. staked
9. appurtenances
1. finely designed
2. well adjusted
3. elegant design
4. marginal gloss

HAMLET   Sir, I will walk here in the hall. If it please his majesty, it is the breathing time[5] of day with me. Let the foils be brought, the gentleman willing, and the king hold his purpose; I will win for him an I can. If not, I will gain nothing but my shame and the 160 odd hits.

OSRIC   Shall I deliver you so?

HAMLET   To this effect, sir, after what flourish your nature will.

OSRIC   I commend my duty to your lordship.

HAMLET   Yours, yours. [*Exit* OSRIC.] He does well to commend it 165 himself; there are no tongues else for's turn.

HORATIO   This lapwing runs away with the shell on his head.[6]

HAMLET   'A did comply,[7] sir, with his dug[8] before 'a sucked it. Thus has he, and many more of the same bevy that I know the drossy age dotes on, only got the tune of the time; and out of an habit of en- 170 counter, a kind of yesty[9] collection which carries them through and through the most fanned and winnowed opinions; and do but blow them to their trial, the bubbles are out.

> *Enter a* LORD.

LORD   My lord, his majesty commended him to you by young Osric, who brings back to him that you attend[1] him in the hall. He sends 175 to know if your pleasure hold to play with Laertes, or that you will take longer time.

HAMLET   I am constant to my purposes; they follow the king's pleasure. If his fitness speaks, mine is ready; now or whensoever, provided I be so able as now.   180

LORD   The king and queen and all are coming down.

HAMLET   In happy time.

LORD   The queen desires you to use some gentle entertainment[2] to Laertes before you fall to play.

HAMLET   She well instructs me.   *Exit* LORD. 185

HORATIO   You will lose this wager, my lord.

HAMLET   I do not think so. Since he went into France I have been in continual practice. I shall win at the odds. But thou wouldst not think how ill[3] all's here about my heart. But it is no matter.

HORATIO   Nay, good my lord—   190

HAMLET   It is but foolery, but it is such a kind of gaingiving[4] as would perhaps trouble a woman.

HORATIO   If your mind dislike anything, obey it. I will forestall their repair[5] hither, and say you are not fit.

HAMLET   Not a whit, we defy augury. There is special providence in 195 the fall of a sparrow. If it be now, 'tis not to come; if it be not to come, it will be now; if it be not now, yet it will come. The readiness is all. Since no man of aught he leaves knows, what is't to leave betimes? Let be.

> *A table prepared. Enter* TRUMPETS, DRUMS, *and* OFFICERS *with cushions;* KING, QUEEN, OSRIC *and* ATTENDANTS *with foils, daggers, and* LAERTES.

---

5. time for exercise
6. The lapwing was thought to be so precocious that it could run immediately after being hatched, even as here with bits of the shell still on its head.
7. deal formally
8. mother's breast

9. yeasty
1. await
2. cordiality
3. uneasy
4. misgiving
5. coming

KING   Come, Hamlet, come and take this hand from me.   200

The KING *puts* LAERTES' *hand into* HAMLET'*s.*

HAMLET   Give me your pardon, sir. I have done you wrong,
But pardon 't as you are a gentleman.
This presence[6] knows, and you must needs have heard,
How I am punished with a sore distraction.
What I have done   205
That might your nature, honor, and exception,[7]
Roughly awake, I here proclaim was madness.
Was 't Hamlet wronged Laertes? Never Hamlet.
If Hamlet from himself be ta'en away,
And when he's not himself does wrong Laertes,   210
Then Hamlet does it not, Hamlet denies it.
Who does it then? His madness. If't be so,
Hamlet is of the faction that is wronged;
His madness is poor Hamlet's enemy.
Sir, in this audience,   215
Let my disclaiming from[8] a purposed evil
Free[9] me so far in your most generous thoughts
That I have shot my arrow o'er the house
And hurt my brother.
LAERTES   I am satisfied in nature,
Whose motive in this case should stir me most   220
To my revenge. But in my terms of honor
I stand aloof, and will no reconcilement
Till by some elder masters of known honor
I have a voice[1] and precedent of peace
To keep my name ungored.[2] But till that time   225
I do receive your offered love like love,
And will not wrong it.
HAMLET   I embrace it freely,
And will this brother's wager frankly[3] play.
Give us the foils.
LAERTES   Come, one for me.
HAMLET   I'll be your foil, Laertes. In mine ignorance   230
Your skill shall, like a star i' th' darkest night,
Stick fiery off[4] indeed.
LAERTES   You mock me, sir.
HAMLET   No, by this hand.
KING   Give them the foils, young Osric. Cousin Hamlet,
You know the wager?
HAMLET   Very well, my lord;   235
Your Grace has laid the odds o' th' weaker side.
KING   I do not fear it, I have seen you both;
But since he is bettered,[5] we have therefore odds.
LAERTES   This is too heavy; let me see another.
HAMLET   This likes[6] me well. These foils have all a[7] length?   240

They prepare to play.

6. company
7. resentment
8. denying of
9. absolve
1. authority
2. unshamed

3. without rancor
4. shine brightly
5. reported better
6. suits
7. the same

OSRIC   Ay, my good lord.
KING   Set me the stoups of wine upon that table.
  If Hamlet give the first or second hit,
  Or quit in answer of[8] the third exchange,
  Let all the battlements their ordnance fire.   245
  The king shall drink to Hamlet's better breath,
  And in the cup an union[9] shall he throw,
  Richer than that which four successive kings
  In Denmark's crown have worn. Give me the cups,
  And let the kettle[1] to the trumpet speak,   250
  The trumpet to the cannoneer without,
  The cannons to the heavens, the heaven to earth,
  "Now the king drinks to Hamlet." Come, begin—

  Trumpets the while.

  And you, the judges, bear a wary eye.
HAMLET   Come on, sir.
LAERTES   Come, my lord.   *They play.*
HAMLET   One.
LAERTES   No.
HAMLET   Judgment?   255
OSRIC   A hit, a very palpable hit.

  Drums, trumpets, and shot. Flourish; a piece goes off.

LAERTES   Well, again.
KING   Stay, give me drink. Hamlet, this pearl is thine.
  Here's to thy health. Give him the cup.
HAMLET   I'll play this bout first; set it by awhile.   260
  Come.   *They play.*
  Another hit; what say you?
LAERTES   I do confess't.
KING   Our son shall win.
QUEEN   He's fat,[2] and scant of breath.
  Here, Hamlet, take my napkin, rub thy brows.   265
  The queen carouses to thy fortune, Hamlet.
HAMLET   Good madam!
KING   Gertrude, do not drink.
QUEEN   I will, my lord; I pray you pardon me.
KING [*aside*]   It is the poisoned cup; it is too late.   270
HAMLET   I dare not drink yet, madam; by and by.
QUEEN   Come, let me wipe thy face.
LAERTES   My lord, I'll hit him now.
KING   I do not think't.
LAERTES [*aside*]   And yet it is almost against my conscience.
HAMLET   Come, for the third, Laertes. You do but dally.   275
  I pray you pass[3] with your best violence;
  I am afeard you make a wanton of me.[4]
LAERTES   Say you so? Come on.   *They play.*
OSRIC   Nothing, neither way.
LAERTES   Have at you now!   280

8. repay
9. pearl
1. kettledrum

2. out of shape
3. attack
4. trifle with me

LAERTES *wounds* HAMLET: *then, in scuffling, they change rapiers, and* HAMLET *wounds* LAERTES.

KING   Part them. They are incensed.
HAMLET   Nay, come again.   *The* QUEEN *falls.*
OSRIC   Look to the queen there, ho!
HORATIO   They bleed on both sides. How is it, my lord?
OSRIC   How is't, Laertes?   285
LAERTES   Why, as a woodcock to mine own springe,[5] Osric.
    I am justly killed with mine own treachery.
HAMLET   How does the queen?
KING   She swoons to see them bleed.
QUEEN   No, no, the drink, the drink! O my dear Hamlet!
    The drink, the drink! I am poisoned.   *Dies.* 290
HAMLET   O, villainy! Ho! let the door be locked.
    Treachery! seek it out.
LAERTES   It is here, Hamlet. Hamlet, thou art slain;
    No med'cine in the world can do thee good.
    In thee there is not half an hour's life.   295
    The treacherous instrument is in thy hand,
    Unbated[6] and envenomed. The foul practice
    Hath turned itself on me. Lo, here I lie,
    Never to rise again. Thy mother's poisoned.
    I can no more. The king, the king's to blame.   300
HAMLET   The point envenomed too?
    Then, venom, to thy work.   *Hurts the* KING.
ALL   Treason! treason!
KING   O, yet defend me, friends. I am but hurt.[7]
HAMLET   Here, thou incestuous, murd'rous, damnéd Dane,   305
    Drink off this potion. Is thy union here?
    Follow my mother.   *The* KING *dies.*
LAERTES   He is justly served.
    It is a poison tempered[8] by himself.
    Exchange forgiveness with me, noble Hamlet.
    Mine and my father's death come not upon thee,   310
    Nor thine on me!   *Dies.*
HAMLET   Heaven make thee free of[9] it! I follow thee.
    I am dead, Horatio. Wretched queen, adieu!
    You that look pale and tremble at this chance,[1]
    That are but mutes or audience to this act,   315
    Had I but time, as this fell sergeant Death
    Is strict in his arrest,[2] O, I could tell you—
    But let it be. Horatio, I am dead:
    Thou livest; report me and my cause aright
    To the unsatisfied.[3]
HORATIO   Never believe it.   320
    I am more an antique Roman than a Dane.
    Here's yet some liquor left.
HAMLET   As th'art a man,
    Give me the cup. Let go. By heaven, I'll ha't.

---

5. snare   9. forgive
6. unblunted   1. circumstance
7. wounded   2. summons to court
8. mixed   3. uninformed

O God, Horatio, what a wounded name,
Things standing thus unknown, shall live behind me!⠀⠀⠀⠀325
If thou didst ever hold me in thy heart,
Absent thee from felicity awhile,
And in this harsh world draw thy breath in pain,
To tell my story.⠀⠀⠀⠀⠀⠀⠀⠀⠀⠀*A march afar off.*
⠀⠀⠀⠀⠀⠀⠀What warlike noise is this?
OSRIC⠀⠀Young Fortinbras, with conquest come from Poland,⠀⠀330
To th' ambassadors of England gives
This warlike volley.[4]
HAMLET⠀⠀⠀⠀⠀⠀O, I die, Horatio!
The potent poison quite o'er-crows[5] my spirit.
I cannot live to hear the news from England,
But I do prophesy th' election lights⠀⠀⠀⠀⠀⠀⠀335
On Fortinbras. He has my dying voice.[6]
So tell him, with th' occurrents,[7] more and less,
Which have solicited[8]—the rest is silence.⠀⠀⠀*Dies.*
HORATIO⠀⠀Now cracks a noble heart. Good night, sweet prince,
And flights of angels sing thee to thy rest!⠀⠀*March within.* 340
Why does the drum come hither?

Enter FORTINBRAS, *with the* AMBASSADORS *and with drum,
colors, and* ATTENDANTS.

FORTINBRAS⠀⠀Where is this sight?
HORATIO⠀⠀⠀⠀⠀⠀⠀⠀⠀What is it you would see?
If aught of woe or wonder, cease your search.
FORTINBRAS⠀⠀This quarry cries on havoc.[9] O proud death,
What feast is toward[1] in thine eternal cell⠀⠀⠀⠀⠀345
That thou so many princes at a shot
So bloodily hast struck?
AMBASSADORS⠀⠀⠀⠀⠀The sight is dismal;
And our affairs from England come too late.
The ears are senseless[2] that should give us hearing
To tell him his commandment is fulfilled,⠀⠀⠀⠀⠀350
That Rosencrantz and Guildenstern are dead.
Where should we have our thanks?
HORATIO⠀⠀⠀⠀⠀⠀⠀⠀Not from his mouth,
Had it th' ability of life to thank you.
He never gave commandment for their death.
But since, so jump[3] upon this bloody question,⠀⠀⠀355
You from the Polack wars, and you from England,
Are here arrived, give orders that these bodies
High on a stage be placéd to the view,
And let me speak to th' yet unknowing world
How these things came about. So shall you hear⠀⠀⠀360
Of carnal, bloody, and unnatural acts;

---

4. The staging presents some difficulties here. If Osric is not clairvoyant, he must have left the stage at some point and returned. One possibility is that he might have left to carry out Hamlet's order to lock the door (line 291) and returned when the sound of the distant march is heard.
5. overcomes
6. support
7. circumstances
8. brought about this scene
9. The game killed in the hunt proclaims a slaughter.
1. in preparation
2. without sense of hearing
3. exactly

Of accidental judgments, casual[4] slaughters;
Of deaths put on by cunning and forced cause;
And, in this upshot,[5] purposes mistook
Fall'n on th' inventors' heads. All this can I   365
Truly deliver.
FORTINBRAS   Let us haste to hear it,
And call the noblest to the audience.[6]
For me, with sorrow I embrace my fortune.
I have some rights of memory[7] in this kingdom,
Which now to claim my vantage[8] doth invite me.   370
HORATIO   Of that I shall have also cause to speak,
And from his mouth whose voice will draw on more.
But let this same be presently performed,
Even while men's minds are wild, lest more mischance
On plots and errors happen.
FORTINBRAS   Let four captains   375
Bear Hamlet like a soldier to the stage,
For he was likely, had he been put on,[9]
To have proved most royal; and for his passage
The soldier's music and the rite of war
Speak loudly for him.   380
Take up the bodies. Such a sight as this
Becomes the field, but here shows much amiss.
Go, bid the soldiers shoot.

Exeunt marching. A peal of ordnance shot off.

---

4. brought about by apparent accident   7. succession
5. result   8. position
6. hearing   9. elected king

The Misanthrope*

CHARACTERS

ALCESTE, *in love with Célimène*
PHILINTE, *Alceste's friend*
ORONTE, *in love with Célimène*
CÉLIMÈNE, *Alceste's beloved*
ÉLIANTE, *Célimène's cousin*
ARSINOÉ, *a friend of Célimène's*

ACASTE ⎱
CLITANDRE ⎰ *Marquesses*
BASQUE, *Célimène's servant*
A GUARD *of the Marshalsea*
DUBOIS, *Alceste's valet*

The Scene throughout is in Célimène's house at Paris.

Act 1

SCENE 1. [PHILINTE, ALCESTE]

PHILINTE   Now, what's got into you?
ALCESTE [*seated*]   Kindly leave me alone.
PHILINTE   Come, come, what is it? This lugubrious tone . . .
ALCESTE   Leave me, I said; you spoil my solitude.
PHILINTE   Oh, listen to me, now, and don't be rude.
ALCESTE   I choose to be rude, Sir, and to be hard of hearing.   5
PHILINTE   These ugly moods of yours are not endearing;
  Friends though we are, I really must insist . . .
ALCESTE [*abruptly rising*]   Friends? Friends, you say? Well, cross me
  off your list.
  I've been your friend till now, as you well know;
  But after what I saw a moment ago   10
  I tell you flatly that our ways must part.
  I wish no place in a dishonest heart.
PHILINTE   Why, what have I done, Alceste? Is this quite just?
ALCESTE   My God, you ought to die of self-disgust.
  I call your conduct inexcusable, Sir,   15
  And every man of honor will concur.
  I see you almost hug a man to death,
  Exclaim for joy until you're out of breath,
  And supplement these loving demonstrations
  With endless offers, vows, and protestations;   20
  Then when I ask you "Who was that?" I find
  That you can barely bring his name to mind!
  Once the man's back is turned, you cease to love him,
  And speak with absolute indifference of him!
  By God, I say it's base and scandalous   25
  To falsify the heart's affections thus;
  If I caught myself behaving in such a way,
  I'd hang myself for shame, without delay.
PHILINTE   It hardly seems a hanging matter to me;
  I hope that you will take it graciously   30

* Translated by Richard Wilbur.

If I extend myself a slight reprieve,
And live a little longer, by your leave.
ALCESTE   How dare you joke about a crime so grave?
PHILINTE   What crime? How else are people to behave?
ALCESTE   I'd have them be sincere, and never part   35
With any word that isn't from the heart.
PHILINTE   When someone greets us with a show of pleasure,
It's but polite to give him equal measure,
Return his love the best that we know how,
And trade him offer for offer, vow for vow.   40
ALCESTE   No, no, this formula you'd have me follow,
However fashionable, is false and hollow,
And I despise the frenzied operations
Of all these barterers of protestations,
These lavishers of meaningless embraces,   45
These utterers of obliging commonplaces,
Who court and flatter everyone on earth
And praise the fool no less than the man of worth.
Should you rejoice that someone fondles you,
Offers his love and service, swears to be true,   50
And fills your ears with praises of your name,
When to the first damned fop he'll say the same?
No, no: no self-respecting heart would dream
Of prizing so promiscuous an esteem;
However high the praise, there's nothing worse   55
Than sharing honors with the universe.
Esteem is founded on comparison:
To honor all men is to honor none.
Since you embrace this indiscriminate vice,
Your friendship comes at far too cheap a price;   60
I spurn the easy tribute of a heart
Which will not set the worthy man apart:
I choose, Sir, to be chosen; and in fine,
The friend of mankind is no friend of mine.
PHILINTE   But in polite society, custom decrees   65
That we show certain outward courtesies. . . .
ALCESTE   Ah, no! we should condemn with all our force
Such false and artificial intercourse.
Let men behave like men; let them display
Their inmost hearts in everything they say;   70
Let the heart speak, and let our sentiments
Not mask themselves in silly compliments.
PHILINTE   In certain cases it would be uncouth
And most absurd to speak the naked truth;
With all respect for your exalted notions,   75
It's often best to veil one's true emotions.
Wouldn't the social fabric come undone
If we were wholly frank with everyone?
Suppose you met with someone you couldn't bear;
Would you inform him of it then and there?   80
ALCESTE   Yes.
PHILINTE   Then you'd tell old Emilie it's pathetic
The way she daubs her features with cosmetic
And plays the gay coquette at sixty-four?

ALCESTE   I would.

PHILINTE   And you'd call Dorilas a bore,
And tell him every ear at court is lame   85
From hearing him brag about his noble name?

ALCESTE   Precisely.

PHILINTE   Ah, you're joking.

ALCESTE   *Au contraire:*[1]
In this regard there's none I'd choose to spare.
All are corrupt; there's nothing to be seen
In court or town but aggravates my spleen.   90
I fall into deep gloom and melancholy
When I survey the scene of human folly,
Finding on every hand base flattery,
Injustice, fraud, self-interest, treachery. . . .
Ah, it's too much; mankind has grown so base,   95
I mean to break with the whole human race.

PHILINTE   This philosophic rage is a bit extreme;
You've no idea how comical you seem;
Indeed, we're like those brothers in the play
Called *School for Husbands,* one of whom was prey . . .[2]   100

ALCESTE   Enough, now! None of your stupid similes.

PHILINTE   Then let's have no more tirades, if you please.
The world won't change, whatever you say or do;
And since plain speaking means so much to you,
I'll tell you plainly that by being frank   105
You've earned the reputation of a crank,
And that you're thought ridiculous when you rage
And rant against the manners of the age.

ALCESTE   So much the better; just what I wish to hear.
No news could be more grateful to my ear.   110
All men are so detestable in my eyes,
I should be sorry if they thought me wise.

PHILINTE   Your hatred's very sweeping, is it not?

ALCESTE   Quite right: I hate the whole degraded lot.

PHILINTE   Must all poor human creatures be embraced,   115
Without distinction, by your vast distaste?
Even in these bad times, there are surely a few . . .

ALCESTE   No, I include all men in one dim view:
Some men I hate for being rogues: the others
I hate because they treat the rogues like brothers,   120
And, lacking a virtuous scorn for what is vile,
Receive the villain with a complaisant smile.
Notice how tolerant people choose to be
Toward that bold rascal who's at law with me.
His social polish can't conceal his nature;   125
One sees at once that he's a treacherous creature;
No one could possibly be taken in
By those soft speeches and that sugary grin.
The whole world knows the shady means by which
The low-brow's grown so powerful and rich,   130
And risen to a rank so bright and high
That virtue can but blush, and merit sigh.

1. To the contrary.
2. Molière's play *The School for Hus-*   *bands* (*L'École des Maris*) had been written in 1661.

Whenever his name comes up in conversation,
None will defend his wretched reputation;
Call him knave, liar, scoundrel, and all the rest,   135
Each head will nod, and no one will protest.
And yet his smirk is seen in every house,
He's greeted everywhere with smiles and bows,
And when there's any honor that can be got
By pulling strings, he'll get it, like as not.   140
My God! It chills my heart to see the ways
Men come to terms with evil nowadays;
Sometimes, I swear, I'm moved to flee and find
Some desert land unfouled by humankind.

PHILINTE   Come, let's forget the follies of the times   145
And pardon mankind for its petty crimes;
Let's have an end of rantings and of railings,
And show some leniency toward human failings.
This world requires a pliant rectitude;
Too stern a virtue makes one stiff and rude;   150
Good sense views all extremes with detestation,
And bids us to be noble in moderation.
The rigid virtues of the ancient days
Are not for us; they jar with all our ways
And ask of us too lofty a perfection.   155
Wise men accept their times without objection,
And there's no greater folly, if you ask me,
Than trying to reform society.
Like you, I see each day a hundred and one
Unhandsome deeds that might be better done,   160
But still, for all the faults that meet my view,
I'm never known to storm and rave like you.
I take men as they are, or let them be,
And teach my soul to bear their frailty;
And whether in court or town, whatever the scene,   165
My phlegm's as philosophic as your spleen.[3]

ALCESTE   This phlegm which you so eloquently commend,
Does nothing ever rile it up, my friend?
Suppose some man you trust should treacherously
Conspire to rob you of your property,   170
And do his best to wreck your reputation?
Wouldn't you feel a certain indignation?

PHILINTE   Why, no. These faults of which you so complain
Are part of human nature, I maintain,
And it's no more a matter for disgust   175
That men are knavish, selfish and unjust,
Than that the vulture dines upon the dead,
And wolves are furious, and apes ill-bred.

ALCESTE   Shall I see myself betrayed, robbed, torn to bits,
And not . . . Oh, let's be still and rest our wits.   180
Enough of reasoning, now. I've had my fill.

PHILINTE   Indeed, you would do well, Sir, to be still.
Rage less at your opponent, and give some thought

---

3. According to the psychology of "humors," character was determined by the relative proportions of four body fluids. An oversupply of *phlegm* produced the stolid, unimaginative character which we still call "phlegmatic."

To how you'll win this lawsuit that he's brought.
ALCESTE I assure you I'll do nothing of the sort. 185
PHILINTE Then who will plead your case before the court?
ALCESTE Reason and right and justice will plead for me.
PHILINTE Oh, Lord. What judges do you plan to see?
ALCESTE Why, none. The justice of my cause is clear.
PHILINTE Of course, man; but there's politics to fear. . . . 190
ALCESTE No, I refuse to lift a hand. That's flat.
I'm either right, or wrong.
PHILINTE Don't count on that.
ALCESTE No, I'll do nothing.
PHILINTE Your enemy's influence
Is great, you know . . .
ALCESTE That makes no difference.
PHILINTE It will; you'll see.
ALCESTE Must honor bow to guile? 195
If so, I shall be proud to lose the trial.
PHILINTE Oh, really . . .
ALCESTE I'll discover by this case
Whether or not men are sufficiently base
And impudent and villainous and perverse
To do me wrong before the universe. 200
PHILINTE What a man!
ALCESTE Oh, I could wish, whatever the cost,
Just for the beauty of it, that my trial were lost.
PHILINTE If people heard you talking so, Alceste,
They'd split their sides. Your name would be a jest.
ALCESTE So much the worse for jesters.
PHILINTE May I enquire 205
Whether this rectitude you so admire,
And these hard virtues you're enamored of
Are qualities of the lady whom you love?
It much surprises me that you, who seem
To view mankind with furious disesteem, 210
Have yet found something to enchant your eyes
Amidst a species which you so despise.
And what is more amazing, I'm afraid,
Is the most curious choice your heart has made.
The honest Éliante is fond of you, 215
Arsinoé, the prude, admires you too;
And yet your spirit's been perversely led
To choose the flighty Célimène instead,
Whose brittle malice and coquettish ways
So typify the manners of our days. 220
How is it that the traits you most abhor
Are bearable in this lady you adore?
Are you so blind with love that you can't find them?
Or do you contrive, in her case, not to mind them?
ALCESTE My love for that young widow's not the kind 225
That can't perceive defects; no, I'm not blind.
I see her faults, despite my ardent love,
And all I see I fervently reprove.
And yet I'm weak; for all her falsity,
That woman knows the art of pleasing me, 230

And though I never cease complaining of her,
I swear I cannot manage not to love her.
Her charm outweighs her faults; I can but aim
To cleanse her spirit in my love's pure flame.
PHILINTE   That's no small task; I wish you all success.   235
You think then that she loves you?
ALCESTE   Heavens, yes!
I wouldn't love her did she not love me.
PHILINTE   Well, if her taste for you is plain to see,
Why do these rivals cause you such despair?
ALCESTE   True love, Sir, is possessive, and cannot bear   240
To share with all the world. I'm here today
To tell her she must send that mob away.
PHILINTE   If I were you, and had your choice to make,
Éliante, her cousin, would be the one I'd take;
That honest heart, which cares for you alone,   245
Would harmonize far better with your own.
ALCESTE   True, true: each day my reason tells me so;
But reason doesn't rule in love, you know.
PHILINTE   I fear some bitter sorrow is in store;
This love . . .

SCENE 2. [ORONTE, ALCESTE, PHILINTE]

ORONTE [*to* ALCESTE]   The servants told me at the door   250
That Éliante and Célimène were out,
But when I heard, dear Sir, that you were about,
I came to say, without exaggeration,
That I hold you in the vastest admiration,
And that it's always been my dearest desire   255
To be the friend of one I so admire.
I hope to see my love of merit requited,
And you and I in friendship's bond united.
I'm sure you won't refuse—if I may be frank—
A friend of my devotedness—and rank.   260

> During this speech of ORONTE'S, ALCESTE *is abstracted, and*
> *seems unaware that he is being spoken to. He only breaks off his*
> *reverie when* ORONTE *says:*

It was for you, if you please, that my words were intended.
ALCESTE   For me, Sir?
ORONTE   Yes, for you. You're not offended?
ALCESTE   By no means. But this much surprises me. . . .
The honor comes most unexpectedly. . . .
ORONTE   My high regard should not astonish you;   265
The whole world feels the same. It is your due.
ALCESTE   Sir . . .
ORONTE   Why, in all the State there isn't one
Can match your merits; they shine, Sir, like the sun.
ALCESTE   Sir . . .
ORONTE   You are higher in my estimation
Than all that's most illustrious in the nation.   270
ALCESTE   Sir . . .
ORONTE   If I lie, may heaven strike me dead!

To show you that I mean what I have said,
Permit me, Sir, to embrace you most sincerely,
And swear that I will prize our friendship dearly.
Give me your hand. And now, Sir, if you choose, 275
We'll make our vows.
ALCESTE   Sir . . .
ORONTE   What! You refuse?
ALCESTE   Sir, it's a very great honor you extend:
But friendship is a sacred thing, my friend;
It would be profanation to bestow
The name of friend on one you hardly know. 280
All parts are better played when well-rehearsed;
Let's put off friendship, and get acquainted first.
We may discover it would be unwise
To try to make our natures harmonize.
ORONTE   By heaven! You're sagacious to the core; 285
This speech has made me admire you even more.
Let time, then, bring us closer day by day;
Meanwhile, I shall be yours in every way.
If, for example, there should be anything
You wish at court, I'll mention it to the King. 290
I have his ear, of course; it's quite well known
That I am much in favor with the throne.
In short, I am your servant. And now, dear friend,
Since you have such fine judgment, I intend
To please you, if I can, with a small sonnet 295
I wrote not long ago. Please comment on it,
And tell me whether I ought to publish it.
ALCESTE   You must excuse me, Sir; I'm hardly fit
To judge such matters.
ORONTE   Why not?
ALCESTE   I am, I fear,
Inclined to be unfashionably sincere. 300
ORONTE   Just what I ask; I'd take no satisfaction
In anything but your sincere reaction.
I beg you not to dream of being kind.
ALCESTE   Since you desire it, Sir, I'll speak my mind.
ORONTE   *Sonnet.* It's a sonnet. . . . *Hope* . . . The poem's addressed 305
To a lady who wakened hopes within my breast.
Hope . . . this is not the pompous sort of thing,
Just modest little verses, with a tender ring.
ALCESTE   Well, we shall see.
ORONTE   *Hope* . . . I'm anxious to hear
Whether the style seems properly smooth and clear, 310
And whether the choice of words is good or bad.
ALCESTE   We'll see, we'll see.
ORONTE   Perhaps I ought to add
That it took me only a quarter-hour to write it.
ALCESTE   The time's irrelevant, Sir: kindly recite it.
ORONTE [*reading*]   *Hope comforts us awhile, 'tis true,* 315
       Lulling our cares with careless laughter,
       And yet such joy is full of rue,
       My Phyllis, if nothing follows after.
PHILINTE   I'm charmed by this already; the style's delightful.

ALCESTE [*sotto voce, to* PHILINTE]   How can you say that? Why, the
    thing is frightful.   320
ORONTE   *Your fair face smiled on me awhile,*
                But was it kindness so to enchant me?
                'Twould have been fairer not to smile,
                If hope was all you meant to grant me.
PHILINTE   What a clever thought! How handsomely you phrase it!   325
ALCESTE [*sotto voce, to* PHILINTE]   You know the thing is trash. How
    dare you praise it?
ORONTE   *If it's to be my passion's fate*
                Thus everlastingly to wait,
                Then death will come to set me free:
                For death is fairer than the fair;   330
                Phyllis, to hope is to despair
                When one must hope eternally.
PHILINTE   The close is exquisite—full of feeling and grace.
ALCESTE [*sotto voce, aside*]   Oh, blast the close; you'd better close
    your face
    Before you send your lying soul to hell.   335
PHILINTE   I can't remember a poem I've liked so well.
ALCESTE [*sotto voce, aside*]   Good Lord!
ORONTE [*to* PHILINTE]   I fear you're flattering me a
    bit.
PHILINTE   Oh, no!
ALCESTE [*sotto voce, aside*]   What else d'you call it, you hypocrite?
ORONTE [*to* ALCESTE]   But you, Sir, keep your promise now: don't
    shrink
    From telling me sincerely what you think.   340
ALCESTE   Sir, these are delicate matters; we all desire
    To be told that we've the true poetic fire.
    But once, to one whose name I shall not mention,
    I said, regarding some verse of his invention,
    That gentlemen should rigorously control   345
    That itch to write which often afflicts the soul;
    That one should curb the heady inclination
    To publicize one's little avocation;
    And that in showing off one's works of art
    One often plays a very clownish part.   350
ORONTE   Are you suggesting in a devious way
    That I ought not . . .
ALCESTE   Oh, that I do not say.
    Further, I told him that no fault is worse
    Than that of writing frigid, lifeless verse,
    And that the merest whisper of such a shame   355
    Suffices to destroy a man's good name.
ORONTE   D'you mean to say my sonnet's dull and trite?
ALCESTE   I don't say that. But I went on to cite
    Numerous cases of once-respected men
    Who came to grief by taking up the pen.   360
ORONTE   And am I like them? Do I write so poorly?
ALCESTE   I don't say that. But I told this person, "Surely
    You're under no necessity to compose;
    Why you should wish to publish, heaven knows.
    There's no excuse for printing tedious rot   365

Unless one writes for bread, as you do not.
Resist temptation, then, I beg of you;
Conceal your pastimes from the public view;
And don't give up, on any provocation,
Your present high and courtly reputation,   370
To purchase at a greedy printer's shop
The name of silly author and scribbling fop."
These were the points I tried to make him see.
ORONTE   I sense that they are also aimed at me;
But now—about my sonnet—I'd like to be told . . .   375
ALCESTE   Frankly, that sonnet should be pigeonholed.
You've chosen the worst models to imitate.
The style's unnatural. Let me illustrate:
> For example, *Your fair face smiled on me awhile,*
> Followed by, *'Twould have been fairer not to smile!*   380
> Or this: *such joy is full of rue;*
> Or this: *For death is fairer than the fair;*
> Or, *Phyllis, to hope is to despair*
> > *When one must hope eternally!*

This artificial style, that's all the fashion,   385
Has neither taste, nor honesty, nor passion;
It's nothing but a sort of wordy play,
And nature never spoke in such a way.
What, in this shallow age, is not debased?
Our fathers, though less refined, had better taste;   390
I'd barter all that men admire today
For one old love song I shall try to say:[4]
> *If the King had given me for my own*
> *Paris, his citadel,*
> *And I for that must leave alone*   395
> *Her whom I love so well,*
> *I'd say then to the Crown,*
> *Take back your glittering town;*
> *My darling is more fair, I swear,*
> *My darling is more fair.*   400

The rhyme's not rich, the style is rough and old,
But don't you see that it's the purest gold
Beside the tinsel nonsense now preferred,
And that there's passion in its every word?
> *If the King had given me for my own*   405
> *Paris, his citadel,*
> *And I for that must leave alone*
> *Her whom I love so well,*
> *I'd say then to the Crown,*
> *Take back your glittering town;*   410
> *My darling is more fair, I swear,*
> *My darling is more fair.*

There speaks a loving heart. [*To* PHILINTE.] You're laughing, eh?
Laugh on, my precious wit. Whatever you say,
I hold that song's worth all the bibelots   415
That people hail today with ah's and oh's.
ORONTE   And I maintain my sonnet's very good.

---

4. No origin is known for Alceste's *chanson.*

ALCESTE   It's not at all surprising that you should.
You have your reasons; permit me to have mine
For thinking that you cannot write a line.   420
ORONTE   Others have praised my sonnet to the skies.
ALCESTE   I lack their art of telling pleasant lies.
ORONTE   You seem to think you've got no end of wit.
ALCESTE   To praise your verse, I'd need still more of it.
ORONTE   I'm not in need of your approval, Sir.   425
ALCESTE   That's good; you couldn't have it if you were.
ORONTE   Come now, I'll lend you the subject of my sonnet;
I'd like to see you try to improve upon it.
ALCESTE   I might, by chance, write something just as shoddy;
But then I wouldn't show it to everybody.   430
ORONTE   You're most opinionated and conceited.
ALCESTE   Go find your flatterers, and be better treated.
ORONTE   Look here, my little fellow, pray watch your tone.
ALCESTE   My great big fellow, you'd better watch your own.
PHILINTE   [*stepping between them*]   Oh, please, please, gentlemen!
This will never do.   435
ORONTE   The fault is mine, and I leave the field to you.
I am your servant, Sir, in every way.
ALCESTE   And I, Sir, am your most abject valet.

SCENE 3.   [PHILINTE, ALCESTE]

PHILINTE   Well, as you see, sincerity in excess
Can get you into a very pretty mess;   440
Oronte was hungry for appreciation. . . .
ALCESTE   Don't speak to me.
PHILINTE   What?
ALCESTE   No more conversation.
PHILINTE   Really, now . . .
ALCESTE   Leave me alone.
PHILINTE   If I . . .
ALCESTE   Out of my sight!
PHILINTE   But what . . .
ALCESTE   I won't listen.
PHILINTE   But . . .
ALCESTE   Silence!
PHILINTE   Now, is it polite . . .
ALCESTE   By heaven, I've had enough. Don't follow me.   445
PHILINTE   Ah, you're just joking. I'll keep you company.

Act 2

SCENE 1.   [ALCESTE, CÉLIMÈNE]

ALCESTE   Shall I speak plainly, Madam? I confess
Your conduct gives me infinite distress,
And my resentment's grown too hot to smother.
Soon, I foresee, we'll break with one another.
If I said otherwise, I should deceive you;   5

Sooner or later, I shall be forced to leave you,
And if I swore that we shall never part,
I should misread the omens of my heart.
CÉLIMÈNE.   You kindly saw me home, it would appear,
So as to pour invectives in my ear.   10
ALCESTE   I've no desire to quarrel. But I deplore
Your inability to shut the door
On all these suitors who beset you so.
There's what annoys me, if you care to know.
CÉLIMÈNE   Is it my fault that all these men pursue me?   15
Am I to blame if they're attracted to me?
And when they gently beg an audience,
Ought I to take a stick and drive them hence?
ALCESTE   Madam, there's no necessity for a stick;
A less responsive heart would do the trick.   20
Of your attractiveness I don't complain;
But those your charms attract, you then detain
By a most melting and receptive manner,
And so enlist their hearts beneath your banner.
It's the agreeable hopes which you excite   25
That keep these lovers round you day and night;
Were they less liberally smiled upon,
That sighing troop would very soon be gone.
But tell me, Madam, why it is that lately
This man Clitandre interests you so greatly?   30
Because of what high merits do you deem
Him worthy of the honor of your esteem?
Is it that your admiring glances linger
On the splendidly long nail of his little finger?
Or do you share the general deep respect   35
For the blond wig he chooses to affect?
Are you in love with his embroidered hose?
Do you adore his ribbons and his bows?
Or is it that this paragon bewitches
Your tasteful eye with his vast German breeches?   40
Perhaps his giggle, or his falsetto voice,
Makes him the latest gallant of your choice?
CÉLIMÈNE   You're much mistaken to resent him so.
Why I put up with him you surely know:
My lawsuit's very shortly to be tried,   45
And I must have his influence on my side.
ALCESTE   Then lose your lawsuit, Madam, or let it drop;
Don't torture me by humoring such a fop.
CÉLIMÈNE   You're jealous of the whole world, Sir.
ALCESTE   That's true,
Since the whole world is well-received by you.   50
CÉLIMÈNE   That my good nature is so unconfined
Should serve to pacify your jealous mind;
Were I to smile on one, and scorn the rest,
Then you might have some cause to be distressed.
ALCESTE   Well, if I musn't be jealous, tell me, then,   55
Just how I'm better treated than other men.
CÉLIMÈNE   You know you have my love. Will that not do?
ALCESTE   What proof have I that what you say is true?

CÉLIMÈNE   I would expect, Sir, that my having said it
. Might give the statement a sufficient credit.   60
ALCESTE   But how can I be sure that you don't tell
The selfsame thing to other men as well?
CÉLIMÈNE   What a gallant speech! How flattering to me!
What a sweet creature you make me out to be!
Well then, to save you from the pangs of doubt,   65
All that I've said I hereby cancel out;
Now, none but yourself shall make a monkey of you:
Are you content?
ALCESTE   Why, why am I doomed to love you?
I swear that I shall bless the blissful hour
When this poor heart's no longer in your power!   70
I make no secret of it: I've done my best
To exorcise this passion from my breast;
But thus far all in vain; it will not go;
It's for my sins that I must love you so.
CÉLIMÈNE   Your love for me is matchless, Sir; that's clear.   75
ALCESTE   Indeed, in all the world it has no peer;
Words can't describe the nature of my passion,
And no man ever loved in such a fashion.
CÉLIMÈNE   Yes, it's a brand-new fashion, I agree:
You show your love by castigating me,   80
And all your speeches are enraged and rude.
I've never been so furiously wooed.
ALCESTE   Yet you could calm that fury, if you chose.
Come, shall we bring our quarrels to a close?
. Let's speak with open hearts, then, and begin . . .   85

SCENE 2. [CÉLIMÈNE, ALCESTE, BASQUE]

CÉLIMÈNE   What is it?
BASQUE   Acaste is here.
CÉLIMÈNE   Well, send him in.

SCENE 3. [CÉLIMÈNE, ALCESTE]

ALCESTE   What! Shall we never be alone at all?
You're always ready to receive a call,
And you can't bear, for ten ticks of the clock,
Not to keep open house for all who knock.   90
CÉLIMÈNE   I couldn't refuse him: he'd be most put out.
ALCESTE   Surely that's not worth worrying about.
CÉLIMÈNE   Acaste would never forgive me if he guessed
That I consider him a dreadful pest.
ALCESTE   If he's a pest, why bother with him then?   95
CÉLIMÈNE   Heavens! One can't antagonize such men;
Why, they're the chartered gossips of the court,
And have a say in things of every sort.
One must receive them, and be full of charm;
They're no great help, but they can do you harm,   100
And though your influence be ever so great,
They're hardly the best people to alienate.

ALCESTE   I see, dear lady, that you could make a case
For putting up with the whole human race;
These friendships that you calculate so nicely . . .   105

SCENE 4. [ALCESTE, CÉLIMÈNE, BASQUE]

BASQUE   Madam, Clitandre is here as well.
ALCESTE   Precisely.
CÉLIMÈNE   Where are you going?
ALCESTE   Elsewhere.
CÉLIMÈNE   Stay.
ALCESTE   No, no.
CÉLIMÈNE   Stay, Sir.
ALCESTE   I can't.
CÉLIMÈNE   I wish it.
ALCESTE   No, I must go.
I beg you, Madam, not to press the matter;
You know I have no taste for idle chatter.   110
CÉLIMÈNE   Stay. I command you.
ALCESTE   No, I cannot stay.
CÉLIMÈNE   Very well; you have my leave to go away.

SCENE 5. [ÉLIANTE, PHILINTE, ACASTE, CLITANDRE,
          ALCESTE, CÉLIMÈNE, BASQUE]

ÉLIANTE [*to* CÉLIMÈNE]   The Marquesses have kindly come to call.
Were they announced?
CÉLIMÈNE   Yes. Basque, bring chairs for all.

        BASQUE *provides the chairs, and exits.*

        [*To* ALCESTE.] You haven't gone?

ALCESTE   No; and I shan't depart   115
Till you decide who's foremost in your heart.
CÉLIMÈNE   Oh, hush.
ALCESTE   It's time to choose; take them, or me.
CÉLIMÈNE   You're mad.
ALCESTE   I'm not, as you shall shortly see.
CÉLIMÈNE   Oh?
ALCESTE   You'll decide.
CÉLIMÈNE   You're joking now, dear friend.
ALCESTE   No, no; you'll choose; my patience is at an end.   120
CLITANDRE   Madam, I come from court, where poor Cléonte
Behaved like a perfect fool, as is his wont.
Has he no friend to counsel him, I wonder,
And teach him less unerringly to blunder?
CÉLIMÈNE   It's true, the man's a most accomplished dunce;   125
His gauche behavior charms the eye at once;
And every time one sees him, on my word,
His manner's grown a trifle more absurd.
ACASTE   Speaking of dunces, I've just now conversed
With old Damon, who's one of the very worst;   130

I stood a lifetime in the broiling sun
Before his dreary monologue was done.
CÉLIMÈNE   Oh, he's a wondrous talker, and has the power
To tell you nothing hour after hour:
If, by mistake, he ever came to the point,   135
The shock would put his jawbone out of joint.
ÉLIANTE [*to* PHILINTE]   The conversation takes its usual turn,
And all our dear friends' ears will shortly burn.
CLITANDRE   Timante's a character, Madam.
CÉLIMÈNE   Isn't he, though?
A man of mystery from top to toe,   140
Who moves about in a romantic mist
On secret missions which do not exist.
His talk is full of eyebrows and grimaces;
How tired one gets of his momentous faces;
He's always whispering something confidential   145
Which turns out to be quite inconsequential;
Nothing's too slight for him to mystify;
He even whispers when he says "good-by."
ACASTE   Tell us about Géralde.
CÉLIMÈNE   That tiresome ass.
He mixes only with the titled class,   150
And fawns on dukes and princes, and is bored
With anyone who's not at least a lord.
The man's obsessed with rank, and his discourses
Are all of hounds and carriages and horses;
He uses Christian names with all the great,   155
And the word Milord, with him, is out of date.
CLITANDRE   He's very taken with Bélise, I hear.
CÉLIMÈNE   She is the dreariest company, poor dear.
Whenever she comes to call, I grope about
To find some topic which will draw her out,   160
But, owing to her dry and faint replies,
The conversation wilts, and droops, and dies.
In vain one hopes to animate her face
By mentioning the ultimate commonplace;
But sun or shower, even hail or frost   165
Are matters she can instantly exhaust.
Meanwhile her visit, painful though it is,
Drags on and on through mute eternities,
And though you ask the time, and yawn, and yawn,
She sits there like a stone and won't be gone.   170
ACASTE   Now for Adraste.
CÉLIMÈNE   Oh, that conceited elf
Has a gigantic passion for himself;
He rails against the court, and cannot bear it
That none will recognize his hidden merit;
All honors given to others give offense   175
To his imaginary excellence.
CLITANDRE   What about young Cléon? His house, they say,
Is full of the best society, night and day.
CÉLIMÈNE   His cook has made him popular, not he:
It's Cléon's table that people come to see.   180
ÉLIANTE   He gives a splendid dinner, you must admit.

CÉLIMÈNE   But must he serve himself along with it?
  For my taste, he's a most insipid dish
  Whose presence sours the wine and spoils the fish.
PHILINTE   Damis, his uncle, is admired no end.   185
  What's your opinion, Madam?
CÉLIMÈNE   Why, he's my friend.
PHILINTE   He seems a decent fellow, and rather clever.
CÉLIMÈNE   He works too hard at cleverness, however.
  I hate to see him sweat and struggle so
  To fill his conversation with *bons mots*.[5]   190
  Since he's decided to become a wit
  His taste's so pure that nothing pleases it;
  He scolds at all the latest books and plays,
  Thinking that wit must never stoop to praise,
  That finding fault's a sign of intellect,   195
  That all appreciation is abject,
  And that by damning everything in sight
  One shows oneself in a distinguished light.
  He's scornful even of our conversations:
  Their trivial nature sorely tries his patience;   200
  He folds his arms, and stands above the battle,
  And listens sadly to our childish prattle.
ACASTE   Wonderful, Madam! You've hit him off precisely.
CLITANDRE   No one can sketch a character so nicely.
ALCESTE   How bravely, Sirs, you cut and thrust at all   205
  These absent fools, till one by one they fall:
  But let one come in sight, and you'll at once
  Embrace the man you lately called a dunce,
  Telling him in a tone sincere and fervent
  How proud you are to be his humble servant.   210
CLITANDRE   Why pick on us? *Madame's* been speaking, Sir.
  And you should quarrel, if you must, with her.
ALCESTE   No, no, by God, the fault is yours, because
  You lead her on with laughter and applause,
  And make her think that she's the more delightful   215
  The more her talk is scandalous and spiteful.
  Oh, she would stoop to malice far, far less
  If no such claque approved her cleverness.
  It's flatterers like you whose foolish praise
  Nourishes all the vices of these days.   220
PHILINTE   But why protest when someone ridicules
  Those you'd condemn, yourself, as knaves or fools?
CÉLIMÈNE   Why, Sir? Because he loves to make a fuss.
  You don't expect him to agree with us,
  When there's an opportunity to express   225
  His heaven-sent spirit of contrariness?
  What other people think, he can't abide;
  Whatever they say, he's on the other side;
  He lives in deadly terror of agreeing;
  'Twould make him seem an ordinary being.   230
  Indeed, he's so in love with contradiction,
  He'll turn against his most profound conviction

5. Witticisms, literally "good words" or "good sayings."

And with a furious eloquence deplore it,
If only someone else is speaking for it.
ALCESTE   Go on, dear lady, mock me as you please;   235
You have your audience in ecstasies.
PHILINTE   But what she says is true: you have a way
Of bridling at whatever people say;
Whether they praise or blame, your angry spirit
Is equally unsatisfied to hear it.   240
ALCESTE   Men, Sir, are always wrong, and that's the reason
That righteous anger's never out of season;
All that I hear in all their conversation
Is flattering praise or reckless condemnation.
CÉLIMÈNE   But . . .
ALCESTE   No, no, Madam, I am forced to state   245
That you have pleasures which I deprecate,
And that these others, here, are much to blame
For nourishing the faults which are your shame.
CLITANDRE   I shan't defend myself, Sir; but I vow
I'd thought this lady faultless until now.   250
ACASTE   I see her charms and graces, which are many;
But as for faults, I've never noticed any.
ALCESTE   I see them, Sir; and rather than ignore them,
I strenuously criticize her for them.
The more one loves, the more one should object   255
To every blemish, every least defect.
Were I this lady, I would soon get rid
Of lovers who approved of all I did,
And by their slack indulgence and applause
Endorsed my follies and excused my flaws.   260
CÉLIMÈNE   If all hearts beat according to your measure,
The dawn of love would be the end of pleasure;
And love would find its perfect consummation
In ecstasies of rage and reprobation.
ÉLIANTE   Love, as a rule, affects men otherwise,   265
And lovers rarely love to criticize.
They see their lady as a charming blur,
And find all things commendable in her.
If she has any blemish, fault, or shame,
They will redeem it by a pleasing name.   270
The pale-faced lady's lily-white, perforce;
The swarthy one's a sweet brunette, of course;
The spindly lady has a slender grace;
The fat one has a most majestic pace;
The plain one, with her dress in disarray,   275
They classify as *beauté négligée;*[6]
The hulking one's a goddess in their eyes,
The dwarf, a concentrate of Paradise;
The haughty lady has a noble mind;
The mean one's witty, and the dull one's kind;   280
The chatterbox has liveliness and verve,
The mute one has a virtuous reserve.
So lovers manage, in their passion's cause,
To love their ladies even for their flaws.

---

6. Careless beauty or the beauty of the untended.

ALCESTE   But I still say . . .

CÉLIMÈNE   I think it would be nice   285
To stroll around the gallery once or twice.
What! You're not going, Sirs?

CLITANDRE *and* ACASTE   No, Madam, no.

ALCESTE   You seem to be in terror lest they go.
Do what you will, Sirs; leave, or linger on,
But I shan't go till after you are gone.   290

ACASTE   I'm free to to linger, unless I should perceive
Madame is tired, and wishes me to leave.

CLITANDRE   And as for me, I needn't go today
Until the hour of the King's *coucher*.[7]

CÉLIMÈNE [*to* ALCESTE]   You're joking, surely?

ALCESTE   Not in the least; we'll see   295
Whether you'd rather part with them, or me.

SCENE 6.   [ALCESTE, CÉLIMÈNE, ÉLIANTE, ACASTE,
               PHILINTE, CLITANDRE, BASQUE]

BASQUE [*to* ALCESTE]   Sir, there's a fellow here who bids me state
That he must see you, and that it can't wait.

ALCESTE   Tell him that I have no such pressing affairs.

BASQUE   It's a long tailcoat that this fellow wears,   300
With gold all over.

CÉLIMÈNE [*to* ALCESTE]   You'd best go down and see.
Or—have him enter.

SCENE 7.   [ALCESTE, CÉLIMÈNE, ÉLIANTE, ACASTE,
               PHILINTE, CLITANDRE, GUARD]

ALCESTE [*confronting the* GUARD]   Well, what do you want with me?
Come in, Sir.

GUARD   I've a word, Sir, for your ear.

ALCESTE   Speak it aloud, Sir; I shall strive to hear.

GUARD   The Marshals have instructed me to say   305
You must report to them without delay.[8]

ALCESTE   Who? Me, Sir?

GUARD   Yes, Sir; you.

ALCESTE   But what do they want?

PHILINTE [*to* ALCESTE]   To scotch your silly quarrel with Oronte.

CÉLIMÈNE [*to* PHILINTE]   What quarrel?

PHILINTE   Oronte and he have fallen out
Over some verse he spoke his mind about;   310
The Marshals wish to arbitrate the matter.

ALCESTE   Never shall I equivocate or flatter!

PHILINTE   You'd best obey their summons; come, let's go.

ALCESTE   How can they mend our quarrel, I'd like to know?
Am I to make a cowardly retraction,   315
And praise those jingles to his satisfaction?

7. At the French court during the period of the play there were formal ceremonies connected with both the king's going to bed, *coucher,* and his rising from bed, *lever.*
8. The "Marshals" were high court officers of the period who formed a court to arbitrate arguments of honor among the nobility. By this time they no longer had any military function. The number of marshals varied, reaching a high of twenty around 1700.

I'll not recant; I've judged that sonnet rightly.
It's bad.
PHILINTE   But you might say so more politely. . . .
ALCESTE   I'll not back down; his verses make me sick.
PHILINTE   If only you could be more politic!   320
But come, let's go.
ALCESTE   I'll go, but I won't unsay
A single word.
PHILINTE   Well, let's be on our way.
ALCESTE   Till I am ordered by my lord the King
To praise that poem, I shall say the thing
Is scandalous, by God, and that the poet   325
Ought to be hanged for having the nerve to show it.

To CLITANDRE *and* ACASTE, *who are laughing.*

By heaven, Sirs, I really didn't know
That I was being humorous.
CÉLIMÈNE   Go, Sir, go;
Settle your business.
ALCESTE   I shall, and when I'm through,
I shall return to settle things with you.   330

Act 3

SCENE 1. [CLITANDRE, ACASTE]

CLITANDRE   Dear Marquess, how contented you appear;
All things delight you, nothing mars your cheer.
Can you, in perfect honesty, declare
That you've a right to be so debonair?
ACASTE   By Jove, when I survey myself, I find   5
No cause whatever for distress of mind.
I'm young and rich; I can in modesty
Lay claim to an exalted pedigree;
And owing to my name and my condition
I shall not want for honors and position.   10
Then as to courage, that most precious trait,
I seem to have it, as was proved of late
Upon the field of honor, where my bearing,
They say, was very cool and rather daring.
I've wit, of course; and taste in such perfection   15
That I can judge without the least reflection,
And at the theater, which is my delight,
Can make or break a play on opening night,
And lead the crowd in hisses or bravos,
And generally be known as one who knows.   20
I'm clever, handsome, gracefully polite;
My waist is small, my teeth are strong and white;
As for my dress, the world's astonished eyes
Assure me that I bear away the prize.
I find myself in favor everywhere,   25
Honored by men, and worshiped by the fair;
And since these things are so, it seems to me
I'm justified in my complacency.

CLITANDRE   Well, if so many ladies hold you dear,
   Why do you press a hopeless courtship here?   30
ACASTE   Hopeless, you say? I'm not the sort of fool
   That likes his ladies difficult and cool.
   Men who are awkward, shy, and peasantish
   May pine for heartless beauties, if they wish,
   Grovel before them, bear their cruelties,   35
   Woo them with tears and sighs and bended knees,
   And hope by dogged faithfulness to gain
   What their poor merits never could obtain.
   For men like me, however, it makes no sense
   To love on trust, and foot the whole expense.   40
   Whatever any lady's merits be,
   I think, thank God, that I'm as choice as she;
   That if my heart is kind enough to burn
   For her, she owes me something in return;
   And that in any proper love affair   45
   The partners must invest an equal share.
CLITANDRE   You think, then, that our hostess favors you?
ACASTE   I've reason to believe that that is true.
CLITANDRE   How did you come to such a mad conclusion?
   You're blind, dear fellow. This is sheer delusion.   50
ACASTE   All right, then: I'm deluded and I'm blind.
CLITANDRE   Whatever put the notion in your mind?
ACASTE   Delusion.
CLITANDRE   What persuades you that you're right?
ACASTE   I'm blind.
CLITANDRE   But have you any proofs to cite?
ACASTE   I tell you I'm deluded.
CLITANDRE   Have you, then,   55
   Received some secret pledge from Célimène?
ACASTE   Oh, no: she scorns me.
CLITANDRE   Tell me the truth, I beg.
ACASTE   She just can't bear me.
CLITANDRE   Ah, don't pull my leg.
   Tell me what hope she's given you, I pray.
ACASTE   I'm hopeless, and it's you who win the day.   60
   She hates me thoroughly, and I'm so vexed
   I mean to hang myself on Tuesday next.
CLITANDRE   Dear Marquess, let us have an armistice
   And make a treaty. What do you say to this?
   If ever one of us can plainly prove   65
   That Célimène encourages his love,
   The other must abandon hope, and yield,
   And leave him in possession of the field.
ACASTE   Now, there's a bargain that appeals to me;
   With all my heart, dear Marquess, I agree.   70
   But hush.

SCENE 2. [CÉLIMÈNE, ACASTE, CLITANDRE]

CÉLIMÈNE   Still here?
CLITANDRE   'Twas love that stayed our feet.
CÉLIMÈNE   I think I heard a carriage in the street.
   Whose is it? D'you know?

SCENE 3. [CÉLIMÈNE, ACASTE, CLITANDRE, BASQUE]

BASQUE   Arsinoé is here,
    Madame.
CÉLIMÈNE   Arsinoé, you say? Oh, dear.
BASQUE   Éliante is entertaining her below.   75
CÉLIMÈNE   What brings the creature here, I'd like to know?
ACASTE   They say she's dreadfully prudish, but in fact
    I think her piety . . .
CÉLIMÈNE   It's all an act.
    At heart she's worldly, and her poor success
    In snaring men explains her prudishness.   80
    It breaks her heart to see the beaux and gallants
    Engrossed by other women's charms and talents,
    And so she's always in a jealous rage
    Against the faulty standards of the age.
    She lets the world believe that she's a prude   85
    To justify her loveless solitude,
    And strives to put a brand of moral shame
    On all the graces that she cannot claim.
    But still she'd love a lover; and Alceste
    Appears to be the one she'd love the best.   90
    His visits here are poison to her pride;
    She seems to think I've lured him from her side;
    And everywhere, at court or in the town,
    The spiteful, envious woman runs me down.
    In short, she's just as stupid as can be,   95
    Vicious and arrogant in the last degree,
    And . . .

SCENE 4. [ARSINOÉ, CÉLIMÈNE, CLITANDRE, ACASTE]

CÉLIMÈNE   Ah! What happy chance has brought you here?
    I've thought about you ever so much, my dear.
ARSINOÉ   I've come to tell you something you should know.
CÉLIMÈNE   How good of you to think of doing so!   100

    CLITANDRE *and* ACASTE *go out, laughing.*

SCENE 5. [ARSINOÉ, CÉLIMÈNE]

ARSINOÉ   It's just as well those gentlemen didn't tarry.
CÉLIMÈNE   Shall we sit down?
ARSINOÉ   That won't be necessary.
    Madam, the flame of friendship ought to burn
    Brightest in matters of the most concern,
    And as there's nothing which concerns us more   105
    Than honor, I have hastened to your door
    To bring you, as your friend, some information
    About the status of your reputation.
    I visited last night, some virtuous folk,
    And, quite by chance, it was of you they spoke;   110
    There was, I fear, no tendency to praise
    Your light behavior and your dashing ways.
    The quantity of gentlemen you see

And your by now notorious coquetry
Were both so vehemently criticized   115
By everyone, that I was much surprised.
Of course, I needn't tell you where I stood;
I came to your defense as best I could,
Assured them you were harmless, and declared
Your soul was absolutely unimpaired.   120
But there are some things, you must realize,
One can't excuse, however hard one tries,
And I was forced at last into conceding
That your behavior, Madam, is misleading,
That makes a bad impression, giving rise   125
To ugly gossip and obscene surmise,
And that if you were more *overtly* good,
You wouldn't be so much misunderstood.
Not that I think you've been unchaste—no! no!
The saints preserve me from a thought so low!   130
But mere good conscience never did suffice:
One must avoid the outward show of vice.
Madam, you're too intelligent, I'm sure,
To think my motives anything but pure
In offering you this counsel—which I do   135
Out of a zealous interest in you.
CÉLIMÈNE   Madam, I haven't taken you amiss;
I'm very much obliged to you for this;
And I'll at once discharge the obligation
By telling you about *your* reputation.   140
You've been so friendly as to let me know
What certain people say of me, and so
I mean to follow your benign example
By offering you a somewhat similar sample.
The other day, I went to an affair   145
And found some most distinguished people there
Discussing piety, both false and true.
The conversation soon came round to you.
Alas! Your prudery and bustling zeal
Appeared to have a very slight appeal.   150
Your affectation of a grave demeanor,
Your endless talk of virtue and of honor,
The aptitude of your suspicious mind
For finding sin where there is none to find,
Your towering self-esteem, that pitying face   155
With which you contemplate the human race,
Your sermonizings and your sharp aspersions
On people's pure and innocent diversions—
All these were mentioned, Madam, and, in fact,
Were roundly and concertedly attacked.   160
"What good," they said, "are all these outward shows,
When everything belies her pious pose?
She prays incessantly; but then, they say,
She beats her maids and cheats them of their pay;
She shows her zeal in every holy place,   165
But still she's vain enough to paint her face;
She holds that naked statues are immoral,
But with a naked *man* she'd have no quarrel."

Of course, I said to everybody there
That they were being viciously unfair;   170
But still they were disposed to criticize you,
And all agreed that someone should advise you
To leave the morals of the world alone,
And worry rather more about your own.
They felt that one's self-knowledge should be great   175
Before one thinks of setting others straight;
That one should learn the art of living well
Before one threatens other men with hell,
And that the Church is best equipped, no doubt,
To guide our souls and root our vices out.   180
Madam, you're too intelligent, I'm sure,
To think my motives anything but pure
In offering you this counsel—which I do
Out of a zealous interest in you.

ARSINOÉ   I dared not hope for gratitude, but I   185
Did not expect so acid a reply;
I judge, since you've been so extremely tart,
That my good counsel pierced you to the heart.

CÉLIMÈNE   Far from it, Madam. Indeed, it seems to me
We ought to trade advice more frequently.   190
One's vision of oneself is so defective
That it would be an excellent corrective.
If you are willing, Madam, let's arrange
Shortly to have another frank exchange
In which we'll tell each other, *entre nous,*[9]   195
What you've heard tell of me, and I of you.

ARSINOÉ   Oh, people never censure you, my dear;
It's me they criticize. Or so I hear.

CÉLIMÈNE   Madam, I think we either blame or praise
According to our taste and length of days.   200
There is a time of life for coquetry,
And there's a season, too, for prudery.
When all one's charms are gone, it is, I'm sure,
Good strategy to be devout and pure:
It makes one seem a little less forsaken.   205
Some day, perhaps, I'll take the road you've taken:
Time brings all things. But I have time aplenty,
And see no cause to be a prude at twenty.

ARSINOÉ   You give your age in such a gloating tone
That one would think I was an ancient crone;   210
We're not so far apart, in sober truth,
That you can mock me with a boast of youth!
Madam, you baffle me. I wish I knew
What moves you to provoke me as you do.

CÉLIMÈNE   For my part, Madam, I should like to know   215
Why you abuse me everywhere you go.
Is it my fault, dear lady, that your hand
Is not, alas, in very great demand?
If men admire me, if they pay me court
And daily make me offers of the sort   220

9. Between ourselves, or between the two of us.

You'd dearly love to have them make to you,
How can I help it? What would you have me do?
If what you want is lovers, please feel free
To take as many as you can from me.
ARSINOÉ   Oh, come. D'you think the world is losing sleep   225
Over that flock of lovers which you keep,
Or that we find it difficult to guess
What price you pay for their devotedness?
Surely you don't expect us to suppose
Mere merit could attract so many beaux?   230
It's not your virtue that they're dazzled by;
Nor is it virtuous love for which they sigh.
You're fooling no one, Madam; the world's not blind;
There's many a lady heaven has designed
To call men's noblest, tenderest feelings out,   235
Who has no lovers dogging her about;
From which it's plain that lovers nowadays
Must be acquired in bold and shameless ways,
And only pay one court for such reward
As modesty and virtue can't afford.   240
Then don't be quite so puffed up, if you please,
About your tawdry little victories;
Try, if you can, to be a shade less vain,
And treat the world with somewhat less disdain.
If one were envious of your amours,   245
One soon could have a following like yours;
Lovers are no great trouble to collect
If one prefers them to one's self-respect.
CÉLIMÈNE   Collect them then, my dear; I'd love to see
You demonstrate that charming theory;   250
Who knows, you might . . .
ARSINOÉ   Now, Madam, that will do;
It's time to end this trying interview.
My coach is late in coming to your door,
Or I'd have taken leave of you before.
CÉLIMÈNE   Oh, please don't feel that you must rush away;   255
I'd be delighted, Madam, if you'd stay.
However, lest my conversation bore you,
Let me provide some better company for you;
This gentleman, who comes most apropos,
Will please you more than I could do, I know.   260

SCENE 6. [ALCESTE, CÉLIMÈNE, ARSINOÉ]

CÉLIMÈNE   Alceste, I have a little note to write
Which simply must go out before tonight;
Please entertain *Madame;* I'm sure that she
Will overlook my incivility.

SCENE 7. [ALCESTE, ARSINOÉ]

ARSINOÉ   Well, Sir, our hostess graciously contrives   265
For us to chat until my coach arrives;
And I shall be forever in her debt

For granting me this little *tête-à-tête*.[1]
We women very rightly give our hearts
To men of noble character and parts,   270
And your especial merits, dear Alceste,
Have roused the deepest sympathy in my breast.
Oh, how I wish they had sufficient sense
At court, to recognize your excellence!
They wrong you greatly, Sir. How it must hurt you   275
Never to be rewarded for your virtue!

ALCESTE   Why, Madam, what cause have I to feel aggrieved?
What great and brilliant thing have I achieved?
What service have I rendered to the King
That I should look to him for anything?   280

ARSINOÉ   Not everyone who's honored by the State
Has done great services. A man must wait
Till time and fortune offer him the chance.
Your merit, Sir, is obvious at a glance,
And . . .

ALCESTE   Ah, forget my merit; I'm not neglected.   285
The court, I think, can hardly be expected
To mine men's souls for merit, and unearth
Our hidden virtues and our secret worth.

ARSINOÉ   *Some* virtues, though, are far too bright to hide;
Yours are acknowledged, Sir, on every side.   290
Indeed, I've heard you warmly praised of late
By persons of considerable weight.

ALCESTE   This fawning age has praise for everyone,
And all distinctions, Madam, are undone.
All things have equal honor nowadays,   295
And no one should be gratified by praise.
To be admired, one only need exist,
And every lackey's on the honors list.

ARSINOÉ   I only wish, Sir, that you had your eye
On some position at court, however high;   300
You'd only have to hint at such a notion
For me to set the proper wheels in motion;
I've certain friendships I'd be glad to use
To get you any office you might choose.

ALCESTE   Madam, I fear that any such ambition   305
Is wholly foreign to my disposition.
The soul God gave me isn't of the sort
That prospers in the weather of a court.
It's all too obvious that I don't possess
The virtues necessary for success.   310
My one great talent is for speaking plain;
I've never learned to flatter or to feign;
And anyone so stupidly sincere
Had best not seek a courtier's career.
Outside the court, I know, one must dispense   315
With honors, privilege, and influence;
But still one gains the right, foregoing these,
Not to be tortured by the wish to please.

----

1. A "face-to-face" meeting or conversation; literally "head-to-head."

One needn't live in dread of snubs and slights,
Nor praise the verse that every idiot writes, 320
Nor humor silly Marquesses, nor bestow
Politic sighs on Madam So-and-So.

ARSINOÉ Forget the court, then; let the matter rest.
But I've another cause to be distressed
About your present situation, Sir. 325
It's to your love affair that I refer.
She whom you love, and who pretends to love you,
Is, I regret to say, unworthy of you.

ALCESTE Why, Madam? Can you seriously intend
To make so grave a charge against your friend? 330

ARSINOÉ Alas, I must. I've stood aside too long
And let that lady do you grievous wrong;
But now my debt to conscience shall be paid:
I tell you that your love has been betrayed.

ALCESTE I thank you, Madam; you're extremely kind. 335
Such words are soothing to a lover's mind.

ARSINOÉ Yes, though she *is* my friend, I say again
You're very much too good for Célimène.
She's wantonly misled you from the start.

ALCESTE You may be right; who knows another's heart? 340
But ask yourself if it's the part of charity
To shake my soul with doubts of her sincerity.

ARSINOÉ Well, if you'd rather be a dupe than doubt her,
That's your affair. I'll say no more about her.

ALCESTE Madam, you know that doubt and vague suspicion 345
Are painful to a man in my position;
It's most unkind to worry me this way
Unless you've some real proof of what you say.

ARSINOÉ Sir, say no more: all doubts shall be removed,
And all that I've been saying shall be proved. 350
You've only to escort me home, and there
We'll look into the heart of this affair.
I've ocular evidence which will persuade you
Beyond a doubt, that Célimène's betrayed you.
Then, if you're saddened by that revelation, 355
Perhaps I can provide some consolation.

Act 4

SCENE 1. [ÉLIANTE, PHILINTE]

PHILINTE Madam, he acted like a stubborn child;
I thought they never would be reconciled;
In vain we reasoned, threatened, and appealed;
He stood his ground and simply would not yield.
The Marshals, I feel sure, have never heard 5
An argument so splendidly absurd.
"No, gentlemen," said he, "I'll not retract.
His verse is bad: extremely bad, in fact.
Surely it does the man no harm to know it.
Does it disgrace him, not to be a poet? 10

A gentleman may be respected still,
Whether he writes a sonnet well or ill.
That I dislike his verse should not offend him;
In all that touches honor, I commend him;
He's noble, brave, and virtuous—but I fear   15
He can't in truth be called a sonneteer.
I'll gladly praise his wardrobe; I'll endorse
His dancing, or the way he sits a horse;
But, gentlemen, I cannot praise his rhyme.
In fact, it ought to be a capital crime   20
For anyone so sadly unendowed
To write a sonnet, and read the thing aloud."
At length he fell into a gentler mood
And, striking a concessive attitude,
He paid Oronte the following courtesies: 25
"Sir, I regret that I'm so hard to please,
And I'm profoundly sorry that your lyric
Failed to provoke me to a panegyric."
After these curious words, the two embraced,
And then the hearing was adjourned—in haste.   30
ÉLIANTE   His conduct has been very singular lately;
Still, I confess that I respect him greatly.
The honesty in which he takes such pride
Has—to my mind—its noble, heroic side.
In this false age, such candor seems outrageous;   35
But I could wish that it were more contagious.
PHILINTE   What most intrigues me in our friend Alceste
Is the grand passion that rages in his breast.
The sullen humors he's compounded of
Should not, I think, dispose his heart to love;   40
But since they do, it puzzles me still more
That he should choose your cousin to adore.
ÉLIANTE   It does, indeed, belie the theory
That love is born of gentle sympathy,
And that the tender passion must be based   45
On sweet accords of temper and of taste.
PHILINTE   Does she return his love, do you suppose?
ÉLIANTE   Ah, that's a difficult question, Sir. Who knows?
How can we judge the truth of her devotion?
Her heart's a stranger to its own emotion.   50
Sometimes it thinks it loves, when no love's there;
At other times it loves quite unaware.
PHILINTE   I rather think Alceste is in for more
Distress and sorrow than he's bargained for;
Were he of my mind, Madam, his affection   55
Would turn in quite a different direction,
And we would see him more responsive to
The kind regard which he receives from you.
ÉLIANTE   Sir, I believe in frankness, and I'm inclined,
In matters of the heart, to speak my mind.   60
I don't oppose his love for her; indeed,
I hope with all my heart that he'll succeed,
And were it in my power, I'd rejoice
In giving him the lady of his choice.

But if, as happens frequently enough   65
In love affairs, he meets with a rebuff—
If Célimène should grant some rival's suit—
I'd gladly play the role of substitute;
Nor would his tender speeches please me less
Because they'd once been made without success.   70
PHILINTE   Well, Madam, as for me, I don't oppose
Your hopes in this affair; and heaven knows
That in my conversations with the man
I plead your cause as often as I can.
But if those two should marry, and so remove   75
All chance that he will offer you his love,
Then I'll declare my own, and hope to see
Your gracious favor pass from him to me.
In short, should you be cheated of Alceste,
I'd be most happy to be second best.   80
ÉLIANTE   Philinte, you're teasing.
PHILINTE   Ah, Madam, never fear;
No words of mine were ever so sincere,
And I shall live in fretful expectation
Till I can make a fuller declaration.

SCENE 2. [ALCESTE, ÉLIANTE, PHILINTE]

ALCESTE   Avenge me, Madam! I must have satisfaction.   85
Or this great wrong will drive me to distraction!
ÉLIANTE   Why, what's the matter? What's upset you so?
ALCESTE   Madam, I've had a mortal, mortal blow.
If Chaos repossessed the universe,
I swear I'd not be shaken any worse.   90
I'm ruined. . . . I can say no more. . . . My soul . . .
ÉLIANTE   Do try, Sir, to regain your self-control.
ALCESTE   Just heaven! Why were so much beauty and grace
Bestowed on one so vicious and so base?
ÉLIANTE   Once more, Sir, tell us. . . .
ALCESTE   My world has gone to wrack;   95
I'm—I'm betrayed; she's stabbed me in the back:
Yes, Célimène (who would have thought it of her?)
Is false to me, and has another lover.
ÉLIANTE   Are you quite certain? Can you prove these things?
PHILINTE   Lovers are prey to wild imaginings   100
And jealous fancies. No doubt there's some mistake. . . .
ALCESTE   Mind your own business, Sir, for heaven's sake.

        To ÉLIANTE.

Madam, I have the proof that you demand
Here in my pocket, penned by her own hand.
Yes, all the shameful evidence one could want   105
Lies in this letter written to Oronte—
Oronte! whom I felt sure she couldn't love,
And hardly bothered to be jealous of.
PHILINTE   Still, in a letter, appearances may deceive;
This may not be so bad as you believe.   110
ALCESTE   Once more I beg you, Sir, to let me be;
Tend to your own affairs; leave mine to me.

ÉLIANTE Compose yourself; this anguish that you feel . . .
ALCESTE Is something, Madam, you alone can heal.
My outraged heart, beside itself with grief,   115
Appeals to you for comfort and relief.
Avenge me on your cousin, whose unjust
And faithless nature has deceived my trust;
Avenge a crime your pure soul must detest.
ÉLIANTE But how, Sir?
ALCESTE   Madam, this heart within my breast   120
Is yours; pray take it; redeem my heart from her,
And so avenge me on my torturer.
Let her be punished by the fond emotion,
The ardent love, the bottomless devotion,
The faithful worship which this heart of mine   125
Will offer up to yours as to a shrine.
ÉLIANTE You have my sympathy, Sir, in all you suffer;
Nor do I scorn the noble heart you offer;
But I suspect you'll soon be mollified,
And this desire for vengeance will subside.   130
When some belovèd hand has done us wrong
We thirst for retribution—but not for long;
However dark the deed that she's committed,
A lovely culprit's very soon acquitted.
Nothing's so stormy as an injured lover,   135
And yet no storm so quickly passes over.
ALCESTE No, Madam, no—this is no lovers' spat;
I'll not forgive her; it's gone too far for that;
My mind's made up; I'll kill myself before
I waste my hopes upon her any more.   140
Ah, here she is. My wrath intensifies.
I shall confront her with her tricks and lies,
And crush her utterly, and bring you then
A heart no longer slave to Célimène.

SCENE 3. [CÉLIMÈNE, ALCESTE]

ALCESTE [*aside*] Sweet heaven, help me to control my passion.   145
CÉLIMÈNE [*aside*] Oh, Lord.

    To ALCESTE.

                    Why stand there staring in that fashion?
And what d'you mean by those dramatic sighs,
And that malignant glitter in your eyes?
ALCESTE I mean that sins which cause the blood to freeze
Look innocent beside your treacheries;   150
That nothing Hell's or Heaven's wrath could do
Ever produced so bad a thing as you.
CÉLIMÈNE Your compliments were always sweet and pretty.
ALCESTE Madam, it's not the moment to be witty.
No, blush and hang your head; you've ample reason,   155
Since I've the fullest evidence of your treason.
Ah, this is what my sad heart prophesied;
Now all my anxious fears are verified;
My dark suspicion and my gloomy doubt

Divined the truth, and now the truth is out. 160
For all your trickery, I was not deceived;
It was my bitter stars that I believed.
But don't imagine that you'll go scot-free;
You shan't misuse me with impunity.
I know that love's irrational and blind; 165
I know the heart's not subject to the mind,
And can't be reasoned into beating faster;
I know each soul is free to choose its master;
Therefore had you but spoken from the heart,
Rejecting my attentions from the start, 170
I'd have no grievance, or at any rate
I could complain of nothing but my fate.
Ah, but so falsely to encourage me—
That was a treason and a treachery
For which you cannot suffer too severely, 175
And you shall pay for that behavior dearly.
Yes, now I have no pity, not a shred;
My temper's out of hand; I've lost my head;
Shocked by the knowledge of your double-dealings,
My reason can't restrain my savage feelings; 180
A righteous wrath deprives me of my senses,
And I won't answer for the consequences.

CÉLIMÈNE   What does this outburst mean? Will you please explain?
Have you, by any chance, gone quite insane?

ALCESTE   Yes, yes, I went insane the day I fell 185
A victim to your black and fatal spell,
Thinking to meet with some sincerity
Among the treacherous charms that beckoned me.

CÉLIMÈNE   Pooh. Of what treachery can you complain?

ALCESTE   How sly you are, how cleverly you feign! 190
But you'll not victimize me any more.
Look: here's a document you've seen before.
This evidence, which I acquired today,
Leaves you, I think, without a thing to say.

CÉLIMÈNE   Is this what sent you into such a fit? 195

ALCESTE   You should be blushing at the sight of it.

CÉLIMÈNE   Ought I to blush? I truly don't see why.

ALCESTE   Ah, now you're being bold as well as sly;
Since there's no signature, perhaps you'll claim . . .

CÉLIMÈNE   I wrote it, whether or not it bears my name. 200

ALCESTE   And you can view with equanimity
This proof of your disloyalty to me!

CÉLIMÈNE   Oh, don't be so outrageous and extreme.

ALCESTE   You take this matter lightly, it would seem.
Was it no wrong to me, no shame to you, 205
That you should send Oronte this billet-doux?

CÉLIMÈNE   Oronte! Who said it was for him?

ALCESTE   Why, those
Who brought me this example of your prose.
But what's the difference? If you wrote the letter
To someone else, it pleases me no better. 210
My grievance and your guilt remain the same.

CÉLIMÈNE   But need you rage, and need I blush for shame;

If this was written to a *woman* friend?
ALCESTE   Ah! Most ingenious. I'm impressed no end;
And after that incredible evasion   215
Your guilt is clear. I need no more persuasion.
How dare you try so clumsy a deception?
D'you think I'm wholly wanting in perception?
Come, come, let's see how brazenly you'll try
To bolster up so palpable a lie: 220
Kindly construe this ardent closing section
As nothing more than sisterly affection!
Here, let me read it. Tell me, if you dare to,
That this is for a woman . . .
CÉLIMÈNE   I don't care to.
What right have you to badger and berate me,   225
And so highhandedly interrogate me?
ALCESTE   Now, don't be angry; all I ask of you
Is that you justify a phrase or two . . .
CÉLIMÈNE   No, I shall not. I utterly refuse,
And you may take those phrases as you choose.   230
ALCESTE   Just show me how this letter could be meant
For a woman's eyes, and I shall be content.
CÉLIMÈNE   No, no, it's for Oronte; you're perfectly right.
I welcome his attentions with delight,
I prize his character and his intellect,   235
And everything is just as you suspect.
Come, do your worst now; give your rage free rein;
But kindly cease to bicker and complain.
ALCESTE [*aside*]   Good God! Could anything be more inhuman?
Was ever a heart so mangled by a woman?   240
When I complain of how she has betrayed me,
She bridles, and commences to upbraid me!
She tries my tortured patience to the limit;
She won't deny her guilt; she glories in it!
And yet my heart's too faint and cowardly   245
To break these chains of passion, and be free,
To scorn her as it should, and rise above
This unrewarded, mad, and bitter love.

      To CÉLIMÈNE.

Ah, traitress, in how confident a fashion
You take advantage of my helpless passion,   250
And use my weakness for your faithless charms
To make me once again throw down my arms!
But do at least deny this black transgression;
Take back that mocking and perverse confession;
Defend this letter and your innocence,   255
And I, poor fool, will aid in your defense.
Pretend, pretend, that you are just and true,
And I shall make myself believe in you.
CÉLIMÈNE   Oh, stop it. Don't be such a jealous dunce,
Or I shall leave off loving you at once.   260
Just why should I *pretend*? What could impel me
To stoop so low as that? And kindly tell me
Why, if I loved another, I shouldn't merely

Inform you of it, simply and sincerely!
I've told you where you stand, and that admission   265
Should altogether clear me of suspicion;
After so generous a guarantee,
What right have you to harbor doubts of me?
Since women are (from natural reticence)
Reluctant to declare their sentiments,   270
And since the honor of our sex requires
That we conceal our amorous desires,
Ought any man for whom such laws are broken
To question what the oracle has spoken?
Should he not rather feel an obligation   275
To trust that most obliging declaration?
Enough, now. Your suspicions quite disgust me;
Why should I love a man who doesn't trust me?
I cannot understand why I continue,
Fool that I am, to take an interest in you.   280
I ought to choose a man less prone to doubt,
And give you something to be vexed about.

ALCESTE   Ah, what a poor enchanted fool I am;
These gentle words, no doubt, were all a sham,
But destiny requires me to entrust   285
My happiness to you, and so I must.
I'll love you to the bitter end, and see
How false and treacherous you dare to be.

CÉLIMÈNE   No, you don't really love me as you ought.

ALCESTE   I love you more than can be said or thought;   290
Indeed, I wish you were in such distress
That I might show my deep devotedness.
Yes, I could wish that you were wretchedly poor,
Unloved, uncherished, utterly obscure;
That fate had set you down upon the earth   295
Without possessions, rank, or gentle birth;
Then, by the offer of my heart, I might
Repair the great injustice of your plight;
I'd raise you from the dust, and proudly prove
The purity and vastness of my love.   300

CÉLIMÈNE   This is a strange benevolence indeed!
God grant that I may never be in need. . . .
Ah, here's Monsieur Dubois, in quaint disguise.

SCENE 4. [CÉLIMÈNE, ALCESTE, DUBOIS]

ALCESTE   Well, why this costume? Why those frightened eyes?
What ails you?

DUBOIS   Well, Sir, things are most mysterious.   305

ALCESTE   What do you mean?

DUBOIS   I fear they're very serious.

ALCESTE   What?

DUBOIS   Shall I speak more loudly?

ALCESTE   Yes; speak out.

DUBOIS   Isn't there someone here, Sir?

ALCESTE   Speak, you lout!
Stop wasting time.

DUBOIS	Sir, we must slip away.	
ALCESTE	How's that?	
DUBOIS	We must decamp without delay.	310
ALCESTE	Explain yourself.	
DUBOIS	I tell you we must fly.	
ALCESTE	What for?	
DUBOIS	We mustn't pause to say good-by.	
ALCESTE	Now what d'you mean by all of this, you clown?	
DUBOIS	I mean, Sir, that we've got to leave this town.	

ALCESTE   I'll tear you limb from limb and joint from joint   315
  If you don't come more quickly to the point.
DUBOIS   Well, Sir, today a man in a black suit,
  Who wore a black and ugly scowl to boot,
  Left us a document scrawled in such a hand
  As even Satan couldn't understand.   320
  It bears upon your lawsuit, I don't doubt;
  But all hell's devils couldn't make it out.
ALCESTE   Well, well, go on. What then? I fail to see
  How this event obliges us to flee.
DUBOIS   Well, Sir, an hour later, hardly more,   325
  A gentleman who's often called before
  Came looking for you in an anxious way.
  Not finding you, he asked me to convey
  (Knowing I could be trusted with the same)
  The following message. . . . Now, what *was* his name?   330
ALCESTE   Forget his name, you idiot. What did he say?
DUBOIS   Well, it was one of your friends, Sir, anyway.
  He warned you to begone, and he suggested
  That if you stay, you may well be arrested.
ALCESTE   What? Nothing more specific? Think, man, think!   335
DUBOIS   No, Sir. He had me bring him pen and ink,
  And dashed you off a letter which, I'm sure,
  Will render things distinctly less obscure.
ALCESTE   Well—let me have it!
CÉLIMÈNE   What *is* this all about?
ALCESTE   God knows; but I have hopes of finding out.   340
  How long am I to wait, you blitherer?
DUBOIS [*after a protracted search for the letter*]   I must have left it on
  your table, Sir.
ALCESTE   I ought to . . .
CÉLIMÈNE   No, no, keep your self-control;
  Go find out what's behind his rigmarole.
ALCESTE   It seems to me that fate, no matter what I do,   345
  Has sworn that I may not converse with you;
  But, Madam, pray permit your faithful lover
  To try once more before the day is over.

Act 5

SCENE 1. [ALCESTE, PHILINTE]

ALCESTE   No, it's too much. My mind's made up, I tell you.
PHILINTE   Why should this blow, however hard, compel you . . .
ALCESTE   No, no, don't waste your breath in argument;

Nothing you say will alter my intent;
This age is vile, and I've made up my mind   5
To have no further commerce with mankind.
Did not truth, honor, decency, and the laws
Oppose my enemy and approve my cause?
My claims were justified in all men's sight;
I put my trust in equity and right;   10
Yet, to my horror and the world's disgrace,
Justice is mocked, and I have lost my case!
A scoundrel whose dishonesty is notorious
Emerges from another lie victorious!
Honor and right condone his brazen fraud,   15
While rectitude and decency applaud!
Before his smirking face, the truth stands charmed,
And virtue conquered, and the law disarmed!
His crime is sanctioned by a court decree!
And not content with what he's done to me,   20
The dog now seeks to ruin me by stating
That I composed a book now circulating,
A book so wholly criminal and vicious
That even to speak its title is seditious!
Meanwhile Oronte, my rival, lends his credit   25
To the same libelous tale, and helps to spread it!
Oronte! a man of honor and of rank,
With whom I've been entirely fair and frank;
Who sought me out and forced me, willy-nilly,
To judge some verse I found extremely silly;   30
And who, because I properly refused
To flatter him, or see the truth abused,
Abets my enemy in a rotten slander!
There's the reward of honesty and candor!
The man will hate me to the end of time   35
For failing to commend his wretched rhyme!
And not this man alone, but all humanity
Do what they do from interest and vanity;
They prate of honor, truth, and righteousness,
But lie, betray, and swindle nonetheless.   40
Come then: man's villainy is too much to bear;
Let's leave this jungle and this jackal's lair.
Yes! treacherous and savage race of men,
You shall not look upon my face again.
PHILINTE Oh, don't rush into exile prematurely;   45
    Things aren't as dreadful as you make them, surely.
    It's rather obvious, since you're still at large,
    That people don't believe your enemy's charge.
    Indeed, his tale's so patently untrue
    That it may do more harm to him than you.   50
ALCESTE Nothing could do that scoundrel any harm:
    His frank corruption is his greatest charm,
    And, far from hurting him, a further shame
    Would only serve to magnify his name.
PHILINTE In any case, his bald prevarication   55
    Has done no injury to your reputation,
    And you may feel secure in that regard.
    As for your lawsuit, it should not be hard

To have the case reopened, and contest
This judgment . . .

ALCESTE   No, no, let the verdict rest.   60
Whatever cruel penalty it may bring,
I wouldn't have it changed for anything.
It shows the times' injustice with such clarity
That I shall pass it down to our posterity
As a great proof and signal demonstration   65
Of the black wickedness of this generation.
It may cost twenty thousand francs; but I
Shall pay their twenty thousand, and gain thereby
The right to storm and rage at human evil,
And send the race of mankind to the devil.[2]   70

PHILINTE   Listen to me . . .

ALCESTE . .   Why? What can you possibly say?
Don't argue, Sir; your labor's thrown away.
Do you propose to offer lame excuses
For men's behavior and the times' abuses?

PHILINTE   No, all you say I'll readily concede: 75
This is a low, conniving age indeed;
Nothing but trickery prospers nowadays,
And people ought to mend their shabby ways.
Yes, man's a beastly creature; but must we then
Abandon the society of men?   80
Here in the world, each human frailty
Provides occasion for philosophy,
And that is virtue's noblest exercise;
If honesty shone forth from all men's eyes,
If every heart were frank and kind and just,   85
What could our virtues do but gather dust
(Since their employment is to help us bear
The villainies of men without despair)?
A heart well-armed with virtue can endure. . . .

ALCESTE   Sir, you're a matchless reasoner, to be sure;   90
Your words are fine and full of cogency;
But don't waste time and eloquence on me.
My reason bids me go, for my own good.
My tongue won't lie and flatter as it should;
God knows what frankness it might next commit,   95
And what I'd suffer on account of it.
Pray let me wait for Célimène's return
In peace and quiet. I shall shortly learn,
By her response to what I have in view,
Whether her love for me is feigned or true.   100

PHILINTE   Till then, let's visit Éliante upstairs.

ALCESTE   No, I am too weighed down with somber cares.
Go to her, do; and leave me with my gloom
Here in the darkened corner of this room.

---

2. Since the loss of twenty thousand francs does not apparently threaten Alceste with financial ruin, we may assume that he is rich. Mm. Édouard Lop and André Sauvage, in their edition of the play (*Les Classiques du Peuple*, Paris, Éditions Sociales, 1963) say that in the seventeenth century such a sum would have purchased a small farm near Paris or provided a sufficient dowry for a young woman of the bourgeois to make a marriage which would move her up the social ladder, In Molière's *The Would-Be Gentleman*, the rich and extravagant M. Jourdain, in preparation for the dinner to impress Dorimene, lends Dorante eighteen thousand francs in addition to purchasing a diamond and many other extravagances of his own.

PHILINTE   Why, that's no sort of company, my friend;   105
I'll see if Éliante will not descend.

SCENE 2. [CÉLIMÈNE, ORONTE, ALCESTE]

ORONTE   Yes, Madam, if you wish me to remain
Your true and ardent lover, you must deign
To give me some more positive assurance.
All this suspense is quite beyond endurance.   110
If your heart shares the sweet desires of mine,
Show me as much by some convincing sign;
And here's the sign I urgently suggest:
That you no longer tolerate Alceste,
But sacrifice him to my love, and sever   115
All your relations with the man forever.
CÉLIMÈNE   Why do you suddenly dislike him so?
You praised him to the skies not long ago.
ORONTE   Madam, that's not the point. I'm here to find
Which way your tender feelings are inclined.   120
Choose, if you please, between Alceste and me,
And I shall stay or go accordingly.
ALCESTE [*emerging from the corner*]   Yes, Madam, choose; this gentle-
man's demand
Is wholly just, and I support his stand.
I too am true and ardent; I too am here   125
To ask you that you make your feelings clear.
No more delays, now; no equivocation;
The time has come to make your declaration.
ORONTE   Sir, I've no wish in any way to be
An obstacle to your felicity.   130
ALCESTE   Sir, I've no wish to share her heart with you;
That may sound jealous, but at least it's true.
ORONTE   If, weighing us, she leans in your direction . . .
ALCESTE   If she regards you with the least affection . . .
ORONTE   I swear I'll yield her to you there and then.   135
ALCESTE   I swear I'll never see her face again.
ORONTE   Now, Madam, tell us what we've come to hear.
ALCESTE   Madam, speak openly and have no fear.
ORONTE   Just say which one is to remain your lover.
ALCESTE   Just name one name, and it will all be over.   140
ORONTE   What! Is it possible that you're undecided?
ALCESTE   What! Can your feelings possibly be divided?
CÉLIMÈNE   Enough: this inquisition's gone too far:
How utterly unreasonable you are!
Not that I couldn't make the choice with ease;   145
My heart has no conflicting sympathies;
I know full well which one of you I favor,
And you'd not see me hesitate or waver.
But how can you expect me to reveal
So cruelly and bluntly what I feel?   150
I think it altogther too unpleasant
To choose between two men when both are present;
One's heart has means more subtle and more kind
Of letting its affections be divined,

Nor need one be uncharitably plain   155
To let a lover know he loves in vain.
ORONTE   No, no, speak plainly; I for one can stand it.
I beg you to be frank.
ALCESTE   And I demand it.
The simple truth is what I wish to know,
And there's no need for softening the blow.   160
You've made an art of pleasing everyone,
But now your days of coquetry are done:
You have no choice now, Madam, but to choose,
For I'll know what to think if you refuse;
I'll take your silence for a clear admission   165
That I'm entitled to my worst suspicion.
ORONTE   I thank you for this ultimatum, Sir,
And I may say I heartily concur.
CÉLIMÈNE   Really, this foolishness is very wearing:
Must you be so unjust and overbearing?   170
Haven't I told you why I must demur?
Ah, here's Éliante; I'll put the case to her.

SCENE 3. [ÉLIANTE, PHILINTE, CÉLIMÈNE, ORONTE,
        ALCESTE]

CÉLIMÈNE   Cousin, I'm being persecuted here
By these two persons, who, it would appear,
Will not be satisfied till I confess   175
Which one I love the more, and which the less,
And tell the latter to his face that he
Is henceforth banished from my company.
Tell me, has ever such a thing been done?
ÉLIANTE   You'd best not turn to me; I'm not the one   180
To back you in a matter of this kind:
I'm all for those who frankly speak their mind.
ORONTE   Madam, you'll search in vain for a defender.
ALCESTE   You're beaten, Madam, and may as well surrender.
ORONTE   Speak, speak, you must; and end this awful strain.   185
ALCESTE   Or don't, and your position will be plain.
ORONTE   A single word will close this painful scene.
ALCESTE   But if you're silent, I'll know what you mean.

SCENE 4. [ARSINOÉ, CÉLIMÈNE, ÉLIANTE, ALCESTE,
        PHILINTE, ACASTE, CLITANDRE, ORONTE]

ACASTE [*to* CÉLIMÈNE]   Madam, with all due deference, we two
Have come back to pick a little bone with you.   190
CLITANDRE [*to* ORONTE *and* ALCESTE]   I'm glad you're present, Sirs,
        as you'll soon learn,
Our business here is also your concern.
ARSINOÉ [*to* CÉLIMÈNE]   Madam, I visit you so soon again
Only because of these two gentlemen,
Who came to me indignant and aggrieved   195
About a crime too base to be believed.
Knowing your virtue, having such confidence in it,
I couldn't think you guilty for a minute,

In spite of all their telling evidence;
And, rising above our little difference,   200
I've hastened here in friendship's name to see
You clear yourself of this great calumny.
ACASTE   Yes, Madam, let us see with what composure
You'll manage to respond to this disclosure.
You lately sent Clitandre this tender note.   205
CLITANDRE   And this one, for Acaste, you also wrote.
ACASTE [*to* ORONTE *and* ALCESTE]   You'll recognize this writing, Sirs, I
   think;
The lady is so free with pen and ink
That you must know it all too well, I fear.
But listen: this is something you should hear.   210
   "How absurd you are to condemn my lightheartedness in society,
and to accuse me of being happiest in the company of others.
Nothing could be more unjust; and if you do not come to me in-
stantly and beg pardon for saying such a thing, I shall never forgive
you as long as I live. Our big bumbling friend the Viscount . . ."   215
What a shame that he's not here.
   "Our big bumbling friend the Viscount, whose name stands first
in your complaint, is hardly a man to my taste; and ever since the
day I watched him spend three-quarters of an hour spitting into a
well, so as to make circles in the water, I have been unable to think   220
highly of him. As for the little Marquess . . ."
In all modesty, gentlemen, that is I.
   "As for the little Marquess, who sat squeezing my hand for such
a long while yesterday, I find him in all respects the most trifling
creature alive; and the only things of value about him are his cape   225
and his sword. As for the man with the green ribbons . . ."
[*To* ALCESTE.]   It's your turn now, Sir.
   "As for the man with the green ribbons, he amuses me now and
then with his bluntness and his bearish ill-humor; but there are
many times indeed when I think him the greatest bore in the world.   230
And as for the sonneteer . . ."
[*To* ORONTE.]   Here's your helping.
   "And as for the sonneteer, who has taken it into his head to be
witty, and insists on being an author in the teeth of opinion, I
simply cannot be bothered to listen to him, and his prose wearies   235
me quite as much as his poetry. Be assured that I am not always so
well entertained as you suppose; that I long for your company, more
than I dare to say, at all these entertainments to which people drag
me; and that the presence of those one loves is the true and perfect
seasoning to all one's pleasures."   240
CLITANDRE   And now for me.
   "Clitandre, whom you mention, and who so pesters me with his
saccharine speeches, is the last man on earth for whom I could feel
any affection. He is quite mad to suppose that I love him, and so are
you, to doubt that you are loved. Do come to your senses; exchange   245
your suppositions for his; and visit me as often as possible, to help
me bear the annoyance of his unwelcome attentions."
It's a sweet character that these letters show,
And what to call it, Madam, you well know.
Enough. We're off to make the world acquainted   250
With this sublime self-portrait that you've painted.

ACASTE   Madam, I'll make you no farewell oration;
No, you're not worthy of my indignation.
Far choicer hearts than yours, as you'll discover,
Would like this little Marquess for a lover.   255

SCENE 5. [CÉLIMÈNE, ÉLIANTE, ARSINOÉ, ALCESTE,
        ORONTE, PHILINTE]

ORONTE   So! After all those loving letters you wrote,
You turn on me like this, and cut my throat!
And your dissembling, faithless heart, I find,
Has pledged itself by turns to all mankind!
How blind I've been! But now I clearly see;   260
I thank you, Madam, for enlightening me.
My heart is mine once more, and I'm content;
The loss of it shall be your punishment.

        To ALCESTE.

Sir, she is yours; I'll seek no more to stand
Between your wishes and this lady's hand.   265

SCENE 6. [CÉLIMÈNE, ÉLIANTE, ARSINOÉ, ALCESTE,
        PHILINTE]

ARSINOÉ [*to* CÉLIMÈNE]   Madam, I'm forced to speak. I'm far too
        stirred
To keep my counsel, after what I've heard.
I'm shocked and staggered by your want of morals.
It's not my way to mix in others' quarrels;
But really, when this fine and noble spirit,   270
This man of honor and surpassing merit,
Laid down the offering of his heart before you,
How *could* you . . .
ALCESTE   Madam, permit me, I implore you,
To represent myself in this debate.
Don't bother, please, to be my advocate.   275
My heart, in any case, could not afford
To give your services their due reward;
And if I chose, for consolation's sake,
Some other lady, 'twould not be you I'd take.
ARSINOÉ   What makes you think you could, Sir? And how dare you   280
Imply that I've been trying to ensnare you?
If you can for a moment entertain
Such flattering fancies, you're extremely vain.
I'm not so interested as you suppose
In Célimène's discarded gigolos.   285
Get rid of that absurd illusion, do.
Women like me are not for such as you.
Stay with this creature, to whom you're so attached;
I've never seen two people better matched.

SCENE 7. [CÉLIMÈNE, ÉLIANTE, ALCESTE, PHILINTE]

ALCESTE [*to* CÉLIMÈNE]   Well, I've been still throughout this exposé,   290
Till everyone but me has said his say.

Come, have I shown sufficient self-restraint?
And may I now . . .

CÉLIMÈNE   Yes, make your just complaint.
Reproach me freely, call me what you will;
You've every right to say I've used you ill.   295
I've wronged you, I confess it; and in my shame
I'll make no effort to escape the blame.
The anger of those others I could despise;
My guilt toward you I sadly recognize.
Your wrath is wholly justified, I fear;   300
I know how culpable I must appear,
I know all things bespeak my treachery,
And that, in short, you've grounds for hating me.
Do so; I give you leave.

ALCESTE   Ah, traitress—how,
How should I cease to love you, even now?   305
Though mind and will were passionately bent
On hating you, my heart would not consent.

> *To* ÉLIANTE *and* PHILINTE.

Be witness to my madness, both of you;
See what infatuation drives one to;
But wait; my folly's only just begun,   310
And I shall prove to you before I'm done
How strange the human heart is, and how far
From rational we sorry creatures are.

> *To* CÉLIMÈNE.

Woman, I'm willing to forget your shame,
And clothe your treacheries in a sweeter name;   315
I'll call them youthful errors, instead of crimes,
And lay the blame on these corrupting times.
My one condition is that you agree
To share my chosen fate, and fly with me
To that wild, trackless, solitary place   320
In which I shall forget the human race.
Only by such a course can you atone
For those atrocious letters; by that alone
Can you remove my present horror of you,
And make it possible for me to love you.   325

CÉLIMÈNE   What! *I* renounce the world at my young age,
And die of boredom in some hermitage?

ALCESTE   Ah, if you really loved me as you ought,
You wouldn't give the world a moment's thought;
Must you have me, and all the world beside?   330

CÉLIMÈNE   Alas, at twenty one is terrified
Of solitude. I fear I lack the force
And depth of soul to take so stern a course.
But if my hand in marriage will content you,
Why, there's a plan which I might well consent to,   335
And . . .

ALCESTE   No, I detest you now. I could excuse
Everything else, but since you thus refuse
To love me wholly, as a wife should do,
And see the world in me, as I in you,

Go! I reject your hand, and disenthrall   340
My heart from your enchantments, once for all.

SCENE 8. [ÉLIANTE, ALCESTE, PHILINTE]

ALCESTE [*to* ÉLIANTE] Madam, your virtuous beauty has no peer;
Of all this world you only are sincere;
I've long esteemed you highly, as you know;
Permit me ever to esteem you so,   345
And if I do not now request your hand,
Forgive me, Madam, and try to understand.
I feel unworthy of it; I sense that fate
Does not intend me for the married state,
That I should do you wrong by offering you   350
My shattered heart's unhappy residue,
And that in short . . .
ÉLIANTE   Your argument's well taken:
Nor need you fear that I shall feel forsaken.
Were I to offer him this hand of mine,
Your friend Philinte, I think, would not decline.   355
PHILINTE Ah, Madam, that's my heart's most cherished goal,
For which I'd gladly give my life and soul.
ALCESTE [*to* ÉLIANTE *and* PHILINTE] May you be true to all you now
      profess,
And so deserve unending happiness.
Meanwhile, betrayed and wronged in everything,   360
I'll flee this bitter world where vice is king,
And seek some spot unpeopled and apart
Where I'll be free to have an honest heart.
PHILINTE Come, Madam, let's do everything we can
To change the mind of this unhappy man.   365

HENRIK IBSEN

The Wild Duck*

CHARACTERS

HÅKON WERLE, *businessman, industrialist, etc.*
GREGERS WERLE, *his son*
OLD EKDAL
HJALMAR EKDAL, *his son, a photographer*
GINA EKDAL, *Hjalmar's wife*
HEDVIG, *their fourteen-year-old daughter*
MRS. SØRBY, *housekeeper to Håkon Werle*
RELLING, *a doctor*

MOLVIK, *a one-time theological student*
PETTERSEN, *Håkon Werle's servant*
GRÅBERG, *Håkon Werle's bookkeeper*
JENSEN, *a hired waiter*
A FLABBY GENTLEMAN
A THIN-HAIRED GENTLEMAN
A NEARSIGHTED GENTLEMAN
SIX OTHER GENTLEMEN, *Håkon Werle's guests*
SEVERAL HIRED SERVANTS

The first act takes place at the home of HÅKON WERLE; *the four following acts at* HJALMAR EKDAL'S.

Act 1

At HÅKON WERLE'S *house. The study, expensively and comfortably appointed; bookcases and upholstered furniture; in the middle of the room a desk with papers and documents; subdued lighting from lamps with green shades. In the rear, open folding doors with portières drawn back reveal a large, elegant drawing room, brilliantly lit by lamps and candelabra. Front right in study, a small baize-covered door to the office wing. Front left, a fireplace with glowing coal fire. Farther back on left wall, double doors to the dining room.*

* PETTERSEN, WERLE'S servant, in livery, and the hired waiter* JENSEN, *in black, are putting the study in order. In the drawing room, two or three other hired waiters are busy arranging for the guests and lighting more candles. The hum of conversation and the laughter of many voices can be heard from the dining room. Somebody taps his wine glass with a knife to signal he is about to make a speech; silence follows; a toast is proposed; cheers, and again the hum of conversation.*

PETTERSEN [*lights a lamp on mantlepiece and sets shade on*]   Say, just listen to them, Jensen. That's the old man on his feet now, making a long toast to Mrs. Sørby.
JENSEN [*moving an armchair forward*]   Do you think it's true, what they're saying—that there's something between them?
PETTERSEN   Devil knows.
JENSEN   I guess he must've been quite a guy in his day.
PETTERSEN   Could be.
JENSEN   They say he's giving this dinner for his son.
PETTERSEN   That's right. His son came home yesterday.

---

* Translated by Dounia Christiani.

JENSEN   I never even knew old Werle had a son.

PETTERSEN   Oh, yes, he's got a son all right. But you can't budge him from the works up at Højdal. He's never once been to town in all the years I've worked in this house.

A HIRED WAITER [*in doorway to drawing room*]   Say, Pettersen, there's an old fellow here . . .

PETTERSEN [*grumbling*]   Oh damn. Who'd want to come at this time!

> OLD EKDAL *appears from the right in drawing room. He is dressed in a shabby overcoat with high collar, and woolen mittens. He has a stick and a fur cap in his hand; a parcel wrapped in brown paper under his arm. Wears a dirty reddish-brown wig and has a little gray mustache.*

PETTERSEN [*going toward him*]   Good God! What are you doing here?

EKDAL [*in doorway*]   Absolutely must get into the office, Pettersen.

PETTERSEN   The office closed an hour ago, and . . .

EKDAL   They told me that at the gate, old man. But Gråberg's still in there. Be a good sport, Pettersen, and let me slip in through here. [*Points to baize door.*] Been this way before.

PETTERSEN   Well, all right then, go ahead. [*Opens door.*] But just be sure you go out the right way. We've got company.

EKDAL   Know that—hm! Thanks, Pettersen, old chap! Good old friend. Thanks. [*Mutters to himself.*] Ass! [*Exit into office.* PETTERSEN *shuts door after him.*]

JENSEN   Does he work in the office?

PETTERSEN   No, they just give him some copying to do at home when they're rushed. Not that he hasn't been a somebody in his day, old Ekdal.

JENSEN   Yes, he looked like there's something about him.

PETTERSEN   Yes, indeed. I want you to know he was once a lieutenant.[1]

JENSEN   Go on—him a lieutenant!

PETTERSEN   So help me, he was. But then he switched over to the timber business, or whatever it was. They say he's supposed to have played a dirty low-down trick on Mr. Werle once. The two of them were in on the Højdal works together then, you see. Oh, I know old Ekdal well, I do. Many's the time we've had a bitters and beer together down at Ma Eriksen's place.

JENSEN   Him? He sure can't have much money to throw around?

PETTERSEN   Lord, Jensen, no. It's me that stands treat, naturally. Seems to me we owe a little respect to them that's come down in the world.

JENSEN   Oh, so he went bankrupt?

PETTERSEN   Worse than that. He was sentenced to hard labor.

JENSEN   Hard labor!

PETTERSEN   Anyway, he went to jail . . . [*Listening.*] Sh! They're getting up from the table now.

> *The dining room doors are thrown open from within by two servants.* MRS. SØRBY *comes out, in conversation with two gentlemen. The rest of the party, among them* HÅKON WERLE, *follow shortly thereafter. Last come* HJALMAR EKDAL *and* GREGERS WERLE.

1. See the note on European titles, p. 229.

MRS. SØRBY [*to the servant, in passing*] Pettersen, will you have the coffee served in the music room, please.

PETTERSEN Very good, Mrs. Sørby.

She and the two gentlemen exit into drawing room and thence off to right. PETTERSEN *and* JENSEN *exit the same way.*

A FLABBY GENTLEMAN [*to a* THIN-HAIRED ONE] Whew! What a dinner! *That* was something to tuck away!

THE THIN-HAIRED GENTLEMAN Oh, with a little good will it's incredible what one can manage in three hours' time.

THE FLABBY GENTLEMAN Yes, but afterwards, my dear sir, afterwards!

A THIRD GENTLEMAN I hear the coffee and liqueurs are being served in the music room.

THE FLABBY GENTLEMAN Splendid! Then perhaps Mrs. Sørby will play something for us.

THE THIN-HAIRED GENTLEMAN [*in an undertone*] As long as Mrs. Sørby doesn't play something *on* us, one of these days.

THE FLABBY GENTLEMAN Oh, Berta wouldn't do that. She isn't the type to cast off her old friends. [*They laugh and exit into drawing room.*]

WERLE [*in a low, depressed tone*] I don't think anybody noticed, Gregers.

GREGERS [*looks at him*] Noticed what?

WERLE Didn't you notice either?

GREGERS What was I supposed to notice?

WERLE We were thirteen at table.

GREGERS Really? Were there thirteen?

WERLE [*with a glance toward* HJALMAR EKDAL] As a rule we are always twelve. [*To the others.*] In here if you please, Gentlemen!

He and the remaining guests, except HJALMAR *and* GREGERS, *exit rear right.*

HJALMAR [*who had heard what was said*] You shouldn't have sent me that invitation, Gregers.

GREGERS What! This party is supposed to be for *me*. And I'm not to invite my best, my only friend?

HJALMAR But I don't think your father approves. I never come to this house any other time.

GREGERS So I hear. But I had to see you and have a talk with you. Because I expect to be leaving again soon.—Yes, we two old school chums, we've certainly drifted far apart, haven't we. It must be sixteen-seventeen years since we saw each other.

HJALMAR Is it as long as all that?

GREGERS It is indeed. Well now, how are you getting along? You look fine. You've put on weight, you're even a bit stout.

HJALMAR Hm, stout is hardly the word. But I suppose I do look a bit more of a man than I did in the old days.

GREGERS Yes, you do. Outwardly you don't seem to have suffered much harm.

HJALMAR [*in a gloomy voice*] But inwardly, Gregers! That's a different story, believe me. You know, of course, how terribly everything collapsed for me and mine since we last saw each other.

GREGERS [*more softly*] How are things now with your father?

HJALMAR Ah, let's not go into that. Naturally, my poor unfortunate father makes his home with me. He hasn't anyone else in the world to turn to. But look, it's so desperately hard for me to talk about this. —Tell me instead how you've been, up there at the works.

GREGERS   Delightfully lonely, that's how I've been. Plenty of opportunity to think about all sorts of things.—Come over here; let's make ourselves comfortable.

He sits down in an armchair by the fireplace and draws HJALMAR *into another beside him.*

HJALMAR [*with sentiment*]   I do want to thank you, all the same, Gregers, for asking me to your father's party. Because now I can see you don't have anything against me anymore.

GREGERS [*in surprise*]   Whatever gave you the idea I had anything against you?

HJALMAR   Why, you did have, you know, the first few years.

GREGERS   What first few years?

HJALMAR   After the great disaster. And it was only natural that you should. After all, it was only by a hair that your father himself missed being dragged into that . . . oh, that terrible business!

GREGERS   And because of that I'm supposed to have a grudge against you? Whoever gave you that idea?

HJALMAR   I *know* you did, Gregers. Your father told me himself.

GREGERS [*startled*]   My father! Oh, I see. Hm.—Was that the reason I never heard from you afterwards—not a single word?

HJALMAR   Yes.

GREGERS   Not even when you went and became a photographer.

HJALMAR   Your father said it would be better not to write you about anything at all.

GREGERS [*absently*]   Well, well, maybe he was right, at that.—But tell me, Hjalmar—are you pretty well satisfied now with things as they are?

HJALMAR [*with a light sigh*]   Why, yes, on the whole I can't complain, really. At first, as you can imagine, it was all pretty strange. My whole world shot to pieces. But then, so was everything else. That terrible calamity of Father's—the shame and disgrace, Gregers . . .

GREGERS [*shaken*]   I know, I know.

HJALMAR   Of course I couldn't possibly think of continuing my studies. There wasn't a penny left. On the contrary, there were debts—mostly to your father, I believe.

GREGERS   Hm . . .

HJALMAR   Well, so I thought it best to make a clean break, you know—drop my old life and all my connections. It was your father especially who advised me to do that; and since he put himself out to be so helpful to me . . .

GREGERS   My father did?

HJALMAR   Yes, surely you know that? Where could *I* have got the money to learn photography and equip a studio and set up in business? Things like that are expensive, let me tell you.

GREGERS   And my *father* paid for it all?

HJALMAR   Why, of course, didn't you know? I understood him to say he'd written and told you.

GREGERS   Not a word about its being *him*. He must have forgotten. We've never exchanged anything but business letters. So it was my *father* . . . !

HJALMAR   It certainly was. He never wanted it to get around, but it was him, all right. And of course it was also he who put me in a position to get married. Or maybe you didn't know about that either?

GREGERS   No, I certainly did not. [*Clapping him on the arm.*] But my dear Hjalmar, I can't tell you how delighted I am to hear all this—and remorseful too. I may have been unjust to my father after all—on a few points. Because this does reveal a kind heart, doesn't it. It's as if, in a way, he had a conscience . . .

HJALMAR   A conscience . . . ?

GREGERS   Well, well, whatever you want to call it, then. No, I really can't tell you how glad I am to hear this about my father.—So you're a married man, Hjalmar. That's more than I'm ever likely to be. Well, I trust you are happy in your marriage?

HJALMAR   Yes, indeed I am. She's as capable and fine a wife as any man could ask for. And she's by no means without culture.

GREGERS   [*a little surprised*]   Why no, I don't suppose she is.

HJALMAR   Life itself is an education, you see. Her daily contact with me . . . besides which there's a couple of very intelligent fellows we see regularly. I assure you, you wouldn't know Gina now.

GREGERS   Gina?

HJALMAR   Why yes, don't you remember her name is Gina?

GREGERS   Whose name is Gina? I haven't the faintest idea what . . .

HJALMAR   But don't you remember she was employed here in this house for a time?

GREGERS   [*looking at him*]   You mean Gina Hansen . . . ?

HJALMAR   Yes, of course I mean Gina Hansen.

GREGERS   . . . who kept house for us the last year of my mother's illness?

HJALMAR   Well of course. But my dear fellow, I know for a fact that your father wrote and told you I had got married.

GREGERS   [*who has risen*]   Yes, he did that, all right. But not that . . . [*Pacing floor.*] Wait a minute—perhaps after all—now that I think about it. But my father always writes me such short letters. [*Sits on arm of chair.*] Listen, Hjalmar, tell me—this is interesting— how did you happen to meet Gina—your wife, that is?

HJALMAR   Oh, quite simply. Gina didn't stay very long here in this house. There was so much trouble here at the time, what with your mother's illness . . . Gina couldn't take all that, so she gave notice and left. That was the year before your mother died—or maybe it was the same year.

GREGERS   It was the same year. I was up at the works at the time. But afterwards?

HJALMAR   Well, Gina went to live with her mother, a Mrs. Hansen, a most capable and hard-working woman who ran a little eating place. She also had a room for rent, a really nice, comfortable room.

GREGERS   And you, I suppose, were lucky enough to find it?

HJALMAR   Yes, as a matter of fact it was your father who gave me the lead. And it was there—you see—that's where I really got to know Gina.

GREGERS   And so you got engaged?

HJALMAR   Yes. You know how easily young people get to care for each other—Hm . . .

GREGERS   [*rises and walks around*]   Tell me—when you had got engaged—was it then that my father got you to . . . I mean—was it then that you started to take up photography?

HJALMAR   Yes, exactly. Because I did so want to get settled and have a home of my own, the sooner the better. And both your father and I felt that this photography business was the best idea. And Gina thought so too. Oh yes, there was another reason as well. It so happened that Gina had just taken up retouching.

GREGERS   *That* fitted in marvelously well.

HJALMAR   [*pleased, rises*]   Yes, didn't it though? It *did* fit in marvelously well, don't you think?

GREGERS   Yes, I must say. Why, my father seems to have been a kind of Providence for you.

HJALMAR   [*moved*]   He did not forsake his old friend's son in the hour of need. For he's a man with *heart*, you see.

MRS. SØRBY   [*entering arm in arm with* HÅKON WERLE]   Not another word, my dear Mr. Werle. You must not stay in there any longer staring at all those lights. It's not good for you.

WERLE   [*letting go her arm and passing his hand over his eyes*]   I rather think you are right.

PETTERSEN *and* JENSEN, *the hired waiter, enter with trays.*

MRS. SØRBY   [*to guests in other room*]   Punch is served, Gentlemen. If anybody wants some he'll have to come in here and get it.

THE FLABBY GENTLEMAN   [*walking over to* MRS. SØRBY]   Good heavens, it is true you've abrogated our precious right to smoke?

MRS. SØRBY   Yes, my dear Chamberlain, here in Mr. Werle's private domain it is forbidden.

THE THIN-HAIRED GENTLEMAN   And when did you introduce this harsh restriction into our cigar regulations, Mrs. Sørby?

MRS. SØRBY   After our last dinner, Chamberlain. I'm afraid certain persons allowed themselves to overstep the bounds.

THE THIN-HAIRED GENTLEMAN   And is one not allowed to overstep the bounds just a little, Madame Berta? Not even the least little bit?

MRS. SØRBY   Under no circumstances, Chamberlain Balle.

Most of the guests are now assembled in WERLE's *study; the waiters hand around glasses of punch.*

WERLE   [*to* HJALMAR, *standing over by a table*]   What's that you're so engrossed in, Ekdal?

HJALMAR   It's just an album, Mr. Werle.

THE THIN-HAIRED GENTLEMAN   [*drifting about*]   Ah yes, photographs! That's in your line, of course.

THE FLABBY GENTLEMAN   [*in an armchair*]   Haven't you brought along any of your own?

HJALMAR   No, I haven't.

THE FLABBY GENTLEMAN   You should have. It's so good for the digestion, don't you know, to sit and look at pictures.

THE THIN-HAIRED GENTLEMAN   Besides contributing a mite to the general entertainment, you know.

A NEARSIGHTED GENTLEMAN   And all contributions are gratefully accepted.

MRS. SØRBY   The gentlemen mean, when you're invited out, you're expected to work a little for your dinner, Ekdal.

THE FLABBY GENTLEMAN   With a cuisine like this, *that* is an absolute pleasure.

THE THIN-HAIRED GENTLEMAN   Good Lord, if it's a question of the struggle for existence . . .

MRS. SØRBY You're so right!

They continue the conversation, laughing and joking.

GREGERS [*quietly*] You must join in, Hjalmar.

HJALMAR [*with a squirm*] What am I to talk about?

THE FLABBY GENTLEMAN Don't you agree, Mr. Werle, that Tokay may be regarded as a relatively healthy wine for the stomach?

WERLE [*by the fireplace*] I can vouch for the Tokay you had today, at any rate; it is one of the very finest vintages. But of course you must have noticed that yourself.

THE FLABBY GENTLEMAN Yes, it had a remarkably delicate bouquet.

HJALMAR [*uncertainly*] Does the vintage make a difference?

THE FLABBY GENTLEMAN [*laughs*] That's a good one!

WERLE [*smiling*] There's certainly no point in putting a noble wine in front of *you*.

THE THIN-HAIRED GENTLEMAN It's the same with Tokay as with photographs, Mr. Ekdal. Both must have sunlight. Or am I mistaken?

HJALMAR Oh no. In photography, the light is everything.

MRS. SØRBY Why, its exactly the same with chamberlains. They also depend on sunshine, as the saying goes—royal sunshine.

THE THIN-HAIRED GENTLEMAN Ouch! That's a tired old joke.

THE NEARSIGHTED GENTLEMAN The lady is in great form . . .

THE FLABBY GENTLEMAN . . . and at our expense, too. [*Wagging his finger.*] Madame Berta! Madame Berta!

MRS. SØRBY Well, but it *is* perfectly true that vintages can differ enormously. The old vintages are the best.

THE NEARSIGHTED GENTLEMAN Do you count *me* among the old ones?

MRS. SØRBY Oh, far from it.

THE THIN-HAIRED GENTLEMAN Listen to that! But what about *me*, dear Mrs. Sørby?

THE FLABBY GENTLEMAN Yes, and me! Where do you put us?

MRS. SØRBY You, among the sweet vintages, Gentlemen.

She sips a glass of punch; the chamberlains laugh and flirt with her.

WERLE Mrs. Sørby always finds a way out—when she wants to. But Gentlemen, you aren't drinking! Pettersen, see to . . . ! Gregers, I think we might take a glass together. [GREGERS *does not move.*] Won't you join us, Ekdal? I didn't get a chance to have a toast with you at table.

GRÅBERG, *the bookkeeper, looks in at baize door.*

GRÅBERG Excuse me, Mr. Werle, but I can't get out.

WERLE What, have they locked you in again?

GRÅBERG Yes, and Flakstad's gone home with the keys . . .

WERLE Well, just come through here, then.

GRÅBERG But there's somebody else . . .

WERLE Come on, come on, both of you. Don't be shy.

GRÅBERG *and* OLD EKDAL *enter from the office.*

WERLE [*involuntarily*] What the . . . !

Laughter and chatter of guests die down. HJALMAR *gives a start at the sight of his father, puts down his glass, and turns away toward the fireplace.*

EKDAL [*does not look up, but makes quick little bows to both sides as he crosses, mumbling*]   Beg pardon. Came the wrong way. Gate's locked . . . gate's locked. Beg pardon.

He and GRÅBERG *go off, rear right.*

WERLE [*between his teeth*]   Damn that Gråberg!

GREGERS [*staring open-mouthed, to* HJALMAR]   Don't tell me that was . . . !

THE FLABBY GENTLEMAN   What's going on? Who was that?

GREGERS   Oh, nobody. Just the bookkeeper and another man.

THE NEARSIGHTED GENTLEMAN [*to* HJALMAR]   Did you know the man?

HJALMAR   I don't know . . . I didn't notice . . .

THE FLABBY GENTLEMAN [*getting up*]   What the devil's the matter, anyway? [*He walks over to some of the others, who are talking in lowered voices.*]

MRS. SØRBY [*whispers to the servant*]   Slip him something outside, something *really* good.

PETTERSEN [*nods his head*]   I'll do that. [*Goes out.*]

GREGERS [*in a low, shocked voice, to* HJALMAR]   Then it really was he!

HJALMAR   Yes.

GREGERS   And you stood here and denied you knew him!

HJALMAR [*whispers vehemently*]   But how *could* I . . . ?

GREGERS   . . . acknowledge your own father?

HJALMAR [*bitterly*]   Oh, if you were in my place, maybe . . .

The conversation among the guests, which has been conducted in low voices, now changes to forced gaiety.

THE THIN-HAIRED GENTLEMAN [*approaching* HJALMAR *and* GREGERS *in a friendly manner*]   Ah, are we reminiscing about old student days, Gentlemen? Eh? Don't you smoke, Mr. Ekdal? Can I give you a light? Oh, no, that's right. We are not allowed . . .

HJALMAR   Thank you, I don't smoke.

THE FLABBY GENTLEMAN   Don't you have some nice bit of poetry you could recite for us, Mr. Ekdal? You used to do that so charmingly.

HJALMAR   I'm afraid I can't remember any.

THE FLABBY GENTLEMAN   Oh, what a pity. Well, Balle, what shall we do now?

Both men cross and go into the drawing room.

HJALMAR [*gloomily*]   Gregers—I'm going! You see, when once a man has felt the crushing blow of fate . . . Say good-bye to your father for me.

GREGERS   Yes, of course. Are you going straight home?

HJALMAR   Yes. Why?

GREGERS   I thought I might drop in later on.

HJALMAR   No, don't do that. Not at my home. My house is a sad place, Gregers—especially after a brilliant banquet like this. We can always meet somewhere in town.

MRS. SØRBY [*has come up to them; in a low voice*]   Are you leaving, Mr. Ekdal?

HJALMAR   Yes.

MRS. SØRBY   Give my best to Gina.

HJALMAR   Thanks.

MRS. SØRBY   And tell her I'll be up to see her one of these days.

HJALMAR   Thanks, I'll do that. [*To* GREGERS.] Don't bother to see me out. I want to slip away unnoticed. [*He crosses room, then into drawing room, and goes off, right.*]

MRS. SØRBY [*softly to the servant, who has returned*]   Well, did you give the old man something?

PETTERSEN   Oh yes; I slipped him a bottle of brandy.

MRS. SØRBY   Oh, you might have thought of something better than that.

PETTERSEN   Not at all, Mrs. Sørby. There's nothing he likes better than brandy.

THE FLABBY GENTLEMAN [*in the doorway, with a sheet of music in his hand*]   What do you say we play something together, Mrs. Sørby?

MRS. SØRBY   Yes, let's do that.

GUESTS   Bravo! Bravo!

> *She and all the guests cross room and go off, right.* GREGERS *remains standing by fireplace.* WERLE *searches for something on the desk and seems to wish* GREGERS *to leave. As* GREGERS *does not move,* WERLE *starts toward the drawing room door.*

GREGERS   Father, do you have a moment?

WERLE [*stops*]   What is it?

GREGERS   I'd like a word with you.

WERLE   Can't it wait till we're alone?

GREGERS   No, it can't. Because we might very well never be alone.

WERLE [*coming closer*]   And what is that supposed to mean?

> *During the following, the sound of a piano is distantly heard from the music room.*

GREGERS   How could people here let that family go to the dogs like that?

WERLE   I suppose you mean the Ekdals?

GREGERS   Yes, I mean the Ekdals. After all, Lieutenant Ekdal was once your close friend.

WERLE   Alas, yes—all too close. Years and years I had to smart for it. He's the one I can thank for the fact that my good name and reputation were blemished in a way, mine too.

GREGERS [*quietly*]   Was he in fact the only guilty one?

WERLE   Who else do you think!

GREGERS   After all, you and he were both in that big timber deal together . . .

WERLE   But was it not Ekdal who drew up the survey map of the area —that fraudulent map? He was the one who did all that illegal felling of timber on State property. In fact, he was in charge of the entire operation up there. I had no idea what Lieutenant Ekdal was up to.

GREGERS   I doubt Lieutenant Ekdal himself knew what he was doing.

WERLE   Maybe so. But the fact remains that he was found guilty and I was acquitted.

GREGERS   Yes, I'm well aware there was no evidence.

WERLE   Acquittal is acquittal. Why do you have to rake up all that miserable old business that turned my hair gray before its time? Is this the sort of stuff you've gone and brooded over all those years up there? I can assure you, Gregers, here in town that whole story was forgotten ages ago—as far as it concerns me.

GREGERS   But what about the poor Ekdals!

WERLE   What exactly do you want me to do for those people? When Ekdal was released he was a broken man, altogether beyond help. There are people in this world who sink to the bottom the minute they get a couple of slugs in them, and they never come up again. You can take my word for it, Gregers, I've put myself out as far as I possibly could, short of encouraging all kinds of talk and suspicion . . .

GREGERS   Suspicion? Oh, I see.

WERLE   I have given Ekdal copying to do for the office, and I pay him far, far more for his work than it is worth . . .

GREGERS   [*without looking at him*]   Hm; I don't doubt *that.*

WERLE   What's the joke? Don't you think I'm telling you the truth? Naturally, you won't find anything about it in my books. I never enter expenses like that.

GREGERS   [*with a cold smile*]   No, I daresay certain expenses are best not accounted for.

WERLE   [*starts*]   What do you mean by *that?*

GREGERS   [*with forced courage*]   Did you enter what it cost you to have Hjalmar Ekdal learn photography?

WERLE   I? What do you mean—enter?

GREGERS   I know now it was you who paid for it. And I also know it was you who set him up so cozily.

WERLE   There, and still I'm supposed to have done nothing for the Ekdals! I assure you, those people have certainly put me to enough expense.

GREGERS   Have you entered any of those expenses?

WERLE   Why do you keep asking that?

GREGERS   Oh, I have my reasons. Look, tell me—that time, when you took such a warm interest in your old friend's son—wasn't it exactly when he was about to get married?

WERLE   What the devil—how can I remember, after all these years . . . ?

GREGERS   You wrote me a letter at the time—a business letter, naturally—and in a postscript it said, nothing more, that Hjalmar Ekdal had married a Miss Hansen.

WERLE   That's right. That was her name.

GREGERS   But you neglected to mention that this Miss Hansen was Gina Hansen—our former maid.

WERLE   [*with a scornful but forced laugh*]   No, because it certainly never occurred to me that you were particularly interested in our former maid.

GREGERS   I wasn't. But—[*lowers his voice*] there were others in this house who *were.*

WERLE   What do you mean by *that?* [*Flaring up.*] Don't tell me you're referring to *me!*

GREGERS   [*quietly but firmly*]   Yes, I'm referring to you.

WERLE   And you dare . . . ! You have the insolence to . . . ! And that ingrate, that, that—photographer! How dare he come here with such accusations!

GREGERS   Hjalmar never said a word about this. I don't think he has the slightest suspicion of anything of the kind.

WERLE   Then where have you got it from? Whoever could have said a thing like that?

GREGERS   My poor, unhappy mother said it. The last time I saw her.

WERLE   Your mother! I might have guessed as much. You and she—you always stuck together. It was she that turned you against me from the start.

GREGERS   No, it was all the things she had to bear, till at last she gave way and went to pieces.

WERLE   Oh, she didn't have anything to bear! No more than plenty of others do, anyway. But there's no way of getting along with morbid, neurotic people—that's a lesson *I* learned, all right. And now here you are, nursing a suspicion like that—mixing up in all kinds of ancient rumors and slander against your own father. Listen here, Gregers, I honestly think that at your age you could find something more useful to do.

GREGERS   Yes, perhaps it is about time.

WERLE   Then maybe you wouldn't take things so seriously as you seem to do now. What's the point in your sitting up there at the works year in year out, slaving away like a common office clerk, refusing to draw a cent more than the standard wage? It's plain silly.

GREGERS   I wish I were so sure about that.

WERLE   Not that I don't understand you. You want to be independent, want to be under no obligation to me. Well, here is your chance to get your independence, to be your own master in everything.

GREGERS   Really? And in what way . . . ?

WERLE   When I wrote you it was urgent that you come to town at once—hm . . .

GREGERS   Yes, what exactly is it you want me for? I have been waiting all day to hear.

WERLE   I propose that you become a partner in the firm.

GREGERS   Me? A partner in your firm?

WERLE   Yes. It needn't mean we'd have to be together all the time. You could take over the business here in town, and I would move up to the works.

GREGERS   *You* would?

WERLE   Well, you see, I don't have the capacity for work that I once had. I've got to go easy on my eyes, Gregers; they've started to get a bit weak.

GREGERS   They've always been that way.

WERLE   Not like now. And besides . . . circumstances might perhaps make it desirable for me to live up there—at any rate for a time.

GREGERS   I never dreamed of anything like that.

WERLE   Look, Gregers—I know we differ on a great many things. But after all, we *are* father and son. Surely we ought to be able to reach some sort of understanding.

GREGERS   To all outward appearances, I take it you mean?

WERLE   Well, even that would be something. Think it over, Gregers. Don't you think it could be done? Eh?

GREGERS [*looks at him coldly*]   There's something behind all this.

WERLE   What do you mean?

GREGERS   There must be something you want to use me for.

WERLE   In a relationship as close as ours surely one can always be of use to the other.

GREGERS   Yes, so they say.

WERLE   I should like to have you home now for a while. I'm a lonely man, Gregers; I've always felt lonely, all my life, but especially now that I'm getting along in years. I need somebody around me.

GREGERS   You've got Mrs. Sørby.

WERLE   Yes, so I have. And she's become just about indispensable to
me. She's bright, she's easygoing, she livens up the house—and that
I need pretty badly.

GREGERS   Well, then. In that case you've got just what you want.

WERLE   Yes, but I'm afraid it can't last. A woman in this kind of
situation can easily have her position misconstrued. For that matter,
it doesn't do the man much good either.

GREGERS   Oh, when a man gives such dinner parties as you do, I
daresay he can take quite a few risks.

WERLE   Yes, but what about *her*, Gregers? I'm afraid she won't put
up with it much longer. And even if she did—even if, out of devotion to me, she ignored the gossip and the aspersions and such . . . ?
Do you really feel, Gregers, you with your strong sense of justice . . .

GREGERS   [*interrupts him*]   Get to the point. Are you thinking of
marrying her?

WERLE   Supposing I were? What then?

GREGERS   Yes, that's what I'm asking, too. What then?

WERLE   Would you be so dead set against it?

GREGERS   No, not at all. By no means.

WERLE   You see, I didn't know if perhaps, out of regard for the
memory of your mother . . .

GREGERS   I am not neurotic.

WERLE   Well, whatever you may or may not be, you've taken a great
load off my mind. I can't tell you how glad I am that I can count
on your support in this matter.

GREGERS   [*looks fixedly at him*]   Now I see what you want to use me
for.

WERLE   Use you for? What an expression!

GREGERS   Oh, let's not be so particular in our choice of words—not
when we are alone, at any rate. [*Short laugh.*] So that's it! That's
why I had to make a personal appearance in town, come hell or high
water. To put up a show of family life in this house for Mrs. Sørby's
sake. Touching little tableau between father and son! *That* would be
something new!

WERLE   How dare you talk like that!

GREGERS   When was there ever any family life around here? Never
as long as I can remember! But now, all of a sudden, we could use
a touch of home-sweet-home. Just think, the fine effect when it can
be reported how the son hastened home—on wings of filial piety—
to the aging father's wedding feast. *Then* what remains of all the
rumors about what the poor dead wife had to put up with? Not a
breath. Why, her own son snuffs them out.

WERLE   Gregers—I don't think there's a man on earth you hate as
much as me.

GREGERS   [*quietly*]   I've seen you too close up.

WERLE   You have seen me through your mother's eyes. [*Drops his
voice a little.*] But don't forget that those eyes were—clouded, now
and then.

GREGERS   [*with trembling voice*]   I know what you're getting at. But
who's to blame for Mother's tragic failing? *You*, and all those . . . !
The last of them was that female you palmed off on Hjalmar Ekdal
when you yourself no longer . . . ugh!

WERLE   [*shrugs his shoulders*]   Word for word as though it were your
mother talking.

GREGERS [*paying no attention*] . . . And there he is now, that great trusting, childlike soul, engulfed in treachery—living under the same roof with such a creature. With no idea that what he calls his home is founded on a lie! [*Comes a step closer.*] When I look back upon your long career, it's as if I saw a battlefield strewn at every turn with shattered lives.

WERLE I almost think the gulf between us is too wide.

GREGERS [*bows stiffly*] So I have observed. Therefore I'll take my hat and go.

WERLE Go? Leave the house?

GREGERS Yes. For now at last I see an objective to live for.

WERLE What objective is that?

GREGERS You'd only laugh if I told you.

WERLE Laughter doesn't come so easily to a lonely man, Gregers.

GREGERS [*pointing to the rear*] Look, Father—your guests are playing Blind Man's Buff with Mrs. Sørby. Goodnight and good-bye.

He goes off, rear right. Laughter and banter are heard from the party, which comes into view in the drawing room.

WERLE [*mutters contemptuously after* GREGERS] Huh! Poor devil. And *he* says he's not neurotic!

Act 2

HJALMAR EKDAL'*s studio. The room, which is quite large, is apparently part of an attic. On the right is a pitched roof with a big skylight, half covered by a blue curtain. In the right corner at the rear is the entrance door; downstage on the same side, a door to the living room. On the left there are likewise two doors, with an iron stove between them. In the rear wall, wide double sliding doors. The studio is cheaply but comfortably furnished and arranged. Between the doors on the right and a little out from the wall stand a sofa and table and some chairs; on the table, a lighted lamp with shade; near the stove, an old armchair. Various pieces of photographic equipment here and there about the room. In the rear, left of the sliding doors, a bookcase containing a few books, some boxes and bottles of chemicals, various instruments, tools, and other objects. Photographs and small items such as brushes, paper, and the like are lying on the table.*

GINA EKDAL *is sitting at the table, sewing.* HEDVIG *is sitting on the sofa reading a book, her hands shading her eyes, her thumbs plugging her ears.*

GINA [*after glancing at her several times as if with suppressed anxiety*] Hedvig! [HEDVIG *does not hear.*]

GINA [*louder*] Hedvig!

HEDVIG [*takes away her hands and looks up*] Yes, Mother?

GINA Hedvig, darling, you mustn't sit and read so long.

HEDVIG Oh, please, Mother, can't I read a little more? Just a little!

GINA No, no. Now you put that book away. Your father doesn't like it; he never reads at night himself.

HEDVIG [*shuts the book*] No, Father doesn't care much for reading.

GINA [*puts her sewing aside and picks up a pencil and a small note-*

book from the table]   Can you remember how much we paid for
the butter today?

HEDVIG   It was one crown sixty-five.[2]

GINA   That's right. [*Writes it down.*] The amount of butter we go
through in this house! Then there was the sausage and the cheese
. . . let me see . . . [*makes a note*] . . . and then the ham . . .
hm . . . [*Adding up.*] Yes, that already comes to . . .

HEDVIG   And the beer.

GINA   That's right, of course. [*Notes it down.*] It does mount up.
But what can you do.

HEDVIG   But then you and I didn't need anything hot for dinner, since
Father was going to be out.

GINA   Yes, that was a help. And besides I did take in eight crowns
fifty for the pictures.

HEDVIG   My! As much as that?

GINA   Eight crowns fifty exactly.

Silence. GINA *takes up her sewing again.* HEDVIG *takes paper
and pencil and starts to draw, her left hand shading her eyes.*

HEDVIG   Isn't it nice to think that Father's at a big dinner party at
Mr. Werle's?

GINA   You can't say he's at Mr. Werle's, really. It was the son that
invited him. [*Short pause.*] We've got nothing to do with old
Mr. Werle.

HEDVIG   I can't wait till Father comes home. He promised to ask
Mrs. Sørby for something good for me.

GINA   Oh yes, there's plenty of good things in *that* house, all right.

HEDVIG [*still drawing*]   Besides, I am just a bit hungry.

OLD EKDAL *enters right rear, a bundle of papers under his arm
and another parcel in his coat pocket.*

GINA   How late you are tonight, Grandpa.

EKDAL   They had locked up the office. Had to wait in Gråberg's room.
Then I had to go through . . . hm.

HEDVIG   Did they give you any more copying to do, Grandfather?

EKDAL   This whole bundle. Just look.

GINA   Well, that's nice.

HEDVIG   And you've got another bundle in your pocket.

EKDAL   What? Nonsense, that isn't anything. [*Stands his walking
stick away in the corner.*] This will keep me busy a long time, Gina.
[*Draws one of the sliding doors in the rear wall a little to one side.*]
Shhh! [*Peeks into the attic a while, then carefully slides the door to.*]
Heh-heh! They're sound asleep, the whole lot of 'em. And she has
settled in the basket by herself. Heh-heh!

HEDVIG   Are you sure she won't be cold in that basket, Grandfather?

EKDAL   Cold? What an idea! In all that straw? [*Walks toward rear
door on left.*] Any matches in my room?

2. Statements about the comparative purchasing power are difficult to make accurately,
but at the time of the play one American dollar was worth three crowns, seventy-five öre,
approximately (one crown = 100 öre). At that time in America, the New York *Times*
could be purchased for two cents daily (three cents on Sundays), and theater tickets ran
as high as $1.50. Room and board in a college rooming home was two dollars a week,
and first-class steamship passage from New York to Liverpool ranged from $60 to $100.
In Act 4, Hedvig's legacy of 100 crowns a month was worth less than $27, but a dollar
had considerably more purchasing power than it does today.

GINA   On the dresser.

EKDAL *goes into his room.*

HEDVIG   Isn't it nice Grandfather got all that copying to do.

GINA   Yes, poor old thing. Now he can make himself a little pocket money.

HEDVIG   Besides, he won't be able to sit all morning in that nasty café of Mrs. Eriksen's.

GINA   Yes, that's another thing.

A short silence.

HEDVIG   Do you think they're still sitting at the table?

GINA   Lord knows. I guess they could be, though.

HEDVIG   Just think, all the delicious things Father must be having! I'm sure he'll be in a good mood when he gets home. Don't you think so, Mother?

GINA   Oh yes. Now, if only we could tell him we got the room rented.

HEDVIG   But we don't need that tonight.

GINA   Oh, it would come in very handy, you know. It's no use to us just standing there empty.

HEDVIG   No, I mean it's not necessary because Father will be in a good mood tonight anyway. It's better to have the news about the room for another time.

GINA [*looks across at her*]   You like having something nice to tell your father when he gets home evenings?

HEDVIG   Certainly, it makes things more cheerful.

GINA [*thinking this over*]   Why yes, I guess there's something in that.

OLD EKDAL *enters from his room and makes for the door on front left.*

GINA [*turning half around in her chair*]   Do you want something in the kitchen, Grandpa?

EKDAL   Yes. Don't get up. [*Goes out.*]

GINA   I hope he's not messing with the fire out there! [*Waits a moment.*] Hedvig, go see what he's up to.

EKDAL *returns with a little mug of steaming water.*

HEDVIG   Are you getting hot water, Grandfather?

EKDAL   Yes, I am. Need it for something. I've got writing to do, and the ink's gone as thick as mud—hm.

GINA   But you ought to eat your supper first, Grandpa. It's all set out for you.

EKDAL   Can't be bothered with supper, Gina. Terribly busy, I tell you. I don't want anybody coming into my room. Not anybody—hm.

He goes into his room. GINA *and* HEDVIG *look at each other.*

GINA [*in a low voice*]   Where on earth do you suppose he got the money?

HEDVIG   I guess from Gråberg.

GINA   No, impossible. Gråberg always sends the money to me.

HEDVIG   Then he must have got a bottle on credit somewhere.

GINA   Poor old soul. Who'd give *him* anything on credit?

HJALMAR EKDAL, *in topcoat and gray felt hat, enters right.*

GINA [*throws down her sewing and gets up*]   Why, Hjalmar, you're back already!

HEDVIG [*simultaneously jumping up*]   Father, what a surprise!

HJALMAR [*lays down his hat*]   Most of them seemed to be leaving.

HEDVIG   So early?

HJALMAR   Well, it was a dinner party, you know. [*About to take off his topcoat.*]

GINA   Let me help you.

HEDVIG   Me too.

They help him off with his coat. GINA hangs it up on the rear wall.

HEDVIG   Were there many there, Father?

HJALMAR   Not too many. There were about twelve or fourteen of us at table.

GINA   Did you get to talk to everybody?

HJALMAR   Oh yes, a little. But actually Gregers monopolized me most of the evening.

GINA   Is Gregers as ugly as ever?

HJALMAR   Well, he isn't exactly a beauty. Hasn't the old man come home?

HEDVIG   Yes, Grandfather's in his room writing.

HJALMAR   Did he say anything?

GINA   No, what about?

HJALMAR   He didn't mention anything about . . . ? I thought I heard he'd been to see Gråberg. I think I'll go in and see him a moment.

GINA   No, no, I wouldn't do that . . .

HJALMAR   Why not? Did he say he didn't want to see me?

GINA   I guess he doesn't want *anybody* in there this evening . . .

HEDVIG [*making signs*]   Ahem—ahem!

GINA [*not noticing*]   . . . he's been out and got himself some hot water.

HJALMAR   Aha, is he sitting and . . . ?

GINA   Yes, that's probably it.

HJALMAR   Dear me—my poor old white-haired father!—Well, let him be, let him get what pleasure he can out of life.

OLD EKDAL, *in dressing gown and with lighted pipe, enters from his room.*

EKDAL   You back? *Thought* it was you I heard talking.

HJALMAR   I just got in this minute.

EKDAL   Guess you didn't see me, did you?

HJALMAR   No. But they said you'd gone through—so I thought I'd catch up with you.

EKDAL   Hm, good of you, Hjalmar. Who were they, all those people?

HJALMAR   Oh, different ones. There was Chamberlain Flor and Chamberlain Balle and Chamberlain Kaspersen and Chamberlain this-that-and-the-other; I don't know . . .

EKDAL [*nodding his head*]   Hear that, Gina? He's been hobnobbing with nothing but chamberlains.

GINA   Yes, I guess they're mighty high-toned in that house now.

HEDVIG   Did the chamberlains sing, Father? Or give recitations?

HJALMAR   No, they just talked nonsense. They did try to get me to recite something for them, but they couldn't make me.

EKDAL   They couldn't make you, eh?

GINA Seems to me you could just as well have done it.

HJALMAR No. One should not be at everybody's beck and call. [*Taking a turn about the room.*] I, at any rate, am not.

EKDAL No, no. *Hjalmar's* not that obliging.

HJALMAR I don't see why *I* should be expected to provide the entertainment the one evening I'm out. Let the others exert themselves. Those fellows do nothing but go from one spread to the next, feasting and drinking day in and day out. Let *them* do something in return for all the good food they get.

GINA I hope you didn't tell them that?

HJALMAR [*humming*] Hm . . . hm . . . hm . . . Well, they were told a thing or two.

EKDAL What, the chamberlains!

HJALMAR And why not? [*Casually.*] Then we had a little controversy over Tokay.

EKDAL Tokay, eh? Say, that's a grand wine.

HJALMAR [*pauses*] It *can* be. But let me tell you, not all vintages are equally fine. It all depends on how much sunshine the grapes have had.

GINA Why, Hjalmar, if you don't know just about everything!

EKDAL They started arguing about that?

HJALMAR They tried to. But then they were given to understand that it's exactly the same with chamberlains. Not all vintages are equally good in their case either—it was pointed out.

GINA Honest, the things you come up with!

EKDAL Heh-heh! So they had to put *that* in their pipes and smoke it!

HJALMAR They got it straight in the face.

EKDAL Hear that, Gina? He said it straight to the chamberlains' faces.

GINA Imagine, straight in their face.

HJALMAR Yes, but I don't want it talked about. You don't repeat this kind of thing. Besides, the whole thing went off in the friendliest possible manner, of course. They were all decent, warm-hearted people—why should I hurt their feelings? No!

EKDAL Still, straight in the face . . .

HEDVIG [*ingratiatingly*] How nice it is to see you all dressed up, Father. You do look nice in a tailcoat.

HJALMAR Yes, don't you think so? And this one really doesn't fit too badly. It could almost have been made to order for me—a trifle tight in the armholes, maybe . . . Give me a hand, Hedvig. [*Takes the tailcoat off.*] I'll put on my jacket instead. Where'd you put my jacket, Gina?

GINA Here it is. [*Brings the jacket and helps him on with it.*]

HJALMAR There we are! Now don't forget to let Molvik have the tails back first thing in the morning.

GINA [*putting tailcoat aside*] I'll take care of it.

HJALMAR [*stretching*] Aaahh, that's more like it. And this type of loose-fitting casual house jacket really suits my style better. Don't you think so, Hedvig?

HEDVIG Oh yes, Father!

HJALMAR And if I pull out my tie like this into two flowing ends . . . look! Eh?

HEDVIG Yes, it goes so well with your mustache and your thick curly hair.

HJALMAR I wouldn't exactly call my hair curly. Wavy, rather.

HEDVIG   Yes, because the curls are so big.

HJALMAR   Waves, actually.

HEDVIG [*after a moment, tugs at his jacket*]   Father!

HJALMAR   Well, what is it?

HEDVIG   Oh, you know as well as I.

HJALMAR   Why no, I certainly don't.

HEDVIG [*half-laughing, half-whimpering*]   Oh yes you do, Daddy! Stop teasing!

HJALMAR   But what is it?

HEDVIG [*shaking him*]   Come on, give it to me, Daddy. You know, the good things you promised me.

HJALMAR   Oh, dear. Imagine, I completely forgot!

HEDVIG   Now you're just trying to fool me, Daddy! That's not very nice! Where did you hide it?

HJALMAR   No, honest, I really did forget. But wait a minute! I've got something else for you, Hedvig. [*Goes across and searches his coat pockets.*]

HEDVIG [*jumping and clapping her hands*]   Oh Mother, Mother!

GINA   See? If you just give him time . . .

HJALMAR [*with a sheet of paper*]   Look, here it is.

HEDVIG   That? It's just a piece of paper.

HJALMAR   It's the menu, Hedvig, the entire menu. Look, they had it specially printed.

HEDVIG   Haven't you got anything else?

HJALMAR   I forgot the rest, I tell you. But take my word for it, it's no great treat all that fancy stuff. Now, why don't you sit down at the table and read the menu, and later on I'll tell you what the different courses taste like, Here you are, Hedvig.

HEDVIG [*swallowing her tears*]   Thanks.

> She sits down but does not read. GINA *makes signs to her, which* HJALMAR *notices.*

HJALMAR [*pacing the floor*]   It's really incredible the things a family man is expected to keep in mind. And just let him forget the least little thing—right away he gets a lot of sour looks. Oh well, that's another thing you get used to. [*Stops by the stove, where* OLD EKDAL *is sitting.*] Have you looked in there this evening, Father?

EKDAL   You bet I have. She's asleep in her basket.

HJALMAR   No, really? In her basket! She's beginning to get used to it, then.

EKDAL   Sure, I told you she would. But now, you know, there are still one or two other little things . . .

HJALMAR   Improvements, yes.

EKDAL   They've got to be done, you know.

HJALMAR   Yes, let's have a little chat about these improvements, Father. Come over here and we'll sit down on the sofa.

EKDAL   Right! Hm, think I'll just fill my pipe first . . . Got to clean it, too. Hm. [*Goes into his room.*]

GINA [*smiles to* HJALMAR]   Clean his pipe—I'll bet.

HJALMAR   Oh well, Gina, let him be—poor shipwrecked old man. —Yes, those improvements—we'd better get them out of the way tomorrow.

GINA   You won't have time tomorrow, Hjalmar.

HEDVIG [*interrupting*]   Yes he will, Mother!

GINA   Don't forget those prints that need to be retouched. They keep coming around for them.

HJALMAR   What! Those prints again? Don't worry, they'll be ready. Any new orders come in?

GINA   No, worse luck. Tomorrow I've got nothing but that double sitting I told you about.

HJALMAR   Is that all? Well, of course, if one doesn't make an effort . . .

GINA   But what more can I do? I'm advertising in the papers as much as we can afford, seems to me.

HJALMAR   Oh, the papers, the papers—you see for yourself what good *they* are. And I suppose there hasn't been anybody to look at the room, either?

GINA   No, not yet.

HJALMAR   That was only to be expected. If people don't show any initiative, well . . . ! One's got to make a determined effort, Gina!

HEDVIG [*going toward him*]   Couldn't I bring you your flute, Father?

HJALMAR   No, no flute for me. *I* need no pleasures in this world. [*Pacing about.*] All right, you'll see how I'll get down to work tomorrow, don't you worry. You can be sure I shall work as long as my strength holds out . . .

GINA   But, Hjalmar dear, I didn't mean it that way.

HEDVIG   Father, how about a bottle of beer?

HJALMAR   No, certainly not. I don't need anything . . . [*Stops.*] Beer? Was it beer you said?

HEDVIG [*gaily*]   Yes, Father, nice cold beer.

HJALMAR   Well—if you insist, you might bring in a bottle.

GINA   Yes, do that. That'll be nice and cozy.

> HEDVIG *runs toward the kitchen door.* HJALMAR, *by the stove, stops her, looks at her, takes her face between his hands, and presses her to him.*

HJALMAR   Hedvig! Hedvig!

HEDVIG [*happy and in tears*]   Daddy darling!

HJALMAR   No, don't call me that. There I sat indulging myself at the rich man's table—sat and gorged myself at the groaning board—and I couldn't even . . . !

GINA [*seated by the table*]   Oh, don't talk nonsense, Hjalmar.

HJALMAR   No, it's the truth. But you mustn't judge me too harshly. You know I love you, all the same.

HEDVIG [*throwing her arms around him*]   And we love you too, Daddy —so much!

HJALMAR   And if I *am* unreasonable once in a while, well—heavens above—remember I am a man beset by a host of cares. Ah, well! [*Drying his eyes.*] No beer, no, not at such a moment. Give me my flute.

> HEDVIG *runs to the bookcase and fetches it.*

HJALMAR   Thanks! That's right, yes. With flute in hand and you two at my side—ah!

> HEDVIG *sits down at the table beside* GINA. HJALMAR *walks up and down and begins a Bohemian folk dance, playing it with vigor but in a slow elegiac tempo and with sentimental interpretation.*

HJALMAR [*breaks off the tune, holds out his left hand to* GINA, *and says with strong emotion*] What if this place *is* cramped and shoddy, Gina. It's still our home. And this I will say: here is my heart's abode.

> *He starts to play again. Soon after, there is a knock on the hall door.*

GINA [*getting up*] Shhh, Hjalmar—I think somebody's coming.

HJALMAR [*putting the flute on the shelf*] Wouldn't you just know!

> GINA *walks over and opens the door.*

GREGERS WERLE [*out in the hall*] I beg your pardon . . .

GINA [*recoiling slightly*] Oh!

GREGERS   . . . isn't this where Mr. Ekdal the photographer lives?

GINA   Yes, it is.

HJALMAR [*going toward the door*] Gregers! You came after all? Well, come in then.

GREGERS [*entering*] I told you I would drop in to see you.

HJALMAR   But tonight . . . ? You left the party?

GREGERS   Both the party and my father's house. —Good evening, Mrs. Ekdal. I don't suppose you recognize me.

GINA   Oh yes. You're not so hard to recognize, Mr. Werle.

GREGERS   No, I resemble my mother, of course. And no doubt you remember her.

HJALMAR   Did I hear you say you left the house?

GREGERS   Yes, I've taken a room at a hotel.

HJALMAR   Really? Well, as long as you're here, take off your coat and sit down.

GREGERS   Thanks. [*Removes his overcoat. He has changed into a plain gray country suit.*]

HJALMAR   Here, on the sofa. Make yourself comfortable.

> GREGERS *sits down on the sofa,* HJALMAR *on a chair by the table.*

GREGERS   So this is where you keep yourself, Hjalmar. This is your place.

HJALMAR   This is the studio, as you can see . . .

GINA   But it's roomier in here, so this is mostly where we stay.

HJALMAR   We had a nicer place before, but this apartment has one great advantage—there's such a lot of splendid extra space.

GINA   And then we've got a room across the hall that we can rent out.

GREGERS [*to* HJALMAR] Well, well—so you've got roomers besides.

HJALMAR   No, not yet. It's not so easily done as all that, you know; it calls for initiative. [*To* HEDVIG.] What about that beer?

> HEDVIG *nods and goes out to the kitchen.*

GREGERS   Your daughter, I take it?

HJALMAR   Yes, that's Hedvig.

GREGERS   Your only child?

HJALMAR   Our only one, yes. She is our greatest joy in the world, and—[*lowers his voice*] she's also our deepest sorrow, Gregers.

GREGERS   What are you saying!

HJALMAR   Yes, Gregers. She's in grave danger of losing her eyesight.

GREGERS   Going blind!

HJALMAR   Yes. So far, there are only the first signs, and things may still be all right for some time yet. But the doctor has warned us. It's inevitable.

GREGERS But this is a terrible misfortune. How did she get like that?

HJALMAR [*sighs*] Heredity, most likely.

GREGERS [*with a start*] Heredity?

GINA Yes, Hjalmar's mother also had bad eyesight.

HJALMAR That's what Father says. I can't remember her myself.

GREGERS Poor child. How does she take it?

HJALMAR Oh, as you can imagine, we don't have the heart to tell her. She doesn't suspect a thing. Happy and carefree, chirping like a little bird, she is fluttering into life's eternal night. [*Overcome.*] Oh, Gregers, it's heartbreaking for me.

> HEDVIG *enters carrying a tray with beer and glasses, which she sets down on the table.*

HJALMAR [*stroking her head*] Thank you, thank you, Hedvig.

> HEDVIG *puts her arms around his neck and whispers in his ear.*

HJALMAR No, no sandwiches just now. [*Looks across.*] That is, unless Gregers would care for some?

GREGERS [*declining*] No, no thanks.

HJALMAR [*with continued pathos*] Oh well, perhaps you might bring in a few, after all. A crust would be nice, if you happen to have one. Just make sure there's plenty of butter on it.

> HEDVIG *nods delightedly and goes out again to the kitchen.*

GREGERS [*who has followed her with his eyes*] She looks strong and healthy enough to me in all other respects.

GINA Yes, thank God. Otherwise there's nothing the matter with her.

GREGERS She's going to look like you in time, Mrs. Ekdal. How old might she be now?

GINA Hedvig's just fourteen; it's her birthday the day after tomorrow.

GREGERS A big girl for her age.

GINA Yes, she certainly shot up this last year.

GREGERS The young ones growing up make us realize how old we ourselves are getting.—How long is it now you've been married?

GINA We've been married already fifteen years—just about.

GREGERS Imagine, is it that long!

GINA [*becomes attentive; looks at him*] Yes, that's what it is, all right.

HJALMAR Yes, it must be all of that. Fifteen years, give or take a couple of months. [*Changing the subject.*] They must have been long years for you, Gregers, up there at the works.

GREGERS They seemed long while I was living through them—now, looking back, I hardly know where all that time went.

> OLD EKDAL *enters from his room, without his pipe, but with his old-fashioned lieutenant's cap on his head. His gait is a bit unsteady.*

EKDAL All right, Hjalmar, now we can sit down and talk about that . . . hm . . . What was it again?

HJALMAR [*going toward him*] Father, there's somebody here. Gregers Werle . . . I don't know if you remember him.

EKDAL [*looks at* GREGERS, *who has risen*] Werle? Is that the son? What does he want with me?

HJALMAR   Nothing. It's me he's come to see.

EKDAL   Oh. So there's nothing the matter?

HJALMAR   No, of course not.

EKDAL   [*swinging his arm*]   Not that I care, you know. I'm not scared . . .

GREGERS   [*goes up to him*]   I just wanted to bring you greetings from your old hunting grounds, Lieutenant Ekdal.

EKDAL   Hunting grounds?

GREGERS   Yes, up there around the Højdal works.

EKDAL   Oh, up there. Oh yes, I used to know my way around up there at one time.

GREGERS   You were a mighty hunter in those days.

EKDAL   So I was. True enough. You're looking at my officer's cap. I don't ask anybody's permission to wear it here in the house. Just as long as I don't go outside with it . . .

HEDVIG *brings a plate of open-faced sandwiches, which she sets on the table.*

HJALMAR   Come sit down now, Father, and have a glass of beer. Help yourself, Gregers.

EKDAL *mutters and hobbles over to the sofa.* GREGERS *sits down on the chair nearest him,* HJALMAR *on the other side of* GREGERS. GINA *sits a little away from the table, sewing;* HEDVIG *stands beside her father.*

GREGERS   Do you remember, Lieutenant Ekdal, how Hjalmar and I used to come up and visit you summers and at Christmas?

EKDAL   Did you? No, no, no, that I can't recollect. But I *was* a crack shot, if I do say so myself. Even used to shoot bears. Got nine of 'em, no less.

GREGERS   [*looking sympathetically at him*]   And now your hunting days are over.

EKDAL   Oh, I wouldn't say *that,* old chap. Still manage a bit of shooting now and then. Of course, not in the old way. Because the forest, you know . . . the forest, the forest . . . ! [*Drinks.*] Is the forest in good shape up there now?

GREGERS   Not so fine as in your day. There's been a lot of cutting down.

EKDAL   Cutting down? [*Lowers his voice as if afraid.*] That's risky business, that. You don't get away with it. The forest takes revenge.

HJALMAR [*filling his glass*]   Here, Father, have a little more.

GREGERS   How can a man like you—such a lover of the great outdoors —how can you live in the middle of a stuffy city, shut in here by four walls?

EKDAL [*gives a little laugh and glances at* HJALMAR]   Oh, it's not so bad here. Not so bad at all.

GREGERS   But all those things that were once so much a part of you— the cool sweeping breeze, the free life in the forest and on the moors, among birds and beasts . . . ?

EKDAL [*smiling*]   Hjalmar, shall we show it to him?

HJALMAR [*quickly, a little embarrassed*]   No, no, Father. Not tonight.

GREGERS   What does he want to show me?

HJALMAR   Oh, it's only a kind of . . . You can see it another time.

GREGERS [*continues to the old man*]   Well, let me tell you what I had in mind, Lieutenant Ekdal. Why don't you come up to Højdal with me. I'll probably be going back soon. You could easily get some copying to do up there as well. While here you don't have a thing in the world to liven you up or amuse you.

EKDAL [*staring at him in astonishment*]   Me? Not a thing in the world to . . . !

GREGERS   Of course, you have Hjalmar. But then he has his own family. And a man like you, who has always been drawn to what is free and untamed . . .

EKDAL [*strikes the table*]   Hjalmar, he's *got* to see it now!

HJALMAR   But, Father, do you really think so? It's dark . . .

EKDAL   Nonsense! It's moonlight. [*Gets up.*] I tell you he's got to see it. Let me pass. Come on and help me, Hjalmar!

HEDVIG   Oh yes, go on, Father!

HJALMAR [*gets up*]   Well, all right.

GREGERS [*to* GINA]   What is it?

GINA   Oh, don't expect anything special.

> EKDAL *and* HJALMAR *have gone to the rear wall and each slides one of the double doors aside.* HEDVIG *helps the old man;* GREGERS *remains standing by the sofa;* GINA *sits unconcerned, sewing. Through the open doors can be seen a long, irregular-shaped attic with nooks and crannies and a couple of free-standing chimneys. Bright moonlight falls through skylights on some parts of the attic, while others are in deep shadow.*

EKDAL [*to* GREGERS]   You're welcome to come right up close.

GREGERS [*goes up to them*]   But what *is* it?

EKDAL   Look and see. Hm.

HJALMAR [*somewhat embarrassed*]   All this belongs to Father, you understand.

GREGERS [*at the door, looking into the attic*]   Why, Lieutenant Ekdal, you keep poultry!

EKDAL   Should hope to say we keep poultry. They're roosting now. But you ought to see this poultry by daylight!

HEDVIG   And then there's . . .

EKDAL   Sh! Sh! Don't say anything yet.

GREGERS   And I see you've got pigeons, too.

EKDAL   Yes indeed, we've got pigeons all right! They have their nesting boxes up under the eaves, they do. Pigeons like to roost high, you see.

HJALMAR   They aren't all of them just ordinary pigeons.

EKDAL   Ordinary! Should say not! We've got tumblers, and a couple of pouters, too. But come over here! Do you see that hutch over there by the wall?

GREGERS   Yes. What do you use that for?

EKDAL   That's where the rabbits sleep at night, old chap.

GREGERS   Oh, so you have rabbits too?

EKDAL   You're damn right we have rabbits! He wants to know if we've got rabbits, Hjalmar! Hm! But now we come to the *real* thing! Now it comes! Move, Hedvig. Come and stand here; that's right! Now, look down there.—Can you see a basket with straw in it?

GREGERS   Why yes. And I see there's a bird sitting in the basket.

EKDAL   Hm—"a bird" . . .

GREGERS   Isn't it a duck?

EKDAL [*offended*]   Well, obviously it's a duck.

HJALMAR   But what *kind* of duck do you suppose it is?

HEDVIG   It's no common ordinary duck . . .

EKDAL   Hush!

GREGERS   And it's not a muscovy duck either.

EKDAL   No, Mr.—Werle, it's not a muscovy duck. It's a wild duck.

GREGERS   What, is it really? A wild duck?

EKDAL   Yessir, that's what it is. That "bird," as you called it—that's the wild duck. Our wild duck, old chap.

HEDVIG   My wild duck. It belongs to me.

GREGERS   And it can really live here in the attic? And thrive?

EKDAL   Of course, you understand, she's got a trough of water to splash around in.

HJALMAR   Fresh water every other day.

GINA [*turning to* HJALMAR]   Hjalmar, please, it's getting freezing cold in here.

EKDAL   Hm, let's shut the door then. Better not to disturb them when they're settled for the night, anyhow. Hedvig, lend a hand.

HJALMAR *and* HEDVIG *slide the attic door shut.*

EKDAL   You can take a good look at her some other time. [*Sits down in the armchair by the stove.*] Oh, they're most remarkable, let me tell you, these wild ducks.

GREGERS   But how did you ever catch it, Lieutenant Ekdal?

EKDAL   Wasn't me that caught it. There's a certain man here in town we have to thank for her.

GREGERS [*struck by a thought*]   That man wouldn't happen to be my father, would he?

EKDAL   Oh yes indeed. Precisely your father. Hm.

HJALMAR   Funny you should guess that, Gregers.

GREGERS   Well, you told me before that you owed such a lot to my father, so it occurred to me that . . .

GINA   But we didn't get the duck from Mr. Werle personally . . .

EKDAL   It's Håkon Werle we have to thank for her just the same, Gina. [*To* GREGERS.] He was out in a boat, you see, and took a shot at her. But it happens his sight isn't so good anymore, your father's. Hm. So she was only winged.

GREGERS   I see. She got some shot in her.

HJALMAR   Yes, a few.

HEDVIG   It was in the wing, so she couldn't fly.

GREGERS   So she dived to the bottom, I suppose?

EKDAL [*sleepily, his voice thick*]   Goes without saying. Always do that, wild ducks. Plunge to the bottom—as deep as they can get, old chap—bite themselves fast in the weeds and tangle—and all the other damn mess down there. And never come up again.

GREGERS   But, Lieutenant Ekdal, *your* wild duck did come up again.

EKDAL   He had such an absurdly clever dog, your father . . . And that dog—it dived after and fetched the duck up again.

GREGERS [*turning to* HJALMAR]   And so you brought it here?

HJALMAR   Not right away. First it was taken to your father's house. But it didn't seem to thrive there, so Pettersen was told to do away with it . . .

EKDAL [*half asleep*]   Hm . . . yes, Pettersen . . . Ass . . .

HJALMAR [*lowering his voice*]   That was how we got it, you see.

Father knows Pettersen slightly, and when he heard all this about the wild duck, he managed to get it turned over to him.

GREGERS   And now it's thriving perfectly well there in the attic.

HJALMAR   Yes, incredibly well. It's got quite plump. Of course, it's been in there so long now, it's forgotten what real wild life is like. That's the whole secret.

GREGERS   You're probably right, Hjalmar. Just don't ever let it catch sight of sea or sky . . . But I mustn't stay any longer, I think your father's asleep.

HJALMAR   Oh, don't worry about that . . .

GREGERS   But incidentally—didn't you say you had a room for rent— a vacant room?

HJALMAR   Yes, why? Do you happen to know somebody . . . ?

GREGERS   May I have that room?

HJALMAR   You?

GINA   You, Mr. Werle?

GREGERS   May I have the room? I could move in first thing tomorrow morning.

HJALMAR   Sure, with the greatest pleasure . . .

GINA   No, really, Mr. Werle, it's not in the least no room for you.

HJALMAR   Why Gina, how can you say that?

GINA   Well, that room's neither big enough or light enough, and . . .

GREGERS   That doesn't matter too much, Mrs. Ekdal.

HJALMAR   I think it's quite a nice room, myself, and not so badly furnished, either.

GINA   But don't forget those two downstairs.

GREGERS   Who are they?

GINA   Oh, there's one that used to be a private tutor . . .

HJALMAR   That's Molvik. He studied to be a pastor, once.

GINA   . . . and then there's a doctor called Relling.

GREGERS   Relling? I know him slightly; he practiced for a while up at Højdal.

GINA   They're a couple of characters, those two. Out on a binge as often as not, and then they come home all hours of the night, and they're not always what you'd call . . .

GREGERS   One soon gets accustomed to things like that. I hope I shall be like the wild duck . . .

GINA   Hm. I think you'd better sleep on it, all the same.

GREGERS   You certainly don't seem anxious to have me in the house, Mrs. Ekdal.

GINA   For heaven's sake, whatever gives you *that* idea?

HJALMAR   Yes, Gina, you really are being strange. [*To* GREGERS.] But tell me, does this mean you'll be staying in town for a while?

GREGERS   [*putting on his overcoat*]   Yes, now I think I'll stay.

HJALMAR   But not at your father's? What do you intend to do?

GREGERS   Ah, if only I knew that, Hjalmar—it wouldn't be so bad. But when you're cursed with a name like Gregers . . . ! "Gregers"— and then "Werle" on top of that! Have you ever heard anything so ghastly?

HJALMAR   Why, I don't think so at all.

GREGERS   Ugh! Phew! I could spit on a man with a name like that. But since it's my cross in life to be Gregers Werle—such as I am . . .

HJALMAR   [*laughing*]   Ha-ha! Suppose you weren't Gregers Werle, what would you choose to be?

GREGERS   If I had the choice, I'd like most of all to be a clever dog.

GINA   A dog!

HEDVIG [*involuntarily*]   Oh no!

GREGERS   Yes, a really absurdly clever dog. The kind that goes in after ducks when they plunge and fasten themselves in the weeds and the tangle in the mud.

HJALMAR   Honestly now, Gregers—what *are* you talking about.

GREGERS   Oh well, it probably doesn't make much sense. Well then, first thing tomorrow morning—I'm moving in. [*To* GINA.] I won't be any trouble to you; I do everything for myself. [*To* HJALMAR.] The rest we'll talk about tomorrow.—Goodnight, Mrs. Ekdal. [*Nods to* HEDVIG.] Goodnight.

GINA   Goodnight, Mr. Werle.

HEDVIG   Goodnight.

HJALMAR [*who has lit a candle*]   Wait a minute, I'd better see you down, it's sure to be dark on the stairs.

GREGERS *and* HJALMAR *leave by the hall door.*

GINA [*gazing ahead, her sewing on her lap*]   Wasn't that crazy talk, wanting to be a dog?

HEDVIG   You know what, Mother—I think he meant something else.

GINA   What else could he mean?

HEDVIG   Oh, I don't know. But it was just as though he meant something different from what he was saying—the whole time.

GINA   You think so? Well, it sure was queer though.

HJALMAR [*returning*]   The light was still on. [*Blows out candle and puts it down.*] Ah, at last a man can get a bite to eat. [*Starts on the sandwiches.*] Well, there you see, Gina—if only you keep your eyes open . . .

GINA   What do you mean, keep your eyes open?

HJALMAR   Well, wasn't it lucky we finally got the room rented? And then imagine, to somebody like Gregers—a dear old friend.

GINA   Well, I don't know what to say, myself.

HEDVIG   Oh, Mother, it will be nice, you'll see.

HJALMAR   You *are* funny, you know. First you were so set on getting it rented, and now you don't like it.

GINA   Well, Hjalmar, if only it had been somebody else. . . . What do you think Mr. Werle's going to say?

HJALMAR   Old Werle? It's none of his business.

GINA   But can't you see there's something the matter between them again, since the young one is moving out? You know what those two are like with each other.

HJALMAR   Yes, that could be, but . . .

GINA   And now maybe Mr. Werle will think you were behind it . . .

HJALMAR   Let him think what he wants! Mr. Werle has done a great deal for me—God knows, I'm the first to admit it. But that doesn't mean I've got to be under his thumb all my life.

GINA   But Hjalmar, dear, he could take it out on Grandpa. Suppose he loses the little money he makes working for Gråberg.

HJALMAR   I almost wish he would! Isn't it rather humiliating for a man like me to see his poor old white-haired father treated like dirt? But now the fullness of time is at hand, I feel. [*Helps himself to another sandwich.*] As sure as I have a mission in life, I shall fulfill it!

HEDVIG   Oh yes, Father, do!

GINA Shhh! Don't wake him up.

HJALMAR [*in a lower voice*] I shall fulfill it, I tell you. The day will come, when . . . That's why it's such a good thing we got the room rented; it puts me in a more independent position. And independent is one thing a man with a mission in life has got to be. [*Over by the armchair, with feeling.*] My poor old white-haired Father . . . Trust in your Hjalmar! He has broad shoulders—strong shoulders, anyway. One fine day you'll wake up and . . . [*To* GINA.] Maybe you don't believe that?

GINA [*getting up*] Sure, I believe it. But let's see about getting him to bed first.

HJALMAR Yes, let's.

They carefully lift the old man.

Act 3

HJALMAR EKDAL's *studio. It is morning; light is coming through the large window in the sloping roof; the curtain is drawn back.*
HJALMAR *is sitting at the table, busy retouching a photograph; several more pictures are lying in front of him. After a while,* GINA, *in coat and hat, enters by the hall door; she has a covered basket on her arm.*

HJALMAR Back already, Gina?

GINA Oh, yes. I've got no time to waste. [*Puts the basket on a chair and takes off her outdoor things.*]

HJALMAR Did you look in on Gregers?

GINA I sure did. And a fine sight it is in there. He certainly fixed the place up the minute he moved in.

HJALMAR Oh?

GINA Yes, he wanted to manage for himself, he said. So he decides to light the fire, and what does he do but turn down the damper so the whole room gets filled with smoke. Phew, there's a smell in there like . . .

HJALMAR Oh dear.

GINA And that's not the worst of it. Next he wants to put out the fire, so he goes and dumps all the water from the washbasin into the stove, so the whole floor's a stinking mess.

HJALMAR What a nuisance.

GINA I got the janitor's wife to clean up after him, the pig, but the place won't be fit to go into again till this afternoon.

HJALMAR What's he doing with himself meanwhile?

GINA He's going out for a while, he said.

HJALMAR I also dropped in on him for a minute—while you were gone.

GINA So I heard. You've gone and invited him to lunch.

HJALMAR Just for a little snack, that's all. After all, it's his first day—we can hardly do less. You must have something in the house.

GINA I'd better see what I can find.

HJALMAR Make sure there's plenty, though. Because I think Relling and Molvik are also coming up. I happened to run into Relling on the stairs, you see, so of course I had to . . .

GINA Well, so we've got to have those two besides?

HJALMAR   Good Lord—one more or less, what difference does that make?

OLD EKDAL [*opens his door and looks in*]   I say, Hjalmar . . . [*Notices* GINA.] Never mind.

GINA   Is there something you want, Grandpa?

EKDAL   No, no, it doesn't matter. Hm! [*Goes back inside his room.*]

GINA [*takes the basket*]   Make sure you keep an eye on him, so he don't go out.

HJALMAR   All right, all right, I will.—Say, Gina, a little herring salad would be very nice. Because I suspect Relling and Molvik were out on a binge last night.

GINA   If only they don't barge in before I can . . .

HJALMAR   No, of course they won't. Take your time.

GINA   Well, all right. Meantime you can get a little work done.

HJALMAR   I *am* working, can't you see? I'm working as hard as I can!

GINA   That way you'll get that off your hands, that's all I meant. [*She goes into the kitchen, with the basket.*]

> HJALMAR *sits a while, working on the photograph with a brush, laboring slowly and with distaste.*

EKDAL [*peeps in, looks around the studio, and says in a low voice*] You busy, Hjalmar?

HJALMAR   Yes, can't you see I'm sitting here struggling with these pictures?

EKDAL   All right, all right. Goodness' sake, if you're all that busy—hm! [*Goes back inside his room; the door remains open.*]

HJALMAR [*continues working in silence for a while, then puts down his brush and walks over to the door*]   Are *you* busy, Father?

EKDAL [*grumbling, inside his room*]   If you're so busy, then I'm busy too. Hm!

HJALMAR   Oh, all right. [*Returns to his work.*]

EKDAL [*after a while, appears again at his door*]   Hm, look, Hjalmar, I'm not really as busy as all *that*.

HJALMAR   I thought you were writing.

EKDAL   What the hell, that Gråberg can wait a day or two, can't he? I don't suppose it's a matter of life and death.

HJALMAR   Of course not. And besides, you're not a slave.

EKDAL   And then there was this other thing in there . . .

HJALMAR   That's just what I was thinking. Do you want to go in? Shall I open the door for you?

EKDAL   Wouldn't really be such a bad idea.

HJALMAR [*getting up*]   Then we'd have *that* off our hands.

EKDAL   Yes, exactly. It was supposed to be ready first thing tomorrow. It *is* tomorrow, isn't it? Hm?

HJALMAR   Oh, yes, it's tomorrow, all right.

> HJALMAR *and* EKDAL *each pull aside one of the double doors. The morning sun is shining in through the skylights. A few pigeons are flying back and forth; others are cooing on the rafters; from farther back in the attic, now and then, can be heard the clucking of hens.*

HJALMAR   There, now you can go ahead with it, Father.

EKDAL [*going in*]   Aren't you coming along?

HJALMAR   Well, you know—I rather think . . . [*Sees* GINA *at the kitchen door.*] Who, me? No, I have no time, I've got work to do. —Now, how about this contraption of ours . . .

> *He pulls a cord, and inside the door a curtain comes down. Its lower part consists of a strip of old canvas, its upper part of a piece of fishing net stretched taut. The attic floor is thus no longer visible.*

HJALMAR [*going across to the table*]   There. Maybe now I can have a few minutes' peace.

GINA   Does he have to go messing around in there again?

HJALMAR   I suppose you'd rather see him running down to Ma Eriksen's place? [*Sitting down.*] Do you want something? I thought you said . . .

GINA   I was only going to ask if you think we could set the table in here.

HJALMAR   Why not? I don't suppose there are any appointments this early?

GINA   No, I'm only expecting that engaged couple that want to be taken together.

HJALMAR   Damn! Couldn't they be taken together some other day!

GINA   But, Hjalmar, dear, I especially booked them for this afternoon, while you're taking your nap.

HJALMAR   Oh, that's all right then. Yes, let's eat in here.

GINA   All right. But there's no rush about setting the table, you can go on using it for a while yet.

HJALMAR   Well, can't you see I *am* using it for all I'm worth?

GINA   Then you'll be free later on, you see. [*Returns to the kitchen.*]

> *Short pause.*

EKDAL [*in the attic door, behind the net*]   Hjalmar!

HJALMAR   What?

EKDAL   Afraid we'll have to move the water trough after all.

HJALMAR   Well, that's just what I've been saying all along.

EKDAL   Hm . . . hm . . . hm . . . [*Disappears inside again.*]

> HJALMAR *works a little while, glances toward the attic, and half gets up.* HEDVIG *enters from the kitchen.*

HJALMAR [*sits down again quickly*]   What is it you want?

HEDVIG   I only wanted to be with you, Father.

HJALMAR [*after a while*]   I have a feeling you're kind of snooping around. Were you told to check up on me by any chance?

HEDVIG   No, of course not.

HJALMAR   What's your mother doing out there?

HEDVIG   Oh, she's busy making the herring salad. [*Walks over to the table.*] Isn't there some little thing I could help you with, Father?

HJALMAR   No, no. It's best I do it all myself—so long as my strength holds out. There's no need, Hedvig; so long as your father manages to preserve his health . . .

HEDVIG   Oh, come on, Daddy, you mustn't say such awful things.

> *She wanders around a little, stops by the opening to the attic, and looks inside.*

HJALMAR   What's he doing, Hedvig?

HEDVIG   Looks like he's making a new path up to the water trough.

HJALMAR He'll never manage that by himself, never in the world! And here am I, condemned to sit here . . . !

HEDVIG [*going up to him*] Let me have the brush, Father; I can do it.

HJALMAR Nonsense; you'll only ruin your eyes.

HEDVIG No I won't. Come on, give me the brush.

HJALMAR [*getting up*] Well, it shouldn't take more than a minute or two.

HEDVIG Pooh, take your time. [*Takes the brush.*] There. [*Sits down.*] And here's one I can copy from.

HJALMAR But don't you dare strain your eyes! You hear? I'm not taking any responsibility; you'll have to take the responsibility yourself. I'm just telling you.

HEDVIG [*retouching*] Yes, yes, of course I will.

HJALMAR My, you're good at it, Hedvig. Just for a couple of minutes, you understand.

He sneaks past the edge of the curtain into the attic, HEDVIG *sits at her work.* HJALMAR *and* EKDAL *are heard debating inside.*

HJALMAR [*appears behind the netting*] Oh, Hedvig, hand me those pliers on the shelf, will you? And the chisel, please. [*Turns to face into attic.*] Now you'll see, Father. Just give me a chance first to show you what I have in mind. [HEDVIG *fetches the tools he wanted from the shelf and reaches them in to him.*] That's it, thanks. Well, it certainly was a good thing I came.

He moves away from the opening. They can be heard carpentering and chatting within. HEDVIG *stands watching them. Presently there is a knock on the hall door; she does not notice it.* GREGERS WERLE *enters and stands by the door a moment; he is bareheaded and without overcoat.*

GREGERS Ahem . . . !

HEDVIG [*turns and goes toward him*] Good morning. Please, come right in.

GREGERS Thank you. [*Looks toward the attic.*] Sounds like you've got workmen in the house.

HEDVIG No, it's only Father and Grandfather. I'll tell them you're here.

GREGERS No, no, don't do that; I'd rather wait a while. [*Sits down on the sofa.*]

HEDVIG Everything is in such a mess . . . [*Starting to clear away the photographs.*]

GREGERS Oh, just leave it. Are those photographs that have to be finished?

HEDVIG Yes, a little job I'm helping Father with.

GREGERS Please don't let me disturb you.

HEDVIG Not a bit.

She moves the things back into her reach and settles down to work. GREGERS *watches her in silence.*

GREGERS Did the wild duck sleep well last night?

HEDVIG Yes, thank you, I think so.

GREGERS [*turning toward the attic*] It looks quite different by day from what it did last night by moonlight.

HEDVIG Yes, it can change such a lot. In the morning it looks differ-

ent than in the afternoon, and when it's raining it looks different
from when it's sunny.

GREGERS   Have you noticed that?

HEDVIG   Sure, anybody can see it.

GREGERS   Do you like to stay in there with the wild duck too?

HEDVIG   Yes, whenever I can.

GREGERS   I don't suppose you have much spare time, though. You go
to school, of course?

HEDVIG   No, not any more. Father's afraid I'll hurt my eyes reading.

GREGERS   Oh, so he gives you lessons himself, then.

HEDVIG   He promised he would, but he hasn't had the time yet.

GREGERS   But isn't there anybody else to help you a little?

HEDVIG   Well, there's Mr. Molvik. But he isn't always, you know . . .
er . . .

GREGERS   You mean he drinks?

HEDVIG   I guess so.

GREGERS   Well, in that case you've got time for all sorts of things. And
in there, it must be like a world all its own—I imagine.

HEDVIG   Absolutely all of its own. And there are such a lot of strange
things in there.

GREGERS   Really?

HEDVIG   Yes, big cases with books in them, and lots of the books have
pictures.

GREGERS   Aha!

HEDVIG   Then there's an old writing desk with drawers and secret
compartments, and a big clock with figures that are supposed to pop
out on the hour. Only the clock doesn't work any more.

GREGERS   So time has stopped in there—in the wild duck's domain.

HEDVIG   Yes. And then there are old paint-boxes and things like that.
And all those books.

GREGERS   And do you ever read the books?

HEDVIG   Oh yes, whenever I get the chance. But most of them are in
English, and I can't read that. But then I look at the pictures. There's
a great big book called *Harrison's History of London;* it must be a
hundred years old, and there's an enormous lot of pictures in it. In
front there's a picture of Death with an hourglass, and a girl. I think
that's horrible. But then there's all the other pictures of churches
and castles and streets and big ships sailing on the sea.

GREGERS   But tell me, where did all those wonderful things come
from?

HEDVIG   Oh, an old sea captain used to live here once, and he brought
them back with him. They called him "The Flying Dutchman."
That's funny, because he wasn't a Dutchman at all.

GREGERS   He wasn't?

HEDVIG   No. But finally he didn't come back, and everything just
stayed here.

GREGERS   Tell me something . . . When you sit in there looking at
pictures, don't you wish you could go abroad and see the real wide
world itself?

HEDVIG   Not at all! I want to stay here at home always and help my
father and mother.

GREGERS   Retouching photographs?

HEDVIG   Well, not only that. Most of all I'd like to learn how to en-
grave pictures like the ones in the English books.

GREGERS   Hm. What does your father say to that?

HEDVIG   I don't think Father likes the idea. He's funny about things like that. Imagine, he talks about me learning basket-weaving and braiding straw! I certainly don't think much of that.

GREGERS   No, neither do I.

HEDVIG   Still, he's right when he says that if I'd learned basket-weaving I could have made the new basket for the wild duck.

GREGERS   You could have, true. And of course you'd have been just the right person for the job.

HEDVIG   Because it's *my* wild duck.

GREGERS   Of course it is.

HEDVIG   Oh yes. I own it. But Daddy and Grandfather can borrow it as often as they like.

GREGERS   I see. What do they do with it?

HEDVIG   Oh, they look after it and build things for it, and things like that.

GREGERS   I understand. Because the wild duck must be the most important creature in there.

HEDVIG   Of course, because she's a *real* wild bird. And besides, it's such a pity for her, poor thing. She's got nobody at all to keep her company.

GREGERS   No family, like the rabbits . . .

HEDVIG   No. The chickens also have plenty of others they grew up together with from the time they were baby chicks. But she's completely cut off from her own kind, poor thing. Everything's so strange about the wild duck, too. Nobody knows her and nobody knows where she comes from, either.

GREGERS   And then she has been down in the depths of the sea.

HEDVIG   [*glances quickly at him, suppresses a smile, and asks*]   Why do you say "the depths of the sea"?

GREGERS   Why, what *should* I say?

HEDVIG   You could say "the bottom of the sea"—or "the sea bottom."

GREGERS   Can't I just as well say "the depths of the sea"?

HEDVIG   Yes, But it sounds so strange to hear other people say "the depths of the sea."

GREGERS   Why is that? Tell me.

HEDVIG   No, I won't. It's something silly.

GREGERS   Oh, I'm sure it isn't. Come on, tell me why you smiled.

HEDVIG   Well, it's because every time I happen to think about the way it is in there—when it kind of comes in a flash through my mind—it always seems to me that the whole room and everything in it is called "the depths of the sea." But that's just silly.

GREGERS   I wouldn't say so at all.

HEDVIG   Well, it's only an attic.

GREGERS   [*looking intently at her*]   Are you so sure of that?

HEDVIG   [*astonished*]   That it's an attic?

GREGERS   Yes, do you know that for sure?

HEDVIG *is silent, looking at him open-mouthed.* GINA *enters from the kitchen with a tablecloth and silverware.*

GREGERS   [*getting up*]   I'm afraid I've descended on you too early.

GINA   Oh well, you got to be someplace. Anyhow, everything's just about ready. Clear the table, Hedvig.

HEDVIG *clears up; she and* GINA *lay the table during the follow-ing dialogue.* GREGERS *sits down in the armchair and starts leaf-ing through an album of photographs.*

GREGERS   I hear you know how to do retouching, Mrs. Ekdal.

GINA [*with a sidelong glance*]   Yes, I know how.

GREGERS   That was indeed most fortunate.

GINA   How do you mean—"fortunate"?

GREGERS   Seeing that Hjalmar became a photographer, I mean.

HEDVIG   Mother knows how to take pictures, too.

GINA   Oh yes, I managed to pick that up, all right.

GREGERS   So perhaps it is really you that carries on the business?

GINA   Well, when Hjalmar hasn't got the time himself . . .

GREGERS   He's very much taken up with his old father, I would imag-ine.

GINA   Yes. Besides it's no job for a man like Hjalmar, taking pictures of every Tom, Dick and Harry that comes along.

GREGERS   I quite agree. Still, once he's gone in for that line of work, shouldn't he . . .

GINA   Sure, Mr. Werle, you don't imagine Hjalmar is just a common ordinary photographer.

GREGERS   True enough. Nevertheless . . . [*A shot is fired inside the attic.*]

GREGERS [*jumps up*]   What was that!

GINA   Ugh, they're shooting again!

GREGERS   Do they *shoot* in there?

HEDVIG   They go hunting.

GREGERS   What on earth . . . ! [*Over by the door into the attic.*] Are you hunting, Hjalmar?

HJALMAR [*behind the netting*]   Oh, you're here? I had no idea, I was so busy . . . [*To* HEDVIG.] You might let a person know! [*Enters studio.*]

GREGERS   You go around shooting in the attic?

HJALMAR [*showing him a double-barreled pistol*]   Oh, only with this thing.

GINA   Yes, one of these days you and Grandpa's going to have an ac-cident yet, with that pissle.

HJALMAR [*annoyed*]   I believe I have told you that a firearm such as this is called a pi*stol.*

GINA   Well, I can't see it makes it any safer, whatever you call it.

GREGERS   So you too have taken up hunting, Hjalmar?

HJALMAR   Only a bit of rabbit shooting now and then. Mostly for Father's sake, you understand.

GINA   Ain't men the limit—always got to have *some*thing to detract theirself with.

HJALMAR [*grimly*]   Yes, yes, we always have to distract ourselves with something.

GINA   That's just what I said.

HJALMAR   Hm. Oh well . . . [*To* GREGERS.] Yes, as I was about to say, by a lucky chance the attic is so situated that nobody can hear us shoot. [*Places the pistol on the top shelf.*] Don't touch the pistol, Hedvig! One of the barrels is loaded, remember that.

GREGERS [*looking in through the net*]   You have a hunting rifle too, I see.

HJALMAR   That's Father's old rifle. It's no good anymore, something's gone wrong with the lock. Still, it's fun to have around; we take it apart and clean it once in a while and grease it and put it together again. Of course, it's mostly Father that plays around with that sort of thing.

HEDVIG [*standing by* GREGERS]   Now you can really see the wild duck.

GREGERS   Yes, I was just looking at it. One of her wings droops a bit, it seems to me.

HJALMAR   Well, that's not so strange. After all, she was hit.

GREGERS   And she's dragging one foot slightly. Or am I mistaken?

HJALMAR   Perhaps, just a wee bit.

HEDVIG   Yes, that's the foot the dog got hold of.

HJALMAR   But aside from that there's not a thing the matter with her —which is really remarkable, considering she's got a charge of shot in her and that she's been between the teeth of a dog . . .

GREGERS [*with a glance at* HEDVIG]   . . . and has been in "the depths of the sea"—for so long.

HEDVIG [*smiles*]   Yes.

GINA [*busy at the table*]   My goodness, that blessed wild duck. You sure make a fuss over her.

HJALMAR   Hm.—Lunch ready soon?

GINA   Yes, right away. Hedvig, come give me a hand.

GINA *and* HEDVIG *go out to the kitchen.*

HJALMAR [*in an undertone*]   I don't think you'd better stand there watching Father. He doesn't like it.

GREGERS *moves from attic door.*

HJALMAR   Maybe I ought to close this door anyhow, before the others get here. [*Clapping his hand to scare the birds.*] Shoo, shoo—beat it! [*Lifting the curtain and pulling the doors together.*] This gadget here is my own invention. It's really quite amusing to have something like this to putter around with and fix up when it gets out of order. Besides which, of course, it's absolutely necessary; Gina doesn't want rabbits and chickens running around in the studio.

GREGERS   No, of course not. And I suppose it's your wife who's in charge here?

HJALMAR   As a rule I leave the routine business to her. That way I can retire to the living room and think about more important things.

GREGERS   What things actually, Hjalmar? Tell me.

HJALMAR   I wonder you didn't ask that sooner. Or maybe you haven't heard about the invention?

GREGERS   Invention? No.

HJALMAR   Really? You haven't? Well, of course, up there in the wilderness . . .

GREGERS   So you've made an invention!

HJALMAR   Not quite *made*, just yet—but I'm busy on it. As you can imagine, when I decided to devote myself to photography it was not merely in order to take pictures of a lot of nobodies . . .

GREGERS   Of course not. Your wife was just saying the same thing.

HJALMAR   I vowed that if I was going to dedicate my powers to this calling, I would raise it so high that it would become both a science and an art. And so I decided to work on this remarkable invention.

GREGERS   What does the invention consist of? What is it going to do?

HJALMAR   Come, come, my dear Gregers, you mustn't ask for details yet. It takes time, you know. Another thing—don't imagine it's vanity that spurs me on. I'm certainly not working for my own sake. Oh no, it is my life's mission that stands before me night and day.

GREGERS   What mission?

HJALMAR   Have you forgotten the silver-haired old man?

GREGERS   Your poor father, yes. But what can you actually do for him?

HJALMAR   I can restore his self-respect by raising the name of Ekdal once again to honor and dignity.

GREGERS   So that is your life's mission.

HJALMAR   Yes, I will rescue the shipwrecked old man. For shipwrecked he was, the moment the storm broke over him. By the time of that terrible investigation he was no longer himself. That pistol there, Gregers—the one we use to shoot rabbits—that has played a role in the tragedy of the House of Ekdal.

GREGERS   The pistol? Really?

HJALMAR   When sentence had been pronounced and he was to be imprisoned—he took that pistol in his hand . . .

GREGERS   He meant to . . . !

HJALMAR   Yes—but didn't dare. Lost his nerve. So broken, so demoralized was he already then. Oh, can you conceive it! He, an army officer, a man who had shot nine bears. He, who was descended from two lieutenant colonels—one after the other, naturally—. Can you conceive it, Gregers?

GREGERS   Yes, very well.

HJALMAR   Not I. Then, once again, the pistol figured in our family chronicle. When he had put on the gray prison uniform and sat behind bars . . . Oh, that was a terrible time for me, let me tell you. I kept the shades down on both my windows. When I peeped out, there was the sun, shining as usual. I couldn't grasp it. I saw people walking in the street, laughing and chatting about trivialities. I could not grasp it. It seemed to me that the whole of existence ought to come to a standstill, like an eclipse.

GREGERS   That's just how I felt, when my mother died.

HJALMAR   In such an hour did Hjalmar Ekdal point the pistol at his own breast.

GREGERS   You also thought of . . . !

HJALMAR   Yes.

GREGERS   But you did not fire.

HJALMAR   No. In the decisive moment I won the victory over myself. I chose to live. And believe me, it takes courage to choose life under those circumstances.

GREGERS   Well, that depends on how you look at it.

HJALMAR   No, my friend, no doubt about it. But it was all for the best. Because now I'll soon perfect my invention, and then Dr. Relling thinks, just as I do, that Father will be allowed to wear his uniform again. I will demand that as my sole reward.

GREGERS   So it's about wearing the uniform that he . . . ?

HJALMAR   Yes, that's what he yearns and pines for most of all. You have no idea how my heart bleeds for him. Every time we celebrate some little family occasion—like Gina's and my wedding anniversary, or whatever it may be—in trots the old man wearing his uniform of happier days. But just let him hear so much as a knock on the door—because he doesn't dare show himself like that in front of strangers, you see—back into his room he scurries as fast as his old legs will carry him. Think, Gregers, how heart-rending it is for a son to see such things!

GREGERS   About how soon do you think the invention will be perfected?

HJALMAR   Good lord, you mustn't ask me for details like dates. An invention is not a thing entirely under one's control. It's largely a matter of inspiration—of a sudden insight—and it's next to impossible to figure out in advance just when that may come.

GREGERS   But you *are* making progress?

HJALMAR   Of course I'm making progress. I grapple every single day with the invention, I'm filled with it. Every afternoon, right after dinner, I shut myself in the living room, where I can concentrate in peace. But I simply must not be rushed; that doesn't do a bit of good. That's what Relling says, too.

GREGERS   And you don't think all this business in the attic there draws you away from your work, and distracts you too much?

HJALMAR   No, no, no. Quite the reverse. You mustn't say such things. After all, I can't go around day in day out everlastingly poring over the same exhausting problems. I must have something to occupy me during the waiting period. The inspiration, the intuition—look, when it's ready to come, it will come, and that's all.

GREGERS   My dear Hjalmar, I almost think there is something of the wild duck in you.

HJALMAR   The wild duck? How do you mean?

GREGERS   You have dived down and bitten yourself fast into the undergrowth.

HJALMAR   Are you by any chance alluding to the all but fatal shot that maimed my father—and me as well?

GREGERS   Not exactly. I wouldn't say that you are maimed. But you have landed in a poisonous swamp, Hjalmar; an insidious blight has got hold of you, and you have sunk down to the depths to die in darkness.

HJALMAR   I? Die in darkness! Now look here, Gregers, you'd really better quit talking such nonsense.

GREGERS   Don't worry, I'll get you up again. You see, I too have got a mission in life now. I found it yesterday.

HJALMAR   That's all very well, but just you leave me out of it. I can assure you that—apart from my understandable melancholy, of course—I am as content as any man could wish to be.

GREGERS   The fact that you are content is itself a result of the poison.

HJALMAR   Look, my dear Gregers, will you please cut out all this rot about blight and poison. I am not at all used to that sort of talk; in my house nobody ever talks to me about unpleasant things.

GREGERS   That I can well believe.

HJALMAR   No, because it's not good for me. And there are no swamp vapors here, as you put it. The roof may be low in the poor photographer's home, that I know—and my means are slender. But I am an inventor, man—and a breadwinner as well. That raises me above my humble circumstances . . . Ah, here comes our lunch!

GINA *and* HEDVIG *enter with bottles of beer, a decanter of schnapps, glasses, and other things for the lunch. At the same time,* RELLING *and* MOLVIK *enter from the hallway, both without hat or overcoat.* MOLVIK *is dressed in black.*

GINA [*setting things on table*] Well, here they come right on the dot.

RELLING Once Molvik got the idea he could smell herring salad, there was no holding him.—Good morning again, Ekdal.

HJALMAR Gregers, may I present Mr. Molvik; Dr. . . . that's right, you know Relling, don't you?

GREGERS Slightly.

RELLING Oh, it's Mr. Werle junior. Yes indeed, we once had a couple of skirmishes up at the Højdal works. You just moved in?

GREGERS This morning.

RELLING Molvik and I live on the floor below, so you're not far from doctor or parson, should you have need of either.

GREGERS Thanks, it's not unlikely I may—yesterday we were thirteen at table.

HJALMAR Oh, don't start on that creepy talk again!

RELLING Relax, Ekdal. You can be damn sure it won't be you.

HJALMAR I hope not, for my family's sake. Well, come sit down and let's eat, drink, and be merry.

GREGERS Aren't we going to wait for your father?

HJALMAR No, he'll have a bite later on in his room. Do sit down!

The men sit down at the table, and eat and drink. GINA *and* HEDVIG *go in and out, waiting on them.*

RELLING Molvik really tied one on last night, Mrs. Ekdal.

GINA Yeah? Again?

RELLING Didn't you hear him when I brought him home?

GINA No, I can't say I did.

RELLING That's good—because last night Molvik really was awful.

GINA Is it true, Molvik?

MOLVIK Let us draw a veil over last night's proceedings. Such episodes are totally foreign to my better self.

RELLING [*to* GREGERS] It comes over him like a sort of possession, so I am obliged to take him out on a binge. Because Mr. Molvik, you see, is dæmonic.

GREGERS Dæmonic?

RELLING Molvik is dæmonic, yes.

GREGERS Hm.

RELLING And dæmonic natures are not made for the straight and narrow; they've got to kick over the traces once in a while.—Well, so you're still sticking it out up there at those ghastly dark works?

GREGERS I have till now.

RELLING Say, did you ever collect on that claim you used to go around with?

GREGERS Claim? [*Grasps his meaning.*] Oh, that.

HJALMAR Were you a bill collector, Gregers?

GREGERS Oh, nonsense.

RELLING He certainly was. He used to go around to all the workmen's shacks presenting something he called "the claim of the ideal."

GREGERS   I was young in those days.

RELLING   You bet you were. Mighty young. And that claim of the ideal—you never did get it honored as long as I was up there.

GREGERS   Nor afterwards, either.

RELLING   Well, then I imagine you've got the sense by now to knock a little off the bill.

GREGERS   Never—not when I'm dealing with an authentic human being.

HJALMAR   Well, that sounds reasonable enough.—Some butter, Gina.

RELLING   And a slice of pork for Molvik.

MOLVIK   Ugh, not pork!

Knocking inside the attic door.

HJALMAR   Open up, Hedvig; Father wants to come out.

HEDVIG *goes and opens the door a little;* OLD EKDAL *enters, carrying a fresly flayed rabbit skin; she closes the door after him.*

EKDAL   Good morning, Gentlemen! Good hunting today. Bagged a beauty.

HJALMAR   And you went and skinned it without waiting for me!

EKDAL   Salted it down, too. Good tender meat, rabbit. Sweet, too, tastes like sugar. Hearty appetite, Gentlemen! [*Goes into his room.*]

MOLVIK [*rising*]   Excuse me . . . I can't . . . I must get downstairs at once . . .

RELLING   Drink some soda water, man!

MOLVIK [*hurrying*]   Uh . . . uh! [*Exit through the hall door.*]

RELLING [*to* HJALMAR]   Let us drain a glass to the old Nimrod.[3]

HJALMAR [*clinks glasses with him*]   Yes, to the sportsman on the brink of the grave.

RELLING   To the gray-headed . . . [*Drinks.*] By the way—is it gray hair he's got, or is it white?

HJALMAR   Sort of betwixt and between, I'd say. As a matter of fact, not much of either any more.

RELLING   Oh well, life can be good enough under a toupee. Yes, Ekdal, when you come right down to it, you are a lucky man. You have your beautiful goal to strive for . . .

HJALMAR   And I do strive, believe me.

RELLING   And then you've got your excellent wife, waddling so cozily in and out in her felt slippers, swaying her hips and making everything nice and comfortable for you.

HJALMAR   Yes, Gina . . . [*nods to her*] you are a good companion to have on life's journey.

GINA   Oh, don't sit there bisecting me.

RELLING   And then your Hedvig, Ekdal, what?

HJALMAR [*moved*]   The child, yes! First and foremost, the child. Hedvig, come here to me. [*Stroking her hair.*] What day is it tomorrow, eh?

HEDVIG [*shaking him*]   Oh, don't say anything about that, Father.

HJALMAR   It pierces me to the heart to think how little we can do— only a little celebration in the attic . . .

HEDVIG   Oh, but that'll be just lovely!

RELLING   And wait till the marvelous invention comes out, Hedvig!

---

3. Nimrod is described in *Genesis* 10:9 as "a mighty hunter before the Lord."

HJALMAR Yes indeed—*then* you shall see! Hedvig, I am resolved to secure your future. You shall want for nothing as long as you live. For you, I shall demand . . . something or other. That will be the poor inventor's sole reward.

HEDVIG [*whispers, her arms around his neck*] Oh you dear, dear Daddy!

RELLING [*to* GREGERS] Well, now, don't you think it's nice, for a change, to sit at a well-laid table in a happy family circle?

HJALMAR Yes, I really appreciate these meal-times.

GREGERS I, for my part, do not thrive in swamp vapors.

RELLING Swamp vapors?

HJALMAR Oh, don't start on *that* again!

GINA God knows there's no swamp vapors around here, Mr. Werle. I air the house out every blessed day.

GREGERS [*leaving the table*] The stench I have in mind, you can hardly air out.

HJALMAR Stench!

GINA Yes, Hjalmar, how do you like that!

RELLING Pardon me—I don't suppose it could be yourself that brought the stink with you from the pits up north?

GREGERS It's just like you to call what I bring to this house a stink.

RELLING [*goes up to him*] Listen here, Mr. Werle junior, I have a strong suspicion you are still carrying around that "claim of the ideal" unabridged in your back pocket.

GREGERS I carry it in my heart.

RELLING Well wherever the hell you carry it, I advise you not to play bill collector here as long as *I'm* around.

GREGERS And suppose I do?

RELLING You'll be sent head first down the stairs. Now you know.

HJALMAR [*rising*] No, Relling, really . . . !

GREGERS Go ahead, throw me out . . .

GINA [*interposing*] You can't do that, Relling. But I must say, Mr. Werle, you've got a nerve to talk to *me* about smells, after the mess you made with your stove.

> *There is a knock on the hall door.*

HEDVIG Mother, somebody's knocking.

HJALMAR Darn! Now all we need is customers barging in.

GINA I'll go . . . [*Goes and opens the door; gives a start; draws back.*] Oh! What the . . . !

> HÅKON WERLE, *in a fur coat, takes a step into the room.*

WERLE I beg your pardon, but I believe my son is staying here.

GINA [*gulping*] Yes.

HJALMAR [*coming forward*] Sir, won't you do us the honor to . . . ?

WERLE Thanks, I just want a word with my son.

GREGERS Yes, what is it? Here I am.

WERLE I wish to talk with you in your room.

GREGERS In my room—all right . . . [*About to go.*]

GINA God, no. It's not fit in there for . . .

WERLE Very well, out in the hall, then. I want to talk to you in private.

HJALMAR You can do it right here, Mr. Werle. Relling, come into the living room.

HJALMAR *and* RELLING *exit right.* GINA *takes* HEDVIG *off with her to the kitchen.*

GREGERS [*after a brief pause*]   Well, now we are alone.

WERLE   You let drop certain remarks last night . . . And in view of the fact that you've gone and moved in with the Ekdals, I can only assume that you have something or other in mind against me.

GREGERS   I intend to open Hjalmar Ekdal's eyes. He must see his position for what it is—that's all.

WERLE   Is that the objective in life you spoke of yesterday?

GREGERS   Yes. You have left me no other.

WERLE   Is it I, then, who twisted your mind, Gregers?

GREGERS   You've twisted my whole life. I'm not thinking of all that concerning Mother . . . But it's you I have to thank that I am forever driven and tormented by a guilty conscience.

WERLE   Aha, your conscience! So that's your trouble.

GREGERS   I should have stood up to you that time the trap was laid for Lieutenant Ekdal. I should have warned him—for I suspected well enough how it was all going to end.

WERLE   Yes, in that case you certainly ought to have spoken out.

GREGERS   I didn't dare. That's what a frightened coward I was. I was so unspeakably afraid of you—not only then but long after.

WERLE   You've got over that fear now, it appears.

GREGERS   Yes, fortunately. The crime committed against old Ekdal, both by myself and by—others—that can never be redeemed. But Hjalmar I can still rescue from all the lies and deceit that threaten to destroy him.

WERLE   Do you think you'll be doing him a favor?

GREGERS   I *know* it.

WERLE   I suppose you think our good photographer is the kind of man to thank you for such a friendly service?

GREGERS   Yes! He certainly is.

WERLE   Hm . . . we'll see.

GREGERS   And besides . . . if I am to go on living, I must find some cure for my sick conscience.

WERLE   It will never be well. Your conscience has been sickly right from childhood. It is a legacy from your mother, Gregers—the only thing she ever left you.

GREGERS [*with a contemptuous half-smile*]   So you still haven't swallowed your disappointment that she didn't bring you the dowry you counted on?

WERLE   Let us keep to the point.—Are you quite resolved to set young Ekdal on what you assume to be the right track?

GREGERS   Yes, quite resolved.

WERLE   Well, in that case I could have saved myself the trouble of coming up here. Then I suppose it's no use asking you to come back home?

GREGERS   No.

WERLE   And you won't join the firm, either?

GREGERS   No.

WERLE   Very well. But since I intend to marry again, your share of my estate will be turned over to you at once.[4]

---

4. As a widower, the elder Werle coud not remarry without securing some part of his estate to surviving children of his previous marriage.

GREGERS [*quickly*]   No, I don't want that.

WERLE   You don't want it?

GREGERS   No, I don't dare. My conscience won't let me.

WERLE [*after a pause*]   Are you going up to the works again?

GREGERS   No, I consider myself released from your service.

WERLE   But what are you going to do?

GREGERS   Accomplish my mission. That's all.

WERLE   All right, but afterwards? What are you going to live on?

GREGERS   I've put aside a little of my salary.

WERLE   Yes, but how long will *that* last!

GREGERS   I think it will last out my time.

WERLE   What's that supposed to mean?

GREGERS   I'm answering no more questions.

WERLE   Good-bye, then, Gregers.

GREGERS   Good-bye.

> HÅKON WERLE *goes.*

HJALMAR [*peeping in*]   Has he gone?

GREGERS   Yes.

> HJALMAR *and* RELLING *enter; also* GINA *and* HEDVIG, *from the kitchen.*

RELLING   Well, that fixed *that* lunch.

GREGERS   Put on your things, Hjalmar. You're coming with me for a long walk.

HJALMAR   Gladly. What did your father want? Anything to do with me?

GREGERS   Just come. We must have a little talk. I'll go get my coat. [*Goes out by the hall door.*]

GINA   You shouldn't go with him, Hjalmar.

RELLING   No, don't you do it, old man. Stay where you are.

HJALMAR [*getting his coat and hat*]   What! When an old friend feels the need to open his heart to me in private . . . !

RELLING   But damn it!—can't you see the fellow is mad, cracked, off his rocker!

GINA   There, what did I tell you? His mother used to get these here fits and conniptions too.

HJALMAR   All the more reason he needs a friend's watchful eye. [*To* GINA.] Be sure and have dinner ready on time. So long. [*Goes out by the hall door.*]

RELLING   What a calamity that fellow didn't go straight to hell down one of the Højdal pits.

GINA   Good God!—what makes you say that?

RELLING [*muttering*]   Oh, I have my reasons.

GINA   Do you think young Werle is really crazy?

RELLING   No, worse luck; he's no more crazy than most. But there's one bug he certainly has got in his system.

GINA   What's the matter with him, anyway?

RELLING   Well, I'll tell you, Mrs. Ekdal. He's got a severe case of inflamed integrity.

GINA   Inflamed integrity?

HEDVIG   Is that a kind of disease?

RELLING   Oh yes. It's a national disease. But it only breaks out sporadically. [*Nods to* GINA.] Thanks for lunch!

> He goes out by the hall door.

GINA [*pacing the floor, disturbed*] Ugh, that Gregers Werle—he always *was* a queer fish.

HEDVIG [*standing by the table and looking searchingly at her*] I think this is all so strange.

Act 4

HJALMAR EKDAL's *studio. Photographs have apparently just been taken; a camera covered with a cloth, a stand, two chairs, a console, and other portrait materials are set out in the middle of the room. Afternoon light; the sun is about to set; after a while it begins to get dark.*

GINA is standing at the open hall door with a dark slide and a wet photographic plate in her hand. She is speaking to somebody outside.

GINA Yes, positively. When I make a promise, I keep it. The first dozen will be ready on Monday.—Good-bye now, good-bye!

Footsteps can be heard going down the stairs. GINA *shuts the door, puts the plate in the slide, and inserts the slide in the covered camera.*

HEDVIG [*entering from the kitchen*] Did they leave?
GINA [*tidying up*] Yes, thank goodness. I finally got rid of them.
HEDVIG Can you understand why Father isn't back yet?
GINA You're sure he's not down at Relling's?
HEDVIG No, he's not there. I just went down the back stairs and asked.
GINA And his dinner standing there getting cold.
HEDVIG Imagine! And Father's always so punctual about dinner.
GINA Well, he'll be here soon, don't worry.
HEDVIG Oh, I wish he'd come. Everything seems so strange.
GINA [*calls out*] There he is!

HJALMAR EKDAL *comes in through the hall door.*

HEDVIG [*up to him*] Father! We've been waiting and waiting for you!
GINA [*glancing across*] You sure have been out a long time, Hjalmar.
HJALMAR [*without looking at her*] I suppose I have, yes. [*He takes off his overcoat.* GINA *and* HEDVIG *try to help him; he waves them aside.*]
GINA Maybe you ate someplace with Werle?
HJALMAR [*hanging up his coat*] No.
GINA [*going toward the kitchen door*] Then I'll go get your dinner.
HJALMAR No, never mind. I don't want anything now.
HEDVIG [*coming closer*] Aren't you feeling well, Father?
HJALMAR Feeling well? Oh yes, tolerably. We had a tiring walk together, Gregers and I.
GINA You shouldn't do that, Hjalmar, you're not used to it.
HJALMAR Hm. There are lots of things a man must get used to in this world. [*Paces up and down.*] Did anybody come while I was out?
GINA Only the engaged couple.
HJALMAR No new orders?

GINA   No, not today.

HEDVIG   There'll be some tomorrow, Father, you'll see.

HJALMAR   I hope you're right, because tomorrow I mean to get down to work in real earnest.

HEDVIG   Tomorrow! Don't you remember what day it is tomorrow?

HJALMAR   Oh, that's right . . . Well, the day after tomorrow, then. From now on I intend to do everything myself; I want to do all the work entirely on my own.

GINA   What on earth for, Hjalmar? You'd only make your life a misery. I can still manage the photography; you go on with the invention.

HEDVIG   And what about the wild duck—and all the chickens and rabbits . . .

HJALMAR   Don't talk to me about that junk! I'm never setting foot in that attic again.

HEDVIG   But Father, you promised me there'd be a party tomorrow . . .

HJALMAR   Hm, that's right. Well, starting the day after tomorrow, then. That damn wild duck, I'd like to wring its neck!

HEDVIG [*cries out*]   The wild duck!

GINA   Well, I never!

HEDVIG [*shaking him*]   But Father, it's *my* wild duck!

HJALMAR   That's the only thing that stops me. I haven't the heart— for your sake, Hedvig, I haven't got the heart. But deep down I feel I ought to do it. I ought not tolerate under my roof any creature that has been in that man's hands.

GINA   Goodness sake, just because Grandpa got it off that good-for-nothing Pettersen . . .

HJALMAR [*walking up and down*]   There are certain demands . . . what shall I call them? Let us say—demands of the ideal—certain claims that a man cannot disregard without peril to his soul.

HEDVIG [*following him about*]   But think, the wild duck—that poor wild duck!

HJALMAR [*halts*]   I *told* you I'll spare it—for your sake. Not a hair of its head shall be . . . hm. As I said, I shall spare it. I have more important things to think about now. But now you ought to go for a little walk, Hedvig; the twilight is just right for you.

HEDVIG   I don't care to go out now.

HJALMAR   Yes, go on. Seems to me you're blinking your eyes a lot. It's not good for you, all these fumes in here. The air is close under this roof.

HEDVIG   Well, all right, I'll run down the kitchen way and walk around a little. My hat and coat . . . ? That's right, they're in my room. Father—promise you won't do anything to the wild duck while I'm gone.

HJALMAR   Not a feather of its head shall be touched. [*Presses her to him.*] You and I, Hedvig—we two . . . ! Well, run along now.

HEDVIG *nods to her parents and goes out through the kitchen.*

HJALMAR [*walks up and down without looking up*]   Gina.

GINA   Yes?

HJALMAR   As of tomorrow . . . or, let us say as of the day after tomorrow—I wish to keep the household accounts myself.

GINA   You want to keep the accounts also?

HJALMAR   Yes, keep track of what we take in, at any rate.

GINA   Oh, God help us, *that's* soon done.

HJALMAR   I wonder. It seems to me you make the money go a remarkably long way. [*Halts and looks at her.*] How do you do it?

GINA   That's because Hedvig and I need so little.

HJALMAR   Is it true that Father is highly paid for the copying he does for Mr. Werle?

GINA   I don't know if it's all that high. I don't know what the rates are for things like that.

HJALMAR   Well, roughly what *does* he get? I want to know.

GINA   It differs. I guess it comes to about what he costs us, and a little pocket money.

HJALMAR   What he *costs* us! You never told me that before!

GINA   No, how could I. It made you so happy to think he got everything from you.

HJALMAR   And in fact it comes from Mr. Werle!

GINA   Oh, don't worry. He can afford it.

HJALMAR   Light me the lamp!

GINA [*lighting the lamp*]   Besides, how can we tell if it actually comes from him; it could easily be Gråberg . . .

HJALMAR   Why do you suddenly drag Gråberg into this?

GINA   Well, I don't know, I just thought . . .

HJALMAR   Hm!

GINA   Anyway, it wasn't me that got Grandpa the copying to do. You know yourself it was Berta, the time she took service there.

HJALMAR   It seems to me your voice is trembling.

GINA [*putting the shade on the lamp*]   Is it?

HJALMAR   And your hands are shaking. Aren't they?

GINA [*firmly*]   Say it straight out, Hjalmar. What's he gone and told you about me?

HJALMAR   Is it true—*can* it be true—that there was something between you and Mr. Werle while you were working in his house?

GINA   It's not true. Not then, there wasn't. He was after me all right, that I will say. And the Missus thought there was something going on, and she made such a fuss and a hullaballoo about it and went for me tooth and nail. She sure did.—So I quit.

HJALMAR   But then, afterwards . . . !

GINA   Well, *you* know, I went home. And my mother . . . she wasn't exactly as straight as you thought she was, Hjalmar. Anyway, she got after me about this, that, and the other. Because by that time Werle was a widower.

HJALMAR   All right! And then?

GINA   Well, I guess you might as well know it. He wouldn't give up till he had his way.

HJALMAR [*striking his hands together*]   And this is the mother of my child! How could you keep a thing like that from me!

GINA   Yes, I know it was wrong. I should've told you long ago, I guess.

HJALMAR   Right at the *start* you should have told me—then I'd have known the sort of woman you were.

GINA   But would you have married me, just the same?

HJALMAR   What do *you* think?

GINA   There you are, that's why I didn't dare tell you at the time. You know how much I'd come to care for you. So how could I go and make my own life a misery?

HJALMAR [*pacing about*]   And this is my Hedvig's mother! And to realize that everything I lay my eyes on . . . [*kicks a chair*] . . . my entire home . . . I owe to a favored predecessor! Oh, that old lecher!

GINA   Do you regret the fourteen-fifteen years we've had together?

HJALMAR [*fronting her*]   Tell me, have you not—every day, every hour—regretted this web of deceit you've spun around me, like a spider? Answer me! Have you really gone around here and not suffered agonies of remorse and shame?

GINA   Bless you, Hjalmar, I've had enough to think about just running the house and everything . . .

HJALMAR   You mean you never even give a thought to your past?

GINA   No, God knows I'd just about forgotten that old business.

HJALMAR   Oh, this dull, apathetic calm! That's what I find so outrageous. Imagine—not even a twinge of remorse!

GINA   But just tell me, Hjalmar—what would've become of you, if you hadn't had a wife like me?

HJALMAR   Like you!

GINA   Well, you've got to admit I've always been kind of more practical and with my feet on the ground than you. Well, of course I *am* a couple of years older.

HJALMAR   What would have become of me!

GINA   Because you weren't exactly living right when you first met me; you can't deny that.

HJALMAR   Is that what you call not living right? Oh, what would you know about a man's feelings when he falls into grief and despair— especially a man of my fiery temperament.

GINA   All right, all right, have it your way. Anyhow, I don't want to make no song and dance about it. Because you certainly turned out to be a real good man, once you got your own home and family. And now we'd got things so nice and comfortable here, and Hedvig and me was just thinking that soon we could spend a little on ourselves in the way of food and clothes.

HJALMAR   In this swamp of deceit, yes.

GINA   Oh, why did that nasty creature have to come poking his nose in here for!

HJALMAR   I, too, thought our home a happy one. What a delusion! And now where am I to find the inner force I need in order to bring forth my invention? Perhaps it will die with me. And then it will have been your past, Gina, that killed it.

GINA [*about to weep*]   Please, Hjalmar, you mustn't say a thing like that. When all my days I only tried to make everything the best for you!

HJALMAR   I ask you—what happens now to the breadwinner's dream? As I would lie there on the sofa, pondering the invention, I suspected full well that it would drain the last drop of my strength. Well I knew that the day I held the patent in my hands, that day would mark my—final hour. And so it was my dream that you would be left the well-to-do widow of the late inventor.

GINA [*drying her tears*]   Hjalmar, don't talk like that. God forbid I should ever live to see the day I'm left a widow!

HJALMAR   Oh well, what's the difference. It's all over now, anyway. All over!

GREGERS WERLE *cautiously opens the hall door and looks in.*

GREGERS   May I come in?

HJALMAR   Yes, come in.

GREGERS [*advances, his face radiant with joy, and reaches out his hands to them*] Well, you two dear people . . . ! [*Looks from the one to the other and whispers to* HJALMAR.] You haven't done it yet?

HJALMAR [*aloud*]   It is done.

GREGERS   It is?

HJALMAR   I have lived through the bitterest hour of my life.

GREGERS   But also, I trust, the most sublime.

HJALMAR   Anyway, for the time being it's done and over with.

GINA   God forgive you, Mr. Werle.

GREGERS [*in great amazement*]   But I don't understand this.

HJALMAR   What don't you understand?

GREGERS   So great an accounting—an accounting that a whole new way of life is to be founded on—a way of life, a partnership in truth, free of all deception . . .

HJALMAR   Yes, yes, I know. I know all that.

GREGERS   I was absolutely confident that when I came through that door I would be met by a radiance of transfiguration shining from the faces of both husband and wife. And all I see is this dull, heavy, gloomy . . .

GINA   Is that it. [*Takes the shade off the lamp.*]

GREGERS   You're not trying to understand me, Mrs. Ekdal. Well, well, I suppose you'll need time . . . But *you*, now, Hjalmar? Surely *you* must feel exalted by this great reckoning.

HJALMAR   Yes, naturally I do. That is—in a kind of way.

GREGERS   For surely nothing in the world can compare to finding forgiveness in one's heart for one who has erred, and raising her up to you with love.

HJALMAR   Do you think a man so easily gets over the bitter cup I just drained?

GREGERS   No, not an ordinary man, perhaps. But a man like *you* . . . !

HJALMAR   All right, I know, I know. But don't push me, Gregers. It takes time.

GREGERS   There is much of the wild duck in you, Hjalmar.

RELLING *has entered by the hall door.*

RELLING   What's this? Are we back to the wild duck again?

HJALMAR   Yes. The damaged trophy of Mr. Werle's sport.

RELLING   Werle senior? Is it him you're talking about?

HJALMAR   Him and . . . the rest of us.

RELLING [*to* GREGERS, *under his breath*]   Damn you to hell!

HJALMAR   What's that you're saying?

RELLING   I was expressing the fervent wish that this quack here would take himself off where he belongs. If he stays around here much longer, he's quite capable of messing you both up.

GREGERS   These two are not going to be "messed up," Mr. Relling. I need not speak for Hjalmar. Him we know. But she too must surely have, deep down inside, something worthy of trust, something of integrity . . .

GINA [*on the point of tears*]   Then why couldn't you leave me be like I was.

RELLING [*to* GREGERS]   Would it be impertinent to ask what it is exactly you want in this house?

GREGERS   I want to lay the foundation for a true marriage.

RELLING   So you don't think the Ekdals' marriage is good enough as it is?

GREGERS   It's probably as good a marriage as most, I regret to say. But a true marriage it has yet to become.

HJALMAR   You never did have an eye for the claim of the ideal, Relling.

RELLING   Nonsense, my boy!—Begging your pardon, Mr. Werle, but how many—at a rough guess—how many true marriages have you seen in your life?

GREGERS   Hardly a single one.

RELLING   Neither have I.

GREGERS   But I *have* seen innumerable marriages of the opposite sort. And I had occasion to observe at close quarters the havoc such a marriage can wreak on both partners.

HJALMAR   A man's whole moral foundation can crumble under his feet; that's the terrible thing.

RELLING   Well, of course I've never been exactly married myself, so I can't judge about that. But this I do know, that the child is part of a marriage too. And you had better leave the child in peace.

HJALMAR   Oh—Hedvig! My poor Hedvig!

RELLING   Yes, see to it you keep Hedvig out of this. You two are grown people. In God's name, go ahead and muck up your own affairs to your heart's content. But I'm warning you—go easy with Hedvig, or you may end by doing her serious injury.

HJALMAR   Injury!

RELLING   Yes, or else she might do herself one—and maybe not only to herself.

GINA   How can you tell a thing like that, Relling?

HJALMAR   There's no immediate danger to her eyes, is there?

RELLING   This has nothing to do with her eyes. But Hedvig is at a difficult age. There's no telling *what* wild ideas she can get into her head.

GINA   Say, that's right! Lately she's started to fool around in such a peculiar way with the stove out in the kitchen. "Playing house on fire," she calls it. Sometimes I'm scared she *will* burn down the house.

RELLING   There you are; I knew it.

GREGERS [*to* RELLING]   But how do you explain a thing like that?

RELLING [*sullenly*]   Puberty, man.

HJALMAR   As long as the child has me! As long as I'm above the ground . . . !

There is a knock on the door.

GINA   Shhh, Hjalmar, there's somebody outside. [*Calls.*] Come in!

Enter MRS. SØRBY, *in outdoor clothes.*

MRS. SØRBY   Good evening!

GINA [*going toward her*]   Why, Berta, it's *you*!

MRS. SØRBY   It certainly is. Have I come at an inconvenient time?

HJALMAR   Gracious, no—a messenger from that house . . .

MRS. SØRBY [*to* GINA]   To tell the truth I hoped I wouldn't find your menfolk at home this time of day. So I dropped in to have a little chat with you and say good-bye.

GINA   Oh? Why? Are you going away?

MRS. SØRBY   Yes, tomorrow early—up to Højdal. Mr. Werle left this afternoon. [*Casually, to* GREGERS.] He send his regards.

GINA   Imagine!

HJALMAR   So Mr. Werle has left? And you're following him?

MRS. SØRBY   Yes, Ekdal, what do you say to that?

HJALMAR   I say—beware!

GREGERS   Let me explain. My father is marrying Mrs. Sørby.

HJALMAR   Marrying her!

GINA   Oh, Berta—finally!

RELLING [*his voice trembling slightly*]   Surely this can't be true?

MRS. SØRBY   Yes, my dear Relling, it's quite true.

RELLING   You are going to get married again?

MRS. SØRBY   It looks like it. Werle has got a special license, and we're going to have a quiet wedding up at the works.

GREGERS   Then I suppose I must wish you joy, like a good stepson.

MRS. SØRBY   Thank you, if you really mean it. I do hope it will lead to happiness for both Werle and myself.

RELLING   You have every reason for hope. Mr. Werle never gets drunk —at least not to my knowledge. And I doubt he's in the habit of beating his wives, either, like the late lamented horse-doctor.

MRS SØRBY   Oh, come now, let Sørby rest in peace. He had his good points too.

RELLING   Mr. Werle has better ones, I'm sure.

MRS. SØRBY   At any rate he didn't go and throw away the best that was in him. The man who does that must take the consequences.

RELLING   Tonight I will go out with Molvik.

MRS. SØRBY   Don't do that, Relling. Don't—for my sake.

RELLING   Can't be helped. [*To* HJALMAR.] Come along too, if you like.

GINA   No, thanks. Hjalmar don't go on such disserpations.

HJALMAR [*angrily, in an undertone*]   Oh, be still!

RELLING   Good-bye, Mrs.—Werle. [*Exit through hall door.*]

GREGERS [*to* MRS. SØRBY]   It appears that you and Dr. Relling are rather intimately acquainted.

MRS. SØRBY   Yes, we've known each other a good many years. As a matter of fact, at one time something or other might have even come of it.

GREGERS   It was certainly lucky for you it didn't.

MRS. SØRBY   You may well say that. But I have always been careful not to act on impulse. After all, a woman can't afford to throw herself away.

GREGERS   Aren't you the least bit afraid I might drop a hint to my father about this old friendship?

MRS. SØRBY   You may be quite sure I told him myself.

GREGERS   Oh?

MRS. SØRBY   Your father knows every last thing that anyone could possibly say about me with any truth. I've told him everything of that kind. It was the first thing I did when I realized what he had in mind.

GREGERS   Then I'd say you are exceptionally frank.

MRS. SØRBY   I have always been frank. For us women it's the best policy.

HJALMAR   What do you say to that, Gina?

GINA   Oh, us women can't all be the same. Some's made one way and some another.

MRS. SØRBY Well, Gina, I do think it's best to go about things as I did. And Werle hasn't kept back anything about himself, either. You know, that's mainly what brought us together. With me he can sit and talk as openly as a child. He never got a chance to do that before. Imagine, a healthy, vigorous man like him, listening all his youth and the best years of his life to nothing but hell-fire sermons. And many a time sermons about completely imaginary offenses—to judge by what I've heard.

GINA That's God's truth, all right.

GREGERS If you ladies are going to embark on that topic, you'll have to excuse me.

MRS. SØRBY There's no need to go on that account. I won't say another word. But I wanted you to know that I haven't hushed up a thing or done anything underhanded. People may say I'm making quite a catch—and so I am, in a way. But still, I don't think I'm getting any more than I'm giving. I will never let him down. And I can look after him and help him as nobody else can, now that he'll soon be helpless.

HJALMAR Soon be helpless?

GREGERS [*to* MRS. SØRBY] All right, all right, don't talk about it here.

MRS. SØRBY It's no use trying to hide it any more, much as he'd like to. He's going blind.

HJALMAR [*struck*] Going blind? But how extraordinary. He too?

GINA Well, lots of people do.

MRS. SØRBY And you can imagine what that means for a businessman. Well, I'll try to use my eyes for him as best I can. But now I really must be going, I've got a thousand things to do.—Oh yes, Ekdal, I was to tell you that if there's anything at all Mr. Werle can do for you, just get in touch with Gråberg.

GREGERS That offer you may be sure Hjalmar Ekdal will decline with thanks.

MRS. SØRBY Really? I didn't have the impression in the past . . .

GINA No, Berta, Hjalmar don't need anything more from Mr. Werle.

HJALMAR [*slowly and with emphasis*] Will you pay my respects to your intended husband and tell him that in the very near future I propose to call on Gråberg . . .

GREGERS What! You want to do *that*!

HJALMAR . . . to call on Gråberg, I repeat, and demand an account of what I owe his employer. I will pay that debt of honor . . . Ha-ha-ha, "debt of honor," that's a good joke! But enough of that. I will pay it all, with five per cent interest.

GINA But Hjalmar, dear, God knows we haven't got the money for that.

HJALMAR Will you inform your intended that I am working indefatigably on my invention. Tell him that what sustains me in that exhausting labor is the wish to free myself from a painful burden of debt. This is my motive for the invention. The entire proceeds shall be used to release me from my pecuniary obligations to your future spouse.

MRS. SØRBY Something has happened in this house.

HJALMAR Yes, so it has.

MRS. SØRBY Well, good-bye then. I still had something I wanted to talk to you about, Gina, but it will have to wait for another time. Good-bye.

HJALMAR *and* GREGERS *bow silently;* GINA *follows* MRS. SØRBY *to the door.*

HJALMAR   Not a step beyond the threshold, Gina!

MRS. SØRBY *leaves;* GINA *shuts the door after her.*

HJALMAR   There, Gregers; now I've got that load of debt off my mind.
GREGERS   Soon, anyway.
HJALMAR   I believe my attitude may be called correct.
GREGERS   You are the man I always took you for.
HJALMAR   In certain cases it is impossible to disregard the claim of the ideal. As provider for my family, naturally I'm bound to writhe and groan. Believe me, it's no joke for a man without private means to pay off a debt of many years' standing—a debt over which, so to speak, the dust of oblivion had already settled. But never mind. My human dignity also demands its rights.
GREGERS   [*laying his hand on his shoulder*]   Dear Hjalmar—wasn't it a good thing that I came?
HJALMAR   Yes.
GREGERS   Getting your whole situation clarified—wasn't that a good thing?
HJALMAR   [*a bit impatiently*]   Yes, of course it was. But there's one thing that outrages my sense of justice.
GREGERS   And what is that?
HJALMAR   It's this, that . . . Well, I don't know if I ought to speak so freely about your father.
GREGERS   Don't hesitate in the least on *my* account.
HJALMAR   Well, then. Can't you see . . . I think it's absolutely outrageous, to realize it turns out that it's not I but *he* who will achieve the true marriage.
GREGERS   How can you say such a thing!
HJALMAR   Because it's so. Aren't your father and Mrs. Sørby entering upon a marriage built on full confidence, built on complete and unconditional frankness on both sides? They sweep nothing under the carpet, nothing is hushed up between them. There has been declared between them, if I may so put it, mutual forgiveness of sin.
GREGERS   All right, what about it?
HJALMAR   Well—then it's all *there.* You said yourself this was the difficulty in founding the true marriage.
GREGERS   But Hjalmar, that's entirely different. Surely you're not going to compare either yourself or her with those two . . . ? Oh, *you* know what I mean.
HJALMAR   All the same, I can't get over the fact that there's something in all this that offends my sense of justice. Why, it looks exactly as if there were no divine Providence in the world.
GINA   For God's sake, Hjalmar, don't talk like that.
GREGERS   Hm; let's not get involved in those questions.
HJALMAR   Though on the other hand, I think I'm beginning to make out the hand of fate after all. He *is* going blind.
GINA   Oh, maybe it's not so certain.
HJALMAR   There's no doubt about it. At least we *ought* not to doubt it, because precisely in that fact lies the proof of just retribution. He blinded the eyes of a trusting fellow being once.
GREGERS   Alas, he has blinded many.

HJALMAR   And now comes Nemesis, mysterious and inexorable, and demands the man's own eyes.[5]

GINA   Don't say such awful things! It scares me.

HJALMAR   It profits a man to immerse himself, once in a while, in the dark side of existence.

HEDVIG, *in her hat and coat, comes in through the hall door, happy and breathless.*

GINA   Are you back already?

HEDVIG   Yes, I didn't feel like walking any more. It was lucky, too, because I just met somebody outside the house.

HJALMAR   That Mrs. Sørby, I suppose.

HEDVIG   Yes.

HJALMAR   [*pacing the floor*]   I hope you have seen her for the last time.

Silence. HEDVIG *looks timidly from one to the other as though trying to gauge their mood.*

HEDVIG   [*approaching* HJALMAR, *ingratiatingly*]   Daddy . . . ?

HJALMAR   Well—what is it, Hedvig?

HEDVIG   Mrs. Sørby brought something for me.

HJALMAR   [*halts*]   For you?

HEDVIG   Yes. It's something for tomorrow.

GINA   Berta always brings some little thing for your birthday.

HJALMAR   What is it?

HEDVIG   No, you're not supposed to find out yet. Mother is to bring it to me in bed first thing in the morning.

HJALMAR   All these intrigues; all these secrets . . . !

HEDVIG   [*hastily*]   Oh, you can see it if you want. It's a big letter. [*Takes the letter out of her coat pocket.*]

HJALMAR   A letter too?

HEDVIG   The letter is all there is. The other thing is coming later on, I guess. But imagine—a letter! I never got a letter before. And it says "Miss" on the outside. [*Reads.*] "Miss Hedvig Ekdal." Imagine —that's me!

HJALMAR   Let me see that letter.

HEDVIG   [*handing it to him*]   There, you see?

HJALMAR   It's Mr. Werle's handwriting.

GINA   Are you sure, Hjalmar?

HJALMAR   See for yourself.

GINA   What would *I* know about it?

HJALMAR   Hedvig, may I open the letter—and read it?

HEDVIG   Yes, of course you may, if you want to.

GINA   Not tonight, Hjalmar. You know it's meant for tomorrow.

HEDVIG   [*in a low voice*]   Oh, why not let him read it! It's bound to be something nice, then he'll be glad and everything will be all right again.

HJALMAR   I may open it, then?

HEDVIG   Yes, please do, Father. It will be fun to find out what it is.

HJALMAR   Very well. [*Opens the letter, reads it, and appears bewildered.*] What *is* this . . . ?

GINA   Why, what does it say?

5. Nemesis was the Greek goddess of revenge, and the term is used still, as here, for providential retribution.

HEDVIG   Please, Father—tell us!

HJALMAR   Be quiet. [*Reads it through again. He has turned pale, but speaks with control.*] It's a bequest, Hedvig, a deed of gift.

HEDVIG   Really? What do I get?

HJALMAR   Read it yourself.

HEDVIG *goes over to the lamp and reads.*

HJALMAR [*in an undertone, clenching his fists*]   The eyes! The eyes— and now this letter!

HEDVIG [*interrupts her reading*]   Yes, but it looks to me like it's Grand-father who's getting it.

HJALMAR [*takes the letter from her*]   You, Gina—can you understand this?

GINA   I don't know the first thing about it. Why don't you just *tell* me?

HJALMAR   Mr. Werle writes to Hedvig that her old grandfather need not trouble himself any more about the copying but that from now on he can draw a hundred crowns every month from the office . . .

GREGERS   Aha!

HEDVIG   A hundred crowns, Mother! I read that part.

GINA   That will be nice for Grandpa.

HJALMAR   . . . one hundred crowns, for as long as he needs it— naturally that means till he passes on.

GINA   Well, that's him provided for, poor old soul.

HJALMAR   But then it comes. You didn't read far enough, Hedvig. Afterwards, the gift passes to you.

HEDVIG   To me? All of it?

HJALMAR   You are assured the same amount for the rest of your life, he writes. Do you hear that, Gina?

GINA   Yes, I hear.

HEDVIG   Imagine—all the money I'm going to get! [*Shaking him.*] Father, Father, aren't you glad?

HJALMAR [*disengages himself from her*]   Glad! [*Walking about.*] Oh, what vistas, what perspectives open up before me! It's Hedvig— *she's* the one he's providing for so amply!

GINA   Naturally. She's the one with the birthday . . .

HEDVIG   Oh, but you'll get it anyway, Father! Don't you know I'll give it all to you and Mother?

HJALMAR   To your mother, yes! There we have it.

GREGERS   Hjalmar, this is a trap that's being set for you.

HJALMAR   Another trap, you think?

GREGERS   When he was here this morning, he said: "Hjalmar Ekdal is not the man you think he is."

HJALMAR   Not the man . . . !

GREGERS   "Just wait, you'll see," he said.

HJALMAR   See that I would let myself be bought off with a bribe . . . !

HEDVIG   Mother, what *is* this all about?

GINA   Go and take off your things.

HEDVIG, *about to cry, goes out by the kitchen door.*

GREGERS   Yes, Hjalmar, now we see who is right—he or I.

HJALMAR [*slowly tears the letter in two and lays the pieces on the table*]   Here is my answer.

GREGERS   Just as I thought.

HJALMAR [*goes over to* GINA, *who is standing by the stove, and speaks in a low voice*]   Now, I want the whole truth. If everything was over between you and him when you—"got to care" for me, as you call it—why did he arrange things so we could afford to get married?

GINA   I guess he thought he'd be able to come and go here as he liked.

HJALMAR   Only that? Wasn't he afraid of a certain possibility?

GINA   I don't know what you mean.

HJALMAR   I want to know if—your child has the right to live under my roof.

GINA [*drawing herself up, her eyes flashing*]   You ask me that!

HJALMAR   I want a straight answer. Is Hedvig mine—or . . .   Well?

GINA [*looks at him with cold defiance*]   I don't know.

HJALMAR [*quavering*]   You don't know!

GINA   How should *I* know? A woman like me . . .

HJALMAR [*quietly, turning away from her*]   Then I have nothing more to do in this house.

GREGERS   Think well what you're doing, Hjalmar!

HJALMAR [*putting on his overcoat*]   There's nothing to think about, for a man like me.

GREGERS   On the contrary, there's everything in the world to think about. You three must stay together if you are to win through to the sublime spirit of sacrifice and forgiveness.

HJALMAR   I don't *want* to! Never! Never! My hat! [*Takes his hat.*] My house lies in ruins about me. [*Bursts into tears.*] Gregers, I have no child!

HEDVIG [*who has opened the kitchen door*]   What are you saying! [*Up to him.*] Father! Father!

GINA   *Now* look what you did!

HJALMAR   Don't come near me, Hedvig. Get away from me. I can't bear to look at you. Oh, those eyes . . . ! Good-bye. [*He makes for the door.*]

HEDVIG [*clinging to him, cries out*]   No! No! Don't leave me!

GINA [*shouts*]   Look at the child, Hjalmar! Look at the child!

HJALMAR   I won't! I can't! I must get out—away from all this. [*He tears himself loose from HEDVIG and goes.*]

HEDVIG [*despair in her eyes*]   He's leaving us, Mother! He's leaving us! He'll never come back any more!

GINA   Don't you cry, Hedvig. Your father's coming back, you'll see.

HEDVIG [*throws herself sobbing on the sofa*]   No, no, he's never coming back to us again.

GREGERS   You do believe I meant it all for the best, Mrs. Ekdal?

GINA   Yes, I imagine you did. But God forgive you all the same.

HEDVIG [*on the sofa*]   Oh, I just want to die! What did I do to him! Mother, you've got to get him home again!

GINA   Yes, yes, yes. Just calm down and I'll go out and look for him. [*Putting on her coat.*] Maybe he's gone down to Relling. But you mustn't lie there bawling like that. Promise?

HEDVIG [*sobbing convulsively*]   All right, I'll stop. If only Father comes back.

GREGERS [*to GINA, who is about to leave*]   Wouldn't it perhaps be better if you first let him go through his ordeal?

GINA   Oh, he can do that after. First of all we have to get the child quieted down. [*Goes out by hall door.*]

HEDVIG [*sitting up, drying her tears*]   Now you've got to tell me what's the matter. Why doesn't my father want me any more?

GREGERS   You're not to ask that till you're all grown up.

HEDVIG [*with little catches in her breath*]   But I can't go on feeling so awful all the time till I'm grown up.—I know what it is. Maybe I'm not really Father's child.

GREGERS [*uneasily*]   How could that be?

HEDVIG   Mother could have found me somewhere. And now maybe Father got to know about it. I've read about things like that.

GREGERS   Well, even in that case . . .

HEDVIG   You'd think he could care for me just the same. Even more, almost. After all, we got the wild duck as a present too, and look how much I love her.

GREGERS [*glad to change the subject*]   Yes, that's right, the wild duck. Let's talk a little about the wild duck, Hedvig.

HEDVIG   That poor wild duck. He can't stand the sight of her either, any more. Imagine, he wanted to wring her neck!

GREGERS   Oh, he wouldn't do that.

HEDVIG   No, but he *said* it. And I think it's an awful thing to say, because I pray for the wild duck every night, that she should be safe from death and everything bad.

GREGERS [*looking at her*]   Do you say your prayers every night?

HEDVIG   Oh yes.

GREGERS   Who taught you that?

HEDVIG   Myself. One time when Father was terribly sick and had leeches on his neck, and he said he was lying at death's door.

GREGERS   Really?

HEDVIG   So I prayed for him when I went to bed. And I've kept it up ever since.

GREGERS   And now you pray for the wild duck too?

HEDVIG   I thought I'd better include her, because she was so sick in the beginning.

GREGERS   Do you also say your prayers in the morning?

HEDVIG   Of course not.

GREGERS   Why *not* in the morning, as well?

HEDVIG   Why, it's light in the morning, so what's there to be afraid of.

GREGERS   And that wild duck you love so much, your father wanted to wring its neck . . .

HEDVIG   No, he said he *ought* to do it, but that he would spare her for my sake. That was nice of him.

GREGERS [*drawing closer to her*]   But supposing now that you of your own free will sacrificed the wild duck for *his* sake?

HEDVIG [*rising*]   The wild duck!

GREGERS   Supposing you were ready to sacrifice for him the most precious thing you have in the world?

HEDVIG   Do you think that would help?

GREGERS   Try it, Hedvig.

HEDVIG [*softly, with eyes shining*]   Yes—I will.

GREGERS   Have you will power enough for that, do you think?

HEDVIG   I'll ask Grandfather to shoot her for me.

GREGERS   Yes, do that. But not a word about this to your mother!

HEDVIG   Why not?

GREGERS   She doesn't understand us.

HEDVIG   The wild duck . . . ? I'll do it in the morning!

GINA *enters by the hall door.*

HEDVIG [*up to her*]   Did you find him, Mother?

GINA   No, but I heard he'd been down to Relling and gone out with him.

GREGERS   Are you sure?

GINA   Yes, the janitor's wife said so. Molvik went with them too, she said.

GREGERS   At a time like this, when his soul so desperately needs to struggle in solitude . . . !

GINA [*taking off her coat*]   Yes, men sure are something. God only knows where Relling dragged him off to. I ran across to Ma Eriksen's, but they're not there.

HEDVIG [*fighting back her tears*]   What if he never comes back!

GREGERS   *He'll* come back. I shall get word to him in the morning, and then you'll *see* how he comes back. You can count on that. Sleep well, Hedvig. Goodnight. [*Goes out by hall door.*]

HEDVIG [*throws her arms around* GINA's *neck, sobbing*]   Mother! Mother!

GINA [*patting her back, sighing*]   Ah, yes. Relling knew what he was talking about, all right. This is what you get when these here maniacs get after you with their "claim of the ordeal."

Act 5

HJALMAR EKDAL's *studio in the cold gray light of morning. There is wet snow on the big panes of the skylight.*

GINA, *aproned and carrying a broom and dust cloth, enters from the kitchen and goes toward the living room door. At the same moment,* HEDVIG *rushes in from the hall.*

GINA [*stops*]   Well?

HEDVIG   Yes, Mother, I think he is down at Relling's . . .

GINA   What did I tell you!

HEDVIG   . . . because the janitor's wife said she heard Relling bring home two others when he came back last night.

GINA   I thought as much.

HEDVIG   But what good does it do, if he won't come up to us.

GINA   Well, at least I can go down and talk to him.

OLD EKDAL, *in dressing gown and slippers and smoking his pipe, appears at the door of his room.*

EKDAL   Say, Hjalmar . . . Isn't Hjalmar home?

GINA   No, he's gone out.

EKDAL   So early? In this blizzard? All right, suit yourself, I can do the morning tour without you.

He slides the attic door open. HEDVIG *helps him. He goes in, and she closes the door after him.*

HEDVIG [*in a low voice*]   Mother, just think, when poor Grandfather finds out that Father wants to leave us.

GINA   Silly! Grandpa mustn't hear anything about it. What a godsend he wasn't home yesterday in all that hullaballoo.

HEDVIG   Yes, but . . .

GREGERS *enters through the hall door.*

GREGERS　Well? Any trace of him?

GINA　He's downstairs at Relling's, from what I hear.

GREGERS　At Relling's! Has he really been out with those two?

GINA　Looks like it.

GREGERS　How *could* he—just when he desperately needed to be alone and really pull himself together . . . !

GINA　You can say *that* again.

RELLING *enters from the hall.*

HEDVIG [*up to him*]　Is Father with you?

GINA [*at the same time*]　Is he there?

RELLING　Yes, he's there all right.

HEDVIG　And you never told us!

RELLING　I know, I'm a bea-east. But first I had to look after that other bea-east, the dæmonic one, I mean. And then I dropped off into such a heavy sleep that . . .

GINA　What's Hjalmar got to say today?

RELLING　Not a thing.

HEDVIG　Isn't he talking at all?

RELLING　Not a blessed word.

GREGERS　Ah, no. I understand that so well.

GINA　What's he doing with himself then?

RELLING　He's lying on the sofa, snoring.

GINA　Oh? Yes, Hjalmar snores something terrific.

HEDVIG　He's asleep? Can he sleep now?

RELLING　Looks damn well like it.

GREGERS　It's understandable, after the spiritual upheaval he's been through . . .

GINA　And him not used to gallivantin' nights, either.

HEDVIG　Maybe it's a good thing he's getting some sleep, Mother.

GINA　That's what I'm thinking too. But in that case we'd better not wake him up too soon. Thanks a lot, Relling. Well, first I'll get the house cleaned and straightened up, and then . . . Come and help me, Hedvig.

GINA *and* HEDVIG *go into the living room.*

GREGERS [*turns to* RELLING]　How would you describe the spiritual turmoil going on in Hjalmar Ekdal?

RELLING　I'm damned if I've noticed any spiritual turmoil in him.

GREGERS　What! At such a turning point, when his whole life has acquired a new foundation . . . ! How can you imagine that with a character like Hjalmar's . . . ?

RELLING　Character! *Him*? If he ever had a tendency to anything as abnormal as you mean by "character," I assure you it was cleared out of him root and branch while he was still a boy.

GREGERS　That would indeed be strange—considering the tender up-bringing he enjoyed.

RELLING　By those two crackpot, hysterical maiden aunts of his, you mean?

GREGERS　Let me tell you, *there* were women who never lost sight of the claim of the ideal . . . all right, now I suppose you'll start being funny again.

RELLING　No, I'm not in the mood. Besides, I know what I'm talking about, he has certainly spouted enough rhetoric about those "twin soul-mothers" of his. Personally, I don't think he has much to thank them for. Ekdal's misfortune is that in his own little circle he has always been taken for a shining light . . .

GREGERS   And you don't think he is? Deep down inside, I mean.

RELLING   I never noticed anything of the kind. That his father thought so—that doesn't mean a thing. The old Lieutenant always *was* a bit simple.

GREGERS   He's always been a man with the innocence of a child. That's what you don't understand.

RELLING   All right, all right. But then when our dear sweet Hjalmar managed to get into the University—after a fashion—right away he became the light of the future for his fellow students too. Of course, he was good-looking, the rascal—pink and white—just the type the girls fall for. And as he had that easy sentimentality and that appealing something in his voice, and a pretty knack for declaiming other people's poetry and other people's ideas . . .

GREGERS   [*indignantly*]   Is it Hjalmar Ekdal you're talking about like this?

RELLING   Yes, with your permission. For that's what he looks like inside, this idol you are groveling to.

GREGERS   I hardly think I'm as blind as all that.

RELLING   Well, you're not far from it. You see, you are a sick man, too.

GREGERS   There you are right.

RELLING   Yes indeed. Yours is a complicated case. First there's this pesky fever of integrity you suffer from. And then, what's even worse, you're forever going around in a delirium of adoration—forever butting in where you don't belong, looking for something to admire.

GREGERS   Well, I certainly won't find anything of the sort where I do belong.

RELLING   The trouble is, you're so shockingly mistaken about those fabulous beings you dream up around you. Here you are at it again, coming to a tenement with your claim of the ideal. Nobody in this house is solvent.

GREGERS   If that's all you think of Hjalmar Ekdal, how can you take pleasure in being everlastingly in his company?

RELLING   Good Lord, I'm supposed to be a doctor of sorts, though I'm ashamed to say it. The least I can do is look after the sick I live in the same house with.

GREGERS   Really! Is Hjalmar Ekdal sick too?

RELLING   Pretty nearly everybody is sick, I'm afraid.

GREGERS   And what treatment are you giving Hjalmar?

RELLING   The usual. I see to it that his life-lie is kept going.

GREGERS   Life—lie? Did I hear you right . . . ?

RELLING   That's right, I said life-lie. You see, the life-lie is the stimulating principle.

GREGERS   May I ask what life-lie you're injecting into Hjalmar?

RELLING   Sorry, I don't betray professional secrets to quacks. You'd be in a position to mess him up for me even worse than you have. But the method is tried and true. I've used it on Molvik as well. Him I made "dæmonic"—that's *his* shot in the arm.

GREGERS   Then he's *not* dæmonic?

RELLING   What the devil does it mean, to be dæmonic? It's just some nonsense I hit on to keep life in him. If I hadn't done that, the poor harmless slob would have succumbed to self-contempt and despair years ago. Same with the old Lieutenant. Though he managed to find his treatment by himself.

GREGERS   Lieutenant Ekdal? What about him?

RELLING   Well, what do *you* think? He, the great bear-hunter, stalking rabbits in that dark attic. And there's not a happier sportsman alive than that old man when he's playing around in there with all that rubbish. The four or five dried-up Christmas trees he saved up, to him they're the same as the whole great living Højdal forest. The rooster and chickens, why, they're wild fowl in the treetops; and the rabbits bumping around underfoot, they are bears he grapples with, the lusty old Nimrod.

GREGERS   Poor, unfortunate old Lieutenant Ekdal—yes. He has certainly had to renounce the ideals of his youth.

RELLING   While I think of it, Mr. Werle junior—don't use this fancy word "ideals." We have a perfectly good plain one: lies.

GREGERS   Are you trying to say the two things are related?

RELLING   Yes, about like typhus and typhoid fever.

GREGERS   Dr. Relling, I won't give up till I have rescued Hjalmar from your clutches!

RELLING   So much the worse for him. Take away the life-lie from the average person, and you take his happiness along with it. [*To* HEDVIG, *who enters from the living room.*] Well, little duck-mother, I'll go down and see if Papa is still lying there pondering on that remarkable invention. [*Goes out by the hall door.*]

GREGERS   [*approaching* HEDVIG]   I can see by your look that it's not yet accomplished.

HEDVIG   What? Oh, about the wild duck. No.

GREGERS   Your courage failed you, I suppose, when it came to the point.

HEDVIG   No, it's not that. But when I woke up this morning and remembered what we had talked about, it seemed so queer.

GREGERS   Queer?

HEDVIG   Yes, I don't know . . . Last night, right when you said it, I thought there was something so lovely about the idea; but after I slept and it all came back to me again, it didn't seem like anything much.

GREGERS   Ah no, you could hardly be expected to grow up in this house without being the worse for it in some way.

HEDVIG   I don't care anything about that. If only my father would come back . . .

GREGERS   Ah, had your eyes but been opened to what really makes life worthwhile—had you the true, joyful, courageous spirit of sacrifice, then you would see how fast he'd come back to you.—But I still have faith in you, Hedvig. [*He goes out through hall door.*]

> HEDVIG *wanders about the room. She is about to go into the kitchen, when there is a knocking from within the attic.* HEDVIG *goes and opens the door a little way.* OLD EKDAL *comes out; she pushes the door to again.*

EKDAL   Hm, not much fun going for your morning walk by yourself.

HEDVIG   Wouldn't you like to go hunting, Grandfather?

EKDAL   It's not hunting weather today. So *dark*. You can hardly see in front of you.

HEDVIG   Don't you ever feel like shooting something besides rabbits?

EKDAL   Why, aren't the rabbits good enough, maybe?

HEDVIG   Yes, but how about the wild duck?

EKDAL   Ho, ho, so you're scared I'll go and shoot your wild duck? Never in the world, child. Never.

HEDVIG   No, I guess you couldn't. It's supposed to be very hard to shoot wild ducks.

EKDAL   Couldn't I? Should hope to say I could.

HEDVIG   How would you go about it, Grandfather?—I don't mean with *my* wild duck, but with some other one.

EKDAL   Would aim to get the shot in just below the breast, you know. That's the surest. And then you've got to shoot *against* the lie of the feathers, see, not *with*.

HEDVIG   Do they die then, Grandfather?

EKDAL   Damn right they die—if you shoot 'em properly. Well, got to go and spruce up. Hm . . . you know why . . . hm. [*Goes into his room.*]

> HEDVIG *waits a moment, glances toward the living room door, goes to the bookcase, and, standing on tiptoe, takes the double-barreled pistol down off the shelf and looks at it.* GINA, *with broom and dust cloth, enters from the living room.* HEDVIG *hastily puts back the pistol, without* GINA *noticing.*

GINA   Don't go fooling with your father's things, Hedvig.

HEDVIG [*moving away from the bookcase*]   I only wanted to straighten up a little.

GINA   Why don't you go in the kitchen and see if the coffee is still hot, I'm taking a tray down to him when I go.

> HEDVIG *goes out.* GINA *begins to clear the studio. Presently the hall door is hesitantly opened, and* HJALMAR EKDAL *looks in. He has his overcoat on, but no hat. He looks unwashed and unkempt; his eyes are sleepy and dull.*

GINA [*stops in the midst of sweeping and looks at him*]   Bless me, Hjalmar—are you back after all?

HJALMAR [*enters, answers in a dull voice*]   I come—only to depart at once.

GINA   Yes, yes, I imagine. But, gosh sakes! Don't you look a sight!

HJALMAR   A sight?

GINA   And just look at your good winter coat! Well, that's had it.

HEDVIG [*at the kitchen door*]   Mother, do you want me . . . [*Sees* HJALMAR, *gives a shout of joy and runs toward him.*] Father! Father!

HJALMAR [*turns aside and waves her away*]   Go away! Go away! [*To* GINA.] Get her away from me, I tell you!

GINA [*in a low voice*]   Go in the living room, Hedvig.

> HEDVIG *goes in silently.*

HJALMAR [*busy, pulling out the table drawer*]   I must have my books with me. Where are my books?

GINA   What books?

HJALMAR   My scientific works, naturally—the technical journals I use for my invention.

GINA [*looking in the bookcase*]   Is it these here that there's no covers on?

HJALMAR   Yes, of course.

GINA [*puts a pile of unbound volumes on the table*]   Shouldn't I get Hedvig to cut the pages for you?

HJALMAR   Nobody needs to cut pages for me.

Short silence.

GINA   So you've made up your mind to leave us, Hjalmar?

HJALMAR [*rummaging among the books*]   That goes without saying, I should think.

GINA   All right.

HJALMAR [*vehemently*]   You expect me to stay around here and have a knife twisted in my heart every minute of the day?

GINA   God forgive you for thinking I could be that bad.

HJALMAR   Prove to me . . . !

GINA   Seems to me *you're* the one that's got something to prove.

HJALMAR   With a past like yours? There are certain claims . . . I am tempted to call them claims of the ideal . . .

GINA   And what about Grandpa? What's to become of *him*, poor old thing?

HJALMAR   I know my duty. The helpless old man comes with me. I must go into town and make the necessary arrangements . . . Hm . . . [*Hesitantly.*] Has anybody found my hat on the stairs?

GINA   No. Did you lose your hat?

HJALMAR   Of course I had it on when I came back last night, there's no doubt about that. But now I can't find it.

GINA   Gosh sakes, wherever did you go with them two rowdies?

HJALMAR   Oh, don't bother me with trivialities. Do you think I'm in a mood to remember details?

GINA   I only hope you didn't catch a cold, Hjalmar. [*Goes into kitchen.*]

HJALMAR [*talking angrily to himself in a low voice as he empties the drawer*]   You're a scoundrel, Relling!—A villain is what you are! You rotten traitor!—If I could just get somebody to murder you!

> He puts some old letters to one side, finds the torn gift document of the day before, picks it up and looks at the pieces. As GINA *enters, he quickly puts them down again.*

GINA [*setting a laden coffee tray on the table*]   Here's a drop of something hot, in case you'd like it. And some cold cuts.

HJALMAR [*glances at the tray*]   Cold cuts? Never again, under this roof! True, I've taken no solid nourishment for nearly twenty-four hours, but never mind.—My notes! The beginning of my memoirs! Where have you put my diary and all my important papers? [*Opens the door to the living room, but draws back.*] There she is again!

GINA   For God's sake, Hjalmar, the child's got to be *some*place.

HJALMAR   Get out.

He stands back. HEDVIG, *terrified, comes into the studio.*

HJALMAR [*his hand on the doorknob, to* GINA]   As I spend these last moments in what was once my home, I wish to be spared the presence of intruders . . . [*Goes into the living room.*]

HEDVIG [*darting towards her mother, asks in a low and trembling voice*]   Does he mean me?

GINA   Stay in the kitchen, Hedvig. Or no—better go to your own room.

[*To* HJALMAR, *as she goes in to him.*] Wait a minute, Hjalmar, don't mess up the whole bureau. I know where everything is.

HEDVIG [*stands motionless for a moment, in terror and confusion, biting her lips to keep from crying. Then she clenches her hands convulsively and says softly*] The wild duck!

> She steals across and takes the pistol from the shelf, opens the attic door a little, slips in and pulls it shut after her. HJALMAR *and* GINA *begin arguing in the living room.*

HJALMAR [*appears with some notebooks and a pile of old sheets of paper, which he puts on the table*] Oh, what good will the valise do! There are a thousand things I've got to drag along with me.

GINA [*follows with the valise*]   Well, leave the rest for the time being, just take a clean shirt and some underwear.

HJALMAR   Phew! All these exhausting preparations! [*Takes off his overcoat and throws it on the sofa.*]

GINA   Meantime your coffee's standing there getting cold.

HJALMAR   Hm. [*Without thinking, he takes a mouthful, and then another.*]

GINA [*dusting the backs of the chairs*]   Your worst job will be finding another attic big enough for the rabbits.

HJALMAR   What! Am I expected to drag along all those rabbits too?

GINA   Well, Grandpa can't do without his rabbits, you know that.

HJALMAR   He'll just have to get used to it. There are more important things in life than rabbits that I have to give up.

GINA [*dusting the bookcase*]   Should I put your flute in the bag for you?

HJALMAR   No. No flute for me. But give me the pistol.

GINA   You want to take that old gun with you?

HJALMAR   Yes. My loaded pistol.

GINA [*looking for it*]   It's gone. He must have taken it in with him.

HJALMAR   Is he in the attic?

GINA   Sure he's in the attic.

HJALMAR   Hm. Poor lonely old man. [*He eats an open-face sandwich, finishes his cup of coffee.*]

GINA   If only we hadn't rented out the room, you could've moved in there.

HJALMAR   And stay under the same roof as . . . ! Never! Never!

GINA   But couldn't you move into the living room for a day or two? There you could have everything all to yourself.

HJALMAR   Never, within these walls!

GINA   Well, how about moving in with Relling and Molvik, then?

HJALMAR   Don't mention their names to me! I get sick just thinking about them. Oh no, I must out into the storm and the snowdrifts— go from house to house seeking shelter for my father and myself.

GINA   But Hjalmar, you haven't got a hat! You lost your hat, remember?

HJALMAR   Oh, that despicable pair, those depraved villains! A hat must be procured. [*Takes another sandwich.*] Arrangements must be made. After all, I don't propose to catch my death of cold. [*Looks for something on the tray.*]

GINA   What are you looking for?

HJALMAR   Butter.

GINA   In a minute. [*Goes into the kitchen.*]

HJALMAR [*calls after her*]   Oh, don't bother. Dry bread is good enough for me.

GINA [*bringing a butter dish*]   Here you are. It's fresh churned, they told me.

> *She pours him another cup of coffee. He sits down on the sofa, spreads more butter on his bread, eats and drinks in silence for a while.*

HJALMAR   Could I, without being interfered with by anyone—and I mean *anyone*—stay in the living room a day or two, do you suppose?

GINA   Sure you could, if you wanted.

HJALMAR   Because I don't see much likelihood of moving all of Father's things in such a rush.

GINA   And another thing, too. First you'll have to tell him you're not going to live with us others no more.

HJALMAR [*pushes his cup away*]   That too, yes. To have to go into all these complicated matters all over again . . . I must consider ways and means. I must have breathing space. I can't take on all these burdens in a single day.

GINA   No, and in such rotten weather, too.

HJALMAR [*moving Werle's letter*]   I see this paper is still lying around.

GINA   Yes, *I* didn't touch it.

HJALMAR   Not that that scrap of paper concerns me . . .

GINA   Well, *I* certainly don't intend to use it.

HJALMAR   . . . still, I don't suppose we should just let it get destroyed. In all the confusion while I'm moving out it could easily . . .

GINA   I'll take care of it, Hjalmar.

HJALMAR   After all, the letter belongs to Father in the first place; it's his business whether he wants to make use of it or not.

GINA [*sighing*]   Yes, poor old Father . . .

HJALMAR   Just to be on the safe side . . . Where will I find some paste?

GINA [*goes to the bookshelf*]   Here's the paste.

HJALMAR   And a brush?

GINA   The brush is here too. [*Brings him the things.*]

HJALMAR [*picks up a pair of scissors*]   Just a strip of paper along the back . . . [*Cutting and pasting.*] Far be it from me to lay hands on somebody else's property—least of all a penniless old man's. —Well, or on—the other person's, either . . . There we are. Let it stay there a while. And when it's dry—remove it. I don't wish to lay eyes on that document again. Ever!

> GREGERS WERLE *enters from the hall.*

GREGERS [*a little surprised*]   What—you sitting here, Hjalmar?

HJALMAR [*gets up quickly*]   I sank down from sheer exhaustion.

GREGERS   I see you've had breakfast, though.

HJALMAR   The body, too, makes claims on us occasionally.

GREGERS   What have you decided to do?

HJALMAR   For a man like myself there is but one way open. I am in the process of gathering together my most important possessions. But you realize it takes time.

GINA [*a bit impatient*]   Well, do I get the room ready for you, or do I pack the bag?

HJALMAR [*after an irritated glance at* GREGERS]   Pack—and get the room ready.

GINA [*takes the valise*]   All right. I'll put in the shirt and the other things, then. [*Goes into the living room and shuts the door behind her.*]

GREGERS [*after a short pause*]   I never dreamed it would end like this. Is it really necessary for you to leave house and home?

HJALMAR [*paces restlessly up and down*]   What do you expect me to do?—I'm not made for unhappiness, Gregers. I must have things nice and secure and peaceful around me.

GREGERS   But *can't* you stay? Just try. To my mind you now have a firm foundation to build on—so start all over again. And remember, you have your invention to live for, besides.

HJALMAR   Oh, don't talk about the invention. It may be a long way off yet.

GREGERS   Really?

HJALMAR   For God's sake, what do you expect me to invent, anyway? They've already invented just about everything. It gets to be more difficult every day . . .

GREGERS   After all the work you've put into it . . . !

HJALMAR   It was that dissolute Relling who got me into it.

GREGERS   Relling?

HJALMAR   Yes, he was the one who first called attention to my talent for making some marvelous invention or other in photography.

GREGERS   Aha! . . . It was Relling!

HJALMAR   Oh, what deep satisfaction I got out of that thing. Not so much the invention itself, but because Hedvig believed in it—believed with all the faith and fervor of a child . . . that is, like a fool I went around imagining she believed in it.

GREGERS   Can you really think that Hedvig deceived you!

HJALMAR   I'm ready to think anything now. It's Hedvig that stands in the way. She'll end up shutting the sun out of my life forever.

GREGERS   Hedvig! You mean Hedvig? How could *she* do anything like that?

HJALMAR [*without answering*]   It's beyond words, how I loved that child. Beyond words, how happy I was every time I came home to my humble rooms and she would run to greet me, with her sweet blinking eyes. Oh, credulous fool that I was! I loved her so unutterably—and so I persuaded myself of the fiction that she loved me the same.

GREGERS   Are you saying it wasn't true?

HJALMAR   How can I tell? Gina I can't get a word out of. And anyway she has absolutely no conception of the principles involved in the situation. But I do feel the need to unburden myself to you, Gregers. It's this terrible doubt . . . Maybe Hedvig never really loved me at all.

GREGERS   You may yet have proof that she did. [*Listening.*] What's that? The wild duck's cry?

HJALMAR   She's quacking. Father's in there.

GREGERS   Is he! [*Joy lights up his face.*] I tell you, you may yet have proof that your poor misunderstood Hedvig loves you!

HJALMAR   Oh, what proof can she give me! I don't dare believe in any assurance from *that* quarter.

GREGERS   Surely Hedvig is incapable of deception.

HJALMAR   Oh, Gregers, that's just what isn't so certain. Who knows what Gina and that Mrs. Sørby have sat here whispering and tittle-tattling about? And nothing escapes Hedvig, believe me. It could even be that the birthday gift wasn't such a surprise. As a matter of fact, I thought I noticed something of the kind.

GREGERS   What on earth has got into you!

HJALMAR   My eyes have been opened. Just you watch—you'll see, the gift is only a beginning. Mrs. Sørby always did have a great lik-ing for Hedvig, and now of course she's in a position to do whatever she wants for the child. They can take her away from me any time they like.

GREGERS   Hedvig would never leave you. Never.

HJALMAR   Don't be too sure. With them standing and beckoning to her with full hands? And I who have loved her so unutterably . . . ! I, whose greatest joy it would have been to take her gently by the hand and lead her, as one leads a child that's afraid of the dark through a great empty room! —I feel it now with painful certainty— the poor photographer in his attic apartment never really meant any-thing to her. She was just shrewd enough to play along with him till the time was ripe.

GREGERS   Hjalmar, you don't believe that yourself.

HJALMAR   The terrible thing is just that I don't know what to believe —that I can *never* know. But do you really doubt that I'm right? Hoho, my dear Gregers, you count too much on the claim of the ideal! Just let the others come with overflowing hands and call to the child: Leave him; life awaits you here with us . . .

GREGERS [*quickly*]   Yes, what then, do you think?

HJALMAR   If I asked her then: Hedvig, are you willing to turn your back on life for me? [*Laughs scornfully.*] Thanks a lot—you'd soon hear the answer I'd get!

A pistol shot is heard from within the attic.

GREGERS [*shouts with joy*]   Hjalmar!

HJALMAR   Damn! He *would* have to go hunting now!

GINA [*entering*]   Ugh, Hjalmar, it sounds like the old man's banging away in there by himself.

HJALMAR   I'll go have a look . . .

GREGERS [*quickly, excitedly*]   Wait! Do you know what that was?

HJALMAR   Of course I know.

GREGERS   No, you don't. But *I* know. That was the proof!

HJALMAR   What proof?

GREGERS   It was a child's act of sacrifice. She's got your father to shoot the wild duck.

HJALMAR   Shoot the wild duck!

GINA   Imagine . . . !

HJALMAR   Whatever for?

GREGERS   She wanted to sacrifice to you the most precious thing she had in the world. Because then, she thought, you would be sure to love her again.

HJALMAR [*softly, with emotion*]   Oh, that child!

GINA   The things she'll think of!

GREGERS   All she wanted was to have your love again, Hjalmar. She felt she couldn't live without it.

GINA [*fighting back her tears*]   There you see, Hjalmar.

HJALMAR   Gina, where is she?

GINA [*sniffling*]   Poor little thing, sitting out in the kitchen, I guess.

HJALMAR [*crosses, and throws open the kitchen door*]   Hedvig—come! Come to me! [*Looks around.*] No, she's not in here.

GINA   Then she must be in her little room. [HJALMAR *walks out.*]

HJALMAR [*offstage*]   No, she's not here either. [*Re-enters the studio.*] She must have gone out.

GINA   Well, you wouldn't let her stay anyplace in the house.

HJALMAR   Oh, if only she'd come home soon—so I can tell her . . . Everything will be all right now, Gregers. Now I really believe we can start life over again.

GREGERS [*quietly*]   I knew it. Redemption would come through the child.

> OLD EKDAL *appears at the door of his room. He is in full uniform, and is busy trying to buckle on his saber.*

HJALMAR [*astonished*]   Father! You *there?*

GINA   You were shooting in your *room?*

EKDAL [*approaches indignantly*]   So, now you go hunting without me, do you, Hjalmar?

HJALMAR [*tense, bewildered*]   You mean it wasn't you that fired the shot in the attic?

EKDAL   Me? Hm!

GREGERS [*calls out to* HJALMAR]   She has shot the wild duck herself!

HJALMAR   What *is* all this? [*Rushes to the attic door, tears it open, looks in, and screams.*] Hedvig!

GINA [*running to the door*]   My God, what is it?

HJALMAR [*going inside*]   She's lying on the floor!

GREGERS   Hedvig? On the floor? [*Follows* HJALMAR *in.*]

GINA [*at the same time*]   Hedvig! [*Enters the attic.*] No! No! No!

EKDAL   Ho-ho, so *she's* taken to hunting too, now.

> HJALMAR, GINA, *and* GREGERS *carry* HEDVIG *into the studio. Her right hand hangs down, the fingers still gripping the pistol.*

HJALMAR [*dazed*]   The pistol went off. She's been hit. Call for help! Help!

GINA [*runs out into the hall and shouts down*]   Relling! Relling! Dr. Relling, come up here quick!

> HJALMAR *and* GREGERS *lay* HEDVIG *down on the sofa.*

EKDAL [*quietly*]   The forest's revenge.

HJALMAR [*on his knees beside* HEDVIG]   She'll come to, right away. She's coming to—yes, yes, yes.

GINA [*having returned*]   Where is she hit? I can't see a thing . . .

> RELLING *hurries in, followed closely by* MOLVIK. *The latter is without vest or collar, and his jacket is unbuttoned.*

RELLING   What's going on here?

GINA   They say Hedvig shot herself.

HJALMAR   Come here and help!

RELLING   Shot herself! [*He pushes the table aside and starts to examine her.*]

HJALMAR [*still kneeling, looking anxiously up at him*]   Surely it can't be serious? What, Relling? She's hardly bleeding at all. Surely it can't be serious?

RELLING   How did this happen?

HJALMAR   Oh, how do I know . . .

GINA   She wanted to shoot the wild duck.

RELLING   The wild duck?

HJALMAR   The pistol must have gone off by itself.

RELLING   Hm. Indeed.

EKDAL   The forest's revenge. Still, I'm not afraid. [*Goes into the attic and shuts himself in.*]

HJALMAR   Well, Relling . . . why don't you *say* something?

RELLING   The bullet entered the chest.

HJALMAR   Yes, but she's coming to!

RELLING   Can't you see? Hedvig is dead.

GINA [*bursts into tears*]   Oh, my baby! My baby!

GREGERS [*huskily*]   In the depths of the sea . . .

HJALMAR [*springing up*]   No, no, she's got to live! Oh dear God, Relling—just for a moment—just long enough so I can tell her how unutterably I loved her the whole time!

RELLING   The heart's been hit. Internal hemorrhage. She died instantly.

HJALMAR   And I drove her away from me like an animal! And in terror she crept into the attic and died for love of me. [*Sobbing.*] Never to be able to make up for it! Never to be able to tell her . . . ! [*Clenches his hands and cries to heaven.*] Oh, Thou above . . . ! If Thou *art* there! Why hast Thou done this thing to me . . .

GINA   Hush, hush, you mustn't carry on like this. I guess maybe we didn't have the right to keep her.

MOLVIK   The child is not dead. She but sleeps.

RELLING   Nonsense.

HJALMAR [*quiets down, goes over to the sofa, folds his arms, and looks at* HEDVIG]   There she lies, so stiff and still.

RELLING [*trying to free the pistol*]   It's so tight, so tight.

GINA   No, no, Relling, don't hurt her fingers. Leave the gun be.

HJALMAR   She shall take it with her.

GINA   Yes, let her. But the child's not going to lie out here for a show. She'll go into her own little room, that's what. Give me a hand, Hjalmar.

> HJALMAR *and* GINA *take* HEDVIG *between them.*

HJALMAR [*as they carry her out*]   Oh, Gina, Gina, can you bear this!

GINA   We'll have to help each other. Now she's as much yours as mine.

MOLVIK [*stretching forth his arms and mumbling*]   Praised be the name of the Lord. Dust unto dust . . . dust unto dust . . .

RELLING [*whispers*]   Shut up, man! You're drunk.

> HJALMAR *and* GINA *carry the body out by the kitchen door.* RELLING *shuts it after them.* MOLVIK *slinks out into the hall.*

RELLING [*crosses to* GREGERS]   No one will ever persuade me that this was an accident.

GREGERS [*who has stood horror-stricken, twitching convulsively*]   Who can say how this terrible thing happened.

RELLING   There were powder burns on her dress. She must have pressed the muzzle right against her chest and fired.

GREGERS Hedvig has not died in vain. Did you see how this sorrow brought out all the nobility in him?

RELLING Most people become noble when they stand in the presence of death. But how long do you think this glory of his will last?

GREGERS Surely it will last and flourish for the rest of his life!

RELLING Before the year is out little Hedvig will be nothing more to him than a theme for pretty declamations.

GREGERS You dare say that about Hjalmar Ekdal!

RELLING We'll talk about it again when the first grass has withered on her grave. *Then* listen to the vomit about "the child untimely torn from its father's breast," *then* watch him wallow in sentimentality and self-admiration and self-pity. Just you wait!

GREGERS If *you* are right, and *I* am wrong, then life's not worth living.

RELLING Oh, life wouldn't be too bad if it weren't for these blessed bill collectors who come pestering us poor folk with their claims of the ideal.

GREGERS [*staring into space*] In that case, I'm glad my destiny is what it is.

RELLING And may I ask—what *is* your destiny?

GREGERS [*on the point of leaving*] To be the thirteenth man at the table.

RELLING The devil it is.

EUROPEAN TITLES

In reading a play like *The Wild Duck*, one should remember that certain titles or forms of address carried a different implication for the nineteenth-century European than they would for twentieth-century Americans. Three used in the play require some elucidation.

When Pettersen tells the hired servant that old Ekdal was once a lieutenant, the response of the hired servant depends on the fact that the title indicated other than the kind of callow incompetent implied in our familiar term "shavetail." Officers of all ranks were generally members of distinguished and well-to-do families, sometimes younger sons who were destined for the army from birth. Understanding this about old Ekdal, we can better appreciate Hjalmar's sense of disgrace in the fallen fortunes of his family and his comments to Gregers about Gina, which imply that he had married beneath him.

At this period titles of nobility had been abolished in Norway, but the title "chamberlain" (*Kammerherr*) was used to indicate officers of the royal court, in many cases certainly honorary officers.

The term "Miss" (*Frøken*), which Hedvig is pleased to find before her name on the letter containing the deed of gift, implied not only that she was growing up but also a certain amount of social status, as the same term implies in the title of Strindberg's *Fröken Julie* (variously translated "Miss Julie" or "Lady Julia").

II

LUIGI PIRANDELLO

Six Characters in Search of an Author [*]

A COMEDY IN THE MAKING

CHARACTERS OF THE COMEDY IN THE MAKING

THE FATHER	THE BOY
THE MOTHER	THE CHILD
THE STEPDAUGHTER	(*The last two do not speak.*)
THE SON	MADAME PACE

ACTORS OF THE COMPANY

THE MANAGER	PROPERTY MAN
LEADING LADY	PROMPTER
LEADING MAN	MACHINIST
SECOND LADY LEAD	MANAGER'S SECRETARY
L'INGÉNUE	DOORKEEPER
JUVENILE LEAD	SCENE-SHIFTERS
OTHER ACTORS AND ACTRESSES	

SCENE: *Daytime. The stage of a theater.*

N. B. *The Comedy is without acts or scenes. The performance is interrupted once, without the curtain being lowered, when the manager and the chief characters withdraw to arrange the scenario. A second interruption of the action takes place when, by mistake, the stage hands let the curtain down.*

Act 1

The spectators will find the curtain raised and the stage as it usually is during the day time. It will be half dark, and empty, so that from the beginning the public may have the impression of an impromptu performance.

Prompter's box and a small table and chair for the MANAGER. *Two other small tables and several chairs scattered about as during rehearsals.*

The ACTORS *and* ACTRESSES *of the company enter from the back of the stage: first one, then another, then two together; nine or ten in all. They are about to rehearse a Pirandello play: Mixing It Up.[1] Some of the company move off towards their dressing rooms. The* PROMPTER, *who has the "book" under his arm, is waiting for the* MANAGER *in order to begin the rehearsal.*

[*] Translated by Edward Storer.

1. The play referred to is Pirandello's *Il Giuoco delle Parti* (1918).

The ACTORS *and* ACTRESSES, *some standing, some sitting, chat and smoke. One perhaps reads a paper; another cons his part.*

Finally, the MANAGER *enters and goes to the table prepared for him. His* SECRETARY *brings him his mail, through which he glances. The* PROMPTER *takes his seat, turns on a light, and opens the "book."*

THE MANAGER [*throwing a letter down on the table*]   I can't see. [*To* PROPERTY MAN.] Let's have a little light, please!

PROPERTY MAN   Yes sir, yes, at once. [*A light comes down on to the stage.*]

THE MANAGER [*clapping his hands*]   Come along! Come along! Second act of "Mixing It Up." [*Sits down.*]

The ACTORS *and* ACTRESSES *go from the front of the stage to the wings, all except the three who are to begin the rehearsal.*

THE PROMPTER [*reading the "book"*]   "Leo Gala's house. A curious room serving as dining-room and study."

THE MANAGER [*to* PROPERTY MAN]   Fix up the old red room.

PROPERTY MAN [*noting it down*]   Red set. All right!

THE PROMPTER [*continuing to read from the "book"*]   "Table already laid and writing desk with books and papers. Book-shelves. Exit rear to Leo's bedroom. Exit left to kitchen. Principal exit to right."

THE MANAGER [*energetically*]   Well, you understand: The principal exit over there; here, the kitchen. [*Turning to actor who is to play the part of* SOCRATES.] You make your entrances and exits here. [*To* PROPERTY MAN.] The baize doors at the rear, and curtains.

PROPERTY MAN [*noting it down*]   Right!

PROMPTER [*reading as before*]   "When the curtain rises, Leo Gala, dressed in cook's cap and apron, is busy beating an egg in a cup. Philip, also dressed as a cook, is beating another egg. Guido Venanzi is seated and listening."

LEADING MAN [*to* MANAGER]   Excuse me, but must I absolutely wear a cook's cap?

THE MANAGER [*annoyed*]   I imagine so. It says so there anyway. [*Pointing to the "book."*]

LEADING MAN   But it's ridiculous!

THE MANAGER [*jumping up in a rage*]   Ridiculous? Ridiculous? Is it my fault if France won't send us any more good comedies, and we are reduced to putting on Pirandello's works, where nobody understands anything, and where the author plays the fool with us all? [*The* ACTORS *grin. The* MANAGER *goes to* LEADING MAN *and shouts.*] Yes sir, you put on the cook's cap and beat eggs. Do you suppose that with all this egg-beating business you are on an ordinary stage? Get that out of your head. You represent the shell of the eggs you are beating! [*Laughter and comments among the* ACTORS.] Silence! and listen to my explanations, please! [*To* LEADING MAN.] "The empty form of reason without the fullness of instinct, which is blind."—You stand for reason, your wife is instinct. It's a mixing up of the parts, according to which you who act your own part become the puppet of yourself. Do you understand?

LEADING MAN   I'm hanged if I do.

THE MANAGER   Neither do I. But let's get on with it. It's sure to be a glorious failure anyway. [*Confidentially.*] But I say, please face three-quarters. Otherwise, what with the abstruseness of the dialogue, and the public that won't be able to hear you, the whole thing will go to hell. Come on! come on!

PROMPTER   Pardon sir, may I get into my box? There's a bit of a draught.

THE MANAGER   Yes, yes, of course!

At this point, the DOORKEEPER *has entered from the stage door and advances towards the* MANAGER'S *table, taking off his braided cap. During this maneuver, the* SIX CHARACTERS *enter, and stop by the door at back of stage, so that when the* DOORKEEPER *is about to announce their coming to the* MANAGER, *they are already on the stage. A tenuous light surrounds them, almost as if irradiated by them—the faint breath of their fantastic reality.*

This light will disappear when they come forward toward the actors. They preserve, however, something of the dream lightness in which they seem almost suspended; but this does not detract from the essential reality of their forms and expressions.

He who is known as the FATHER *is a man of about 50: hair, reddish in color, thin at the temples; he is not bald, however; thick mustaches, falling over his still fresh mouth, which often opens in an empty and uncertain smile. He is fattish, pale; with an especially wide forehead. He has blue, oval-shaped eyes, very clear and piercing. Wears light trousers and a dark jacket. He is alternatively mellifluous and violent in his manner.*

The MOTHER *seems crushed and terrified as if by an intolerable weight of shame and abasement. She is dressed in modest black and wears a thick widow's veil of crêpe. When she lifts this, she reveals a wax-like face. She always keeps her eyes downcast.*

The STEPDAUGHTER *is dashing, almost impudent, beautiful. She wears mourning too, but with great elegance. She shows contempt for the timid half-frightened manner of the wretched* BOY (14 *years old, and also dressed in black); on the other hand, she displays a lively tenderness for her little sister, the* CHILD (*about four*), *who is dressed in white, with a black silk sash at the waist.*

The SON (22) *tall, severe in his attitude of contempt for the* FATHER, *supercilious and indifferent to the* MOTHER. *He looks as if he had come on the stage against his will.*

DOORKEEPER [*cap in hand*]   Excuse me, sir . . .

THE MANAGER [*rudely*]   Eh? What is it?

DOORKEEPER [*timidly*]   These people are asking for you, sir.

THE MANAGER [*furious*]   I am rehearsing, and you know perfectly well no one's allowed to come in during rehearsals! [*Turning to the* CHARACTERS.] Who are you, please? What do you want?

THE FATHER [*coming forward a little, followed by the others who seem embarrassed*]   As a matter of fact . . . we have come here in search of an author . . .

THE MANAGER [*half angry, half amazed*]   An author? What author?

THE FATHER   Any author, sir.

THE MANAGER But there's no author here. We are not rehearsing a new piece.

THE STEPDAUGHTER [*vivaciously*] So much the better, so much the better! We can be your new piece.

AN ACTOR [*coming forward from the others*] Oh, do you hear that?

THE FATHER [*to* STEPDAUGHTER] Yes, but if the author isn't here . . . [*to* MANAGER] unless you would be willing . . .

THE MANAGER You are trying to be funny.

THE FATHER No, for Heaven's sake, what are you saying? We bring you a drama, sir.

THE STEPDAUGHTER We may be your fortune.

THE MANAGER Will you oblige me by going away? We haven't time to waste with mad people.

THE FATHER [*mellifluously*] Oh sir, you know well that life is full of infinite absurdities, which, strangely enough, do not even need to appear plausible, since they are true.

THE MANAGER What the devil is he talking about?

THE FATHER I say that to reverse the ordinary process may well be considered a madness: that is, to create credible situations, in order that they may appear true. But permit me to observe that if this be madness, it is the sole *raison d'être*[2] of your profession, gentlemen. [*The* ACTORS *look hurt and perplexed.*]

THE MANAGER [*getting up and looking at him*] So our profession seems to you one worthy of madmen then?

THE FATHER Well, to make seem true that which isn't true . . . without any need . . . for a joke as it were . . . Isn't that your mission, gentlemen: to give life to fantastic characters on the stage?

THE MANAGER [*interpreting the rising anger of the* COMPANY] But I would beg you to believe, my dear sir, that the profession of the comedian is a noble one. If today, as things go, the playwrights give us stupid comedies to play and puppets to represent instead of men, remember we are proud to have given life to immortal works here on these very boards! [*The* ACTORS, *satisfied, applaud their* MANAGER.]

THE FATHER [*interrupting furiously*] Exactly, perfectly, to living beings more alive than those who breathe and wear clothes: beings less real perhaps, but truer! I agree with you entirely. [*The* ACTORS *look at one another in amazement.*]

THE MANAGER But what do you mean? Before, you said . . .

THE FATHER No, excuse me, I meant it for you, sir, who were crying out that you had no time to lose with madmen, while no one better than yourself knows that nature uses the instrument of human fantasy in order to pursue her high creative purpose.

THE MANAGER Very well,—but where does all this take us?

THE FATHER Nowhere! It is merely to show you that one is born to life in many forms, in many shapes, as tree, or as stone, as water, as butterfly, or as woman. So one may also be born a character in a play.

THE MANAGER [*with feigned comic dismay*] So you and these other friends of yours have been born characters?

THE FATHER Exactly, and alive as you see! [MANAGER *and* ACTORS *burst out laughing.*]

---

2. French expression meaning justification; literally, reason to be.

THE FATHER [*hurt*]   I am sorry you laugh, because we carry in us a drama, as you can guess from this woman here veiled in black.

THE MANAGER [*losing patience at last and almost indignant*]   Oh, chuck it! Get away please! Clear out of here! [*To* PROPERTY MAN.] For Heaven's sake, turn them out!

THE FATHER [*resisting*]   No, no, look here, we . . .

THE MANAGER [*roaring*]   We come here to work, you know.

LEADING ACTOR   One cannot let oneself be made such a fool of.

THE FATHER [*determined, coming forward*]   I marvel at your incredulity, gentlemen. Are you not accustomed to see the characters created by an author spring to life in yourselves and face each other? Just because there is no "book" [*pointing to the* PROMPTER'S *box*] which contains us, you refuse to believe . . .

THE STEPDAUGHTER [*advances towards* MANAGER, *smiling and coquettish*]   Believe me, we are really six most interesting characters, sir; side-tracked however.

THE FATHER   Yes, that is the word! [*To* MANAGER *all at once.*] In the sense, that is, that the author who created us alive no longer wished, or was no longer able, materially to put us into a work of art. And this was a real crime, sir; because he who has had the luck to be born a character can laugh even at death. He cannot die. The man, the writer, the instrument of the creation will die, but his creation does not die. And to live for ever, it does not need to have extraordinary gifts or to be able to work wonders. Who was Sancho Panza? Who was Don Abbondio?[3] Yet they live eternally because—live germs as they were—they had the fortune to find a fecundating matrix, a fantasy which could raise and nourish them: make them live forever!

THE MANAGER   That is quite all right. But what do you want here, all of you?

THE FATHER   We want to live.

THE MANAGER [*ironically*]   For eternity?

THE FATHER   No, sir, only for a moment . . . in you.

AN ACTOR   Just listen to him!

LEADING LADY   They want to live, in us. . . .

JUVENILE LEAD [*pointing to the* STEPDAUGHTER]   I've no objection, as far as that one is concerned!

THE FATHER   Look here! look here! The comedy has to be made. [*To the* MANAGER.] But if you and your actors are willing, we can soon concert it among ourselves.

THE MANAGER [*annoyed*]   But what do you want to concert? We don't go in for concerts here. Here we play dramas and comedies!

THE FATHER   Exactly! That is just why we have come to you.

THE MANAGER   And where is the "book"?

THE FATHER   It is in us! [*The* ACTORS *laugh.*] The drama is in us, and we are the drama. We are impatient to play it. Our inner passion drives us on to this.

THE STEPDAUGHTER [*disdainful, alluring, treacherous, full of impudence*]   My passion, sir! Ah, if you only knew! My passion for him! [*Points to the* FATHER *and makes a pretense of embracing him. Then she breaks out into a loud laugh.*]

---

3. Sancho Panza is Don Quixote's squire in Cervantes' famous novel. Don Abbondio is a priest in Manzoni's *I Promessi Sposi* (The Fiancés), one of the most famous works of Italian literature.

THE FATHER [*angrily*]   Behave yourself! And please don't laugh in that fashion.

THE STEPDAUGHTER   With your permission, gentlemen, I, who am a two months' orphan, will show you how I can dance and sing. [*Sings and then dances* Prends garde à Tchou-Tchin-Tchou.][4]

> Les chinois sont un peuple malin,
> De Shangaî à Pékin,
> Ils ont mis des écriteaux partout:
> Prenez garde à Tchou-Tchin-Tchou.

ACTORS *and* ACTRESSES   Bravo! Well done! Tip-top!

THE MANAGER   Silence! This isn't a café concert, you know! [*Turning to the* FATHER *in consternation.*] Is she mad?

THE FATHER   Mad? No, she's worse than mad.

THE STEPDAUGHTER [*to* MANAGER]   Worse? Worse? Listen! Stage this drama for us at once! Then you will see that at a certain moment I . . . when this little darling here. . . . [*Takes the* CHILD *by the hand and leads her to the* MANAGER.] Isn't she a dear? [*Takes her up and kisses her.*] Darling! Darling! [*Puts her down again and adds feelingly.*] Well, when God suddenly takes this dear little child away from that poor mother there; and this imbecile here [*seizing hold of the* BOY *roughly and pushing him forward*] does the stupidest things, like the fool he is, you will seè me run away. Yes, gentlemen, I shall be off. But the moment hasn't arrived yet. After what has taken place between him and me [*indicates the* FATHER *with a horrible wink*] I can't remain any longer in this society, to have to witness the anguish of this mother here for that fool. . . . [*Indicates the* SON.] Look at him! Look at him! See how indifferent, how frigid he is, because he is the legitimate son. He despises me, despises him [*pointing to the* BOY], despises this baby here; because . . . we are bastards. [*Goes to the* MOTHER *and embraces her.*] And he doesn't want to recognize her as his mother—she who is the common mother of us all. He looks down upon her as if she were only the mother of us three bastards. Wretch! [*She says all this very rapidly, excitedly. At the word "bastards" she raises her voice, and almost spits out the final "Wretch!"*]

THE MOTHER [*to the* MANAGER, *in anguish*]   In the name of these two little children, I beg you. . . . [*She grows faint and is about to fall.*] Oh God!

THE FATHER [*coming forward to support her as do some of the* ACTORS] Quick, a chair, a chair for this poor widow!

THE ACTORS   Is it true? Has she really fainted?

THE MANAGER   Quick, a chair! Here!

One of the ACTORS *brings a chair, the* OTHERS *proffer assistance. The* MOTHER *tries to prevent the* FATHER *from lifting the veil which covers her face.*

THE FATHER   Look at her! Look at her!

THE MOTHER   No, no; stop it please!

THE FATHER [*raising her veil*]   Let them see you!

---

4. The French words of this song mean "The Chinese are a wicked people, from Shanghai to Peking, they have put up posters everywhere: 'Watch out for Tchou-Tchin-Tchou.' " This is a French adaptation of a song called "Chu-Chin-Chow," music by Dave Stamper and words by Gene Buck, which first appeared in the Ziegfeld Follies of 1917.

THE MOTHER [*rising and covering her face with her hands, in desperation*]   I beg you, sir, to prevent this man from carrying out his plan which is loathsome to me.

THE MANAGER [*dumbfounded*]   I don't understand at all. What is the situation? Is this lady your wife? [*To the* FATHER.]

THE FATHER   Yes, gentlemen: my wife!

THE MANAGER   But how can she be a widow if you are alive? [*The* ACTORS *find relief for their astonishment in a loud laugh.*]

THE FATHER   Don't laugh! Don't laugh like that, for Heaven's sake. Her drama lies just here in this: she has had a lover, a man who ought to be here.

THE MOTHER [*with a cry*]   No! No!

THE STEPDAUGHTER   Fortunately for her, he is dead. Two months ago as I said. We are in mourning, as you see.

THE FATHER   He isn't here, you see, not because he is dead. He isn't here—look at her a moment and you will understand—because her drama isn't a drama of the love of two men for whom she was incapable of feeling anything except possibly a little gratitude—gratitude not for me but for the other. She isn't a woman, she is a mother, and her drama—powerful, sir, I assure you—lies, as a matter of fact, all in these four children she has had by two men.

THE MOTHER   I had them? Have you got the courage to say that I wanted them? [*To the* COMPANY.] It was his doing. It was he who gave me to that other man, who forced me to go away with him.

THE STEPDAUGHTER   It isn't true.

THE MOTHER [*startled*]   Not true, isn't it?

THE STEPDAUGHTER   No, it isn't true, it just isn't true.

THE MOTHER   And what can you know about it?

THE STEPDAUGHTER   It isn't true. Don't believe it. [*To* MANAGER.] Do you know why she says so? For that fellow there. [*Indicates the* SON.] She tortures herself, destroys herself on account of the neglect of that son there; and she wants him to believe that if she abandoned him when he was only two years old, it was because he [*indicates the* FATHER] made her do so.

THE MOTHER [*vigorously*]   He forced me to it, and I call God to witness it. [*To the* MANAGER.] Ask him [*indicates* HUSBAND] if it isn't true. Let him speak. You [*to* DAUGHTER] are not in a position to know anything about it.

THE STEPDAUGHTER   I know you lived in peace and happiness with my father while he lived. Can you deny it?

THE MOTHER   No, I don't deny it. . . .

THE STEPDAUGHTER   He was always full of affection and kindness for you. [*To the* BOY, *angrily.*] It's true, isn't it? Tell them! Why don't you speak, you little fool?

THE MOTHER   Leave the poor boy alone. Why do you want to make me appear ungrateful, daughter? I don't want to offend your father. I have answered him that I didn't abandon my house and my son through any fault of mine, nor from any wilful passion.

THE FATHER   It is true. It was my doing.

LEADING MAN [*to the* COMPANY]   What a spectacle!

LEADING LADY   We are the audience this time.

JUVENILE LEAD   For once, in a way.

THE MANAGER [*beginning to get really interested*]   Let's hear them out. Listen!

THE SON   Oh yes, you're going to hear a fine bit now. He will talk to you of the Demon of Experiment.

THE FATHER   You are a cynical imbecile. I've told you so already a hundred times. [*To the* MANAGER.] He tries to make fun of me on account of this expression which I have found to excuse myself with.

THE SON [*with disgust*]   Yes, phrases! phrases!

THE FATHER   Phrases! Isn't everyone consoled when faced with a trouble or fact he doesn't understand, by a word, some simple word, which tells us nothing and yet calms us?

THE STEPDAUGHTER   Even in the case of remorse. In fact, especially then.

THE FATHER   Remorse? No, that isn't true. I've done more than use words to quiet the remorse in me.

THE STEPDAUGHTER   Yes, there was a bit of money too. Yes, yes, a bit of money. There were the hundred lire he was about to offer me in payment, gentlemen. . . . [*Sensation of horror among the* ACTORS.]

THE SON [*to the* STEPDAUGHTER]   This is vile.

THE STEPDAUGHTER   Vile? There they were in a pale blue envelope on a little mahogany table in the back of Madame Pace's shop. You know Madame Pace—one of those ladies who attract poor girls of good family into their ateliers, under the pretext of their selling *robes et manteaux*.[5]

THE SON   And she thinks she has bought the right to tyrannize over us all with those hundred lire he was going to pay; but which, fortunately—note this, gentlemen—he had no chance of paying.

THE STEPDAUGHTER   It was a near thing, though, you know! [*Laughs ironically.*]

THE MOTHER [*protesting*]   Shame, my daughter, shame!

THE STEPDAUGHTER   Shame indeed! This is my revenge! I am dying to live that scene. . . . The room . . . I see it. . . . Here is the window with the cloaks on display, there the divan, the looking-glass, a screen, there in front of the window the little mahogany table with the blue envelope containing one hundred lire. I see it. I see it. I could take hold of it. . . . But you, gentlemen, you ought to turn your backs now: I am almost nude, you know. But I don't blush: I leave that to him. [*Indicating* FATHER.]

THE MANAGER   I don't understand this at all.

THE FATHER   Naturally enough. I would ask you, sir, to exercise your authority a little here, and let me speak before you believe all she is trying to blame me with. Let me explain.

THE STEPDAUGHTER   Ah yes, explain it in your own way.

THE FATHER   But don't you see that the whole trouble lies here? In words, words. Each one of us has within him a whole world of things, each man of us his own special world. And how can we ever come to an understanding if I put in the words I utter the sense and value of things as I see them; while you who listen to me must inevitably translate them according to the conception of things each one of you has within himself. We think we understand each other, but we never really do. Look here! This woman [*indicating the* MOTHER] takes all my pity for her as a specially ferocious form of cruelty.

THE MOTHER   But you drove me away.

5. French for "dresses and coats (or capes)."

THE FATHER   Do you hear her? I drove her away! She believes I really
sent her away.

THE MOTHER   You know how to talk, and I don't; but, believe me, sir
[to MANAGER], after he had married me . . . who knows why? . . . I
was a poor insignificant woman. . . .

THE FATHER   But, good Heavens! it was just for your humility that I
married you. I loved this simplicity in you. [He stops when he sees
she makes signs to contradict him, opens his arms wide in sign of
desperation seeing how hopeless it is to make himself understood.]
You see she denies it. Her mental deafness, believe me, is phenom-
enal, the limit: [touches his forehead] deaf, deaf, mentally deaf! She
has plenty of feeling. Oh yes, a good heart for the children; but the
brain—deaf, to the point of desperation—!

THE STEPDAUGHTER   Yes, but ask him how his intelligence has helped
us.

THE FATHER   If we could see all the evil that may spring from good,
what should we do? [At this point the LEADING LADY, who is biting
her lips with rage at seeing the LEADING MAN flirting with the STEP-
DAUGHTER, comes forward and speaks to the MANAGER.]

LEADING LADY   Excuse me, but are we going to rehearse today?

MANAGER   Of course, of course; but let's hear them out.

JUVENILE LEAD   This is something quite new.

L'INGÉNUE   Most interesting!

LEADING LADY   Yes, for the people who like that kind of thing. [Casts
a glance at LEADING MAN.]

THE MANAGER [to FATHER]   You must please explain yourself quite
clearly. [Sits down.]

THE FATHER   Very well then: listen! I had in my service a poor man,
a clerk, a secretary of mine, full of devotion, who became friends
with her. [Indicating the MOTHER.] They understood one another,
were kindred souls in fact, without, however, the least suspicion of
any evil existing. They were incapable even of thinking of it.

THE STEPDAUGHTER   So he thought of it—for them!

THE FATHER   That's not true. I meant to do good to them—and to
myself, I confess, at the same time. Things had come to the point
that I could not say a word to either of them without their making
a mute appeal, one to the other, with their eyes. I could see them
silently asking each other how I was to be kept in countenance,
how I was to be kept quiet. And this, believe me, was just about
enough of itself to keep me in a constant rage, to exasperate me
beyond measure.

THE MANAGER   And why didn't you send him away then—this secretary of yours?

THE FATHER   Precisely what I did, sir. And then I had to watch this
poor woman drifting forlornly about the house like an animal
without a master like an animal one has taken in out of pity.

THE MOTHER   Ah yes . . . !

THE FATHER [suddenly turning to the MOTHER]   It's true about the
son anyway, isn't it?

THE MOTHER   He took my son away from me first of all.

THE FATHER   But not from cruelty. I did it so that he should grow up
healthy and strong by living in the country.

THE STEPDAUGHTER [pointing to him ironically]   As one can see.

THE FATHER [quickly]   Is it my fault if he has grown up like this?

I sent him to a wet nurse in the country, a peasant, as *she* did not seem to me strong enough, though she is of humble origin. That was, anyway, the reason I married her. Unpleasant all this may be, but how can it be helped? My mistake possibly, but there we are! All my life I have had these confounded aspirations towards a certain solid moral sanity. [*At this point, the* STEPDAUGHTER *bursts into a noisy laugh.*] Oh, stop it! Stop it! I can't stand it.

THE MANAGER   Yes, please stop it, for Heaven's sake.

THE STEPDAUGHTER   But imagine moral sanity from him, if you please —the client of certain ateliers like that of Madame Pace!

THE FATHER   Fool! That is the proof that I am a man! This seeming contradiction, gentlemen, is the strongest proof that I stand here a live man before you. Why, it is just for this very incongruity in my nature that I have had to suffer what I have. I could not live by the side of that woman [*indicating the* MOTHER] any longer; but not so much for the boredom she inspired me with as for the pity I felt for her.

THE MOTHER   And so he turned me out—

THE FATHER   —well provided for! Yes, I sent her to that man, gentlemen . . . to let her go free of me.

THE MOTHER   And to free himself.

THE FATHER   Yes, I admit it. It was also a liberation for me. But great evil has come of it. I meant well when I did it; and I did it more for her sake than mine. I swear it. [*Crosses his arms on his chest; then turns suddenly to the* MOTHER.] Did I ever lose sight of you until that other man carried you off to another town, like the angry fool he was? And on account of my pure interest in you . . . my pure interest, I repeat, that had no base motive in it. . . . I watched with the tenderest concern the new family that grew up around her. She can bear witness to this. [*Points to the* STEPDAUGHTER.]

THE STEPDAUGHTER   Oh yes, that's true enough. When I was a kiddie, so so high, you know, with plaits over my shoulders and panties longer than my skirts, I used to see him waiting outside the school for me to come out. He came to see how I was growing up.

THE FATHER   This is infamous, shameful!

THE STEPDAUGHTER   No. Why?

THE FATHER   Infamous! infamous! [*Then excitedly to* MANAGER *explaining.*] After she [*indicating* MOTHER] went away, my house seemed suddenly empty. She was my incubus, but she filled my house. I was like a dazed fly alone in the empty rooms. This boy here [*indicating the* SON] was educated away from home, and when he came back, he seemed to me to be no more mine. With no mother to stand between him and me, he grew up entirely for himself, on his own, apart, with no tie of intellect or affection binding him to me. And then—strange but true—I was driven, by curiosity at first and then by some tender sentiment, towards her family, which had come into being through my will. The thought of her began gradually to fill up the emptiness I felt all around me. I wanted to know if she were happy in living out the simple daily duties of life. I wanted to think of her as fortunate and happy because far away from the complicated torments of my spirit. And so, to have proof of this, I used to watch that child coming out of school.

THE STEPDAUGHTER   Yes, yes. True. He used to follow me in the street and smiled at me, waved his hand, like this. I would look at him with interest, wondering who he might be. I told my mother, who guessed at once. [*The* MOTHER *agrees with a nod.*] Then she didn't want to send me to school for some days; and when I finally went back, there he was again—looking so ridiculous—with a paper parcel in his hands. He came close to me, caressed me, and drew out a fine straw hat from the parcel, with a bouquet of flowers—all for me!

THE MANAGER   A bit discursive this, you know!

THE SON [*contemptuously*]   Literature! Literature!

THE FATHER   Literature indeed! This is life, this is passion!

THE MANAGER   It may be, but it won't act.

THE FATHER   I agree. This is only the part leading up. I don't suggest this should be staged. She [*pointing to the* STEPDAUGHTER], as you see, is no longer a little girl with plaits down her back—.

THE STEPDAUGHTER   —and the panties showing below the skirt!

THE FATHER   The drama is coming now, sir; something new, complex, most interesting.

THE STEPDAUGHTER   As soon as my father died . . .

THE FATHER   —there was absolute misery for them. They came back here, unknown to me. Through her stupidity! [*Pointing to the* MOTHER.] It is true she can barely write her own name; but she could anyhow have got her daughter to write to me that they were in need . . .

THE MOTHER   And how was I to divine all this sentiment in him?

THE FATHER   That is exactly your mistake, never to have guessed any of my sentiments.

THE MOTHER   After so many years apart, and all that had happened . . .

THE FATHER   Was it my fault if that fellow carried you away? It happened quite suddenly; for after he had obtained some job or other, I could find no trace of them; and so, not unnaturally, my interest in them dwindled. But the drama culminated unforeseen and violent on their return, when I was impelled by my miserable flesh that still lives. . . . Ah! what misery, what wretchedness is that of the man who is alone and disdains debasing *liaisons!* Not old enough to do without women, and not young enough to go and look for one without shame. Misery? It's worse than misery; it's a horror; for no woman can any longer give him love; and when a man feels this. . . . One ought to do without, you say? Yes, yes, I know. Each of us when he appears before his fellows is clothed in a certain dignity. But every man knows what unconfessable things pass within the secrecy of his own heart. One gives way to the temptation, only to rise from it again, afterwards, with a great eagerness to re-establish one's dignity, as if it were a tombstone to place on the grave of one's shame, and a monument to hide and sign the memory of our weaknesses. Everybody's in the same case. Some folks haven't the courage to say certain things, that's all!

THE STEPDAUGHTER   All appear to have the courage to do them though.

THE FATHER   Yes, but in secret. Therefore, you want more courage to say these things. Let a man but speak these things out, and folks at once label him a cynic. But it isn't true. He is like all the others, better indeed, because he isn't afraid to reveal with the light of the intelligence the red shame of human bestiality on which most men close their eyes so as not to see it.

Woman—for example, look at her case! She turns tantalizing

inviting glances on you. You seize her. No sooner does she feel herself in your grasp than she closes her eyes. It is the sign of her mission, the sign by which she says to man: "Blind yourself, for I am blind."

THE STEPDAUGHTER   Sometimes she can close them no more: when she no longer feels the need of hiding her shame to herself, but dry-eyed and dispassionately, sees only that of the man who has blinded himself without love. Oh, all these intellectual complications make me sick, disgust me—all this philosophy that uncovers the beast in man, and then seeks to save him, excuse him . . . I can't stand it, sir. When a man seeks to "simplify" life bestially, throwing aside every relic of humanity, every chaste aspiration, every pure feeling, all sense of ideality, duty, modesty, shame . . . then nothing is more revolting and nauseous than a certain kind of remorse—crocodiles' tears, that's what it is.

THE MANAGER   Let's come to the point. This is only discussion.

THE FATHER   Very good, sir! But a fact is like a sack which won't stand up when it is empty. In order that it may stand up, one has to put into it the reason and sentiment which have caused it to exist. I couldn't possibly know that after the death of that man, they had decided to return here, that they were in misery, and that she [*pointing to the* MOTHER] had gone to work as a modiste, and at a shop of the type of that of Madame Pace.

THE STEPDAUGHTER   A real high-class modiste, you must know, gentlemen. In appearance, she works for the leaders of the best society; but she arranges matters so that these elegant ladies serve her purpose . . . without prejudice to other ladies who are . . . well . . . only so so.

THE MOTHER   You will believe me, gentlemen, that it never entered my mind that the old hag offered me work because she had her eye on my daughter.

THE STEPDAUGHTER   Poor mamma! Do you know, sir, what that woman did when I brought her back the work my mother had finished? She would point out to me that I had torn one of my frocks, and she would give it back to my mother to mend. It was I who paid for it, always I; while this poor creature here believed she was sacrificing herself for me and these two children here, sitting up at night sewing Madame Pace's gowns.

THE MANAGER   And one day you met there . . .

THE STEPDAUGHTER   Him, him. Yes sir, an old client. There's a scene for you to play! Superb!

THE FATHER   She, the Mother arrived just then . . .

THE STEPDAUGHTER   [*treacherously*]   Almost in time!

THE FATHER   [*crying out*]   No, in time! in time! Fortunately I recognized her . . . in time. And I took them back home with me to my house. You can imagine now her position and mine; she, as you see her; and I who cannot look her in the face.

THE STEPDAUGHTER   Absurd! How can I possibly be expected—after that—to be a modest young miss, a fit person to go with his confounded aspirations for "a solid moral sanity"?

THE FATHER   For the drama lies all in this—in the conscience that I have, that each one of us has. We believe this conscience to be a single thing, but it is many-sided. There is one for this person, and another for that. Diverse consciences. So we have this illusion of being one person for all, of having a personality that is unique in all our acts. But it isn't true. We perceive this when, tragically perhaps, in something we do, we are as it were, suspended, caught up in the air on a kind of hook. Then we perceive that all of us was not in that act, and that it would be an atrocious injustice to judge us by that action alone, as if all our existence were summed up in that one deed. Now do you understand the perfidy of this girl? She surprised me in a place, where she ought not to have known me, just as I could not exist for her; and she now seeks to attach to me a reality such as I could never suppose I should have to assume for her in a shameful and fleeting moment of my life. I feel this above all else. And the drama, you will see, acquires a tremendous value from this point. Then there is the position of the others . . . his. . . . [*Indicating the* son.]

THE SON [*shrugging his shoulders scornfully*]   Leave me alone! I don't come into this.

THE FATHER   What? You don't come into this?

THE SON   I've got nothing to do with it, and don't want to have; because you know well enough I wasn't made to be mixed up in all this with the rest of you.

THE STEPDAUGHTER   We are only vulgar folk! He is the fine gentleman. You may have noticed, Mr. Manager, that I fix him now and again with a look of scorn while he lowers his eyes—for he knows the evil he has done me.

THE SON [*scarcely looking at her*]   I?

THE STEPDAUGHTER   You! you! you! I owe my life on the streets to you. Did you or did you not deny us, with your behavior, I won't say the intimacy of home, but even that mere hospitality which makes guests feel at their ease? We were intruders who had come to disturb the kingdom of your legitimacy. I should like to have you witness, Mr. Manager, certain scenes between him and me. He says I have tyrannized over everyone. But it was just his behavior which made me insist on the reason for which I had come into the house— this reason he calls "vile"—into his house, with my mother who is his mother too. And I came as mistress of the house.

THE SON   It's easy for them to put me always in the wrong. But imagine, gentlemen, the position of a son, whose fate it is to see arrive one day at his home a young woman of impudent bearing, a young woman who inquires for his father, with whom who knows what business she has. This young man has then to witness her return bolder than ever, accompanied by that child there. He is obliged to watch her treat his father in an equivocal and confidential manner. She asks money of him in a way that lets one suppose he must give it to her, *must*, do you understand, because he has every obligation to do so.

THE FATHER   But I have, as a matter of fact, this obligation. I owe it to your mother.

THE SON   How should I know? When had I ever seen or heard of her? One day there arrive with her [*indicating* STEPDAUGHTER] that lad and this baby here. I am told: "This is *your* mother too, you know." I divine from her manner [*indicating* STEPDAUGHTER *again*] why it is they have come home. I had rather not say what I feel and think about it. I shouldn't even care to confess to myself. No action can therefore be hoped for from me in this affair. Believe me, Mr. Manager, I am an "unrealized" character, dramatically speaking; and I find myself not at all at ease in their company. Leave me out of it, I beg you.

THE FATHER   What? It is just because you are so that . . .

THE SON   How do you know what I am like? When did you ever bother your head about me?

THE FATHER   I admit it. I admit it. But isn't that a situation in itself? This aloofness of yours which is so cruel to me and to your mother, who returns home and sees you almost for the first time grown up, who doesn't recognize you but knows you are her son . . . [*Pointing out the* MOTHER *to the* MANAGER.] See, she's crying!

THE STEPDAUGHTER   [*angrily, stamping her foot*]   Like a fool!

THE FATHER   [*indicating* STEPDAUGHTER]   She can't stand him, you know. [*Then referring again to the* SON.] He says he doesn't come into the affair, whereas he is really the hinge of the whole action. Look at that lad who is always clinging to his mother, frightened and humiliated. It is on account of this fellow here. Possibly his situation is the most painful of all. He feels himself a stranger more than the others. The poor little chap feels himself mortified, humiliated at being brought into a home out of charity as it were. [*In confidence.*] He is the image of his father. Hardly talks at all. Humble and quiet.

THE MANAGER   Oh, we'll cut him out. You've no notion what a nuisance boys are on the stage. . . .

THE FATHER   He disappears soon, you know. And the baby too. She is the first to vanish from the scene. The drama consists finally in this: when that mother re-enters my house, her family born outside of it, and shall we say superimposed on the original, ends with the death of the little girl, the tragedy of the boy and the flight of the elder daughter. It cannot go on, because it is foreign to its surroundings. So after much torment, we three remain: I, the mother, that son. Then, owing to the disappearance of that extraneous family, we too find ourselves strange to one another. We find we are living in an atmosphere of mortal desolation which is the revenge, as he [*indicating* SON] scornfully said of the Demon of Experiment, that unfortunately hides in me. Thus, sir, you see when faith is lacking, it becomes impossible to create certain states of happiness, for we lack the necessary humility. Vaingloriously, we try to substitute ourselves for this faith, creating thus for the rest of the world a reality which we believe after their fashion, while, actually, it doesn't exist. For each one of us has his own reality to be respected before God, even when it is harmful to one's very self.

THE MANAGER   There is something in what you say. I assure you all this interests me very much. I begin to think there's the stuff for a drama in all this, and not a bad drama either.

THE STEPDAUGHTER   [*coming forward*]   When you've got a character like me.

THE FATHER   [*shutting her up, all excited to learn the decision of the* MANAGER]   You be quiet!

THE MANAGER   [*reflecting, heedless of interruption*]   It's new . . . hem . . . yes. . . .

THE FATHER   Absolutely new!

THE MANAGER   You've got a nerve though, I must say, to come here and fling it at me like this. . . .

THE FATHER   You will understand, sir, born as we are for the stage . . .

THE MANAGER   Are you amateur actors then?

THE FATHER   No. I say born for the stage, because . . .

THE MANAGER   Oh, nonsense. You're an old hand, you know.

THE FATHER   No sir, no. We act that role for which we have been cast, that role which we are given in life. And in my own case, passion itself, as usually happens, becomes a trifle theatrical when it is exalted.

THE MANAGER   Well, well, that will do. But you see, without an author . . . I could give you the address of an author if you like. . . .

THE FATHER   No, no. Look here! You must be the author.

THE MANAGER   I? What are you talking about?

THE FATHER   Yes, you, you! Why not?

THE MANAGER   Because I have never been an author: that's why.

THE FATHER   Then why not turn author now? Everybody does it. You don't want any special qualities. Your task is made much easier by the fact that we are all here alive before you. . . .

THE MANAGER   It won't do.

THE FATHER   What? When you see us live our drama . . .

THE MANAGER   Yes, that's all right. But you want someone to write it.

THE FATHER   No, no. Someone to take it down, possibly, while we play it, scene by scene! It will be enough to sketch it out at first, and then try it over.

THE MANAGER   Well . . . I am almost tempted. It's a bit of an idea. One might have a shot at it.

THE FATHER   Of course. You'll see what scenes will come out of it. I can give you one, at once . . .

THE MANAGER   By Jove, it tempts me. I'd like to have a go at it. Let's try it out. Come with me to my office. [*Turning to the* ACTORS.] You are at liberty for a bit, but don't step out of the theatre for long. In a quarter of an hour, twenty minutes, all back here again! [*To the* FATHER.] We'll see what can be done. Who knows if we don't get something really extraordinary out of it?

THE FATHER   There's no doubt about it. They [*indicating the* CHAR- ACTERS] had better come with us too, hadn't they?

THE MANAGER   Yes, yes. Come on! come on! [*Moves away and then turning to the* ACTORS.] Be punctual, please! [MANAGER *and the* SIX CHARACTERS *cross the stage and go off. The other* ACTORS *remain, looking at one another in astonishment.*]

LEADING MAN   Is he serious? What the devil does he want to do?

JUVENILE LEAD   This is rank madness.

THIRD ACTOR   Does he expect to knock off a drama in five minutes?

JUVENILE LEAD   Like the improvisers!

LEADING LADY   If he thinks that I'm going to take part in a joke like this . . .

JUVENILE LEAD   I'm out of it anyway.

FOURTH ACTOR   I should like to know who they are. [*Alludes to* CHAR- ACTERS.]

THIRD ACTOR   What do you suppose? Madmen or rascals!

JUVENILE LEAD   And he takes them seriously!

L'INGÉNUE   Vanity! He fancies himself as an author now.

LEADING MAN   It's absolutely unheard of. If the stage has come to this . . . well I'm . . .

FIFTH ACTOR   It's rather a joke.

THIRD ACTOR   Well, we'll see what's going to happen next.

Thus talking, the ACTORS *leave the stage; some going out by the little door at the back; others retiring to their dressing-rooms. The curtain remains up. The action of the play is suspended for twenty minutes.*

Act 2

The stage call-bells ring to warn the company that the play is about to begin again.

The STEPDAUGHTER *comes out of the* MANAGER's *office along with the* CHILD *and the* BOY. *As she comes out of the office, she cries:*

THE STEPDAUGHTER   Nonsense! nonsense! Do it yourselves! I'm not going to mix myself up in this mess. [*Turning to the* CHILD *and coming quickly with her on to the stage.*] Come on, Rosetta, let's run!

The BOY *follows them slowly, remaining a little behind and seeming perplexed.*

THE STEPDAUGHTER [*stops, bends over the* CHILD *and takes the latter's face between her hands*]   My little darling! You're frightened, aren't you? You don't know where we are, do you? [*Pretending to reply to a question of the* CHILD.] What is the stage? It's a place, baby, you know, where people play at being serious, a place where they act comedies. We've got to act a comedy now, dead serious, you know; and you're in it also, little one. [*Embraces her, pressing the little head to her breast, and rocking the* CHILD *for a moment.*] Oh darling, darling, what a horrid comedy you've got to play! What a wretched part they've found for you! A garden . . . a fountain . . . look . . . just suppose, kiddie, it's here. Where, you say? Why, right here in the middle. It's all pretense you know. That's the trouble, my pet: it's all make-believe here. It's better to imagine it though, because if they fix it up for you, it'll only be painted cardboard, painted cardboard for the rockery, the water, the plants. . . . Ah, but I think a baby like this one would sooner have a make-believe fountain than a real one, so she could play with it. What a joke it'll be for the others! But for you, alas! not quite such a joke: you who are real, baby dear, and really play by a real fountain that is big and green and beautiful, with ever so many bamboos around it that are reflected in the water, and a whole lot of little ducks swimming about. . . . No, Rosetta, no, your mother doesn't bother about you on account of that wretch of a son there. I'm in the devil of a temper, and as for that lad . . . [*Seizes* BOY *by the arm to force him to take one of his hands out of his pockets.*] What have you got there? What are you hiding? [*Pulls his hand out of his pocket, looks into it and catches the glint of a revolver.*] Ah! where did you get this? [*The* BOY, *very pale in the face, looks at her, but does not answer.*] Idiot! If I'd been in your place, instead of killing myself, I'd have shot one of those two, or both of them: father and son.

The FATHER *enters from the office, all excited from his work. The* MANAGER *follows him.*

THE FATHER Come on, come on dear! Come here for a minute! We've arranged everything. It's all fixed up.

THE MANAGER [*also excited*] If you please, young lady, there are one or two points to settle still. Will you come along?

THE STEPDAUGHTER [*following him towards the office*] Ouff! what's the good, if you've arranged everything.

> *The* FATHER, MANAGER, *and* STEPDAUGHTER *go back into the office again for a moment. At the same time, the* SON, *followed by the* MOTHER, *comes out.*

THE SON [*looking at the three entering office*] Oh this is fine, fine! And to think I can't even get away!

> *The* MOTHER *attempts to look at him, but lowers her eyes immediately when he turns away from her. She then sits down. The* BOY *and the* CHILD *approach her. She casts a glance again at the* SON, *and speaks with humble tones, trying to draw him into conversation.*

THE MOTHER And isn't my punishment the worst of all? [*Then seeing from the* SON's *manner that he will not bother himself about her.*] My God! Why are you so cruel? Isn't it enough for one person to support all this torment? Must you then insist on others seeing it also?

THE SON [*half to himself, meaning the* MOTHER *to hear, however*] And they want to put it on the stage! If there was at least a reason for it! He thinks he has got at the meaning of it all. Just as if each one of us in every circumstance of life couldn't find his own explanation of it! [*Pauses.*] He complains he was discovered in a place where he ought not to have been seen, in a moment of his life which ought to have remained hidden and kept out of the reach of that convention which he has to maintain for other people. And what about my case? Haven't I had to reveal what no son ought ever to reveal: how father and mother live and are man and wife for themselves quite apart from that idea of father and mother which we give them? When this idea is revealed, our life is then linked at one point only to that man and that woman; and as such it should shame them, shouldn't it?

> *The* MOTHER *hides her face in her hands. From the dressing-rooms and the little door at the back of the stage the* ACTORS *and* STAGE MANAGER *return, followed by the* PROPERTY MAN, *and the* PROMPTER. *At the same moment, the* MANAGER *comes out of his office, accompanied by the* FATHER *and the* STEP-DAUGHTER.

THE MANAGER Come on, come on, ladies and gentlemen! Heh! you there, machinist!

MACHINIST Yes sir?

THE MANAGER Fix up the white parlor with the floral decorations. Two wings and a drop with a door will do. Hurry up!

> *The* MACHINIST *runs off at once to prepare the scene, and arranges it while the* MANAGER *talks with the* STAGE MANAGER, *the* PROPERTY MAN, *and the* PROMPTER *on matters of detail.*

THE MANAGER [*to* PROPERTY MAN] Just have a look, and see if there isn't a sofa or divan in the wardrobe . . .

PROPERTY MAN There's the green one.

THE STEPDAUGHTER No no! Green won't do. It was yellow, ornamented with flowers—very large! and most comfortable!

PROPERTY MAN There isn't one like that.

THE MANAGER It doesn't matter. Use the one we've got.

THE STEPDAUGHTER Doesn't matter? It's most important!

THE MANAGER We're only trying it now. Please don't interfere. [*To* PROPERTY MAN.] See if we've got a shop window—long and narrowish.

THE STEPDAUGHTER And the little table! The little mahogany table for the pale blue envelope!

PROPERTY MAN [*to* MANAGER] There's that little gilt one.

THE MANAGER That'll do fine.

THE FATHER A mirror.

THE STEPDAUGHTER And the screen! We must have a screen. Otherwise how can I manage?

PROPERTY MAN That's all right, Miss. We've got any amount of them.

THE MANAGER [*to the* STEPDAUGHTER] We want some clothes pegs too, don't we?

THE STEPDAUGHTER Yes, several, several!

THE MANAGER See how many we've got and bring them all.

PROPERTY MAN All right!

> The PROPERTY MAN *hurries off to obey his orders. While he is putting the things in their places, the* MANAGER *talks to the* PROMPTER *and then with the* CHARACTERS *and the* ACTORS.

THE MANAGER [*to* PROMPTER] Take your seat. Look here: this is the outline of the scenes, act by act. [*Hands him some sheets of paper.*] And now I'm going to ask you to do something out of the ordinary.

PROMPTER Take it down in shorthand?

THE MANAGER [*pleasantly surprised*] Exactly! Can you do shorthand?

PROMPTER Yes, a little.

THE MANAGER Good! [*Turning to a* STAGE HAND.] Go and get some paper from my office, plenty, as much as you can find.

> The STAGE HAND *goes off, and soon returns with a handful of paper which he gives to the* PROMPTER.

THE MANAGER [*to* PROMPTER] You follow the scenes as we play them, and try and get the points down, at any rate the most important ones. [*Then addressing the* ACTORS.] Clear the stage, ladies and gentlemen! Come over here [*pointing to the left*] and listen attentively.

LEADING LADY But, excuse me, we . . .

THE MANAGER [*guessing her thought*] Don't worry! You won't have to improvise.

LEADING MAN What have we to do then?

THE MANAGER Nothing. For the moment you just watch and listen. Everybody will get his part written out afterwards. At present we're going to try the thing as best we can. They're going to act now.

THE FATHER [*as if fallen from the clouds into the confusion of the stage*] We? What do you mean, if you please, by a rehearsal?

THE MANAGER A rehearsal for them. [*Points to the* ACTORS.]

THE FATHER But since we are the characters . . .

THE MANAGER All right: "characters" then, if you insist on calling yourselves such. But here, my dear sir, the characters don't act. Here the actors do the acting. The characters are there, in the "book" [*pointing towards* PROMPTER's *box*]—when there is a "book"!

THE FATHER   I won't contradict you; but excuse me, the actors aren't the characters. They want to be, they pretend to be, don't they? Now if these gentlemen here are fortunate enough to have us alive before them . . .

THE MANAGER   Oh this is grand! You want to come before the public yourselves then?

THE FATHER   As we are. . . .

THE MANAGER   I can assure you it would be a magnificent spectacle!

LEADING MAN   What's the use of us here anyway then?

THE MANAGER   You're not going to pretend that you can act? It makes me laugh! [*The* ACTORS *laugh.*] There, you see, they are laughing at the notion. But, by the way, I must cast the parts. That won't be difficult. They cast themselves. [*To the* SECOND LADY LEAD.] You play the Mother. [*To the* FATHER.] We must find her a name.

THE FATHER   Amalia, sir.

THE MANAGER   But that is the real name of your wife. We don't want to call her by her real name.

THE FATHER   Why ever not, if it is her name? . . . Still, perhaps, if that lady must. . . . [*Makes a slight motion of the hand to indicate the* SECOND LADY LEAD.] I see this woman here [*means the* MOTHER] as Amalia. But do as you like. [*Gets more and more confused.*] I don't know what to say to you. Already, I begin to hear my own words ring false, as if they had another sound. . . .

THE MANAGER   Don't you worry about it. It'll be our job to find the right tones. And as for her name, if you want her Amalia, Amalia it shall be; and if you don't like it, we'll find another! For the moment though, we'll call the characters in this way. [*To* JUVENILE LEAD.] You are the Son. [*To the* LEADING LADY.] You naturally are the Stepdaughter. . . .

THE STEPDAUGHTER   [*excitedly*]   What? what? I, that woman there? [*Bursts out laughing.*]

THE MANAGER   [*angry*]   What is there to laugh at?

LEADING LADY   [*indignant*]   Nobody has ever dared to laugh at me. I insist on being treated with respect; otherwise I go away.

THE STEPDAUGHTER   No, no, excuse me . . . I am not laughing at you. . . .

THE MANAGER   [*to* STEPDAUGHTER]   You ought to feel honored to be played by . . .

LEADING LADY   [*at once, contemptuously*]   "That woman there" . . .

THE STEPDAUGHTER   But I wasn't speaking of you, you know. I was speaking of myself—whom I can't see at all in you! That is all. I don't know . . . but . . . you . . . aren't in the least like me. . . .

THE FATHER   True. Here's the point. Look here, sir, our temperaments, our souls . . .

THE MANAGER   Temperament, soul, be hanged! Do you suppose the spirit of the piece is in you? Nothing of the kind!

THE FATHER   What, haven't we our own temperaments, our own souls?

THE MANAGER   Not at all. Your soul or whatever you like to call it takes shape here. The actors give body and form to it, voice and gesture. And my actors—I may tell you—have given expression to much more lofty material than this little drama of yours, which may or may not hold up on the stage. But if it does, the merit of it, believe me, will be due to my actors.

THE FATHER   I don't dare contradict you, sir; but, believe me, it is a terrible suffering for us who are as we are, with these bodies of ours, these features to see . . .

THE MANAGER [*cutting him short and out of patience*]   Good heavens! The make-up will remedy all that, man, the make-up. . . .

THE FATHER   Maybe. But the voice, the gestures . . .

THE MANAGER   Now, look here! On the stage, you as yourself, cannot exist. The actor here acts you, and that's an end to it!

THE FATHER   I understand. And now I think I see why our author who conceived us as we are, all alive, didn't want to put us on the stage after all. I haven't the least desire to offend your actors. Far from it! But when I think that I am to be acted by . . . I don't know by whom. . . .

LEADING MAN [*on his dignity*]   By me, if you've no objection!

THE FATHER [*humbly, mellifluously*]   Honored, I assure you, sir. [*Bows.*] Still, I must say that try as this gentleman may, with all his good will and wonderful art, to absorb me into himself . . .

LEADING MAN   Oh chuck it! "Wonderful art!" Withdraw that, please!

THE FATHER   The performance he will give, even doing his best with make-up to look like me . . .

LEADING MAN   It will certainly be a bit difficult! [*The* ACTORS *laugh.*]

THE FATHER   Exactly! It will be difficult to act me as I really am. The effect will be rather—apart from the make-up—according as to how he supposes I am, as he senses me—if he does sense me—and not as I inside of myself feel myself to be. It seems to me then that account should be taken of this by everyone whose duty it may become to criticize us. . . .

THE MANAGER   Heavens! The man's starting to think about the critics now! Let them say what they like. It's up to us to put on the play if we can. [*Looking around.*] Come on! come on! Is the stage set? [*To the* ACTORS *and* CHARACTERS.] Stand back—stand back! Let me see, and don't let's lose any more time! [*To the* STEPDAUGHTER.] Is it all right as it is now?

THE STEPDAUGHTER   Well, to tell the truth, I don't recognize the scene.

THE MANAGER   My dear lady, you can't possibly suppose that we can construct that shop of Madame Pace piece by piece here? [*To the* FATHER.] You said a white room with flowered wall paper, didn't you?

THE FATHER   Yes.

THE MANAGER   Well then. We've got the furniture right more or less. Bring that little table a bit further forward. [*The* STAGE HANDS *obey the order. To* PROPERTY MAN.] You go and find an envelope, if possible, a pale blue one; and give it to that gentleman. [*Indicates* FATHER.]

PROPERTY MAN   An ordinary envelope?

MANAGER *and* FATHER   Yes, yes, an ordinary envelope.

PROPERTY MAN   At once, sir. [*Exit.*]

THE MANAGER   Ready, everyone! First scene—the Young Lady. [*The* LEADING LADY *comes forward.*] No, no, you must wait. I meant her. [*Indicating the* STEPDAUGHTER.] You just watch—

THE STEPDAUGHTER [*adding at once*]   How I shall play it, how I shall live it! . . .

LEADING LADY [*offended*]   I shall live it also, you may be sure, as soon as I begin!

THE MANAGER [*with his hands to his head*]   Ladies and gentlemen, if you please! No more useless discussions! Scene I: the young lady with Madame Pace. Oh! [*Looks around as if lost.*] And this Madame Pace, where is she?

THE FATHER   She isn't with us, sir.

THE MANAGER   Then what the devil's to be done?

THE FATHER   But she is alive too.

THE MANAGER   Yes, but where is she?

THE FATHER   One minute. Let me speak! [*Turning to the* ACTRESSES.] If these ladies would be so good as to give me their hats for a moment. . . .

THE ACTRESSES [*half surprised, half laughing, in chorus*]   What? Why? Our hats? What does he say?

THE MANAGER   What are you going to do with the ladies' hats? [*The* ACTORS *laugh.*]

THE FATHER   Oh nothing. I just want to put them on these pegs for a moment. And one of the ladies will be so kind as to take off her cloak. . . .

THE ACTORS   Oh, what d'you think of that? Only the cloak? He must be mad.

SOME ACTRESSES   But why? Cloaks as well?

THE FATHER   To hang them up here for a moment. Please be so kind, will you?

THE ACTRESSES [*taking off their hats, one or two also their cloaks, and going to hang them on the racks*]   After all, why not? There you are! This is really funny. We've got to put them on show.

THE FATHER   Exactly; just like that, on show.

THE MANAGER   May we know why?

THE FATHER   I'll tell you. Who knows if, by arranging the stage for her, she does not come here herself, attracted by the very articles of her trade? [*Inviting the* ACTORS *to look towards the exit at back of stage.*] Look! Look!

> The door at the back of stage opens and MADAME PACE *enters and takes a few steps forward. She is a fat, oldish woman with crudely dyed hair. She is rouged and powdered, dressed with a comical elegance in black silk. Round her waist is a long silver chain from which hangs a pair of scissors. The* STEPDAUGHTER *runs over to her at once amid the stupor of the* ACTORS.

THE STEPDAUGHTER [*turning towards her*]   There she is! There she is!

THE FATHER [*radiant*]   It's she! I said so, didn't I? There she is!

THE MANAGER [*conquering his surprise, and then becoming indignant*]   What sort of a trick is this?

LEADING MAN [*almost at the same time*]   What's going to happen next?

JUVENILE LEAD   Where does *she* come from?

L'INGÉNUE   They've been holding her in reserve, I guess.

LEADING LADY   A vulgar trick!

THE FATHER [*dominating the protests*]   Excuse me, all of you! Why are you so anxious to destroy in the name of a vulgar, commonplace sense of truth, this reality which comes to birth attracted and formed by the magic of the stage itself, which has indeed more right to live here than you, since it is much truer than you—if you don't mind my saying so? Which is the actress among you who is to play Madame Pace? Well, here is Madame Pace herself. And you will allow, I fancy, that the actress who acts her will be less true than this woman here, who is herself in person. You see my daughter recognized her and went over to her at once. Now you're going to witness the scene!

> But the scene between the STEPDAUGHTER *and* MADAME PACE *has already begun despite the protest of the actors and the reply of the* FATHER. *It has begun quietly, naturally, in a manner impossible for the stage. So when the* ACTORS, *called to attention by the* FATHER, *turn round and see* MADAME PACE, *who has placed one hand under the* STEPDAUGHTER'S *chin to raise her head, they observe her at first with great attention, but hearing her speak in an unintelligible manner their interest begins to wane.*

THE MANAGER   Well? well?

LEADING MAN   What does she say?

LEADING LADY   One can't hear a word.

JUVENILE LEAD   Louder! Louder please!

THE STEPDAUGHTER [*leaving* MADAME PACE, *who smiles a Sphinxlike smile, and advancing towards the* ACTORS]   Louder? Louder? What are you talking about? These aren't matters which can be shouted at the top of one's voice. If I have spoken them out loud, it was to shame him and have my revenge. [*Indicates* FATHER.] But for Madame it's quite a different matter.

THE MANAGER   Indeed? indeed? But here, you know, people have got to make themselves heard, my dear. Even we who are on the stage can't hear you. What will it be when the public's in the theatre? And anyway, you can very well speak up now among yourselves, since we shan't be present to listen to you as we are now. You've got to pretend to be alone in a room at the back of a shop where no one can hear you.

> The STEPDAUGHTER *coquettishly and with a touch of malice makes a sign of disagreement two or three times with her finger.*

THE MANAGER   What do you mean by no?

THE STEPDAUGHTER [*sotto voce, mysteriously*]   There's someone who will hear us if she [*indicating* MADAME PACE] speaks out loud.

THE MANAGER [*in consternation*]   What? Have you got someone else to spring on us now? [*The* ACTORS *burst out laughing.*]

THE FATHER   No, no sir. She is alluding to me. I've got to be here— there behind that door, in waiting; and Madame Pace knows it. In fact, if you will allow me, I'll go there at once, so I can be quite ready. [*Moves away.*]

THE MANAGER [*stopping him*]   No! Wait! wait! We must observe the conventions of the theatre. Before you are ready . . .

THE STEPDAUGHTER [*interrupting him*]   No, get on with it at once! I'm just dying, I tell you, to act this scene. If he's ready, I'm more than ready.

THE MANAGER [*shouting*]   But, my dear young lady, first of all, we must have the scene between you and this lady. . . . [*Indicates* MADAME PACE.] Do you understand? . . .

THE STEPDAUGHTER   Good Heavens! She's been telling me what you

know already: that mamma's work is badly done again, that the
material's ruined; and that if I want her to continue to help us in our
misery I must be patient. . . .

MADAME PACE [*coming forward with an air of great importance*]   Yes
indeed, sir, I no wanta take advantage of her, I no wanta be hard. . . .

> *Note.* MADAME PACE *is supposed to talk in a jargon half Italian,
> half English.*

THE MANAGER [*alarmed*]   What? What? She talks like that? [*The*
ACTORS *burst out laughing again.*]

THE STEPDAUGHTER [*also laughing*]   Yes yes, that's the way she talks,
half English, half Italian! Most comical it is!

MADAME PACE   Itta seem not verra polite gentlemen laugha atta me
eeff I trya best speaka English.

THE MANAGER   *Diamine!*[6] Of course! Of course! Let her talk like that!
Just what we want. Talk just like that, Madame, if you please! The
effect will be certain. Exactly what was wanted to put a little comic
relief into the crudity of the situation. Of course she talks like that!
Magnificent!

THE STEPDAUGHTER   Magnificent? Certainly! When certain suggestions
are made to one in language of that kind, the effect is certain, since it
seems almost a joke. One feels inclined to laugh when one hears her
talk about an "old signore" "who wanta talka nicely with you." Nice
old signore,[7] eh, Madame?

MADAME PACE   Not so old my dear, not so old! And even if you no
lika him, he won't make any scandal!

THE MOTHER [*jumping up amid the amazement and consternation of
the* ACTORS *who had not been noticing her. They move to restrain
her*]   You old devil! You murderess!

THE STEPDAUGHTER [*running over to calm her* MOTHER]   Calm yourself, Mother, calm yourself! Please don't. . . .

THE FATHER [*going to her also at the same time*]   Calm yourself! Don't
get excited! Sit down now!

THE MOTHER   Well then, take that woman away out of my sight!

THE STEPDAUGHTER [*to* MANAGER]   It is impossible for my mother to
remain here.

THE FATHER [*to* MANAGER]   They can't be here together. And for this
reason, you see: that woman there was not with us when we came.
. . . If they are on together, the whole thing is given away inevitably,
as you see.

THE MANAGER   It doesn't matter. This is only a first rough sketch—
just to get an idea of the various points of the scene, even con-
fusedly. . . . [*Turning to the* MOTHER *and leading her to her chair.*]
Come along, my dear lady, sit down now, and let's get on with the
scene. . . .

> *Meanwhile, the* STEPDAUGHTER, *coming forward again, turns
> to* MADAME PACE.

THE STEPDAUGHTER   Come on, Madame, come on!

MADAME PACE [*offended*]   No, no, *grazie.*[8] I not do anything witha
your mother present.

---

6. An Italian exclamation, equivalent to
"The deuce!" or "The devil!"

7. "Signore" is Italian for "gentleman."
8. Italian for "Thank you" or "Thanks."

THE STEPDAUGHTER   Nonsense! Introduce this "old signore" who wants to talk nicely to me. [*Addressing the* COMPANY *imperiously.*] We've got to do this scene one way or another, haven't we? Come on! [*To* MADAME PACE.] You can go!

MADAME PACE   Ah yes! I go'way! I go'way! Certainly! [*Exits furious.*]

THE STEPDAUGHTER   [*to the* FATHER]   Now you make your entry. No, you needn't go over there. Come here. Let's suppose you've already come in. Like that, yes! I'm here with bowed head, modest like. Come on! Out with your voice! Say "Good morning, Miss" in that peculiar tone, that special tone. . . .

THE MANAGER   Excuse me, but are you the Manager, or am I? [*To the* FATHER, *who looks undecided and perplexed.*] Get on with it, man! Go down there to the back of the stage. You needn't go off. Then come right forward here.

> The FATHER *does as he is told, looking troubled and perplexed at first. But as soon as he begins to move, the reality of the action affects him, and he begins to smile and to be more natural. The* ACTORS *watch intently.*

THE MANAGER   [*sotto voce, quickly to the* PROMPTER *in his box*]   Ready! ready? Get ready to write now.

THE FATHER   [*coming forward and speaking in a different tone*]   Good afternoon, Miss!

THE STEPDAUGHTER   [*head bowed down slightly, with restrained disgust*]   Good afternoon!

THE FATHER   [*looks under her hat which partly covers her face. Perceiving she is very young, he makes an exclamation, partly of surprise, partly of fear lest he compromise himself in a risky adventure*]   Ah . . . but . . . ah . . . I say . . . this is not the first time that you have come here, is it?

THE STEPDAUGHTER   [*modestly*]   No sir.

THE FATHER   You've been here before, eh? [*Then seeing her nod agreement.*] More than once? [*Waits for her to answer, looks under her hat, smiles, and then says.*] Well then, there's no need to be so shy, is there? May I take off your hat?

THE STEPDAUGHTER   [*anticipating him and with veiled disgust*]   No sir . . . I'll do it myself. [*Takes it off quickly.*]

> The MOTHER, *who watches the progress of the scene with the* SON *and the other two children who cling to her, is on thorns; and follows with varying expressions of sorrow, indignation, anxiety, and horror the words and actions of the other two. From time to time she hides her face in her hands and sobs.*

THE MOTHER   Oh, my God, my God!

THE FATHER   [*playing his part with a touch of gallantry*]   Give it to me! I'll put it down. [*Takes hat from her hands.*] But a dear little head like yours ought to have a smarter hat. Come and help me choose one from the stock, won't you?

L'INGÉNUE   [*interrupting*]   I say . . . those are our hats you know.

THE MANAGER   [*furious*]   Silence! silence! Don't try and be funny, if you please. . . . We're playing the scene now I'd have you notice. [*To the* STEPDAUGHTER.] Begin again, please!

THE STEPDAUGHTER   [*continuing*]   No thank you, sir.

THE FATHER   Oh, come now. Don't talk like that. You must take it.

I shall be upset if you don't. There are some lovely little hats here; and then—Madame will be pleased. She expects it, anyway, you know.

THE STEPDAUGHTER   No, no! I couldn't wear it!

THE FATHER   Oh, you're thinking about what they'd say at home if they saw you come in with a new hat? My dear girl, there's always a way round these little matters, you know.

THE STEPDAUGHTER   [*all keyed up*]   No, it's not that. I couldn't wear it because I am . . . as you see . . . you might have noticed . . . [*Showing her black dress.*]

THE FATHER   . . . in mourning! Of course: I beg your pardon: I'm frightfully sorry. . . .

THE STEPDAUGHTER   [*forcing herself to conquer her indignation and nausea*]   Stop! Stop! It's I who must thank you. There's no need for you to feel mortified or specially sorry. Don't think any more of what I've said. [*Tries to smile.*] I must forget that I am dressed so. . . .

THE MANAGER   [*interrupting and turning to the* PROMPTER]   Stop a minute! Stop! Don't write that down. Cut out that last bit. [*Then to the* FATHER *and* STEPDAUGHTER.] Fine! it's going fine! [*To the* FATHER *only.*] And now you can go on as we arranged. [*To the* ACTORS.] Pretty good that scene, where he offers her the hat, eh?

THE STEPDAUGHTER   The best's coming now. Why can't we go on?

THE MANAGER   Have a little patience! [*To the* ACTORS.] Of course, it must be treated rather lightly.

LEADING MAN   Still, with a bit of go in it!

LEADING LADY   Of course! It's easy enough! [*To* LEADING MAN.] Shall you and I try it now?

LEADING MAN   Why, yes! I'll prepare my entrance. [*Exit in order to make his entrance.*]

THE MANAGER   [*to* LEADING LADY]   See here! The scene between you and Madame Pace is finished. I'll have it written out properly after. You remain here . . . oh, where are you going?

LEADING LADY   One minute. I want to put my hat on again. [*Goes over to hat-rack and puts her hat on her head.*]

THE MANAGER   Good! You stay here with your head bowed down a bit.

THE STEPDAUGHTER   But she isn't dressed in black.

LEADING LADY   But I shall be, and much more effectively than you.

THE MANAGER   [*to* STEPDAUGHTER]   Be quiet please, and watch! You'll be able too learn something. [*Clapping his hands.*] Come on! come on! Entrance, please!

The door at rear of stage opens, and the LEADING MAN *enters with the lively manner of an old gallant. The rendering of the scene by the* ACTORS *from the very first words is seen to be quite a different thing, though it has not in any way the air of a parody. Naturally, the* STEPDAUGHTER *and the* FATHER, *not being able to recognize themselves in the* LEADING LADY *and the* LEADING MAN, *who deliver their words in different tones and with a different psychology, express, sometimes with smiles, sometimes with gestures, the impression they receive.*

LEADING MAN   Good afternoon, Miss. . . .

THE FATHER   [*at once unable to contain himself*]   No! no!

The STEPDAUGHTER, *noticing the way the* LEADING MAN *enters, bursts out laughing.*

THE MANAGER [*furious*]   Silence! And you please just stop that laughing. If we go on like this, we shall never finish.

THE STEPDAUGHTER   Forgive me, sir, but it's natural enough. This lady [*indicating* LEADING LADY] stands there still; but if she is supposed to be me, I can assure you that if I heard anyone say "Good afternoon" in that manner and in that tone, I should burst out laughing as I did.

THE FATHER   Yes, yes, the manner, the tone. . . .

THE MANAGER   Nonsense! Rubbish! Stand aside and let me see the action.

LEADING MAN   If I've got to represent an old fellow who's coming into a house of an equivocal character . . .

THE MANAGER   Don't listen to them, for Heaven's sake! Do it again! It goes fine. [*Waiting for the* ACTORS *to begin again.*] Well?

LEADING MAN   Good afternoon, Miss.

LEADING LADY   Good afternoon.

LEADING MAN [*imitating the gesture of the* FATHER *when he looked under the hat, and then expressing quite clearly first satisfaction and then fear*]   Ah, but . . . I say . . . this is not the first time that you have come here, is it?

THE MANAGER   Good, but not quite so heavily. Like this. [*Acts himself.*] "This isn't the first time that you have come here." . . . [*To* LEADING LADY.]   And you say: "No, sir."

LEADING LADY   No, sir.

LEADING MAN   You've been here before, more than once.

THE MANAGER   No, no, stop! Let her nod "yes" first. "You've been here before, eh?" [*The* LEADING LADY *lifts up her head slightly and closes her eyes as though in disgust. Then she inclines her head twice.*]

THE STEPDAUGHTER [*unable to contain herself*]   Oh my God! [*Puts a hand to her mouth to prevent herself from laughing.*]

THE MANAGER [*turning round*]   What's the matter?

THE STEPDAUGHTER   Nothing, nothing!

THE MANAGER [*to* LEADING MAN]   Go on!

LEADING MAN   You've been here before, eh? Well then, there's no need to be so shy, is there? May I take off your hat?

The LEADING MAN *says this last speech in such a tone and with such gestures that the* STEPDAUGHTER, *though she has her hand to her mouth, cannot keep from laughing.*

LEADING LADY [*indignant*]   I'm not going to stop here to be made a fool of by that woman there.

LEADING MAN   Neither am I! I'm through with it!

THE MANAGER [*shouting to* STEPDAUGHTER]   Silence! for once and all, I tell you!

THE STEPDAUGHTER   Forgive me! forgive me!

THE MANAGER   You haven't any manners: that's what it is! You go too far.

THE FATHER [*endeavoring to intervene*]   Yes, it's true, but excuse her. . . .

THE MANAGER   Excuse what? It's absolutely disgusting.

THE FATHER   Yes, sir, but believe me, it has such a strange effect when . . .

THE MANAGER   Strange? Why strange? Where is it strange?

THE FATHER   No, sir; I admire your actors—this gentleman here, this lady; but they are certainly not us!

THE MANAGER   I should hope not. Evidently they cannot be you, if they are actors.

THE FATHER   Just so: actors! Both of them act our parts exceedingly well. But, believe me, it produces quite a different effect on us. They want to be us, but they aren't, all the same.

THE MANAGER   What is it then anyway?

THE FATHER   Something that is . . . that is theirs—and no longer ours . . .

THE MANAGER   But naturally, inevitably. I've told you so already.

THE FATHER   Yes, I understand . . . I understand. . . .

THE MANAGER   Well then, let's have no more of it! [*Turning to the* ACTORS.] We'll have the rehearsals by ourselves, afterwards, in the ordinary way. I never could stand rehearsing with the author present. He's never satisfied! [*Turning to* FATHER *and* STEPDAUGHTER.] Come on! Let's get on with it again; and try and see if you can't keep from laughing.

THE STEPDAUGHTER   Oh, I shan't laugh any more. There's a nice little bit coming for me now: you'll see.

THE MANAGER   Well then: when she says "Don't think any more of what I've said, I must forget, etc.," you [*addressing the* FATHER] come in sharp with "I understand, I understand"; and then you ask her . . .

THE STEPDAUGHTER [*interrupting*]   What?

THE MANAGER   Why she is in mourning.

THE STEPDAUGHTER   Not at all! See here: when I told him that it was useless for me to be thinking about my wearing mourning, do you know how he answered me? "Ah well," he said, "then let's take off this little frock."

THE MANAGER   Great! Just what we want, to make a riot in the theatre!

THE STEPDAUGHTER   But it's the truth!

THE MANAGER   What does that matter? Acting is our business here. Truth up to a certain point, but no further.

THE STEPDAUGHTER   What do you want to do then?

THE MANAGER   You'll see, you'll see! Leave it to me.

THE STEPDAUGHTER   No sir! What you want to do is to piece together a little romantic sentimental scene out of my disgust, out of all the reasons, each more cruel and viler than the other, why I am what I am. He is to ask me why I'm in mourning; and I'm to answer with tears in my eyes, that it is just two months since papa died. No sir, no! He's got to say to me; as he did say: "Well, let's take off this little dress at once." And I, with my two months' mourning in my heart, went there behind that screen, and with these fingers tingling with shame . . .

THE MANAGER [*running his hands through his hair*]   For Heaven's sake! What are you saying?

THE STEPDAUGHTER [*crying out excitedly*]   The truth! The truth!

THE MANAGER   It may be. I don't deny it, and I can understand all your horror; but you must surely see that you can't have this kind of thing on the stage. It won't go.

THE STEPDAUGHTER   Not possible, eh? Very well! I'm much obliged to you—but I'm off!

THE MANAGER   Now be reasonable! Don't lose your temper!

THE STEPDAUGHTER   I won't stop here! I won't! I can see you've fixed it all up with him in your office. All this talk about what is possible for the stage . . . I understand! He wants to get at his complicated "cerebral drama," to have his famous remorses and torments acted; but I want to act my part, *my part!*

THE MANAGER [*annoyed, shaking his shoulders*]   Ah! Just *your* part! But, if you will pardon me, there are other parts than yours: His [*indicating the* FATHER] and hers! [*Indicating the* MOTHER.] On the stage you can't have a character becoming too prominent and overshadowing all the others. The thing is to pack them all into a neat little framework and then act what is actable. I am aware of the fact that everyone has his own interior life which he wants very much to put forward. But the difficulty lies in this fact: to set out just so much as is necessary for the stage, taking the other characters into consideration, and at the same time hint at the unrevealed interior life of each. I am willing to admit, my dear young lady, that from your point of view it would be a fine idea if each character could tell the public all his troubles in a nice monologue or a regular one hour lecture. [*Good humoredly.*] You must restrain yourself, my dear, and in your own interest, too; because this fury of yours, this exaggerated disgust you show, may make a bad impression, you know. After you have confessed to me that there were others before him at Madame Pace's and more than once . . .

THE STEPDAUGHTER [*bowing her head, impressed*]   It's true. But remember those others mean him for me all the same.

THE MANAGER [*not understanding*]   What? The others? What do you mean?

THE STEPDAUGHTER   For one who has gone wrong, sir, he who was responsible for the first fault is responsible for all that follow. He is responsible for my faults, was, even before I was born. Look at him, and see if it isn't true!

THE MANAGER   Well, well! And does the weight of so much responsibility seem nothing to you? Give him a chance to act it, to get it over!

THE STEPDAUGHTER   How? How can he act all his "noble remorses," all his "moral torments," if you want to spare him the horror of being discovered one day—after he had asked her what he did ask her—in the arms of her, that already fallen woman, that child, sir, that child he used to watch come out of school? [*She is moved.*]

> The MOTHER *at this point is overcome with emotion, and breaks out into a fit of crying. All are touched. A long pause.*

THE STEPDAUGHTER [*as soon as the* MOTHER *becomes a little quieter, adds resolutely and gravely*]   At present, we are unknown to the public. Tomorrow, you will act us as you wish, treating us in your own manner. But do you really want to see drama, do you want to see it flash out as it really did?

THE MANAGER   Of course! That's just what I do want, so I can use as much of it as is possible.

THE STEPDAUGHTER   Well then, ask that Mother there to leave us.

THE MOTHER [*changing her low plaint into a sharp cry*]   No! No! Don't permit it, sir, don't permit it!

THE MANAGER   But it's only to try it.

THE MOTHER   I can't bear it. I can't.

THE MANAGER   But since it has happened already . . . I don't understand!

THE MOTHER   It's taking place now. It happens all the time. My torment isn't a pretended one. I live and feel every minute of my torture. Those two children there—have you heard them speak? They can't speak any more. They cling to me to keep up my torment actual and vivid for me. But for themselves, they do not exist, they aren't any more. And she [*indicating the* STEPDAUGHTER] has run away, she has left me, and is lost. If I now see her here before me, it is only to renew for me the tortures I have suffered for her too.

THE FATHER   The eternal moment! She [*indicating the* STEPDAUGHTER] is here to catch me, fix me, and hold me eternally in the stocks for that one fleeting and shameful moment of my life. She can't give it up! And you sir, cannot either fairly spare me it.

THE MANAGER   I never said I didn't want to act it. It will form, as a matter of fact, the nucleus of the whole first act right up to her surprise. [*Indicates the* MOTHER.]

THE FATHER   Just so! This is my punishment: the passion in all of us that must culminate in her final cry.

THE STEPDAUGHTER   I can hear it still in my ears. It's driven me mad, that cry!—You can put me on as you like; it doesn't matter. Fully dressed, if you like—provided I have at least the arm bare; because, standing like this [*she goes close to the* FATHER *and leans her head on his breast*] with my head so, and my arms round his neck, I saw a vein pulsing in my arm here; and then, as if that live vein had awakened disgust in me, I closed my eyes like this, and let my head sink on his breast. [*Turning to the* MOTHER.] Cry out, mother! Cry out! [*Buries head in* FATHER's *breast, and with her shoulders raised as if to prevent her hearing the cry, adds in tones of intense emotion.*] Cry out as you did then!

THE MOTHER   [*coming forward to separate them*]   No! My daughter, my daughter! [*And after having pulled her away from him.*] You brute! you brute! She is my daughter! Don't you see she's my daughter?

THE MANAGER   [*walking backwards towards footlights*]   Fine! fine! Damned good! And then, of course—curtain!

THE FATHER   [*going towards him excitedly*]   Yes, of course, because that's the way it really happened.

THE MANAGER   [*convinced and pleased*]   Oh, yes, no doubt about it. Curtain here, curtain!

> At the reiterated cry of the MANAGER, the MACHINIST lets the curtain down, leaving the MANAGER and the FATHER in front of it before the footlights.

THE MANAGER   The darned idiot! I said "curtain" to show the act should end there, and he goes and lets it down in earnest. [*To the* FATHER, *while he pulls the curtain back to go on to the stage again.*] Yes, yes, it's all right. Effect certain! That's the right ending. I'll guarantee the first act at any rate.

Act 3

*When the curtain goes up again, it is seen that the stage hands
have shifted the bit of scenery used in the last part, and have
rigged up instead at the back of the stage a drop, with some
trees, and one or two wings. A portion of a fountain basin is
visible. The* MOTHER *is sitting on the right with the two children by her side. The* SON *is on the same side, but away from the
others. He seems bored, angry, and full of shame. The* FATHER
and the STEPDAUGHTER *are also seated toward the right front. On
the other side (left) are the* ACTORS, *much in the positions they
occupied before the curtain was lowered. Only the* MANAGER *is
standing up in the middle of the stage, with his hand closed over
his mouth in the act of meditating.*

THE MANAGER [*shaking his shoulders after a brief pause*]   Ah yes: the
second act! Leave it to me, leave it all to me as we arranged, and
you'll see! It'll go fine!

THE STEPDAUGHTER   Our entry into his house [*indicates* FATHER]
in spite of him. . . . [*Indicates the* SON.]

THE MANAGER [*out of patience*]   Leave it to me, I tell you!

THE STEPDAUGHTER   Do let it be clear, at any rate, that it is in spite
of my wishes.

THE MOTHER [*from her corner, shaking her head*]   For all the good
that's come of it. . . .

THE STEPDAUGHTER [*turning toward her quickly*]   It doesn't matter.
The more harm done us, the more remorse for him.

THE MANAGER [*impatiently*]   I understand! Good Heavens! I understand! I'm taking it into account.

THE MOTHER [*supplicatingly*]   I beg you, sir, to let it appear quite
plain that for conscience' sake I did try in every way . . .

THE STEPDAUGHTER [*interrupting indignantly and continuing for the
MOTHER*]   . . . to pacify me, to dissuade me from spiting him. [*To
MANAGER.*] Do as she wants: satisfy her, because it is true! I enjoy it
immensely. Anyhow, as you can see, the meeker she is, the more she
tries to get at his heart, the more distant and aloof does he become.

THE MANAGER   Are we going to begin this second act or not?

THE STEPDAUGHTER   I'm not going to talk any more now. But I must
tell you this: you can't have the whole action take place in the
garden, as you suggest. It isn't possible!

THE MANAGER   Why not?

THE STEPDAUGHTER   Because he [*indicates the* SON *again*] is always
shut up alone in his room. And then there's all the part of that poor
dazed-looking boy there which takes place indoors.

THE MANAGER   Maybe! On the other hand, you will understand—we
can't change scenes three or four times in one act.

THE LEADING MAN   They used to once.

THE MANAGER   Yes, when the public was up to the level of that child
there.

THE LEADING LADY   It makes the illusion easier.

THE FATHER [*irritated*]   The illusion! For Heaven's sake, don't say
illusion. Please don't use that word, which is particularly painful
for us.

THE MANAGER [*astounded*]   And why, if you please?

THE FATHER   It's painful, cruel, really cruel; and you ought to understand that.

THE MANAGER   But why? What ought we to say then? The illusion, I tell you, sir, which we've got to create for the audience. . . .

THE LEADING MAN   With our acting.

THE MANAGER   The illusion of a reality.

THE FATHER   I understand; but you, perhaps, do not understand us. Forgive me! You see . . . here for you and your actors, the thing is only—and rightly so . . . a kind of game. . . .

THE LEADING LADY [*interrupting indignantly*]   A game! We're not children here, if you please! We are serious actors.

THE FATHER   I don't deny it. What I mean is the game, or play, of your art, which has to give, as the gentleman says, a perfect illusion of reality.

THE MANAGER   Precisely—!

THE FATHER   Now, if you consider the fact that we [*indicates himself and the other five* CHARACTERS], as we are, have no other reality outside of this illusion. . . .

THE MANAGER [*astonished, looking at his* ACTORS, *who are also amazed*]   And what does that mean?

THE FATHER [*after watching them for a moment with a wan smile*]   As I say, sir, that which is a game of art for you is our sole reality. [*Brief pause. He goes a step or two nearer the* MANAGER *and adds.*] But not only for us, you know, by the way. Just you think it over well. [*Looks him in the eyes.*] Can you tell me who you are?

THE MANAGER [*perplexed, half smiling*]   What? Who am I? I am myself.

THE FATHER   And if I were to tell you that that isn't true, because you and I . . . ?

THE MANAGER   I should say you were mad—! [*The* ACTORS *laugh.*]

THE FATHER   You're quite right to laugh: because we are all making believe here. [*To* MANAGER.] And you can therefore object that it's only for a joke that that gentleman there [*indicates the* LEADING MAN], who naturally is himself, has to be me, who am on the contrary myself—this thing you see here. You see I've caught you in a trap! [*The* ACTORS *laugh.*]

THE MANAGER [*annoyed*]   But we've had all this over once before. Do you want to begin again?

THE FATHER   No, no! That wasn't my meaning! In fact, I should like to request you to abandon this game of art [*looking at the* LEADING LADY *as if anticipating her*] which you are accustomed to play here with your actors, and to ask you seriously once again: who are you?

THE MANAGER [*astonished and irritated, turning to his* ACTORS]   If this fellow here hasn't got a nerve! A man who calls himself a character comes and asks me who I am!

THE FATHER [*with dignity, but not offended*]   A character, sir, may always ask a man who he is. Because a character has really a life of his own, marked with his especial characteristics; for which reason he is always "somebody." But a man—I'm not speaking of you now—may very well be "nobody."

THE MANAGER   Yes, but you are asking these questions of me, the boss, the manager! Do you understand?

THE FATHER   But only in order to know if you, as you really are now, see yourself as you once were with all the illusions that were yours then, with all the things both inside and outside of you as they seemed to you—as they were then indeed for you. Well, sir, if you think of all those illusions that mean nothing to you now, of all those things which don't even *seem* to you to exist any more, while once they *were* for you, don't you feel that—I won't say these boards—but the very earth under your feet is sinking away from you when you reflect that in the same way this *you* as you feel it to-day—all this present reality of yours—is fated to seem a mere illusion to you tomorrow?

THE MANAGER [*without having understood much, but astonished by the specious argument*]   Well, well! And where does all this take us anyway?

THE FATHER   Oh, nowhere! It's only to show you that if we [*indicating the* CHARACTERS] have no other reality beyond the illusion, you too must not count overmuch on your reality as you feel it today, since, like that of yesterday, it may prove an illusion for you tomorrow.

THE MANAGER [*determining to make fun of him*]   Ah, excellent! Then you'll be saying next that you, with this comedy of yours that you brought here to act, are truer and more real than I am.

THE FATHER [*with the greatest seriousness*]   But of course; without doubt!

THE MANAGER   Ah, really?

THE FATHER   Why, I thought you'd understand that from the beginning.

THE MANAGER   More real than I?

THE FATHER   If your reality can change from one day to another. . .

THE MANAGER   But everyone knows it can change. It is always changing, the same as anyone else's.

THE FATHER [*with a cry*]   No, sir, not ours! Look here! That is the very difference! Our reality doesn't change: it can't change! It can't be other than what it is, because it is already fixed for ever. It's terrible. Ours is an immutable reality which should make you shudder when you approach us if you are really conscious of the fact that your reality is a mere transitory and fleeting illusion, taking this form today and that tomorrow, according to the conditions, according to your will, your sentiments, which in turn are controlled by an intellect that shows them to you today in one manner and to-morrow. . . . Who knows how? . . . Illusions of reality represented in this fatuous comedy of life that never ends, nor can ever end! Because if tomorrow it were to end . . . then why, all would be finished.

THE MANAGER   Oh for God's sake, will you *at least* finish with this philosophizing and let us try and shape this comedy which you yourself have brought me here? You argue and philosophize a bit too much, my dear sir. You know you seem to me almost, almost. . . . [*Stops and looks him over from head to foot.*] Ah, by the way, I think you introduced yourself to me as a—what shall . . . we say—a "character," created by an author who did not afterward care to make a drama of his own creations.

THE FATHER   It is the simple truth, sir.

THE MANAGER   Nonsense! Cut that out, please! None of us believes it, because it isn't a thing, as you must recognize yourself, which one can believe seriously. If you want to know, it seems to me you are trying to imitate the manner of a certain author whom I heartily

detest—I warn you—although I have unfortunately bound myself
to put on one of his works.[9] As a matter of fact, I was just starting
to rehearse it, when you arrived. [*Turning to the* ACTORS.] And this
is what we've gained—out of the frying-pan into the fire!

THE FATHER   I don't know to what author you may be alluding, but
believe me I feel what I think; and I seem to be philosophizing only
for those who do not think what they feel, because they blind themselves with their own sentiment. I know that for many people this
self-blinding seems much more "human"; but the contrary is really
true. For man never reasons so much and becomes so introspective as
when he suffers; since he is anxious to get at the cause of his sufferings, to learn who has produced them, and whether it is just or
unjust that he should have to bear them. On the other hand, when
he is happy, he takes his happiness as it comes and doesn't analyze
it, just as if happiness were his right. The animals suffer without reasoning about their sufferings. But take the case of a man who suffers
and begins to reason about it. Oh no! it can't be allowed! Let him
suffer like an animal, and then—ah yet, he is "human"!

THE MANAGER   Look here! Look here! You're off again, philosophizing
worse than ever.

THE FATHER   Because I suffer, sir! I'm not philosophizing: I'm crying
aloud the reason of my sufferings.

THE MANAGER [*makes brusque movement as he is taken with a new
idea*]   I should like to know if anyone has ever heard of a character
who gets right out of his part and perorates and speechifies as you
do. Have you ever heard of a case? I haven't.

THE FATHER   You have never met such a case, sir, because authors,
as a rule, hide the labor of their creations. When the characters
are really alive before their author, the latter does nothing but
follow them in their action, in their words, in the situations which
they suggest to him; and he has to will them the way they will
themselves—for there's trouble if he doesn't. When a character
is born, he acquires at once such an independence, even of his own
author, that he can be imagined by everybody even in many other
situations where the author never dreamed of placing him; and so
he acquires for himself a meaning which the author never thought
of giving him.

THE MANAGER   Yes, yes, I know this.

THE FATHER   What is there then to marvel at in us? Imagine such a
misfortune for characters as I have described to you: to be born
of an author's fantasy, and be denied life by him; and then answer
me if these characters left alive, and yet without life, weren't right
in doing what they did do and are doing now, after they have
attempted everything in their power to persuade him to give them
their stage life. We've all tried him in turn, I, she [*indicating the*
STEPDAUGHTER] and she. [*Indicating the* MOTHER.]

THE STEPDAUGHTER   It's true. I too have sought to tempt him, many,
many times, when he has been sitting at his writing table, feeling
a bit melancholy, at the twilight hour. He would sit in his armchair too lazy to switch on the light, and all the shadows that crept
into his room were full of our presence coming to tempt him. [*As
if she saw herself still there by the writing table, and was annoyed*

9. The "certain author" is Pirandello himself.

by the presence of the ACTORS.] Oh, if you would only go away,
go away and leave us alone—mother here with that son of hers—
I with that child—that boy there always alone—and then I
with him [*just hints at the* FATHER]—and then I alone, alone . . .
in those shadows! [*Makes a sudden movement as if in the vision she
has of herself illuminating those shadows she wanted to seize hold
of herself.*] Ah! my life! my life! Oh, what scenes we proposed to him
—and I tempted him more than any of the others!

THE FATHER   Maybe. But perhaps it was your fault that he refused to
give us life: because you were too insistent, too troublesome.

THE STEPDAUGHTER   Nonsense! Didn't he make me so himself? [*Goes
close to the* MANAGER *to tell him as if in confidence.*] In my opinion
he abandoned us in a fit of depression, of disgust for the ordinary
theatre as the public knows it and likes it.

THE SON   Exactly what it was, sir; exactly that!

THE FATHER   Not at all! Don't believe it for a minute. Listen to me!
You'll be doing quite right to modify, as you suggest, the excesses
both of this girl here, who wants to do too much, and of this young
man, who won't do anything at all.

THE SON   No, nothing!

THE MANAGER   You too get over the mark occasionally, my dear sir, if
I may say so.

THE FATHER   I? When? Where?

THE MANAGER   Always! Continuously! Then there's this insistence of
yours in trying to make us believe you are a character. And then too,
you must really argue and philosophize less, you know, much less.

THE FATHER   Well, if you want to take away from me the possibility
of representing the torment of my spirit which never gives me peace,
you will be suppressing me: that's all. Every true man, sir, who is a
little above the level of the beasts and plants does not live for the
sake of living, without knowing how to live; but he lives so as to give
a meaning and a value of his own to life. For me this is *everything*.
I cannot give up this, just to represent a mere fact as she [*indicating
the* STEPDAUGHTER] wants. It's all very well for her, since her "ven-
detta" lies in the "fact." I'm not going to do it. It destroys my *raison
d'être*.

THE MANAGER   Your *raison d'être!* Oh, we're going ahead fine! First
she starts off, and then you jump in. At this rate, we'll never finish.

THE FATHER   Now, don't be offended! Have it your own way—provided, however, that within the limits of the parts you assign us each
one's sacrifice isn't too great.

THE MANAGER   You've got to understand that you can't go on arguing
at your own pleasure. Drama is action, sir, action and not confounded philosophy.

THE FATHER   All right. I'll do just as much arguing and philosophizing
as everybody does when he is considering his own torments.

THE MANAGER   If the drama permits! But for Heaven's sake, man,
let's get along and come to the scene.

THE STEPDAUGHTER   It seems to me we've got too much action with
our coming into his house. [*Indicating* FATHER.] You said, before,
you couldn't change the scene every five minutes.

THE MANAGER   Of course not. What we've got to do is to combine
and group up all the facts in one simultaneous, close-knit, action.
We can't have it as you want, with your little brother wandering

like a ghost from room to room, hiding behind doors and meditating a project which—what did you say it did to him?

THE STEPDAUGHTER   Consumes him, sir, wastes him away!

THE MANAGER   Well, it may be. And then at the same time, you want the little girl there to be playing in the garden . . . one in the house, and the other in the garden: isn't that it?

THE STEPDAUGHTER   Yes, in the sun, in the sun! That is my only pleasure: to see her happy and careless in the garden after the misery and squalor of the horrible room where we all four slept together. And I had to sleep with her—I, do you understand?—with my vile contaminated body next to hers; with her folding me fast in her loving little arms. In the garden, whenever she spied me, she would run to take me by the hand. She didn't care for the big flowers, only the little ones; and she loved to show me them and pet me.

THE MANAGER   Well then, we'll have it in the garden. Everything shall happen in the garden; and we'll group the other scenes there. [*Calls a* STAGE HAND.] Here, a backcloth with trees and something to do as a fountain basin. [*Turning round to look at the back of the stage.*] Ah, you've fixed it up. Good! [*To* STEPDAUGHTER.] This is just to give an idea, of course. The Boy, instead of hiding behind the doors, will wander about here in the garden, hiding behind the trees. But it's going to be rather difficult to find a child to do that scene with you where she shows you the flowers. [*Turning to the* BOY.] Come forward a little, will you please? Let's try it now! Come along! come along! [*Then seeing him come shyly forward, full of fear and looking lost.*] It's a nice business, this lad here. What's the matter with him? We'll have to give him a word or two to say. [*Goes close to him, puts a hand on his shoulders, and leads him behind one of the trees.*] Come on! come on! Let me see you a little! Hide here . . . yes, like that. Try and show your head just a little as if you were looking for someone. . . . [*Goes back to observe the effect, when the* BOY *at once goes through the action.*] Excellent! fine! [*Turning to* STEPDAUGHTER.] Suppose the little girl there were to surprise him as he looks round, and run over to him, so we could give him a word or two to say?

THE STEPDAUGHTER   It's useless to hope he will speak, as long as that fellow there is here. . . . [*Indicates the* SON.] You must send him away first.

THE SON [*jumping up*]   Delighted! Delighted! I don't ask for anything better. [*Begins to move away.*]

THE MANAGER [*at once stopping him*]   No! No! Where are you going? Wait a bit!

> The MOTHER *gets up alarmed and terrified at the thought that he is really about to go away. Instinctively she lifts her arms to prevent him, without, however, leaving her seat.*

THE SON [*to* MANAGER *who stops him*]   I've got nothing to do with this affair. Let me go please! Let me go!

THE MANAGER   What do you mean by saying you've got nothing to do with this?

THE STEPDAUGHTER [*calmly, with irony*]   Don't bother to stop him: he won't go away.

THE FATHER   He has to act the terrible scene in the garden with his mother.

THE SON [*suddenly resolute and with dignity*]   I shall act nothing at all. I've said so from the very beginning. [*To the* MANAGER.] Let me go!

THE STEPDAUGHTER [*going over to the* MANAGER]   Allow me? [*Puts down the* MANAGER's *arm which is restraining the* SON.] Well, go away then, if you want to! [*The* SON *looks at her with contempt and hatred. She laughs and says.*] You see, he can't, he can't go away! He is obliged to stay here, indissolubly bound to the chain. If I, who fly off when that happens which has to happen, because I can't bear him—if I am still here and support that face and expression of his, you can well imagine that he is unable to move. He has to remain here, has to stop with that nice father of his, and that mother whose only son he is. [*Turning to the* MOTHER.] Come on, mother, come along! [*Turning to* MANAGER *to indicate her.*] You see, she was getting up to keep him back. [*To the* MOTHER, *beckoning her with her hand.*] Come on! come on! [*Then to* MANAGER.] You can imagine how little she wants to show these actors of yours what she really feels; but so eager is she to get near him that. . . . There, you see? She is willing to act her part. [*And in fact, the* MOTHER *approaches him; and as soon as the* STEPDAUGHTER *has finished speaking, opens her arms to signify that she consents.*]

THE SON [*suddenly*]   No! no! If I can't go away, then I'll stop here; but I repeat: I act nothing!

THE FATHER [to MANAGER *excitedly*]   You can force him, sir.

THE SON   Nobody can force me.

THE FATHER   I can.

THE STEPDAUGHTER   Wait a minute, wait. . . . First of all, the baby has to go to the fountain. . . . [*Runs to take the* CHILD *and leads her to the fountain.*]

THE MANAGER   Yes, yes of course; that's it. Both at the same time.

> The SECOND LADY LEAD *and the* JUVENILE LEAD *at this point separate themselves from the group of* ACTORS. *One watches the* MOTHER *attentively; the other moves about studying the movements and manner of the* SON *whom he will have to act.*

THE SON [*to* MANAGER]   What do you mean by both at the same time? It isn't right. There was no scene between me and her. [*Indicates the* MOTHER.] Ask her how it was!

THE MOTHER   Yes, it's true. I had come into his room. . . .

THE SON   Into my room, do you understand? Nothing to do with the garden.

THE MANAGER   It doesn't matter. Haven't I told you we've got to group the action?

THE SON [*observing the* JUVENILE LEAD *studying him*]   What do you want?

THE JUVENILE LEAD   Nothing! I was just looking at you.

THE SON [*turning toward the* SECOND LADY LEAD]   Ah! she's at it too: to re-act her part! [*Indicating the* MOTHER.]

THE MANAGER   Exactly! And it seems to me that you ought to be grateful to them for their interest.

THE SON   Yes, but haven't you yet perceived that it isn't possible to live in front of a mirror which not only freezes us with the image of ourselves, but throws our likeness back at us with a horrible grimace?

THE FATHER   That is true, absolutely true. You must see that.

THE MANAGER [*to* SECOND LADY LEAD *and* JUVENILE LEAD]   He's right!
Move away from them!

THE SON   Do as you like. I'm out of this!

THE MANAGER   Be quiet, you, will you? And let me hear your mother!
[*To* MOTHER.] You were saying you had entered. . . .

THE MOTHER   Yes, into his room, because I couldn't stand it any
longer. I went to empty my heart to him of all the anguish that tortures me. . . . But as soon as he saw me come in. . . .

THE SON   Nothing happened! There was no scene. I went away, that's
all! I don't care for scenes!

THE MOTHER   It's true, true. That's how it was.

THE MANAGER   Well now, we've got to do this bit between you and
him. It's indispensable.

THE MOTHER   I'm ready . . . when you are ready. If you could only
find a chance for me to tell him what I feel here in my heart.

THE FATHER [*going to* SON *in a great rage*]   You'll do this for your
mother, for your mother, do you understand?

THE SON [*quite determined*]   I do nothing!

THE FATHER [*taking hold of him and shaking him*]   For God's sake, do
as I tell you! Don't you hear your mother asking you for a favor?
Haven't you even got the guts to be a son?

THE SON [*taking hold of the* FATHER]   No! No! And for God's sake
stop it, or else. . . . [*General agitation. The* MOTHER, *frightened, tries
to separate them.*]

THE MOTHER [*pleading*]   Please! please!

THE FATHER [*not leaving hold of the* SON]   You've got to obey, do you
hear?

THE SON [*almost crying from rage*]   What does it mean, this madness
you've got? [*They separate.*] Have you no decency, that you insist on
showing everyone our shame? I won't do it! I won't! And I stand for
the will of our author in this. He didn't want to put us on the stage,
after all!

THE MANAGER   Man alive! You came here . . .

THE SON [*indicating* FATHER]   He did! I didn't!

THE MANAGER   Aren't you here now?

THE SON   It was his wish, and he dragged us along with him. He's
told you not only the things that did happen, but also things that
have never happened at all.

THE MANAGER   Well, tell me then what did happen. You went out of
your room without saying a word?

THE SON   Without a word, so as to avoid a scene!

THE MANAGER   And then what did you do?

THE SON   Nothing . . . walking in the garden. . . . [*Hesitates for a
moment with expression of gloom.*]

THE MANAGER [*coming closer to him, interested by his extraordinary
reserve*]   Well, well . . . walking in the garden. . . .

THE SON [*exasperated*]   Why on earth do you insist? It's horrible!

The MOTHER *trembles, sobs, and looks towards the fountain.*

THE MANAGER [*slowly observing the glance and turning toward the*
SON *with increasing apprehension*]   The baby?

THE SON   There in the fountain. . . .

THE FATHER [*pointing with tender pity to the* MOTHER]   She was following him at the moment. . . .

THE MANAGER [*to the* SON *anxiously*]   And then you. . . .

THE SON   I ran over to her; I was jumping in to drag her out when I saw something that froze my blood . . . the boy standing stock still, with eyes like a madman's, watching his little drowned sister, in the fountain! [*The* STEPDAUGHTER *bends over the fountain to hide the* CHILD. *She sobs.*] Then. . . . [*A revolver shot rings out behind the trees where the* BOY *is hidden.*]

THE MOTHER [*with a cry of terror runs over in that direction together with several of the* ACTORS *amid general confusion*]   My son! My son! [*Then amid the cries and exclamations one hears her voice.*] Help! Help!

THE MANAGER [*pushing the* ACTORS *aside while they lift up the* BOY *and carry him off*]   Is he really wounded?

SOME ACTORS   He's dead! dead!

OTHER ACTORS   No, no, it's only make-believe, it's only pretense!

THE FATHER [*with a terrible cry*]   Pretense? Reality, sir, reality!

THE MANAGER   Pretense? Reality? To hell with it all! Never in my life has such a thing happened to me. I've lost a whole day over these people, a whole day!

A View from the Bridge

CHARACTERS

LOUIS	RODOLPHO
MIKE	FIRST IMMIGRATION OFFICER
ALFIERI	SECOND IMMIGRATION OFFICER
EDDIE	MR. LIPARI
CATHERINE	MRS. LIPARI
BEATRICE	TWO "SUBMARINES"[1]
MARCO	NEIGHBORS
TONY	

Act 1

*The street and house front of a tenement building. The front is
skeletal entirely. The main acting area is the living room-dining
room of* EDDIE's *apartment. It is a worker's flat, clean, sparse,
homely. There is a rocker down front; a round dining table at
center, with chairs; and a portable phonograph.*

*At back are a bedroom door and an opening to the kitchen;
none of these interiors are seen.*

At the right, forestage, a desk. This is MR. ALFIERI's *law office.*

*There is also a telephone booth. This is not used until the last
scenes, so it may be covered or left in view.*

*A stairway leads up to the apartment, and then farther up to
the next story, which is not seen.*

*Ramps, representing the street, run upstage and off to right
and left.*

As the curtain rises, LOUIS *and* MIKE, *longshoremen, are pitch-
ing coins against the building at left.*

A distant foghorn blows.

Enter ALFIERI, *a lawyer in his fifties turning gray; he is portly,
good-humored, and thoughtful. The two pitchers nod to him as
he passes. He crosses the stage to his desk, removes his hat, runs
his fingers through his hair, and grinning, speaks to the audience.*

ALFIERI   You wouldn't have known it, but something amusing has just
happened. You see how uneasily they nod to me? That's because I
am a lawyer. In this neighborhood to meet a lawyer or a priest on
the street is unlucky. We're only thought of in connection with disasters, and they'd rather not get too close.

I often think that behind that suspicious little nod of theirs lie
three thousand years of distrust. A lawyer means the law, and in
Sicily, from where their fathers came, the law has not been a friendly
idea since the Greeks were beaten.

I am inclined to notice the ruins in things, perhaps because I was
born in Italy. . . . I only came here when I was twenty-five. In those
days, Al Capone, the greatest Carthaginian of all, was learning his

---

1. Immigrants who have entered the United States and remain in the country illegally.

trade on these pavements, and Frankie Yale himself was cut precisely in half by a machine gun on the corner of Union Street, two blocks away, Oh, there were many here who were justly shot by unjust men. Justice is very important here.[2]

But this is Red Hook, not Sicily. This is the slum that faces the bay on the seaward side of Brooklyn Bridge. This is the gullet of New York swallowing the tonnage of the world. And now we are quite civilized, quite American. Now we settle for half, and I like it better. I no longer keep a pistol in my filing cabinet.

And my pratice is entirely unromantic.

My wife has warned me, so have my friends; they tell me the people in this neighborhood lack elegance, glamour. After all, who have I dealt with in my life? Longshoremen and their wives, and fathers and grandfathers, compensation cases, evictions, family squabbles—the petty troubles of the poor—and yet . . . every few years there is still a case, and as the parties tell me what the trouble is, the flat air in my office suddenly washes in with the green scent of the sea, the dust in this air is blown away and the thought comes that in some Caesar's year, in Calabria perhaps or on the cliff at Syracuse, another lawyer, quite differently dressed, heard the same complaint and sat there as powerless as I, and watched it run its bloody course.

> EDDIE *has appeared and has been pitching coins with the men and is highlighted among them. He is forty—a husky, slightly overweight longshoreman.*

This one's name was Eddie Carbone, a longshoreman working the docks from Brooklyn Bridge to the breakwater where the open sea begins. [ALFIERI *walks into darkness.*]

EDDIE [*moving up steps into doorway*] Well, I'll see ya, fellas.

> CATHERINE *enters from kitchen, crosses down to window, looks out.*

LOUIS You workin' tomorrow?

EDDIE Yeah, there's another day yet on that ship. See ya, Louis.

> EDDIE *goes into the house, as light rises in the apartment.* CATHERINE *is waving to* LOUIS *from the window and turns to him.*

CATHERINE Hi, Eddie!

> EDDIE *is pleased and therefore shy about it; he hangs up his cap and jacket.*

EDDIE Where you goin' all dressed up?

CATHERINE [*running her hands over her skirt*] I just got it. You like it?

EDDIE Yeah, it's nice. And what happened to your hair?

CATHERINE You like it? I fixed it different. [*Calling to kitchen.*] He's here, B.!

EDDIE Beautiful. Turn around, lemme see in the back. [*She turns for him.*] Oh, if your mother was alive to see you now! She wouldn't believe it.

CATHERINE You like it, huh?

2. See the note on Italians in America, p. 314.

EDDIE   You look like one of them girls that went to college. Where you goin'?

CATHERINE [*taking his arm*]   Wait'll B. comes in, I'll tell you something. Here, sit down. [*She is walking him to the armchair. Calling offstage.*] Hurry up, will you, B.?

EDDIE [*sitting*]   What's goin' on?

CATHERINE   I'll get you a beer, all right?

EDDIE   Well, tell me what happened. Come over here, talk to me.

CATHERINE   I want to wait till B. comes in. [*She sits on her heels beside him.*] Guess how much we paid for the skirt.

EDDIE   I think it's too short, ain't it?

CATHERINE [*standing*]   No! not when I stand up.

EDDIE   Yeah, but you gotta sit down sometimes.

CATHERINE   Eddie, it's the style now. [*She walks to show him.*] I mean, if you see me walkin' down the street—

EDDIE   Listen, you been givin' me the willies the way you walk down the street, I mean it.

CATHERINE   Why?

EDDIE   Catherine, I don't want to be a pest, but I'm tellin' you you're walkin' wavy.

CATHERINE   I'm walkin' wavy?

EDDIE   Now don't aggravate me, Katie, you are walkin' wavy! I don't like the looks they're givin' you in the candy store. And with them new high heels on the sidewalk—clack, clack, clack. The heads are turnin' like windmills.

CATHERINE   But those guys look at all the girls, you know that.

EDDIE   You ain't "all the girls."

CATHERINE [*almost in tears because he disapproves*]   What do you want me to do? You want me to—

EDDIE   Now don't get mad, kid.

CATHERINE   Well, I don't know what you want from me.

EDDIE   Katie, I promised your mother on her deathbed. I'm responsible for you. You're a baby, you don't understand these things. I mean like when you stand here by the window, wavin' outside.

CATHERINE   I was wavin' to Louis!

EDDIE   Listen, I could tell you things about Louis which you wouldn't wave to him no more.

CATHERINE [*trying to joke him out of his warning*]   Eddie, I wish there was one guy you couldn't tell me things about!

EDDIE   Catherine, do me a favor, will you? You're gettin' to be a big girl now, you gotta keep yourself more, you can't be so friendly, kid. [*Calls.*] Hey, B., what're you doin' in there? [*To* CATHERINE.] Get her in here, will you? I got news for her.

CATHERINE [*starting out*]   What?

EDDIE   Her cousins landed.

CATHERINE [*clapping her hands together*]   No! [*She turns instantly and starts for the kitchen.*] B.! Your cousins!

BEATRICE *enters, wiping her hands with a towel.*

BEATRICE [*in the face of* CATHERINE's *shout*]   What?

CATHERINE   Your cousins got in!

BEATRICE [*astounded, turns to* EDDIE]   What are you talkin' about? Where?

EDDIE   I was just knockin' off work before and Tony Bereli come over to me; he says the ship is in the North River.

BEATRICE   [*her hands are clasped at her breast; she seems half in fear, half in unutterable joy*]   They're all right?

EDDIE   He didn't see them yet, they're still on board. But as soon as they get off he'll meet them. He figures about ten o'clock they'll be here,

BEATRICE   [*sits, almost weak from tension*]   And they'll let them off the ship all right? That's fixed, heh?

EDDIE   Sure, they give them regular seamen papers and they walk off with the crew. Don't worry about it, B., there's nothin' to it. Couple of hours they'll be here.

BEATRICE   What happened? They wasn't supposed to be till next Thursday.

EDDIE   I don't know; they put them on any ship they can get them out on. Maybe the other ship they was supposed to take there was some danger—What you cryin' about?

BEATRICE   [*astounded and afraid*]   I'm—I just—I can't believe it! I didn't even buy a new tablecloth; I was gonna wash the walls—

EDDIE   Listen, they'll think it's a millionaire's house compared to the way they live. Don't worry about the walls. They'll be thankful. [*To* CATHERINE.]   Whyn't you run down buy a tablecloth. Go ahead, here. [*He is reaching into his pocket.*]

CATHERINE   There's no stores open now.

EDDIE   [*to* BEATRICE]   You was gonna put a new cover on the chair.

BEATRICE   I know—well, I thought it was gonna be next week! I was gonna clean the walls, I was gonna wax the floors. [*She stands disturbed.*]

CATHERINE   [*pointing upward*]   Maybe Mrs. Dondero upstairs—

BEATRICE   [*of the tablecloth*]   No, hers is worse than this one. [*Suddenly.*]   My God, I don't even have nothin' to eat for them! [*She starts for the kitchen.*]

EDDIE   [*reaching out and grabbing her arm*]   Hey, hey! Take it easy.

BEATRICE   No, I'm just nervous, that's all. [*To* CATHERINE.]   I'll make the fish.

EDDIE   You're savin' their lives, what're you worryin' about the tablecloth? They probably didn't see a tablecloth in their whole life where they come from.

BEATRICE   [*looking into his eyes*]   I'm just worried about you, that's all I'm worried.

EDDIE   Listen, as long as they know where they're gonna sleep.

BEATRICE   I told them in the letters. They're sleepin' on the floor.

EDDIE   Beatrice, all I'm worried about is you got such a heart that I'll end up on the floor with you, and they'll be in our bed.

BEATRICE   All right, stop it.

EDDIE   Because as soon as you see a tired relative, I end up on the floor.

BEATRICE   When did you end up on the floor?

EDDIE   When your father's house burned down I didn't end up on the floor?

BEATRICE   Well, their house burned down!

EDDIE   Yeah, but it didn't keep burnin' for two weeks!

BEATRICE   All right, look, I'll tell them to go someplace else. [*She starts into the kitchen.*]

EDDIE   Now wait a minute. Beatrice! [*She halts. He goes to her.*] I just don't want you bein' pushed around, that's all. You got too big a heart. [*He touches her hand.*] What're you so touchy?

BEATRICE   I'm just afraid if it don't turn out good you'll be mad at me.

EDDIE   Listen, if everybody keeps his mouth shut, nothin' can happen. They'll pay for their board.

BEATRICE   Oh, I told them.

EDDIE   Then what the hell. [*Pause. He moves.*] It's an honor, B. I mean it. I was just thinkin' before, comin' home, suppose my father didn't come to this country, and I was starvin' like them over there . . . and I had people in America could keep me a couple of months? The man would be honored to lend me a place to sleep.

BEATRICE   [*there are tears in her eyes. She turns to* CATHERINE] You see what he is? [*She turns and grabs* EDDIE's *face in her hands.*] Mmm! You're an angel! God'll bless you. [*He is gratefully smiling.*] You'll see, you'll get a blessing for this!

EDDIE   [*laughing*]   I'll settle for my own bed.

BEATRICE   Go, Baby, set the table.

CATHERINE   We didn't tell him about me yet.

BEATRICE   Let him eat first, then we'll tell him. Bring everything in.

> *She hurries* CATHERINE *out.*

EDDIE   [*sitting at the table*]   What's all that about? Where's she goin'?

BEATRICE   Noplace. It's very good news, Eddie. I want you to be happy.

EDDIE   What's goin' on?

> CATHERINE *enters with plates, forks.*

BEATRICE   She's got a job.

> *Pause.* EDDIE *looks at* CATHERINE, *then back to* BEATRICE.

EDDIE   What job? She's gonna finish school.

CATHERINE   Eddie, you won't believe it—

EDDIE   No—no, you gonna finish school. What kinda job, what do you mean? All of a sudden you—

CATHERINE   Listen a minute, it's wonderful.

EDDIE   It's not wonderful. You'll never get nowheres unless you finish school. You can't take no job. Why didn't you ask me before you take a job?

BEATRICE   She's askin' you now, she didn't take nothin' yet.

CATHERINE   Listen a minute! I came to school this morning and the principal called me out of the class, see? To go to his office.

EDDIE   Yeah?

CATHERINE   So I went in and he says to me he's got my records, y'know? And there's a company wants a girl right away. It ain't exactly a secretary, it's a stenographer first, but pretty soon you get to be secretary. And he says to me that I'm the best student in the whole class—

BEATRICE   You hear that?

EDDIE   Well why not? Sure she's the best.

CATHERINE   I'm the best student, he says, and if I want, I should take the job and the end of the year he'll let me take the examination and he'll give me the certificate. So I'll save practically a year!

EDDIE   [*strangely nervous*]   Where's the job? What company?

CATHERINE   It's a big plumbing company over Nostrand Avenue.
EDDIE   Nostrand Avenue and where?
CATHERINE   It's someplace by the Navy Yard.
BEATRICE   Fifty dollars a week, Eddie.
EDDIE [*to* CATHERINE, *surprised*]   Fifty?[3]
CATHERINE   I swear.

> *Pause.*

EDDIE   What about all the stuff you wouldn't learn this year, though?
CATHERINE   There's nothin' more to learn, Eddie, I just gotta practice from now on. I know all the symbols and I know the keyboard. I'll just get faster, that's all. And when I'm workin' I'll keep gettin' better and better, you see?
BEATRICE   Work is the best practice anyway.
EDDIE   That ain't what I wanted, though.
CATHERINE   Why! It's a great big company—
EDDIE   I don't like that neighborhood over there.
CATHERINE   It's a block and half from the subway, he says.
EDDIE   Near the Navy Yard plenty can happen in a block and a half. And a plumbin' company! That's one step over the water front. They're practically longshoremen.
BEATRICE   Yeah, but she'll be in the office, Eddie.
EDDIE   I know she'll be in the office, but that ain't what I had in mind.
BEATRICE   Listen, she's gotta go to work sometime.
EDDIE   Listen, B., she'll be with a lotta plumbers? And sailors up and down the street? So what did she go to school for?
CATHERINE   But it's fifty a week, Eddie.
EDDIE   Look, did I ask you for money? I supported you this long I support you a little more. Please, do me a favor, will ya? I want you to be with different kind of people. I want you to be in a nice office. Maybe a lawyer's office someplace in New York in one of them nice buildings. I mean if you're gonna get outa here then get out; don't go practically in the same kind of neighborhood.

> *Pause.* CATHERINE *lowers her eyes.*

BEATRICE   Go, Baby, bring in the supper. [CATHERINE *goes out.*] Think about it a little bit, Eddie. Please. She's crazy to start work. It's not a little shop, it's a big company. Someday she could be a secretary. They picked her out of the whole class. [*He is silent, staring down at the tablecloth, fingering the pattern.*] What are you worried about? She could take care of herself. She'll get out of the subway and be in the office in two minutes.
EDDIE [*somehow sickened*]   I know that neighborhood, B., I don't like it.
BEATRICE   Listen, if nothin' happened to her in this neighborhood it ain't gonna happen noplace else. [*She turns his face to her.*] Look, you gotta get used to it, she's no baby no more. Tell her to take it. [*He turns his head away.*] You hear me? [*She is angering.*] I don't

---

3. Catherine's prospective salary indicates that the play takes place in the early 1950s. A little later in the play Eddie tells Marco and Rodolpho that a longshoreman can expect to earn an average of $30 to $40 a week. Some comparative prices: the New York *Times* cost five cents daily in the New York area and 15 cents elsewhere. Theater tickets ranged in cost from $1.20 to $6. Men's shoes could be purchased for $9.95 to $22.95, and bedsheets from $2.79 to $3.19.

understand you; she's seventeen years old, you gonna keep her in the house all her life?

EDDIE [*insulted*]   What kinda remark is that?

BEATRICE [*with sympathy but insistent force*]   Well, I don't understand when it ends. First is was gonna be when she graduated high school, so she graduated high school. Then it was gonna be when she learned stenographer, so she learned stenographer. So what're we gonna wait for now? I mean it, Eddie, sometimes I don't understand you; they picked her out of the whole class, it's an honor for her.

> CATHERINE *enters with food, which she silently sets on the table. After a moment of watching her face,* EDDIE *breaks into a smile, but it almost seems that tears will form in his eyes.*

EDDIE   With your hair that way you look like a madonna, you know that? You're the madonna type. [*She doesn't look at him, but continues ladling out food onto the plates.*] You wanna go to work, heh, Madonna?

CATHERINE [*softly*]   Yeah.

EDDIE [*with a sense of her childhood, her babyhood, and the years*] All right, go to work. [*She looks at him, then rushes and hugs him.*] Hey, hey! Take it easy! [*He holds her face away from him to look at her.*] What're you cryin' about? [*He is affected by her, but smiles his emotion away.*]

CATHERINE [*sitting at her place*]   I just—[*Bursting out.*] I'm gonna buy all new dishes with my first pay! [*They laugh warmly.*] I mean it. I'll fix up the whole house! I'll buy a rug!

EDDIE   And then you'll move away.

CATHERINE   No, Eddie!

EDDIE [*grinning*]   Why not? That's life. And you'll come visit on Sundays, then once a month, then Christmas and New Year's, finally.

CATHERINE [*grasping his arm to reassure him and to erase the accusation*]   No, please!

EDDIE [*smiling but hurt*]   I only ask you one thing—don't trust nobody. You got a good aunt but she's got too big a heart, you learned bad from her. Believe me.

BEATRICE   Be the way you are, Katie, don't listen to him.

EDDIE [*to* BEATRICE—*strangely and quickly resentful*]   You lived in a house all your life, what do you know about it? You never worked in your life.

BEATRICE   She likes people. What's wrong with that?

EDDIE   Because most people ain't people. She's goin' to work; plumbers; they'll chew her to pieces if she don't watch out. [*To* CATHERINE.] Believe me, Katie, the less you trust, the less you be sorry.

> EDDIE *crosses himself and the women do the same, and they eat.*

CATHERINE   First thing I'll buy is a rug, heh, B.?

BEATRICE   I don't mind. [*To* EDDIE.] I smelled coffee all day today. You unloadin' coffee today?

EDDIE   Yeah, a Brazil ship.

CATHERINE   I smelled it too. It smelled all over the neighborhood.

EDDIE   That's one time, boy, to be a longshoreman is a pleasure. I could work coffee ships twenty hours a day. You go down in the hold, y'know? It's like flowers, that smell. We'll bust a bag tomorrow, I'll bring you some.

BEATRICE   Just be sure there's no spiders in it, will ya? I mean it. [*She directs this to* CATHERINE, *rolling her eyes upward.*] I still remember that spider coming out of that bag he brung home. I nearly died.

EDDIE   You call that a spider? You oughta see what comes outa the bananas sometimes.

BEATRICE   Don't talk about it!

EDDIE   I seen spiders could stop a Buick.

BEATRICE [*clapping her hands over her ears*]   All right, shut up!

EDDIE [*laughing and taking a watch out of his pocket*]   Well, who started with spiders?

BEATRICE   All right, I'm sorry, I didn't mean it. Just don't bring none home again. What time is it?

EDDIE   Quarter nine. [*Puts watch back in his pocket. They continue eating in silence.*]

CATHERINE   He's bringin' them ten o'clock, Tony?

EDDIE   Around, yeah. [*He eats.*]

CATHERINE   Eddie, suppose somebody asks if they're livin' here. [*He looks at her as through already she had divulged something publicly. Defensively.*] I mean if they ask.

EDDIE   Now look, Baby, I can see we're gettin' mixed up again here.

CATHERINE   No, I just mean . . . people'll see them goin' in and out.

EDDIE   I don't care who sees them goin' in and out as long as you don't see them goin' in and out. And this goes for you too, B. You don't see nothin' and you don't know nothin'.

BEATRICE   What do you mean? I understand.

EDDIE   You don't understand; you still think you can talk about this to somebody just a little bit. Now lemme say it once and for all, because you're makin' me nervous again, both of you. I don't care if somebody comes in the house and sees them sleepin' on the floor, it never comes out of your mouth who they are or what they're doin' here.

BEATRICE   Yeah, but my mother'll know—

EDDIE   Sure she'll know, but just don't you be the one who told her, that's all. This is the United States government you're playin' with now, this is the Immigration Bureau. If you said it you knew it, if you didn't say it you didn't know it.

CATHERINE   Yeah, but Eddie, suppose somebody—

EDDIE   I don't care what question it is. You—don't—know—nothin'. They got stool pigeons all over this neighborhood they're payin' them every week for information, and you don't know who they are. It could be your best friend. You hear? [*To* BEATRICE.] Like Vinny Bolzano, remember Vinny?

BEATRICE   Oh, yeah. God forbid.

EDDIE   Tell her about Vinny. [*To* CATHERINE.] You think I'm blowin' steam here? [*To* BEATRICE.] Go ahead, tell her. [*To* CATHERINE.] You was a baby then. There was a family lived next door to her mother, he was about sixteen—

BEATRICE   No, he was no more than fourteen, cause I was to his confirmation in Saint Agnes. But the family had an uncle that they were hidin' in the house, and he snitched to the Immigration.

CATHERINE   The kid snitched?

EDDIE   On his own uncle!

CATHERINE   What, was he crazy?

EDDIE   He was crazy after, I tell you that, boy.

BEATRICE   Oh, it was terrible. He had five brothers and the old father. And they grabbed him in the kitchen and pulled him down the stairs —three flights his head was bouncin' like a coconut. And they spit on him in the street, his own father and his brothers. The whole neighborhood was cryin'.

CATHERINE   Ts! So what happened to him?

BEATRICE   I think he went away. [*To* EDDIE.] I never seen him again, did you?

EDDIE   [*rises during this, taking out his watch*]   Him? You'll never see him no more, a guy do a thing like that? How's he gonna show his face? [*To* CATHERINE, *as he gets up uneasily.*] Just remember, kid, you can quicker get back a million dollars that was stole than a word that you gave away. [*He is standing now, stretching his back.*]

CATHERINE   Okay, I won't say a word to nobody, I swear.

EDDIE   Gonna rain tomorrow. We'll be slidin' all over the decks. Maybe you oughta put something on for them, they be here soon.

BEATRICE   I only got fish, I hate to spoil it if they ate already. I'll wait, it only takes a few minutes; I could broil it.

CATHERINE   What happens, Eddie, when that ship pulls out and they ain't on it, though? Don't the captain say nothin'?

EDDIE   [*slicing an apple with his pocket knife*]   Captain's pieced off, what do you mean?

CATHERINE   Even the captain?

EDDIE   What's the matter, the captain don't have to live? Captain gets a piece, maybe one of the mates, piece for the guy in Italy who fixed the papers for them, Tony here'll get a little bite. . . .

BEATRICE   I just hope they get work here, that's all I hope.

EDDIE   Oh, the syndicate'll fix jobs for them; till they pay 'em off they'll get them work every day. It's after the pay-off, then they'll have to scramble like the rest of us.

BEATRICE   Well, it be better than they got there.

EDDIE   Oh sure, well, listen. So you gonna start Monday, heh, Madonna?

CATHERINE   [*embarrassed*]   I'm supposed to, yeah.

> EDDIE *is standing facing the two seated women. First* BEATRICE *smiles, then* CATHERINE, *for a powerful emotion is on him, a childish one and a knowing fear, and the tears show in his eyes —and they are shy before the avowal.*

EDDIE   [*sadly smiling, yet somehow proud of her*]   Well . . . I hope you have good luck. I wish you the best. You know that, kid.

CATHERINE   [*rising, trying to laugh*]   You sound like I'm goin' a million miles!

EDDIE   I know. I guess I just never figured on one thing.

CATHERINE   [*smiling*]   What?

EDDIE   That you would ever grow up. [*He utters a soundless laugh at himself, feeling his breast pocket of his shirt.*] I left a cigar in my other coat, I think. [*He starts for the bedroom.*]

CATHERINE   Stay there! I'll get it for you.

> *She hurries out. There is a slight pause, and* EDDIE *turns to* BEATRICE, *who has been avoiding his gaze.*

EDDIE   What are you mad at me lately?

BEATRICE   Who's mad? [*She gets up, clearing the dishes.*] I'm not mad. [*She picks up the dishes and turns to him.*] You're the one is mad. [*She turns and goes into the kitchen as* CATHERINE *enters from the bedroom with a cigar and a pack of matches.*]

CATHERINE   Here! I'll light it for you! [*She strikes a match and holds it to his cigar. He puffs. Quietly.*] Don't worry about me, Eddie, heh?

EDDIE   Don't burn yourself. [*Just in time she blows out the match.*] You better go in help her with the dishes.

CATHERINE   [*turns quickly to the table, and, seeing the table cleared, she says, almost guiltily*] Oh! [*She hurries into the kitchen, and as she exits there.*] I'll do the dishes, B.!

> Alone, EDDIE *stands looking toward the kitchen for a moment. Then he takes out his watch, glances at it, replaces it in his pocket, sits in the armchair, and stares at the smoke flowing out of his mouth.*
> *The lights go down, then come up on* ALFIERI, *who has moved onto the forestage.*

ALFIERI   He was as good a man as he had to be in a life that was hard and even. He worked on the piers when there was work, he brought home his pay, and he lived. And toward ten o'clock of that night, after they had eaten, the cousins came.

> *The lights fade on* ALFIERI *and rise on the street. Enter* TONY, *escorting* MARCO *and* RODOLPHO, *each with a valise.* TONY *halts, indicates the house. They stand for a moment looking at it.*

MARCO   [*he is a square-built peasant of thirty-two, suspicious, tender, and quiet-voiced*]   Thank you.

TONY   You're on your own now. Just be careful, that's all. Ground floor.

MARCO   Thank you.

TONY   [*indicating the house*]   I'll see you on the pier tomorrow. You'll go to work.

> MARCO *nods.* TONY *continues on walking down the street.*

RODOLPHO   This will be the first house I ever walked into in America! Imagine! She said they were poor!

MARCO   Ssh! Come. [*They go to door.*]

> MARCO *knocks. The lights rise in the room.* EDDIE *goes and opens the door. Enter* MARCO *and* RODOLPHO, *removing their caps.* BEATRICE *and* CATHERINE *enter from the kitchen. The lights fade in the street.*

EDDIE   You Marco?

MARCO   Marco.

EDDIE   Come on in! [*He shakes* MARCO's *hand.*]

BEATRICE   Here, take the bags!

MARCO   [*nods, looks to the women and fixes on* BEATRICE. *Crosses to* BEATRICE]   Are you my cousin? [*She nods. He kisses her hand.*]

BEATRICE   [*above the table, touching her chest with her hand*]   Beatrice. This is my husband, Eddie. [*All nod.*] Catherine, my sister Nancy's daughter. [*The brothers nod.*]

MARCO [*indicating* RODOLPHO] My brother. Rodolpho. [RODOLPHO *nods.* MARCO *comes with a certain formal stiffness to* EDDIE.] I want to tell you now Eddie—when you say go, we will go.

EDDIE Oh, no . . . [*Takes* MARCO's *bag.*]

MARCO I see it's a small house, but soon, maybe, we can have our own house.

EDDIE You're welcome, Marco, we got plenty of room here. Katie, give them supper, heh? [*Exits into bedroom with their bags.*]

CATHERINE Come here, sit down. I'll get you some soup.

MARCO [*as they go to the table*] We ate on the ship. Thank you. [*To* EDDIE, *calling off to bedroom.*] Thank you.

BEATRICE Get some coffee. We'll all have coffee. Come sit down.

RODOLPHO *and* MARCO *sit, at the table.*

CATHERINE [*wondrously*] How come he's so dark and you're so light, Rodolpho?

RODOLPHO [*ready to laugh*] I don't know. A thousand years ago, they say, the Danes invaded Sicily.

BEATRICE *kisses* RODOLPHO. *They laugh as* EDDIE *enters.*

CATHERINE [*to* BEATRICE] He's practically blond!

EDDIE How's the coffee doin'?

CATHERINE [*brought up*] I'm gettin' it. [*She hurries out to kitchen.*]

EDDIE [*sits on his rocker*] Yiz have a nice trip?

MARCO The ocean is always rough. But we are good sailors.

EDDIE No trouble gettin' here?

MARCO No. The man brought us. Very nice man.

RODOLPHO [*to* EDDIE] He says we start to work tomorrow. Is he honest?

EDDIE [*laughing*] No. But as long as you owe them money, they'll get you plenty of work. [*To* MARCO.] Yiz ever work on the piers in Italy?

MARCO Piers? Ts!—no.

RODOLPHO [*smiling at the smallness of his town*] In our town there are no piers, only the beach, and little fishing boats.

BEATRICE So what kinda work did yiz do?

MARCO [*shrugging shyly, even embarrassed*] Whatever there is, anything.

RODOLPHO Sometimes they build a house, or if they fix the bridge— Marco is a mason and I bring him the cement. [*He laughs.*] In harvest time we work in the fields . . . if there is work. Anything.

EDDIE Still bad there, heh?

MARCO Bad, yes.

RODOLPHO [*laughing*] It's terrible! We stand around all day in the piazza listening to the fountain like birds. Everybody waits only for the train.

BEATRICE What's on the train?

RODOLPHO Nothing. But if there are many passengers and you're lucky you make a few lire to push the taxi up the hill.

Enter CATHERINE; *she listens.*

BEATRICE You gotta push a taxi?

RODOLPHO [*laughing*] Oh, sure! It's a feature in our town. The horses in our town are skinnier than goats. So if there are too many passengers we help to push the carriages up to the hotel. [*He laughs.*] In our town the horses are only for show.

CATHERINE Why don't they have automobile taxis?

RODOLPHO There is one. We push that too. [*They laugh.*] Everything in our town you gotta push!

BEATRICE [*to* EDDIE] How do you like that!

EDDIE [*to* MARCO] So what're you wanna do, you gonna stay here in this country or you wanna go back?

MARCO [*surprised*] Go back?

EDDIE Well, you're married, ain't you?

MARCO Yes. I have three children.

BEATRICE Three! I thought only one.

MARCO Oh, no. I have three now. Four years, five years, six years.

BEATRICE Ah . . . I bet they're cryin' for you already, heh?

MARCO What can I do? The older one is sick in his chest. My wife—she feeds them from her own mouth. I tell you the truth, if I stay there they will never grow up. They eat the sunshine.

BEATRICE My God. So how long you want to stay?

MARCO With your permission, we will stay maybe a—

EDDIE She don't mean in this house, she means in the country.

MARCO Oh. Maybe four, five, six years, I think.

RODOLPHO [*smiling*] He trusts his wife.

BEATRICE Yeah, but maybe you'll get enough, you'll be able to go back quicker.

MARCO I hope. I don't know. [*To* EDDIE.] I understand it's not so good here either.

EDDIE Oh, you guys'll be all right—till you pay them off, anyway. After that, you'll have to scramble, that's all. But you'll make better here than you could there.

RODOLPHO How much? We hear all kinds of figures. How much can a man make? We work hard, we'll work all day, all night—

MARCO *raises a hand to hush him.*

EDDIE [*he is coming more and more to address* MARCO *only*] On the average a whole year? Maybe—well, it's hard to say, see. Sometimes we lay off, there's no ships three four weeks.

MARCO Three, four weeks!—Ts!

EDDIE But I think you could probably—thirty, forty a week, over the whole twelve months of the year.

MARCO [*rises, crosses to* EDDIE] Dollars.

EDDIE Sure dollars.

MARCO *puts an arm round* RODOLPHO *and they laugh.*

MARCO If we can stay here a few months, Beatrice—

BEATRICE Listen, you're welcome, Marco—

MARCO Because I could send them a little more if I stay here.

BEATRICE As long as you want, we got plenty a room.

MARCO [*his eyes are showing tears*] My wife—[*To* EDDIE.] My wife —I want to send right away maybe twenty dollars—

EDDIE You could send them something next week already.

MARCO [*he is near tears*] Eduardo . . . [*He goes to* EDDIE, *offering his hand.*]

EDDIE Don't thank me. Listen, what the hell, it's no skin off me. [*To* CATHERINE.] What happened to the coffee?

CATHERINE I got it on. [*To* RODOLPHO.] You married too? No.

RODOLPHO [*rises*] Oh, no . . .

BEATRICE [*to* CATHERINE] I told you he—

CATHERINE   I know, I just thought maybe he got married recently.

RODOLPHO   I have no money to get married. I have a nice face, but no money. [*He laughs.*]

CATHERINE [*to* BEATRICE]   He's a real blond!

BEATRICE [*to* RODOLPHO]   You want to stay here too, heh? For good?

RODOLPHO   Me? Yes, forever! Me, I want to be an American. And then I want to go back to Italy when I am rich, and I will buy a motor-cycle. [*He smiles.* MARCO *shakes him affectionately.*]

CATHERINE   A motorcycle!

RODOLPHO   With a motorcycle in Italy you will never starve any more.

BEATRICE   I'll get you coffee. [*She exits to the kitchen.*]

EDDIE   What you do with a motorcycle?

MARCO   He dreams, he dreams.

RODOLPHO [*to* MARCO]   Why? [*To* EDDIE.] Messages! The rich people in the hotel always need someone who will carry a message. But quickly, and with a great noise. With a blue motorcycle I would station myself in the courtyard of the hotel, and in a little while I would have messages.

MARCO   When you have no wife you have dreams.

EDDIE   Why can't you just walk, or take a trolley or sump'm?

Enter BEATRICE *with coffee.*

RODOLPHO   Oh, no, the machine, the machine is necessary. A man comes into a great hotel and says, I am a messenger. Who is this man? He disappears walking, there is no noise, nothing. Maybe he will never come back, maybe he will never deliver the message. But a man who rides up on a great machine, this man is responsible, this man exists. He will be given messages. [*He helps* BEATRICE *set out the coffee things.*] I am also a singer, though.

EDDIE   You mean a regular—?

RODOLPHO   Oh, yes. One night last year Andreola got sick. Baritone. And I took his place in the garden of the hotel. Three arias I sang without a mistake! Thousand-lire notes they threw from the tables, money was falling like a storm in the treasury.[4] It was magnificent. We lived six months on that night, eh, Marco?

MARCO *nods doubtfully.*

MARCO   Two months.

EDDIE *laughs.*

BEATRICE   Can't you get a job in that place?

RODOLPHO   Andreola got better. He's a baritone, very strong.

BEATRICE *laughs.*

MARCO [*regretfully, to* BEATRICE]   He sang too loud.

RODOLPHO   Why too loud?

MARCO   Too loud. The guests in that hotel are all Englishmen. They don't like too loud.

RODOLPHO [*to* CATHERINE]   Nobody ever said it was too loud!

MARCO   I say. It was too loud. [*To* BEATRICE.] I knew it as soon as he started to sing. Too loud.

RODOLPHO   Then why did they throw so much money?

---

4. At the time of the play one thousand lire were worth about $1.60. In Italy a news-paper cost 20 lire, a 100-watt light bulb 300 lire, and a five-tube radio 39,500 lire.

MARCO   They paid for your courage. The English like courage. But once is enough.

RODOLPHO [*to all but* MARCO]   I never heard anybody say it was too loud.

CATHERINE   Did you ever hear of jazz?

RODOLPHO   Oh, sure! I *sing* jazz.

CATHERINE [*rises*]   You could sing jazz?

RODOLPHO   Oh, I sing Napolidan, jazz, bel canto—I sing "Paper Doll," you like "Paper Doll"?[5]

CATHERINE   Oh, sure, I'm crazy for "Paper Doll." Go ahead, sing it.

RODOLPHO [*takes his stance after getting a nod of permission from* MARCO, *and with a high tenor voice begins singing*]
"I'll tell you boys it's tough to be alone,
And it's tough to love a doll that's not your own.
I'm through with all of them,
I'll never fall again,
Hey, boy, what you gonna do?
I'm gonna buy a paper doll that I can call my own,
A doll that other fellows cannot steal.

  EDDIE *rises and moves upstage.*

And then those flirty, flirty guys
With their flirty, flirty eyes
Will have to flirt with dollies that are real—"

EDDIE   Hey, kid—hey, wait a minute—

CATHERINE [*enthralled*]   Leave him finish, it's beautiful! [*To* BEA-TRICE.] He's terrific! It's terrific, Rodolpho.

EDDIE   Look, kid; you don't want to get picked up, do ya?

MARCO   No—no! [*He rises.*]

EDDIE [*indicating the rest of the building*]   Because we never had no singers here . . . and all of a sudden there's a singer in the house, y'know what I mean?

MARCO   Yes, yes. You'll be quiet, Rodolpho.

EDDIE [*he is flushed*]   They got guys all over the place, Marco. I mean.

MARCO   Yes. He'll be quiet. [*To* RODOLPHO.] You'll be quiet.

  RODOLPHO *nods.* EDDIE *has risen, with iron control, even a smile.*
  He moves to CATHERINE.

EDDIE   What's the high heels for, Garbo?

CATHERINE   I figured for tonight—

EDDIE   Do me a favor, will you? Go ahead.

  Embarrassed now, angered, CATHERINE *goes out into the bed-*
  room. BEATRICE *watches her go and gets up; in passing, she*
  gives EDDIE *a cold look, restrained only by the strangers, and*
  goes to the table to pour coffee.

EDDIE [*striving to laugh, and to* MARCO, *but directed as much to* BEA-TRICE]   All actresses they want to be around here.

RODOLPHO [*happy about it*]   In Italy too! All the girls.

5. "Paper Doll" (1942) is an American popular song with words and music by Johnny S. Black. "Napolidan" or Neapolitan songs are a popular Italian form, character-ized by sentimentality in the lyrics, music, and performance. "Bel canto" (literally, beautiful singing) is a style of operatic singing which emphasizes beauty of sound and brilliance of execution over dramatic expression of emotions appropriate to the text.

CATHERINE *emerges from the bedroom in low-heel shoes, comes to the table.* RODOLPHO *is lifting a cup.*

EDDIE [*he is sizing up* RODOLPHO, *and there is a concealed suspicion*] Yeah, heh?

RODOLPHO Yes! [*Laughs, indicating* CATHERINE.] Especially when they are so beautiful!

CATHERINE You like sugar?

RODOLPHO Sugar? Yes! I like sugar very much!

EDDIE *is downstage, watching as she pours a spoonful of sugar into his cup, his face puffed with trouble, and the room dies. Lights rise on* ALFIERI.

ALFIERI Who can ever know what will be discovered? Eddie Carbone had never expected to have a destiny. A man works, raises his family, goes bowling, eats, gets old, and then he dies. Now, as the weeks passed, there was a future, there was a trouble that would not go away.

The lights fade on ALFIERI, *then rise on* EDDIE *standing at the doorway of the house.* BEATRICE *enters on the street. She sees* EDDIE, *smiles at him. He looks away. She starts to enter the house when* EDDIE *speaks.*

EDDIE It's after eight.

BEATRICE Well, it's a long show at the Paramount.

EDDIE They must've seen every picture in Brooklyn by now. He's supposed to stay in the house when he ain't working. He ain't supposed to go advertising himself.

BEATRICE Well that's his trouble, what do you care? If they pick him up they pick him up, that's all. Come in the house.

EDDIE What happened to the stenography? I don't see her practice no more.

BEATRICE She'll get back to it. She's excited, Eddie.

EDDIE She tell you anything?

BEATRICE [*comes to him, now the subject is opened*] What's the matter with you? He's a nice kid, what do you want from him?

EDDIE That's a nice kid? He gives me the heeby-jeebies.

BEATRICE [*smiling*] Ah, go on, you're just jealous.

EDDIE Of *him?* Boy, you don't think much of me.

BEATRICE I don't understand you. What's so terrible about him?

EDDIE You mean it's all right with you? That's gonna be her husband?

BEATRICE Why? He's a nice fella, hard workin', he's a good-lookin' fella.

EDDIE He sings on the ships, didja know that?

BEATRICE What do you mean, he sings?

EDDIE Just what I said, he sings. Right on the deck, all of a sudden, a whole song comes out of his mouth—with motions. You know what they're callin' him now? Paper Doll they're callin' him, Canary. He's like a weird. He comes out on the pier, one-two-three, it's a regular free show.

BEATRICE Well, he's a kid; he don't know how to behave himself yet.

EDDIE And with that wacky hair; he's like a chorus girl or sump'm.

BEATRICE So he's blond, so—

EDDIE I just hope that's his regular hair, that's all I hope.

BEATRICE   You crazy or sump'm? [*She tries to turn him to her.*]

EDDIE [*he keeps his head turned away*]   What's so crazy? I don't like his whole way.

BEATRICE   Listen, you never seen a blond guy in your life? What about Whitey Balso?

EDDIE [*turning to her victoriously*]   Sure, but Whitey don't sing; he don't do like that on the ships.

BEATRICE   Well, maybe that's the way they do in Italy.

EDDIE   Then why don't his brother sing? Marco goes around like a man; nobody kids Marco. [*He moves from her, halts. She realizes there is a campaign solidified in him.*] I tell you the truth I'm surprised I have to tell you all this. I mean I'm surprised, B.

BEATRICE [*she goes to him with purpose now*]   Listen, you ain't gonna start nothin' here.

EDDIE   I ain't startin' nothin', but I ain't gonna stand around lookin' at that. For that character I didn't bring her up. I swear, B., I'm surprised at you; I sit there waitin' for you to wake up but everything is great with you.

BEATRICE   No, everything ain't great with me.

EDDIE   No?

BEATRICE   No. But I got other worries.

EDDIE   Yeah. [*He is already weakening.*]

BEATRICE   Yeah, you want me to. tell you?

EDDIE [*in retreat*]   Why? What worries you got?

BEATRICE   When am I gonna be a wife again, Eddie?

EDDIE   I ain't been feelin' good. They bother me since they came.

BEATRICE   It's almost three months you don't feel good; they're only here a couple of weeks. It's three months, Eddie.

EDDIE   I don't know, B. I don't want to talk about it.

BEATRICE   What's the matter, Eddie, you don't like me, heh?

EDDIE   What do you mean, I don't like you? I said I don't feel good, that's all.

BEATRICE   Well, tell me, am I doing something wrong? Talk to me.

EDDIE [*pause. He can't speak, then*]   I can't. I can't talk about it.

BEATRICE   Well tell me what—

EDDIE   I got nothin' to say about it!

> She stands for a moment; he is looking off; she turns to go into the house.

EDDIE   I'll be all right, B.; just lay off me, will ya? I'm worried about her.

BEATRICE   The girl is gonna be eighteen years old, it's time already.

EDDIE   B., he's taking her for a ride!

BEATRICE   All right, that's her ride. What're you gonna stand over her till she's forty? Eddie, I want you to cut it out now, you hear me? I don't like it! Now come in the house.

EDDIE   I want to take a walk, I'll be in right away.

BEATRICE   They ain't goin' to come any quicker if you stand in the street. It ain't nice, Eddie.

EDDIE   I'll be in right away. Go ahead. [*He walks off.*]

> She goes into the house. EDDIE *glances up the street, sees* LOUIS *and* MIKE *coming, and sits on an iron railing.* LOUIS *and* MIKE *enter.*

LOUIS   Wanna go bowlin' tonight?

EDDIE   I'm too tired. Goin' to sleep.

LOUIS   How's your two submarines?

EDDIE   They're okay.

LOUIS   I see they're gettin' work allatime.

EDDIE   Oh yeah, they're doin' all right.

MIKE   That's what we oughta do. We oughta leave the country and come in under the water. Then we get work.

EDDIE   You ain't kiddin'.

LOUIS   Well, what the hell. Y'know?

EDDIE   Sure.

LOUIS   [*sits on railing beside* EDDIE]   Believe me, Eddie, you got a lotta credit comin' to you.

EDDIE   Aah, they don't bother me, don't cost me nutt'n.

MIKE   That older one, boy, he's a regular bull. I seen him the other day liftin' coffee bags over the Matson Line. They leave him alone he woulda load the whole ship by himself.[6]

EDDIE   Yeah, he's a strong guy, that guy. Their father was a regular giant, supposed to be.

LOUIS   Yeah, you could see. He's a regular slave.

MIKE   [*grinning*]   That blond one, though—[EDDIE *looks at him.*] He's got a sense of humor. [LOUIS *snickers.*]

EDDIE   [*searchingly*]   Yeah. He's funny—

MIKE   [*starting to laugh*]   Well he ain't exackly funny, but he's always like makin' remarks like, y'know? He comes around, everybody's laughin'. [LOUIS *laughs.*]

EDDIE   [*uncomfortably, grinning*]   Yeah, well . . . he's got a sense of humor.

MIKE   [*laughing*]   Yeah, I mean, he's always makin' like remarks, like, y'know?

EDDIE   Yeah, I know. But he's a kid yet, y'know? He—he's just a kid, that's all.

MIKE   [*getting hysterical with* LOUIS]   I know. You take one look at him—everybody's happy. [LOUIS *laughs.*] I worked one day with him last week over the Moore-MacCormack Line, I'm tellin' you they was all hysterical. [LOUIS *and he explode in laughter.*]

EDDIE   Why? What'd he do?

MIKE   I don't know . . . he was just humorous. You never can remember what he says, y'know? But it's the way he says it. I mean he gives you a look sometimes and you start laughin'!

EDDIE   Yeah. [*Troubled.*] He's got a sense of humor.

MIKE   [*gasping*]   Yeah.

LOUIS   [*rising*]   Well, we see ya, Eddie.

EDDIE   Take it easy.

LOUIS   Yeah. See ya.

MIKE   If you wanna come bowlin' later we're goin' Flatbush Avenue.

> *Laughing, they move to exit, meeting* RODOLPHO *and* CATHERINE *entering on the street. Their laughter rises as they see* RODOLPHO, *who does not understand but joins in.* EDDIE *moves to enter the house as* LOUIS *and* MIKE *exit.* CATHERINE *stops him at the door.*

---

6. The Matson Line and the Moore-MacCormack Line (see below) are shipping companies whose names are used to designate the piers where their ships are usually docked.

CATHERINE   Hey, Eddie—what a picture we saw! Did we laugh!

EDDIE [*he can't help smiling at sight of her*]   Where'd you go?

CATHERINE   Paramount. It was with those two guys, y'know? That—

EDDIE   Brooklyn Paramount?

CATHERINE [*with an edge of anger, embarrassed before* RODOLPHO] Sure, the Brooklyn Paramount. I told you we wasn't goin' to New York.

EDDIE [*retreating before the threat of her anger*]   All right, I only asked you. [*To* RODOLPHO.] I just don't want her hangin' around Times Square, see? It's full of tramps over there.

RODOLPHO   I would like to go to Broadway once, Eddie. I would like to walk with her once where the theaters are and the opera. Since I was a boy I see pictures of those lights.

EDDIE [*his little patience waning*]   I want to talk to her a minute, Rodolpho. Go inside, will you?

RODOLPHO   Eddie, we only walk together in the streets. She teaches me.

CATHERINE   You know what he can't get over? That there's no fountains in Brooklyn!

EDDIE [*smiling unwillingly*]   Fountains? [RODOLPHO *smiles at his own naïveté.*]

CATHERINE   In Italy he says, every town's got fountains, and they meet there. And you know what? They got oranges on the trees where he comes from, and lemons. Imagine—on the trees? I mean it's interesting. But he's crazy for New York.

RODOLPHO [*attempting familiarity*]   Eddie, why can't we go once to Broadway—?

EDDIE   Look, I gotta tell her something—

RODOLPHO   Maybe you can come too. I want to see all those lights. [*He sees no response in* EDDIE's *face. He glances at* CATHERINE.] I'll walk by the river before I go to sleep. [*He walks off down the street.*]

CATHERINE   Why don't you talk to him, Eddie? He blesses you, and you don't talk to him hardly.

EDDIE [*enveloping her with his eyes*]   I bless you and you don't talk to me. [*He tries to smile.*]

CATHERINE   *I* don't talk to you? [*She hits his arm.*] What do you mean?

EDDIE   I don't see you no more. I come home you're runnin' around someplace—

CATHERINE   Well, he wants to see everything, that's all, so we go. . . . You mad at me?

EDDIE   No. [*He moves from her, smiling sadly.*] It's just I used to come home, you was always there. Now, I turn around, you're a big girl. I don't know how to talk to you.

CATHERINE   Why?

EDDIE   I don't know, you're runnin', you're runnin', Katie. I don't think you listening any more to me.

CATHERINE [*going to him*]   Ah, Eddie, sure I am. What's the matter? You don't like him?

Slight pause.

EDDIE [*turns to her*]   You like him, Katie?

CATHERINE [*with a blush but holding her ground*]   Yeah. I like him.

EDDIE [*his smile goes*]   You like him.
CATHERINE [*looking down*]   Yeah. [*Now she looks at him for the consequences, smiling but tense. He looks at her like a lost boy.*] What're you got against him? I don't understand. He only blesses you.
EDDIE [*turns away*]   He don't bless me, Katie.
CATHERINE   He does! You're like a father to him!
EDDIE [*turns to her*]   Katie.
CATHERINE   What, Eddie?
EDDIE   You gonna marry him?
CATHERINE   I don't know. We just been . . . goin' around, that's all. [*Turns to him.*] What're you got against him, Eddie? Please, tell me. What?
EDDIE   He don't respect you.
CATHERINE   Why?
EDDIE   Katie . . . if you wasn't an orphan, wouldn't he ask your father's permission before he run around with you like this?
CATHERINE   Oh, well, he didn't think you'd mind.
EDDIE   He knows I mind, but it don't bother him if I mind, don't you see that?
CATHERINE   No, Eddie, he's got all kinds of respect for me. And you too! We walk across the street he takes my arm—he almost bows to me! You got him all wrong, Eddie; I mean it, you—
EDDIE   Katie, he's only bowin' to his passport.
CATHERINE   His passport!
EDDIE   That's right. He marries you he's got the right to be an American citizen. That's what's goin' on here.

She is puzzled and surprised.

You understand what I'm tellin' you? The guy is lookin' for his break, that's all he's lookin' for.
CATHERINE [*pained*]   Oh, no, Eddie, I don't think so.
EDDIE   You don't think so! Katie, you're gonna make me cry here. Is that a workin' man? What does he do with his first money? A snappy new jacket he buys, records, a pointy pair new shoes and his brother's kids are starvin' over there with tuberculosis? That's a hit-and-run guy, baby; he's got bright lights in his head, Broadway. Them guys don't think of nobody but theirself! You marry him and the next time you see him it'll be for divorce!
CATHERINE [*steps toward him*]   Eddie, he never said a word about his papers or—
EDDIE   You mean he's supposed to tell you that?
CATHERINE   I don't think he's even thinking about it.
EDDIE   What's better for him to think about! He could be picked up any day here and he's back pushin' taxis up the hill!
CATHERINE   No, I don't believe it.
EDDIE   Katie, don't break my heart, listen to me.
CATHERINE   I don't want to hear it.
EDDIE   Katie, listen . . .
CATHERINE   He loves me!
EDDIE [*with deep alarm*]   Don't say that, for God's sake! This is the oldest racket in the country—
CATHERINE [*desperately, as though he had made his imprint*]   I don't believe it! [*She rushes to the house.*]

EDDIE [*following her*]   They been pullin' this since the Immigration Law was put in! They grab a green kid that don't know nothin' and they—

CATHERINE [*sobbing*]   I don't believe it and I wish to hell you'd stop it!

EDDIE   Katie!

> *They enter the apartment. The lights in the living room have risen and* BEATRICE *is there. She looks past the sobbing* CATHERINE *at* EDDIE, *who, in the presence of his wife, makes an awkward gesture of eroded command, indicating* CATHERINE.

EDDIE   Why don't you straighten her out?

BEATRICE [*inwardly angered at his flowing emotion, which in itself alarms her*]   When are you going to leave her alone?

EDDIE   B., the guy is no good!

BEATRICE [*suddenly, with open fright and fury*]   You going to leave her alone? Or you gonna drive me crazy?

> *He turns, striving to retain his dignity, but nevertheless in guilt walks out of the house, into the street and away.* CATHERINE *starts into a bedroom.*

Listen, Catherine.

> CATHERINE *halts, turns to her sheepishly.*

What are you going to do with yourself?

CATHERINE   I don't know.

BEATRICE   Don't tell me you don't know; you're not a baby any more, what are you going to do with yourself?

CATHERINE   He won't listen to me.

BEATRICE   I don't understand this. He's not your father, Catherine. I don't understand what's going on here.

CATHERINE [*as one who herself is trying to rationalize a buried impulse*]   What am I going to do, just kick him in the face with it?

BEATRICE   Look, honey, you wanna get married, or don't you wanna get married? What are you worried about, Katie?

CATHERINE [*quietly, trembling*]   I don't know, B. It just seems wrong if he's against it so much.

BEATRICE [*never losing her aroused alarm*]   Sit down, honey, I want to tell you something. Here, sit down. Was there ever any fella he liked for you? There wasn't, was there?

CATHERINE   But he says Rodolpho's just after his papers.

BEATRICE   Look, he'll say anything. What does he care what he says? If it was a prince came here for you it would be no different. You know that, don't you?

CATHERINE   Yeah, I guess.

BEATRICE   So what does that mean?

CATHERINE [*slowly turns her head to* BEATRICE]   What?

BEATRICE   It means you gotta be your own self more. You still think you're a little girl, honey. But nobody else can make up your mind for you any more, you understand? You gotta give him to understand that he can't give you orders no more.

CATHERINE   Yeah, but how am I going to do that? He thinks I'm a baby.

BEATRICE   Because *you* think you're a baby. I told you fifty times already, you can't act the way you act. You still walk around in front of him in your slip—

CATHERINE   Well I forgot.

BEATRICE   Well you can't do it. Or like you sit on the edge of the bathtub talkin' to him when he's shavin' in his underwear.

CATHERINE   When'd I do that?

BEATRICE   I seen you in there this morning.

CATHERINE   Oh . . . well, I wanted to tell him something and I—

BEATRICE   I know, honey. But if you act like a baby and he be treatin' you like a baby. Like when he comes home sometimes you throw yourself at him like when you was twelve years old.

CATHERINE   Well I like to see him and I'm happy so I—

BEATRICE   Look, I'm not tellin' you what to do honey, but—

CATHERINE   No, you could tell me, B.! Gee, I'm all mixed up. See, I— He looks so sad now and it hurts me.

BEATRICE   Well look Katie, if it's goin' to hurt you so much you're gonna end up an old maid here.

CATHERINE   No!

BEATRICE   I'm tellin' you, I'm not makin' a joke. I tried to tell you a couple of times in the last year or so. That's why I was so happy you were going to go out and get work, you wouldn't be here so much, you'd be a little more independent. I mean it. It's wonderful for a whole family to love each other, but you're a grown woman and you're in the same house with a grown man. So you'll act different now, heh?

CATHERINE   Yeah, I will. I'll remember.

BEATRICE   Because it ain't only up to him, Katie, you understand? I told him the same thing already.

CATHERINE   [*quickly*]   What?

BEATRICE   That he should let you go. But, you see, if only I tell him, he thinks I'm just bawlin' him out, or maybe I'm jealous or somethin', you know?

CATHERINE   [*astonished*]   He said you was jealous?

BEATRICE   No, I'm just sayin' maybe that's what he thinks. [*She reaches over to* CATHERINE's *hand; with a strained smile.*] You think I'm jealous of you, honey?

CATHERINE   No! It's the first I thought of it.

BEATRICE   [*with a quiet sad laugh*]   Well you should have thought of it before . . . but I'm not. We'll be all right. Just give him to understand; you don't have to fight, you're just—You're a woman, that's all, and you got a nice boy, and now the time came when you said good-by. All right?

CATHERINE   [*strangely moved at the prospect*]   All right. . . . If I can.

BEATRICE   Honey . . . you gotta.

> CATHERINE, *sensing now an imperious demand, turns with some fear, with a discovery, to* BEATRICE. *She is at the edge of tears, as though a familiar world had shattered.*

CATHERINE   Okay.

> *Lights out on them and up on* ALFIERI, *seated behind his desk.*

ALFIERI   It was at this time that he first came to me. I had represented his father in an accident case some years before, and I was acquainted with the family in a casual way. I remember him now as he walked through my doorway—

Enter EDDIE *down right ramp.*

His eyes were like tunnels; my first thought was that he had committed a crime.

EDDIE *sits beside the desk, cap in hand, looking out.*

But soon I saw it was only a passion that had moved into his body, like a stranger. [ALFIERI *pauses, looks down at his desk, then to* EDDIE *as though he were continuing a conversation with him.*] I don't quite understand what I can do for you. Is there a question of law somewhere?

EDDIE   That's what I want to ask you.

ALFIERI   Because there's nothing illegal about a girl falling in love with an immigrant.

EDDIE   Yeah, but what about it if the only reason for it is to get his papers?

ALFIERI   First of all you don't know that.

EDDIE   I see it in his eyes; he's laughin' at her and he's laughin' at me.

ALFIERI   Eddie, I'm a lawyer. I can only deal in what's provable. You understand that, don't you? Can you prove that?

EDDIE   *I know what's in his mind, Mr. Alfieri!*

ALFIERI   Eddie, even if you could prove that—

EDDIE   Listen . . . will you listen to me a minute? My father always said you was a smart man. I want you to listen to me.

ALFIERI   I'm only a lawyer, Eddie.

EDDIE   Will you listen a minute? I'm talkin' about the law. Lemme just bring out what I mean. A man, which he comes into the country illegal, don't it stand to reason he's gonna take every penny and put it in the sock? Because they don't know from one day to another, right?

ALFIERI   All right.

EDDIE   He's spendin'. Records he buys now. Shoes. Jackets. Y'understand me? This guy ain't worried. This guy is *here.* So it must be that he's got it all laid out in his mind already—he's stayin'. Right?

ALFIERI   Well? What about it?

EDDIE   All right. [*He glances at* ALFIERI, *then down to the floor.*] I'm talking to you confidential, ain't I?

ALFIERI   Certainly.

EDDIE   I mean it don't go no place but here. Because I don't like to say this about anybody. Even my wife I didn't exactly say this.

ALFIERI   What is it?

EDDIE   [*takes a breath and glances briefly over each shoulder*]   The guy ain't right, Mr. Alfieri.

ALFIERI   What do you mean?

EDDIE   I mean he ain't right.

ALFIERI   I don't get you.

EDDIE   [*shifts to another position in the chair*]   Dja ever get a look at him?

ALFIERI   Not that I know of, no.

EDDIE   He's a blond guy. Like . . . platinum. You know what I mean?

ALFIERI   No.

EDDIE   I mean if you close the paper fast—you could blow him over.

ALFIERI   Well that doesn't mean—

EDDIE   Wait a minute, I'm tellin' you sump'm. He sings, see. Which is—I mean it's all right, but sometimes he hits a note, see. I turn around. I mean—high. You know what I mean?

ALFIERI   Well, that's a tenor.

EDDIE   I know a tenor, Mr. Alfieri. This ain't no tenor. I mean if you came in the house and you didn't know who was singin', you wouldn't be lookin' for him you be lookin' for her.

ALFIERI   Yes, but that's not—

EDDIE   I'm tellin' you sump'm, wait a minute. Please, Mr. Alfieri. I'm tryin' to bring out my thoughts here. Couple of nights ago my niece brings out a dress which it's too small for her, because she shot up like a light this last year. He takes the dress, lays it on the table, he cuts it up; one-two-three, he makes a new dress. I mean he looked so sweet there, like an angel—you could kiss him he was so sweet.

ALFIERI   Now look, Eddie—

EDDIE   Mr. Alfieri, they're laughin' at him on the piers. I'm ashamed. Paper Doll they call him. Blondie now. His brother thinks it's because he's got a sense of humor, see—which he's got—but that ain't why they're laughin'. Which they're not goin' to come out with it because they know he's my relative, which they have to see me if they make a crack, y'know? But I know what they're laughin' at, and when I think of that guy layin' his hands on her I could—I mean it's eatin' me out, Mr. Alfieri, because I struggled for that girl. And now he comes in my house and—

ALFIERI   Eddie, look—I have my own children. I understand you. But the law is very specific. The law does not . . .

EDDIE   [*with a fuller flow of indignation*]   You mean to tell me that there's no law that a guy which he ain't right can go to work and marry a girl and—?

ALFIERI   You have no recourse in the law, Eddie.

EDDIE   Yeah, but if he ain't right, Mr. Alfieri, you mean to tell me—

ALFIERI   There is nothing you can do, Eddie, believe me.

EDDIE   Nothin'.

ALFIERI   Nothing at all. There's only one legal question here.

EDDIE   What?

ALFIERI   The manner in which they entered the country. But I don't think you want to do anything about that, do you?

EDDIE   You mean—?

ALFIERI   Well, they entered illegally.

EDDIE   Oh, Jesus, no, I wouldn't do nothin' about that, I mean—

ALFIERI   All right, then, let me talk now, eh?

EDDIE   Mr. Alfieri, I can't believe what you tell me. I mean there must be some kinda law which—

ALFIERI   Eddie, I want you to listen to me. [*Pause.*] You know, sometimes God mixes up the people. We all love somebody, the wife, the kids—every man's got somebody that he loves, heh? But sometimes . . . there's too much. You know? There's too much, and it goes where it mustn't. A man works hard, he brings up a child, sometimes it's a niece, sometimes, even a daughter, and he never realizes it, but through the years—there is too much love for the daughter, there is too much love for the niece. Do you understand what I'm saying to you?

EDDIE [*sardonically*] What do you mean, I shouldn't look out for her good?

ALFIERI Yes, but these things have to end, Eddie, that's all. The child has to grow up and go away, and the man has to learn to forget. Because after all, Eddie—what other way can it end? [*Pause.*] Let her go. That's my advice. You did your job, now it's her life; wish her luck, and let her go. [*Pause.*] Will you do that? Because there's no law, Eddie; make up your mind to it; the law is not interested in this.

EDDIE You mean to tell me, even if he's a punk? If he's—

ALFIERI There's nothing you can do.

    EDDIE *stands.*

EDDIE Well, all right, thanks. Thanks very much.

ALFIERI What are you going to do?

EDDIE [*with a helpless but ironic gesture*] What can I do? I'm a patsy, what can a patsy do? I worked like a dog twenty years so a punk could have her, so that's what I done. I mean, in the worst times, in the worst, when there wasn't a ship comin' in the harbor, I didn't stand around lookin' for relief—I hustled. When there was empty piers in Brooklyn I went to Hoboken, Staten Island, the West Side, Jersey, all over—because I made a promise. I took out of my own mouth to give to her. I took out of my wife's mouth. I walked hungry plenty days in this city! [*It begins to break through.*] And now I gotta sit in my own house and look at a son-of-a-bitch punk like that —which he came out of nowhere! I give him my house to sleep! I take the blankets off my bed for him, and he takes and puts his dirty filthy hands on her like a goddam thief!

ALFIERI [*rising*] But, Eddie, she's a woman now.

EDDIE He's stealing from me!

ALFIERI She wants to get married, Eddie. She can't marry you, can she?

EDDIE [*furiously*] What're you talkin' about, marry me! I don't know what the hell you're talkin' about!

    Pause.

ALFIERI I gave you my advice, Eddie. That's it.

    EDDIE *gathers himself. A pause.*

EDDIE Well, thanks. Thanks very much. It just—it's breakin' my heart, y'know. I—

ALFIERI I understand. Put it out of your mind. Can you do that?

EDDIE I'm—[*He feels the threat of sobs, and with a helpless wave.*] I'll see you around. [*He goes out up the right ramp.*]

ALFIERI [*sits on desk*] There are times when you want to spread an alarm, but nothing has happened. I knew, I knew then and there— I could have finished the whole story that afternoon. It wasn't as though there was a mystery to unravel. I could see every step coming, step after step, like a dark figure walking down a hall toward a certain door. I knew where he was heading for, I knew where he was going to end. And I sat here many afternoons asking myself why, being an intelligent man, I was so powerless to stop it. I even went to a certain old lady in the neighborhood, a very wise old woman, and I told her, and she only nodded, and said, "Pray for him . . ." And so I—waited here.

As lights go out on ALFIERI, *they rise in the apartment where all are finishing dinner.* BEATRICE *and* CATHERINE *are clearing the table.*

CATHERINE   You know where they went?
BEATRICE   Where?
CATHERINE   They went to Africa once. On a fishing boat.

EDDIE *glances at her.*

It's true, Eddie.

BEATRICE *exits into the kitchen with dishes.*

EDDIE   I didn't say nothin'. [*He goes to his rocker, picks up a newspaper.*]
CATHERINE   And I was never even in Staten Island.
EDDIE [*sitting with the paper*]   You didn't miss nothin'.

Pause. CATHERINE *takes dishes out.*

How long that take you, Marco—to get to Africa?
MARCO [*rising*]   Oh . . . two days. We go all over.
RODOLPHO [*rising*]   Once we went to Yugoslavia.
EDDIE [*to* MARCO]   They pay all right on them boats?

BEATRICE *enters. She and* RODOLPHO *stack the remaining dishes.*

MARCO   If they catch fish they pay all right. [*Sits on a stool.*]
RODOLPHO   They're family boats, though. And nobody in our family owned one. So we only worked when one of the families was sick.
BEATRICE   Y'know, Marco, what I don't understand—there's an ocean full of fish and yiz are all starvin'.
EDDIE   They gotta have boats, nets, you need money.

CATHERINE *enters.*

BEATRICE   Yeah, but couldn't they like fish from the beach? You see them down Coney Island—
MARCO   Sardines.
EDDIE   Sure. [*Laughing.*] How you gonna catch sardines on a hook?
BEATRICE   Oh, I didn't know they're sardines. [*To* CATHERINE.] They're sardines!
CATHERINE   Yeah, they follow them all over the ocean, Africa, Yugoslavia . . . [*She sits and begins to look through a movie magazine.* RODOLPHO *joins her.*]
BEATRICE [*to* EDDIE]   It's funny, y'know. You never think of it, that sardines are swimming in the ocean! [*She exits to kitchen with dishes.*]
CATHERINE   I know. It's like oranges and lemons on a tree. [*To* EDDIE.] I mean you ever think of oranges and lemons on a tree?
EDDIE   Yeah, I know. It's funny. [*To* MARCO.] I heard that they paint the oranges to make them look orange.

BEATRICE *enters.*

MARCO [*he has been reading a letter*]   Paint?
EDDIE   Yeah, I heard that they grow like green.
MARCO   No, in Italy the oranges are orange.
RODOLPHO   Lemons are green.

EDDIE [*resenting his instruction*]   I know lemons are green, for Christ's sake, you see them in the store they're green sometimes. I said oranges they paint, I didn't say nothin' about lemons.

BEATRICE [*sitting; diverting their attention*]   Your wife is gettin' the money all right, Marco?

MARCO   Oh, yes. She bought medicine for my boy.

BEATRICE   That's wonderful. You feel better, heh?

MARCO   Oh, yes! But I'm lonesome.

BEATRICE   I just hope you ain't gonna do like some of them around here. They're here twenty-five years, some men, and they didn't get enough together to go back twice.

MARCO   Oh, I know. We have many families in our town, the children never saw the father. But I will go home. Three, four years, I think.

BEATRICE   Maybe you should keep more here. Because maybe she thinks it comes so easy you'll never get ahead of yourself.

MARCO   Oh, no, she saves. I send everything. My wife is very lonesome. [*He smiles shyly.*]

BEATRICE   She must be nice. She pretty? I bet, heh?

MARCO [*blushing*]   No, but she understand everything.

RODOLPHO   Oh, he's got a clever wife!

EDDIE   I betcha there's plenty surprises sometimes when those guys get back there, heh?

MARCO   Surprises?

EDDIE [*laughing*]   I mean, you know—they count the kids and there's a couple extra than when they left?

MARCO   No—no . . . The women wait, Eddie. Most. Most. Very few surprises.

RODOLPHO   It's more strict in our town.

EDDIE *looks at him now.*

It's not so free.

EDDIE [*rises, paces up and down*]   It ain't so free here either, Rodolpho, like you think. I seen greenhorns sometimes get in trouble that way—they think just because a girl don't go around with a shawl over her head that she ain't strict, y'know? Girl don't have to wear black dress to be strict. Know what I mean—

RODOLPHO   Well, I always have respect—

EDDIE   I know, but in your town you wouldn't just drag off some girl without permission, I mean. [*He turns.*] You know what I mean, Marco? It ain't that much different here.

MARCO [*cautiously*]   Yes.

BEATRICE   Well, he didn't exactly drag her off though, Eddie.

EDDIE   I know, but I seen some of them get the wrong idea sometimes. [*To* RODOLPHO.] I mean it might be a little more free here but it's just as strict.

RODOLPHO   I have respect for her, Eddie. I do anything wrong?

EDDIE   Look, kid, I ain't her father, I'm only her uncle—

BEATRICE   Well then, be an uncle then.

EDDIE *looks at her, aware of her criticizing force.*

I *mean.*

MARCO   No, Beatrice, if he does wrong you must tell him. [*To* EDDIE.] What does he do wrong?

EDDIE Well, Marco, till he came here she was never out on the street twelve o'clock at night.

MARCO [*to* RODOLPHO] You come home early now.

BEATRICE [*to* CATHERINE] Well, you said the movie ended late, didn't you?

CATHERINE Yeah.

BEATRICE Well, tell him, honey. [*To* EDDIE.] The movie ended late.

EDDIE Look, B., I'm just sayin'—he thinks she always stayed out like that.

MARCO You come home early now, Rodolpho.

RODOLPHO [*embarrassed*] All right, sure. But I can't stay in the house all the time, Eddie.

EDDIE Look, kid, I'm not only talkin' about her. The more you run around like that the more chance you're takin'. [*To* BEATRICE.] I mean suppose he gets hit by a car or something. [*To* MARCO.] Where's his papers, who is he? Know what I mean?

BEATRICE Yeah, but who is he in the daytime, though? It's the same chance in the daytime.

EDDIE [*holding back a voice full of anger*] Yeah, but he don't have to go lookin' for it, Beatrice. If he's here to work, then he should work; if he's here for a good time then he could fool around! [*To* MARCO.] But I understood, Marco, that you was both comin' to make a livin' for your family. You understand me, don't you, Marco? [*He goes to his rocker.*]

MARCO I beg your pardon, Eddie.

EDDIE I mean, that's what I understood in the first place, see.

MARCO Yes. That's why we came.

EDDIE [*sits on his rocker*] Well, that's all I'm askin'.

> EDDIE *reads his paper. There is a pause, an awkwardness. Now* CATHERINE *gets up and puts a record on the phonograph—"Paper Doll."*

CATHERINE [*flushed with revolt*] You wanna dance, Rodolpho?

> EDDIE *freezes.*

RODOLPHO [*in deference to* EDDIE] No, I—I'm tired.

BEATRICE Go ahead, dance, Rodolpho.

CATHERINE Ah, come on. They got a beautiful quartet, those guys. Come.

> *She has taken his hand and he stiffly rises, feeling* EDDIE'S *eyes on his back, and they dance.*

EDDIE [*to* CATHERINE] What's that, a new record?

CATHERINE It's the same one. We bought it the other day.

BEATRICE [*to* EDDIE] They only bought three records. [*She watches them dance;* EDDIE *turns his head away.* MARCO *just sits there, waiting. Now* BEATRICE *turns to* EDDIE.] Must be nice to go all over in one of them fishin' boats. I would like that myself. See all them other countries?

EDDIE Yeah.

BEATRICE [*to* MARCO] But the women don't go along, I bet.

MARCO No, not on the boats. Hard work.

BEATRICE What're you got, a regular kitchen and everything?

MARCO Yes, we eat very good on the boats—especially when Rodolpho comes along; everybody gets fat.

BEATRICE Oh, he cooks?

MARCO Sure, very good cook. Rice, pasta, fish, everything.

EDDIE *lowers his paper.*

EDDIE He's a cook, too! [*Looks at* RODOLPHO.] He sings, he cooks . . .

RODOLPHO *smiles thankfully.*

BEATRICE Well it's good, he could always make a living.

EDDIE It's wonderful. He sings, he cooks, he could make dresses . . .

CATHERINE They get some high pay, them guys. The head chefs in all the big hotels are men. You read about them.

EDDIE That's what I'm sayin'.

CATHERINE *and* RODOLPHO *continue dancing.*

CATHERINE Yeah, well, I mean.

EDDIE [*to* BEATRICE] He's lucky, believe me. [*Slight pause. He looks away, then back to* BEATRICE.] That's why the waterfront is no place for him. [*They stop dancing.* RODOLPHO *turns off phonograph.*] I mean like me—I can't cook, I can't sing, I can't make dresses, so I'm on the waterfront. But if I could cook, if I could sing, if I could make dresses, I wouldn't be on the waterfront. [*He has been unconsciously twisting the newspaper into a tight roll. They are all regarding him now; he senses he is exposing the issue and he is driven on.*] I would be someplace else. I would be like in a dress store. [*He has bent the rolled paper and it suddenly tears in two. He suddenly gets up and pulls his pants up over his belly and goes to* MARCO.] What do you say, Marco, we go to the bouts next Saturday night. You never seen a fight, did you?

MARCO [*uneasily*] Only in the moving pictures.

EDDIE [*going to* RODOLPHO] I'll treat yiz. What do you say, Danish? You wanna come along? I'll buy the tickets.

RODOLPHO Sure. I like to go.

CATHERINE [*goes to* EDDIE; *nervously happy now*] I'll make some coffee, all right?

EDDIE Go ahead, make some! Make it nice and strong. [*Mystified, she smiles and exits to kitchen. He is weirdly elated, rubbing his fists into his palms. He strides to* MARCO.] You wait, Marco, you see some real fights here. You ever do any boxing?

MARCO No, I never.

EDDIE [*to* RODOLPHO] Betcha you have done some, heh?

RODOLPHO No.

EDDIE Well, come on, I'll teach you.

BEATRICE What's he got to learn that for?

EDDIE Ya can't tell, one a these days somebody's liable to step on his foot or sump'm. Come on, Rodolpho, I show you a couple a passes. [*He stands below table.*]

BEATRICE Go ahead, Rodolpho. He's a good boxer, he could teach you.

RODOLPHO [*embarrassed*] Well, I don't know how to—[*He moves down to* EDDIE.]

EDDIE Just put your hands up. Like this, see? That's right. That's very good, keep your left up, because you lead with the left, see, like this. [*He gently moves his left into* RODOLPHO's *face.*] See? Now what you gotta do is you gotta block me, so when I come in like that you— [RODOLPHO *parries his left.*] Hey, that's very good! [RODOLPHO *laughs.*] All right, now come into me. Come on.

RODOLPHO   I don't want to hit you, Eddie.

EDDIE   Don't pity me, come on. Throw it, I'll show you how to block it. [RODOLPHO *jabs at him, laughing. The others join.*] 'At's it. Come on again. For the jaw right here. [RODOLPHO *jabs with more assurance.*] Very good!

BEATRICE [*to* MARCO]   He's very good!

> EDDIE *crosses directly upstage of* RODOLPHO.

EDDIE   Sure, he's great! Come on, kid, put sump'm behind it, you can't hurt me. [RODOLPHO, *more seriously, jabs at* EDDIE's *jaw and grazes it.*] Attaboy.

> CATHERINE *comes from the kitchen, watches.*

Now I'm gonna hit you, so block me, see?

CATHERINE [*with beginning alarm*]   What are they doin'?

> *They are lightly boxing now.*

BEATRICE [*she senses only the comradeship in it now*]   He's teachin' him; he's very good!

EDDIE   Sure, he's terrific! Look at him go! [RODOLPHO *lands a blow.*] 'At's it! Now, watch out, here I come, Danish! [*He feints with his left hand and lands with his right. It mildly staggers* RODOLPHO. MARCO *rises.*]

CATHERINE [*rushing to* RODOLPHO]   Eddie!

EDDIE   Why? I didn't hurt him. Did I hurt you, kid? [*He rubs the back of his hand across his mouth.*]

RODOLPHO   No, no, he didn't hurt me. [*To* EDDIE *with a certain gleam and a smile.*] I was only surprised.

BEATRICE [*pulling* EDDIE *down into the rocker*]   That's enough, Eddie; he did pretty good, though.

EDDIE   Yeah. [*Rubbing his fists together.*] He could be very good, Marco. I'll teach him again.

> MARCO *nods at him dubiously.*

RODOLPHO   Dance, Catherine. Come. [*He takes her hand; they go to phonograph and start it. It plays "Paper Doll."*]

> RODOLPHO *takes her in his arms. They dance.* EDDIE *in thought sits in his chair, and* MARCO *takes a chair, places it in front of* EDDIE, *and looks down at it.* BEATRICE *and* EDDIE *watch him.*

MARCO   Can you lift this chair?

EDDIE   What do you mean?

MARCO   From here. [*He gets on one knee with one hand behind his back, and grasps the bottom of one of the chair legs but does not raise it.*]

EDDIE   Sure, why not? [*He comes to the chair, kneels, grasps the leg, raises the chair one inch, but it leans over to the floor.*] Gee, that's hard, I never knew that. [*He tries again, and again fails.*] It's on an angle, that's why, heh?

MARCO   Here.

> MARCO *kneels, grasps, and with strain slowly raises the chair higher and higher, getting to his feet now.* RODOLPHO *and* CATHERINE *have stopped dancing as* MARCO *raises the chair over his head.*

> MARCO *is face to face with* EDDIE, *a strained tension gripping his eyes and jaw, his neck stiff, the chair raised like a weapon over* EDDIE's *head—and he transforms what might appear like a glare of warning into a smile of triumph, and* EDDIE's *grin vanishes as he absorbs his look.*

CURTAIN

Act 2

Light rises on ALFIERI *at his desk.*

ALFIERI   On the twenty-third of that December a case of Scotch whisky slipped from a net while being unloaded—as a case of Scotch whisky is inclined to do on the twenty-third of December on Pier Forty-one. There was no snow, but it was cold, his wife was out shopping. Marco was still at work. The boy had not been hired that day; Catherine told me later that this was the first time they had been alone together in the house.

> *Light is rising on* CATHERINE *in the apartment.* RODOLPHO *is watching as she arranges a paper pattern on cloth spread on the table.*

CATHERINE   You hungry?

RODOLPHO   Not for anything to eat. [*Pause.*] I have nearly three hundred dollars. Catherine?

CATHERINE   I heard you.

RODOLPHO   You don't like to talk about it any more?

CATHERINE   Sure, I don't mind talkin' about it.

RODOLPHO   What worries you, Catherine?

CATHERINE   I been wantin' to ask you about something. Could I?

RODOLPHO   All the answers are in my eyes, Catherine. But you don't look in my eyes lately. You're full of secrets. [*She looks at him. She seems withdrawn.*] What is the question?

CATHERINE   Suppose I wanted to live in Italy.

RODOLPHO [*smiling at the incongruity*]   You going to marry somebody rich?

CATHERINE   No, I mean live there—you and me.

RODOLPHO [*his smile vanishing*]   When?

CATHERINE   Well . . . when we get married.

RODOLPHO [*astonished*]   You want to be an Italian?

CATHERINE   No, but I could live there without being Italian. Americans live there.

RODOLPHO   Forever?

CATHERINE   Yeah.

RODOLPHO [*crosses to rocker*]   You're fooling.

CATHERINE   No, I mean it.

RODOLPHO   Where do you get such an idea?

CATHERINE   Well, you're always saying it's so beautiful there, with the mountains and the ocean and all the—

RODOLPHO   You're fooling me.

CATHERINE   I mean it.

RODOLPHO [*goes to her slowly*]   Catherine, if I ever brought you home with no money, no business, nothing, they would call the priest and the doctor and they would say Rodolpho is crazy.

CATHERINE   I know, but I think we would be happier there.

RODOLPHO   Happier! What would you eat? You can't cook the view!

CATHERINE   Maybe you could be a singer, like in Rome or—

RODOLPHO   Rome! Rome is full of singers.

CATHERINE   Well, I could work then.

RODOLPHO   Where?

CATHERINE   God, there must be jobs somewhere!

RODOLPHO   There's nothing! Nothing, nothing, nothing. Now tell me what you're talking about. How can I bring you from a rich country to suffer in a poor country? What are you talking about? [*She searches for words.*] I would be a criminal stealing your face. In two years you would have an old, hungry face. When my brother's babies cry they give them water, water that boiled a bone. Don't you believe that?

CATHERINE [*quietly*]   I'm afraid of Eddie here.

Slight pause.

RODOLPHO [*steps closer to her*]   We wouldn't live here. Once I am a citizen I could work anywhere and I would find better jobs and we would have a house, Catherine. If I were not afraid to be arrested I would start to be something wonderful here!

CATHERINE [*steeling herself*]   Tell me something. I mean just tell me, Rodolpho—would you still want to do it if it turned out we had to go live in Italy? I mean just if it turned out that way.

RODOLPHO   This is your question or his question?

CATHERINE   I would like to know, Rodolpho. I mean it.

RODOLPHO   To go there with nothing.

CATHERINE   Yeah.

RODOLPHO   No. [*She looks at him wide-eyed.*] No.

CATHERINE   You wouldn't?

RODOLPHO   No; I will not marry you to live in Italy. I want you to be my wife, and I want to be a citizen. Tell him that, or I will. Yes. [*He moves about angrily.*] And tell him also, and tell yourself, please, that I am not a beggar, and you are not a horse, a gift, a favor for a poor immigrant.

CATHERINE   Well, don't get mad!

RODOLPHO   I am furious! [*Goes to her.*] Do you think I am so desperate? My brother is desperate, not me. You think I would carry on my back the rest of my life a woman I didn't love just to be an American? It's so wonderful? You think we have no tall buildings in Italy? Electric lights? No wide streets? No flags? No automobiles? Only work we don't have. I want to be an American so I can work, that is the only wonder here—work! How can you insult me, Catherine?

CATHERINE   I didn't mean that—

RODOLPHO   My heart dies to look at you. Why are you so afraid of him?

CATHERINE [*near tears*]   I don't know!

RODOLPHO   Do you trust me, Catherine? You?

CATHERINE   It's only that I—He was good to me, Rodolpho. You don't know him; he was always the sweetest guy to me. Good. He razzes me all the time but he don't mean it. I know. I would—just feel ashamed if I made him sad. 'Cause I always dreamt that when I got married he would be happy at the wedding, and laughin'— and now he's—mad all the time and nasty—[*She is weeping.*] Tell him you'd live in Italy—just tell him, and maybe he would start to trust you a little, see? Because I want him to be happy; I mean—I like him, Rodolpho—and I can't stand it!

RODOLPHO   Oh, Catherine—oh, little girl.

CATHERINE   I love you, Rodolpho, I love you.

RODOLPHO   Then why are you afraid? That he'll spank you?

CATHERINE   Don't, don't laugh at me! I've been here all my life. . . . Every day I saw him when he left in the morning and when he came home at night. You think it's so easy to turn around and say to a man he's nothin' to you no more?

RODOLPHO   I know, but—

CATHERINE   You don't know; nobody knows! I'm not a baby, I know a lot more than people think I know. Beatrice says to be a woman, but—

RODOLPHO   Yes.

CATHERINE   Then why don't she be a woman? If I was a wife I would make a man happy instead of goin' at him all the time. I can tell a block away when he's blue in his mind and just wants to talk to somebody quiet and nice. . . . I can tell when he's hungry or wants a beer before he even says anything. I know when his feet hurt him, I mean I *know* him and now I'm supposed to turn around and make a stranger out of him? I don't know why I have to do that, I mean.

RODOLPHO   Catherine. If I take in my hands a little bird. And she grows and wishes to fly. But I will not let her out of my hands because I love her so much, is that right for me to do? I don't say you must hate him; but anyway you must go, mustn't you? Catherine?

CATHERINE [*softly*]   Hold me.

RODOLPHO [*clasping her to him*]   Oh, my little girl.

CATHERINE   Teach me. [*She is weeping.*] I don't know anything, teach me, Rodolpho, hold me.

RODOLPHO   There's nobody here now. Come inside. Come. [*He is leading her toward the bedrooms.*] And don't cry any more.

Light rises on the street. In a moment EDDIE *appears. He is unsteady, drunk. He mounts the stairs. He enters the apartment, looks around, takes out a bottle from one pocket, puts it on the table. Then another bottle from another pocket, and a third from an inside pocket. He sees the pattern and cloth, goes over to it and touches it, and turns toward upstage.*

EDDIE   Beatrice? [*He goes to the open kitchen door and looks in.*] Beatrice? Beatrice?

CATHERINE *enters from bedroom; under his gaze she adjusts her dress.*

CATHERINE   You got home early.

EDDIE   Knocked off for Christmas early. [*Indicating the pattern.*] Rodolpho makin' you a dress?

CATHERINE   No, I'm makin' a blouse.

RODOLPHO *appears in the bedroom doorway.* EDDIE *sees him and his arm jerks slightly in shock.* RODOLPHO *nods to him testingly.*

RODOLPHO   Beatrice went to buy presents for her mother.

Pause.

EDDIE   Pack it up. Go ahead. Get your stuff and get outa here. [CATHERINE *instantly turns and walks toward the bedroom, and* EDDIE *grabs her arm.*] Where you goin'?

CATHERINE [*trembling with fright*]   I think I have to get out of here, Eddie.

EDDIE   No, you ain't goin' nowheres, he's the one.

CATHERINE   I think I can't stay here no more. [*She frees her arm, steps back toward the bedroom.*] I'm sorry, Eddie. [*She sees the tears in his eyes.*] Well, don't cry. I'll be around the neighborhood; I'll see you. I just can't stay here no more. You know I can't. [*Her sobs of pity and love for him break her composure.*] Don't you know I can't? You know that, don't you? [*She goes to him.*] Wish me luck. [*She clasps her hands prayerfully.*] Oh, Eddie, don't be like that!

EDDIE   You ain't goin' nowheres.

CATHERINE   Eddie, I'm not gonna be a baby any more! You—

He reaches out suddenly, draws her to him, and as she strives to free herself he kisses her on the mouth.

RODOLPHO   Don't! [*He pulls on* EDDIE'S *arm.*] Stop that! Have respect for her!

EDDIE [*spun round by* RODOLPHO]   You want something?

RODOLPHO   Yes! She'll be my wife. That is what I want. My wife!

EDDIE   But what're you gonna be?

RODOLPHO   I show you what I be!

CATHERINE   Wait outside; don't argue with him!

EDDIE   Come on, show me! What're you gonna be? Show me!

RODOLPHO [*with tears of rage*]   Don't say that to me!

RODOLPHO *flies at him in attack.* EDDIE *pins his arms, laughing, and suddenly kisses him.*

CATHERINE   Eddie! Let go, ya hear me! I'll kill you! Leggo of him!

She tears at EDDIE'S *face and* EDDIE *releases* RODOLPHO. EDDIE *stands there with tears rolling down his face as he laughs mockingly at* RODOLPHO. *She is staring at him in horror.* RODOLPHO *is rigid. They are like animals that have torn at one another and broken up without a decision, each waiting for the other's mood.*

EDDIE [*to* CATHERINE]   You see? [*To* RODOLPHO.] I give you till tomorrow, kid. Get outa here. Alone. You hear me? Alone.

CATHERINE I'm going with him, Eddie. [*She starts toward* RODOL-
PHO.]

EDDIE [*indicating* RODOLPHO *with his head*] Not with that. [*She
halts, frightened. He sits, still panting for breath, and they watch
him helplessly as he leans toward them over the table.*] Don't make
me do nuttin', Catherine. Watch your step, submarine. By rights
they oughta throw you back in the water. But I got pity for you.
[*He moves unsteadily toward the door, always facing* RODOLPHO.]
Just get outa here and don't lay another hand on her unless you
wanna go out feet first. [*He goes out of the apartment.*]

   The lights go down, as they rise on ALFIERI.

ALFIERI On December twenty-seventh I saw him next. I normally go
home well before six, but that day I sat around looking out my
window at the bay, and when I saw him walking through my doorway, I knew why I had waited. And if I seem to tell this like a
dream, it was that way. Several moments arrived in the course of
the two talks we had when it occurred to me how—almost transfixed I had come to feel. I had lost my strength somewhere. [EDDIE
enters, removing his cap, sits in the chair, looks thoughtfully out.]
I looked in his eyes more than I listened—in fact, I can hardly
remember the conversation. But I will never forget how dark the
room became when he looked at me; his eyes were like tunnels. I
kept wanting to call the police, but nothing had happened. Nothing
at all had really happened. [*He breaks off and looks down at the
desk. Then he turns to* EDDIE.] So in other words, he won't leave?

EDDIE My wife is talkin' about renting a room upstairs for them. An
old lady on the top floor is got an empty room.

ALFIERI What does Marco say?

EDDIE He just sits there. Marco don't say much.

ALFIERI I guess they didn't tell him, heh? What happened?

EDDIE I don't know; Marco don't say much.

ALFIERI What does your wife say?

EDDIE [*unwilling to pursue this*] Nobody's talkin' much in the house.
So what about that?

ALFIERI But you didn't prove anything about him. It sounds like he
just wasn't strong enough to break your grip.

EDDIE I'm tellin' you I know—he ain't right. Somebody that don't
want it can break it. Even a mouse, if you catch a teeny mouse and
you hold it in your hand, that mouse can give you the right kind of
fight. He didn't give me the right kind of fight, I know it, Mr.
Alfieri, the guy ain't right.

ALFIERI What did you do that for, Eddie?

EDDIE To show her what he is! So she would see, once and for all!
Her mother'll turn over in the grave! [*He gathers himself almost
peremptorily.*] So what do I gotta do now? Tell me what to do.

ALFIERI She actually said she's marrying him?

EDDIE She told me, yeah. So what do I do?

   Slight pause.

ALFIERI This is my last word, Eddie, take it or not, that's your business. Morally and legally you have no rights, you cannot stop it; she
is a free agent.

EDDIE [*angering*] Didn't you hear what I told you?

ALFIERI [*with a tougher tone*]   I heard what you told me, and I'm telling you what the answer is. I'm not only telling you now, I'm warning you—the law is nature. The law is only a word for what has a right to happen. When the law is wrong it's because it's unnatural, but in this case it is natural and a river will drown you if you buck it now. Let her go. And bless her. [*A phone booth begins to glow on the opposite side of the stage; a faint, lonely blue.* EDDIE *stands up, jaws clenched.*] Somebody had to come for her, Eddie, sooner or later. [EDDIE *starts turning to go and* ALFIERI *rises with new anxiety.*] You won't have a friend in the world, Eddie! Even those who understand will turn against you, even the ones who feel the same will despise you! [EDDIE *moves off.*] Put it out of your mind! Eddie! [*He follows into the darkness, calling desperately.*]

> EDDIE *is gone. The phone is glowing in light now. Light is out on* ALFIERI. EDDIE *has at the same time appeared beside the phone.*

EDDIE   Give me the number of the Immigration Bureau. Thanks. [*He dials.*] I want to report something. Illegal immigrants. Two of them. That's right. Four-forty-one Saxon Street, Brooklyn, yeah. Ground floor. Heh? [*With greater difficulty.*] I'm just around the neighborhood, that's all. Heh?

> *Evidently he is being questioned further, and he slowly hangs up. He leaves the phone just as* LOUIS *and* MIKE *come down the street.*

LOUIS   Go bowlin', Eddie?

EDDIE   No, I'm due home.

LOUIS   Well, take it easy.

EDDIE   I'll see yiz.

> *They leave him, exiting right, and he watches them go. He glances about, then goes up into the house. The lights go on in the apartment.* BEATRICE *is taking down Christmas decorations and packing them in a box.*

EDDIE   Where is everybody? [BEATRICE *does not answer.*] I says where is everybody?

BEATRICE [*looking up at him, wearied with it, and concealing a fear of him*]   I decided to move them upstairs with Mrs. Dondero.

EDDIE   Oh, they're all moved up there already?

BEATRICE   Yeah.

EDDIE   Where's Catherine? She up there?

BEATRICE   Only to bring pillow cases.

EDDIE   She ain't movin' in with them.

BEATRICE   Look, I'm sick and tired of it. I'm sick and tired of it!

EDDIE   All right, all right, take it easy.

BEATRICE   I don't wanna hear no more about it, you understand? Nothin'!

EDDIE   What're you blowin' off about? Who brought them in here?

BEATRICE   All right, I'm sorry; I wish I'd a drop dead before I told them to come. In the ground I wish I was.

EDDIE   Don't drop dead, just keep in mind who brought them in here, that's all. [*He moves about restlessly.*] I mean I got a couple of rights here. [*He moves, wanting to beat down her evident disapproval of him.*] This is my house here not their house.

BEATRICE What do you want from me? They're moved out; what do you want now?

EDDIE I want my respect!

BEATRICE So I moved them out, what more do you want? You got your house now, you got your respect.

EDDIE [*he moves about biting his lip*] I don't like the way you talk to me, Beatrice.

BEATRICE I'm just tellin' you I done what you want!

EDDIE I don't like it! The way you talk to me and the way you look at me. This is my house. And she is my niece and I'm responsible for her.

BEATRICE So that's why you done that to him?

EDDIE I done what to him?

BEATRICE What you done to him in front of her; you know what I'm talkin' about. She goes around shakin' all the time, she can't go to sleep! That's what you call responsible for her?

EDDIE [*quietly*] The guy ain't right, Beatrice. [*She is silent.*] Did you hear what I said?

BEATRICE Look, I'm finished with it. That's all. [*She resumes her work.*]

EDDIE [*helping her to pack the tinsel*] I'm gonna have it out with you one of these days, Beatrice.

BEATRICE Nothin' to have out with me, it's all settled. Now we gonna be like it never happened, that's all.

EDDIE I want my respect, Beatrice, and you know what I'm talkin' about.

BEATRICE What?

Pause.

EDDIE [*finally his resolution hardens*] What I feel like doin' in the bed and what I don't feel like doin'. I don't want no—

BEATRICE When'd I say anything about that?

EDDIE You said, you said, I ain't deaf. I don't want no more conversations about that, Beatrice. I do what I feel like doin' or what I don't feel like doin'.

BEATRICE Okay.

Pause.

EDDIE You used to be different, Beatrice. You had a whole different way.

BEATRICE *I'm* no different.

EDDIE You didn't used to jump me all the time about everything. The last year or two I come in the house I don't know what's gonna hit me. It's a shootin' gallery in here and I'm the pigeon.

BEATRICE Okay, okay.

EDDIE Don't tell me okay, okay, I'm tellin' you the truth. A wife is supposed to believe the husband. If I tell you that guy ain't right don't tell me he is right.

BEATRICE But how do you know?

EDDIE Because I know. I don't go around makin' accusations. He give me the heeby-jeebies the first minute I seen him. And I don't like you sayin' I don't want her marryin' anybody. I broke my back payin' her stenography lessons so she could go out and meet a better class of people. Would I do that if I didn't want her to get married? Sometimes you talk like I was a crazy man or sump'm.

BEATRICE   But she likes him.

EDDIE   Beatrice, she's a baby, how is she gonna know what she likes?

BEATRICE   Well, you kept her a baby, you wouldn't let her go out. I told you a hundred times.

Pause.

EDDIE   All right. Let her go out, then.

BEATRICE   She don't wanna go out now. It's too late, Eddie.

Pause.

EDDIE   Suppose I told her to go out. Suppose I—

BEATRICE   They're going to get married next week, Eddie.

EDDIE [*his head jerks around to her*]   She said that?

BEATRICE   Eddie, if you want my advice, go to her and tell her good luck. I think maybe now that you had it out you learned better.

EDDIE   What's the hurry next week?

BEATRICE   Well, she's been worried about him bein' picked up; this way he could start to be a citizen. She loves him, Eddie. [*He gets up, moves about uneasily, restlessly.*] Why don't you give her a good word? Because I still think she would like you to be a friend, y'know? [*He is standing, looking at the floor.*] I mean like if you told her you'd go to the wedding.

EDDIE   She asked you that?

BEATRICE   I know she would like it. I'd like to make a party here for her. I mean there oughta be some kinda send-off. Heh? I mean she'll have trouble enough in her life, let's start it off happy. What do you say? Cause in her heart she still loves you, Eddie. I know it. [*He presses his fingers against his eyes.*] What're you, cryin'? [*She goes to him holds his face.*] Go . . . whyn't you go tell her you're sorry?

> CATHERINE *is seen on the upper landing of the stairway, and they hear her descending.*

There . . . she's comin' down. Come on, shake hands with her.

EDDIE [*moving with suppressed suddenness*]   No, I can't, I can't talk to her.

BEATRICE   Eddie, give her a break; a wedding should be happy!

EDDIE   I'm goin', I'm goin' for a walk.

> *He goes upstage for his jacket.* CATHERINE *enters and starts for the bedroom door.*

BEATRICE   Katie? . . . Eddie, don't go, wait a minute. [*She embraces* EDDIE's *arm with warmth.*] Ask him, Katie. Come on, honey.

EDDIE   It's all right, I'm—[*He starts to go and she holds him.*]

BEATRICE   No, she wants to ask you. Come on, Katie, ask him. We'll have a party! What're we gonna do, hate each other? Come on!

CATHERINE   I'm gonna get married, Eddie. So if you wanna come, the wedding be on Saturday.

Pause.

EDDIE   Okay. I only wanted the best for you, Katie. I hope you know that.

CATHERINE   Okay. [*She starts out again.*]

EDDIE   Catherine? [*She turns to him.*] I was just tellin' Beatrice . . . if you wanna go out, like . . . I mean I realize maybe I kept you home too much. Because he's the first guy you ever knew, y'know? I mean now that you got a job, you might meet some fellas, and you get a different idea, y'know? I mean you could always come back to him, you're still only kids, the both of yiz. What's the hurry? Maybe you'll get around a little bit, you grow up a little more, maybe you'll see different in a couple of months. I mean you be surprised, it don't have to be him.

CATHERINE   No, we made it up already.

EDDIE [*with increasing anxiety*]   Katie, wait a minute.

CATHERINE   No, I made up my mind.

EDDIE   But you never knew no other fella, Katie! How could you make up your mind?

CATHERINE   Cause I did. I don't want nobody else.

EDDIE   But, Katie, suppose he gets picked up.

CATHERINE   That's why we gonna do it right away. Soon as we finish the wedding he's goin' right over and start to be a citizen. I made up my mind, Eddie. I'm sorry. [*To* BEATRICE.] Could I take two more pillow cases for the other guys?

BEATRICE   Sure, go ahead. Only don't let her forget where they came from.

CATHERINE *goes into a bedroom.*

EDDIE   She's got other boarders up there?

BEATRICE   Yeah, there's two guys that just came over.

EDDIE   What do you mean, came over?

BEATRICE   From Italy. Lipari the butcher—his nephew. They come from Bari, they just got here yesterday. I didn't even know till Marco and Rodolpho moved up there before.

CATHERINE *enters, going toward exit with two pillow cases.*

It'll be nice, they could all talk together.

EDDIE   Catherine! [*She halts near the exit door. He takes in* BEATRICE *too.*] What're you, got no brains? You put them up there with two other submarines?

CATHERINE   Why?

EDDIE [*in a driving fright and anger*]   Why! How do you know they're not trackin' these guys? They'll come up for them and find Marco and Rodolpho! Get them out of the house!

BEATRICE   But they been here so long already—

EDDIE   How do you know what enemies Lipari's got? Which they'd love to stab him in the back?

CATHERINE   Well what'll I do with them?

EDDIE   The neighborhood is full of rooms. Can't you stand to live a couple of blocks away from him? Get them out of the house!

CATHERINE   Well maybe tomorrow night I'll—

EDDIE   Not tomorrow, do it now. Catherine, you never mix yourself with somebody else's family! These guys get picked up, Lipari's liable to blame you or me and we got his whole family on our head. They got a temper, that family.

Two men in overcoats appear outside, start into the house.

CATHERINE   How'm I gonna find a place tonight?

EDDIE   Will you stop arguin' with me and get them out! You think I'm always tryin' to fool you or sump'm? What's the matter with you, don't you believe I could think of your good? Did I ever ask sump'm for myself? You think I got no feelin's? I never told you nothin' in my life that wasn't for your good. Nothin'! And look at the way you talk to me! Like I was an enemy! Like I— [*A knock on the door. His head swerves. They all stand motionless. Another knock.* EDDIE, *in a whisper, pointing upstage.*] Go up the fire escape, get them out over the back fence.

CATHERINE *stands motionless, uncomprehending.*

FIRST OFFICER [*in the hall*]   Immigration! Open up in there!

EDDIE   Go, go. Hurry up! [*She stands a moment staring at him in a realized horror.*] Well, what're you lookin' at!

FIRST OFFICER   Open up!

EDDIE [*calling toward door*]   Who's that there?

FIRST OFFICER   Immigration, open up.

EDDIE *turns, looks at* BEATRICE. *She sits. Then he looks at* CATHERINE. *With a sob of fury* CATHERINE *streaks into a bedroom. Knock is repeated.*

EDDIE   All right, take it easy, take it easy. [*He goes and opens the door. The* OFFICER *steps inside.*] What's all this?

FIRST OFFICER   Where are they?

SECOND OFFICER *sweeps past and, glancing about, goes into the kitchen.*

EDDIE   Where's who?

FIRST OFFICER   Come on, come on, where are they? [*He hurries into the bedrooms.*]

EDDIE   Who? We got nobody here. [*He looks at* BEATRICE, *who turns her head away. Pugnaciously, furious, he steps toward* BEATRICE.] What's the matter with *you?*

FIRST OFFICER *enters from the bedroom, calls to the kitchen.*

FIRST OFFICER   Dominick?

Enter SECOND OFFICER *from kitchen.*

SECOND OFFICER   Maybe it's a different apartment.

FIRST OFFICER   There's only two more floors up there. I'll take the front, you go up the fire escape. I'll let you in. Watch your step up there.

SECOND OFFICER   Okay, right, Charley. [FIRST OFFICER *goes out apartment door and runs up the stairs.*] This is Four-forty-one isn't it?

EDDIE   That's right.

SECOND OFFICER *goes out into the kitchen.* EDDIE *turns to* BEATRICE. *She looks at him now and sees his terror.*

BEATRICE [*weakened with fear*]   Oh, Jesus, Eddie.

EDDIE   What's the matter with *you?*

BEATRICE [*pressing her palms against her face*]   Oh, my God, my God.

EDDIE What're you, accusin' me?

BEATRICE [*her final thrust is to turn toward him instead of running from him*] My God, what did you do?

> Many steps on the outer stair draw his attention. We see the FIRST OFFICER descending, with MARCO, behind him RODOLPHO, and CATHERINE and the two strange immigrants, followed by SECOND OFFICER. BEATRICE hurries to door.

CATHERINE [*backing down stairs, fighting with* FIRST OFFICER; *as they appear on the stairs*] What do yiz want from them? They work, that's all. They're boarders upstairs, they work on the piers.

BEATRICE [*to* FIRST OFFICER] Ah, Mister, what do you want from them, who do they hurt?

CATHERINE [*pointing to* RODOLPHO] They ain't no submarines, he was born in Philadelphia.

FIRST OFFICER Step aside, lady.

CATHERINE What do you mean? You can't just come in a house and—

FIRST OFFICER All right, take it easy. [*To* RODOLPHO.] What street were you born in Philadelphia?

CATHERINE What do you mean, what street? Could you tell me what street you were born?

FIRST OFFICER Sure. Four blocks away, One-eleven Union Street. Let's go fellas.

CATHERINE [*fending him off* RODOLPHO] No, you can't! Now, get outa here!

FIRST OFFICER Look, girlie, if they're all right they'll be out tomorrow. If they're illegal they go back where they came from. If you want, get yourself a lawyer, although I'm tellin' you now you're wasting your money. Let's get them in the car, Dom. [*To the men.*] Andiamo, Andiamo, let's go.[7]

> The men start, but MARCO hangs back.

BEATRICE [*from doorway*] Who're they hurtin', for God's sake, what do you want from them? They're starvin' over there, what do you want! Marco!

> MARCO suddenly breaks from the group and dashes into the room and faces EDDIE; BEATRICE and FIRST OFFICER rush in as MARCO spits into EDDIE's face.
>
> CATHERINE runs into hallway and throws herself into RODOLPHO's arms. EDDIE, with an enraged cry, lunges for MARCO.

EDDIE Oh, you mother's—!

> FIRST OFFICER quickly intercedes and pushes EDDIE from MARCO, who stands there accusingly.

FIRST OFFICER [*between them, pushing* EDDIE *from* MARCO] Cut it out!

EDDIE [*over the* FIRST OFFICER's *shoulder, to* MARCO] I'll kill you for that, you son of a bitch!

FIRST OFFICER Hey! [*Shakes him.*] Stay in here now, don't come out, don't bother him. You hear me? Don't come out, fella.

---

7. *Andiamo* is Italian for "let's go."

For an instant there is silence. Then FIRST OFFICER *turns and takes* MARCO's *arm and then gives a last, informative look at* EDDIE. *As he and* MARCO *are going out into the hall,* EDDIE *erupts.*

EDDIE   I don't forget that, Marco! You hear what I'm sayin'?

Out in the hall, FIRST OFFICER *and* MARCO *go down the stairs. Now, in the street,* LOUIS, MIKE, *and several neighbors including the butcher,* LIPARI—*a stout, intense, middle-aged man—are gathering around the stoop.*

LIPARI, *the butcher, walks over to the two strange men and kisses them. His wife, keening, goes and kisses their hands.* EDDIE *is emerging from the house shouting after* MARCO. BEATRICE *is trying to restrain him.*

EDDIE   That's the thanks I get? Which I took the blankets off my bed for yiz? You gonna apologize to me, Marco! *Marco!*

FIRST OFFICER [*in the doorway with* MARCO]   All right, lady, let them go. Get in the car, fellas, it's right over there.

RODOLPHO *is almost carrying the sobbing* CATHERINE *off up the street, left.*

CATHERINE   He was born in Philadelphia! What do you want from him?

FIRST OFFICER   Step aside, lady, come on now . . .

The SECOND OFFICER *has moved off with the two strange men.* MARCO, *taking advantage of the* FIRST OFFICER's *being occupied with* CATHERINE, *suddenly frees himself and points back at* EDDIE.

MARCO   That one! I accuse that one!

EDDIE *brushes* BEATRICE *aside and rushes out to the stoop.*

FIRST OFFICER [*grabbing him and moving him quickly off up the left street*]   Come on!

MARCO [*as he is taken off, pointing back at* EDDIE]   That one! He killed my children! That one stole the food from my children!

MARCO *is gone. The crowd has turned to* EDDIE.

EDDIE [*to* LIPARI *and wife*]   He's crazy! I give him the blankets off my bed. Six months I kept them like my own brothers!

LIPARI, *the butcher, turns and starts up left with his arm around his wife.*

EDDIE   Lipari! [*He follows* LIPARI *up left.*] For Christ's sake, I kept them, I give them the blankets off my bed!

LIPARI *and wife exit.* EDDIE *turns and starts crossing down right to* LOUIS *and* MIKE.

EDDIE   Louis! *Louis!*

LOUIS *barely turns, then walks off and exits down right with* MIKE. *Only* BEATRICE *is left on the stoop.* CATHERINE *now returns, blank-eyed, from offstage and the car.* EDDIE *calls after* LOUIS *and* MIKE.

EDDIE   He's gonna take that back. He's gonna take that back or I'll kill him! You hear me? I'll kill him! I'll kill him! [*He exits up street calling.*]

> *There is a pause of darkness before the lights rise, on the reception room of a prison.* MARCO *is seated;* ALFIERI, CATHERINE, *and* RODOLPHO *standing.*

ALFIERI   I'm waiting, Marco, what do you say?

RODOLPHO   Marco never hurt anybody.

ALFIERI   I can bail you out until your hearing comes up. But I'm not going to do it, you understand me? Unless I have your promise. You're an honorable man, I will believe your promise. Now what do you say?

MARCO   In my country he would be dead now. He would not live this long.

ALFIERI   All right, Rodolpho—you come with me now.

RODOLPHO   No! Please, mister. Marco—promise the man. Please, I want you to watch the wedding. How can I be married and you're in here? Please, you're not going to do anything; you know you're not.

MARCO *is silent.*

CATHERINE [*kneeling left of* MARCO]   Marco, don't you understand? He can't bail you out if you're gonna do something bad. To hell with Eddie. Nobody is gonna talk to him again if he lives to a hundred. Everybody knows you spit in his face, that's enough, isn't it? Give me the satisfaction—I want you at the wedding. You got a wife and kids, Marco. You could be workin' till the hearing comes up, instead of layin' around here.

MARCO [*to* ALFIERI]   I have no chance?

ALFIERI [*crosses to behind* MARCO]   No, Marco. You're going back. The hearing is a formality, that's all.

MARCO   But him? There is a chance, eh?

ALFIERI   When she marries him he can start to become an American. They permit that, if the wife is born here.

MARCO [*looking at* RODOLPHO]   Well—we did something. [*He lays a palm on* RODOLPHO's *arm and* RODOLPHO *covers it.*]

RODOLPHO   Marco, tell the man.

MARCO [*pulling his hand away*]   What will I tell him? He knows such a promise is dishonorable.

ALFIERI   To promise not to kill is not dishonorable.

MARCO [*looking at* ALFIERI]   No?

ALFIERI   No.

MARCO [*gesturing with his head—this is a new idea*]   Then what is done with such a man?

ALFIERI   Nothing. If he obeys the law, he lives. That's all.

MARCO [*rises, turns to* ALFIERI]   The law? All the law is not in a book.

ALFIERI   Yes. In a book. There is no other law.

MARCO [*his anger rising*]   He degraded my brother. My blood. He robbed my children, he mocks my work. I work to come here, mister!

ALFIERI   I know, Marco—

MARCO   There is no law for that? Where is the law for that?

ALFIERI   There is none.

MARCO [*shaking his head, sitting*]   I don't understand this country.
ALFIERI   Well? What is your answer? You have five or six weeks you
could work. Or else you sit here. What do you say to me?
MARCO [*lowers his eyes. It almost seems he is ashamed*]   All right.
ALFIERI   You won't touch him. This is your promise.

> *Slight pause.*

MARCO   Maybe he wants to apologize to me.

> MARCO *is staring away.* ALFIERI *takes one of his hands.*

ALFIERI   This is not God, Marco. You hear? Only God makes justice.
MARCO   All right.
ALFIERI [*nodding, not with assurance*]   Good! Catherine, Rodolpho,
Marco, let us go.

> CATHERINE *kisses* RODOLPHO *and* MARCO, *then kisses* ALFIERI'S
> *hand.*

CATHERINE   I'll get Beatrice and meet you at the church. [*She leaves
quickly.*]

> MARCO *rises.* RODOLPHO *suddenly embraces him.* MARCO *pats
> him on the back and* RODOLPHO *exits after* CATHERINE. MARCO
> faces ALFIERI.

ALFIERI   Only God, Marco.

> MARCO *turns and walks out.* ALFIERI *with a certain processional
> tread leaves the stage. The lights dim out.*
> *The lights rise in the apartment.* EDDIE *is alone in the rocker,
> rocking back and forth in little surges. Pause. Now* BEATRICE
> *emerges from a bedroom. She is in her best clothes, wearing a
> hat.*

BEATRICE [*with fear, going to* EDDIE]   I'll be back in about an hour,
Eddie. All right?
EDDIE [*quietly, almost inaudibly, as though drained*]   What, have I
been talkin' to myself?
BEATRICE   Eddie, for God's sake, it's her wedding.
EDDIE   Didn't you hear what I told you? You walk out that door to
that wedding you ain't comin' back here, Beatrice.
BEATRICE   Why! What do you want?
EDDIE   I want my respect. Didn't you ever hear of that? From my wife?

> CATHERINE *enters from bedroom.*

CATHERINE   It's after three; we're supposed to be there already,
Beatrice. The priest won't wait.
BEATRICE   Eddie. It's her wedding. There'll be nobody there from her
family. For my sister let me go. I'm goin' for my sister.
EDDIE [*as though hurt*]   Look, I been arguin' with you all day already,
Beatrice, and I said what I'm gonna say. He's gonna come here and
apologize to me or nobody from this house is goin' into that church
today. Now if that's more to you than I am, then go. But don't come
back. You be on my side or on their side, that's all.
CATHERINE [*suddenly*]   Who the hell do you think you are?
BEATRICE   Sssh!
CATHERINE   You got no more right to tell nobody nothin'! Nobody!
The rest of your life, nobody!

BEATRICE   Shut up, Katie! [*She turns* CATHERINE *around.*]

CATHERINE   You're gonna come with me!

BEATRICE   I can't Katie, I can't . . .

CATHERINE   How can you listen to him? This rat!

BEATRICE [*shaking* CATHERINE]   Don't you call him that!

CATHERINE [*clearing from* BEATRICE]   What're you scared of? He's a rat! He belongs in the sewer!

BEATRICE   Stop it!

CATHERINE [*weeping*]   He bites people when they sleep! He comes when nobody's lookin' and poisons decent people. In the garbage he belongs!

> EDDIE *seems about to pick up the table and fling it at her.*

BEATRICE   No, Eddie! Eddie! [*To* CATHERINE.] Then we all belong in the garbage. You, and me too. Don't say that. Whatever happened we all done it, and don't you ever forget it, Catherine. [*She goes to* CATHERINE.] Now go, go to your wedding, Katie, I'll stay home. Go. God bless you, God bless your children.

> *Enter* RODOLPHO.

RODOLPHO   Eddie?

EDDIE   Who said you could come in here? Get outa here!

RODOLPHO   Marco is coming, Eddie.

> *Pause.* BEATRICE *raises her hands in terror.*

He's praying in the church. You understand? [*Pause.* RODOLPHO *advances into the room.*] Catherine, I think it is better we go. Come with me.

CATHERINE   Eddie, go away, please.

BEATRICE [*quietly*]   Eddie. Let's go someplace. Come. You and me.

> *He has not moved.*

I don't want you to be here when he comes. I'll get your coat.

EDDIE   Where? Where am I goin'? This is my house.

BEATRICE [*crying out*]   What's the use of it! He's crazy now, you know the way they get, what good is it! You got nothin' against Marco, you always liked Marco!

EDDIE   I got nothin' against Marco? Which he called me a rat in front of the whole neighborhood? Which he said I killed his children! Where you been?

RODOLPHO [*quite suddenly, stepping up to* EDDIE]   It is my fault, Eddie. Everything. I wish to apologize. It was wrong that I do not ask your permission. I kiss your hand. [*He reaches for* EDDIE's *hand, but* EDDIE *snaps it away from him.*]

BEATRICE   Eddie, he's apologizing!

RODOLPHO   I have made all our troubles. But you have insult me too. Maybe God understand why you did that to me. Maybe you did not mean to insult me at all—

BEATRICE   Listen to him! Eddie, listen what he's tellin' you!

RODOLPHO   I think, maybe when Marco comes, if we can tell him we are comrades now, and we have no more argument between us. Then maybe Marco will not—

EDDIE   Now, listen—

CATHERINE   Eddie, give him a chance!

BEATRICE   What do you want! Eddie, what do you want!

EDDIE   I want my name! He didn't take my name; he's only a punk. Marco's got my name—[*to* RODOLPHO] and you can run tell him, kid, that he's gonna give it back to me in front of this neighborhood, or we have it out. [*Hoisting up his pants.*] Come on, where is he? Take me to him.

BEATRICE   Eddie, listen—

EDDIE   I heard enough! Come on, let's go!

BEATRICE   Only blood is good? He kissed your hand!

EDDIE   What he does don't mean nothin' to nobody! [*To* RODOLPHO.] Come on!

BEATRICE   [*barring his way to the stairs*]   What's gonna mean somethin'? Eddie, listen to me. Who could give you your name? Listen to me, I love you, I'm talkin' to you, I love you; if Marco'll kiss your hand outside, if he goes on his knees, what is he got to give you? That's not what you want.

EDDIE   Don't bother me!

BEATRICE   You want somethin' else, Eddie, and you can never have her!

CATHERINE   [*in horror*]   B.!

EDDIE   [*shocked, horrified, his fists clenching*]   Beatrice!

MARCO *appears outside, walking toward the door from a distant point.*

BEATRICE   [*crying out, weeping*]   The truth is not as bad as blood, Eddie! I'm tellin' you the truth—tell her good-by forever!

EDDIE   [*crying out in agony*]   That's what you think of me—that I would have such a thought? [*His fists clench his head as though it will burst.*]

MARCO   [*calling near the door outside*]   Eddie Carbone!

EDDIE *swerves about; all stand transfixed for an instant. People appear outside.*

EDDIE   [*as though flinging his challenge*]   Yeah, Marco! Eddie Carbone. Eddie Carbone. Eddie Carbone. [*He goes up the stairs and emerges from the apartment.* RODOLPHO *streaks up and out past him and runs to* MARCO.]

RODOLPHO   No, Marco, please! Eddie, please, he has children! You will kill a family!

BEATRICE   Go in the house! Eddie, go in the house!

EDDIE   [*he gradually comes to address the people*]   Maybe he come to apologize to me. Heh, Marco? For what you said about me in front of the neighborhood? [*He is incensing himself and little bits of laughter even escape him as his eyes are murderous and he cracks his knuckles in his hands with a strange sort of relaxation.*] He knows that ain't right. To do like that? To a man? Which I put my roof over their head and my food in their mouth? Like in the Bible? Strangers I never seen in my whole life? To come out of the water and grab a girl for a passport? To go and take from your own family like from the stable—and never a word to me? And now accusations in the bargain! [*Directly to* MARCO.] Wipin' the neighborhood with my name like a dirty rag! I want my name, Marco. [*He is moving now, carefully, toward* MARCO.] Now gimme my name and we go together to the wedding.

BEATRICE *and* CATHERINE   [*keening*]   Eddie! Eddie, don't! Eddie!

EDDIE   No, Marco knows what's right from wrong. Tell the people, Marco, tell them what a liar you are! [*He has his arms spread and* MARCO *is spreading his.*] Come on, liar, you know what you done! [*He lunges for* MARCO *as a great hushed shout goes up from the people.*]

> MARCO *strikes* EDDIE *beside the neck.*

MARCO   Animal! You go on your knees to me!

> EDDIE *goes down with the blow and* MARCO *starts to raise a foot to stomp him when* EDDIE *springs a knife into his hand and* MARCO *steps back.* LOUIS *rushes in toward* EDDIE.

LOUIS   Eddie, for Christ's sake!

> EDDIE *raises the knife and* LOUIS *halts and steps back.*

EDDIE   You lied about me, Marco. Now say it. Come on now, say it!
MARCO   Anima-a-a-l!

> EDDIE *lunges with the knife.* MARCO *grabs his arm, turning the blade inward and pressing it home as the women and* LOUIS *and* MIKE *rush in and separate them, and* EDDIE, *the knife still in his hand, falls to his knees before* MARCO. *The two women support him for a moment, calling his name again and again.*

CATHERINE   Eddie I never meant to do nothing bad to you.
EDDIE   Then why—Oh, B.!
BEATRICE   Yes, yes!
EDDIE   My B.!

> *He dies in her arms, and* BEATRICE *covers him with her body.* ALFIERI, *who is in the crowd, turns out to the audience. The lights have gone down, leaving him in a glow, while behind him the dull prayers of the people and the keening of the women continue.*

ALFIERI   Most of the time now we settle for half and I like it better. But the truth is holy, and even as I know how wrong he was, and his death useless, I tremble, for I confess that something perversely pure calls to me from his memory—not purely good, but himself purely, for he allowed himself to be wholly known and for that I think I will love him more than all my sensible clients. And yet, it is better to settle for half, it must be! And so I mourn him—I admit it—with a certain . . . alarm.

CURTAIN

ITALIANS IN AMERICA

The early Italian immigrants to the United States were mostly from Sicily and Southern Italy (perhaps as many as 80 percent), and many of the stereotyped notions about Italian-Americans are based on our understanding of Italian-Americans of Sicilian or Southern Italian origin. Miller makes use of several of these stereotypes in his play.

Italian-Americans are pictured, for example, as a closely knit group which lives in an uneasy truce with the law and which has its own code of behavior, its own *mores,* which are more carefully observed than the law. A part of this is due to the history of Sicily and Southern Italy, which is different from that of the rest of the peninsula. The region was originally settled by Greeks and had therefore a different cultural background from the central and northern parts of Italy. For many centuries, the Kingdom of the Two Sicilies with its capital at Naples was a separate political entity with its own history (including Norse raids and dominance at times). In modern times the South of Italy has tended to be agricultural and poor in contrast to the industrial and relatively affluent North.

Another stereotyped notion about Italian-Americans which is used in the play is their association with organized crime and with violent gangland murders, such as the famous St. Valentine's Day Massacre. Various names—the Mafia, the Syndicate and the Cosa Nostra—have been used for the reputed monolithic organization of criminals, largely controlled by Sicilians, Southern Italians, and their descendants. In the play the illegal entry of Marco and Rodolpho is arranged by the "Syndicate." Two Mafiosi are mentioned in the play. Alphonse or Alfonso (Al) Capone, also known as "Scarface," who was born in Naples in 1899, was believed to be one of the most important leaders of the "Mafia" during the 1920s, particularly in Chicago bootlegging circles. He died in Miami in 1947, having served eight years (1931–39) in federal prison for income tax evasion. Francesco ("Frankie Yale") Uale, a less important figure, was driving along a Brooklyn street on Sunday afternoon, July 1, 1928, when four men in another car opened fire on him. Uale, who had been associated with Capone, had a splendid funeral including such a macabre touch as a silver casket valued at $15,000,

Further, all of the Italian place names in the play refer to Sicily or Southern Italy. Syracuse is a city in Sicily, Bari a seaport near Naples, and Calabria a province of Southern Italy.

III

GEORGE BERNARD SHAW

Caesar and Cleopatra*

A HISTORY

CHARACTERS

RA, *as prologue*
JULIUS CAESAR, *Roman military and political leader*
RUFIO, *one of his officers*
A ROMAN CENTURION
BRITANNUS, *a British slave, secretary to Caesar*
CLEOPATRA, *Queen of Egypt*
FTATATEETA, *her Chief Nurse*
IRAS ⎱ *two of Cleopatra's*
CHARMIAN ⎰ *attendants*
PTOLEMY DIONYSUS, *King of Egypt, husband and brother of Cleopatra*

PHOTINUS, *a eunuch and principal attendant of Ptolemy*
ACHILLAS, *a general and member of Ptolemy's faction*
THEODOTUS, *Ptolemy's tutor*
BELZANOR, *a Captain of the Guards*
THE PERSIAN, *a Guardsman*
BEL AFFRIS, *an Egyptian soldier*
LUCIUS SEPTIMIUS, *a former Roman officer*
APOLLODORUS, *a Sicilian merchant*

GUARDSMEN, EGYPTIAN AND ROMAN SOLDIERS, A MAJOR-DOMO, A PRIEST, A MUSICIAN, A BOATMAN, PORTERS, COURT OFFICIALS, COURTIERS, WOMEN ATTENDING CLEOPATRA, SLAVES

PROLOGUE

In the doorway of the temple of Ra[1] in Memphis. Deep gloom. An august personage with a hawk's head is mysteriously visible by his own light in the darkness within the temple. He surveys the modern audience with great contempt; and finally speaks the following words to them:

Peace! Be silent and hearken unto me, ye quaint little islanders. Give ear, ye men with white paper on your breasts and nothing written thereon (to signify the innocence of your minds). Hear me, ye women who adorn yourselves alluringly and conceal your thoughts from your men, leading them to believe that ye deem them wondrous strong and masterful whilst in truth ye hold them in your hearts as children without judgment. Look upon my hawk's head; and know that I am Ra, who was once in Egypt a mighty god. Ye cannot kneel nor prostrate yourselves; for ye are packed in rows without freedom to move, obstructing one another's vision; neither do any of ye regard it as seemly to do ought until ye see all the rest

---

* See note on Shaw's spelling, p. 459.   1. An Egyptian sun god.

do so too; wherefore it commonly happens that in great emergencies ye do nothing though each telleth his fellow that something must be done. I ask you not for worship, but for silence. Let not your men speak nor your women cough; for I am come to draw you back two thousand years over the graves of sixty generations. Ye poor posterity, think not that ye are the first. Other fools before ye have seen the sun rise and set, and the moon change her shape and her hour. As they were so ye are; and yet not so great; for the pyramids my people built stand to this day; whilst the dustheaps on which ye slave, and which ye call empires, scatter in the wind even as ye pile your dead sons' bodies on them to make yet more dust.

Hearken to me then, oh ye compulsorily educated ones. Know that even as there is an old England and a new, and ye stand perplexed between the twain; so in the days when I was worshipped was there an old Rome and a new, and men standing perplexed between them. And the old Rome was poor and little, and greedy and fierce, and evil in many ways; but because its mind was little and its work was simple, it knew its own mind and did its own work; and the gods pitied it and helped it and strengthened it and shielded it; for the gods are patient with littleness. Then the old Rome, like the beggar on horseback, presumed on the favor of the gods, and said, "Lo! there is neither riches nor greatness in our littleness: the road to riches and greatness is through robbery of the poor and slaughter of the weak." So they robbed their own poor until they became great masters of that art, and knew by what laws it could be made to appear seemly and honest. And when they had squeezed their own poor dry, they robbed the poor of other lands, and added those lands to Rome until there came a new Rome, rich and huge. And I, Ra, laughed; for the minds of the Romans remained the same size whilst their dominion spread over the earth.

Now mark me, that ye may understand what ye are presently to see. Whilst the Romans still stood between the old Rome and the new, there arose among them a mighty soldier: Pompey the Great.[2] And the way of the soldier is the way of death; but the way of the gods is the way of life; and so it comes that a god at the end of his way is wise and a soldier at the end of his way is a fool. So Pompey held by the old Rome, in which only soldiers could become great; but the gods turned to the new Rome, in which any man with wit enough could become what he would. And Pompey's friend Julius Caesar was on the side of the gods; for he saw that Rome had passed beyond the control of the little old Romans. This Caesar was a great talker and a politician: he bought men with words and with gold, even as ye are bought. And when they would not be satisfied with words and gold, and demanded also the glories of war, Caesar in his middle age turned his hand to that trade; and they that were against him when he sought their welfare, bowed down before him when he became a slayer and a conqueror; for such is the nature of you mortals. And as for Pompey, the gods grew tired of his triumphs and his airs of being himself a god; for he talked of law and duty and other matters that concerned not a mere human worm. And the gods smiled on Caesar; for he lived the life they had given him boldly, and was not forever rebuking us for our indecent ways of creation, and hiding our handiwork as a shameful thing. Ye know well what I mean; for this is one of your own sins.

---

2. Gnaeus Pompeius, surnamed Magnus (106–48 B.C.), was a prominent Roman soldier and politician for some 35 years. At one time he was allied with Caesar and married to Caesar's daughter; later the two men fell out. After Pompey was defeated by Caesar at Pharsalia in 48 B.C., he escaped to Egypt, where he was killed by one of his own men.

And thus it fell out between the old Rome and the new, that Caesar said, "Unless I break the law of old Rome, I cannot take my share in ruling her; and the gift of ruling that the gods gave me will perish without fruit." But Pompey said, "The law is above all; and if thou break it thou shalt die." Then said Caesar, "I will break it: kill me who can." And he broke it. And Pompey went for him, as ye say, with a great army to slay him and uphold the old Rome. So Caesar fled across the Adriatic sea; for the high gods had a lesson to teach him, which lesson they shall also teach you in due time if ye continue to forget them and to worship that cad among gods, Mammon.[3] Therefore before they raised Caesar to be master of the world, they were minded to throw him down into the dust, even beneath the feet of Pompey, and blacken his face before the nations. And Pompey they raised higher than ever, he and his laws and his high mind that aped the gods, so that his fall might be the more terrible. And Pompey followed Caesar, and overcame him with all the majesty of old Rome, and stood over him and over the whole world even as ye stand over it with your fleet that covers thirty miles of the sea. And when Caesar was brought down to utter nothingness, he made a last stand to die honorably, and did not despair; for he said, "Against me there is Pompey, and the old Rome, and the law and the legions: all all against me; but high above these are the gods; and Pompey is a fool." And the gods laughed and approved; and on the field of Pharsalia the impossible came to pass; the blood and iron ye pin your faith on fell before the spirit of man; for the spirit of man is the will of the gods; and Pompey's power crumbled in his hand, even as the power of imperial Spain crumbled when it was set against your fathers in the days when England was little, and knew her own mind, and had a mind to know instead of a circulation of newspapers. Wherefore look to it, lest some little people whom ye would enslave rise up and become in the hand of God the scourge of your boastings and your injustices and your lusts and stupidities.

And now, would ye know the end of Pompey, or will ye sleep while a god speaks? Heed my words well; for Pompey went where ye have gone, even to Egypt, where there was a Roman occupation even as there was but now a British one.[4] And Caesar pursued Pompey to Egypt; a Roman fleeing, and a Roman pursuing: dog eating dog. And the Egyptians said, "Lo: those Romans which have lent money to our kings and levied a distraint upon us with their arms, call for ever upon us to be loyal to them by betraying our country to them. But now behold two Romes! Pompey's Rome and Caesar's Rome! To which of the twain shall we pretend to be loyal?" So they turned in their perplexity to a soldier that had once served Pompey, and that knew the ways of Rome and was full of her lusts. And they said to him, "Lo: in thy country dog eats dog; and both dogs are coming to eat us: what counsel hast thou to give us?" And this soldier, whose name was Lucius Septimius, and whom ye shall presently see before ye, replied, "Ye shall diligently consider which is the bigger dog of the two; and ye shall kill the other dog for his sake and thereby earn his favor." And the Egyptians said, "Thy counsel is expedient; but if we kill a man outside the law we set ourselves in the place of the gods; and this we dare not do. But thou, being a Roman, art accustomed to this kind of killing; for thou hast imperial instincts. Wilt thou therefore kill the lesser dog for us?" And he said, "I will; for I have made my home in Egypt; and I

3. The personification of riches and greed.

4. British troops occupied Egyptian territory in 1882 and remained until the 1950s.

desire consideration and influence among you." And they said, "We knew well thou wouldst not do it for nothing: thou shalt have thy reward." Now when Pompey came, he came alone in a little galley, putting his trust in the law and the constitution. And it was plain to the people of Egypt that Pompey was now but a very small dog. So when he set his foot on the shore he was greeted by his old comrade Lucius Septimius, who welcomed him with one hand and with the other smote off his head, and kept it as it were a pickled cabbage to make a present to Caesar. And mankind shuddered; but the gods laughed; for Septimius was but a knife that Pompey had sharpened; and when it turned against his own throat they said that Pompey had better have made Septimius a ploughman than so brave and ready-handed a slayer. Therefore again I bid you beware, ye who would all be Pompeys if ye dared; for war is a wolf that may come to your own door.

Are ye impatient with me? Do ye crave for a story of an unchaste woman? Hath the name of Cleopatra tempted ye hither? Ye foolish ones; Cleopatra is as yet but a child that is whipped by her nurse. And what I am about to shew you for the good of your souls is how Caesar, seeking Pompey in Egypt, found Cleopatra; and how he received that present of a pickled cabbage that was once the head of Pompey; and what things happened between the old Caesar and the child queen before he left Egypt and battled his way back to Rome to be slain there as Pompey was slain, by men in whom the spirit of Pompey still lived. All this ye shall see; and ye shall marvel, after your ignorant manner, that men twenty centuries ago were already just such as you, and spoke and lived as ye speak and live, no worse and no better, no wiser and no sillier. And the two thousand years that have past are to me, the god Ra, but a moment; nor is this day any other than the day in which Caesar set foot in the land of my people. And now I leave you; for ye are a dull folk, and instruction is wasted on you; and I had not spoken so much but that it is in the nature of a god to struggle for ever with the dust and the darkness, and to drag from them, by the force of his longing for the divine, more life and more light. Settle ye therefore in your seats and keep silent; for ye are about to hear a man speak, and a great man he was, as ye count greatness. And fear not that I shall speak to you again: the rest of the story must ye learn from them that lived it. Farewell; and do not presume to applaud me.

The temple vanishes in utter darkness.

AN ALTERNATIVE TO THE PROLOGUE

An October night on the Syrian border of Egypt towards the end of the XXXIII Dynasty, in the year 706 by Roman computation, afterwards reckoned by Christian computation as 48 B.C. A great radiance of silver fire, the dawn of a moonlit night, is rising in the east. The stars and the cloudless sky are our own contemporaries, nineteen and a half centuries younger than we know them; but you would not guess that from their appearance. Below them are two notable drawbacks of civilization: a palace, and soldiers. The palace, an old, low, Syrian building of whitened mud, is not so ugly as Buckingham Palace; and the officers in the courtyard are more highly civilized than modern English officers: for example, they do not dig up the corpses of their dead enemies and mutilate them, as we dug up Cromwell and the Mahdi.[5] *They are in two groups: one intent on the gambling of their captain* BELZANOR, *a warrior of fifty, who, with his spear on the ground beside his knee, is stooping to throw dice with a sly-looking young* PERSIAN *recruit; the other gathered about a guardsman who has just finished telling a naughty story (still current in English barracks) at which they are laughing uproariously. They are about a dozen in number, all highly aristocratic young Egyptian* GUARDSMEN, *handsomely equipped with weapons and armor, very unEnglish in point of not being ashamed of and uncomfortable in their professional dress; on the contrary, rather ostentatiously and arrogantly warlike, as valuing themselves on their military caste.*

BELZANOR *is a typical veteran, tough and wilful; prompt, capable and crafty where brute force will serve; helpless and boyish when it will not: an effective sergeant, an incompetent general, a deplorable dictator. Would, if influentially connected, be employed in the two last capacities by a modern European State on the strength of his success in the first. Is rather to be pitied just now in view of the fact that* JULIUS CAESAR *is invading his country. Not knowing this, is intent on his game with the* PERSIAN, *whom, as a foreigner, he considers quite capable of cheating him.*

His subalterns are mostly handsome young fellows whose interest in the game and the story symbolize with tolerable completeness the main interests in life of which they are conscious. Their spears are leaning against the walls, or lying on the ground ready to their hands. The corner of the courtyard forms a triangle of which one side is the front of the palace, with a doorway, the other a wall with a gateway. The storytellers are on the palace side: the gamblers, on the gateway side. Close to the gateway, against the wall, is a stone block high enough to enable a Nubian SENTINEL, *standing on it, to look over the wall. The yard is lighted by a torch stuck in the wall. As the laughter from the group round the storyteller dies away, the kneeling* PERSIAN, *winning the throw, snatches up the stake from the ground.*

BELZANOR   By Apis,[6] Persian, thy gods are good to thee.

PERSIAN   Try yet again, O captain. Double or quits!

BELZANOR   No more. I am not in the vein.

SENTINEL [*poising his javelin as he peers over the wall*]   Stand. Who goes there?

They all start, listening. A strange VOICE *replies from without.*

VOICE   The bearer of evil tidings.

BELZANOR [*calling to the sentry*]   Pass him.

SENTINEL [*grounding his javelin*]   Draw near, O bearer of evil tidings.

BELZANOR [*pocketing the dice and picking up his spear*]   Let us receive this man with honor. He bears evil tidings.

5. At the Restoration in 1660, the body of Oliver Cromwell (1599–1658), leader of the Puritans, was taken from his tomb in Westminster Abbey. His bones were hung up on Tyburn gallows, and his head was placed on a pole at Westminster Hall. Mohammed Ahmed (called the Madhi, or chosen one) led a rebellion in the Sudan and set up an independent republic after his defeat of the British at Khartoum in 1885. He died that same year. In 1898 the British, while regaining control of the Sudan, captured his tomb at Omdurman. The tomb was destroyed, the body thrown in the river, and the head sent to Cairo.

6. An Egyptian god, often pictured with the body of a man and the head of a bull. He represented the image or soul of the principal Egyptian god Osiris.

The GUARDSMEN *seize their spears and gather about the gate, leaving a way through for the* NEW COMER.

PERSIAN [*rising from his knee*]   Are evil tidings, then, so honorable?

BELZANOR   O barbarous Persian, hear my instruction. In Egypt the bearer of good tidings is sacrificed to the gods as a thank offering; but no god will accept the blood of the messenger of evil. When we have good tidings, we are careful to send them in the mouth of the cheapest slave we can find. Evil tidings are borne by young noblemen who desire to bring themselves into notice. [*They join the rest at the gate.*]

SENTINEL   Pass, O young captain; and bow the head in the House of the Queen.

VOICE   Go anoint thy javelin with fat of swine, O Blackamoor; for before morning the Romans will make thee eat it to the very butt.

> *The owner of the* VOICE, *a fairhaired dandy, dressed in a different fashion from that affected by the* GUARDSMEN, *but no less extravagantly, comes through the gateway laughing. He is somewhat battlestained; and his left forearm, bandaged, comes through a torn sleeve. In his right hand he carries a Roman sword in its sheath. He swaggers down the courtyard, the* PERSIAN *on his right,* BELZANOR *on his left, and the* GUARDSMEN *crowding down behind him.*

BELZANOR   Who are thou that laughest in the House of Cleopatra the Queen, and in the teeth of Belzanor, the captain of her guard?

NEW COMER   I am Bel Affris, descended from the gods.

BELZANOR [*ceremoniously*]   Hail, cousin!

ALL [*except the* PERSIAN]   Hail, cousin!

PERSIAN   All the Queen's guards are descended from the gods, O stranger, save myself. I am Persian, and descended from many kings.

BEL AFFRIS [*to the* GUARDSMEN]   Hail, cousins! [*To the* PERSIAN, *condescendingly.*] Hail, mortal!

BELZANOR   You have been in battle, Bel Affris; and you are a soldier among soldiers. You will not let the Queen's women have the first of your tidings.

BEL AFFRIS   I have no tidings, except that we shall have our throats cut presently, women, soldiers, and all.

PERSIAN [*to* BELZANOR]   I told you so.

SENTINEL [*who has been listening*]   Woe, alas!

BEL AFFRIS [*calling to him*]   Peace, peace, poor Ethiop: destiny is with the gods who painted thee black. [*To* BELZANOR.] What has this mortal [*indicating the* PERSIAN] told you?

BELZANOR   He says that the Roman Julius Caesar, who has landed on our shores with a handful of followers, will make himself master of Egypt. He is afraid of the Roman soldiers. [*The* GUARDSMEN *laugh with boisterous scorn.*] Peasants, brought up to scare crows and follow the plough! Sons of smiths and millers and tanners! And we nobles, consecrated to arms, descended from the gods!

PERSIAN   Belzanor: the gods are not always good to their poor relations.

BELZANOR [*hotly, to the* PERSIAN]   Man to man, are we worse than the slaves of Caesar?

BEL AFFRIS [*stepping between them*] Listen, cousin. Man to man, we Egyptians are as gods above the Romans.

GUARDSMEN [*exultantly*] Aha!

BEL AFFRIS But this Caesar does not pit man against man: he throws a legion at you where you are weakest as he throws a stone from a catapult; and that legion is as a man with one head, a thousand arms, and no religion. I have fought against them; and I know.

BELZANOR [*derisively*] Were you frightened, cousin?

> The GUARDSMEN *roar with laughter, their eyes sparkling at the wit of their captain.*

BEL AFFRIS No, cousin; but I was beaten. They were frightened (perhaps); but they scattered us like chaff.

> The GUARDSMEN, *much damped, utter a growl of contemptuous disgust.*

BELZANOR Could you not die?

BEL AFFRIS No: that was too easy to be worthy of a descendant of the gods. Besides, there was no time: all was over in a moment. The attack came just where we least expected it.

BELZANOR That shews that the Romans are cowards.

BEL AFFRIS They care nothing about cowardice, these Romans: they fight to win. The pride and honor of war are nothing to them.

PERSIAN Tell us the tale of the battle. What befell?

GUARDSMEN [*gathering eagerly round* BEL AFFRIS] Ay: the tale of the battle.

BEL AFFRIS Know then, that I am a novice in the guard of the temple of Ra in Memphis, serving neither Cleopatra nor her brother Ptolemy, but only the high gods. We went a journey to inquire of Ptolemy why he had driven Cleopatra into Syria, and how we of Egypt should deal with the Roman Pompey, newly come to our shores after his defeat by Caesar at Pharsalia. What, think ye, did we learn? Even that Caesar is coming also in hot pursuit of his foe, and that Ptolemy has slain Pompey, whose severed head he holds in readiness to present to the conqueror. [*Sensation among the* GUARDSMEN.] Nay, more: we found that Caesar is already come; for we had not made half a day's journey on our way back when we came upon a city rabble flying from his legions, whose landing they had gone out to withstand.

BELZANOR And ye, the temple guard! did ye not withstand these legions?

BEL AFFRIS What man could that we did. But there came the sound of a trumpet whose voice was as the cursing of a black mountain. Then saw we a moving wall of shields coming towards us. You know how the heart burns when you charge a fortified wall; but how if the fortified wall were to charge y o u ?

PERSIAN [*exulting in having told them so*] Did I not say it?

BEL AFFRIS When the wall came nigh, it changed into a line of men —common fellows enough, with helmets, leather tunics, and breastplates. Every man of them flung his javelin: the one that came my way drove through my shield as through a papyrus—lo there! [*he points to the bandage on his left arm*] and would have gone through my neck had I not stooped. They were charging at the double then, and were upon us with short swords almost as soon as their javelins.

When a man is close to you with such a sword, you can do nothing with our weapons: they are all too long.

PERSIAN   What did you do?

BEL AFFRIS   Doubled my fist and smote my Roman on the sharpness of his jaw. He was but mortal after all: he lay down in a stupor; and I took his sword and laid it on. [*Drawing the sword.*] Lo! a Roman sword with Roman blood on it!

GUARDSMEN [*approvingly*]   Good! [*They take the sword and hand it round, examining it curiously.*]

PERSIAN   And your men?

BEL AFFRIS   Fled. Scattered like sheep.

BELZANOR [*furiously*]   The cowardly slaves! Leaving the descendants of the gods to be butchered!

BEL AFFRIS [*with acid coolness*]   The descendants of the gods did not stay to be butchered, cousin. The battle was not to the strong; but the race was to the swift. The Romans, who have no chariots, sent a cloud of horsemen in pursuit, and slew multitudes. Then our high priest's captain rallied a dozen descendants of the gods and exhorted us to die fighting. I said to myself: surely it is safer to stand than to lose my breath and be stabbed in the back; so I joined our captain and stood. Then the Romans treated us with respect; for no man attacks a lion when the field is full of sheep, except for the pride and honor of war, of which these Romans know nothing. So we escaped with our lives; and I am come to warn you that you must open your gates to Caesar; for his advance guard is scarce an hour behind me; and not an Egyptian warrior is left standing between you and his legions.

SENTINEL   Woe, alas! [*He throws down his javelin and flies into the palace.*]

BELZANOR   Nail him to the door, quick! [*The* GUARDSMEN *rush for him with their spears; but he is too quick for them.*] Now this news will run through the palace like fire through stubble.

BEL AFFRIS   What shall we do to save the women from the Romans?

BELZANOR   Why not kill them?

PERSIAN   Because we should have to pay blood money for some of them. Better let the Romans kill them: it is cheaper.

BELZANOR [*awestruck at his brain power*]   O subtle one! O serpent!

BEL AFFRIS   But your Queen?

BELZANOR   True: we must carry off Cleopatra.

BEL AFFRIS   Will ye not await her command?

BELZANOR   Command! a girl of sixteen! Not we. At Memphis ye deem her a Queen: here we know better. I will take her on the crupper of my horse. When we soldiers have carried her out of Caesar's reach, then the priests and the nurses and the rest of them can pretend she is a Queen again, and put their commands into her mouth.

PERSIAN   Listen to me, Belzanor.

BELZANOR   Speak, O subtle beyond thy years.

PERSIAN   Cleopatra's brother Ptolemy is at war with her. Let us sell her to him.

GUARDSMEN   O subtle one! O serpent!

BELZANOR   We dare not. We are descended from the gods; but Cleopatra is descended from the river Nile; and the lands of our fathers will grow no grain if the Nile rises not to water them. Without our father's gifts we should live the lives of dogs.

PERSIAN   It is true: the Queen's guard cannot live on its pay. But hear me further, O ye kinsmen of Osiris.

GUARDSMEN   Speak, O subtle one. Hear the serpent-begotten!

PERSIAN   Have I heretofore spoken truly to you of Caesar, when you thought I mocked you?

GUARDSMEN   Truly, truly.

BELZANOR [*reluctantly admitting it*]   So Bel Affris says.

PERSIAN   Hear more of him, then. This Caesar is a great lover of women: he makes them his friends and counsellors.

BELZANOR   Faugh! This rule of women will be the ruin of Egypt!

PERSIAN   Let it rather be the ruin of Rome! Caesar grows old now: he is past fifty and full of labors and battles. He is too old for the young women; and the old women are too wise to worship him.

BEL AFFRIS   Take heed, Persian. Caesar is by this time almost within earshot.

PERSIAN   Cleopatra is not yet a woman: neither is she wise. But she already troubles men's wisdom.

BELZANOR   Ay: that is because she is descended from the river Nile and a black kitten of the sacred White Cat. What then?

PERSIAN   Why, sell her secretly to Ptolemy, and then offer ourselves to Caesar as volunteers to fight for the overthrow of her brother and the rescue of our Queen, the Great Granddaughter of the Nile.

GUARDSMEN   O serpent!

PERSIAN   He will listen to us if we come with her picture in our mouths. He will conquer and kill her brother, and reign in Egypt with Cleopatra for his Queen. And we shall be her guard.

GUARDSMEN   O subtlest of all the serpents! O admiration! O wisdom!

BEL AFFRIS   He will also have arrived before you have done talking, O word spinner.

BELZANOR   That is true. [*An affrighted uproar in the palace interrupts him.*] Quick: the flight has begun: guard the door. [*They rush to the door and form a cordon before it with their spears. A mob of women-servants and nurses surges out. Those in front recoil from the spears, screaming to those behind to keep back.* BELZANOR's *voice dominates the disturbance as he shouts.*] Back there. In again, unprofitable cattle.

GUARDSMEN   Back, unprofitable cattle.

BELZANOR   Send us out Ftatateeta, the Queen's chief nurse.

THE WOMEN [*calling into the palace*]   Ftatateeta, Ftatateeta. Come, come. Speak to Belzanor.

A WOMAN   Oh, keep back. You are thrusting me on the spearheads.

A huge grim woman, her face covered with a network of tiny wrinkles, and her eyes old, large, and wise; sinewy handed, very tall, very strong; with the mouth of a bloodhound and the jaws of a bulldog, appears on the threshold. She is dressed like a person of consequence in the palace, and confronts the GUARDSMEN *insolently.*

FTATATEETA   Make way for the Queen's chief nurse.

BELZANOR [*with solemn arrogance*]   Ftatateeta: I am Belzanor, the captain of the Queen's guard, descended from the gods.

FTATATEETA [*retorting his arrogance with interest*]   Belzanor: I am Ftatateeta, the Queen's chief nurse; and your divine ancestors were proud to be painted on the wall in the pyramids of the kings whom my fathers served.

The WOMEN *laugh triumphantly.*

BELZANOR [*with grim humor*]   Ftatateeta: daughter of a long-tongued, swivel-eyed chameleon, the Romans are at hand. [*A cry of terror from the* WOMEN: *they would fly but for the spears.*] Not even the descendants of the gods can resist them; for they have each man seven arms, each carrying seven spears. The blood in their veins is boiling quicksilver; and their wives become mothers in three hours, and are slain and eaten the next day.

A shudder of horror from the WOMEN. FTATATEETA, *despising them and scorning the soldiers, pushes her way through the crowd and confronts the spear points undismayed.*

FTATATEETA   Then fly and save yourselves, O cowardly sons of the cheap clay gods that are sold to fish porters; and leave us to shift for ourselves.

BELZANOR   Not until you have first done our bidding, O terror of manhood. Bring out Cleopatra the Queen to us; and then go whither you will.

FTATATEETA [*with a derisive laugh*]   Now I know why the gods have taken her out of our hands. [*The* GUARDSMEN *start and look at one another.*] Know, thou foolish soldier, that the Queen has been missing since an hour past sundown.

BELZANOR [*furious*]   Hag: you have hidden her to sell to Caesar or her brother. [*He grasps her by the left wrist, and drags her, helped by a few of the* GUARD, *to the middle of the courtyard, where, as they fling her on her knees, he draws a murderous looking knife.*] Where is she? Where is she? or—[*He threatens to cut her throat.*]

FTATATEETA [*savagely*]   Touch me, dog; and the Nile will not rise on your fields for seven times seven years of famine.

BELZANOR [*frightened, but desperate*]   I will sacrifice. I will pay. Or stay. [*To the* PERSIAN.] You, O subtle one: your father's lands lie far from the Nile. Slay her.

PERSIAN [*threatening her with his knife*]   Persia has but one god; yet he loves the blood of old women. Where is Cleopatra?

FTATATEETA   Persian: as Osiris lives, I do not know. I chid her for bringing evil days upon us by talking to the sacred cats of the priests, and carrying them in her arms. I told her she would be left alone here when the Romans came as a punishment for her disobedience. And now she is gone—run away—hidden. I speak the truth. I call Osiris to witness—

THE WOMEN [*protesting officiously*]   She speaks the truth, Belzanor.

BELZANOR   You have frightened the child: she is hiding. Search— quick—into the palace—search every corner.

The GUARDS, *led by* BELZANOR, *shoulder their way into the palace through the flying crowd of* WOMEN, *who escape through the courtyard gate.*

FTATATEETA [*screaming*]   Sacrilege! Men in the Queen's chambers! Sa—[*Her voice dies away as the* PERSIAN *put his knife to her throat.*]

BEL AFFRIS [*laying a hand on* FTATATEETA's *left shoulder*]   Forbear her yet a moment, Persian. [*To* FTATATEETA, *very significantly.*] Mother: your gods are asleep or away hunting; and the sword is at your throat. Bring us to where the Queen is hid, and you shall live.

FTATATEETA [*contemptuously*] Who shall stay the sword in the hand of a fool, if the high gods put it there? Listen to me, ye young men without understanding. Cleopatra fears me; but she fears the Romans more. There is but one power greater in her eyes than the wrath of the Queen's nurse and the cruelty of Caesar; and that is the power of the Sphinx that sits in the desert watching the way to the sea. What she would have it know, she tells into the ears of the sacred cats; and on her birthday she sacrifices to it and decks it with poppies. Go ye therefore into the desert and seek Cleopatra in the shadow of the Sphinx; and on your heads see to it that no harm comes to her.

BEL AFFRIS [*to the* PERSIAN] May we believe this, O subtle one?

PERSIAN Which way come the Romans?

BEL AFFRIS Over the desert, from the sea, by this very Sphinx.

PERSIAN [*to* FTATATEETA] O mother of guile! O aspic's tongue! You have made up this tale so that we two may go into the desert and perish on the spears of the Romans. [*Lifting his knife.*] Taste death.

FTATATEETA Not from thee, baby. [*She snatches his ankle from under him and flies stooping along the palace wall, vanishing in the darkness within its precinct.* BEL AFFRIS *roars with laughter as the* PERSIAN *tumbles. The* GUARDSMEN *rush out of the palace with* BELZANOR *and a mob of fugitives, mostly carrying bundles.*]

PERSIAN Have you found Cleopatra?

BELZANOR She is gone. We have searched every corner.

SENTINEL [*appearing at the door of the palace*] Woe! Alas! Fly, fly!

BELZANOR What is the matter now?

SENTINEL The sacred white cat has been stolen.

ALL Woe! woe! [*General panic. They all fly with cries of consternation. The torch is thrown down and extinguished in the rush. The noise of the fugitives dies away. Darkness and dead silence.*]

Act 1

The same darkness into which the temple of Ra and the Syrian palace vanished. The same silence. Suspense. Then the blackness and stillness break softly into silver mist and strange airs as the wind-swept harp of Memnon plays at the dawning of the moon.[7] *It rises full over the desert; and a vast horizon comes into relief, broken by a huge shape which soon reveals itself in the spreading radiance as a Sphinx*[8] *pedestalled on the sands. The light still clears, until the upraised eyes of the image are distinguished looking straight forward and upward in infinite fearless vigil, and a mass of color between its great paws defines itself as a heap of red poppies on which a girl lies motionless, her silken vest heaving gently and regularly with the breathing of a dreamless sleeper, and*

---

7. In *The Iliad* Memnon, a king of Ethiopia and son of the dawn goddess Eos (Aurora), fought with the Trojans and was killed by Achilles. The Greeks gave his name to a colossal statue near the Egyptian city of Thebes which was reputed to "sing"

at dawn.

8. A monster with the head of a woman and the body of a lion. Many statues in this form are found in Egypt, including the great one near Giza for which Caesar mistakes this one.

her braided hair glittering in a shaft of moonlight like a bird's wing.

Suddenly there comes from afar a vaguely fearful sound (it might be the bellow of a Minotaur[9] softened by great distance) and Memnon's music stops. Silence: then a few faint high-ringing trumpet notes. Then silence again. Then a man comes from the south with stealing steps, ravished by the mystery of the night, all wonder, and halts, lost in contemplation, opposite the left flank of the Sphinx, whose bosom, with its burden, is hidden from him by its massive shoulder.

THE MAN   Hail, Sphinx: saluation from Julius Caesar! I have wandered in many lands, seeking the lost regions from which my birth into this world exiled me, and the company of creatures such as I myself. I have found flocks and pastures, men and cities, but no other Caesar, no air native to me, no man kindred to me, none who can do my day's deed, and think my night's thought. In the little world yonder, Sphinx, my place is as high as yours in this great desert; only I wander, and you sit still; I conquer, and you endure; I work and wonder, you watch and wait; I look up and am dazzled, look down and am darkened, look round and am puzzled, whilst your eyes never turn from looking out—out of the world—to the lost region—the home from which we have strayed. Sphinx, you and I, strangers to the race of men, are no strangers to one another: have I not been conscious of you and of this place since I was born? Rome is a madman's dream: this is my Reality. These starry lamps of yours I have seen from afar in Gaul, in Britain, in Spain, in Thessaly, signalling great secrets to some eternal sentinel below, whose post I never could find. And here at last is their sentinel—an image of the constant and immortal part of my life, silent, full of thoughts, alone in the silver desert. Sphinx, Sphinx: I have climbed mountains at night to hear in the distance the stealthy footfall of the winds that chase your sands in forbidden play—our invisible children, O Sphinx, laughing in whispers. My way hither was the way of destiny; for I am he of whose genius you are the symbol: part brute, part woman, and part god—nothing of man in me at all. Have I read your riddle, Sphinx?

THE GIRL   [*who has wakened, and peeped cautiously from her nest to see who is speaking*]   Old gentleman.

CAESAR   [*starting violently, and clutching his sword*]   Immortal gods!

THE GIRL   Old gentleman: dont run away.

CAESAR   [*stupefied*]   "Old gentleman: dont run away"!!! This! to Julius Caesar!

THE GIRL   [*urgently*]   Old gentleman.

CAESAR   Sphinx: you presume on your centuries. I am younger than you, though your voice is but a girl's voice as yet.

THE GIRL   Climb up here, quickly; or the Romans will come and eat you.

CAESAR   [*running forward past the Sphinx's shoulder, and seeing her*]   A child at its breast! a divine child!

THE GIRL   Come up quickly. You must get up at its side and creep round.

CAESAR   [*amazed*]   Who are you?

9. A monster with the head of a bull and the body of a man. The Labyrinth at Cnossus in Crete was reputedly constructed to contain him.

THE GIRL   Cleopatra, Queen of Egypt.

CAESAR   Queen of the Gypsies, you mean.[1]

CLEOPATRA   You must not be disrespectful to me, or the Sphinx will let the Romans eat you. Come up. It is quite cosy here.

CAESAR [*to himself*]   What a dream! What a magnificent dream! Only let me not wake, and I will conquer ten continents to pay for dreaming it out to the end. [*He climbs to the Sphinx's flank, and presently reappears to her on the pedestal, stepping round its right shoulder.*]

CLEOPATRA   Take care. Thats right. Now sit down: you may have its other paw. [*She seats herself comfortably on its left paw.*] It is very powerful and will protect us; but [*shivering, and with plaintive loneliness*] it would not take any notice of me or keep me company. I am glad you have come: I was very lonely. Did you happen to see a white cat anywhere?

CAESAR [*sitting slowly down on the right paw in extreme wonderment*] Have you lost one?

CLEOPATRA   Yes: the sacred white cat: is it not dreadful? I brought him here to sacrifice him to the Sphinx; but when we got a little way from the city a black cat called him, and he jumped out of my arms and ran away to it. Do you think that the black cat can have been my great-great-great-grandmother?

CAESAR [*staring at her*]   Your great-great-great-grandmother! Well, why not? Nothing would surprise me on this night of nights.

CLEOPATRA   I think it must have been. My great-grandmother's great-grandmother was a black kitten of the sacred white cat; and the river Nile made her his seventh wife. That is why my hair is so wavy. And I always want to be let do as I like, no matter whether it is the will of the gods or not: that is because my blood is made with Nile water.

CAESAR   What are you doing here at this time of night? Do you live here?

CLEOPATRA   Of course not: I am the Queen; and I shall live in the palace at Alexandria when I have killed my brother, who drove me out of it. When I am old enough I shall do just what I like. I shall be able to poison the slaves and see them wriggle, and pretend to Ftatateeta that she is going to be put into the fiery furnace.

CAESAR   Hm! Meanwhile why are you not at home and in bed?

CLEOPATRA   Because the Romans are coming to eat us all. You are not at home and in bed either.

CAESAR [*with conviction*]   Yes I am. I live in a tent; and I am now in that tent, fast asleep and dreaming. Do you suppose that I believe you are real, you impossible little dream witch?

CLEOPATRA [*giggling and leaning trustfully towards him*]   You are a funny old gentleman. I like you.

CAESAR   Ah, that spoils the dream. Why dont you dream that I am young?

CLEOPATRA   I wish you were; only I think I should be more afraid of you. I like men, especially young men with round strong arms; but I am afraid of them. You are old and rather thin and stringy; but you have a nice voice; and I like to have somebody to talk to, though I think you are a little mad. It is the moon that makes you talk to yourself in that silly way.

---

1. "Gypsies" are so called because they were formerly believed to be of Egyptian origin, but Caesar is really expressing, somewhat anachronistically, his distrust of Cleopatra's claim to be Queen of the Egyptians.

CAESAR   What! you heard that, did you? I was saying my prayers to the great Sphinx.

CLEOPATRA   But this isnt the great Sphinx.

CAESAR [*much disappointed, looking up at the statue*]   What!

CLEOPATRA   This is only a dear little kitten of a Sphinx. Why, the great Sphinx is so big that it has a temple between its paws. This is my pet Sphinx. Tell me: do you think the Romans have any sorcerers who could take us away from the Sphinx by magic?

CAESAR   Why? Are you afraid of the Romans?

CLEOPATRA [*very seriously*]   Oh, they would eat us if they caught us. They are barbarians. Their chief is called Julius Caesar. His father was a tiger and his mother a burning mountain; and his nose is like an elephant's trunk. [CAESAR *involuntarily rubs his nose.*] They all have long noses, and ivory tusks, and little tails, and seven arms with a hundred arrows in each; and they live on human flesh.

CAESAR   Would you like me to shew you a real Roman?

CLEOPATRA [*terrified*]   No. You are frightening me.

CAESAR   No matter: this is only a dream—

CLEOPATRA [*excitedly*]   It is not a dream: it is not a dream. See, see.

>   She plucks a pin from her hair and jabs it repeatedly into his arm.

CAESAR   Ffff—Stop. [*Wrathfully.*] How dare you?

CLEOPATRA [*abashed*]   You said you were dreaming. [*Whimpering.*] I only wanted to shew you—

CAESAR [*gently*]   Come, come: dont cry. A queen mustnt cry. [*He rubs his arm, wondering at the reality of the smart.*] Am I awake? [*He strikes his hand against the Sphinx to test its solidity. It feels so real that he begins to be alarmed, and says perplexedly.*] Yes, I— [*quite panic-stricken*] no: impossible: madness, madness! [*Desperately.*] Back to camp—to camp. [*He rises to spring down from the pedestal.*]

CLEOPATRA [*flinging her arms in terror round him*]   No: you shant leave me. No, no, no: dont go. I'm afraid—afraid of the Romans.

CAESAR [*as the conviction that he is really awake forces itself on him*]   Cleopatra: can you see my face well?

CLEOPATRA   Yes. It is so white in the moonlight.

CAESAR   Are you sure it is the moonlight that makes me look whiter than an Egyptian? [*Grimly.*] Do you notice that I have a rather long nose?

CLEOPATRA [*recoiling, paralysed by a terrible suspicion*]   Oh!

CAESAR   It is a Roman nose, Cleopatra.

CLEOPATRA   Ah! [*With a piercing scream she springs up; darts round the left shoulder of the Sphinx; scrambles down to the sand; and falls on her knees in frantic supplication, shrieking.*] Bite him in two, Sphinx: bite him in two. I meant to sacrifice the white cat—I did indeed—I—[CAESAR, *who has slipped down from the pedestal, touches her on the shoulder.*] Ah! [*She buries her head in her arms.*]

CAESAR   Cleopatra: Shall I teach you a way to prevent Caesar from eating you?

CLEOPATRA [*clinging to him piteously*]   Oh do, do, do. I will steal Ftatateeta's jewels and give them to you. I will make the river Nile water your lands twice a year.

CAESAR   Peace, peace, my child. Your gods are afraid of the Romans:

you see the Sphinx dare not bite me, nor prevent me carrying you
off to Julius Caesar.

CLEOPATRA [*in pleading murmurings*]   You wont, you wont. You said
you wouldnt.

CAESAR   Caesar never eats women.

CLEOPATRA [*springing up full of hope*]   What!

CAESAR [*impressively*]   But he eats girls [*she relapses*] and cats. Now
you are a silly little girl; and you are descended from the black
kitten. You are both a girl and a cat.

CLEOPATRA [*trembling*]   And will he eat m e?

CAESAR   Yes; unless you make him believe that you are a woman.

CLEOPATRA   Oh, you must get a sorcerer to make a woman of me.
Are you a sorcerer?

CAESAR   Perhaps. But it will take a long time; and this very night you
must stand face to face with Caesar in the palace of your fathers.

CLEOPATRA   No, no. I darent.

CAESAR   Whatever dread may be in your soul—however terrible
Caesar may be to you—you must confront him as a brave woman
and a great queen; and you must feel no fear. If your hand shakes:
if your voice quavers; then—night and death! [*She moans.*] But if
he thinks you worthy to rule, he will set you on the throne by his
side and make you the real ruler of Egypt.

CLEOPATRA [*despairingly*]   No: he will find me out: he will find me
out.

CAESAR [*rather mournfully*]   He is easily deceived by women. Their
eyes dazzle him; and he sees them not as they are, but as he wishes
them to appear to him.

CLEOPATRA [*hopefully*]   Then we will cheat him. I will put on Ftatateeta's head-dress; and he will think me quite an old woman.

CAESAR   If you do that he will eat you at one mouthful.

CLEOPATRA   But I will give him a cake with my magic opal and seven
hairs of the white cat baked in it; and—

CAESAR [*abruptly*]   Pah! you are a little fool. He will eat your cake and
you too. [*He turns contemptuously from her.*]

CLEOPATRA [*running after him and clinging to him*]   Oh please,
p l e a s e! I will do whatever you tell me. I will be good. I will be
your slave. [*Again the terrible bellowing note sounds across the
desert, now closer at hand. It is the bucina, the Roman war trumpet.*]

CAESAR   Hark!

CLEOPATRA [*trembling*]   What was that?

CAESAR   Caesar's voice.

CLEOPATRA [*pulling at his hand*]   Let us run away. Come. Oh, come.

CAESAR   You are safe with me until you stand on your throne to receive
Caesar. Now lead me thither.

CLEOPATRA [*only too glad to get away*]   I will, I will. [*Again the
bucina.*] Oh come, come, come: the gods are angry. Do you feel
the earth shaking?

CAESAR   It is the tread of Caesar's legions.

CLEOPATRA [*drawing him away*]   This way, quickly. And let us look
for the white cat as we go. It is he that has turned you into a Roman.

CAESAR   Incorrigible, oh, incorrigible! Away! [*He follows her, the
bucina sounding louder as they steal across the desert. The moonlight wanes: the horizon again shows black against the sky, broken
only by the fantastic silhouette of the Sphinx. The sky itself vanishes*

in darkness, from which there is no relief until the gleam of a distant torch falls on great Egyptian pillars supporting the roof of a majestic corridor. At the further end of this corridor a Nubian slave appears carrying the torch. CAESAR, *still led by* CLEOPATRA, *follows him. They come down the corridor,* CAESAR *peering keenly about at the strange architecture, and at the pillar shadows between which, as the passing torch makes them hurry noiselessly backwards, figures of men with wings and hawks' heads, and vast black marble cats, seem to flit in and out of ambush. Further along, the wall turns a corner and makes a spacious transept in which* CAESAR *sees, on his right, a throne, and behind the throne a door. On each side of the throne is a slender pillar with a lamp on it.*]

CAESAR   What place is this?

CLEOPATRA   This is where I sit on the throne when I am allowed to wear my crown and robes. [*The slave holds his torch to shew the throne.*]

CAESAR   Order the slave to light the lamps.

CLEOPATRA [*shyly*]   Do you think I may?

CAESAR   Of course. You are the Queen. [*She hesitates.*] Go on.

CLEOPATRA [*timidly, to the slave*]   Light all the lamps.

FTATATEETA [*suddenly coming from behind the throne*]   Stop. [*The slave stops. She turns sternly to* CLEOPATRA, *who quails like a naughty child.*] Who is this you have with you; and how dare you order the lamps to be lighted without my permission? [CLEOPATRA *is dumb with apprehension.*]

CAESAR   Who is she?

CLEOPATRA   Ftatateeta.

FTATATEETA [*arrogantly*]   Chief nurse to—

CAESAR [*cutting her short*]   I speak to the Queen. Be silent. [*To* CLEOPATRA.] Is this how your servants know their places? Send her away; and do you [*to the slave*] do as the Queen has bidden. [*The slave lights the lamps. Meanwhile* CLEOPATRA *stands hesitating, afraid of* FTATATEETA.] You are the Queen: send her away.

CLEOPATRA [*cajoling*]   Ftatateeta, dear: you must go away—just for a little.

CAESAR   You are not commanding her to go away: you are begging her. You are no Queen. You will be eaten. Farewell. [*He turns to go.*]

CLEOPATRA [*clutching him*]   No, no, no. Dont leave me.

CAESAR   A Roman does not stay with queens who are afraid of their slaves.

CLEOPATRA   I am not afraid. Indeed I am not afraid.

FTATATEETA   We shall see who is afraid here. [*Menacingly.*] Cleopatra—

CAESAR   On your knees, woman: am I also a child that you dare trifle with me? [*He points to the floor at* CLEOPATRA's *feet.* FTATATEETA, *half cowed, half savage, hesitates.* CAESAR *calls to the* NUBIAN.] Slave. [*The* NUBIAN *comes to him.*] Can you cut off a head? [*The* NUBIAN *nods and grins ecstatically, shewing all his teeth.* CAESAR *takes his sword by the scabbard, ready to offer the hilt to the* NUBIAN, *and turns again to* FTATATEETA, *repeating his gesture.*] Have you remembered yourself, mistress?

FTATATEETA, *crushed, kneels before* CLEOPATRA, *who can hardly believe her eyes.*

FTATATEETA [*hoarsely*]   O Queen, forget not thy servant in the days of thy greatness.

CLEOPATRA [*blazing with excitement*]   Go. Begone. Go away. [FTATATEETA *rises with stooped head, and moves backward towards the door.* CLEOPATRA *watches her submission eagerly, almost clapping her hands, which are trembling. Suddenly she cries.*] Give me something to beat her with. [*She snatches a snake-skin from the throne and dashes after* FTATATEETA, *whirling it like a scourge in the air.* CAESAR *makes a bound and manages to catch her and hold her while* FTATATEETA *escapes.*]

CAESAR   You scratch, kitten, do you?

CLEOPATRA [*breaking from him*]   I w i l l beat somebody. I will beat h i m. [*She attacks the slave.*] There, there, there! [*The slave flies for his life up the corridor and vanishes. She throws the snake-skin away and jumps on the step of the throne with her arms waving, crying.*] I am a real Queen at last—a real, real Queen! Cleopatra the Queen! [CAESAR *shakes his head dubiously, the advantage of the change seeming open to question from the point of view of the general welfare of Egypt. She turns and looks at him exultantly. Then she jumps down from the steps, runs to him, and flings her arms around him rapturously, crying.*] Oh, I love you for making me a Queen.

CAESAR   But queens love only kings.

CLEOPATRA   I will make all the men I love kings. I will make you a king. I will have many young kings, with round, strong arms; and when I am tired of them I will whip them to death; but you shall always be my king: my nice, kind, wise, good old king.

CAESAR   Oh, my wrinkles, my wrinkles! And my child's heart! You will be the most dangerous of all Caesar's conquests.

CLEOPATRA [*appalled*]   Caesar! I forgot Caesar. [*Anxiously.*] You will tell him that I am a Queen, will you not?—a real Queen. Listen! [*stealthily coaxing him*] let us run away and hide until Caesar is gone.

CAESAR   If you fear Caesar, you are no true queen; and though you were to hide beneath a pyramid, he would go straight to it and lift it with one hand. And then—! [*He chops his teeth together.*]

CLEOPATRA [*trembling*]   Oh!

CAESAR   Be afraid if you dare. [*The note of the bucina resounds again in the distance. She moans with fear.* CAESAR *exults in it, exclaiming.*] Aha! Caesar approaches the throne of Cleopatra. Come: take your place. [*He takes her hand and leads her to the throne. She is too downcast to speak.*] Ho, there, Teetatota. How do you call your slaves?

CLEOPATRA [*spiritlessly, as she sinks on the throne and cowers there, shaking*]   Clap your hands.

He claps his hands. FTATATEETA *returns.*

CAESAR   Bring the Queen's robes, and her crown, and her women; and prepare her.

CLEOPATRA [*eagerly—recovering herself a little*]   Yes, the crown, Ftatateeta: I shall wear the crown.

FTATATEETA   For whom must the Queen put on her state?

CAESAR   For a citizen of Rome. A king of kings, Totateeta.

CLEOPATRA [*stamping at her*]   How dare you ask questions? Go and do as you are told. [FTATATEETA *goes out with a grim smile.* CLEO-

PATRA *goes on eagerly, to* CAESAR.] Caesar will know that I am a Queen when he sees my crown and robes, will he not?

CAESAR   No. How shall he know that you are not a slave dressed up in the Queen's ornaments?

CLEOPATRA   You must tell him.

CAESAR   He will not ask me. He will know Cleopatra by her pride, her courage, her majesty, and her beauty. [*She looks very doubtful.*] Are you trembling?

CLEOPATRA [*shivering with dread*]   No, I—I—[*In a very sickly voice.*] No.

FTATATEETA *and three* WOMEN *come in with the regalia.*

FTATATEETA   Of all the Queen's women, these three alone are left. The rest are fled. [*They begin to deck* CLEOPATRA, *who submits, pale and motionless.*]

CAESAR   Good, good. Three are enough. Poor Caesar generally has to dress himself.

FTATATEETA [*contemptuously*]   The Queen of Egypt is not a Roman barbarian. [*To* CLEOPATRA.] Be brave, my nursling. Hold up your head before this stranger.

CAESAR [*admiring* CLEOPATRA, *and placing the crown on her head*]   Is it sweet or bitter to be a Queen, Cleopatra?

CLEOPATRA   Bitter.

CAESAR   Cast out fear; and you will conquer Caesar. Tota: are the Romans at hand?

FTATATEETA   They are at hand; and the guard has fled.

THE WOMEN [*wailing subduedly*]   Woe to us!

The NUBIAN *comes running down the hall.*

NUBIAN   The Romans are in the courtyard. [*He bolts through the door. With a shriek, the* WOMEN *fly after him.* FTATATEETA's *jaw expresses savage resolution: she does not budge.* CLEOPATRA *can hardly restrain herself from following them.* CAESAR *grips her wrist, and looks steadfastly at her. She stands like a martyr.*]

CAESAR   The Queen must face Caesar alone. Answer "So be it."

CLEOPATRA [*white*]   So be it.

CAESAR [*releasing her*]   Good.

A tramp and tumult of armed men is heard. CLEOPATRA's *terror increases. The bucina sounds close at hand, followed by a formidable clangor of trumpets. This is too much for* CLEOPATRA: *she utters a cry and darts towards the door.* FTATATEETA *stops her ruthlessly.*

FTATATEETA   You are my nursling. You have said "So be it"; and if you die for it, you must make the Queen's word good. [*She hands* CLEOPATRA *to* CAESAR, *who takes her back, almost beside herself with apprehension, to the throne.*]

CAESAR   Now, if you quail—! [*He seats himself on the throne.*]

She stands on the step, all but unconscious, waiting for death. The Roman soldiers troop in tumultuously through the corridor, headed by their ensign with his eagle, and their bucinator, a burly fellow with his instrument coiled round his body, its brazen bell shaped like the head of a howling wolf. When they reach the transept, they stare in amazement at the throne; dress into ordered rank opposite it; draw their swords and lift them in the air with a shout of H a i l ,   C a e s a r . CLEO-PATRA *turns and stares wildly at* CAESAR; *grasps the situation; and, with a great sob of relief, falls into his arms.*

Act 2

Alexandria. A hall on the first floor of the Palace, ending in a loggia approached by two steps. Through the arches of the loggia the Mediterranean can be seen, bright in the morning sun. The clean lofty walls, painted with a procession of the Egyptian theocracy, presented in profile as flat ornament, and the absence of mirrors, sham perspectives, stuffy upholstery and textiles, make the place handsome, wholesome, simple and cool, or, as a rich English manufacturer would express it, poor, bare, ridiculous and unhomely. For Tottenham Court Road civilization is to this Egyptian civilization as glass bead and tattoo civilization is to Tottenham Court Road.[2]

The young king PTOLEMY DIONYSUS *(aged ten) is at the top of the steps, on his way in through the loggia, led by his guardian* POTHINUS, *who has him by the hand. The court is assembled to receive him. It is made up of men and women (some of the women being officials) of various complexions and races, mostly Egyptian; some of them, comparatively fair, from lower Egypt, some, much darker, from upper Egypt; with a few Greeks and Jews. Prominent in a group on* PTOLEMY'S *right hand is* THEODOTUS, PTOLEMY'S *tutor. Another group, on* PTOLEMY'S *left, is headed by* ACHILLAS, *the general of* PTOLEMY'S *troops.* THEODOTUS *is a little old man, whose features are as cramped and wizened as his limbs, except his tall straight forehead, which occupies more space than all the rest of his face. He maintains an air of magpie keenness and profundity, listening to what the others say with the sarcastic vigilance of a philosopher listening to the exercises of his disciples.* ACHILLAS *is a tall handsome man of thirty-five, with a fine black beard curled like the coat of a poodle. Apparently not a clever man, but distinguished and dignified.* POTHINUS *is a vigorous man of fifty, a eunuch, passionate, energetic and quick witted, but of common mind and character; impatient and unable to control his temper. He has fine tawny hair, like fur.* PTOLEMY, *the King, looks much older than an English boy of ten; but he has the childish air, the habit of being in leading strings, the mixture of impotence and petulance, the appearance of being excessively washed, combed and dressed by other hands, which is exhibited by court-bred princes of all ages.*

All receive the King with reverences. He comes down the steps to a chair of state which stands a little to his right, the only seat in the hall. Taking his place before it, he looks nervously for instructions to POTHINUS, *who places himself at his left hand.*

---

2. A heavily commercial street in Central London. It is a northern continuation of Charing Cross Road, beginning at Oxford Street.

POTHINUS   The King of Egypt has a word to speak.

THEODOTUS   [*in a squeak which he makes impressive by sheer self-opinionativeness*]   Peace for the King's word!

PTOLEMY   [*without any vocal inflexions: he is evidently repeating a lesson*]   Take notice of this all of you. I am the first-born son of Auletes the Flute Blower who was your King. My sister Berenice drove him from his throne and reigned in his stead but—but— [*He hesitates.*]

POTHINUS   [*stealthily prompting*]   —but the gods would not suffer—

PTOLEMY   Yes—the gods would not suffer—not suffer—[*He stops; then, crestfallen.*] I forget what the gods would not suffer.

THEODOTUS   Let Pothinus, the King's guardian, speak for the King.

POTHINUS   [*suppressing his impatience with difficulty*]   The King wished to say that the gods would not suffer the impiety of his sister to go unpunished.

PTOLEMY   [*hastily*]   Yes: I remember the rest of it. [*He resumes his monotone.*] Therefore the gods sent a stranger one Mark Antony a Roman captain of horsemen across the sands of the desert and he set my father again upon the throne. And my father took Berenice my sister and struck her head off. And now that my father is dead yet another of his daughters my sister Cleopatra would snatch the kingdom from me and reign in my place. But the gods would not suffer—[POTHINUS *coughs admonitorily*]—the gods—the gods would not suffer—

POTHINUS   [*prompting*]   —will not maintain—

PTOLEMY   Oh yes—will not maintain such iniquity they will give her head to the axe even as her sister's. But with the help of the witch Ftatateeta she hath cast a spell on the Roman Julius Caesar to make him uphold her false pretence to rule in Egypt. Take notice then that I will not suffer—that I will not suffer—[*Pettishly, to* POTHINUS.] What is it that I will not suffer?

POTHINUS   [*suddenly exploding with all the force and emphasis of political passion*]   The King will not suffer a foreigner to take from him the throne of our Egypt. [*A shout of applause.*] Tell the King, Achillas, how many soldiers and horsemen follow the Romans?

THEODOTUS   Let the King's general speak!

ACHILLAS   But two Roman legions, O King. Three thousand soldiers and scarce a thousand horsemen.

> The court breaks into derisive laughter; and a great chattering begins, amid which RUFIO, a Roman officer, appears in the loggia. He is a burly, black-bearded man of middle age, very blunt, prompt and rough, with small clear eyes, and plump nose and cheeks, which, however, like the rest of his flesh, are in iron-hard condition.

RUFIO   [*from the steps*]   Peace, ho! [*The laughter and chatter cease abruptly.*] Caesar approaches.

THEODOTUS   [*with much presence of mind*]   The King permits the Roman commander to enter!

> CAESAR, plainly dressed, but wearing an oak wreath to conceal his baldness, enters from the loggia, attended by BRITANNUS, his secretary, a Briton, about forty, tall, solemn, and already slightly bald, with a heavy, drooping, hazel-coloured moustache

*trained so as to lose its ends in a pair of trim whiskers. He is
carefully dressed in blue, with portfolio, inkhorn, and reed pen
at his girdle. His serious air and sense of the importance of the
business in hand is in marked contrast to the kindly interest of*
CAESAR, *who looks at the scene, which is new to him, with the
frank curiosity of a child, and then turns to the King's chair:*
BRITANNUS *and* RUFIO *posting themselves near the steps at the
other side.*

CAESAR [*looking at* POTHINUS *and* PTOLEMY] Which is the King? the
man or the boy?

POTHINUS I am Pothinus, the guardian of my lord the King.

CAESAR [*patting* PTOLEMY *kindly on the shoulder*] So you are the
King. Dull work at your age, eh? [*To* POTHINUS.] Your servant,
Pothinus. [*He turns away unconcernedly and comes slowly along the
middle of the hall, looking from side to side at the courtiers until he
reaches* ACHILLAS.] And this gentleman?

THEODOTUS Achillas, the King's general.

CAESAR [*to* ACHILLAS, *very friendly*] A general, eh? I am a general
myself. But I began too old, too old. Health and many victories,
Achillas!

ACHILLAS As the gods will, Caesar.

CAESAR [*turning to* THEODOTUS] And you, sir, are—?

THEODOTUS Theodotus, the King's tutor.

CAESAR You teach men how to be kings, Theodotus. That is very
clever of you. [*Looking at the gods on the walls as he turns away
from* THEODOTUS *and goes up again to* POTHINUS.] And this place?

POTHINUS The council chamber of the chancellors of the King's
treasury, Caesar.

CAESAR Ah! that reminds me. I want some money.

POTHINUS The King's treasury is poor, Caesar.

CAESAR Yes: I notice that there is but one chair in it.

RUFIO [*shouting gruffly*] Bring a chair there, some of you, for Caesar.

PTOLEMY [*rising shyly to offer his chair*] Caesar—

CAESAR [*kindly*] No, no, my boy: that is your chair of state. Sit down.

> *He makes* PTOLEMY *sit down again. Meanwhile* RUFIO, *looking
> about him, sees in the nearest corner an image of the god Ra,
> represented as a seated man with the head of a hawk. Before the
> image is a bronze tripod, about as large as a three-legged stool,
> with a stick of incense burning on it.* RUFIO, *with Roman re-
> sourcefulness and indifference to foreign superstitions, promptly
> seizes the tripod; shakes off the incense; blows away the ash;
> and dumps it down behind* CAESAR, *nearly in the middle of the
> hall.*

RUFIO Sit on that, Caesar.

> *A shiver runs through the court, followed by a hissing whisper of
> Sacrilege!*

CAESAR [*seating himself*] Now, Pothinus, to business. I am badly in
want of money.

BRITANNUS [*disapproving of these informal expressions*] My master
would say that there is a lawful debt due to Rome by Egypt, contracted by the King's deceased father to the Triumvirate; and that

it is Caesar's duty to his country to require immediate payment.

CAESAR [*blandly*] Ah, I forgot. I have not made my companions known here. Pothinus: this is Britannus, my secretary. He is an islander from the western end of the world, a day's voyage from Gaul. [BRITANNUS *bows stiffly.*] This gentleman is Rufio, my comrade in arms. [RUFIO *nods.*] Pothinus: I want 1,600 talents.

> The courtiers, appalled, murmur loudly, and THEODOTUS and ACHILLAS appeal mutely to one another against so monstrous a demand.

POTHINUS [*aghast*] Forty million sesterces! Impossible. There is not so much money in the King's treasury.

CAESAR [*encouragingly*] O n l y 1,600 talents, Pothinus. Why count it in sesterces? A sestertius is only worth a loaf of bread.

POTHINUS And a talent is worth a racehorse. I say it is impossible. We have been at strife here, because the King's sister Cleopatra falsely claims his throne. The King's taxes have not been collected for a whole year.

CAESAR Yes they have, Pothinus. My officers have been collecting them all morning. [*Renewed whisper and sensation, not without some stifled laughter, among the courtiers.*]

RUFIO [*bluntly*] You must pay, Pothinus. Why waste words? You are getting off cheaply enough.

POTHINUS [*bitterly*] Is it possible that Caesar, the conqueror of the world, has time to occupy himself with such a trifle as our taxes?

CAESAR My friend: taxes are the chief business of a conqueror of the world.

POTHINUS Then take warning, Caesar. This day, the treasures of the temple and the gold of the King's treasury shall be sent to the mint to be melted down for our ransom in the sight of the people. They shall see us sitting under bare walls and drinking from wooden cups. And their wrath be on your head, Caesar, if you force us to this sacrilege!

CAESAR Do not fear, Pothinus: the people know how well wine tastes in wooden cups. In return for your bounty, I will settle this dispute about the throne for you, if you will. What say you?

POTHINUS If I say no, will that hinder you?

RUFIO [*defiantly*] No.

CAESAR You say the matter has been at issue for a year, Pothinus. May I have ten minutes at it?

POTHINUS You will do your pleasure, doubtless.

CAESAR Good! But first, let us have Cleopatra here.

THEODOTUS She is not in Alexandria: she is fled into Syria.

CAESAR I think not. [*To* RUFIO.] Call Totateeta.

RUFIO [*calling*] Ho there, Teetatota.

> FTATATEETA enters the loggia, and stands arrogantly at the top of the steps.

FTATATEETA Who pronounces the name of Ftatateeta, the Queen's chief nurse?

CAESAR Nobody can pronounce it, Tota, except yourself. Where is your mistress?

CLEOPATRA, *who is hiding behind* FTATATEETA, *peeps out at them laughing.* CAESAR *rises.*

CAESAR   Will the Queen favor us with her presence for a moment?

CLEOPATRA [*pushing* FTATATEETA *aside and standing haughtily on the brink of the steps*]   Am I to behave like a Queen?

CAESAR   Yes.

CLEOPATRA *immediately comes down to the chair of state; seizes* PTOLEMY; *drags him out of his seat; then takes his place in the chair.* FTATATEETA *seats herself on the step of the loggia, and sits there, watching the scene with sibylline intensity.*

PTOLEMY [*mortified, and struggling with his tears*]   Caesar: this is how she treats me always. If I am a king why is she allowed to take everything from me?

CLEOPATRA   You are not to be King, you little cry-baby. You are to be eaten by the Romans.

CAESAR [*touched by* PTOLEMY's *distress*]   Come here, my boy, and stand by me.

PTOLEMY *goes over to* CAESAR, *who, resuming his seat on the tripod, takes the boy's hand to encourage him.* CLEOPATRA, *furiously jealous, rises and glares at them.*

CLEOPATRA [*with flaming cheeks*]   Take your throne: I dont want it. [*She flings away from the chair, and approaches* PTOLEMY, *who shrinks from her.*] Go this instant and sit down in your place.

CAESAR   Go, Ptolemy. Always take a throne when it is offered to you.

RUFIO   I hope you will have the good sense to follow your own advice when we return to Rome, Caesar.

PTOLEMY *slowly goes back to the throne, giving* CLEOPATRA *a wide berth, in evident fear of her hands. She takes his place beside* CAESAR.

CAESAR   Pothinus—

CLEOPATRA [*interrupting him*]   Are you not going to speak to me?

CAESAR   Be quiet. Open your mouth again before I give you leave and you shall be eaten.

CLEOPATRA   I am not afraid. A queen must not be afraid. Eat my husband there, if you like: h e is afraid.

CAESAR [*starting*]   Your husband! What do you mean?

CLEOPATRA [*pointing to* PTOLEMY]   That little thing.

The two Romans and the Briton stare at one another in amazement.

THEODOTUS   Caesar: you are a stranger here, and not conversant with our laws. The kings and queens of Egypt may not marry except with their own royal blood. Ptolemy and Cleopatra are born king and consort just as they are born brother and sister.

BRITANNUS [*shocked*]   Caesar: this is not proper.

THEODOTUS [*outraged*]   How!

CAESAR [*recovering his self-possession*]   Pardon him, Theodotus: he is a barbarian, and thinks that the customs of his tribe and island are the laws of nature.

BRITANNUS   On the contrary, Caesar, it is these Egyptians who are barbarians; and you do wrong to encourage them. I say it is a scandal.

CAESAR   Scandal or not, my friend, it opens the gate of peace. [*He addresses* POTHINUS *seriously.*] Pothinus: hear what I propose.

RUFIO   Hear Caesar there.

CAESAR   Ptolemy and Cleopatra shall reign jointly in Egypt.

ACHILLAS   What of the King's younger brother and Cleopatra's younger sister?

RUFIO [*explaining*]   There is another little Ptolemy, Caesar: so they tell me.

CAESAR   Well, the little Ptolemy can marry the other sister; and we will make them both a present of Cyprus.

POTHINUS [*impatiently*]   Cyprus is of no use to anybody.

CAESAR   No matter: you shall have it for the sake of peace.

BRITANNUS [*unconsciously anticipating a later statesman*]   Peace with honor, Pothinus.[3]

POTHINUS [*mutinously*]   Caesar: be honest. The money you demand is the price of our freedom. Take it; and leave us to settle our own affairs.

THE BOLDER COURTIERS [*encouraged by* POTHINUS's *tone and* CAESAR's *quietness*]   Yes, yes. Egypt for the Egyptians!

> *The conference now becomes an altercation, the Egyptians becoming more and more heated.* CAESAR *remains unruffled; but* RUFIO *grows fiercer and doggeder, and* BRITANNUS *haughtily indignant.*

RUFIO [*contemptuously*]   Egypt for the Egyptians! Do you forget that there is a Roman army of occupation here, left by Aulus Gabinius when he set up your toy king for you?

ACHILLAS [*suddenly asserting himself*]   And now under m y command. *I* am the Roman general here, Caesar.

CAESAR [*tickled by the humor of the situation*]   And also the Egyptian general, eh?

POTHINUS [*triumphantly*]   That is so, Caesar.

CAESAR [*to* ACHILLAS]   So you can make war on the Egyptians in the name of Rome, and on the Romans—on me, if necessary—in the name of Egypt?

ACHILLAS   That is so, Caesar.

CAESAR   And which side are you on at present, if I may presume to ask, general?

ACHILLAS   On the side of the right and of the gods.

CAESAR   Hm! How many men have you?

ACHILLAS   That will appear when I take the field.

RUFIO [*truculently*]   Are your men Romans? If not, it matters not how many there are, provided you are no stronger than 500 to ten.

POTHINUS   It is useless to try to bluff us, Rufio. Caesar has been defeated before and may be defeated again. A few weeks ago Caesar was flying for his life before Pompey: a few months hence he may

---

3. The "later statesman" is Disraeli, who in 1878 returning from a meeting of European powers in Berlin, aimed at stopping Russia from increasing its influence in Europe, told Parliament, "Lord Salisbury and myself have brought you back peace—but a peace, I hope, with honor."

by flying for his life before Cato and Juba of Numidia, the African King.[4]

ACHILLAS [*following up* POTHINUS's *speech menacingly*]   What can you do with 4,000 men?

THEODOTUS [*following up* ACHILLAS's *speech with a raucous squeak*] And without money? Away with you.

ALL THE COURTIERS [*shouting fiercely and crowding towards* CAESAR] Away with you. Egypt for the Egyptians! Begone.

> RUFIO *bites his beard, too angry to speak.* CAESAR *sits as comfortably as if he were at breakfast, and the cat were clamoring for a piece of Finnan-haddie.*

CLEOPATRA   Why do you let them talk to you like that, Caesar? Are you afraid?

CAESAR   Why, my dear, what they say is quite true.

CLEOPATRA   But if you go away, I shall not be Queen.

CAESAR   I shall not go away until you are Queen.

POTHINUS   Achillas: if you are not a fool, you will take that girl whilst she is under your hand.

RUFIO [*daring them*]   Why not take Caesar as well, Achillas?

POTHINUS [*retorting the defiance with interest*]   Well said, Rufio. Why not?

RUFIO   Try, Achillas. [*Calling.*] Guard there.

> *The loggia immediately fills with* CAESAR's *soldiers, who stand, sword in hand, at the top of the steps, waiting the word to charge from their centurion, who carries a cudgel. For a moment the Egyptians face them proudly: then they retire sullenly to their former places.*

BRITANNUS   You are Caesar's prisoners, all of you.

CAESAR [*benevolently*]   Oh no, no, no. By no means. Caesar's guests, gentlemen.

CLEOPATRA   Wont you cut their heads off?

CAESAR   What! Cut off your brother's head?

CLEOPATRA   Why not? He would cut off mine, if he got the chance. Wouldnt you, Ptolemy?

PTOLEMY [*pale and obstinate*]   I would. I will, too, when I grow up.

> CLEOPATRA *is rent by a struggle between her newly-acquired dignity as a queen, and a strong impulse to put out her tongue at him. She takes no part in the scene which follows, but watches it with curiosity and wonder, fidgeting with the restlessness of a child, and sitting down on* CAESAR's *tripod when he rises.*

POTHINUS   Caesar: if you attempt to detain us—

RUFIO   He will succeed, Egyptian: make up your mind to that. We hold the palace, the beach, and the eastern harbor. The road to Rome is open; and you shall travel it if Caesar chooses.

CAESAR [*courteously*]   I could do no less, Pothinus, to secure the re-

---

4. Marcus Porcius Cato (95–46 B.C.) called Uticensis, the great-grandson of Cato the Censor, and Juba I (85–46 B.C.), the king of Numidia, were among the enemies of Caesar in the Civil War. They were defeated by Caesar at the battle of Thapsus (46 B.C.). Juba had himself killed by one of his servants; Cato committed suicide at Utica shortly thereafter.

treat of my own soldiers. I am accountable for every life among them. But you are free to go. So are all here, and in the palace.

RUFIO [*aghast at this clemency*]   What! Renegades and all?

CAESAR [*softening the expression*]   Roman army of occupation and all, Rufio.

POTHINUS [*bewildered*]   But—but—but—

CAESAR   Well, my friend?

POTHINUS   You are turning us out of our own palace into the streets; and you tell us with a grand air that we are free to go! It is for you to go.

CAESAR   Your friends are in the street, Pothinus. You will be safer there.

POTHINUS   This is a trick. I am the King's guardian: I refuse to stir. I stand on my right here. Where is your right?

CAESAR   It is in Rufio's scabbard, Pothinus. I may not be able to keep it there if you wait too long.

Sensation.

POTHINUS [*bitterly*]   And this is Roman justice!

THEODOTUS   But not Roman gratitude, I hope.

CAESAR   Gratitude! Am I in your debt for any service, gentlemen?

THEODOTUS   Is Caesar's life of so little account to him that he forgets that we have saved it?

CAESAR   My life! Is that all?

THEODOTUS   Your life. Your laurels. Your future.

POTHINUS   It is true. I can call a witness to prove that but for us, the Roman army of occupation, led by the greatest soldier in the world, would now have Caesar at its mercy. [*Calling through the loggia.*] Ho, there, Lucius Septimius [CAESAR *starts, deeply moved*]: if my voice can reach you, come forth and testify before Caesar.

CAESAR [*shrinking*]   No, no.

THEODOTUS   Yes, I say. Let the military tribune bear witness.

LUCIUS SEPTIMIUS, *a clean-shaven, trim athlete of about 40, with symmetrical features, resolute mouth, and handsome, thin Roman nose, in the dress of a Roman officer, comes in through the loggia and confronts* CAESAR, *who hides his face with his robe for a moment; then, mastering himself, drops it, and confronts the tribune with dignity.*

POTHINUS   Bear witness, Lucius Septimius. Caesar came hither in pursuit of his foe. Did we shelter his foe?

LUCIUS   As Pompey's foot touched the Egyptian shore, his head fell by the stroke of my sword.

THEODOTUS [*with viperish relish*]   Under the eyes of his wife and child! Remember that, Caesar! They saw it from the ship he had just left. We have given you a full and sweet measure of vengeance.

CAESAR [*with horror*]   Vengeance!

POTHINUS   Our first gift to you, as your galley came into the roadstead, was the head of your rival for the empire of the world. Bear witness, Lucius Septimius: is it not so?

LUCIUS   It is so. With this hand, that slew Pompey, I placed his head at the feet of Caesar.

CAESAR   Murderer! So would you have slain Caesar, had Pompey been victorious at Pharsalia.

LUCIUS   Woe to the vanquished, Caesar! When I served Pompey, I slew as good men as he, only because he conquered them. His turn came at last.

THEODOTUS [*flatteringly*]   The deed was not yours, Caesar, but ours—nay, mine; for it was done by my counsel. Thanks to us, you keep your reputation for clemency, and have your vengeance too.

CAESAR   Vengeance! Vengeance!! Oh, if I could stoop to vengeance, what would I not exact from you as the price of this murdered man's blood? [*They shrink back, appalled and disconcerted.*] Was he not my son-in-law, my ancient friend, for 20 years the master of great Rome, for 30 years the compeller of victory? Did not I, as a Roman, share his glory? Was the Fate that forced us to fight for the mastery of the world, of our making? Am I Julius Caesar, or am I a wolf, that you fling to me the grey head of the old soldier, the laurelled conqueror, the mighty Roman, treacherously struck down by this callous ruffian, and then claim my gratitude for it! [*To* LUCIUS SEPTIMIUS.] Begone: you fill me with horror.

LUCIUS [*cold and undaunted*]   Pshaw! You have seen severed heads before, Caesar, and severed right hands too, I think; some thousands of them, in Gaul, after you vanquished Vercingetorix.[5] Did you spare him, with all your clemency? Was that vengeance?

CAESAR   No, by the gods! would that it had been! Vengeance at least is human. No, I say: those severed right hands, and the brave Vercingetorix basely strangled in a vault beneath the Capitol, were [*with shuddering satire*] a wise severity, a necessary protection to the commonwealth, a duty of statesmanship—follies and fictions ten times bloodier than honest vengeance! What a fool was I then! To think that men's lives should be at the mercy of such fools! [*Humbly.*] Lucius Septimius, pardon me: why should the slayer of Vercingetorix rebuke the slayer of Pompey? You are free to go with the rest. Or stay if you will: I will find a place for you in my service.

LUCIUS   The odds are against you, Caesar. I go. [*He turns to go out through the loggia.*]

RUFIO [*full of wrath at seeing his prey escaping*]   That means that he is a Republican.

LUCIUS [*turning defiantly on the loggia steps*]   And what are you?

RUFIO   A Caesarian, like all Caesar's soldiers.

CAESAR [*courteously*]   Lucius: believe me, Caesar is no Caesarian. Were Rome a true republic, then were Caesar the first of Republicans. But you have made your choice. Farewell.

LUCIUS   Farewell. Come, Achillas, whilst there is yet time.

> CAESAR, *seeing that* RUFIO's *temper threatens to get the worse of him, puts his hand on his shoulder and brings him down the hall out of harm's way,* BRITANNUS *accompanying them and posting himself on* CAESAR's *right hand. This movement brings the three in a little group to the place occupied by* ACHILLAS, *who moves haughtily away and joins* THEODOTUS *on the other side.* LUCIUS SEPTIMIUS *goes out through the soldiers in the loggia.* POTHINUS, THEODOTUS *and* ACHILLAS *follow him with the courtiers, very mistrustful of the soldiers, who close up in their rear and go*

---

5. The valiant Gaulish chief Vercingetorix was defeated and captured by Caesar in the Gallic Wars. He was exhibited as a part of Caesar's triumph in 45 B.C. and then put to death. He was still alive at the time of the play's action.

out after them, keeping them moving without much ceremony. The KING *is left in his chair, piteous, obstinate, with twitching face and fingers. During these movements* RUFIO *maintains an energetic grumbling, as follows:*

RUFIO [*as* LUCIUS *departs*]   Do you suppose he would let us go if he had our heads in his hands?

CAESAR   I have no right to suppose that his ways are any baser than mine.

RUFIO   Pshaw!

CAESAR   Rufio: if I take Lucius Septimius for my model, and become exactly like him, ceasing to be Caesar, will you serve me still?

BRITANNUS   Caesar: this is not good sense. Your duty to Rome demands that her enemies should be prevented from doing further mischief.

> CAESAR, *whose delight in the moral eye-to-business of his British secretary is inexhaustible, smiles indulgently.*

RUFIO   It is no use talking to him, Britannus: you may save your breath to cool your porridge. But mark this, Caesar. Clemency is very well for you; but what is it for your soldiers, who have to fight tomorrow the men you spared yesterday? You may give what orders you please; but I tell you that your next victory will be a massacre, thanks to your clemency. I, for one, will take no prisoners. I will kill my enemies in the field; and then you can preach as much clemency as you please: I shall never have to fight them again. And now, with your leave, I will see these gentry off the premises. [*He turns to go.*]

CAESAR [*turning also and seeing* PTOLEMY]   What! have they left the boy alone! Oh shame, shame!

RUFIO [*taking* PTOLEMY's *hand and making him rise*]   Come, your majesty!

PTOLEMY [*to* CAESAR, *drawing away his hand from* RUFIO]   Is he turning me out of my palace?

RUFIO [*grimly*]   You are welcome to stay if you wish.

CAESAR [*kindly*]   Go, my boy. I will not harm you but you will be safer away, among your friends. Here you are in the lion's mouth.

PTOLEMY [*turning to go*]   It is not the lion I fear, but [*looking at* RUFIO] the jackal. [*He goes out through the loggia.*]

CAESAR [*laughing approvingly*]   Brave boy!

CLEOPATRA [*jealous of* CAESAR's *approbation, calling after* PTOLEMY] Little silly. You think that very clever.

CAESAR   Britannus: attend the King. Give him in charge to that Pothinus fellow. [BRITANNUS *goes out after* PTOLEMY.]

RUFIO [*pointing to* CLEOPATRA] · And this piece of goods? What is to be done with h e r? However, I suppose I may leave that to you. [*He goes out through the loggia.*]

CLEOPATRA [*flushing suddenly and turning on* CAESAR]   Did you mean me to go with the rest?

CAESAR [*a little preoccupied, goes with a sigh to* PTOLEMY's *chair, whilst she waits for his answer with red cheeks and clenched fist*] You are free to do just as you please, Cleopatra.

CLEOPATRA   Then you do not care whether I stay or not?

CAESAR [*smiling*]   Of course I had rather you stayed.

CLEOPATRA   Much, m u c h rather?

CAESAR [*nodding*]   Much, much rather.

CLEOPATRA   Then I consent to stay, because I am asked. But I do not want to, mind.

CAESAR   That is quite understood. [*Calling.*] Totateeta.

> FTATATEETA, *still seated, turns her eyes on him with a sinister expression, but does not move.*

CLEOPATRA [*with a splutter of laughter*]   Her name is not Totateeta: it is Ftatateeta. [*Calling.*] Ftatateeta. [FTATATEETA *instantly rises and comes to* CLEOPATRA.]

CAESAR [*stumbling over the name*]   Tfatafeeta will forgive the erring tongue of a Roman. Tota: the Queen will hold her state here in Alexandria. Engage women to attend upon her; and do all that is needful.

FTATATEETA   Am I then the mistress of the Queen's household?

CLEOPATRA [*sharply*]   No: *I* am the mistress of the Queen's household. Go and do as you are told, or I will have you thrown into the Nile this very afternoon, to poison the poor crocodiles.

CAESAR [*shocked*]   Oh no, no.

CLEOPATRA   Oh yes, yes. You are very sentimental, Caesar; but you are clever; and if you do as I tell you, you will soon learn to govern.

> CAESAR, *quite dumbfounded by this impertinence, turns in his chair and stares at her.* FTATATEETA, *smiling grimly, and shewing a splendid set of teeth, goes, leaving them alone together.*

CAESAR   Cleopatra: I really think I must eat you, after all.

CLEOPATRA [*kneeling beside him and looking at him with eager interest, half real, half affected to shew how intelligent she is*]   You must not talk to me now as if I were a child.

CAESAR   You have been growing up since the Sphinx introduced us the other night; and you think you know more than I do already.

CLEOPATRA [*taken down, and anxious to justify herself*]   No: that would be very silly of me: of course I know that. But—[*suddenly*] are you angry with me?

CAESAR   No.

CLEOPATRA [*only half believing him*]   Then why are you so thoughtful?

CAESAR [*rising*]   I have work to do, Cleopatra.

CLEOPATRA [*drawing back*]   Work! [*Offended.*] You are tired of talking to me; and that is your excuse to get away from me.

CAESAR [*sitting down again to appease her*]   Well, well: another minute. But then—work!

CLEOPATRA   Work! what nonsense! You must remember that you are a king now: I have made you one. Kings dont work.

CAESAR   Oh! Who told you that, little kitten? Eh?

CLEOPATRA   My father was King of Egypt; and he never worked. But he was a great king, and cut off my sister's head because she rebelled against him and took the throne from him.

CAESAR   Well; and how did he get his throne back again?

CLEOPATRA [*eagerly, her eyes lighting up*]   I will tell you. A beautiful young man, with strong round arms, came over the desert with many horsemen, and slew my sister's husband and gave my father back his throne. [*Wistfully.*] I was only twelve then. Oh, I wish he would come again, now that I am a queen. I would make him my husband.

CAESAR   It might be managed, perhaps; for it was I who sent that beautiful young man to help your father.

CLEOPATRA [*enraptured*]   You know him!

CAESAR [*nodding*]   I do.

CLEOPATRA   Has he come with you? [CAESAR *shakes his head: she is cruelly disappointed.*] Oh, I wish he had, I wish he had. If only I were a little older; so that he might not think me a mere kitten, as you do! But perhaps that is because y o u are old. He is many, m a n y years younger than you, is he not?

CAESAR [*as if swallowing a pill*]   He is somewhat younger.

CLEOPATRA   Would he be my husband, do you think, if I asked him?

CAESAR   Very likely.

CLEOPATRA   But I should not like to ask him. Could you not persuade him to ask me—without knowing that I wanted him to?

CAESAR [*touched by her innocence of the beautiful young man's character*]   My poor child!

CLEOPATRA   Why do you say that as if you were sorry for me? Does he love anyone else?

CAESAR   I am afraid so.

CLEOPATRA [*tearfully*]   Then I shall not be his first love.

CAESAR   Not quite the first. He is greatly admired by women.

CLEOPATRA   I wish I could be the first. But if he loves me, I will make him kill all the rest. Tell me: is he still beautiful? Do his strong round arms shine in the sun like marble?

CAESAR   He is in excellent condition—considering how much he eats and drinks.

CLEOPATRA   Oh, you must not say common, earthly things about him; for I love him. He is a god.

CAESAR   He is a great captain of horsemen, and swifter of foot than any other Roman.

CLEOPATRA   What is his real name?

CAESAR [*puzzled*]   His r e a l name?

CLEOPATRA   Yes. I always call him Horus, because Horus is the most beautiful of our gods.[6] But I want to know his real name.

CAESAR   His name is Mark Antony.

CLEOPATRA [*musically*]   Mark Antony. Mark Antony, Mark Antony! What a beautiful name! [*She throws her arms round* CAESAR's *neck.*] Oh, how I love you for sending him to help my father! Did you love my father very much?

CAESAR   No, my child; but your father, as you say, never worked. I always work. So when he lost his crown he had to promise me 16,000 talents to get it back for him.

CLEOPATRA   Did he ever pay you?

CAESAR   Not in full.

CLEOPATRA   He was quite right: it was too dear. The whole world is not worth 16,000 talents.

CAESAR   That is perhaps true, Cleopatra. Those Egyptians who work paid as much of it as he could drag from them. The rest is still due. But as I most likely shall not get it, I must go back to my work. So you must run away for a little and send my secretary to me.

6. Horus was an Egyptian sky god, the son of Isis and Osiris, frequently represented as a falcon. One of his attributes was the winged sun disk, and the Greeks (and Cleopatra was a Greek) identified him with Apollo, the sun god.

CLEOPATRA [*coaxing*]   No: I want to stay and hear you talk about Mark Antony.

CAESAR   But if I do not get to work, Pothinus and the rest of them will cut us off from the harbor; and then the way from Rome will be blocked.

CLEOPATRA   No matter: I dont want you to go back to Rome.

CAESAR   But you want Mark Antony to come from it.

CLEOPATRA [*springing up*]   Oh yes, yes, yes: I forgot. Go quickly and work, Caesar; and keep the way over the sea open for my Mark Antony. [*She runs out through the loggia, kissing her hand to Mark Antony across the sea.*]

CAESAR [*going briskly up the middle of the hall to the loggia steps*] Ho, Britannus. [*He is startled by the entry of a wounded Roman* SOLDIER, *who confronts him from the upper step.*] What now?

SOLDIER [*pointing to his bandaged head*]   This, Caesar; and two of my comrades killed in the market place.

CAESAR [*quiet, but attending*]   Ay. Why?

SOLDIER   There is an army come to Alexandria, calling itself the Roman army.

CAESAR   The Roman army of occupation. Ay?

SOLDIER   Commanded by one Achillas.

CAESAR   Well?

SOLDIER   The citizens rose against us when the army entered the gates. I was with two others in the market place when the news came. They set upon us. I cut my way out; and here I am.

CAESAR   Good. I am glad to see you alive. [RUFIO *enters the loggia hastily, passing behind the soldier to look out through one of the arches at the quay beneath.*] Rufio: we are besieged.

RUFIO   What! Already?

CAESAR   Now or to-morrow: what does it matter? We s h a l l be besieged.

BRITANNUS *runs in.*

BRITANNUS   Caesar—

CAESAR [*anticipating him*]   Yes: I know. [RUFIO *and* BRITANNUS *come down the hall from the loggia at opposite sides, past* CAESAR, *who waits for a moment near the step to say to the soldier:*] Comrade: give the word to turn out on the beach and stand by the boats. Get your wound attended to. Go. [*The* SOLDIER *hurries out.* CAESAR *comes down the hall between* RUFIO *and* BRITANNUS.] Rufio: we have some ships in the west harbor. Burn them.

RUFIO [*staring*]   Burn them!!

CAESAR   Take every boat we have in the east harbor, and seize the Pharos—that island with the lighthouse.[7] Leave half our men behind to hold the beach and the quay outside this palace: that is the way home.

RUFIO [*disapproving strongly*]   Are we to give up the city?

CAESAR   We have not got it, Rufiio. This palace we have; and—what is that building next door?

RUFIO   The theatre.

7. Pharos was an island in Alexandria harbor, site of the famous lighthouse of Alexandria, one of the Seven Wonders of the Ancient World. The name was also applied to the lighthouse itself.

CAESAR　We will have that too: it commands the strand. For the rest, Egypt for the Egyptians!

RUFIO　Well, you know best, I suppose. Is that all?

CAESAR　That is all. Are those ships burnt yet?

RUFIO　Be easy: I shall waste no more time. [*He runs out.*]

BRITANNUS　Caesar: Pothinus demands speech of you. In my opinion he needs a lesson. His manner is most insolent.

CAESAR　Where is he?

BRITANNUS　He waits without.

CAESAR　Ho there! admit Pothinus.

> POTHINUS *appears in the loggia, and comes down the hall very haughtily to* CAESAR's *left hand.*

CAESAR　Well, Pothinus?

POTHINUS　I have brought you our ultimatum, Caesar.

CAESAR　Ultimatum! The door was open: you should have gone out through it before you declared war. You are my prisoner now. [*He goes to the chair and loosens his toga.*]

POTHINUS　[*scornfully*]　I y o u r prisoner! Do you know that you are in Alexandria, and that King Ptolemy, with an army outnumbering your little troop a hundred to one, is in possession of Alexandria?

CAESAR　[*unconcernedly taking off his toga and throwing it on the chair*] Well, my friend, get out if you can. And tell your friends not to kill any more Romans in the market place. Otherwise my soldiers, who do not share my celebrated clemency, will probably kill you. Britannus: pass the word to the guard; and fetch my armor. [BRITANNUS *runs out,* RUFIO *returns.*] Well?

RUFIO　[*pointing from the loggia to a cloud of smoke drifting over the harbor*]　See there! [POTHINUS *runs eagerly up the steps to look out.*]

CAESAR　What, ablaze already! Impossible!

RUFIO　Yes, five good ships, and a barge laden with oil grappled to each. But it is not my doing: the Egyptians have saved me the trouble. They have captured the west harbor.

CAESAR　[*anxiously*]　And the east harbor? The lighthouse, Rufio?

RUFIO　[*with a sudden splutter of raging ill usage, coming down to* CAESAR *and scolding him*]　Can I embark a legion in five minutes? The first cohort is already on the beach. We can do no more. If you want faster work, come and do it yourself.

CAESAR　[*soothing him*]　Good, good. Patience, Rufio, patience.

RUFIO　Patience! Who is impatient here, you or I? Would I be here, if I could not oversee them from that balcony?

CAESAR　Forgive me, Rufio; and [*anxiously*] hurry them as much as—

> He is interrupted by an outcry as of an old man in the extremity of misfortune. It draws near rapidly; and THEODOTUS *rushes in, tearing his hair, and squeaking the most lamentable exclamations.* RUFIO *steps back to stare at him, amazed at his frantic condition.* POTHINUS *turns to listen.*

THEODOTUS　[*on the steps, with uplifted arms*]　Horror unspeakable! Woe, alas! Help!

RUFIO　What now?

CAESAR　[*frowning*]　Who is slain?

THEODOTUS　Slain! Oh, worse than the death of ten thousand men! Loss irreparable to mankind!

RUFIO   What has happened, man?

THEODOTUS [*rushing down the hall between them*]   The fire has spread from your ships. The first of the seven wonders of the world perishes. The library of Alexandria is in flames.

RUFIO   Pshaw! [*Quite relieved, he goes up to the loggia and watches the preparations of the troops on the beach.*]

CAESAR   Is that all?

THEODOTUS [*unable to believe his senses*]   All! Caesar: will you go down to posterity as a barbarous soldier too ignorant to know the value of books?

CAESAR   Theodotus: I am an author myself; and I tell you it is better that the Egyptians should live their lives than dream them away with the help of books.

THEODOTUS [*kneeling, with genuine literary emotion: the passion of the pedant*]   Caesar: once in ten generations of men, the world gains an immortal book.

CEASAR [*inflexible*]   If it did not flatter mankind, the common executioner would burn it.

THEODOTUS   Without history, death will lay you beside your meanest soldier.

CAESAR   Death will do that in any case. I ask no better grave.

THEODOTUS   What is burning there is the memory of mankind.

CAESAR   A shameful memory. Let it burn.

THEODOTUS [*wildly*]   Will you destroy the past?

CAESAR   Ay, and build the future with its ruins. [THEODOTUS, *in despair, strikes himself on the temples with his fists.*] But hearken, Theodotus, teacher of kings: you who valued Pompey's head no more than a shepherd values an onion, and who now kneel to me, with tears in your old eyes, to plead for a few sheepskins scrawled with errors. I cannot spare you a man or a bucket of water just now; but you shall pass freely out of the palace. Now, away with you to Achillas; and borrow his legions to put out the fire. [*He hurries him to the steps.*]

POTHINUS [*significantly*]   You understand. Theodotus: I remain a prisoner.

THEODOTUS   A prisoner!

CAESAR   Will you stay to talk whilst the memory of mankind is burning? [*Calling through the loggia.*] Ho there! Pass Theodotus out. [*To* THEODOTUS.] Away with you.

THEODOTUS [*to* POTHINUS]   I must go to save the library. [*He hurries out.*]

CAESAR   Follow him to the gate, Pothinus. Bid him urge your people to kill no more of my soldiers, for your sake.

POTHINUS   My life will cost you dear if you take it, Caesar. [*He goes out after* THEODOTUS.]

> RUFIO, *absorbed in watching the embarkation, does not notice the departure of the two Egyptians.*

RUFIO [*shouting from the loggia to the beach*]   All ready, there?

CENTURION [*from below*]   All ready. We wait for Caesar.

CAESAR   Tell them Caesar is coming—the rogues! [*Calling.*] Britannicus. [*This magniloquent version of his secretary's name is one of* CAESAR's *jokes. In later years it would have meant, quite seriously and officially, Conqueror of Britain.*]

RUFIO [*calling down*]   Push off, all except the longboat. Stand by it to embark, Caesar's guard there. [*He leaves the balcony and comes down into the hall.*] Where are those Egyptians? Is this more clemency? Have you let them go?

CAESAR [*chuckling*]   I have let Theodotus go to save the library. We must respect literature, Rufio.

RUFIO [*raging*]   Folly on folly's head! I believe if you could bring back all the dead of Spain, Gaul, and Thessaly to life, you would do it that we might have the trouble of fighting them over again.

CAESAR   Might not the gods destroy the world if their only thought were to be at peace next year? [RUFIO, *out of all patience, turns away in anger.* CAESAR *suddenly grips his sleeve, and adds slyly in his ear.*] Besides, my friend: every Egyptian we imprison means imprisoning two Roman soldiers to guard him. Eh?

RUFIO   Agh! I might have known there was some fox's trick behind your fine talking. [*He gets away from* CAESAR *with an ill-humored shrug, and goes to the balcony for another look at the preparations; finally goes out.*]

CAESAR   Is Britannus asleep? I sent him for my armor an hour ago. [*Calling.*] Britannicus, thou British islander. Britannicus!

> CLEOPATRA *runs in through the loggia with* CAESAR's *helmet and sword, snatched from* BRITANNUS, *who follows her with a cuirass and greaves. They come down to* CAESAR, *she to his left hand,* BRITANNUS *to his right.*

CLEOPATRA   I am going to dress you, Caesar. Sit down. [*He obeys.*] These Roman helmets are so becoming! [*She takes off his wreath.*] Oh! [*She bursts out laughing at him.*]

CAESAR   What are you laughing at?

CLEOPATRA   Youre bald. [*Beginning with a big B, and ending with a splutter.*]

CAESAR [*almost annoyed*]   Cleopatra! [*He rises, for the convenience of* BRITANNUS, *who puts the cuirass on him.*]

CLEOPATRA   So that is why you wear the wreath—to hide it.

BRITANNUS   Peace, Egyptian: they are the bays of the conqueror. [*He buckles the cuirass.*]

CLEOPATRA   Peace, thou: islander! [*To* CAESAR.] You should rub your head with strong spirits of sugar, Caesar. That will make it grow.

CAESAR [*with a wry face*]   Cleopatra: do you like to be reminded that you are very young?

CLEOPATRA [*pouting*]   No.

CAESAR [*sitting down again, and setting out his leg for* BRITANNUS, *who kneels to put on his greaves*]   Neither do I like to be reminded that I am—middle aged. Let me give you ten of my superfluous years. That will make you 26, and leave me only—no matter. Is it a bargain?

CLEOPATRA   Agreed. 26, mind. [*She puts the helmet on him.*] Oh! How nice! You look only about 50 in it!

BRITANNUS [*looking up severely at* CLEOPATRA]   You must not speak in this manner to Caesar.

CLEOPATRA   Is it true that when Caesar caught you on that island, you were painted all over blue?

BRITANNUS   Blue is the colour worn by all Britons of good standing. In war we stain our bodies blue; so that though our enemies may strip us of our clothes and our lives, they cannot strip us of our respectability. [*He rises.*]

CLEOPATRA [*with* CAESAR's *sword*] Let me hang this on. Now you look splendid. Have they made any statues of you in Rome?

CAESAR Yes, many statues.

CLEOPATRA You must send for one and give it to me.

RUFIO [*coming back into the loggia, more impatient than ever*] Now Caesar: have you done talking? The moment your foot is aboard there will be no holding our men back: the boats will race one another for the lighthouse.

CAESAR [*drawing his sword and trying the edge*] Is this well set today, Britannicus? At Pharsalia it was as blunt as a barrel-hoop.

BRITANNUS It will split one of the Egyptian's hairs today, Caesar. I have set it myself.

CLEOPATRA [*suddenly throwing her arms in terror round* CAESAR] Oh, you are not really going into battle to be killed?

CAESAR No, Cleopatra. No man goes to battle to be killed.

CLEOPATRA But they d o get killed. My sister's husband was killed in battle. You must not go. Let h i m go. [*Pointing to* RUFIO. *They all laugh at her.*] Oh please, p l e a s e, dont go. What will happen to me if you never come back?

CAESAR [*gravely*] Are you afraid?

CLEOPATRA [*shrinking*] No.

CAESAR [*with quiet authority*] Go to the balcony; and you shall see us take the Pharos. You must learn to look on battles. Go. [*She goes, downcast, and looks out from the balcony.*] That is well. Now, Rufio. March.

CLEOPATRA [*suddenly clapping her hands*] Oh, you will not be able to go!

CAESAR Why? What now?

CLEOPATRA They are drying up the harbor with buckets—a multitude of soldiers—over there [*pointing out across the sea to her left*] —they are dipping up the water.

RUFIO [*hastening to look*] It is true. The Egyptian army! Crawling over the edge of the west harbor like locusts. [*With sudden anger he strides down to* CAESAR.] This is your accursed clemency, Caesar. Theodotus has brought them.

CAESAR [*delighted at his own cleverness*] I meant him to, Rufio. They have come to put out the fire. The library will keep them busy whilst we seize the lighthouse. Eh? [*He rushes out buoyantly through the loggia, followed by* BRITANNUS.]

RUFIO [*disgustedly*] More foxing! Agh! [*He rushes off. A shout from the soldiers announces the appearance of* CAESAR *below.*]

CENTURION [*below*] All aboard. Give way there. [*Another shout.*]

CLEOPATRA [*waving her scarf through the loggia arch*] Goodbye, goodbye, dear Caesar. Come back safe. Goodbye!

Act 3

The edge of the quay in front of the palace, looking out west over the east harbor of Alexandria to Pharos island, just off the end of which, and connected with it by a narrow mole, is the famous lighthouse, a gigantic square tower of white marble diminishing in

*size story by story to the top, on which stands a cresset beacon.
The island is joined to the main land by the Heptastadium, a great
mole or causeway five miles long bounding the harbor on the
south.*

In the middle of the quay a Roman SENTINEL *stands on guard
pilum in hand, looking out to the lighthouse with strained attention, his left hand shading his eyes. The pilum is a stout wooden
shaft 4½ feet long, with an iron spit about three feet long fixed in
it. The* SENTINEL *is so absorbed that he does not notice the approach from the north end of the quay of four Egyptian market*
PORTERS *carrying rolls of carpet, preceded by* FTATATEETA *and*
APOLLODORUS *the Sicilian.* APOLLODORUS *is a dashing young man
of about 24, handsome and debonair, dressed with deliberate aes-
theticism in the most delicate purples and dove greys, with ornaments of bronze, oxidized silver, and stones of jade and agate. His
sword, designed as carefully as a medieval cross, has a blued blade
showing through an openwork scabbard of purple leather and fili-
gree. The* PORTERS, *conducted by* FTATATEETA, *pass along the quay
behind the* SENTINEL *to the steps of the palace, where they put
down their bales and squat on the ground.* APOLLODORUS *does not
pass along with them: he halts, amused by the preoccupation of
the* SENTINEL.

APOLLODORUS [*calling to the* SENTINEL]   Who goes there, eh?

SENTINEL [*starting violently and turning with his pilum at the charge,
revealing himself as a small, wiry, sandy-haired, conscientious young
man with an elderly face*]   What's this? Stand. Who are you?

APOLLODORUS   I am Apollodorus the Sicilian. Why, man, what are you
dreaming of? Since I came through the lines beyond the theatre
there, I have brought my caravan past three sentinels, all so busy
staring at the lighthouse that not one of them challenged me. Is this
Roman discipline?

SENTINEL   We are not here to watch the land but the sea. Caesar has
just landed on the Pharos. [*Looking at* FTATATEETA.] What have
you here? Who is this piece of Egyptian crockery?

FTATATEETA   Apollodorus: rebuke this Roman dog; and bid him bridle
his tongue in the presence of Ftatateeta, the mistress of the Queen's
household.

APOLLODORUS   My friend: this is a great lady, who stands high with
Caesar.

SENTINEL [*not at all impressed, pointing to the carpets*]   And what is
all this truck?

APOLLODORUS   Carpets for the furnishing of the Queen's apartments
in the palace. I have picked them from the best carpets in the world;
and the Queen shall choose the best of my choosing.

SENTINEL   So you are the carpet merchant?

APOLLODORUS [*hurt*]   My friend: I am a patrician.

SENTINEL   A patrician! A patrician keeping a shop instead of following
arms!

APOLLODORUS   I do not keep a shop. Mine is a temple of the arts. I am
a worshipper of beauty. My calling is to choose beautiful things for
beautiful queens. My motto is Art for Art's sake.

SENTINEL   That is not the password.

APOLLODORUS   It is a universal password.

SENTINEL   I know nothing about universal passwords. Either give me the password for the day or get back to your shop.

> FTATATEETA, *roused by his hostile tone, steals towards the edge of the quay with the step of a panther, and gets behind him.*

APOLLODORUS   How if I do neither?

SENTINEL   Then I will drive this pilum through you.

APOLLODORUS   At your service, my friend. [*He draws his sword, and springs to his guard with unruffled grace.*]

FTATATEETA [*suddenly seizing the* SENTINEL'S *arms from behind*] Thrust your knife into the dog's throat, Apollodorus. [*The chivalrous* APOLLODORUS *laughingly shakes his head; breaks ground away from the* SENTINEL *towards the palace; and lowers his point.*]

SENTINEL [*struggling vainly*]   Curse on you! Let me go. Help ho!

FTATATEETA [*lifting him from the ground*]   Stab the little Roman reptile. Spit him on your sword.

> *A couple of Roman soldiers, with a* CENTURION, *come running along the edge of the quay from the north end. They rescue their comrade, and throw off* FTATATEETA, *who is sent reeling away on the left hand of the* SENTINEL.

CENTURION [*an unattractive man of fifty, short in his speech and manners, with a vinewood cudgel in his hand*]   How now? What is all this?

FTATATEETA [*to* APOLLODORUS]   Why did you not stab him? There was time!

APOLLODORUS   Centurion: I am here by order of the Queen to—

CENTURION [*interrupting him*]   The Queen! Yes, yes: [*to the* SENTINEL] pass him in. Pass all these bazaar people in to the Queen, with their goods. But mind you pass no one out that you have not passed in—not even the Queen herself.

SENTINEL   This old woman is dangerous: she is as strong as three men. She wanted the merchant to stab me.

APOLLODORUS   Centurion: I am not a merchant. I am a patrician and a votary of art.

CENTURION   Is the woman your wife?

APOLLODORUS [*horrified*]   No, no! [*Correcting himself politely.*] Not that the lady is not a striking figure in her own way. But [*emphatically*] she is n o t my wife.

FTATATEETA [*to the* CENTURION]   Roman: I am Ftatateeta, the mistress of the Queen's household.

CENTURION   Keep your hands off our men, mistress; or I will have you pitched into the harbor, though you were as strong as ten men. [*To his men.*] To your posts: march! [*He returns with his men the way they came.*]

FTATATEETA [*looking malignantly after him*]   We shall see whom Isis[8] loves best: her servant Ftatateeta or a dog of a Roman.

SENTINEL [*to* APOLLODORUS, *with a wave of his pilum towards the palace*]   Pass in there; and keep your distance. [*Turning to* FTATA-

---

8. An Egyptian fertility goddess, the sister and wife of Osiris. She was frequently pictured as cow-headed.

TEETA.] Come within a yard of me, you old crocodile; and I will give you this [*the pilum*] in your jaws.

CLEOPATRA [*calling from the palace*]   Ftatateeta, Ftatateeta.

FTATATEETA [*looking up, scandalized*]   Go from the window, go from the window. There are men here.

CLEOPATRA   I am coming down.

FTATATEETA [*distracted*]   No, no. What are you dreaming of? O ye gods, ye gods! Apollodorus: bid your men pick up your bales; and in with me quickly.

APOLLODORUS   Obey the mistress of the Queen's household.

FTATATEETA [*impatiently, as the porters stoop to lift the bales*]   Quick, quick: she will be out upon us. [CLEOPATRA *comes from the palace and across the quay to* FTATATEETA.] Oh that ever I was born!

CLEOPATRA [*eagerly*]   Ftatateeta: I have thought of something. I want a boat—at once.

FTATATEETA   A boat! No, no: you cannot. Apollodorus: speak to the Queen.

APOLLODORUS [*gallantly*]   Beautiful queen: I am Apollodorus the Sicilian, your servant, from the bazaar. I have brought you the three most beautiful Persian carpets in the world to choose from.

CLEOPATRA   I have no time for carpets to-day. Get me a boat.

FTATATEETA   What whim is this? You cannot go on the water except in the royal barge.

APOLLODORUS   Royalty, Ftatateeta, lies not in the barge but in the Queen. [*To* CLEOPATRA.] The touch of your majesty's foot on the gunwhale of the meanest boat in the harbor will make it royal. [*He turns to the harbor and calls seaward.*] Ho there, boatman! Pull in to the steps.

CLEOPATRA   Apollodorus: you are my perfect knight; and I will always buy my carpets through you. [APOLLODORUS *bows joyously. An oar appears above the quay; and the* BOATMAN, *a bullet-headed, vivacious, grinning fellow, burnt almost black by the sun, comes up a flight of steps from the water on the* SENTINEL's *right, oar in hand, and waits at the top.*] Can you row, Apollodorus?

APOLLODORUS   My oars shall be your majesty's wings. Whither shall I row my Queen?

CLEOPATRA   To the lighthouse. Come. [*She makes for the steps.*]

SENTINEL [*opposing her with his pilum at the charge*]   Stand. You cannot pass.

CLEOPATRA [*flushing angrily*]   How dare you? Do you know that I am the Queen?

SENTINEL   I have my orders. You cannot pass.

CLEOPATRA   I will make Caesar have you killed if you do not obey me.

SENTINEL   He will do worse to me if I disobey my officer. Stand back.

CLEOPATRA   Ftatateeta: strangle him.

SENTINEL [*alarmed—looking apprehensively at* FTATATEETA, *and brandishing his pilum*]   Keep off, there.

CLEOPATRA [*running to* APOLLODORUS]   Apollodorus: make your slaves help us.

APOLLODORUS   I shall not need their help, lady. [*He draws his sword.*] Now, soldier: choose which weapon you will defend yourself with. Shall it be sword against pilum, or sword against sword?

SENTINEL   Roman against Sicilian, curse you. Take that. [*He hurls his pilum at* APOLLODORUS, *who drops expertly on one knee. The pilum*

passes whizzing over his head and falls harmless. APOLLODORUS, *with
a cry of triumph, springs up and attacks the* SENTINEL, *who draws his
sword and defends himself, crying.*] Ho there, guard. Help!

> CLEOPATRA, *half frightened, half delighted, takes refuge near
> the palace, where the porters are squatting among the bales.
> The* BOATMAN, *alarmed, hurries down the steps out of harm's
> way, but stops, with his head just visible above the edge of the
> quay, to watch the fight. The* SENTINEL *is handicapped by his
> fear of an attack in the rear from* FTATATEETA. *His swordsman-
> ship, which is of a rough and ready sort, is heavily taxed, as he
> has occasionally to strike at her to keep her off between a blow
> and a guard with* APOLLODORUS. *The* CENTURION *returns with
> several soldiers.* APOLLODORUS *springs back towards* CLEOPATRA
> *as this reinforcement confronts him.*

CENTURION [*coming to the* SENTINEL's *right hand*]   What is this? What
now?

SENTINEL [*panting*]   I could do well enough by myself if it werent for
the old woman. Keep her off me: that is all the help I need.

CENTURION   Make your report, soldier. What has happened?

FTATATEETA   Centurion: he would have slain the Queen.

SENTINEL [*bluntly*]   I would, sooner than let her pass. She wanted to
take boat, and go—so she said—to the lighthouse. I stopped her,
as I was ordered to; and she set this fellow on me. [*He goes to pick
up his pilum and returns to his place with it.*]

CENTURION [*turning to* CLEOPATRA]   Cleopatra: I am loth to offend
you; but without Caesar's express order we dare not let you pass beyond the Roman lines.

APOLLODORUS   Well, Centurion; and has not the lighthouse been within the Roman lines since Caesar landed there?

CLEOPATRA   Yes, yes. Answer that, if you can.

CENTURION [*to* APOLLODORUS]   As for you, Apollodorus, you may thank
the gods that you are not nailed to the palace door with a pilum for
your meddling.

APOLLODORUS [*urbanely*]   My military friend, I was not born to be
slain by so ugly a weapon. When I fall, it will be [*holding up his
sword*] by this white queen of arms, the only weapon fit for an artist.
And now that you are convinced that we do not want to go beyond
the lines, let me finish killing your sentinel and depart with the
Queen.

CENTURION [*as the* SENTINEL *makes an angry demonstration*]   Peace
there, Cleopatra: I must abide by my orders, and not by the subtle-
ties of this Sicilian. You must withdraw into the palace and examine
your carpets there.

CLEOPATRA [*pouting*]   I will not: I am the Queen. Caesar does not
speak to me as you do. Have Caesar's centurions changed manners
with his scullions?

CENTURION [*sulkily*]   I do my duty. That is enough for me.

APOLLODORUS   Majesty: when a stupid man is doing something he is
ashamed of, he always declares that it is his duty.

CENTURION [*angry*]   Apollodorus—

APOLLODORUS [*interrupting him with defiant elegance*]   I will make
amends for that insult with my sword at fitting time and place. Who
says artist, says duellist. [*To* CLEOPATRA.] Hear my counsel, star of

the east. Until word comes to these soldiers from Caesar himself, you are a prisoner. Let me go to him with a message from you, and a present; and before the sun has stooped half way to the arms of the sea, I will bring you back Caesar's order of release.

CENTURION [*sneering at him*]   And you will sell the Queen the present, no doubt.

APOLLODORUS   Centurion: the Queen shall have from me, without payment, as the unforced tribute of Sicilian taste to Egyptian beauty, the richest of these carpets for her present to Caesar.

CLEOPATRA [*exultantly, to the* CENTURION]   Now you see what an ignorant common creature you are!

CENTURION [*curtly*]   Well, a fool and his wares are soon parted. [*He turns to his men.*] Two more men to this post here; and see that no one leaves the palace but this man and his merchandise. If he draws his sword again inside the lines, kill him. To your posts. March.

He goes out, leaving two AUXILIARY SENTINELS *with the other.*

APOLLODORUS [*with polite goodfellowship*]   My friends: will you not enter the palace and bury our quarrel in a bowl of wine? [*He takes out his purse, jingling the coins in it.*] The Queen has presents for you all.

SENTINEL [*very sulkily*]   You heard our orders. Get about your business.

FIRST AUXILIARY   Yes: you ought to know better. Off with you.

SECOND AUXILIARY [*looking longingly at the purse—this sentinel is a hooknosed man, unlike his comrade, who is squab faced*]   Do not tantalize a poor man.

APOLLODORUS [*to* CLEOPATRA]   Pearl of Queens: the centurion is at hand; and the Roman soldier is incorruptible when his officer is looking. I must carry your word to Caesar.

CLEOPATRA [*who has been meditating among the carpets*]   Are these carpets very heavy?

APOLLODORUS   It matters not how heavy. There are plenty of porters.

CLEOPATRA   How do they put the carpets into boats? Do they throw them down?

APOLLODORUS   Not into small boats, majesty. It would sink them.

CLEOPATRA   Not into that man's boat, for instance? [*Pointing to the* BOATMAN.]

APOLLODORUS   No. Too small.

CLEOPATRA   But you can take a carpet to Caesar in it if I send one?

APOLLODORUS   Assuredly.

CLEOPATRA   And you will have it carried gently down the steps and take great care of it?

APOLLODORUS   Depend on me.

CLEOPATRA   Great, g r e a t care?

APOLLODORUS   More than of my own body.

CLEOPATRA   You will promise me not to let the porters drop it or throw it about?

APOLLODORUS   Place the most delicate glass goblet in the palace in the heart of the roll, Queen; and if it be broken, my head shall pay for it.

CLEOPATRA   Good. Come, Ftatateeta. [FTATATEETA *comes to her.* APOLLODORUS *offers to squire them into the palace.*] No, Apollodorus, you must not come. I will choose a carpet for myself. You must wait here. [*She runs into the palace.*]

APOLLODORUS [*to the* PORTERS]   Follow this lady [*indicating* FTATA-TEETA]; and obey her.

The PORTERS *rise and take up their bales.*

FTATATEETA [*addressing the* PORTERS *as if they were vermin*]   This way. And take your shoes off before you put your feet on those stairs.

She goes in, followed by the PORTERS *with the carpets. Meanwhile* APOLLODORUS *goes to the edge of the quay and looks out over the harbor. The* SENTINELS *keep their eyes on him malignantly.*

APOLLODORUS [*addressing the* SENTINEL]   My friend—

SENTINEL [*rudely*]   Silence there.

FIRST AUXILIARY   Shut your muzzle, you.

SECOND AUXILIARY [*in a half whisper, glancing apprehensively towards the north end of the quay*]   Cant you wait a bit?

APOLLODORUS   Patience, worthy three-headed donkey. [*They mutter ferociously; but he is not at all intimidated.*] Listen: were you set here to watch me, or to watch the Egyptians?

SENTINEL   We know our duty.

APOLLODORUS   Then why dont you do it? There is something going on over there. [*Pointing southwestward to the mole.*]

SENTINEL [*sulkily*]   I do not need to be told what to do by the like of you.

APOLLODORUS   Blockhead. [*He begins shouting.*] Ho there, Centurion. Hoiho!

SENTINEL   Curse your meddling. [*Shouting.*] Hoiho! Alarm! Alarm!

FIRST AND SECOND AUXILIARIES   Alarm! Alarm! Hoiho!

The CENTURION *comes running in with his guard.*

CENTURION   What now? Has the old woman attacked you again? [*Seeing* APOLLODORUS.] Are y o u here still?

APOLLODORUS [*pointing as before*]   See there. The Egyptians are moving. They are going to recapture the Pharos. They will attack by sea and land: by land along the great mole; by sea from the west harbor. Stir yourselves, my military friends: the hunt is up. [*A clangor of trumpets from several points along the quay.*] Aha! I told you so.

CENTURION [*quickly*]   The two extra men pass the alarm to the south posts. One man keep guard here. The rest with me—quick.

The two AUXILIARY SENTINELS *run off to the south. The* CENTURION *and his guard run off northward; and immediately afterwards the bucina sounds. The four* PORTERS *come from the palace carrying a carpet, followed by* FTATATEETA.

SENTINEL [*handling his pilum apprehensively*]   You again! [*The* PORTERS *stop.*]

FTATATEETA   Peace, Roman fellow: you are now singlehanded. Apollodorus: this carpet is Cleopatra's present to Caesar. It has rolled up in it ten precious goblets of the thinnest Iberian crystal, and a hundred eggs of the sacred blue pigeon. On your honor, let not one of them be broken.

APOLLODORUS   On my head be it! [*To the* PORTERS.] Into the boat with them carefully.

The PORTERS *carry the carpet to the steps.*

FIRST PORTER [*looking down at the boat*]   Beware what you do, sir. Those eggs of which the lady speaks must weigh more than a pound apiece. This boat is too small for such a load.

BOATMAN [*excitedly rushing up the steps*]   Oh thou injurious porter! Oh thou unnatural son of a she-camel! [*To* APOLLODORUS.] My boat, sir, hath often carried five men. Shall it not carry your lordship and a bale of pigeon's eggs? [*To the* PORTER.] Thou mangy dromedary, the gods shall punish thee for this envious wickedness.

FIRST PORTER [*stolidly*]   I cannot quit this bale now to beat thee; but another day I will lie in wait for thee.

APOLLODORUS [*going between them*]   Peace there. If the boat were but a single plank, I would get to Caesar on it.

FTATATEETA [*anxiously*]   In the name of the gods, Apollodorus, run no risks with that bale.

APOLLODORUS   Fear not, thou venerable grotesque: I guess its great worth. [*To the* PORTERS.] Down with it, I say; and gently; or ye shall eat nothing but stick for ten days.[9]

> *The* BOATMAN *goes down the steps, followed by the* PORTERS *with the bale:* FTATATEETA *and* APOLLODORUS *watching from the edge.*

APOLLODORUS   Gently, my sons, my children—[*with sudden alarm*] gently, ye dogs. Lay it level in the stern—so—tis well.

FTATATEETA [*screaming down at one of the* PORTERS]   Do not step on it, do not step on it. Oh thou brute beast!

FIRST PORTER [*ascending*]   Be not excited, mistress: all is well.

FTATATEETA [*panting*]   All well! Oh, thou hast given my heart a turn! [*She clutches her side, gasping.*]

> *The four* PORTERS *have now come up and are waiting at the stairhead to be paid.*

APOLLODORUS   Here, ye hungry ones. [*He gives money to the* FIRST PORTER, *who holds it in his hand to shew to the others. They crowd greedily to see how much it is, quite prepared, after the Eastern fashion, to protest to heaven against their patron's stinginess. But his liberality overpowers them.*]

FIRST PORTER   O bounteous prince!

SECOND PORTER   O lord of the bazaar!

THIRD PORTER   O favored of the gods!

FOURTH PORTER   O father to all the porters of the market!

SENTINEL [*enviously, threatening them fiercely with his pilum*]   Hence, dogs: off. Out of this. [*They fly before him northward along the quay.*]

APOLLODORUS   Farewell, Ftatateeta. I shall be at the lighthouse before the Egyptians. [*He descends the steps.*]

FTATATEETA   The gods speed thee and protect my nursling!

> *The* SENTRY *returns from chasing the* PORTERS *and looks down at the boat, standing near the stairhead lest* FTATATEETA *should attempt to escape.*

---

9. "To eat stick" means to be beaten (with a stick).

APOLLODORUS [*from beneath, as the boat moves off*]   Farewell, valiant pilum pitcher.

SENTINEL   Farewell, shopkeeper.

APOLLODORUS   Ha, ha! Pull, thou brave boatman, pull. Soho-o-o-o-o! [*He begins to sing in bacarolle measure to the rhythm of the oars.*]

> My heart, my heart, spread out thy wings:
> Shake off thy heavy load of love—

Give me the oars, O son of a snail.

SENTINEL [*threatening* FTATATEETA]   Now mistress: back to your henhouse. In with you.

FTATATEETA [*falling on her knees and stretching her hands over the waters*]   Gods of the seas, bear her safely to the shore!

SENTINEL   Bear w h o safely? What do you mean?

FTATATEETA [*looking darkly at him*]   Gods of Egypt and of Vengeance, let this Roman fool be beaten like a dog by his captain for suffering her to be taken over the waters.

SENTINEL   Accursed one: is she then in the boat? [*He calls over the sea.*] Hoiho, there, boatman! Hoiho!

APOLLODORUS [*singing in the distance*]

> My heart, my heart, be whole and free:
> Love is thine only enemy.

Meanwhile RUFIO, *the morning's fighting done, sits munching dates on a faggot of brushwood outside the door of the lighthouse, which towers gigantic to the clouds on his left. His helmet, full of dates, is between his knees; and a leathern bottle of wine is by his side. Behind him the great stone pedestal of the lighthouse is shut in from the open sea by a low stone parapet, with a couple of steps in the middle to the broad coping. A huge chain with a hook hangs down from the lighthouse crane above his head. Faggots like the one he sits on lie beneath it ready to be drawn up to feed the beacon.* CAESAR *is standing on the step at the parapet looking out anxiously, evidently ill at ease.* BRITANNUS *comes out of the lighthouse door.*

RUFIO   Well, my British islander. Have you been up to the top?

BRITANNUS   I have. I reckon it at 200 feet high.

RUFIO   Anybody up there?

BRITANNUS   One elderly Tyrian to work the crane; and his son, a well conducted youth of 14.

RUFIO [*looking at the chain*]   What! An old man and a boy work that! Twenty men, you mean.

BRITANNUS   Two only, I assure you. They have counterweights, and a machine with boiling water in it which I do not understand: it is not of British design. They use it to haul up barrels of oil and faggots to burn in the brazier on the roof.

RUFIO   But—

BRITANNUS   Excuse me: I came down because there are messengers coming along the mole to us from the island. I must see what their business is. [*He hurries out past the lighthouse.*]

CAESAR [*coming away from the parapet, shivering and out of sorts*]   Rufio: this has been a mad expedition. We shall be beaten. I wish I knew how our men are getting on with that barricade across the great mole.

RUFIO [*angrily*]   Must I leave my food and go starving to bring you a report?

CAESAR [*soothing him nervously*]   No, Rufio, no. Eat, my son, eat. [*He takes another turn,* RUFIO *chewing dates meanwhile.*] The Egyptians cannot be such fools as not to storm the barricade and swoop down on us here before it is finished. It is the first time I have ever run an avoidable risk. I should not have come to Egypt.

RUFIO   An hour ago you were all for victory.

CAESAR [*apologetically*]   Yes: I was a fool—rash, Rufio—boyish.

RUFIO   Boyish! Not a bit of it. Here. [*Offering him a handful of dates.*]

CAESAR   What are these for?

RUFIO   To eat. Thats whats the matter with you. When a man comes to your age, he runs down before his midday meal. Eat and drink; and then have another look at our chances.

CAESAR [*taking the dates*]   My age! [*He shakes his head and bites a date.*] Yes, Rufio: I am an old man—worn out now—true, quite true. [*He gives way to melancholy contemplation, and eats another date.*] Achillas is still in his prime: Ptolemy is a boy. [*He eats another date, and plucks up a little.*] Well, every dog has his day; and I have had mine: I cannot complain. [*With sudden cheerfulness.*] These dates are not bad, Rufio. [BRITANNUS *returns, greatly excited, with a leathern bag.* CAESAR *is himself again in a moment.*] What now?

BRITANNUS [*triumphantly*]   Our brave Rhodian mariners have captured a treasure. There! [*He throws the bag down at* CAESAR's *feet.*] Our enemies are delivered into our hands.

CAESAR   In that bag?

BRITANNUS   Wait till you hear, Caesar. This bag contains all the letters which have passed between Pompey's party and the army of occupation here.

CAESAR   Well?

BRITANNUS [*impatient of* CAESAR's *slowness to grasp the situation*] Well, we shall now know who your foes are. The name of every man who has plotted against you since you crossed the Rubicon may be in these papers, for all we know.

CAESAR   Put them in the fire.

BRITANNUS   Put them—[*he gasps*]!!!!

CAESAR   In the fire. Would you have me waste the next three years of my life in proscribing and condemning men who will be my friends when I have proved that my friendship is worth more than Pompey's was—than Cato's is. O incorrigible British islander: am I a bull dog, to seek quarrels merely to shew how stubborn my jaws are?

BRITANNUS   But your honor—the honor of Rome—

CAESAR   I do not make human sacrifices to my honor, as your Druids do. Since you will not burn these, at least I can drown them. [*He picks up the bag and throws it over the parapet into the sea.*]

BRITANNUS   Caesar: this is mere eccentricity. Are traitors to be allowed to go free for the sake of a paradox?

RUFIO [*rising*]   Caesar: when the islander has finished preaching, call me again. I am going to have a look at the boiling water machine.

He goes into the lighthouse.

BRITANNUS [*with genuine feeling*]   O Caesar, my great master, if I could but persuade you to regard life seriously, as men do in my country!

CAESAR   Do they truly do so, Britannus?

BRITANNUS   Have you not been there? Have you not seen them? What Briton speaks as you do in your moments of levity? What Briton neglects to attend the services at the sacred grove? What Briton wears clothes of many colors as you do, instead of plain blue, as all solid, well esteemed men should? These are moral questions with us.

CAESAR   Well, well, my friend: someday I shall settle down and have a blue toga, perhaps. Meanwhile, I must get on as best I can in my flippant Roman way. [APOLLODORUS *comes past the lighthouse.*] What now?

BRITANNUS [*turning quickly, and challenging the stranger with official haughtiness*]   What is this? Who are you? How did you come here?

APOLLODORUS   Calm yourself, my friend: I am not going to eat you. I have come by boat, from Alexandria, with precious gifts for Caesar.

CAESAR   From Alexandria!

BRITANNUS [*severely*]   That is Caesar, sir.

RUFIO [*appearing at the lighthouse door*]   Whats the matter now?

APOLLODORUS   Hail, great Caesar! I am Apollodorus the Sicilian, an artist.

BRITANNUS   An artist! Why have they admitted this vagabond?

CAESAR   Peace, man. Apollodorus is a famous patrician amateur.

BRITANNUS [*disconcerted*]   I crave the gentleman's pardon. [*To* CAESAR.] I understood him to say that he was a professional. [*Somewhat out of countenance, he allows* APOLLODORUS *to approach* CAESAR, *changing places with him.* RUFIO, *after looking* APOLLODORUS *up and down with marked disparagement, goes to the other side of the platform.*]

CAESAR   You are welcome, Apollodorus. What is your business?

APOLLODORUS   First, to deliver to you a present from the Queen of Queens.

CAESAR   Who is that?

APOLLODORUS   Cleopatra of Egypt.

CAESAR [*taking him into his confidence in his most winning manner*]   Apollodorus: this is no time for playing with presents. Pray you, go back to the Queen, and tell her that if all goes well I shall return to the palace this evening.

APOLLODORUS   Caesar: I cannot return. As I approached the lighthouse, some fool threw a great leathern bag into the sea. It broke the nose of my boat; and I had hardly time to get myself and my charge to the shore before the poor little cockleshell sank.

CAESAR   I am sorry, Apollodorus. The fool shall be rebuked. Well, well: what have you brought me? The Queen will be hurt if I do not look at it.

RUFIO   Have we time to waste on this trumpery? The Queen is only a child.

CAESAR   Just so: that is why we must not disappoint her. What is the present, Apollodorus?

APOLLODORUS   Caesar: it is a Persian carpet—a beauty! And in it are —so I am told—pigeons' eggs and crystal goblets and fragile precious things. I dare not for my head have it carried up that narrow ladder from the causeway.

RUFIO   Swing it up by the crane, then. We will send the eggs to the cook, drink our wine from the goblets; and the carpet will make a bed for Caesar.

APOLLODORUS   The crane! Caesar: I have sworn to tender this bale of carpets as I tender my own life.

CAESAR [*cheerfully*]   Then let them swing you up at the same time; and if the chain breaks, you and the pigeons' eggs will perish together.

> He goes to the chain and looks up along it, examining it curiously.

APOLLODORUS [*to* BRITANNUS]   Is Caesar serious?

BRITANNUS   His manner is frivolous because he is an Italian; but he means what he says.

APOLLODORUS   Serious or not, he spake well. Give me a squad of soldiers to work the crane.

BRITANNUS   Leave the crane to me. Go and await the descent of the chain.

APOLLODORUS   Good. You will presently see me there [*turning to them all and pointing with an eloquent gesture to the sky above the parapet*] rising like the sun with my treasure.

> He goes back the way he came. BRITANNUS goes into the lighthouse.

RUFIO [*ill-humoredly*]   Are you really going to wait here for this foolery, Caesar?

CAESAR [*backing away from the crane as it gives signs of working*] Why not?

RUFIO   The Egyptians will let you know why not if they have the sense to make a rush from the shore end of the mole before our barricade is finished. And here we are waiting like children to see a carpet full of pigeons' eggs.

> The chain rattles, and is drawn up high enough to clear the parapet. It then swings round out of sight behind the lighthouse.

CAESAR   Fear not, my son Rufio. When the first Egyptian takes his first step along the mole, the alarm will sound; and we two will reach the barricade from our end before the Egyptians reach it from their end—we two, Rufio: I, the old man, and you, his biggest boy. And the old man will be there first. So peace; and give me some more dates.

APOLLODORUS [*from the causeway below*]   Soho, haul away. So-ho-o-o-o! [*The chain is drawn up and comes round again from behind the lighthouse.* APOLLODORUS *is swinging in the air with his bale of carpet at the end of it. He breaks into song as he soars above the parapet.*]

> Aloft, aloft, behold the blue
> That never shone in woman's eyes—

Easy there: stop her. [*He ceases to rise.*] Further round! [*The chain comes forward above the platform.*]

RUFIO [*calling up*]   Lower away there. [*The chain and its load begin to descend.*]

APOLLODORUS [*calling up*] Gently—slowly—mind the eggs.
RUFIO [*calling up*] Easy there—slowly—slowly.

> APOLLODORUS *and the bale are deposited safely on the flags in the middle of the platform.* RUFIO *and* CAESAR *help* APOLLODORUS *to cast off the chain from the bale.*

RUFIO Haul up.

> *The chain rises clear of their heads with a rattle.* BRITANNUS *comes from the lighthouse and helps them to uncord the carpet.*

APOLLODORUS [*when the cords are loose*] Stand off, my friends: let Caesar see. [*He throws the carpet open.*]
RUFIO Nothing but a heap of shawls. Where are the pigeons' eggs?
APOLLODORUS Approach, Caesar; and search for them among the shawls.
RUFIO [*drawing his sword*] Ha, treachery. Keep back, Caesar: I saw the shawl move: there is something alive there.
BRITANNUS [*drawing his sword*] It is a serpent.
APOLLODORUS Dares Caesar thrust his hand into the sack where the serpent moves?
RUFIO [*turning on him*] Treacherous dog—
CAESAR Peace. Put up your swords. Apollodorus: your serpent seems to breathe very regularly. [*He thrusts his hand under the shawls and draws out a bare arm.*] This is a pretty little snake.
RUFIO [*drawing out the other arm*] Let us have the rest of you.

> *They pull* CLEOPATRA *up by the wrists into a sitting position.* BRITANNUS, *scandalized, sheathes his sword with a drive of protest.*

CLEOPATRA [*gasping*] Oh, I'm smothered. Oh, Caesar, a man stood on me in the boat; and a great sack of something fell upon me out of the sky; and then the boat sank; and then I was swung up into the air and bumped down.
CAESAR [*petting her as she rises and takes refuge on his breast*] Well, never mind: here you are safe and sound at last.
RUFIO Ay, and now that she i s here, what are we to do with her?
BRITANNUS She cannot stay here, Caesar, without the companionship of some matron.
CLEOPATRA [*jealously, to* CAESAR, *who is obviously perplexed*] Arnt you glad to see me?
CAESAR Yes, yes; I am very glad. But Rufio is very angry; and Britannus is shocked.
CLEOPATRA [*contemptuously*] You can have their heads cut off, can you not?
CAESAR They would not be so useful with their heads cut off as they are now, my sea bird.
RUFIO [*to* CLEOPATRA] We shall have to go away presently and cut some of your Egyptians' heads off. How will you like being left here with the chance of being captured by that little brother of yours if we are beaten?
CLEOPATRA But you mustnt leave me alone. Caesar: you will not leave me alone, will you?
RUFIO What! not when the trumpet sounds and all our lives depend on Caesar's being at the barricade before the Egyptians reach it? Eh?

CLEOPATRA   Let them lose their lives: they are only soldiers.

CAESAR [*gravely*]   Cleopatra: when that trumpet sounds, we must take every man his life in his hand, and throw it in the face of Death. And of my soldiers who have trusted me there is not one whose hand I shall not hold more sacred than your head. [CLEOPATRA *is overwhelmed. Her eyes fill with tears.*] Apollodorus: you must take her back to the palace.

APOLLODORUS   Am I a dolphin, Caesar, to cross the seas with young ladies on my back? My boat is sunk: all yours are either at the barricade or have returned to the city. I will hail one if I can: that is all I can do. [*He goes back to the causeway.*]

CLEOPATRA [*struggling with her tears*]   It does not matter. I will not go back. Nobody cares for me.

CAESAR   Cleopatra—

CLEOPATRA   You want me to be killed.

CAESAR [*still more gravely*]   My poor child: your life matters little here to anyone but yourself. [*She gives way altogether at this, casting herself down on the faggots weeping. Suddenly a great tumult is heard in the distance, bucinas and trumpets sounding through a storm of shouting.* BRITANNUS *rushes to the parapet and looks along the mole.* CAESAR *and* RUFIO *turn to one another with quick intelligence.*]

CAESAR   Come, Rufio.

CLEOPATRA [*scrambling to her knees and clinging to him*]   No, no. Do not leave me, Caesar. [*He snatches his skirt from her clutch.*] Oh!

BRITANNUS [*from the parapet*]   Caesar: we are cut off. The Egyptians have landed from the west harbor between us and the barricade!!!

RUFIO [*running to see*]   Curses! It is true. We are caught like rats in a trap.

CAESAR [*ruthfully*]   Rufio, Rufio: my men at the barricade are between the sea party and the shore party. I have murdered them.

RUFIO [*coming back from the parapet to* CAESAR's *right hand*]   Ay: that comes of fooling with this girl here.

APOLLODORUS [*coming up quickly from the causeway*]   Look over the parapet, Caesar.

CAESAR   We have looked, my friend. We must defend ourselves here.

APOLLODORUS   I have thrown the ladder into the sea. They cannot get in without it.

RUFIO   Ay; and we cannot get out. Have you thought of that?

APOLLODORUS   Not get out! Why not? You have ships in the east harbor.

BRITANNUS [*hopefully, at the parapet*]   The Rhodian galleys are standing in towards us already. [CAESAR *quickly joins* BRITANNUS *at the parapet.*]

RUFIO [*to* APOLLODORUS, *impatiently*]   And by what road are we to walk to the galleys, pray?

APOLLODORUS [*with gay, defiant rhetoric*]   By the road that leads everywhere—the diamond path of the sun and moon. Have you never seen the child's shadow play of The Broken Bridge? "Ducks and geese with ease get over"[1]—eh? [*He throws away his cloak and cap, and binds his sword on his back.*]

---

1. During the season 1776–77 the New Ombres Chinoises introduced to England *The Broken Bridge.* The play was one of the most popular "Chinese shadow" plays. "Chinese shadows" were a special kind of puppet, opaque figures silhouetted upon a screen and operated from below.

RUFIO   What are you talking about?

APOLLODORUS   I will shew you. [*Calling to* BRITANNUS.] How far off is the nearest galley?

BRITANNUS   Fifty fathom.

CAESAR   No, no: they are further off than they seem in this clear air to your British eyes. Nearly quarter of a mile, Apollodorus.

APOLLODORUS   Good. Defend yourselves here until I send you a boat from that galley.

RUFIO   Have you wings, perhaps?

APOLLODORUS   Water wings, soldier. Behold!

> *He runs up the steps between* CAESAR *and* BRITANNUS *to the coping of the parapet; springs into the air; and plunges head foremost into the sea.*

CAESAR   [*like a schoolboy—wildly excited*]   Bravo, bravo! [*Throwing off his cloak.*] By Jupiter, I will do that too.

RUFIO   [*seizing him*]   You are mad. You shall not.

CAESAR   Why not? Can I not swim as well as he?

RUFIO   [*frantic*]   Can an old fool dive and swim like a young one? He is twenty-five and you are fifty.

CAESAR   [*breaking loose from* RUFIO]   Old!!!

BRITANNUS   [*shocked*]   Rufio: you forget yourself.

CAESAR   I will race you to the galley for a week's pay, father Rufio.

CLEOPATRA   But me! me!!! me!!! what is going to become of me?

CAESAR   I will carry you on my back to the galley like a dolphin. Rufio: when you see me rise to the surface, throw her in: I will answer for her. And then in with you after her, both of you.

CLEOPATRA   No, no, NO. I shall be drowned.

BRITANNUS   Caesar: I am a man and a Briton, not a fish. I must have a boat. I cannot swim.

CLEOPATRA   Neither can I.

CAESAR   [*to* BRITANNUS]   Stay here, then, alone, until I recapture the lighthouse: I will not forget you. Now, Rufio.

RUFIO   You have made up your mind to this folly?

CAESAR   The Egyptians have made it up for me. What else is there to do? And mind where you jump: I do not want to get your fourteen stone in the small of my back as I come up. [*He runs up the steps and stands on the coping.*]

BRITANNUS   [*anxiously*]   One last word, Caesar. Do not let yourself be seen in the fashionable part of Alexandria until you have changed your clothes.

CAESAR   [*calling over the sea*]   Ho, Apollodorus. [*He points skyward and quotes the barcarolle.*]

The white upon the blue above—

APOLLODORUS   [*swimming in the distance*]

Is purple on the green below—

CAESAR   [*exultantly*]   Aha! [*He plunges into the sea.*]

CLEOPATRA   [*running excitedly to the steps*]   Oh, let me see. He will be drowned. [RUFIO *seizes her.*]—Ah—ah—ah—ah! [*He pitches her screaming into the sea.* RUFIO *and* BRITANNUS *roar with laughter.*]

RUFIO   [*looking down after her*]   He has got her. [*To* BRITANNUS.] Hold the fort, Briton. Caesar will not forget you. [*He springs off.*]

BRITANNUS [*running to the steps to watch them as they swim*]   All safe, Rufio?

RUFIO [*swimming*]   All safe.

CAESAR [*swimming further off*]   Take refuge up there by the beacon; and pile the fuel on the trap door, Britannus.

BRITANNUS [*calling in reply*]   I will first do so, and then commend myself to my country's gods. [*A sound of cheering from the sea.* BRITANNUS *gives full vent to his excitement.*]   The boat has reached him: Hip, hip, hip, hurrah!

Act 4

CLEOPATRA's *sousing in the east harbor of Alexandria was in October 48 B.C. In March 47 she is passing the afternoon in her boudoir in the palace, among a bevy of her ladies, listening to a slave girl who is playing the harp in the middle of the room. The harpist's master, an old* MUSICIAN, *with a lined face, prominent brows, white beard, moustache and eyebrows twisted and horned at the ends, and a consciously keen and pretentious expression, is squatting on the floor close to her on her right, watching her performance.* FTATATEETA *is in attendance near the door, in front of a group of female slaves. Except the harp player all are seated:* CLEOPATRA *in a chair opposite the door on the other side of the room; the rest on the ground.* CLEOPATRA's *ladies are all young, the most conspicuous being* CHARMIAN *and* IRAS, *her favorites.* CHARMIAN *is a hatchet faced, terra cotta colored little goblin, swift in her movements, and neatly finished at the hands and feet.* IRAS *is a plump, goodnatured creature, rather fatuous, with a profusion of red hair, and a tendency to giggle on the slightest provocation.*

CLEOPATRA   Can I—

FTATATEETA [*insolently, to the player*]   Peace, thou! The Queen speaks. [*The player stops.*]

CLEOPATRA [*to the old* MUSICIAN]   I want to learn to play the harp with my own hands. Caesar loves music. Can you teach me?

MUSICIAN   Assuredly I and no one else can teach the Queen. Have I not discovered the lost method of the ancient Egyptians, who could make a pyramid tremble by touching a bass string? All the other teachers are quacks: I have exposed them repeatedly.

CLEOPATRA   Good: you shall teach me. How long will it take?

MUSICIAN   Not very long: only four years. Your Majesty must first become proficient in the philosophy of Pythagoras.[2]

CLEOPATRA   Has she [*indicating the slave*] become proficient in the philosophy of Pythagoras?

MUSICIAN   Oh, she is but a slave. She learns as a dog learns.

CLEOPATRA   Well, then, I will learn as a dog learns; for she plays better than you. You shall give me a lesson every day for a fortnight. [*The* MUSICIAN *hastily scrambles to his feet and bows profoundly.*]

---

2. The Greek philosopher Pythagoras flourished in Southern Italy in the sixth century B.C. He was interested in both mathematics and music and was credited with discovering the relation between musical intervals and arithmetic ratios.

After that, whenever I strike a false note you shall be flogged; and if I strike so many that there is not time to flog you, you shall be thrown into the Nile to feed the crocodiles. Give the girl a piece of gold; and send them away.

MUSICIAN [*much taken aback*] But true art will not be thus forced.

FTATATEETA [*pushing him out*] What is this? Answering the Queen, forsooth. Out with you.

> *He is pushed out by* FTATATEETA, *the girl following with her harp, amid the laughter of the ladies and slaves.*

CLEOPATRA Now, can any of you amuse me? Have you any stories or any news?

IRAS Ftatateeta—

CLEOPATRA Oh, Ftatateeta, Ftatateeta, always Ftatateeta. Some new tale to set me against her.

IRAS No: this time Ftatateeta has been virtuous. [*All the ladies laugh —not the slaves.*] Pothinus has been trying to bribe her to let him speak with you.

CLEOPATRA [*wrathfully*] Ha! you all sell audiences with me, as if I saw whom you please, and not whom I please. I should like to know how much of her gold piece that harp girl will have to give up before she leaves the palace.

IRAS We can easily find out that for you.

> *The ladies laugh.*

CLEOPATRA [*frowning*] You laugh; but take care, take care. I will find out some day how to make myself served as Caesar is served.

CHARMIAN Old hooknose! [*They laugh again.*]

CLEOPATRA [*revolted*] Silence. Charmian: do not you be a silly little Egyptian fool. Do you know why I allow you all to chatter impertinently just as you please, instead of treating you as Ftatateeta would treat you if she were Queen?

CHARMIAN Because you try to imitate Caesar in everything; and he lets everybody say what they please to him.

CLEOPATRA No; but because I asked him one day why he did so; and he said "Let your women talk; and you will learn something from them." What have I to learn from them? I said. "What they are," said he; and oh! you should have seen his eye as he said it. You would have curled up, you shallow things. [*They laugh. She turns fiercely on* IRAS.] At whom are you laughing—at me or at Caesar?

IRAS At Caesar.

CLEOPATRA If you were not a fool, you would laugh at me; and if you were not a coward you would not be afraid to tell me so. [FTATATEETA *returns.*] Ftatateeta: they tell me that Pothinus has offered you a bribe to admit him to my presence.

FTATATEETA [*protesting*] Now by my father's gods—

CLEOPATRA [*cutting her short despotically*] Have I not told you not to deny things? You would spend the day calling your father's gods to witness to your virtues if I let you. Go take the bribe; and bring in Pothinus. [FTATATEETA *is about to reply.*] Dont answer me. Go.

> FTATATEETA *goes out; and* CLEOPATRA *rises and begins to prowl to and fro between her chair and the door, meditating. All rise and stand.*

IRAS [*as she reluctantly rises*]   Heigho! I wish Caesar were back in Rome.

CLEOPATRA [*threateningly*]   It will be a bad day for you all when he goes. Oh, if I were not ashamed to let him see that I am as cruel at heart as my father, I would make you repent that speech! Why do you wish him away?

CHARMIAN   He makes you so terribly prosy and serious and learned and philosophical. It is worse than being religious, at o u r ages. [*The ladies laugh.*]

CLEOPATRA   Cease that endless cackling, will you. Hold your tongues.

CHARMIAN [*with mock resignation*]   Well, well: we must try to live up to Caesar.

> *They laugh again.* CLEOPATRA *rages silently as she continues to prowl to and fro.* FTATATEETA *comes back with* POTHINUS, *who halts on the threshold.*

FTATATEETA [*at the door*]   Pothinus craves the ear of the—

CLEOPATRA   There, there: that will do: let him come in. [*She resumes her seat. All sit down except* POTHINUS, *who advances to the middle of the room.* FTATATEETA *takes her former place.*] Well, Pothinus: what is the latest news from your rebel friends?

POTHINUS [*haughtily*]   I am no friend of rebellion. And a prisoner does not receive news.

CLEOPATRA   You are no more a prisoner than I am—than Caesar is. These six months we have been besieged in this palace by my subjects. You are allowed to walk on the beach among the soldiers. Can I go further myself, or can Caesar?

POTHINUS   You are but a child, Cleopatra, and do not understand these matters.

> *The ladies laugh.* CLEOPATRA *looks inscrutably at him.*

CHARMIAN   I see you do not know the latest news, Pothinus.

POTHINUS   What is that?

CHARMIAN   That Cleopatra is no longer a child. Shall I tell you how to grow much older, and much, m u c h wiser in one day?

POTHINUS   I should prefer to grow wiser without growing older.

CHARMIAN   Well, go up to the top of the lighthouse; and get somebody to take you by the hair and throw you into the sea. [*The ladies laugh.*]

CLEOPATRA   She is right, Pothinus: you will come to the shore with much conceit washed out of you. [*The ladies laugh.* CLEOPATRA *rises impatiently.*] Begone, all of you. I will speak with Pothinus alone. Drive them out, Ftatateeta. [*They run out laughing.* FTATATEETA *shuts the door on them.*] What are y o u waiting for?

FTATATEETA   It is not meet that the Queen remain alone with—

CLEOPATRA [*interrupting her*]   Ftatateeta: must I sacrifice you to your father's gods to teach you that *I* am Queen of Egypt, and not you?

FTATATEETA [*indignantly*]   You are like the rest of them. You want to be what these Romans call a New Woman. [*She goes out, banging the door.*]

CLEOPATRA [*sitting down again*]   Now Pothinus: why did you bribe Ftatateeta to bring you hither?

POTHINUS [*studying her gravely*]   Cleopatra: what they tell me is true. You are changed.

CLEOPATRA   Do you speak with Caesar every day for six months: and y o u will be changed.

POTHINUS   It is the common talk that you are infatuated with this old man?

CLEOPATRA   Infatuated? What does that mean? Made foolish, is it not? Oh no: I wish I were.

POTHINUS   You wish you were made foolish! How so?

CLEOPATRA   When I was foolish, I did what I liked, except when Ftatateeta beat me; and even then I cheated her and did it by stealth. Now that Caesar has made me wise, it is no use my liking or disliking: I do what must be done, and have no time to attend to myself. That is not happiness; but it is greatness. If Caesar were gone, I think I could govern the Egyptians; for what Caesar is to me, I am to the fools around me.

POTHINUS [*looking hard at her*]   Cleopatra: this may be the vanity of youth.

CLEOPATRA   No, no: it is not that I am so clever, but that the others are so stupid.

POTHINUS [*musingly*]   Truly, that is the great secret.

CLEOPATRA   Well, now tell me what you came to say?

POTHINUS [*embarrassed*]   I! Nothing.

CLEOPATRA   Nothing!

POTHINUS   At least—to beg for my liberty: that is all.

CLEOPATRA   For that you would have knelt to Caesar. No, Pothinus: you came with some plan that depended on Cleopatra being a little nursery kitten. Now that Cleopatra is a Queen, the plan is upset.

POTHINUS [*bowing his head submissively*]   It is so.

CLEOPATRA [*exultant*]   Aha!

POTHINUS [*raising his eyes keenly to hers*]   Is Cleopatra then indeed a Queen, and no longer Caesar's prisoner and slave?

CLEOPATRA   Pothinus: we are all Caesar's slaves—all we in this land of Egypt—whether we will or no. And she who is wise enough to know this will reign when Caesar departs.

POTHINUS   You harp on Caesar's departure.

CLEOPATRA   What if I do?

POTHINUS   Does he not love you?

CLEOPATRA   Love me! Pothinus: Caesar loves no one. Who are those we love. Only those whom we do not hate: all people are strangers and enemies to us except those we love. But it is not so with Caesar. He has no hatred in him: he makes friends with everyone as he does with dogs and children. His kindness to me is a wonder; neither mother, father, nor nurse have ever taken so much care for me, or thrown open their thoughts to me so freely.

POTHINUS   Well: is not this love?

CLEOPATRA   What! when he will do as much for the first girl he meets on his way back to Rome? Ask his slave, Britannus: he has been just as good to him. Nay, ask his very horse! His kindness is not for anything in me: it is in his own nature.

POTHINUS   But how can you be sure that he does not love you as men love women?

CLEOPATRA   Because I cannot make him jealous. I have tried.

POTHINUS   Hm! Perhaps I should have asked, then, do y o u love h i m?

CLEOPATRA   Can one love a god? Besides, I love another Roman: one whom I saw long before Caesar—no god, but a man—one who can love and hate—one whom I can hurt and who would hurt me.

POTHINUS   Does Caesar know this?

CLEOPATRA   Yes.

POTHINUS   And he is not angry?

CLEOPATRA   He promises to send him to Egypt to please me!

POTHINUS   I do not understand this man.

CLEOPATRA [*with superb contempt*]   Y o u understand Caesar! How could you? [*Proudly.*] I do—by instinct.

POTHINUS [*deferentially, after a moment's thought*]   Your Majesty caused me to be admitted to-day. What message has the Queen for me?

CLEOPATRA   This. You think that by making my brother king, you will rule in Egypt, because you are his guardian and he is a little silly.

POTHINUS   The Queen is pleased to say so.

CLEOPATRA   The Queen is pleased to say this also. That Caesar will eat up you, and Achillas, and my brother, as a cat eats up mice; and that he will put on this land of Egypt as a shepherd puts on his garment. And when he has done that, he will return to Rome, and leave Cleopatra here as his viceroy.

POTHINUS [*breaking out wrathfully*]   That he shall never do. We have a thousand men to his ten; and we will drive him and his beggarly legions into the sea.

CLEOPATRA [*with scorn, getting up to go*]   You rant like any common fellow. Go, then, and marshal your thousands; and make haste; for Mithridates of Pergamos is at hand with reinforcements for Caesar. Caesar has held you at bay with two legions: we shall see what he will do with twenty.

POTHINUS   Cleopatra—

CLEOPATRA   Enough, enough: Caesar has spoiled me for talking to weak things like you. [*She goes out.* POTHINUS, *with a gesture of rage, is following, when* FTATATEETA *enters and stops him.*]

POTHINUS   Let me go forth from this hateful place.

FTATATEETA   What angers you?

POTHINUS   The curse of all the gods of Egypt be upon her! She has sold her country to the Roman, that she may buy it back from him with her kisses.

FTATATEETA   Fool: did she not tell you that she would have Caesar gone?

POTHINUS   You listened?

FTATATEETA   I took care that some honest woman should be at hand whilst you were with her.

POTHINUS   Now by the gods—

FTATATEETA   Enough of your gods! Caesar's gods are all powerful here It is no use y o u coming to Cleopatra: you are only an Egyptian. She will not listen to any of her own race: she treats us all as children.

POTHINUS   May she perish for it!

FTATATEETA [*balefully*]   May your tongue wither for that wish! Go! send for Lucius Septimius, the slayer of Pompey. He is a Roman: may be she will listen to him. Begone!

POTHINUS [*darkly*]   I know to whom I must go now.

FTATATEETA [*suspiciously*]   To whom, then?

POTHINUS   To a greater Roman than Lucius. And mark this, mistress. You thought, before Caesar came, that Egypt should presently be

ruled by you and your crew in the name of Cleopatra. I set myself
against it—

FTATATEETA [*interrupting him—wrangling*] Ay; that it might be
ruled by you and y o u r crew in the name of Ptolemy.

POTHINUS Better me, or even you, than a woman with a Roman
heart; and that is what Cleopatra is now become. Whilst I live,
she shall never rule. So guide yourself accordingly. [*He goes out.*]

> *It is by this time drawing on to dinner time. The table is laid on
> the roof of the palace; and thither* RUFIO *is now climbing, ush-
> ered by a majestic palace* OFFICIAL, *wand of office in hand, and
> followed by a* SLAVE *carrying an inlaid stool. After many stairs
> they emerge at last into a massive colonnade on the roof. Light
> curtains are drawn between the columns on the north and east
> to soften the westering sun. The* OFFICIAL *leads* RUFIO *to one of
> these shaded sections. A cord for pulling the curtains apart
> hangs down between the pillars.*

OFFICIAL [*bowing*] The Roman commander will await Caesar here.

> *The* SLAVE *sets down the stool near the southernmost column,
> and slips out through the curtains.*

RUFIO [*sitting down, a little blown*] Pouf! That was a climb. How
high have we come?

OFFICIAL We are on the palace roof, O Beloved of Victory!

RUFIO Good! the Beloved of Victory has no more stairs to get up.

> *A* SECOND OFFICIAL *enters from the opposite end, walking back-
> wards.*

SECOND OFFICIAL Caesar approaches.

> CAESAR, *fresh from the bath, clad in a new tunic of purple silk,
> comes in, beaming and festive, followed by two* SLAVES *carrying
> a light couch, which is hardly more than an elaborately de-
> signed bench. They place it near the northmost of the two
> curtained columns. When this is done they slip out through the
> curtains; and the two* OFFICIALS, *formally bowing, follow them.*
> RUFIO *rises to receive* CAESAR.

CAESAR [*coming over to him*] Why, Rufio! [*Surveying his dress with
an air of admiring astonishment.*] A new baldrick! A new golden
pommel to your sword! And you have had your hair cut. But not
your beard—? impossible! [*He sniffs at* RUFIO's *beard.*] Yes, per-
fumed, by Jupiter Olympus!

RUFIO [*growling*] Well: is it to please myself?

CAESAR [*affectionately*] No, my son Rufio, but to please me—to celebrate my birthday.

RUFIO [*contemptuously*] Your birthday! You always have a birthday
when there is a pretty girl to be flattered or an ambassador to be
conciliated. We had seven of them in ten months last year.

CAESAR [*contritely*] It is true, Rufio! I shall never break myself of
these petty deceits.

RUFIO Who is to dine with us—besides Cleopatra?

CAESAR Apollodorus the Sicilian.

RUFIO That popinjay!

CAESAR Come! the popinjay is an amusing dog—tells a story; sings a song; and saves us the trouble of flattering the Queen. What does she care for old politicians and camp-fed bears like us? No: Apollodorus is good company, Rufio, good company.

RUFIO Well, he can swim a bit and fence a bit: he might be worse, if he only knew how to hold his tongue.

CAESAR The gods forbid he should ever learn! Oh, this military life! this tedious, brutal life of action! That is the worst of us Romans: we are mere doers and drudgers: a swarm of bees turned into men. Give me a good talker—one with wit and imagination enough to live without continually doing something!

RUFIO Ay! a nice time he would have of it with you when dinner was over! Have you noticed that I am before my time?

CAESAR Aha! I thought that meant something. What is it?

RUFIO Can we be overheard here?

CAESAR Our privacy invites eavesdropping. I can remedy that. [*He claps his hands twice. The curtains are drawn, revealing the roof garden with a banqueting table set across in the middle for four persons, one at each end, and two side by side. The side next* CAESAR *and* RUFIO *is blocked with golden wine vessels and basins. A gorgeous* MAJOR-DOMO *is superintending the laying of the table by a staff of* SLAVES. *The colonnade goes round the garden at both sides to the further end, where a gap in it, like a great gateway, leaves the view open to the sky beyond the western edge of the roof, except in the middle, where a life size image of Ra, seated on a huge plinth, towers up, with hawk head and crown of asp and disk. His altar, which stands at his feet, is a single white stone.*] Now everybody can see us, nobody will think of listening to us. [*He sits down on the bench left by the two* SLAVES.]

RUFIO [*sitting down on his stool*] Pothinus wants to speak to you. I advise you to see him: there is some plotting going on here among the women.

CAESAR Who is Pothinus?

RUFIO The fellow with hair like squirrel's fur—the little King's bear leader, whom you kept prisoner.

CAESAR [*annoyed*] And has he not escaped?

RUFIO No.

CAESAR [*rising imperiously*] Why not? You have been guarding this man instead of watching the enemy. Have I not told you always to let prisoners escape unless there are special orders to the contrary? Are there not enough mouths to be fed without him?

RUFIO Yes; and if you would have a little sense and let me cut his throat, you would save his rations. Anyhow, he w o n t escape. Three sentries have told him they would put a pilum through him if they saw him again. What more can they do? He prefers to stay and spy on us. So would I if I had to do with generals subject to fits of clemency.

CAESAR [*resuming his seat, argued down*] Hm! And so he wants to see me.

RUFIO Ay. I have brought him with me. He is waiting there [*jerking his thumb over his shoulder*] under guard.

CAESAR And you want me to see him?

RUFIO [*obstinately*] I dont want anything. I daresay you will do what you like. Dont put it on to me.

CAESAR [*with an air of doing it expressly to indulge* RUFIO] Well, well: let us have him.

RUFIO [*calling*] Ho there, guard! Release your man and send him up. [*Beckoning.*] Come along!

> POTHINUS *enters and stops mistrustfully between the two, looking from one to the other.*

CAESAR [*graciously*] Ah, Pothinus! You are welcome. And what is the news this afternoon?

POTHINUS Caesar: I come to warn you of a danger, and to make you an offer.

CAESAR Never mind the danger. Make the offer.

RUFIO Never mind the offer. Whats the danger?

POTHINUS Caesar: you think that Cleopatra is devoted to you.

CAESAR [*gravely*] My friend: I already know what I think. Come to your offer.

POTHINUS I will deal plainly. I know not by what strange gods you have been enabled to defend a palace and a few yards of beach against a city and an army. Since we cut you off from Lake Mareotis, and you dug wells in the salt sea sand and brought up buckets of fresh water from them, we have known that your gods are irresistible, and that you are a worker of miracles. I no longer threaten you—

RUFIO [*sarcastically*] Very handsome of you, indeed.

POTHINUS So be it: you are the master. Our gods sent the north west winds to keep you in our hands; but you have been too strong for them.

CAESAR [*gently urging him to come to the point*] Yes, yes, my friend. But what then?

RUFIO Spit it out, man. What have you to say?

POTHINUS I have to say that you have a traitress in your camp. Cleopatra—

MAJOR-DOMO [*at the table, announcing*] The Queen! [CAESAR *and* RUFIO *rise.*]

RUFIO [*aside to* POTHINUS] You should have spat it out sooner, you fool. Now it is too late.

> CLEOPATRA, *in gorgeous raiment, enters in state through the gap in the colonnade, and comes down past the image of Ra and past the table to* CAESAR. *Her retinue, headed by* FTATATEETA, *joins the staff at the table.* CAESAR *gives* CLEOPATRA *his seat, which she takes.*

CLEOPATRA [*quickly, seeing* POTHINUS] What is h e doing here?

CAESAR [*seating himself beside her, in the most amiable of tempers*] Just going to tell me something about you. You shall hear it. Proceed, Pothinus.

POTHINUS [*disconcerted*] Caesar—[*He stammers.*]

CAESAR Well, out with it.

POTHINUS What I have to say is for your ear, not for the Queen's.

CLEOPATRA [*with subdued ferocity*] There are means of making you speak. Take care.

POTHINUS [*defiantly*] Caesar does not employ those means.

CAESAR My friend: when a man has anything to tell in this world, the difficulty is not to make him tell it, but to prevent him from telling it too often. Let me celebrate my birthday by setting you free. Farewell: we shall not meet again.

CLEOPATRA [*angrily*]   Caesar: this mercy is foolish.

POTHINUS [*to* CAESAR]   Will you not give me a private audience? Your life may depend on it. [CAESAR *rises loftily.*]

RUFIO [*aside to* POTHINUS]   Ass! Now we shall have some heroics.

CAESAR [*oratorically*]   Pothinus—

RUFIO [*interrupting him*]   Caesar: the dinner will spoil if you begin preaching your favorite sermon about life and death.

CLEOPATRA [*priggishly*]   Peace, Rufio. I desire to hear Caesar.

RUFIO [*bluntly*]   Your Majesty has heard it before. You repeated it to Apollodorus last week; and he thought it was all your own. [CAESAR's *dignity collapses. Much tickled, he sits down again and looks roguishly at* CLEOPATRA, *who is furious.* RUFIO *calls as before.*] Ho there, guard! Pass the prisoner out. He is released. [*To* POTHINUS.] Now off with you. You have lost your chance.

POTHINUS [*his temper overcoming his prudence*]   I w i l l speak.

CAESAR [*to* CLEOPATRA]   You see. Torture would not have wrung a word from him.

POTHINUS   Caesar: you have taught Cleopatra the arts by which the Romans govern the world.

CAESAR   Alas! they cannot even govern themselves. What then?

POTHINUS   What then? Are you so besotted with her beauty that you do not see that she is impatient to reign in Egypt alone, and that her heart is set on your departure?

CLEOPATRA [*rising*]   Liar!

CAESAR [*shocked*]   What! Protestations! Contradictions!

CLEOPATRA [*ashamed, but trembling with suppressed rage*]   No. I do not deign to contradict. Let him talk. [*She sits down again.*]

POTHINUS   From her own lips I have heard it. You are to be her catspaw: you are to tear the crown from her brother's head and set it on her own, delivering us all into her hand—delivering yourself also. And then Caesar can return to Rome, or depart through the gate of death, which is nearer and surer.

CAESAR [*calmly*]   Well, my friend; and is not this very natural?

POTHINUS [*astonished*]   Natural! Then you do not resent treachery?

CAESAR   Resent! O thou foolish Egyptian, what have I to do with resentment? Do I resent the wind when it chills me, or the night when it makes me stumble in the darkness? Shall I resent youth when it turns from age, and ambition when it turns from servitude? To tell me such a story as this is but to tell me that the sun will rise tomorrow.

CLEOPATRA [*unable to contain herself*]   But it is false—false. I swear it.

CAESAR   It is true, though you swore it a thousand times, and believed all you swore. [*She is convulsed with emotion. To screen her, he rises and takes* POTHINUS *to* RUFIO, *saying:*] Come, Rufio: let us see Pothinus past the guard. I have a word to say to him. [*Aside to them.*] We must give the Queen a moment to recover herself. [*Aloud.*] Come. [*He takes* POTHINUS *and* RUFIO *out with him, conversing with them meanwhile.*] Tell your friends, Pothinus, that they must not think I am opposed to a reasonable settlement of the country's affairs—[*They pass out of hearing.*]

CLEOPATRA [*in a stifled whisper*]   Ftatateeta, Ftatateeta.

FTATATEETA [*hurrying to her from the table and petting her*] Peace, child: be comforted—

CLEOPATRA [*interrupting her*] Can they hear us?

FTATATEETA No, dear heart, no.

CLEOPATRA Listen to me. If he leaves the Palace alive, never see my face again.

FTATATEETA He? Poth—

CLEOPATRA [*striking her on the mouth*] Strike his life out as I strike his name from your lips. Dash him down from the wall. Break him on the stones. Kill, kill, k i l l him.

FTATATEETA [*shewing all her teeth*] The dog shall perish.

CLEOPATRA Fail in this, and you go out from before me for ever.

FTATATEETA [*resolutely*] So be it. You shall not see my face until his eyes are darkened.

> CAESAR *comes back, with* APOLLODORUS, *exquisitely dressed, and* RUFIO.

CLEOPATRA [*to* FTATATEETA] Come soon—soon. [FTATATEETA *turns her meaning eyes for a moment on her mistress; then goes grimly away past Ra and out.* CLEOPATRA *runs like a gazelle to* CAESAR.] So you have come back to me, Caesar. [*Caressingly.*] I thought you were angry. Welcome, Apollodorus. [*She gives him her hand to kiss, with her other arm about* CAESAR.]

APOLLODORUS Cleopatra grows more womanly beautiful from week to week.

CLEOPATRA Truth, Apollodorus?

APOLLODORUS Far, far short of the truth! Friend Rufio threw a pearl into the sea: Caesar fished up a diamond.

CAESAR Caesar fished up a touch of rheumatism, my friend. Come: to dinner! to dinner! [*They move towards the table.*]

CLEOPATRA [*skipping like a young fawn*] Yes, to dinner. I have ordered s u c h a dinner for you, Caesar!

CAESAR Ay? What are we to have?

CLEOPATRA Peacocks' brains.

CAESAR [*as if his mouth watered*] Peacocks' brains, Apollodorus!

APOLLODORUS Not for me. I prefer nightingales' tongues. [*He goes to one of the two covers set side by side*].

CLEOPATRA Roast boar, Rufio!

RUFIO [*gluttonously*] Good! [*He goes to the seat next* APOLLODORUS, *on his left.*]

CAESAR [*looking at his seat, which is at the end of the table, to Ra's left hand*] What has become of my leathern cushion?

CLEOPATRA [*at the opposite end*] I have got new ones for you.

MAJOR-DOMO These cushions, Caesar, are of Maltese gauze, stuffed with rose leaves.

CAESAR Rose leaves! Am I a caterpillar? [*He throws the cushions away and seats himself on the leather mattress underneath.*]

CLEOPATRA What a shame! My new cushions!

MAJOR-DOMO [*at* CAESAR's *elbow*] What shall we serve to whet Caesar's appetite?

CAESAR What have you got?

MAJOR-DOMO Sea hedgehogs, black and white sea acorns, sea nettles, beccaficoes, purple shellfish—

CAESAR Any oysters?

MAJOR-DOMO　Assuredly.

CAESAR　B r i t i s h oysters?

MAJOR-DOMO [*assenting*]　British oysters, Caesar.

CAESAR　Oysters, then. [*The* MAJOR-DOMO *signs to a* SLAVE *at each order; and the* SLAVE *goes out to execute it.*] I have been in Britain —that western land of romance—the last piece of earth on the edge of the ocean that surrounds the world. I went there in search of its famous pearls. The British pearl was a fable; but in searching for it I found the British oyster.

APOLLODORUS　All posterity will bless you for it. [*To the* MAJOR-DOMO.] Sea hedgehogs for me.

RUFIO　Is there nothing solid to begin with?

MAJOR-DOMO　Fieldfares with asparagus—

CLEOPATRA [*interrupting*]　Fattened fowls! have some fattened fowls, Rufio.

RUFIO　Ay, that will do.

CLEOPATRA [*greedily*]　Fieldfares for me.

MAJOR-DOMO　Caesar will deign to choose his wine? Sicilian, Lesbian, Chian—

RUFIO [*contemptuously*]　All Greek.

APOLLODORUS　Who would drink Roman wine when he could get Greek. Try the Lesbian, Caesar.

CAESAR　Bring me my barley water.

RUFIO [*with intense disgust*]　Ugh! Bring m e my Falernian. [*The Falernian is presently brought to him.*]

CLEOPATRA [*pouting*]　It is waste of time giving you dinners, Caesar. My scullions would not condescend to your diet.

CAESAR [*relenting*]　Well, well: let us try the Lesbian. [*The* MAJOR-DOMO *fills* CAESAR's *goblet; then* CLEOPATRA's *and* APOLLODORUS's.] But when I return to Rome, I will make laws against these extravagances. I will even get the laws carried out.

CLEOPATRA [*coaxingly*]　Never mind. To-day you are to be like other people: idle, luxurious, and kind. [*She stretches her hand to him along the table.*]

CAESAR　Well, for once I will sacrifice my comfort—[*kissing her hand*] there! [*He takes a draught of wine.*] Now are you satisfied?

CLEOPATRA　And you no longer believe that I long for your departure for Rome?

CAESAR　I no longer believe anything. My brains are asleep. Besides, who knows whether I shall return to Rome?

RUFIO [*alarmed*]　How? Eh? What?

CAESAR　What has Rome to shew me that I have not seen already? One year of Rome is like another, except that I grow older, whilst the crowd in the Appian Way is always the same age.

APOLLODORUS　It is no better here in Egypt. The old men, when they are tired of life, say "We have seen everything except the source of the Nile."

CAESAR [*his imagination catching fire*]　And why not see that? Cleopatra: will you come with me and track the flood to its cradle in the heart of the regions of mystery? Shall we leave Rome behind us —Rome, that has achieved greatness only to learn how greatness destroys nations of men who are not great! Shall I make you a new kingdom, and build you a holy city there in the great unknown?

CLEOPATRA [*rapturously*]　Yes, yes. You shall.

RUFIO   Ay: now he will conquer Africa with two legions before we come to the roast boar.

APOLLODORUS   Come: no scoffing. This is a noble scheme: in it Caesar is no longer merely the conquering soldier, but the creative poet-artist. Let us name the holy city, and consecrate it with Lesbian wine,

CAESAR   Cleopatra shall name it herself.

CLEOPATRA   It shall be called Caesar's Gift to his Beloved.

APOLLODORUS   No, no. Something vaster than that—something universal, like the starry firmament.

CAESAR [*prosaically*]   Why not simply The Cradle of the Nile?

CLEOPATRA   No: the Nile is my ancestor; and he is a god. Oh! I have thought of something. The Nile shall name it himself. Let us call upon him. [*To the* MAJOR-DOMO.] Send for him. [*The three men stare at one another; but the* MAJOR-DOMO *goes out as if he had received the most matter-of-fact order.*] And [*to the retinue*] away with you all.

> *The retinue withdraws, making obeisance. A priest enters, carrying a miniature Sphinx with a tiny tripod before it. A morsel of incense is smoking in the tripod. The priest comes to the table and places the image in the middle of it. The light begins to change to the magenta purple of the Egyptian sunset, as if the god had brought a strange colored shadow with him. The three men are determined not to be impressed; but they feel curious in spite of themselves.*

CAESAR   What hocus-pocus is this?

CLEOPATRA   You shall see. And it is n o t hocus-pocus. To do it properly, we should kill something to please him; but perhaps he will answer Caesar without that if we spill some wine to him.

APOLLODORUS [*turning his head to look up over his shoulder at Ra*]   Why not appeal to our hawkheaded friend here?

CLEOPATRA [*nervously*]   Sh! He will hear you and be angry.

RUFIO [*phlegmatically*]   The source of the Nile is out of his district, I expect.

CLEOPATRA   No: I will have my city named by nobody but my dear little Sphinx, because it was in its arms that Caesar found me asleep. [*She languishes at* CAESAR *then turns curtly to the priest.*] Go. I am a priestess, and have power to take your charge from you. [*The priest makes a reverence and goes out.*] Now let us call on the Nile altogether. Perhaps he will rap on the table.

CAESAR   What! table rapping! Are such superstitions still believed in this year 707 of the Republic?

CLEOPATRA   It is no superstition: our priests learn lots of things from the tables. Is it not so, Apollodorus?

APOLLODORUS   Yes: I profess myself a converted man. When Cleopatra is priestess, Apollodorus is devotee. Propose the conjuration.

CLEOPATRA   You must say with me "Send us thy voice, Father Nile."

ALL FOUR [*holding their glasses together before the idol*]   Send us thy voice, Father Nile.

> *The death cry of a man in mortal terror and agony answers them. Appalled, the men set down their glasses, and listen. Silence. The purple deepens in the sky.* CAESAR, *glancing at*

CLEOPATRA, *catches her pouring out her wine before the god, with gleaming eyes, and mute assurances of gratitude and worship,* APOLLODORUS *springs up and runs to the edge of the roof to peer down and listen.*

CAESAR [*looking piercingly at* CLEOPATRA]   What was that?
CLEOPATRA [*petulantly*]   Nothing. They are beating some slave.
CAESAR   Nothing.
RUFIO   A man with a knife in him, I'll swear.
CAESAR [*rising*]   A murder.
APOLLODORUS [*at the back, waving his hand for silence*]   S-sh! Silence. Did you hear that?
CAESAR   Another cry?
APOLLODORUS [*returning to the table*]   No, a thud. Something fell on the beach, I think.
RUFIO [*grimly, as he rises*]   Something with bones in it, eh?
CAESAR [*shuddering*]   Hush, hush, Rufio. [*He leaves the table and returns to the colonnade:* RUFIO *following at his left elbow, and* APOLLODORUS *at the other side.*]
CLEOPATRA [*still in her place at the table*]   Will you leave me, Caesar? Apollodorus: are you going?
APOLLODORUS   Faith, dearest Queen, my appetite is gone.
CAESAR   Go down to the courtyard, Apollodorus; and find out what has happened.

APOLLODORUS *nods and goes out, making for the staircase by which* RUFIO *ascended.*

CLEOPATRA   Your soldiers have killed somebody, perhaps. What does it matter?

The murmur of a crowd rises from the beach below. CAESAR *and* RUFIO *look at one another.*

CAESAR   This must be seen to. [*He is about to follow* APOLLODORUS *when* RUFIO *stops him with a hand on his arm as* FTATATEETA *comes back by the far end of the roof, with dragging steps, a drowsy satiety in her eyes and in the corners of the bloodhound lips. For a moment* CAESAR *suspects that she is drunk with wine. Not so* RUFIO: *he knows well the red vintage that has inebriated her.*]
RUFIO [*in a low tone*]   There is some mischief between those two.
FTATATEETA   The Queen looks again on the face of her servant.

CLEOPATRA *looks at her for a moment with an exultant reflection of her murderous expression. Then she flings her arms round her; kisses her repeatedly and savagely; and tears off her jewels and heaps them on her. The two men turn from the spectacle to look at one another.* FTATATEETA *drags herself sleepily to the altar; kneels before Ra; and remains there in prayer.* CAESAR *goes to* CLEOPATRA, *leaving* RUFIO *in the colonnade.*

CAESAR [*with searching earnestness*]   Cleopatra: what has happened?
CLEOPATRA [*in mortal dread of him, but with her utmost cajolery*] Nothing, dearest Caesar. [*With sickly sweetness, her voice almost failing.*] Nothing. I am innocent. [*She approaches him affectionately.*] Dear Caesar: are you angry with me? Why do you look at

me so? I have been here with you all the time. How can I know what has happened?

CAESAR [*reflectively*]   That is true.

CLEOPATRA [*greatly relieved, trying to caress him*]   Of course it is true. [*He does not respond to the caress.*] Y o u know it is true, Rufio.

The murmur without suddenly swells to a roar and subsides.

RUFIO   I shall know presently. [*He makes for the altar in the burly trot that serves him for a stride, and touches* FTATATEETA *on the shoulder.*] Now, mistress: I shall want you. [*He orders her, with a gesture, to go before him.*]

FTATATEETA [*rising and glowering at him*]   My place is with the Queen.

CLEOPATRA   She has done no harm, Rufio.

CAESAR [*to* RUFIO]   Let her stay.

RUFIO [*sitting down on the altar*]   Very well. Then my place is here too; and you can see what is the matter for yourself. The city is in a pretty uproar, it seems.

CAESAR [*with grave displeasure*]   Rufio: there is a time for obedience.

RUFIO   And there is a time for obstinacy. [*He folds his arms doggedly.*]

CAESAR [*to* CLEOPATRA]   Send her away.

CLEOPATRA [*whining in her eagerness to propitiate him*]   Yes, I will. I will do whatever you ask me, Caesar, always, because I love you. Ftatateeta: go away.

FTATATEETA   The Queen's word is my will. I shall be at hand for the Queen's call. [*She goes out past Ra, as she came.*]

RUFIO [*following her*]   Remember, Caesar, y o u r bodyguard also is within call. [*He follows her out.*]

> CLEOPATRA, *presuming upon* CAESAR'*s submission to* RUFIO, *leaves the table and sits down on the bench in the colonnade.*

CLEOPATRA   Why do you allow Rufio to treat you so? You should teach him his place.

CAESAR   Teach him to be my enemy, and to hide his thoughts from me as you are now hiding yours.

CLEOPATRA [*her fears returning*]   Why do you say that, Caesar? Indeed, indeed, I am not hiding anything. You are wrong to treat me like this. [*She stifles a sob.*] I am only a child; and you turn into stone because you think someone has been killed. I cannot bear it. [*She purposely breaks down and weeps. He looks at her with profound sadness and complete coldness. She looks up to see what effect she is producing. Seeing that he is unmoved, she sits up, pretending to struggle with her emotion and to put it bravely away.*] But there: I know you hate tears: you shall not be troubled with them. I know you are not angry, but only sad; only I am so silly, I cannot help being hurt when you speak coldly. Of course you are quite right: it is dreadful to think of anyone being killed or even hurt; and I hope nothing really serious has—[*Her voice dies away under his contemptuous penetration.*]

CAESAR   What has frightened you into this? What have you done? [*A trumpet sounds on the beach below.*] Aha! that sounds like the answer.

CLEOPATRA [*sinking back trembling on the bench and covering her face with her hands*]   I have not betrayed you, Caesar: I swear it.

CAESAR   I know that. I have not trusted you. [*He turns from her, and is about to go out when* APOLLODORUS *and* BRITANNUS *drag in* LUCIUS SEPTIMIUS *to him.* RUFIO *follows.* CAESAR *shudders.*] Again, Pompey's murderer!

RUFIO   The town has gone mad, I think. They are for tearing the palace down and driving us into the sea straight away. We laid hold of this renegade in clearing them out of the courtyard.

CAESAR   Release him. [*They let go his arms.*] What has offended the citizens, Lucius Septimius?

LUCIUS   What did you expect, Caesar? Pothinus was a favorite of theirs.

CAESAR   What has happened to Pothinus? I set him free, here, not half an hour ago. Did they not pass him out?

LUCIUS   Ay, through the gallery arch sixty feet above ground, with three inches of steel in his ribs. He is as dead as Pompey. We are quits now, as to killing—you and I.

CAESAR [*shocked*]   Assassinated!—our prisoner, our guest! [*He turns reproachfully on* RUFIO.] Rufio—

RUFIO [*emphatically—anticipating the question*]   Whoever did it was a wise man and a friend of yours [CLEOPATRA *is greatly emboldened*]; but none of u s had a hand in it. So it is no use to frown at me. [CAESAR *turns and looks at* CLEOPATRA.]

CLEOPATRA [*violently—rising*]   He was slain by order of the Queen of Egypt. I am not Julius Caesar the dreamer, who allows every slave to insult him. Rufio has said I did well: now the others shall judge me too. [*She turns to the others.*] This Pothinus sought to make me conspire with him to betray Caesar to Achillas and Ptolemy. I refused; and he cursed me and came privily to Caesar to accuse me of his own treachery. I caught him in the act; and he insulted me— m e, the Queen! to my face. Caesar would not avenge me: he spoke him fair and set him free. Was I right to avenge myself? Speak, Lucius.

LUCIUS   I do not gainsay it. But you will get little thanks from Caesar for it.

CLEOPATRA   Speak, Apollodorus. Was I wrong?

APOLLODORUS   I have only one word of blame, most beautiful. You should have called upon me, your knight; and in fair duel I should have slain the slanderer.

CLEOPATRA [*passionately*]   I will be judged by your very slave, Caesar. Britannus: speak. Was I wrong?

BRITANNUS   Were treachery, falsehood, and disloyalty left unpunished, society must become like an arena full of wild beasts, tearing one another to pieces. Caesar is in the wrong.

CAESAR [*with quiet bitterness*]   And so the verdict is against me, it seems.

CLEOPATRA [*vehemently*]   Listen to me, Caesar. If one man in all Alexandria can be found to say that I did wrong, I swear to have myself crucified on the door of the palace by my own slaves.

CAESAR   If one man in all the world can be found, now or forever, to k n o w that you did wrong, that man will have either to conquer the world as I have, or be crucified by it. [*The uproar in the streets again reaches them.*] Do you hear? These knockers at your gate are are also believers in vengeance and in stabbing. You have slain their leader: it is right that they shall slay you. If you doubt it, ask your four counsellors here. And then in the name of that r i g h t [*he em-*

phasizes the word with great scorn] shall I not slay them for murdering their Queen, and be slain in my turn by their countrymen as the invader of their fatherland? Can Rome do less then than slay these slayers, too, to shew the world how Rome avenges her sons and her honor. And so, to the end of history, murder shall breed murder, always in the name of right and honor and peace, until the gods are tired of blood and create a race that can understand. [*Fierce uproar.* CLEOPATRA *becomes white with terror.*] Hearken, you who must not be insulted. Go near enough to catch their words: you will find them bitterer than the tongue of Pothinus. [*Loftily, wrapping himself up in an impenetrable dignity.*] Let the Queen of Egypt now give her orders for vengeance, and take her measures for defence; for she has renounced Caesar. [*He turns to go.*]

CLEOPATRA [*terrified, running to him and falling on her knees*] You will not desert me, Caesar. You will defend the palace.

CAESAR You have taken the powers of life and death upon you. I am only a dreamer.

CLEOPATRA But they will kill me.

CAESAR And why not?

CLEOPATRA In pity—

CAESAR Pity! What! has it come to this so suddenly, that nothing can save you now but pity? Did it save Pothinus?

> *She rises, wringing her hands, and goes back to the bench in despair.* APOLLODORUS *shews his sympathy with her by quietly posting himself behind the bench. The sky has by this time become the most vivid purple, and soon begins to change to a glowing pale orange, against which the colonnade and the great image shew darklier and darklier.*

RUFIO Caesar: enough of preaching. The enemy is at the gate.

CAESAR [*turning on him and giving way to his wrath*] Ay; and what has held him baffled at the gate all these months? Was it my folly, as you deem it, or your wisdom? In this Egyptian Red Sea of blood, whose hand has held all your heads above the waves? [*Turning on* CLEOPATRA.] And yet, when Caesar says to such an one, "Friend, go free," you, clinging for your little life to my sword, dare steal out and stab him in the back? And you, soldiers and gentlemen, and honest servants as you forget that you are, applaud this assassination, and say "Caesar is in the wrong." By the gods, I am tempted to open my hand and let you all sink into the flood.

CLEOPATRA [*with a ray of cunning hope*] But, Caesar, if you do, you will perish yourself.

> CAESAR's *eyes blaze.*

RUFIO [*greatly alarmed*] Now, by great Jove, you filthy little Egyptian rat, that is the very word to make him walk out alone into the city and leave us here to be cut to pieces. [*Desperately, to* CAESAR.] Will you desert us because we are a parcel of fools? I mean no harm by killing: I do it as a dog kills a cat, by instinct. We are all dogs at your heels; but we have served you faithfully.

CAESAR [*relenting*] Alas, Rufio, my son, my son: as dogs we are like to perish now in the streets.

APOLLODORUS [*at his post behind* CLEOPATRA'*s seat*]   Caesar: what you say has an Olympian ring in it: it must be right; for it is fine art. But I am still on the side of Cleopatra. If we must die, she shall not want the devotion of a man's heart nor the strength of a man's arm.

CLEOPATRA [*sobbing*]   But I dont want to die.

CAESAR [*sadly*]   Oh, ignoble, ignoble!

LUCIUS [*coming forward between* CAESAR *and* CLEOPATRA]   Hearken to me, Caesar. It may be ignoble; but I also mean to live as long as I can.

CAESAR   Well, my friend, you are likely to outlive Caesar. Is it any magic of mine, think you, that has kept your army and this whole city at bay for so long? Yesterday, what quarrel had they with me that they should risk their lives against me? But today we have flung them down their hero, murdered; and now every man of them is set upon clearing out this nest of assassins—for such we are and no more. Take courage then; and sharpen your sword. Pompey's head has fallen; and Caesar's head is ripe.

APOLLODORUS   Does Caesar despair?

CAESAR [*with infinite pride*]   He who has never hoped can never despair. Caesar, in good or bad fortune, looks his fate in the face.

LUCIUS   Look it in the face, then; and it will smile as it always has on Caesar.

CAESAR [*with involuntary haughtiness*]   Do you presume to encourage me?

LUCIUS   I offer you my services. I will change sides if you will have me.

CAESAR [*suddenly coming down to earth again, and looking sharply at him, divining that there is something behind the offer*]   What! At this point?

LUCIUS [*firmly*]   At this point.

RUFIO   Do you suppose Caesar is mad, to trust you?

LUCIUS   I do not ask him to trust me until he is victorious. I ask for mv life, and for a command in Caesar's army. And since Caesar is a fair dealer, I will pay in advance.

CAESAR   Pay! How?

LUCIUS   With a piece of good news for you.

CAESAR *divines the news in a flash.*

RUFIO   What news?

CAESAR [*with an elated and buoyant energy which makes* CLEOPATRA *sit up and stare*]   What news! What news, did you say, my son Rufio? The relief has arrived: what other news remains for us? Is it not so, Lucius Septimius? Mithridates of Pergamos is on the march.

LUCIUS   He has taken Pelusium.

CAESAR [*delighted*]   Lucius Septimius: you are henceforth my officer. Rufio: the Egyptians must have sent every soldier from the city to prevent Mithridates crossing the Nile. There is nothing in the streets now but mob—mob!

LUCIUS   It is so. Mithridates is marching by the great road to Memphis to cross above the Delta. Achillas will fight him there.

CAESAR [*all audacity*]   Achillas shall fight Caesar there. See, Rufio. [*He runs to the table; snatches a napkin; and draws a plan on it with his finger dipped in wine, whilst* RUFIO *and* LUCIUS SEPTIMIUS *crowd about him to watch, all looking closely, for the light is now almost gone.*] Here is the palace [*pointing to his plan*]: here is the theatre. You [*to* RUFIO] take twenty men and pretend to go by t h a t street [*pointing it out*]; and whilst they are stoning you, out go the cohorts by this and this. My streets are right, are they, Lucius?

LUCIUS Ay, that is the fig market—

CAESAR [*too much excited to listen to him*] I saw them the day we arrived. Good! [*He throws the napkin on the table, and comes down again into the colonnade.*] Away, Britannus: tell Petronius that within an hour half our forces must take ship for the western lake. See to my horse and armor. [BRITANNUS *runs out.*] With the rest, I shall march round the lake and up the Nile to meet Mithridates. Away, Lucius; and give the word. [LUCIUS *hurries out after* BRITANNUS.] Apollodorus: lend me your sword and your right arm for this campaign.

APOLLODORUS Ay, and my heart and life to boot.

CAESAR [*grasping his hand*] I accept both. [*Mighty handshake.*] Are you ready for work?

APOLLODORUS Ready for Art—the Art of War. [*He rushes out after* LUCIUS, *totally forgetting* CLEOPATRA.]

RUFIO Come! this is something like business.

CAESAR [*buoyantly*] Is it not, my only son? [*He claps his hands. The* SLAVES *hurry in to the table.*] No more of this mawkish revelling: away with all this stuff: shut it out of my sight and be off with you. [*The* SLAVES *begin to remove the table; and the curtains are drawn, shutting in the colonnade.*] You understand about the streets, Rufio?

RUFIO Ay, I think I do. I will get through them, at all events.

The bucina sounds busily in the courtyard beneath.

CAESAR Come, then: we must talk to the troops and hearten them. You down to the beach: I to the courtyard. [*He makes for the staircase.*]

CLEOPATRA [*rising from her seat, where she has been quite neglected all this time, and stretching out her hands timidly to him*] Caesar.

CAESAR [*turning*] Eh?

CLEOPATRA Have you forgotten me?

CAESAR [*indulgently*] I am busy now, my child, busy. When I return your affairs shall be settled. Farewell; and be good and patient.

He goes, preoccupied and quite indifferent. She stands with clenched fists, in speechless rage and humiliation.

RUFIO That game is played and lost, Cleopatra. The woman always gets the worst of it.

CLEOPATRA [*haughtily*] Go. Follow your master.

RUFIO [*in her ear, with rough familiarity*] A word first. Tell your executioner that if Pothinus had been properly killed—in the t h r o a t— he would not have called out. Your man bungled his work.

CLEOPATRA [*enigmatically*] How do you know it was a man?

RUFIO [*startled, and puzzled*] It was not you: you were with us when it happened. [*She turns her back scornfully on him. He shakes his head, and draws the curtains to go out. It is now a magnificent moonlit night. The table has been removed.* FTATATEETA *is seen in the light of the moon and stars, again in prayer before the white altar-stone of Ra.* RUFIO *starts; closes the curtains again softly; and says in a low voice to* CLEOPATRA.] Was it she? with her own hand?

CLEOPATRA [*threateningly*] Whoever it was, let my enemies beware of her. Look to it, Rufio, you who dare make the Queen of Egypt a fool before Caesar.

RUFIO [*looking grimly at her*] I will look to it, Cleopatra. [*He nods in

*confirmation of the promise, and slips out through the curtains,
loosening his sword in its sheath as he goes.*]
ROMAN SOLDIERS [*in the courtyard below*]   Hail, Caesar! Hail, hail!

   CLEOPATRA *listens. The bucina sounds again, followed by several
   trumpets.*

CLEOPATRA [*wringing her hands and calling*]   Ftatateeta. Ftatateeta. It
is dark; and I am alone. Come to me. [*Silence.*] Ftatateeta. [*Louder.*]
Ftatateeta. [*Silence. In a panic she snatches the cord and pulls the
curtains apart.* FTATATEETA *is lying dead on the altar of Ra, with
her throat cut. Her blood deluges the white stone.*]

Act 5

*High noon. Festival and military pageant on the esplanade before
the palace. In the east harbor* CAESAR's *galley, so gorgeously decorated that it seems to be rigged with flowers, is alongside the quay,
close to the steps* APOLLODORUS *descended when he embarked with
the carpet. A Roman* GUARD *is posted there in charge of a gangway, whence a red floorcloth is laid down the middle of the
esplanade turning off to the north opposite the central gate in the
palace front, which shuts in the esplanade on the south side. The
broad steps of the gate, crowded with* CLEOPATRA's *ladies, all in
their gayest attire, are like a flower garden. The façade is lined by
her guard, officered by the same gallants to whom* BEL AFFRIS
announced the coming of CAESAR *six months before in the old
palace on the Syrian border. The north side is lined by Roman
soldiers, with the townsfolk on tiptoe behind them, peering over
their heads at the cleared esplanade, in which the* OFFICERS *stroll
about, chatting. Among these are* BELZANOR *and the* PERSIAN;
also the CENTURION, *vinewood cudgel in hand, battle worn, thick-
booted and much outshone, both socially and decoratively, by the
Egyptian officers.*

   APOLLODORUS *makes his way through the townsfolk and calls
to the officers from behind the Roman line.*

APOLLODORUS   Hullo! May I pass?
CENTURION   Pass Apollodorus the Sicilian there! [*The* SOLDIERS *let him
through.*]
BELZANOR   Is Caesar at hand?
APOLLODORUS   Not yet. He is still in the market place. I could not
stand any more of the roaring of the soldiers! After half an hour of
the enthusiasm of an army, one feels the need of a little sea air.
PERSIAN   Tell us the news. Hath he slain the priests?
APOLLODORUS   Not he. They met him in the market place with ashes
on their heads and their gods in their hands. They placed the gods at
his feet. The only one that was worth looking at was Apis: a miracle
of gold and ivory work. By my advice he offered the chief priest two
talents for it.
BELZANOR [*appalled*]   Apis the all-knowing for two talents! What said
the Priest?
APOLLODORUS   He invoked the mercy of Apis, and asked for five.
BELZANOR   There will be famine and tempest in the land for this.

PERSIAN   Pooh! Why did not Apis cause Caesar to be vanquished by Achillas? Any fresh news from the war, Apollodorus?

APOLLODORUS   The little King Ptolemy was drowned.

BELZANOR   Drowned! How?

APOLLODORUS   With the rest of them. Caesar attacked them from three sides at once and swept them into the Nile. Ptolemy's barge sank.

BELZANOR   A marvellous man, this Caesar! Will he come soon, think you?

APOLLODORUS   He was settling the Jewish question when I left.

> *A flourish of trumpets from the north, and commotion among the townsfolk, announces the approach of* CAESAR.

PERSIAN   He has made short work of them. Here he comes. [*He hurries to his post in front of the Egyptian lines.*]

BELZANOR [*following him*]   Ho there! Caesar comes.

> *The* SOLDIERS *stand at attention, and dress their lines.* APOLLODORUS *goes to the Egyptian line.*

CENTURION [*hurrying to the gangway* GUARD]   Attention there! Caesar comes.

> CAESAR *arrives in state with* RUFIO: BRITANNUS *following. The* SOLDIERS *receive him with enthusiastic shouting.*

CAESAR   I see my ship awaits me. The hour of Caesar's farewell to Egypt has arrived. And now, Rufio, what remains to be done before I go?

RUFIO [*at his left hand*]   You have not yet appointed a Roman governor for this province.

CAESAR [*looking whimsically at him, but speaking with perfect gravity*]   What say you to Mithridates of Pergamos, my reliever and rescuer, the great son of Eupator?

RUFIO   Why, that you will want him elsewhere. Do you forget that you have some three or four armies to conquer on your way home?

CAESAR   Indeed! Well, what say you to yourself?

RUFIO [*incredulously*]   I! I a governor! What are you dreaming of? Do you not know that I am only the son of a freedman?

CAESAR [*affectionately*]   Has not Caesar called you his son? [*Calling to the whole assembly.*]   Peace awhile there; and hear me.

ROMAN SOLDIERS   Hear Caesar.

CAESAR   Hear the service, quality, rank and name of the Roman governor. By service, Caesar's shield; by quality, Caesar's friend; by rank, a Roman soldier. [*The Roman* SOLDIERS *give a triumphant shout.*] By name, Rufio. [*They shout again.*]

RUFIO [*kissing* CAESAR'*s hand*]   Ay: I am Caesar's shield; but of what use shall I be when I am no longer on Caesar's arm? Well, no matter —[*He becomes husky, and turns away to recover himself.*]

CAESAR   Where is that British Islander of mine?

BRITANNUS [*coming forward on* CAESAR'*s right hand*]   Here, Caesar.

CAESAR   Who bade you, pray, thrust yourself into the battle of the Delta, uttering the barbarous cries of your native land, and affirming yourself a match for any four of the Egyptians, to whom you applied unseemly epithets?

BRITANNUS   Caesar: I ask you to excuse the language that escaped me in the heat of the moment.

CAESAR   And how did you, who cannot swim, cross the canal with us when we stormed the camp?

BRITANNUS   Caesar: I clung to the tail of your horse.

CAESAR   These are not the deeds of a slave, Britannicus, but of a free man.

BRITANNUS   Caesar: I was born free.

CAESAR   But they call you Caesar's slave.

BRITANNUS   Only as Caesar's slave have I found real freedom.

CAESAR [*moved*]   Well said. Ungrateful that I am, I was about to set you free; but now I will not part from you for a million talents. [*He claps him friendly on the shoulder.* BRITANNUS, *gratified, but a trifle shamefaced, takes his hand and kisses it sheepishly.*]

BELZANOR [*to the* PERSIAN]   This Roman knows how to make men serve him.

PERSIAN   Ay: men too humble to become dangerous rivals to him.

BELZANOR   O subtle one! O cynic!

CAESAR [*seeing* APOLLODORUS *in the Egyptian corner, and calling to him*]   Apollodorus: I leave the art of Egypt in your charge. Remember: Rome loves art and will encourage it ungrudgingly.

APOLLODORUS   I understand, Caesar. Rome will produce no art itself; but it will buy up and take away whatever the other nations produce.

CAESAR   What! Rome produce no art! Is peace not an art? is war not an art? is government not an art? is civilization not an art? All these we give you in exchange for a few ornaments. You will have the best of the bargain. [*Turning to* RUFIO.] And now, what else have I to do before I embark? [*Trying to recollect.*] There is something I cannot remember: what c a n it be? Well, well: it must remain undone: we must not waste this favorable wind. Farewell, Rufio.

RUFIO   Caesar: I am loth to let you go to Rome without your shield. There are too many daggers there.

CAESAR   It matters not: I shall finish my life's work on my way back; and then I shall have lived long enough. Besides: I have always disliked the idea of dying: I had rather be killed. Farewell.

RUFIO [*with a sigh, raising his hands and giving* CAESAR *up as incorrigible*]   Farewell. [*They shake hands.*]

CAESAR [*waving his hand to* APOLLODORUS]   Farewell, Apollodorus, and my friends, all of you. Aboard!

> *The gangway is run out from the quay to the ship. As* CAESAR *moves towards it,* CLEOPATRA, *cold and tragic, cunningly dressed in black, without ornaments or decoration of any kind, and thus making a striking figure among the brilliantly dressed bevy of ladies as she passes through it, comes from the palace and stands on the steps.* CAESAR *does not see her until she speaks.*

CLEOPATRA   Has Cleopatra no part in this leavetaking?

CAESAR [*enlightened*]   Ah, I k n e w there was something. [*To* RUFIO.] How could you let me forget her, Rufio? [*Hastening to her.*] Had I gone without seeing you, I should never have forgiven myself. [*He takes her hands, and brings her into the middle of the esplanade. She submits stonily.*] Is this mourning for me?

CLEOPATRA   No.

CAESAR [*remorsefully*]   Ah, that was thoughtless of me! It is for your brother.

CLEOPATRA   No.

CAESAR For whom, then?

CLEOPATRA Ask the Roman governor whom you have left us.

CAESAR Rufio?

CLEOPATRA Yes: Rufio. [*She points at him with deadly scorn.*] He who is to rule here in Caesar's name, in Caesar's way, according to Caesar's boasted laws of life.

CAESAR [*dubiously*] He is to rule as he can, Cleopatra. He has taken the work upon him, and will do it in his own way.

CLEOPATRA Not in your way, then?

CAESAR [*puzzled*] What do you mean by my way?

CLEOPATRA Without punishment. Without revenge. Without judgment.

CAESAR [*approvingly*] Ay: that is the right way, the great way, the only possible way in the end. [*To* RUFIO.] Believe it Rufio, if you can.

RUFIO Why, I believe it, Caesar. You have convinced me of it long ago. But look you. You are sailing for Numidia today. Now tell me: if you meet a hungry lion there, you will not punish it for wanting to eat you?

CAESAR [*wondering what he is driving at*] No.

RUFIO Nor revenge upon it the blood of those it has already eaten.

CAESAR No.

RUFIO Nor judge it for its guiltiness.

CAESAR No.

RUFIO What, then, will you do to save your life from it?

CAESAR [*promptly*] Kill it, man, without malice, just as it would kill me. What does this parable of the lion mean?

RUFIO Why, Cleopatra had a tigress that killed men at her bidding. I thought she might bid it to kill you some day. Well, had I not been Caesar's pupil, what pious things might I not have done to that tigress! I might have punished it. I might have revenged Pothinus on it.

CAESAR [*interjects*] Pothinus!

RUFIO [*continuing*] I might have judged it. But I put all these follies behind me; and, without malice, only cut its throat. And that is why Cleopatra comes to you in mourning.

CLEOPATRA [*vehemently*] He has shed the blood of my servant Ftatateeta. On your head be it as upon his, Caesar, if you hold him free of it.

CAESAR [*energetically*] On my head be it, then; for it was well done. Rufio: had you set yourself in the seat of the judge, and with hateful ceremonies and appeals to the gods handed that woman over to some hired executioner to be slain before the people in the name of justice, never again would I have touched your hand without a shudder. But this was natural slaying: I feel no horror at it.

> RUFIO, *satisfied, nods at* CLEOPATRA, *mutely inviting her to mark that.*

CLEOPATRA [*pettish and childish in her impotence*] No: not when a Roman slays an Egyptian. All the world will now see how unjust and corrupt Caesar is.

CAESAR [*taking her hands coaxingly*] Come: do not be angry with me. I am sorry for that poor Totateeta. [*She laughs in spite of herself.*] Aha! you are laughing. Does that mean reconciliation?

CLEOPATRA [*angry with herself for laughing*] No, n o, NO!! But it is so ridiculous to hear you call her Totateeta.

CAESAR   What! As much a child as ever, Cleopatra! Have I not made a woman of you after all?

CLEOPATRA   Oh, it is you who are a great baby: you make me seem silly because you will not behave seriously. But you have treated me badly; and I do not forgive you.

CAESAR   Bid me farewell.

CLEOPATRA   I will not.

CAESAR [*coaxing*]   I will send you a beautiful present from Rome.

CLEOPATRA [*proudly*]   Beauty from Rome to Egypt indeed! What can Rome give m e that Egypt cannot give me?

APOLLODORUS   That is true, Caesar. If the present is to be really beautiful, I shall have to buy it for you in Alexandria.

CAESAR   You are forgetting the treasures for which Rome is most famous, my friend. You cannot buy t h e m in Alexandria.

APOLLODORUS   What are they, Caesar?

CAESAR   Her sons. Come, Cleopatra: forgive me and bid me farewell; and I will send you a man, Roman from head to heel and Roman of the noblest; not old and ripe for the knife, not lean in the arms and cold in the heart; not hiding a bald head under his conqueror's laurels; not stooped with the weight of the world on his shoulders; but brisk and fresh, strong and young, hoping in the morning, fighting in the day, and revelling in the evening. Will you take such an one in exchange for Caesar?

CLEOPATRA [*palpitating*]   His name, his name?

CAESAR   Shall it be Mark Antony? [*She throws herself into his arms.*]

RUFIO   You are a bad hand at a bargain, mistress, if you will swop Caesar for Antony.

CAESAR   So now you are satisfied.

CLEOPATRA   You will not forget.

CAESAR   I will not forget. Farewell: I do not think we shall meet again. Farewell. [*He kisses her on the forehead. She is much affected and begins to sniff. He embarks.*]

ROMAN SOLDIERS [*as he sets his foot on the gangway*]   Hail, Caesar; and farewell!

He reaches the ship and returns RUFIO's *wave of the hand.*

APOLLODORUS [*to* CLEOPATRA]   No tears, dearest Queen: they stab your servant to the heart. He will return some day.

CLEOPATRA   I hope not. But I cant help crying, all the same.

She waves her handkerchief to CAESAR; *and the ship begins to move.*

ROMAN SOLDIERS [*drawing their swords and raising them in the air*]   Hail, Caesar!

SHAW'S NOTES TO CAESAR AND CLEOPATRA

CLEOPATRA'S CURE FOR BALDNESS

For the sake of conciseness in a hurried situation I have made Cleopatra recommend rum. This, I am afraid, is an anachronism: the only real one in the play. To balance it, I give a couple of the remedies she actually believed in. They are quoted by Galen[1] from Cleopatra's book on Cosmetic.

"For bald patches, powder red sulphuret of arsenic and take it up

---

1. A Greek physician and writer on medical subjects (c. 130–200 A.D.), regarded for centuries afterward as a prime authority in medicine.

with oak gum, as much as it will bear. Put on a rag and apply, having soaped the place well first. I have mixed the above with a foam of nitre, and it worked well."

Several other receipts follow, ending with: "The following is the best of all, acting for fallen hairs, when applied with oil or pomatum; acts for falling off of eyelashes or for people getting bald all over. It is wonderful. Of domestic mice burnt, one part; of vine rag burnt, one part; of horse's teeth burnt, one part; of bear's grease one; of deer's marrow one; of reed bark one. To be pounded when dry, and mixed with plenty of honey til it gets the consistency of honey; then the bear's grease and marrow to be mixed (when melted), the medicine to be put in a brass flask, and the bald part rubbed til it sprouts."

Concerning these ingredients, my fellow-dramatist Gilbert Murray, who, as a Professor of Greek, has applied to classical antiquity the methods of high scholarship (my own method is pure divination), writes to me as follows: "Some of this I dont understand, and possibly Galen did not, as he quotes your heroine's own language. Foam of nitre is, I think, something like soapsuds. Reed bark is an odd expression. It might mean the outside membrane of a reed: I do not know what it ought to be called. In the burnt mice receipt I take it that you first mixed the solid powders with honey, and then added the grease. I expect Cleopatra preferred it because in most of the others you have to lacerate the skin, prick it, or rub it till it bleeds. I do not know what vine rag is. I translate literally."

APPARENT ANACHRONISMS

The only way to write a play which shall convey to the general public an impression of antiquity is to make the characters speak blank verse and abstain from reference to steam, telegraphy, or any of the material conditions of their existence. The more ignorant men are, the more convinced are they that their little parish and their little chapel is an apex to which civilization and philosophy has painfully struggled up the pyramid of time from a desert of savagery. Savagery, they think, became barbarism; barbarism became ancient civilization; ancient civilization became Pauline Christianity; Pauline Christianity became Roman Catholicism; Roman Catholicism became the Dark Ages; and the Dark Ages were finally enlightened by the Protestant instincts of the English race. The whole process is summed up as Progress with a capital P. And any elderly gentleman of Progressive temperament will testify that the improvement since he was a boy is enormous.

Now if we count the generations of Progressive elderly gentleman since, say, Plato, and add together the successive enormous improvements to which each of them has testified, it will strike us at once as an unaccountable fact that the world, instead of having been improved in 67 generations out of all recognition, presents, on the whole, a rather less dignified appearance in Ibsen's Enemy of the People than in Plato's Republic. And in truth, the period of time covered by history is far too short to allow of any perceptible progress in the popular sense of Evolution of the Human Species. The notion that there has been any such Progress since Caesar's time (less than 20 centuries) is too absurd for discussion. All the savagery, barbarism, dark ages and the rest of it of which we have any record as existing in the past exists at the present moment. A British carpenter or stonemason may point out that he gets twice as much money for his labor as his father did in the same trade, and that his suburban house, with its bath, its cottage piano, its drawing room suite, and its album of photographs, would have shamed the plainness of his grandmother's. But the descendants of feudal barons, living in squalid lodgings on a salary of fifteen shillings a week instead of in castles on princely revenues, do not congratulate the world on the change. Such changes, in fact, are not to the point. It has been known, as far back as our records go, that man running wild in the woods is different from man kennelled in a city slum; that a dog seems to understand a shepherd better than a hewer of wood and drawer of water can understand an astronomer; and that breeding, gentle nurture, and luxurious food and shelter will produce a kind of man with whom the common laborer is socially incompatible. The same thing is true of horses and dogs. Now there is clearly room for great changes in the world by increasing the percentage of individuals who are carefully bred and gently nurtured, even to finally making the most of every man and woman born. But that possibility existed in the days of the Hittites as much as it does today. It does not give the slightest real support to the common assumption that the civilized contemporaries of the Hittites were unlike their civilized descendants today.

This would appear the tritest commonplace if it were not that the ordinary citizen's ignorance of the past combines with his idealization of the present to mislead and flatter him: Our latest book on the new railway across Asia describes the dulness of the Siberian farmer and the vulgar pursepride of the Siberian man of business without the least consciousness that the string of contemptuous instances given might have been saved by writing simply "Farmers and provincial plutocrats in Siberia are exactly what they are in England." The latest professor descanting on the civilization of the Western Empire in the fifth century feels bound to assume, in the teeth of his own researches, that the Christian was one sort of animal and the Pagan another. It might as well be assumed as indeed it generally is assumed by implication, that a murder committed with a poisoned arrow is different from a murder committed with a Mauser rifle. All such notions are illusions. Go back to the first syllable of recorded time, and there you will find your Christian and your Pagan, your yokel and your poet, helot and hero, Don Quixote and Sancho, Tamino and Papageno, Newton and bushman[2] unable to count eleven, all alive and contemporaneous, and all convinced that they are the heirs of all the ages and the privileged recipients of THE truth (all others damnable heresies), just as you have them today, flourishing in countries each of which is the bravest and best that ever sprang at Heaven's command from out the azure main.

Again, there is the illusion of "increased command over Nature," meaning that cotton is cheap and that ten miles of country road on a bicycle have replaced four on foot. But even if man's increased command over Nature included any increased command over himself (the only sort of command relevant to his evolution into a higher being), the fact remains that it is only by running away from the increased command over Nature to country places where Nature is still in primitive command over Man that he can recover from the effects of the smoke, the stench, the foul air, the overcrowding, the racket, the ugliness, the dirt which the cheap cotton costs us. If manufacturing activity means Progress, the town must be more advanced than the country;

---

2. The first pair of characters are from Cervantes' *Don Quixote;* the second from Mozart's *The Magic Flute.* In both cases the first named represent the spiritual or intellectual man; the second is his servant or companion who represents the physical man. Sir Isaac Newton (1642–1727) was a distinguished English mathematician and physicist.

and the field laborers and village artisans of today must be much less changed from the servants of Job than the proletariat of modern London from the proletariat of Caesar's Rome. Yet the cockney proletarian is so inferior to the village laborer that it is only by steady recruiting from the country that London is kept alive. This does not seem as if the change since Job's time were Progress in the popular sense: quite the reverse. The common stock of discoveries in physics has accumulated a little: that is all.

One more illustration. Is the Englishman prepared to admit that the American is his superior as a human being? I ask this question because the scarcity of labor in America relatively to the demand for it has led to a development of machinery there, and a consequent "increase of command over Nature" which makes many of our English methods appear almost medieval to the up-to-date Chicagoan. This means that the American has an advantage over the Englishman of exactly the same nature that the Englishman has over the contemporaries of Cicero. Is the Englishman prepared to draw the same conclusion in both cases? I think not. The American, of course, will draw it cheerfully; but I must then ask him whether, since a modern negro has a greater "command over Nature" than Washington had, we are also to accept the conclusion, involved in his former one, that humanity has progressed from Washington to the *fin de siècle* negro.

Finally, I would point out that if life is crowned by its success and devotion in industrial organization and ingenuity, we had better worship the ant and the bee (as moralists urge us to do in our childhood), and humble ourselves before the arrogance of the birds of Aristophanes.[3]

My reason then for ignoring the popular conception of Progress in Caesar and Cleopatra is that there is no reason to suppose that any Progress has taken place since their time. But even if I shared the popular delusion, I do not see that I could have made any essential difference in the play. I can only imitate humanity as I know it: Nobody knows whether Shakespear thought that ancient Athenian joiners, weavers, or bellows menders were any different from Elizabethan ones; but it is quite certain that he could not have made them so, unless, indeed, he had played the literary man and made Quince say, not "Is all our company here?" but "Bottom: was not that Socrates that passed us at the Piræus with Glaucon and Polemarchus on his way to the house of Kephalus?"[4] And so on.

CLEOPATRA

Cleopatra was only sixteen when Caesar went to Egypt; but in Egypt sixteen is a riper age than it is in England. The childishness I have ascribed to her, as far as it is childishness of character and not lack of experience, is not a matter of years. It may be observed in our own climate at the present day in many women of fifty. It is a mistake to suppose that the difference between wisdom and folly has anything to do with the difference between physical age and physical youth. Some women are younger at seventy than most women at seventeen.

It must be borne in mind, too, that Cleopatra was a queen, and was therefore not the typical Greek-cultured, educated Egyptian lady of her time. To represent her by any such type would be as absurd as to

3. In his comedy *The Birds*, the Greek dramatist Aristophanes (c. 448–380 B.C.) uses birds as characters.
4. In *A Midsummer's Night's Dream* Shakespeare sets the play in ancient Athens, but he does not attempt to give his Athenian tradesmen, including Bottom and Quince, ancient Greek names or modes of speaking.

represent George IV[5] by a type founded on the attainments of Sir Isaac Newton. It is true that an ordinarily well educated Alexandrian girl of her time would no more have believed bogey stories about the Romans than the daughter of a modern Oxford professor would believe them about the Germans (though, by the way, it is possible to talk great nonsense at Oxford about foreigners when we are at war with them). But I do not feel bound to believe that Cleopatra was well educated. Her father, the illustrious Flute Blower,[6] was not at all a parent of the Oxford professor type. And Cleopatra was a chip of the old block.

BRITANNUS

I find among those who have read this play in manuscript a strong conviction that an ancient Briton could not possibly have been like a modern one. I see no reason to adopt this curious view. It is true that the Roman and Norman conquests must have for a time disturbed the normal British type produced by the climate. But Britannus, born before these events, represents the unadulterated Briton who fought Caesar and impressed Roman observers much as we should expect the ancestors of Mr Podsnap[7] to impress the cultivated Italians of their time.

I am told that it is not scientific to treat national character as a product of climate. This only shews the wide difference between common knowledge and the intellectual game called science. We have men of exactly the same stock, and speaking the same language, growing in Great Britain, in Ireland, and in America. The result is three of the most distinctly marked nationalities under the sun. Racial characteristics are quite another matter. The difference between a Jew and a Gentile has nothing to do with the difference between an Englishman and a German. The characteristics of Britannus are local characteristics, not race characteristics. In an ancient Briton they would, I take it, be exaggerated, since modern Britain, disforested, drained, urbanified and consequently cosmopolized, is presumably less characteristically British than Caesar's Britain.

And again I ask does anyone who, in the light of a competent knowledge of his own age, has studied history from contemporary documents, believe that 67 generations of promiscuous marriage have made any appreciable difference in the human fauna of these isles? Certainly I do not.

JULIUS CAESAR

As to Caesar himself, I have purposely avoided the usual anachronism of going to Caesar's books, and concluding that the style is the man. That is only true of authors who have the specific literary genius, and have practiced long enough to attain complete self-expression in letters. It is not true even on these conditions in an age when literature is conceived as a game of style, and not as a vehicle of self-expression by the author. Now Caesar was an amateur stylist writing books of travel and campaign histories in a style so impersonal that the authenticity of the later volumes is disputed. They reveal some of his qualities just as the Voyage of a Naturalist Round the World reveals some of Darwin's,[8] without expressing his private personality. An Englishman reading them would say that Caesar was a man of great common

5. King of England 1820–30, known for his extravagance and dissolute life.

6. Cleopatra's father was Ptolemy XII, also known as Ptolemy Auletes, Ptolemy the Flute-Blower.

7. A character in Dickens' *Our Mutual Friend*, who expressed his smug certainty of the superiority of his own nation by referring to foreign things and people with his personal phrase of contempt, "Not English."

8. Charles Darwin (1809–1882), British naturalist and writer on natural history, remembered as the discoverer of evolution.

sense and good taste, meaning thereby a man without originality or moral courage.

In exhibiting Caesar as a much more various person than the historian of the Gallic wars, I hope I have not been too much imposed on by the dramatic illusion to which all great men owe part of their reputation and some the whole of it. I admit that reputations gained in war are specially questionable. Able civilians taking up the profession of arms, like Caesar and Cromwell, in middle age, have snatched all its laurels from opponent commanders bred to it, apparently because capable persons engaged in military pursuits are so scarce that the existence of two of them at the same time in the same hemisphere is extremely rare. The capacity of any conqueror is therefore more likely than not to be an illusion produced by the incapacity of his adversary. At all events, Caesar might have won his battles without being wiser than Charles XII or Nelson or Joan of Arc,[9] who were, like most modern "self-made" millionaires, half-witted geniuses, enjoying the worship accorded by all races to certain forms of insanity. But Caesar's victories were only advertisements for an eminence that would never have become popular without them. Caesar is greater off the battle field than on it. Nelson off his quarterdeck was so quaintly out of the question that when his head was injured at the battle of the Nile, and his conduct became for some years openly scandalous, the difference was not important enough to be noticed. It may, however, be said that peace hath her illusory reputations no less than war. And it is certainly true that in civil life mere capacity for work—the power of killing a dozen secretaries under you, so to speak, as a life-or-death courier kills horses—enables men with common ideas and superstitions to distance all competitors in the strife of political ambition. It was this power of work that astonished Cicero as the most prodigious of Caesar's gifts, as it astonished later observers in Napoleon before it wore him out. How if Caesar were nothing but a Nelson and a Gladstone[1] combined! a prodigy of vitality without any special quality of mind; nay, with ideas that were worn out before he was born, as Nelson's and Gladstone's were! I have considered that possibility too, and rejected it. I cannot cite all the stories about Caesar which seem to me to shew that he was genuinely original; but let me at least point out that I have been careful to attribute nothing but originality to him. Originality gives a man an air of frankness, generosity, and magnanimity by enabling him to estimate the value of truth, money, or success in any particular instance quite independently of convention and moral generalization. He therefore will not, in the ordinary Treasury bench fashion, tell a lie which everybody knows to be a lie (and consequently expects him as a matter of good taste to tell). His lies are not found out: they pass for candors. He understands the paradox of money, and gives it away when he can get most for it: in other words, when its value is least, which is just when a common man tries hardest to get it. He knows that the real moment of success is not the moment apparent to the crowd. Hence, in order to produce an impression of complete disinterestedness and magnanimity, he has only to act with entire selfishness; and this is perhaps the only sense in which a man can be said to be *naturally great*. It is in this sense that I have represented Caesar as great. Having virtue, he had no need of goodness.

9. Charles XII (1682–1718), King of Sweden from 1697 to his death; Horatio, Viscount Nelson (1758–1805), British admiral; and Joan of Arc (1412–1431), the French national heroine and saint.

1. William Ewart Gladstone (1809–1898), British statesman who was Victoria's Prime Minister on four occasions.

He is neither forgiving, frank, nor generous, because a man who is too great to resent has nothing to forgive; a man who says things that other people are afraid to say need be no more frank than Bismarck[2] was; and there is no generosity in giving things you do not want to people of whom you intend to make use. This distinction between virtue and goodness is not understood in England: hence the poverty of our drama in heroes. Our stage attempts at them are mere goody-goodies. Goodness, in its popular British sense of self-denial, implies that man is vicious by nature, and that supreme goodness is supreme martyrdom. Not sharing that pious opinion, I have not given countenance to it in any of my plays. In this I follow the precedent of the ancient myths, which represent the hero as vanquishing his enemies, not in fair fight, but with enchanted sword, superequine horse and magical invulnerability, the possession of which, from the vulgar moralistic point of view, robs his exploits of any merit whatever.

As to Caesar's sense of humor, there is no more reason to assume that he lacked it than to assume that he was deaf or blind. It is said that on the occasion of his assassination by a conspiracy of moralists (it is always your moralist who makes assassination a duty, on the scaffold or off it), he defended himself until the good Brutus struck him, when he exclaimed "What! you too, Brutus!" and disdained further fight. If this be true, he must have been an incorrigible comedian. But even if we waive this story, or accept the traditional sentimental interpretation of it, there is still abundant evidence of his lightheartedness and adventurousness. Indeed it is clear from his whole history that what has been called his ambition was an instinct for exploration. He had much more of Columbus and Franklin in him than of Henry V.[3]

However, nobody need deny Caesar a share, at least, of the qualities I have attributed to him. All men, much more Julius Caesars, possess all qualities in some degree. The really interesting question is whether I am right in assuming that the way to produce an impression of greatness is by exhibiting a man, not as mortifying his nature by doing his duty, in the manner which our system of putting little men into great positions (not having enough great men in our influential families to go round) forces us to inculcate, but as simply doing what he naturally wants to do. For this raises the question whether our world has not been wrong in its moral theory for the last 2,500 years or so. It must be a constant puzzle to many of us that the Christian era, so excellent in its intentions, should have been practically such a very discreditable episode in the history of the race. I doubt if this is altogether due to the vulgar and sanguinary sensationalism of our religious legends, with their substitution of gross physical torments and public executions for the passion of humanity. Islam, substituting voluptuousness for torment (a merely superficial difference, it is true) has done no better. It may have been the failure of Christianity to emancipate itself from expiatory theories of moral responsibility, guilt, innocence, reward, punishment, and the rest of it, that baffled its intension of changing the world. But these are bound up in all philosophies of creation as opposed to cosmism. They may therefore be regarded as the price we pay for popular religion.

2. Prince Otto von Bismarck (1815–1898), German statesman and first Chancellor of the German Empire.

3. Henry V, King of England 1413–22, was primarily known as a military leader in contrast to the Italian explorer Christopher Columbus (1451–1506) and the American statesman, writer, inventor, and philosopher Benjamin Franklin (1706–1790).

GEORGE BERNARD SHAW

Major Barbara

CHARACTERS

ANDREW UNDERSHAFT, *a munitions manufacturer*

LADY BRITOMART, *his wife, from whom he lives apart*[1]

STEPHEN
BARBARA   } *their children*
SARAH

ADOLPHUS CUSINS, *a Professor of Greek, in love with Barbara*

CHARLES LOMAX, *a scion of the upper classes, in love with Sarah*

MORRISON, *Lady Britomart's butler*

ROMOLA (RUMMY) MITCHENS
BRONTERRE O'BRIEN (SNOBBY)   } *habitués of the West Ham Shelter of the Salvation Army*
PRICE

JENNY HILL, *a young Salvation Army girl*

PETER SHIRLEY, *an older man who has lost his job*

BILL WALKER, *an intruder at the Shelter*

MRS. BAINES, *a senior officer in the Salvation Army*

BILTON, *a foreman at Undershaft's munitions works*

Act 1

It is after dinner in January 1906, in the library in LADY BRITO-
MART UNDERSHAFT'S *house in Wilton Crescent.*[2] *A large and comfortable settee is in the middle of the room, upholstered in dark
leather. A person sitting on it (it is vacant at present) would have,
on his right,* LADY BRITOMART'S *writing table, with the lady herself
busy at it; a smaller writing table behind him on his left; the door
behind him on* LADY BRITOMART'S *side; and a window with a window seat directly on his left. Near the window is an armchair.*

LADY BRITOMART *is a woman of fifty or thereabouts, well dressed
and yet careless of her dress, well bred and quite reckless of her
breeding, well mannered and yet appallingly outspoken and indifferent to the opinion of her interlocutors, amiable and yet peremp-
tory, arbitrary, and high-tempered to the last bearable degree, and
withal a very typical managing matron of the upper class, treated
as a naughty child until she grew into a scolding mother, and
finally settling down with plenty of practical ability and worldly
experience, limited in the oddest way with domestic and class limi-
tations, conceiving the universe exactly as if it were a large house
in Wilton Crescent, though handling her corner of it very effectively on that assumption, and being quite enlightened and liberal
as to the books in the library, the pictures on the walls, the music
in the portfolios, and the articles in the papers.*

Her son, STEPHEN, comes in. He is a gravely correct young man
under 25, taking himself very seriously, but still in some awe of his

---

1. As the daughter of an earl, Lady Britomart retains her title after her marriage although neither her husband nor children share it.

2. Wilton Crescent is located near Hyde Park Corner in the fashionable section of London called Belgravia.

mother, from childish habit and bachelor shyness rather than from any weakness of character.

STEPHEN Whats the matter?

LADY BRITOMART Presently, Stephen.

> STEPHEN *submissively walks to the settee and sits down. He takes up a Liberal weekly called The Speaker.*[3]

LADY BRITOMART Dont begin to read, Stephen. I shall require all your attention.

STEPHEN It was only while I was waiting—

LADY BRITOMART Dont make excuses, Stephen. [*He puts down The Speaker.*] Now! [*She finishes her writing; rises; and comes to the settee.*] I have not kept you waiting v e r y long, I think.

STEPHEN Not at all, mother.

LADY BRITOMART Bring me my cushion. [*He takes the cushion from the chair at the desk and arranges it for her as she sits down on the settee.*] Sit down. [*He sits down and fingers his tie nervously.*] Dont fiddle with your tie, Stephen: there is nothing the matter with it.

STEPHEN I beg your pardon. [*He fiddles with his watch chain instead.*]

LADY BRITOMART Now are you attending to me, Stephen?

STEPHEN Of course, mother.

LADY BRITOMART No: it's n o t of course. I want something much more than your everyday matter-of-course attention. I am going to speak to you very seriously, Stephen. I wish you would let that chain alone.

STEPHEN [*hastily relinquishing the chain*] Have I done anything to annoy you, mother? If so, it was quite unintentional.

LADY BRITOMART [*astonished*] Nonsense! [*With some remorse.*] My poor boy, did you think I was angry with you?

STEPHEN What is it, then, mother? You are making me very uneasy.

LADY BRITOMART [*squaring herself at him rather aggressively*] Stephen: may I ask how soon you intend to realize that you are a grown-up man, and that I am only a woman?

STEPHEN [*amazed*] Only a—

LADY BRITOMART Dont repeat my words, please: it is a most aggravating habit. You must learn to face life seriously, Stephen. I really cannot bear the whole burden of our family affairs any longer. You must advise me; you must assume the responsibility.

STEPHEN I!

LADY BRITOMART Yes, you, of course. You were 24 last June. Youve been at Harrow and Cambridge. Youve been to India and Japan. You must know a lot of things, now; unless you have wasted your time most scandalously. Well, a d v i s e me.

STEPHEN [*much perplexed*] You know I have never interfered in the household—

LADY BRITOMART No: I should think not. I dont want you to order the dinner.

STEPHEN I mean in our family affairs.

---

3. *The Speaker* first appeared in 1890 and was a left-wing review of politics, letters, science, and the arts. In 1907 it became *The Nation.* In 1931 it merged with *The New Statesman,* founded two decades earlier by Shaw and his Socialist friends, the Webbs. For a time the merged publication was called *The New Statesman and the Nation,* but since 1957 the name *The New Statesman* has been used.

LADY BRITOMART   Well, you must interfere now; for they are getting quite beyond me.

STEPHEN [*troubled*]   I have thought sometimes that perhaps I ought; but really, mother, I know so little about them; and what I do know is so painful! it is so impossible to mention some things to you—[*He stops, ashamed.*]

LADY BRITOMART   I suppose you mean your father.

STEPHEN [*almost inaudibly*]   Yes.

LADY BRITOMART   My dear: we cant go on all our lives not mentioning him. Of course you were quite right not to open the subject until I asked you to; but you are old enough now to be taken into my confidence, and to help me to deal with him about the girls.

STEPHEN   But the girls are all right. They are engaged.

LADY BRITOMART [*complacently*]   Yes: I have made a very good match for Sarah. Charles Lomax will be a millionaire at 35. But that is ten years ahead; and in the meantime his trustees cannot under the terms of his father's will allow him more than £800 a year.[4]

STEPHEN   But the will says also that if he increases his income by his own exertions, they may double the increase.

LADY BRITOMART   Charles Lomax's exertions are much more likely to decrease his income than to increase it. Sarah will have to find at least another £800 a year for the next ten years; and even then they will be as poor as church mice. And what about Barbara? I thought Barbara was going to make the most brilliant career of all of you. And what does she do? Joins the Salvation Army; discharges her maid; lives on a pound a week; and walks in one evening with a professor of Greek whom she has picked up in the street, and who pretends to be a Salvationist, and actually plays the big drum for her in public because he has fallen head over ears in love with her.

STEPHEN   I was certainly rather taken aback when I heard they were engaged. Cusins is a very nice fellow, certainly: nobody would ever guess that he was born in Australia; but—

LADY BRITOMART   Oh, Adolphus Cusins will make a very good husband. After all, nobody can say a word against Greek: it stamps a man at once as an educated gentleman. And my family, thank Heaven, is not a pig-headed Tory one. We are Whigs, and believe in liberty.[5] Let snobbish people say what they please: Barbara shall marry, not the man they like, but the man *I* like.

STEPHEN   Of course I was thinking only of his income. However, he is not likely to be extravagant.

LADY BRITOMART   Dont be too sure of that, Stephen. I know your quiet, simple, refined, poetic people like Adolphus: quite content with the best of everything! They cost more than your extravagant people, who are always as mean as they are second rate. No: Bar-

---

4. At the time of the play and until recently, the units of British currency were the penny (*pl.* pence), the shilling, and the pound or pound sterling. The pound contained 20 shillings, each worth 12 pence. Other terms used to describe British money are guinea (21 shillings), sovereign (a coin worth one pound), crown (five shillings), half crown (coin worth two and one-half shillings), florin (coin worth two shillings), groat (four pence) and farthing (one-fourth of a penny). In some cases, like the farthing, the term remained in the language long after the coin had ceased to circulate. At the time of the play the pound was worth about $4.90 in American money. Some prices of the period: one cent for the daily *New York Times* in the metropolitan area (two cents elsewhere) and five cents on Sunday; coffee sold for 16 to 40 cents per pound, a man's dress shirt for a dollar, and theater tickets from 25 cents to $1.50.

5. Lady Britomart is somewhat out of date politically. The terms "Whig" and "Tory" were generally replaced by Liberal and Conservative after the passage of the First Reform Bill in 1832, almost 75 years prior to the date of the play's action.

bara will need at least £2000 a year. You see it means two additional households. Besides, my dear, y o u must marry soon. I dont
approve of the present fashion of philandering bachelors and late
marriages; and I am trying to arange something for you.

STEPHEN   It's very good of you, mother; but perhaps I had better arrange that for myself.

LADY BRITOMAT   Nonsense! you are much too young to begin match-
making: you would be taken in by some pretty little nobody. Of
course I dont mean that you are not to be consulted: you know that
as well as I do. [STEPHEN *closes his lips and is silent.*] Now dont sulk,
Stephen.

STEPHEN   I am not sulking, mother. What has all this got to do with—
with—with my father?

LADY BRITOMART   My dear Stephen: where is the money to come
from? It is easy enough for you and the other children to live on my
income as long as we are in the same house; but I cant keep four
families in four separate houses. You know how poor my father is:
he has barely seven thousand a year now; and really, if he were not
the Earl of Stevenage, he would have to give up society. He can do
nothing for us. He says, naturally enough, that it is absurd that he
should be asked to provide for the children of a man who is rolling in
money. You see, Stephen, your father must be fabulously wealthy,
because there is always a war going on somewhere.

STEPHEN   You need not remind me of that, mother. I have hardly
ever opened a newspaper in my life without seeing our name in it.
The Undershaft torpedo! The Undershaft quick firers! The Undershaft ten inch! The Undershaft disappearing rampart gun! The Undershaft submarine! and now the Undershaft aerial battleship! At
Harrow they called me the Woolwich Infant. At Cambridge it was
the same. A little brute at King's who was always trying to get up
revivals, spoilt my Bible—your first birthday present to me—by writing under my name, "Son and heir to Undershaft and Lazarus, Death
and Destruction Dealers: address, Christendom and Judea." But that
was not so bad as the way I was kowtowed to everywhere because
my father was making millions by selling cannons.

LADY BRITOMART   It is not only the cannons, but the war loans that
Lazarus arranges under cover of giving credit for the cannons. You
know, Stephen, it's perfectly scandalous. Those two men, Andrew
Undershaft and Lazarus, positively have Europe under their thumbs.
That is why your father is able to behave as he does. He is above
the law. Do you think Bismarck or Gladstone or Disraeli could have
openly defied every social and moral obligation all their lives as your
father has?[6] They simply wouldnt have dared. I asked Gladstone to
take it up. I asked The Times to take it up. I asked the Lord Chamberlain to take it up.[7] But it was just like asking them to declare war
on the Sultan. They w o u l d n t. They said they couldnt touch
him. I believe they were afraid.

STEPHEN   What could they do? He does not actually break the law.

LADY BRITOMART   Not break the law! He is always breaking the law.
He broke the law when he was born: his parents were not married.

6. Prince Otto von Bismarck (1815–
1898), William Ewart Gladstone (1809–
1898) and Benjamin Disraeli (1804–
1881) were among the most distinguished
statemen of the nineteenth century.

7. The Lord Chamberlain, chief officer
of the royal household, would have exerted
little political power. Shaw despised the
office because the Lord Chamberlain was
charged with precensoring plays. Shaw
fought the law, but it remained in force
until 1968. The first play produced without precensorship was the American musical *Hair*.

STEPHEN   Mother! Is that true?

LADY BRITOMART   Of course it's true: that was why we separated.

STEPHEN   He married without letting you know this!

LADY BRITOMART [*rather taken aback by this inference*]   Oh no. To do Andrew justice, that was not the sort of thing he did. Besides, you know the Undershaft motto: Unashamed. Everybody knew.

STEPHEN   But you said that was why you separated.

LADY BRITOMART   Yes, because he was not content with being a foundling himself: he wanted to disinherit you for another foundling. That was what I couldnt stand.

STEPHEN [*ashamed*]   Do you mean for—for—for—

LADY BRITOMART   Dont stammer, Stephen. Speak distinctly.

STEPHEN   But this is so frightful to me, mother. To have to speak to you about such things!

LADY BRITOMART   It's not pleasant for me, either, especially if you are still so childish that you must make it worse by a display of embarrassment. It is only in the middle classes, Stephen, that people get into a state of dumb helpless horror when they find that there are wicked people in the world. In our class, we have to decide what is to be done with wicked people; and nothing should disturb our self-possession. Now ask your question properly.

STEPHEN   Mother: have you no consideration for me? For Heaven's sake either treat me as a child, as you always do, and tell me nothing at all; or tell me everything and let me take it as best I can.

LADY BRITOMART   Treat you as a child! What do you mean? It is most unkind and ungrateful of you to say such a thing. You know I have never treated any of you as children. I have always made you my companions and friends, and allowed you perfect freedom to do and say whatever you liked, so long as you liked what I could approve of.

STEPHEN [*desperately*]   I daresay we have been the very imperfect children of a very perfect mother; but I do beg you to let me alone for once, and tell me about this horrible business of my father wanting to set me aside for another son.

LADY BRITOMART [*amazed*]   Another son! I never said anything of the kind. I never dreamt of such a thing. This is what comes of interrupting me.

STEPHEN   But you said—

LADY BRITOMART [*cutting him short*]   Now be a good boy, Stephen, and listen to me patiently. The Undershafts are descended from a foundling in the parish of St Andrew Undershaft in the city. That was long ago, in the reign of James the First. Well, this foundling was adopted by an armorer and gun-maker. In the course of time the foundling succeeded to the business; and from some notion of gratitude, or some vow or something, he adopted another foundling, and left the business to him. And that foundling did the same. Ever since that, the cannon business has always been left to an adopted foundling named Andrew Undershaft.

STEPHEN   But did they never marry? Were there no legitimate sons?

LADY BRITOMART   Oh yes: they married just as your father did; and they were rich enough to buy land for their own children and leave them well provided for. But they always adopted and trained some foundling to succeed them in the business; and of course they always quarrelled with their wives furiously over it. Your father was adopted in that way; and he pretends to consider himself bound to keep up the tradition and adopt somebody to leave the business to. Of course

I was not going to stand that. There may have been some reason for it when the Undershafts could only marry women in their own class, whose sons were not fit to govern great estates. But there could be no excuse for passing over m y son.

STEPHEN [*dubiously*]   I am afraid I should make a poor hand of managing a cannon foundry.

LADY BRITOMART   Nonsense! you could easily get a manager and pay him a salary.

STEPHEN   My father evidently had no great opinion of my capacity.

LADY BRITOMART   Stuff, child! you were only a baby: it had nothing to do with your capacity. Andrew did it on principle, just as he did every perverse and wicked thing on principle. When my father remonstrated, Andrew actually told him to his face that history tells us of only two successful institutions: one the Undershaft firm, and the other the Roman Empire under the Antonines.[8] That was because the Antonine emperors all adopted their successors. Such rubbish! The Stevenages are as good as the Antonines, I hope; and you are a Stevenage. But that was Andrew all over. There you have the man! Always clever and unanswerable when he was defending nonsense and wickedness: always awkward and sullen when he had to behave sensibly and decently!

STEPHEN   Then it was on my account that your home life was broken up, mother. I am sorry.

LADY BRITOMART   Well, dear, there were other differences. I really cannot bear an immoral man. I am not a Pharisee, I hope; and I should not have minded his merely d o i n g wrong things: we are none of us perfect. But your father didnt exactly d o wrong things: he said them and thought them: that was what was so dreadful. He really had a sort of religion of wrongness. Just as one doesnt mind men practising immorality so long as they own that they are in the wrong by preaching morality; so I couldnt forgive Andrew for preaching immorality while he practised morality. You would all have grown up without principles, without any knowledge of right and wrong, if he had been in the house. You know, my dear, your father was a very attractive man in some ways. Children did not dislike him; and he took advantage of it to put the wickedest ideas into their heads, and make them quite unmanageable. I did not dislike him myself: very far from it; but nothing can bridge over moral disagreement.

STEPHEN   All this simply bewilders me, mother. People may differ about matters of opinion, or even about religion; but how can they differ about right and wrong? Right is right; and wrong is wrong; and if a man cannot distinguish them properly, he is either a fool or a rascal: thats all.

LADY BRITOMART [*touched*]   Thats my own boy! [*She pats his cheek.*] Your father never could answer that: he used to laugh and get out of it under cover of some affectionate nonsense. And now that you understand the situation, what do you advise me to do?

STEPHEN   Well, what c a n you do?

---

8. From 96 A.D. to 180 A.D. the Roman emperors, the so-called Five Good Emperors, were succeeded by persons they had adopted. The five were Nerva (96–98), Trajan (98–117), Hadrian (117–138), Antoninus Pius (138–161), from whose name the term "Antonines" is derived, and Marcus Aurelius (161–180). Commodus, the son and successor of Marcus Aurelius, did not live up to the reputation of his predecessors.

LADY BRITOMART   I must get the money somehow.

STEPHEN   We cannot take money from him. I had rather go and live in some cheap place like Bedford Square or even Hampstead than take a farthing of his money.[9]

LADY BRITOMART   But after all, Stephen, our present income comes from Andrew.

STEPHEN [*shocked*]   I never knew that.

LADY BRITOMART   Well, you surely didnt suppose your grandfather had anything to give me. The Stevenages could not do everything for you. We gave you social position. Andrew had to contribute s o m e t h i n g. He had a very good bargain, I think.

STEPHEN [*bitterly*]   We are utterly dependent on him and his cannons, then?

LADY BRITOMART   Certainly not: the money is settled. But he provided it. So you see it is not a question of taking money from him or not: it is simply a question of how much. I dont want any more for myself.

STEPHEN   Nor do I.

LADY BRITOMART   But Sarah does; and Barbara does. That is, Charles Lomax and Adolphus Cusins will cost them more. So I must put my pride in my pocket and ask for it, I suppose. That is your advice, Stephen, is it not?

STEPHEN   No.

LADY BRITOMART [*sharply*]   Stephen!

STEPHEN   Of course if you are determined—

LADY BRITOMART   I am not determined: I ask your advice; and I am waiting for it. I will not have all the responsibility thrown on my shoulders.

STEPHEN [*obstinately*]   I would die sooner than ask him for another penny.

LADY BRITOMART [*resignedly*]   You mean that *I* must ask him. Very well, Stephen: it shall be as you wish. You will be glad to know that your grandfather concurs. But he thinks I ought to ask Andrew to come here and see the girls. After all, he must have some natural affection for them.

STEPHEN   Ask him here!!!

LADY BRITOMART   Do n o t repeat my words, Stephen. Where else can I ask him?

STEPHEN   I never expected you to ask him at all.

LADY BRITOMART   Now dont tease, Stephen. Come! you see that it is necessary that he should pay us a visit, dont you?

STEPHEN [*reluctantly*]   I suppose so, if the girls cannot do without his money.

LADY BRITOMART   Thank you, Stephen: I knew you would give me the right advice when it was properly explained to you. I have asked your father to come this evening. [STEPHEN *bounds from his seat.*] Dont jump, Stephen: it fidgets me.

STEPHEN [*in utter consternation*]   Do you mean to say that my father is coming here tonight—that he may be here at any moment?

LADY BRITOMART [*looking at her watch*]   I said nine. [*He gasps. She*

9. Hampstead, about four miles northwest of the center of London, and Bloomsbury, which includes Bedford Square as well as the British Museum and the University of London, were less fashionable than Belgravia but hardly poor districts. Many writers and theatrical personalities have been associated with both districts. Shaw is mocking Stephen's anti-intellectualism.

rises.] Ring the bell, please. [STEPHEN *goes to the smaller writing table; presses a button on it; and sits at it with his elbows on the table and his head in his hands, outwitted and overwhelmed.*] It is ten minutes to nine yet; and I have to prepare the girls. I asked Charles Lomax and Adolphus to dinner on purpose that they might be here. Andrew had better see them in case he should cherish any delusions as to their being capable of supporting their wives. [*The butler enters:* LADY BRITOMART *goes behind the settee to speak to him.*] Morrison: go up to the drawing room and tell everybody to come down here at once. [MORRISON *withdraws.* LADY BRITOMART *turns to* STEPHEN.] Now remember, Stephen: I shall need all your countenance and authority. [*He rises and tries to recover some vestige of these attributes.*] Give me a chair, dear. [*He pushes a chair forward from the wall to where she stands, near the smaller writing table. She sits down; and he goes to the armchair, into which he throws himself.*] I dont know how Barbara will take it. Ever since they made her a major in the Salvation Army she has developed a propensity to have her own way and order people about which quite cows me sometimes. It's not ladylike: I'm sure I dont know where she picked it up. Anyhow, Barbara shant bully m e; but still it's just as well that your father should be here before she has time to refuse to meet him or make a fuss. Dont look nervous, Stephen: it will only encourage Barbara to make difficulties. *I* am nervous enough, goodness knows; but I dont shew it.

> SARAH *and* BARBARA *come in with their respective young men,* CHARLES LOMAX *and* ADOLPHUS CUSINS. SARAH *is slender, bored, and mundane.* BARBARA *is robuster, jollier, much more energetic.* SARAH *is fashionably dressed:* BARBARA *is in Salvation Army uniform.* LOMAX, *a young man about town, is like many other young men about town. He is afflicted with a frivolous sense of humor which plunges him at the most inopportune moments into paroxysms of imperfectly suppressed laughter.* CUSINS *is a spectacled student, slight, thin haired, and sweet voiced, with a more complex form of* LOMAX's *complaint. His sense of humor is intellectual and subtle, and is complicated by an appalling temper. The lifelong struggle of a benevolent temperament and a high conscience against impulses of inhuman ridicule and fierce impatience has set up a chronic strain which has visibly wrecked his constitution. He is a most implacable, determined, tenacious, intolerant person who by mere force of character presents himself as—and indeed actually is—considerate, gentle, explanatory, even mild and apologetic, capable possibly of murder, but not of cruelty or coarseness. By the operation of some instinct which is not merciful enough to blind him with the illusions of love, he is obstinately bent on marrying* BARBARA. LOMAX *likes* SARAH *and thinks it will be rather a lark to marry her. Consequently, he has not attempted to resist* LADY BRITOMART's *arrangements to that end.*
>
> All four look as if they had been having a good deal of fun in the drawing room. The girls enter first, leaving the swains outside. SARAH comes to the settee. BARBARA comes in after her and stops at the door.*

BARBARA   Are Cholly and Dolly to come in?

LADY BRITOMART [*forcibly*]   Barbara: I will not have Charles called Cholly: the vulgarity of it positively makes me ill.

BARBARA   It's all right, mother: Cholly is quite correct nowadays. Are they to come in?

LADY BRITOMART   Yes, if they will behave themselves.

BARBARA [*through the door*]   Come in, Dolly; and behave yourself.

> BARBARA *comes to her mother's writing table.* CUSINS *enters smiling, and wanders towards* LADY BRITOMART.

SARAH [*calling*]   Come in, Cholly. [LOMAX *enters, controlling his features very imperfectly, and places himself vaguely between* SARAH *and* BARBARA.]

LADY BRITOMART [*peremptorily*]   Sit down, all of you. [*They sit.* CUSINS *crosses to the window and seats himself there.* LOMAX *takes a chair.* BARBARA *sits at the writing table and* SARAH *on the settee.*] I dont in the least know what you are laughing at, Adolphus. I am surprised at you, though I expected nothing better from Charles Lomax.

CUSINS [*in a remarkably gentle voice*]   Barbara has been trying to teach me the West Ham Salvation March.[1]

LADY BRITOMART   I see nothing to laugh at in that; nor should you if you are really converted.

CUSINS [*sweetly*]   You were not present. It was really funny, I believe.

LOMAX   Ripping.

LADY BRITOMART   Be quiet, Charles. Now listen to me, children. Your father is coming here this evening.

> *General stupefaction.* LOMAX, SARAH, *and* BARBARA *rise:* SARAH *scared, and* BARBARA *amused and expectant.*

LOMAX [*remonstrating*]   Oh I say!

LADY BRITOMART   You are not called on to say anything, Charles.

SARAH   Are you serious, mother?

LADY BRITOMART   Of course I am serious. It is on your account, Sarah, and also on Charles's. [*Silence.* SARAH *sits, with a shrug.* CHARLES *looks painfully unworthy.*] I hope you are not going to object, Barbara.

BARBARA   I! why should I? My father has a soul to be saved like anybody else. He's quite welcome as far as I am concerned. [*She sits on the table, and softly whistles 'Onward, Christian Soldiers.'*]

LOMAX [*still remonstrant*]   But really, dont you know! Oh I say!

LADY BRITOMART [*frigidly*]   What do you wish to convey, Charles?

LOMAX   Well, you must admit that this is a bit thick.

LADY BRITOMART [*turning with ominous suavity to* CUSINS]   Adolphus: you are a professor of Greek. Can you translate Charles Lomax's remarks into reputable English for us?

CUSINS [*cautiously*]   If I may say so, Lady Brit, I think Charles has rather happily expressed what we all feel. Homer, speaking of Autolycus, uses the same phrase. πυκινὸν δόμον ἐλθεῖν [2] means a bit thick.

---

1. West Ham is a poor section in the East End of London and the site of Barbara's good works.

2. The Greek phrase was supplied to Shaw by Gilbert Murray, the Greek scholar to whom the play was dedicated and who was the model for Cusins. The Greek original actually reads πυκινὸν δόμον αντιτορήσας.

LOMAX [*handsomely*]   Not that I mind, you know, if Sarah dont. [*He sits.*]

LADY BRITOMART [*crushingly*]   Thank you. Have I y o u r permission, Adolphus, to invite my own husband to my own house?

CUSINS [*gallantly*]   You have my unhesitating support in everything you do.

LADY BRITOMART   Tush! Sarah: have you nothing to say?

SARAH   Do you mean that he is coming regularly to live here?

LADY BRITOMART   Certainly not. The spare room is ready for him if he likes to stay for a day or two and see a little more of you; but there are limits.

SARAH   Well, he cant eat us, I suppose. *I* dont mind.

LOMAX [*chuckling*]   I wonder how the old man will take it.

LADY BRITOMART   Much as the old woman will, no doubt, Charles.

LOMAX [*abashed*]   I didnt mean—at least—

LADY BRITOMART   You didnt t h i n k, Charles. You never do; and the result is, you never mean anything. And now please attend to me, children. Your father will be quite a stranger to us.

LOMAX   I suppose he hasnt seen Sarah since she was a little kid.

LADY BRITOMART   Not since she was a little kid, Charles, as you express it with that elegance of diction and refinement of thought that seem never to desert you. Accordingly—er— [*Impatiently.*] Now I have forgotten what I was going to say. That comes of your provoking me to be sarcastic, Charles. Adolphus: will you kindly tell me where I was.

CUSINS [*sweetly*]   You were saying that as Mr Undershaft has not seen his children since they were babies, he will form his opinion of the way you have brought them up from their behavior tonight, and that therefore you wish us all to be particularly careful to conduct ourselves well, especially Charles.

LADY BRITOMART [*with emphatic approval*]   Precisely.

LOMAX   Look here, Dolly: Lady Brit didnt say that.

LADY BRITOMART [*vehemently*]   I did, Charles. Adolphus's recollection is perfectly correct. It is most important that you should be good; and I do beg you for once not to pair off into opposite corners and giggle and whisper while I am speaking to your father.

BARBARA   All right, mother. We'll do you credit. [*She comes off the table, and sits in her chair with ladylike elegance.*]

LADY BRITOMART   Remember, Charles, that Sarah will want to feel proud of you instead of ashamed of you.

LOMAX   Oh I say! theres nothing to be exactly proud of, dont you know.

LADY BRITOMART   Well, try and look as if there was.

MORRISON, *pale and dismayed, breaks into the room in unconcealed disorder.*

MORRISON   Might I speak a word to you, my lady?

LADY BRITOMART   Nonsense! Shew him up.

MORRISON   Yes, my lady. [*He goes.*]

LOMAX   Does Morrison know who it is?

LADY BRITOMART   Of course. Morrison has always been with us.

LOMAX   It must be a regular corker for him, dont you know.

LADY BRITOMART   Is this a moment to get on my nerves, Charles, with your outrageous expressions?

LOMAX   But this is something out of the ordinary, really—

MORRISON [*at the door*]   The—er—Mr Undershaft. [*He retreats in confusion.*]

ANDREW UNDERSHAFT *comes in. All rise.* LADY BRITOMART *meets him in the middle of the room behind the settee.*

ANDREW *is, on the surface, a stoutish, easygoing elderly man, with kindly patient manners, and an engaging simplicity of character. But he has a watchful, deliberate, waiting, listening face, and formidable reserves of power, both bodily and mental, in his capacious chest and long head. His gentleness is partly that of a strong man who has learnt by experience that his natural grip hurts ordinary people unless he handles them very carefully, and partly the mellowness of age and success. He is also a little shy in his present very delicate situation.*

LADY BRITOMART   Good evening, Andrew.

UNDERSHAFT   How d'ye do, my dear.

LADY BRITOMART   You look a good deal older.

UNDERSHAFT [*apologetically*]   I a m somewhat older. [*Taking her hand with a touch of courtship.*] Time has stood still with you.

LADY BRITOMART [*throwing away his hand*]   Rubbish! This is your family.

UNDERSHAFT [*surprised*]   Is it so large? I am sorry to say my memory is failing very badly in some things. [*He offers his hand with paternal kindness to* LOMAX.]

LOMAX [*jerkily shaking his hand*]   Ahdedoo.

UNDERSHAFT   I can see you are my eldest. I am very glad to meet you again, my boy.

LOMAX [*remonstrating*]   No, but look here dont you know—[*Overcome.*] Oh I say!

LADY BRITOMART [*recovering from momentary speechlessness*]   Andrew: do you mean to say that you dont remember how many children you have?

UNDERSHAFT   Well, I am afraid I— They have grown so much—er. Am I making any ridiculous mistake? I may as well confess: I recollect only one son. But so many things have happened since, of course —er—

LADY BRITOMART [*decisively*]   Andrew: you are talking nonsense. Of course you have only one son.

UNDERSHAFT   Perhaps you will be good enough to introduce me, my dear.

LADY BRITOMART   That is Charles Lomax, who is engaged to Sarah.

UNDERSHAFT   My dear sir, I beg your pardon.

LOMAX   Notatall. Delighted, I assure you.

LADY BRITOMART   This is Stephen.

UNDERSHAFT [*bowing*]   Happy to make your acquaintance, Mr Stephen. Then [*going to* CUSINS] y o u must be my son. [*Taking* CUSINS' *hands in his.*] How are you, my young friend? [*To* LADY BRITOMART.] He is very like you, my love.

CUSINS   You flatter me, Mr Undershaft. My name is Cusins: engaged to Barbara. [*Very explicitly.*] That is Major Barbara Undershaft, of the Salvation Army. That is Sarah, your second daughter. This is Stephen Undershaft, your son.

UNDERSHAFT   My dear Stephen, I b e g your pardon.

STEPHEN   Not at all.

UNDERSHAFT   Mr Cusins: I am much indebted to you for explaining so precisely. [*Turning to* SARAH.] Barbara, my dear—

SARAH [*prompting him*]   Sarah.

UNDERSHAFT   Sarah, of course. [*They shake hands. He goes over to* BARBARA.] Barbara—I am right this time, I hope?

BARBARA   Quite right. [*They shake hands.*]

LADY BRITOMART [*resuming command*]   Sit down, all of you. Sit down, Andrew. [*She comes forward and sits on the settee.* CUSINS *also brings his chair forward on her left.* BARBARA *and* STEPHEN *resume their seats.* LOMAX *gives his chair to* SARAH *and goes for another.*]

UNDERSHAFT   Thank you, my love.

LOMAX [*conversationally, as he brings a chair forward between the writing table and the settee, and offers it to* UNDERSHAFT]   Takes you some time to find out exactly where you are, dont it?

UNDERSHAFT [*accepting the chair, but remaining standing*]   That is not what embarrasses me, Mr Lomax. My difficulty is that if I play the part of a father, I shall produce the effect of an intrusive stranger; and if I play the part of a discreet stranger, I may appear a callous father.

LADY BRITOMART   There is no need for you to play any part at all, Andrew. You had much better be sincere and natural.

UNDERSHAFT [*submissively*]   Yes, my dear: I daresay that will be best. [*He sits down comfortably.*] Well, here I am. Now what can I do for you all?

LADY BRITOMART   You need not do anything, Andrew. You are one of the family. You can sit with us and enjoy yourself.

> *A painfully conscious pause.* BARBARA *makes a face at* LOMAX, *whose too long suppressed mirth immediately explodes in agonized neighings.*

LADY BRITOMART [*outraged*]   Charles Lomax: if you can behave yourself, behave yourself. If not, leave the room.

LOMAX   I'm awfully sorry, Lady Brit; but really you know, upon my soul! [*He sits on the settee between* LADY BRITOMART *and* UNDERSHAFT, *quite overcome.*]

BARBARA   Why dont you laugh if you want to, Cholly? It's good for your inside.

LADY BRITOMART   Barbara: you have had the education of a lady. Please let your father see that; and dont talk like a street girl.

UNDERSHAFT   Never mind me, my dear. As you know, I am not a gentleman; and I was never educated.

LOMAX [*encouragingly*]   Nobody'd know it, I assure you. You look all right, you know.

CUSINS   Let me advise you to study Greek, Mr Undershaft. Greek scholars are privileged men. Few of them know Greek; and none of them know anything else; but their position is unchallengeable. Other languages are the qualifications of waiters and commercial travellers: Greek is to a man of position what the hallmark is to silver.

BARBARA   Dolly: dont be insincere. Cholly: fetch your concertina and play something for us.

LOMAX [*jumps up eagerly, but checks himself to remark doubtfully to* UNDERSHAFT]   Perhaps that sort of thing isnt in your line, eh?

UNDERSHAFT   I am particularly fond of music.

LOMAX [*delighted*]   Are you? Then I'll get it. [*He goes upstairs for the instrument.*]

UNDERSHAFT   Do you play, Barbara?

BARBARA   Only the tambourine. But Cholly's teaching me the concertina.

UNDERSHAFT   Is Cholly also a member of the Salvation Army?

BARBARA   No: he says it's bad form to be a dissenter.[3] But I dont despair of Cholly. I made him come yesterday to a meeting at the dock gates, and take the collection in his hat.

UNDERSHAFT [*looks whimsically at his wife*]!!

LADY BRITOMART   It is not my doing, Andrew. Barbara is old enough to take her own way. She has no father to advise her.

BARBARA   Oh yes she has. There are no orphans in the Salvation Army.

UNDERSHAFT   Your father there has a great many children and plenty of experience, eh?

BARBARA [*looking at him with quick interest and nodding*]   Just so. How did y o u come to understand that? [LOMAX *is heard at the door trying the concertina.*]

LADY BRITOMART   Come in, Charles. Play us something at once.

LOMAX   Righto! [*He sits down in his former place, and preludes.*]

UNDERSHAFT   One moment, Mr Lomax. I am rather interested in the Salvation Army. Its motto might be my own: Blood and Fire.

LOMAX [*shocked*]   But not your sort of blood and fire, you know.

UNDERSHAFT   My sort of blood cleanses: my sort of fire purifies.

BARBARA   So do ours. Come down tomorrow to my shelter—the West Ham shelter—and see what we're doing. We're going to march to a great meeting in the Assembly Hall at Mile End.[4] Come and see the shelter and then march with us: it will do you a lot of good. Can you play anything?

UNDERSHAFT   In my youth I earned pennies, and even shillings occasionally, in the streets and in public house parlors by my natural talent for stepdancing.[5] Later on, I became a member of the Undershaft orchestral society, and performed passably on the tenor trombone.

LOMAX [*scandalized—putting down the concertina*]   Oh I say!

BARBARA   Many a sinner has played himself into heaven on the trombone, thanks to the Army.

LOMAX [*to* BARBARA, *still rather shocked*]   Yes; but what about the cannon business, dont you know? [*To* UNDERSHAFT.] Getting into heaven is not exactly in your line, is it?

LADY BRITOMART   Charles!!!

LOMAX   Well; but it stands to reason, dont it? The cannon business may be necessary and all that: we cant get on without cannons; but it isnt right, you know. On the other hand, there may be a certain amount of tosh[6] about the Salvation Army—I belong to the Established Church myself—but still you cant deny that it's religion; and you cant go against religion, can you? At least unless youre downright immoral, dont you know.

---

3. A "dissenter" is a Protestant who worships outside the established Anglican church.

4. Mile End is a poor section in the East End of London. Mile End Road is a continuation of Whitechapel Road, beginning one mile to the east of the old City wall. The section is associated with the Salvation Army which began there with outdoor services conducted by William Booth in 1865.

5. Stepdancing is a form intended to display the performer's skill by the use of special steps.

6. Pretension or nonsense.

UNDERSHAFT   You hardly appreciate my position, Mr Lomax—

LOMAX [*hastily*]   I'm not saying anything against you personally—

UNDERSHAFT   Quite so, quite so. But consider for a moment. Here I am, a profiteer in mutilation and murder. I find myself in a specially amiable humor just now because, this morning, down at the foundry, we blew twenty-seven dummy soldiers into fragments with a gun which formerly destroyed only thirteen.

LOMAX [*leniently*]   Well, the more destructive war becomes, the sooner it will be abolished, eh?

UNDERSHAFT   Not at all. The more destructive war becomes the more fascinating we find it. No, Mr Lomax: I am obliged to you for making the usual excuse for my trade; but I am not ashamed of it. I am not one of those men who keep their morals and their business in water-tight compartments. All the spare money my trade rivals spend on hospitals, cathedrals, and other receptacles for conscience money, I devote to experiments and researches in improved methods of destroying life and property. I have always done so; and I always shall. Therefore your Christmas card moralities of peace on earth and goodwill among men are of no use to me. Your Christianity, which enjoins you to resist not evil, and to turn the other cheek, would make me a bankrupt. M y morality—m y religion—must have a place for cannons and torpedoes in it.

STEPHEN [*coldly—almost sullenly*]   You speak as if there were half a dozen moralities and religions to choose from, instead of one true morality and one true religion.

UNDERSHAFT   For me there is only one true morality; but it might not fit you, as you do not manufacture aerial battleships. There is only one true morality for every man; but every man has not the same true morality.

LOMAX [*overtaxed*]   Would you mind saying that again? I didnt quite follow it.

CUSINS   It's quite simple. As Euripides says, one man's meat is another man's poison morally as well as physically.[7]

UNDERSHAFT   Precisely.

LOMAX   Oh, t h a t ! Yes, yes, yes. True. True.

STEPHEN   In other words, some men are honest and some are scoundrels.

BARBARA   Bosh! There are no scoundrels.

UNDERSHAFT   Indeed? Are there any good men?

BARBARA   No. Not one. There are neither good men nor scoundrels: there are just children of one Father; and the sooner they stop calling one another names the better. You neednt talk to me: I know them. Ive had scores of them through my hands: scoundrels, criminals, infidels, philanthropists, missionaries, county councillors, all sorts. Theyre all just the same sort of sinner; and theres the same salvation ready for them all.

UNDERSHAFT   May I ask have you ever saved a maker of cannons?

BARBARA   No. Will you let me try?

7. In his dedication to the play Shaw expressed his admiration for Gilbert Murray's translation of *The Bacchae* of Euripides. If Cusins is referring to a specific passage, he may mean the following from that translation: "For strangely graven / Is the orb of life, that one and another / In gold and power may outpass his brother. / And men in their millions float and flow / And seethe with a million hopes as leaven; / And they win their Will, or they miss their Will, / And the hopes are dead or are pined for still; / But whoe'er can know, / As the long days go, / That to Live is happy, hath found his Heaven!" The passage is quoted with some alterations in Act 2 of this play.

UNDERSHAFT   Well, I will make a bargain with you. If I go to see you tomorrow in your Salvation Shelter, will you come the day after to see me in my cannon works?

BARBARA   Take care. It may end in your giving up the cannons for the sake of the Salvation Army.

UNDERSHAFT   Are you sure it will not end in your giving up the Salvation Army for the sake of the cannons?

BARBARA   I will take my chance of that.

UNDERSHAFT   And I will take my chance of the other. [*They shake hands on it.*] Where is your shelter?

BARBARA   In West Ham. At the sign of the cross. Ask anybody in Canning Town.[8] Where are your works?

UNDERSHAFT   In Perivale St Andrews. At the sign of the sword. Ask anybody in Europe.

LOMAX   Hadnt I better play something?

BARBARA   Yes. Give us Onward, Christian Soldiers.

LOMAX   Well, thats rather a strong order to begin with, dont you know. Suppose I sing Thourt passing hence, my brother. It's much the same tune.

BARBARA   It's too melancholy. You get saved, Cholly; and youll pass hence, my brother, without making such a fuss about it.

LADY BRITOMART   Really, Barbara, you go on as if religion were a pleasant subject. Do have some sense of propriety.

UNDERSHAFT   I do not find it an unpleasant subject, my dear. It is the only one that capable people really care for.

LADY BRITOMART   [*looking at her watch*]   Well, if you are determined to have it, I insist on having it in a proper and respectable way. Charles: ring for prayers.

General amazement. STEPHEN *rises in dismay.*

LOMAX   [*rising*]   Oh I say!

UNDERSHAFT   [*rising*]   I am afraid I must be going.

LADY BRITOMART   You cannot go now, Andrew: it would be most improper. Sit down. What will the servants think?

UNDERSHAFT   My dear: I have conscientious scruples. May I suggest a compromise? If Barbara will conduct a little service in the drawing room, with Mr Lomax as organist, I will attend it willingly. I will even take part, if a trombone can be procured.

LADY BRITOMART   Dont mock, Andrew.

UNDERSHAFT   [*shocked—to* BARBARA]   You dont think I am mocking, my love, I hope.

BARBARA   No, of course not; and it wouldnt matter if you were: half the Army came to their first meeting for a lark. [*Rising.*] Come along. [*She throws her arm round her father and sweeps him out, calling to the others from the threshold.*] Come, Dolly. Come, Cholly.

CUSINS *rises.*

LADY BRITOMART   I will not be disobeyed by everybody. Adolphus: sit down. [*He does not.*] Charles: you may go. You are not fit for prayers: you cannot keep your countenance.

LOMAX   Oh I say! [*He goes out.*]

---

8. Canning Town is a poor area in the East End of London, near the East India docks.

LADY BRITOMART [*continuing*]   But you, Adolphus, can behave yourself if you choose to. I insist on your staying.

CUSINS   My dear Lady Brit: there are things in the family prayer book that I couldnt bear to hear you say.

LADY BRITOMART   What things, pray?

CUSINS   Well, you would have to say before all the servants that we have done things we ought not to have done, and left undone things we ought to have done, and that there is no health in us. I cannot bear to hear you doing yourself such an injustice, and Barbara such an injustice. As for myself, I flatly deny it: I have done my best. I shouldnt dare to marry Barbara—I couldnt look you in the face—if it were true. So I must go to the drawing room.

LADY BRITOMART [*offended*]   Well, go. [*He starts for the door.*] And remember this, Adolphus: [*He turns to listen.*] I have a very strong suspicion that you went to the Salvation Army to worship Barbara and nothing else. And I quite appreciate the very clever way in which you systematically humbug me. I have found you out. Take care Barbara doesnt. Thats all.

CUSINS [*with unruffled sweetness*]   Dont tell on me. [*He steals out.*]

LADY BRITOMART   Sarah: if you want to go, go. Anything's better than to sit there as if you wished you were a thousand miles away.

SARAH [*languidly*]   Very well, mamma. [*She goes.*]

LADY BRITOMART, *with a sudden flounce, gives way to a little gust of tears.*

STEPHEN [*going to her*]   Mother: whats the matter?

LADY BRITOMART [*swishing away her tears with her handkerchief*] Nothing. Foolishness. You can go with him, too, if you like, and leave me with the servants.

STEPHEN   Oh, you mustnt think that, mother. I—I dont like him.

LADY BRITOMART   The others do. That is the injustice of a woman's lot. A woman has to bring up her children; and that means to restrain them, to deny them things they want, to set them tasks, to punish them when they do wrong, to do all the unpleasant things. And then the father, who has nothing to do but pet them and spoil them, comes in when all her work is done and steals their affection from her.

STEPHEN   He has not stolen our affection from you. It is only curiosity.

LADY BRITOMART [*violently*]   I wont be consoled, Stephen. There is nothing the matter with me. [*She rises and goes towards the door.*]

STEPHEN   Where are you going, mother?

LADY BRITOMART   To the drawing room, of course. [*She goes out. Onward, Christian Soldiers, on the concertina, with tambourine accompaniment, is heard when the door opens.*] Are you coming, Stephen?

STEPHEN   No. Certainly not. [*She goes. He sits down on the settee, with compressed lips and an expression of strong dislike.*]

Act 2

The yard of the West Ham shelter of the Salvation Army is a cold place on a January morning. The building itself, an old warehouse, is newly whitewashed. Its gabled end projects into the yard

*in the middle, with a door on the ground floor, and another in the
loft above it without any balcony or ladder, but with a pulley
rigged over it for hoisting sacks. Those who come from this central
gable end into the yard have the gateway leading to the street on
their left, with a stone horse-trough just beyond it, and, on the
right, a penthouse shielding a table from the weather. There are
forms at the table; and on them are seated a man and a woman,
both much down on their luck, finishing a meal of bread (one
thick slice each, with margarine and golden syrup) and diluted
milk.*

*The man, a workman out of employment, is young, agile, a
talker, a poser, sharp enough to be capable of anything in reason
except honesty or altruistic considerations of any kind. The woman
is a commonplace old bundle of poverty and hard-worn humanity.
She looks sixty and probably is forty-five. If they were rich people,
gloved and muffed and well wrapped up in furs and overcoats,
they would be numbed and miserable; for it is a grindingly cold
raw January day; and a glance at the background of grimy ware-
houses and leaden sky visible over the whitewashed walls of the
yard would drive any idle rich person straight to the Mediterranean. But these two, being no more troubled with visions of the
Mediterranean than of the moon, and being compelled to keep
more of their clothes in the pawnshop, and less on their persons, in
winter than in summer, are not depressed by the cold: rather are
they stung into vivacity, to which their meal has just now given an
almost jolly turn. The man takes a pull at his mug, and then gets
up and moves about the yard with his hands deep in his pockets,
occasionally breaking into a stepdance.*

THE WOMAN   Feel better arter your meal, sir?[9]

THE MAN   No. Call that a meal! Good enough for you, praps; but wot
is it to me, an intelligent workin man.

THE WOMAN   Workin man! Wot are you?

THE MAN   Painter.

THE WOMAN [*sceptically*]   Yus, I dessay.

THE MAN   Yus, you dessay! I know. Every loafer that cant do noth-
ink calls isself a painter. Well, I'm a real painter: grainer, finisher,
thirty-eight bob a week when I can get it.[1]

THE WOMAN   Then why dont you go and get it?

THE MAN   I'll tell you why. Fust: I'm intelligent—fffff! it's rotten cold
here [*he dances a step or two*]—yes: intelligent beyond the station
o life into which it has pleased the capitalists to call me; and they
dont like a man that sees through em. Second, an intelligent bein
needs a doo share of appiness; so I drink somethink cruel when I
get the chawnce. Third, I stand by my class and do as little as I can
so's to leave arf the job for me fellow workers. Fourth, I'm fly enough
to know wots inside the law and wots outside it;[2] and inside it I do
as the capitalists do: pinch wot I can lay me ands on. In a proper
state of society I am sober, industrious and honest: in Rome, so to
speak, I do as the Romans do. Wots the consequence? When trade is

9. See note on Shaw's spelling, p. 459.
1. A "grainer" is a craftsman who paints
an imitation of the grain of wood or the
streaks of marble in inferior materials. A

"finisher" puts the final touches on the
paint job.
2. "Fly" is a slang word meaning knowing or aware.

bad—and it's rotten bad just now—and the employers az to sack arf their men, they generally start on me.

THE WOMAN   Whats your name?

THE MAN   Price. Bronterre O'Brien Price. Usually called Snobby Price, for short.

THE WOMAN   Snobby's a carpenter, aint it? You said you was a painter.

PRICE   Not that kind of snob, but the genteel sort. I'm too uppish, owing to my intelligence, and my father being a Chartist[3] and a reading, thinking man: a stationer, too. I'm none of your common hewers of wood and drawers of water; and dont you forget it. [*He returns to his seat at the table, and takes up his mug.*] Wots y o u r name?

THE WOMAN   Rummy Mitchens, sir.

PRICE [*quaffing the remains of his milk to her*]   Your elth, Miss Mitchens.

RUMMY [*correcting him*]   Missis Mitchens.

PRICE   Wot! Oh Rummy, Rummy! Respectable married woman, Rummy, gittin rescued by the Salvation Army by pretendin to be a bad un. Same old game!

RUMMY   What am I to do? I cant starve. Them Salvation lasses is dear good girls; but the better you are, the worse they likes to think you were before they rescued you. Why shouldnt they av a bit o credit, poor loves? theyre worn to rags by their work. And where would they get the money to rescue us if we was to let on we're no worse than other people? You know what ladies and gentlemen are.

PRICE   Thievin swine! Wish I ad their job, Rummy, all the same. Wot does Rummy stand for? Pet name praps?

RUMMY   Short for Romola.[4]

PRICE   For wot!?

RUMMY   Romola. It was out of a new book. Somebody me mother wanted me to grow up like.

PRICE   We're companions in misfortune, Rummy. Both on us got names that nobody cawnt pronounce. Consequently I'm Snobby and youre Rummy because Bill and Sally wasnt good enough for our parents. Such is life!

RUMMY   Who saved you, Mr Price? Was it Major Barbara?

PRICE   No: I come here on my own. I'm goin to be Bronterre O'Brien Price, the converted painter. I know wot they like. I'll tell em how I blasphemed and gambled and wopped my poor old mother—

RUMMY [*shocked*]   Used you to beat your mother?

PRICE   Not likely. She used to beat me. No matter: you come and listen to the converted painter, and youll hear how she was a pious woman that taught me me prayers at er knee, an how I used to come home drunk and drag her out o bed be er snow white airs, an lam into er with the poker.

RUMMY   That whats so unfair to us women. Your confessions is just as big lies as ours: you dont tell what you really done no more than us; but you men can tell your lies right out at the meetins and be made much of for it; while the sort o confessions we az to make az to be wispered to one lady at a time. It aint right, spite of all their piety.

---

3. Chartism was a political movement concerned with electoral and parliamentary reform. It arose in the 1830s and continued with varying success until 1848.

4. The heroine and title character of George Eliot's historical novel about Savonarola, published in 1863.

PRICE   Right! Do you spose the Army'd be allowed if it went and did right? Not much. It combs our air and makes us good little blokes to be robbed and put upon. But I'll play the game as good as any of em. I'll see somebody struck by lightnin, or hear a voice sayin "Snobby Price: where will you spend eternity?" I'll av a time of it, I tell you.

RUMMY   You wont be let drink, though.

PRICE   I'll take it out in gorspellin, then. I dont want to drink if I can get fun enough any other way.

>   JENNY HILL, *a pale, overwrought, pretty Salvation lass of 18, comes in through the yard gate, leading* PETER SHIRLEY, *a half hardened, half worn-out elderly man, weak with hunger.*

JENNY [*supporting him*]   Come! pluck up. I'll get you something to eat. Youll be all right then.

PRICE [*rising and hurrying officiously to take the old man off* JENNY'S *hands*]   Poor old man! Cheer up, brother: youll find rest and peace and appiness ere. Hurry up with the food, miss: e's fair done. [JENNY *hurries into the shelter.*] Ere, buck up, daddy! shes fetchin y'a thick slice o breadn treacle, an a mug o skyblue.[5] [*He seats him at the corner of the table.*]

RUMMY [*gaily*]   Keep up your old art! Never say die!

SHIRLEY   I'm not an old man. I'm only 46. I'm as good as ever I was. The grey patch come in my hair before I was thirty. All it wants is three pennorth o hair dye: am I to be turned on the streets to starve for it? Holy God! Ive worked ten to twelve hours a day since I was thirteen, and paid my way all through; and now am I to be thrown into the gutter and my job given to a young man that can do it no better than me because Ive black hair that goes white at the first change?

PRICE [*cheerfully*]   No good jawrin about it. Youre ony a jumped-up, jerked-off, orspittle-turned-out incurable of an ole workin man: who cares about you? Eh? Make the thievin swine give you a meal: theyve stole many a one from you. Get a bit o your own back. [JENNY *returns with the usual meal.*] There you are, brother. Awsk a blessin an tuck that into you.

SHIRLEY [*looking at it ravenously but not touching it, and crying like a child*]   I never took anything before.

JENNY [*petting him*]   Come, come! the Lord sends it to you: he wasnt above taking bread from his friends; and why should you be? Besides, when we find you a job you can pay us for it if you like.

SHIRLEY [*eagerly*]   Yes, yes: thats true. I can pay you back: its only a loan. [*Shivering.*] Oh Lord! oh Lord! [*He turns to the table and attacks the meal ravenously.*]

JENNY   Well, Rummy, are you more comfortable now?

RUMMY   God bless you, lovey! youve fed my body and saved my soul, havnt you? [JENNY, *touched, kisses her.*] Sit down and rest a bit: you must be ready to drop.

JENNY   Ive been going hard since morning. But theres more work than we can do. I mustnt stop.

RUMMY   Try a prayer for just two minutes. Youll work all the better after.

---

5. "Treacle" is roughly molasses. "Skyblue" is a name for thin or watery milk.

JENNY [*her eyes lighting up*]   Oh isnt it wonderful how a few minutes prayer revives you! I was quite lightheaded at twelve o'clock, I was so tired; but Major Barbara just sent me to pray for five minutes; and I was able to go on as if I had only just begun. [*To* PRICE.] Did you have a piece of bread?

PRICE [*with unction*]   Yes, miss; but Ive got the piece that I value more; and thats the peace that passeth hall hannerstennin.

RUMMY [*fervently*]   Glory Hallelujah!

> BILL WALKER, *a rough customer of about 25, appears at the yard gate and looks malevolently at* JENNY.

JENNY   That makes me so happy. When you say that, I feel wicked for loitering here. I must get to work again.

> *She is hurrying to the shelter, when the new-comer moves quickly up to the door and intercepts her. His manner is so threatening that she retreats as he comes at her truculently, driving her down the yard.*

BILL   Aw knaow you. Youre the one that took awy maw girl. Youre the one that set er agen me. Well, I'm gowin to ev er aht. Not that Aw care a carse for er or you: see? Bat Aw'll let er knaow; and Aw'll let y o u knaow. Aw'm gowing to give her a doin thatll teach er to cat awy from me. Nah in wiv you and tell er to cam aht afore Aw cam in and kick er aht. Tell er Bill Walker wants er. She'll knaow wot thet means; and if she keeps me witin itll be worse. You stop to jawr beck at me; and Aw'll stawt on you: d'ye eah? Theres your wy. In you gow. [*He takes her by the arm and slings her towards the door of the shelter. She falls on her hand and knee.* RUMMY *helps her up again.*]

PRICE [*rising, and venturing irresolutely towards* BILL]   Easy there, mate. She aint doin you no arm.

BILL   Oo are you callin mite? [*Standing over him threateningly.*] Youre gowin to stend ap for er, aw yer? Put ap your ends.

RUMMY [*running indignantly to him to scold him*]   Oh, you great brute—[*He instantly swings his left hand back against her face. She screams and reels back to the trough, where she sits down, covering her bruised face with her hands and rocking herself and moaning with pain.*]

JENNY [*going to her*]   Oh, God forgive you! How could you strike an old woman like that?

BILL [*seizing her by the hair so violently that she also screams, and tearing her away from the old woman*]   You Gawd forgimme again an Aw'll Gawd forgive you one on the jawr thetll stop you pryin for a week. [*Holding her and turning fiercely on* PRICE.] Ev you ennything to sy agen it?

PRICE [*intimidated*]   No, matey: she aint anything to do with me.

BILL   Good job for you! Aw'd pat two meals into you and fawt you with one finger arter, you stawved cur. [*To* JENNY.] Nah are you gowin to fetch aht Mog Ebbijem;[6] or em Aw to knock your fice off you and fetch her meself?

JENNY [*writhing in his grasp*]   Oh please someone go in and tell Major

---

6. Bill's young lady must have been named Margaret (Mag) Habberjam or Habbijam.

Barbara—[*She screams again as he wrenches her head down; and* PRICE *and* RUMMY *flee into the shelter.*]

BILL   You want to gow in and tell your Mijor of me, do you?

JENNY   Oh please dont drag my hair. Let me go.

BILL   Do you or downt you? [*She stifles a scream.*] Yus or nao?

JENNY   God give me strength—

BILL [*striking her with his fist in the face*]   Gow an shaow her thet, and tell her if she wants one lawk it to cam and interfere with me. [JENNY, *crying with pain, goes into the shed. He goes to the form and addresses the old man.*] Eah: finish your mess; an git aht o maw wy.

SHIRLEY [*springing up and facing him fiercely, with the mug in his hand*]   You take a liberty with me, and I'll smash you over the face with the mug and cut your eye out. Aint you satisfied—young whelps like you—·ith takin the bread out o the mouths of your elders that have brought you up and slaved for you, but you must come shovin and cheekin and bullyin in here, where the bread o charity is sickenin in our stummicks?

BILL [*contemptuously, but backing a little*]   Wot good are you, you aold palsy mag?[7] Wot good are you?

SHIRLEY   As good as you and better. I'll do a day's work agen you or any fat young soaker of your age. Go and take my job at Horrockses, where I worked for ten year. They want young men there: they cant afford to keep men over forty-five. Theyre very sorry—give you a character and happy to help you to get anything suited to your years —sure a steady man wont be long out of a job. Well, let em try y o u. Theyll find the differ. What do y o u know? Not as much as how to beeyave yourself—layin your dirty fist across the mouth of a respectable woman!

BILL   Downt provowk me to ly it acrost yours: d'ye eah?

SHIRLEY [*with blighting contempt*]   Yes: you like an old man to hit, dont you, when youve finished with the women. I aint seen you hit a young one yet.

BILL [*stung*]   You loy, you aold soupkitchener, you. There was a yang menn eah. Did Aw offer to itt him or did Aw not?

SHIRLEY   Was he starvin or was he not? Was he a man or only a cross-eyed thief an a loafer? Would you hit my son-in-law's brother?

BILL   Oo's ee?

SHIRLEY   Todger Fairmile o Balls Pond. Him that won £20 off the Japanese wrastler at the music hall by standin out 17 minutes 4 seconds agen him.

BILL [*sullenly*]   Aw'm nao music awl wrastler. Ken he box?

SHIRLEY   Yes: an you cant.

BILL   Wot! Aw cawnt, cawnt Aw? Wots thet you sy? [*Threatening him.*]

SHIRLEY [*not budging an inch*]   Will you box Todger Fairmile if I put him on to you? Say the word.

BILL [*subsiding with a slouch*]   Aw'll stend ap to enny menn alawv, if he was ten Todger Fairmawls. But Aw dont set ap to be a per-feshnal.

SHIRLEY [*looking down on him with unfathomable disdain*]   Y o u box! Slap an old woman with the back o your hand! You hadnt even the sense to hit her where a magistrate couldnt see the mark of it,

---

7. Literally, a palsied, old chatterer (from magpie), but used here as a general term of contempt.

you silly young lump of conceit and ignorance. Hit a girl in the jaw and ony make her cry! If Todger Fairmile'd done it, she wouldnt a got up inside o ten minutes, no more than you would if he got on to you. Yah! I'd set about you myself if I had a week's feedin in me instead o two months' starvation. [*He turns his back on him and sits down moodily at the table.*]

BILL [*following him and stooping over him to drive the taunt in*]   You loy! youve the bread and treacle in you that you cam eah to beg.

SHIRLEY [*bursting into tears*]   Oh God! it's true: I'm only an old pauper on the scrap heap. [*Furiously.*] But youll come to it yourself; and then youll know. Youll come to it sooner than a teetotaller like me, fillin yourself with gin at this hour o the mornin!

BILL   Aw'm nao gin drinker, you oald lawr; bat wen Aw want to give my girl a bloomin good awdin Aw lawk to ev a bit o devil in me: see? An eah Aw emm, talkin to a rotten aold blawter like you sted o givin her wot for. [*Working himself into a rage.*] Aw'm gowin in there to fetch her aht. [*He makes vengefully for the shelter door.*]

SHIRLEY   Youre goin to the station on a stretcher, more likely; and theyll take the gin and the devil out of you there when they get you inside. You mind what youre about: the major here is the Earl o Stevenage's granddaughter.

BILL [*checked*]   Garn![8]

SHIRLEY   Youll see.

BILL [*his resolution oozing*]   Well, Aw aint dan nathin to er.

SHIRLEY   Spose she said you did! who'd believe you?

BILL [*very uneasy, skulking back to the corner of the penthouse[9]*] Gawd! theres no jastice in this cantry. To think wot them people can do! Aw'm as good as er.

SHIRLEY   Tell her so. It's just what a fool like you would do.

> BARBARA, *brisk and businesslike, comes from the shelter with a note book, and addresses herself to* SHIRLEY. BILL, *cowed, sits down in the corner on a form, and turns his back on them.*

BARBARA   Good morning.

SHIRLEY [*standing up and taking off his hat*]   Good morning, miss.

BARBARA   Sit down: make yourself at home. [*He hesitates; but she puts a friendly hand on his shoulder and makes him obey.*] Now then! since youve made friends with us, we want to know all about you. Names and addresses and trades.

SHIRLEY   Peter Shirley. Fitter. Chucked out two months ago because I was too old.

BARBARA [*not at all surprised*]   Youd pass still. Why didnt you dye your hair?

SHIRLEY   I did. Me age come out at a coroner's inquest on me daughter.

BARBARA   Steady?

SHIRLEY   Teetotaller. Never out of a job before. Good worker. And sent to the knackers like an old horse![1]

BARBARA   No matter: if you did your part God will do his.

SHIRLEY [*suddenly stubborn*]   My religion's no concern of anybody but myself.

---

8. A colloquial expression, used by the lower classes, meaning something like "get away with you."

9. A shed or secondary building, usually with a sloping roof and attached to the main structure.

1. A "knacker" bought old or diseased horses and slaughtered them for their hides and hooves and for meat to be used in dog food.

BARBARA [*guessing*]   I know. Secularist?[2]

SHIRLEY [*hotly*]   Did I offer to deny it?

BARBARA   Why should you? My own father's a Secularist, I think. Our Father—yours and mine—fulfils himself in many ways; and I daresay he knew what he was about when he made a Secularist of you. So buck up, Peter! we can always find a job for a steady man like you. [SHIRLEY, *disarmed and a little bewildered, touches his hat. She turns from him to* BILL.] Whats y o u r name?

BILL [*insolently*]   Wots thet to you?

BARBARA [*calmly making a note*]   Afraid to give his name. Any trade?

BILL   Oo's afride to give is nime? [*Doggedly, with a sense of heroically defying the House of Lords in the person of Lord Stevenage.*] If you want to bring a chawge agen me, bring it. [*She waits, unruffled.*] Moy nime's Bill Walker.

BARBARA [*as if the name were familiar: trying to remember how*]   Bill Walker? [*Recollecting.*] Oh, I know: youre the man that Jenny Hill was praying for inside just now. [*She enters his name in her note book.*]

BILL   Oo's Jenny Ill? And wot call as she to pry for me?

BARBARA   I dont know. Perhaps it was you that cut her lip.

BILL [*defiantly*]   Yus, it w a s me that cat her lip. Aw aint afride o y o u.

BARBARA   How could you be, since youre not afraid of God? Youre a brave man, Mr Walker. It takes some pluck to do o u r work here; but none of us dare lift our hand against a girl like that, for fear of her father in heaven.

BILL [*sullenly*]   I want nan o your kentin jawr. I spowse you think Aw cam eah to beg from you, like this demmiged lot eah. Not me. Aw downt want your bread and scripe and ketlep.[3] Aw dont blieve in your Gawd, no more than you do yourself.

BARBARA [*sunnily apologetic and ladylike, as on a new footing with him*]   Oh, I beg your pardon for putting your name down, Mr Walker. I didnt understand. I'll strike it out.

BILL [*taking this as a slight, and deeply wounded by it*]   Eah! you let maw nime alown. Aint it good enaff to be in your book?

BARBARA [*considering*]   Well, you see, theres no use putting down your name unless I can do something for you, is there? Whats your trade?

BILL [*still smarting*]   Thets nao concern o yours.

BARBARA   Just so. [*Very businesslike.*] I'll put you down as [*writing*] the man who—struck—poor little Jenny Hill—in the mouth.

BILL [*rising threateningly*]   See eah. Awve ed enaff o this.

BARBARA [*quite sunny and fearless*]   What did you come to us for?

BILL   Aw cam for maw gel, see? Aw cam to tike her aht o this and to brike er jawr for er.

BARBARA [*complacently*]   You see I was right about your trade. [BILL, *on the point of retorting furiously, finds himself, to his great shame and terror, in danger of crying instead. He sits down again suddenly.*] Whats her name?

BILL [*dogged*]   Er nime's Mog Ebbijem: thets wot her nime is.

---

2. Secularism as a formal movement dates from about 1850 and the teachings of G. J. Holyoake. It taught that man should order and interpret his life in terms of this world, without recourse to a belief in God or the afterlife.

3. "Scripe" (i.e., scrape) is a thin spreading (of butter) on bread. "Ketlep" (i.e., catlap) is tea or some other weak drink fit only for a cat to lap up.

BARBARA   Mog Habbijam! Oh, she's gone to Canning Town, to our barracks there.

BILL   [*fortified by his resentment of Mog's perfidy*]   Is she? [*Vindictively.*] Then Aw'm gowin to Kennintahn arter her. [*He crosses to the gate; hesitates; finally comes back at* BARBARA.] Are you loyin to me to git shat o me?

BARBARA   I dont want to get shut of you. I want to keep you here and save your soul. Youd better stay: youre going to have a bad time today, Bill.

BILL   Oo's gowin to give it to me? Y o u, preps?

BARBARA   Someone you dont believe in. But youll be glad afterwards.

BILL   [*slinking off*]   Aw'll gow to Kennintahn to be aht o reach o your tangue. [*Suddenly turning on her with intense malice.*] And if Aw downt fawnd Mog there, Aw'll cam beck and do two years for you, selp me Gawd if Aw downt!

BARBARA   [*a shade kindlier, if possible*]   It's no use, Bill. She's got another bloke.

BILL   Wot!

BARBARA   One of her own converts. He fell in love with her when he saw her with her soul saved, and her face clean, and her hair washed.

BILL   [*surprised*]   Wottud she wash it for, the carroty slat? It's red.

BARBARA   It's quite lovely now, because she wears a new look in her eyes with it. It's a pity youre too late. The new bloke has put your nose out of joint, Bill.

BILL   Aw'll put his nowse aht o joint for him. Not that Aw care a carse for er, mawnd thet. But Aw'll teach her to drop me as if Aw was dirt. And Aw'll teach him to meddle with maw judy. Wots iz bleedin nime?

BARBARA   Sergeant Todger Fairmile.

SHIRLEY   [*rising with grim joy*]   I'll go with him, miss. I want to see them two meet. I'll take him to the infirmary when it's over.

BILL   [*to* SHIRLEY, *with undissembled misgiving*]   Is thet im you was speakin on?

SHIRLEY   Thats him.

BILL   Im that wrastled in the music awl?

SHIRLEY   The competitions at the National Sportin Club was worth nigh a hundred a year to him. He's gev em up now for religion; so he's a bit fresh for want of the exercise he was accustomed to. He'll be glad to see you. Come along.

BILL   Wots is wight?

SHIRLEY   Thirteen four.[4] [BILL's *last hope expires.*]

BARBARA   Go and talk to him, Bill. He'll convert you.

SHIRLEY   He'll convert your head into a mashed potato.

BILL   [*sullenly*]   Aw aint afride of im. Aw aint afride of ennybody. Bat e can lick me. She's dan me. [*He sits down moodily on the edge of the horse-trough.*]

SHIRLEY   You aint goin. I thought not. [*He resumes his seat.*]

BARBARA   [*calling*]   Jenny!

JENNY   [*appearing at the shelter door with a plaster on the corner of her mouth*]   Yes, Major.

BARBARA   Send Rummy Mitchens out to clear away here.

---

4. In England the weight of human beings is frequently given in terms of the *stone*, a measure equal to fourteen pounds. The Sergeant weighs 186 pounds.

JENNY   I think she's afraid.

BARBARA [*her resemblance to her mother flashing out for a moment*]
Nonsense! she must do as she's told.

JENNY [*calling into the shelter*]   Rummy: the Major says you must
come.

>   JENNY *comes to* BARBARA, *purposely keeping on the side next*
>   BILL, *lest he should suppose that she shrank from him or bore*
>   *malice.*

BARBARA   Poor little Jenny! Are you tired? [*Looking at the wounded*
cheek.] Does it hurt?

JENNY   No: it's all right now. It was nothing.

BARBABA [*critically*]   It was as hard as he could hit, I expect. Poor
Bill! You dont feel angry with him, do you?

JENNY   Oh no, no, no: indeed I dont, Major, bless his poor heart!

>   BARBARA *kisses her; and she runs away merrily into the shelter.* BILL
>   *writhes with an agonizing return of his new and alarming symptoms,*
>   *but says nothing.* RUMMY MITCHENS *comes from the shelter.*

BARBARA [*going to meet* RUMMY]   Now Rummy, bustle. Take in those
mugs and plates to be washed; and throw the crumbs about for the
birds.

>   RUMMY *takes the three plates and mugs; but* SHIRLEY *takes back*
>   *his mug from her, as there is still some milk left in it.*

RUMMY   There aint any crumbs. This aint a time to waste good bread
on birds.

PRICE [*appearing at the shelter door*]   Gentleman come to see the shelter, Major. Says he's your father.

BARBARA   All right. Coming. [SNOBBY *goes back into the shelter, fol-*
lowed by BARBARA.]

RUMMY [*stealing across to* BILL *and addressing him in a subdued voice,*
but with intense conviction]   I'd av the lor of you, you flat eared
pignosed potwalloper,[5] if she'd let me. Youre no gentleman, to hit a
lady in the face. [BILL, *with greater things moving in him, takes no*
notice.]

SHIRLEY [*following her*]   Here! in with you and dont get yourself into
more trouble by talking.

RUMMY [*with hauteur*]   I aint ad the pleasure o being hintroduced to
you, as I can remember. [*She goes into the shelter with the plates.*]

SHIRLEY   Thats the—

BILL [*savagely*]   Downt you talk to me, d'ye eah? You lea me alown,
or Aw'll do you a mischief. Aw'm not dirt under y o u r feet, ennywy.

SHIRLEY [*calmly*]   Dont you be afeerd. You aint such prime company
that you need expect to be sought after. [*He is about to go into the*
shelter when BARBARA *comes out, with* UNDERSHAFT *on her right.*]

BARBARA   Oh, there you are, Mr Shirley! [*Between them.*] This is my
father: I told you he was a Secularist, didnt I? Perhaps youll be able
to comfort one another.

UNDERSHAFT [*startled*]   A Secularist! Not the least in the world: on
the contrary, a confirmed mystic.

---

5. A "potwalloper," originally "potwaller," was a householder, who was therefore
eligible to vote in Parliamentary elections. The word began to be used as a term of contempt early in the nineteenth century.

BARBARA   Sorry, I'm sure. By the way, papa, what i s your religion? in case I have to introduce you again.

UNDERSHAFT   My religion? Well, my dear, I am a Millionaire. That is my religion.

BARBARA   Then I'm afraid you and Mr Shirley wont be able to comfort one another after all. Youre not a Millionaire, are you, Peter?

SHIRLEY   No; and proud of it.

UNDERSHAFT [*gravely*]   Poverty, my friend, is not a thing to be proud of.

SHIRLEY [*angrily*]   Who made your millions for you? Me and my like. Whats kep us poor? Keepin you rich. I wouldnt have your conscience, not for all your income.

UNDERSHAFT   I wouldnt have your income, not for all your conscience, Mr Shirley. [*He goes to the penthouse and sits down on a form.*]

BARBARA [*stopping SHIRLEY adroitly as he is about to retort*]   You wouldnt think he was my father, would you, Peter? Will you go into the shelter and lend the lasses a hand for a while: we're worked off our feet.

SHIRLEY [*bitterly*]   Yes: I'm in their debt for a meal, aint I?

BARBARA   Oh, not because youre in their debt, but for love of them, Peter, for love of them. [*He cannot understand, and is rather scandalized.*] There! dont stare at me. In with you; and give that conscience of yours a holiday. [*Bustling him into the shelter.*]

SHIRLEY [*as he goes in*]   Ah! it's a pity you never was trained to use your reason, miss. Youd have been a very taking lecturer on Secularism.

BARBARA *turns to her father.*

UNDERSHAFT   Never mind me, my dear. Go about your work; and let me watch it for a while.

BARBARA   All right.

UNDERSHAFT   For instance, whats the matter with that out-patient over there?

BARBARA [*looking at BILL, whose attitude has never changed, and whose expression of brooding wrath has deepened*]   Oh, we shall cure him in no time. Just watch. [*She goes over to BILL and waits. He glances up at her and casts his eyes down again, uneasy, but grimmer than ever.*] It w o u l d be nice to just stamp on Mog Habbijam's face, wouldnt it, Bill?

BILL [*starting up from the trough in consternation*]   It's a loy: Aw never said so. [*She shakes her head.*] Oo taold you wot was in moy mawnd?

BARBARA   Only your new friend.

BILL   Wot new friend?

BARBARA   The devil, Bill. When he gets round people they get miserable, just like you.

BILL [*with a heartbreaking attempt at devil-may-care cheerfulness*]   Aw aint miserable. [*He sits down again, and stretches his legs in an attempt to seem indifferent.*]

BARBARA   Well, if youre happy, why dont you look happy, as we do?

BILL [*his legs curling back in spite of him*]   Aw'm eppy enaff, Aw tell you. Woy cawnt you lea me alown? Wot ev I dan to y o u? Aw aint smashed y o u r fice, ev Aw?

BARBARA [*softly: wooing his soul*]   It's not me thats getting at you, Bill.

BILL   Oo else is it?

BARBARA   Somebody that doesn't intend you to smash women's faces, I suppose. Somebody or something that wants to make a man of you.

BILL [*blustering*]   Mike a menn o m e! Aint Aw a menn? eh? Oo sez Aw'm not a menn?

BARBARA   Theres a man in you somewhere, I suppose. But why did he let you hit poor little Jenny Hill? That wasnt very manly of him, was it?

BILL [*tormented*]   Ev dan wiv it, Aw tell you. Chack it. Aw'm sick o your Jenny Ill and er silly little fice.

BARBARA   Then why do you keep thinking about it? Why does it keep coming up against you in your mind? Youre not getting converted, are you?

BILL [*with conviction*]   Not ME. Not lawkly.

BARBARA   Thats right, Bill. Hold out against it. Put out your strength. Dont lets get you cheap. Todger Fairmile said he wrestled for three nights against his salvation harder than he ever wrestled with the Jap at the music hall. He gave in to the Jap when his arm was going to break. But he didnt give in to his salvation until his heart was going to break. Perhaps youll escape that. You havnt any heart, have you?

BILL   Wot d'ye mean? Woy aint Aw got a awt the sime as ennybody else?

BARBARA   A man with a heart wouldnt have bashed poor little Jenny's face, would he?

BILL [*almost crying*]   Ow, w i l l you lea me alown? Ev Aw ever offered to meddle with y o u, that you cam neggin and provowkin me lawk this? [*He writhes convulsively from his eyes to his toes.*]

BARBARA [*with a steady soothing hand on his arm and a gentle voice that never lets him go*]   It's your soul thats hurting you, Bill, and not me. Weve been through it all ourselves. Come with us, Bill. [*He looks wildly round.*] To brave manhood on earth and eternal glory in heaven. [*He is on the point of breaking down.*] Come. [*A drum is heard in the shelter; and* BILL, *with a gasp, escapes from the spell as* BARBARA *turns quickly.* ADOLPHUS *enters from the shelter with a big drum.*] Oh! there you are, Dolly. Let me introduce a new friend of mine, Mr Bill Walker. This is my bloke, Bill: Mr Cusins. [CUSINS *salutes with his drumstick.*]

BILL   Gowin to merry im?

BARBARA   Yes.

BILL [*fervently*]   Gawd elp im! Gaw-aw-aw-awd elp im!

BARBARA   Why? Do you think he wont be happy with me?

BILL   Awve aony ed to stend it for a mawnin: e'll ev to stend it for a lawftawm.

CUSINS   That is a frightful reflection, Mr Walker. But I cant tear myself away from her.

BILL   Well, Aw ken. [*To* BARBARA.] Eah! do you knaow where Aw'm gowin to, and wot Aw'm gowin to do?

BARBARA   Yes: youre going to heaven; and youre coming back here before the week's out to tell me so.

BILL   You loy. Aw'm gowin to Kennintahn, to spit in Todger Fairmawl's eye. Aw beshed Jenny Ill's fice; an nar Aw'll git me aown fice beshed and cam beck and shaow it to er. Ee'll itt me ardern Aw itt er. Thatll mike us square. [*To* ADOLPHUS.] Is thet fair or is it not? Youre a genlmn: you oughter knaow.

BARBARA   Two black eyes wont make one white one, Bill.

BILL   Aw didnt awst y o u. Cawnt you never keep your mahth shat? Oy awst the genlmn.

CUSINS [*reflectively*]   Yes: I think youre right, Mr Walker. Yes: I should do it. It's curious: it's exactly what an ancient Greek would have done.

BARBARA   But what good will it do?

CUSINS   Well, it will give Mr Fairmile some exercise; and it will satisfy Mr Walker's soul.

BILL   Rot! there aint nao sach a thing as a saoul. Ah kin you tell wevver Awve a saoul or not? You never seen it.

BARBARA   Ive seen it hurting you when you went against it.

BILL [*with compressed aggravation*]   If you was maw gel and took the word aht o me mahth lawk thet, Aw'd give you sathink youd feel urtin, Aw would. [*To* ADOLPHUS.] You tike maw tip, mite. Stop er jawr; or youll doy afoah your tawn. [*With intense expression.*] Wore aht: thets wot youll be: wore aht. [*He goes away through the gate.*]

CUSINS [*looking after him*]   I wonder!

BARBARA   Dolly! [*Indignant, in her mother's manner.*]

CUSINS   Yes, my dear, it's very wearing to be in love with you. If it lasts, I quite think I shall die young.

BARBARA   Should you mind?

CUSINS   Not at all. [*He is suddenly softened, and kisses her over the drum, evidently not for the first time, as people cannot kiss over a big drum without practice.* UNDERSHAFT *coughs.*]

BARBARA   It's all right, papa, weve not forgotten you. Dolly: explain the place to papa: I havnt time. [*She goes busily into the shelter.*]

UNDERSHAFT *and* ADOLPHUS *now have the yard to themselves.* UNDERSHAFT, *seated on a form, and still keenly attentive, looks hard at* ADOLPHUS. ADOLPHUS *looks hard at him.*

UNDERSHAFT   I fancy you guess something of what is in my mind, Mr Cusins. [CUSINS *flourishes his drumsticks as if in the act of beating a lively rataplan, but makes no sound.*]   Exactly so. But suppose Barbara finds you out!

CUSINS   You know, I do not admit that I am imposing on Barbara. I am quite genuinely interested in the views of the Salvation Army. The fact is, I am a sort of collector of religions; and the curious thing is that I find I can believe them all. By the way, have you any religion?

UNDERSHAFT   Yes.

CUSINS   Anything out of the common?

UNDERSHAFT   Only that there are two things necessary to Salvation.

CUSINS [*disappointed, but polite*]   Ah, the Church Catechism. Charles Lomax also belongs to the Established Church.

UNDERSHAFT   The two things are—

CUSINS   Baptism and—

UNDERSHAFT   No. Money and gunpowder.

CUSINS [*surprised, but interested*]   That is the general opinion of our governing classes. The novelty is in hearing any man confess it.

UNDERSHAFT   Just so.

CUSINS   Exuse me: is there any place in your religion for honor, justice, truth, love, mercy and so forth?

UNDERSHAFT   Yes: they are the graces and luxuries of a rich, strong, and safe life.

CUSINS   Suppose one is forced to choose between them and money or gunpowder?

UNDERSHAFT   Choose money a n d gunpowder; for without enough of both you cannot afford the others.

CUSINS   That is your religion?

UNDERSHAFT   Yes.

The cadence of this reply makes a full close in the conversation. CUSINS *twists his face dubiously and contemplates* UNDERSHAFT. UNDERSHAFT *contemplates him.*

CUSINS   Barbara wont stand that. You will have to choose between your religion and Barbara.

UNDERSHAFT   So will you, my friend. She will find out that that drum of yours is hollow.

CUSINS   Father Undershaft: you are mistaken: I am a sincere Salvationist. You do not understand the Salvation Army. It is the army of joy, of love, of courage: it has banished the fear and remorse and despair of the old hell-ridden evangelical sects: it marches to fight the devil with trumpet and drum, with music and dancing, with banner and palm, as becomes a sally from heaven by its happy garrison. It picks the waster out of the public house and makes a man of him: it finds a worm wriggling in a back kitchen, and lo! a woman! Men and women of rank too, sons and daughters of the Highest. It takes the poor professor of Greek, the most artificial and self-suppressed of human creatures, from his meal of roots, and lets loose the rhapsodist in him; reveals the true worship of Dionysos to him; sends him down the public street drumming dithyrambs. [*He plays a thundering flourish on the drum.*]

UNDERSHAFT   You will alarm the shelter.

CUSINS   Oh, they are accustomed to these sudden ecstasies. However, if the drum worries you—[*He pockets the drumsticks; unhooks the drum; and stands it on the ground opposite the gateway.*]

UNDERSHAFT   Thank you.

CUSINS   You remember what Euripides says about your money and gunpowder?

UNDERSHAFT   No.

CUSINS [*declaiming*]

One and another
In money and guns may outpass his brother;
And men in their millions float and flow
And seethe with a million hopes as leaven;
And they win their will; or they miss their will;
And their hopes are dead or are pined for still;
But whoe'er can know
As the long days go
That to live is happy, has found h i s heaven.

My translation: what do you think of it?

UNDERSHAFT   I think, my friend, that if you wish to know, as the long days go, that to live is happy, you must first acquire money enough for a decent life, and power enough to be your own master.

CUSINS   You are damnably discouraging. [*He resumes his declamation.*]

> Is it so hard a thing to see
> That the spirit of God—whate'er it be—
> The law that abides and changes not, ages long,
> The Eternal and Nature-born: t h e s e things be strong?
> What else is Wisdom? What of Man's endeavor,
> Or God's high grace so lovely and so great?
> To stand from fear set free? to breathe and wait?
> To hold a hand uplifted over Fate?
> And shall not Barbara be loved for ever?[6]

UNDERSHAFT   Euripides mentions Barbara, does he?

CUSINS   It is a fair translation. The word means Loveliness.

UNDERSHAFT   May I ask—as Barbara's father—how much a year she is to be loved for ever on?

CUSINS   As Barbara's father, that is more your affair than mine. I can feed her by teaching Greek: that is about all.

UNDERSHAFT   Do you consider it a good match for her?

CUSINS   [*with polite obstinacy*]   Mr Undershaft: I am in many ways a weak, timid, ineffectual person; and my health is far from satisfactory. But whenever I feel that I must have anything, I get it, sooner or later. I feel that way about Barbara. I dont like marriage: I feel intensely afraid of it; and I dont know what I shall do with Barbara or what she will do with me. But I feel that I and nobody else must marry her. Please regard that as settled.—Not that I wish to be arbitrary; but why should I waste your time in discussing what is inevitable?

UNDERSHAFT   You mean that you will stick at nothing: not even the conversion of the Salvation Army to the worship of Dionysos.[7]

CUSINS   The business of the Salvation Army is to save, not to wrangle about the name of the pathfinder. Dionysos or another: what does it matter?

UNDERSHAFT   [*rising and approaching him*]   Professor Cusins: you are a young man after my own heart.

CUSINS   Mr Undershaft: you are, as far as I am able to gather, a most infernal old rascal; but you appeal very strongly to my sense of ironic humor.

UNDERSHAFT *mutely offers his hand. They shake.*

UNDERSHAFT   [*suddenly concentrating himself*]   And now to business.

CUSINS   Pardon me. We are discussing religion. Why go back to such an uninteresting and unimportant subject as business?

UNDERSHAFT   Religion is our business at present, because it is through religion alone that we can win Barbara.

CUSINS   Have you, too, fallen in love with Barbara?

UNDERSHAFT   Yes, with a father's love.

CUSINS   A father's love for a grown-up daughter is the most dangerous

6. Both quotations are freely adapted from Gilbert Murray's translation of *The Bacchae*. In the first, Shaw substitutes "money and guns" for "gold and power," and in the second, "Fate" for "Hate" and "Barbara" for "Loveliness."

7. Dionysos, or Dionysus, the Greek god of wine, was associated with a form of worship more ecstatic and emotional than that of the Olympians, which was regarded as an intrusion on the religious scene (as in *The Bacchae*). Some scholars believe that the worship of Dionysus, in fact, represents an older stage of religion.

of all infatuations. I apologize for mentioning my own pale, coy, mistrustful fancy in the same breath with it.

UNDERSHAFT   Keep to the point. We have to win her; and we are neither of us Methodists.

CUSINS   That doesnt matter. The power Barbara wields here—the power that wields Barbara herself—is not Calvinism, not Presbyterianism, not Methodism—[8]

UNDERSHAFT   Not Greek Paganism either, eh?

CUSINS   I admit that. Barbara is quite original in her religion.

UNDERSHAFT [*triumphantly*]   Aha! Barbara Undershaft would be. Her inspiration comes from within herself.

CUSINS   How do you suppose it got there?

UNDERSHAFT [*in towering excitement*]   It is the Undershaft inheritance. I shall hand on my torch to my daughter. She shall make my converts and preach my gospel—

CUSINS   What! Money and gunpowder!

UNDERSHAFT   Yes, money and gunpowder. Freedom and power. Command of life and command of death.

CUSINS [*urbanely: trying to bring him down to earth*]   This is extremely interesting, Mr Undershaft. Of course you know that you are mad.

UNDERSHAFT [*with redoubled force*]   And you?

CUSINS   Oh, mad as a hatter. You are welcome to my secret since I have discovered yours. But I am astonished. Can a madman make cannons?

UNDERSHAFT   Would anyone else than a madman make them? And now [*with surging energy*] question for question. Can a sane man translate Euripides?

CUSINS   No.

UNDERSHAFT [*seizing him by the shoulder*]   Can a sane woman make a man of a waster or a woman of a worm?

CUSINS [*reeling before the storm*]   Father Colossus—Mammoth Millionaire—

UNDERSHAFT [*pressing him*]   Are there two mad people or three in this Salvation shelter today?

CUSINS   You mean Barbara is as mad as we are?

UNDERSHAFT [*pushing him lightly off and resuming his equanimity suddenly and completely*]   Pooh, Professor! let us call things by their proper names. I am a millionaire; you are a poet; Barbara is a savior of souls. What have we three to do with the common mob of slaves and idolaters? [*He sits down again with a shrug of contempt for the mob.*]

CUSINS   Take care! Barbara is in love with the common people. So am I. Have you never felt the romance of that love?

UNDERSHAFT [*cold and sardonic*]   Have you ever been in love with Poverty, like St Francis? Have you ever been in love with Dirt, like St Simeon![9] Have you ever been in love with disease and suffering, like our nurses and philanthropists? Such passions are not virtues,

8. Calvinism refers to the theological teachings of John Calvin (1509–1564), Presbyterianism is a movement, traditionally Calvinistic, which sprang up in the 16th century and which rejected traditional forms of church government. Methodism was a nonconformist movement which began at Oxford in 1729 with preaching of John Wesley, his brother Charles, and others who had been within the established Anglican church.

9. St. Francis of Assisi (1181–1226), the founder of the Franciscan order, and Saint Simeon Stylites the Elder (c. 388–459), who lived atop a column for 36 years and conditioned himself to remain standing throughout Lent, were famous ascetics.

but the most unnatural of all the vices. This love of the common people may please an earl's granddaughter and a university professor; but I have been a common man and a poor man; and it has no romance for me. Leave it to the poor to pretend that poverty is a blessing: leave it to the coward to make a religion of his cowardice by preaching humility: we know better than that. We three must stand together above the common people: how else can we help their children to climb up beside us? Barbara must belong to us, not to the Salvation Army.

CUSINS   Well, I can only say that if you think you will get her away from the Salvation Army by talking to her as you have been talking to me, you dont know Barbara.

UNDERSHAFT   My friend: I never ask for what I can buy.

CUSINS [*in a white fury*]   Do I understand you to imply that you can buy Barbara?

UNDERSHAFT   No; but I can buy the Salvation Army.

CUSINS   Quite impossible.

UNDERSHAFT   You shall see. All religious organizations exist by selling themselves to the rich.

CUSINS   Not the Army. That is the Church of the poor.

UNDERSHAFT   All the more reason for buying it.

CUSINS   I dont think you quite know what the Army does for the poor.

UNDERSHAFT   Oh yes I do. It draws their teeth: that is enough for me as a man of business.

CUSINS   Nonsense! It makes them sober—

UNDERSHAFT   I prefer sober workmen. The profits are larger.

CUSINS   —honest—

UNDERSHAFT   Honest workmen are the most economical.

CUSINS   —attached to their homes—

UNDERSHAFT   So much the better: they will put up with anything sooner than change their shop.

CUSINS   —happy—

UNDERSHAFT   An invaluable safeguard against revolution.

CUSINS   —unselfish—

UNDERSHAFT   Indifferent to their own interests, which suits me exactly.

CUSINS   —with their thoughts on heavenly things—

UNDERSHAFT [*rising*]   And not on Trade Unionism nor Socialism. Excellent.

CUSINS [*revolted*]   You really are an infernal old rascal.

UNDERSHAFT [*indicating* PETER SHIRLEY, *who has just come from the shelter and strolled dejectedly down the yard between them*]   And this is an honest man!

SHIRLEY   Yes; and what av I got by it? [*He passes on bitterly and sits on the form, in the corner of the penthouse.*]

>   SNOBBY PRICE, *beaming sanctimoniously, and* JENNY HILL *with a tambourine full of coppers, come from the shelter and go to the drum, on which* JENNY *begins to count the money.*

UNDERSHAFT [*replying to* SHIRLEY]   Oh, your employers must have got a good deal by it from first to last. [*He sits on the table, with one foot on the side form.* CUSINS, *overwhelmed, sits down on the same form nearer the shelter.* BARBARA *comes from the shelter to the middle of the yard. She is excited and a little overwrought.*]

BARBARA   Weve just had a splendid experience meeting at the other gate in Cripps's Lane. Ive hardly ever seen them so much moved as they were by your confession, Mr Price.

PRICE   I could almost be glad of my past wickedness if I could believe that it would elp to keep hathers stright.

BARBARA   So it will, Snobby. How much, Jenny?

JENNY   Four and tenpence, Major.

BARBARA   Oh Snobby, if you had given your poor mother just one more kick, we should have got the whole five shillings!

PRICE   If she heard you say that, miss, she'd be sorry I didnt. But I'm glad. Oh what a joy it will be to her when she hears I'm saved!

UNDERSHAFT   Shall I contribute the odd twopence, Barbara? The millionaire's mite, eh? [*He takes a couple of pennies from his pocket.*]

BARBARA   How did you make that twopence?

UNDERSHAFT   As usual. By selling cannons, torpedoes, submarines, and my new patent Grand Duke hand grenade.

BARBARA   Put it back in your pocket. You cant buy your salvation here for two pence: you must work it out.

UNDERSHAFT   Is twopence not enough? I can afford a little more, if you press me.

BARBARA   Two million millions would not be enough. There is bad blood on your hands; and nothing but good blood can cleanse them. Money is no use. Take it away. [*She turns to* CUSINS.] Dolly: you must write another letter for me to the papers. [*He makes a wry face.*] Yes: I know you dont like it; but it must be done. The starvation this winter is beating us: everybody is unemployed. The General says we must close this shelter if we cant get more money. I force the collections at the meetings until I am ashamed: dont I, Snobby?

PRICE   It's a fair treat to see you work it, miss. The way you got them up from three-and-six to four-and-ten with that hymn, penny by penny and verse by verse, was a caution. Not a Cheap Jack on Mile End Waste could touch you at it.[1]

BARBARA   Yes; but I wish we could do without it. I am getting at last to think more of the collection than of the people's souls. And what are those hatfuls of pence and halfpence? We want thousands! tens of thousands! hundreds of thousands! I want to convert people, not to be always begging for the Army in a way I'd die sooner than beg for myself.

UNDERSHAFT   [*in profound irony*]   Genuine unselfishness is capable of anything, my dear.

BARBARA   [*unsuspectingly, as she turns away to take the money from the drum and put it in a bag she carries*]   Yes, isnt it? [UNDERSHAFT *looks sardonically at* CUSINS.]

CUSINS   [*aside to* UNDERSHAFT]   Mephistopheles! Machiavelli![2]

BARBARA   [*tears coming into her eyes as she ties the bag and pockets it*]   How are we to feed them? I cant talk religion to a man with bodily hunger in his eyes. [*Almost breaking down.*] It's frightful.

JENNY   [*running to her*]   Major, dear—

BARBARA   [*rebounding*]   No: dont comfort me. It will be all right. We shall get the money.

---

1. A "Cheap Jack" is a street vendor who first puts a high price on his wares and then pretends to be offering a bargain by lowering it.
2. Mephistopheles is the name of a devil, best known as the familiar spirit of Dr. Faustus. Niccolo Machiavelli (1469–1527) was an Italian statesman and political theorist. Both are examples of cunning employed to wicked ends.

UNDERSHAFT   How?

JENNY   By praying for it, of course. Mrs Baines says she prayed for it last night; and she has never prayed for it in vain: never once. [*She goes to the gate and looks out into the street.*]

BARBARA [*who has dried her eyes and regained her composure*]   By the way, dad, Mrs Baines has come to march with us to our big meeting this afternoon; and she is very anxious to meet you, for some reason or other. Perhaps she'll convert you.

UNDERSHAFT   I shall be delighted, my dear.

JENNY [*at the gate: excitedly*]   Major! Major! heres that man back again.

BARBARA   What man?

JENNY   The man that hit me. Oh, I hope he's coming back to join us.

> BILL WALKER, *with frost on his jacket, comes through the gate, his hands deep in his pockets and his chin sunk between his shoulders, like a cleaned-out gambler. He halts between* BAR-BARA *and the drum.*

BARBARA   Hullo, Bill! Back already!

BILL [*nagging at her*]   Bin talkin ever sence, ev you?

BARBARA   Pretty nearly. Well, has Todger paid you out for poor Jenny's jaw?

BILL   Nao e aint.

BARBARA   I thought your jacket looked a bit snowy.

BILL   Sao it is snaowy. You want to knaow where the snaow cam from, downt you?

BARBARA   Yes.

BILL   Well, it cam from orf the grahnd in Pawkinses Corner in Kenintahn. It got rabbed orf be maw shaoulders: see?

BARBARA   Pity you didnt rub some off with your knees. Bill! That would have done you a lot of good.

BILL [*with sour mirthless humor*]   Aw was sivin anather menn's knees at the tawm. E was kneelin on moy ed, e was.

JENNY   Who was kneeling on your head?

BILL   Todger was. E was pryin for me: pryin camfortable wiv me as a cawpet. Sow was Mog. Sao was the aol bloomin meetin. Mog she says "Ow Lawd brike his stabborn sperrit; bat downt urt is dear art." Thet was wot she said. "Downt urt is dear art"! An er blowk— thirteen stun four!—kneelin wiv all is wight on me. Fanny, aint it?

JENNY   Oh no. We're so sorry, Mr Walker.

BARBARA [*enjoying it frankly*]   Nonsense! of course it's funny. Served you right, Bill! You must have done something to him first.

BILL [*doggedly*]   Aw did wot Aw said Aw'd do. Aw spit in is eye. E looks ap at the skoy and sez, "Ow that Aw should be fahnd worthy to be spit upon for the gospel's sike!" e sez; an Mog sez "Glaory Allelloolier!"; an then e called me Braddher, an dahned me as if Aw was a kid and e was me mather worshin me a Setterda nawt. Aw ednt jast nao shaow wiv im at all. Arf the street pryed; an the tather arf larfed fit to split theirselves. [*To* BARBARA.] There! are you settisfawd nah?

BARBARA [*her eyes dancing*]   Wish I'd been there, Bill.

BILL   Yus: youd a got in a hextra bit o talk on me, wouldnt you?

JENNY   I'm so sorry, Mr Walker.

BILL [*fiercely*]   Downt you gow bein sorry for me: youve no call. Listen eah. Aw browk your jawr.

JENNY   No, it didnt hurt me: indeed it didnt, except for a moment. It was only that I was frightened.

BILL   Aw downt want to be forgive be you, or be ennybody. Wot Aw did Aw'll py for. Aw trawd to gat me aown jawr browk to settisfaw you—

JENNY [*distressed*]   Oh no—

BILL [*impatiently*]   Tell y' Aw did: cawnt you listen to wots bein taold you? All Aw got be it was bein mide a sawt of in the pablic street for me pines. Well, if Aw cawnt settisfaw you one wy, Aw ken another. Listen eah! Aw ed two quid sived agen the frost; an Awve a pahnd of it left. A mite o mawn last week ed words with the judy e's gowin to merry. E give er wot-for; an e's bin fawnd fifteen bob. E ed a rawt to itt er cause they was gowin to be merrid; but Aw ednt nao rawt to itt you; sao put another fawv bob on an call it a pahnd's worth. [*He produces a sovereign.*][3] Eahs the manney. Tike it; and lets ev no more o your forgivin an pryin and your Mijor jawrin me. Let wot Aw dan be dan an pide for; and let there be a end of it.

JENNY   Oh, I couldnt take it, Mr Walker. But if you would give a shilling or two to poor Rummy Mitchens! you really did hurt her; and she's old.

BILL [*contemptuously*]   Not lawkly. Aw'd give her anather as soon as look at er. Let her ev the lawr o me as she threatened! S h e aint forgiven me: not mach. Wot Aw dan to er is not on me mawnd— wot she [*indicating* BARBARA] mawt call on me conscience—no more than stickin a pig. It's this Christian gime o yours that Aw wownt ev plyed agen me: this bloomin forgivin an neggin an jawrin that mikes a menn thet sore that iz lawf's a burdn to im. Aw wownt ev it, Aw tell you; sao tike your manney and stop thraowin your silly beshed fice hap agen me.

JENNY   Major: may I take a little of it for the Army?

BARBARA   No: the Army is not to be bought. We want your soul, Bill; and we'll take nothing less.

BILL [*bitterly*]   Aw knaow. Me an maw few shillins is not good enaff for you. Youre a earl's grendorter, you are. Nathink less than a anderd pahnd for you.

UNDERSHAFT   Come, Barbara! you could do a great deal of good with a hundred pounds. If you will set this gentleman's mind at ease by taking his pound, I will give the other ninety-nine.

BILL, *dazed by such opulence, instinctively touches his cap.*

BARBARA   Oh, youre too extravagant, papa. Bill offers twenty pieces of silver. All you need offer is the other ten.[4] That will make the standard price to buy anybody who's for sale. I'm not; and the Army's not. [*To* BILL.] Youll never have another quiet moment, Bill, until you come round to us. You cant stand out against your salvation.

---

3. "Quid" and "bob" are colloquial terms for pound and shilling, respectively. A sovereign is a gold coin worth one pound.

4. Barbara alludes to the betrayal of Jesus by Judas for thirty pieces of silver. Bill's sovereign is the same as twenty shillings.

BILL [*sullenly*]   Aw cawnt stend aht agen music awl wrastlers and awtful tangued women. Awve offered to py. Aw can do no more. Tike it or leave it. There it is. [*He throws the sovereign on the drum, and sits down on the horse-trough. The coin fascinates* SNOBBY PRICE, *who takes an early opportunity of dropping his cap on it.*]

> MRS BAINES *comes from the shelter. She is dressed as a Salvation Army Commissioner. She is an earnest looking woman of about 40, with a caressing, urgent voice, and an appealing manner.*

BARBARA   This is my father, Mrs Baines. [UNDERSHAFT *comes from the table, taking his hat off with marked civility.*] Try what you can do with him. He wont listen to me, because he remembers what a fool I was when I was a baby. [*She leaves them together and chats with* JENNY.]

MRS BAINES   Have you been shewn over the shelter, Mr Undershaft? You know the work we're doing, of course.

UNDERSHAFT [*very civilly*]   The whole nation knows it, Mrs Baines.

MRS BAINES   No, sir: the whole nation does not know it, or we should not be crippled as we are for want of money to carry our work through the length and breadth of the land. Let me tell you that there would have been rioting this winter in London but for us.

UNDERSHAFT   You really think so?

MRS BAINES   I know it. I remember 1886, when you rich gentlemen hardened your hearts against the cry of the poor. They broke the windows of your clubs in Pall Mall.[5]

UNDERSHAFT [*gleaming with approval of their method*]   And the Mansion House Fund went up next day from thirty thousand pounds to seventy-nine thousand! I remember quite well.

MRS BAINES   Well, wont you help me to get at the people? They wont break windows then. Come here, Price. Let me shew you to this gentleman. [PRICE *comes to be inspected.*] Do you remember the window breaking?

PRICE   My ole father thought it was the revolution, maam.

MRS BAINES   Would you break windows now?

PRICE   Oh no, maam. The windows of eaven av bin opened to me. I know now that the rich man is a sinner like myself.

RUMMY [*appearing above at the loft door*]   Snobby Price!

PRICE   Wot is it?

RUMMY   Your mother's askin for you at the other gate in Cripps's Lane. She's heard about your confession. [PRICE *turns pale.*]

MRS BAINES   Go, Mr Price; and pray with her.

JENNY   You can go through the shelter, Snobby.

PRICE [*to* MRS BAINES]   I couldnt face her now, maam, with all the weight of my sins fresh on me. Tell her she'll find her son at ome, waitin for her in prayer. [*He skulks off through the gate, incidentally*

---

5. Pall Mall is a spacious street extending from St. James Street to the foot of the Haymarket, notable for the many fashionable clubs there. (Pepys went "clubbing" there.) Trafalgar Square is nearby, and on February 8, 1886, a meeting in the Square about unemployment was apparently taken over by a group from the Social Democratic Federation, who turned the crowd into a mob and led them through Pall Mall, St. James Street, Piccadilly, and other nearby areas, breaking the windows of clubs, overturning carriages, and committing other acts of vandalism. It was several hours before the police, who had expected no trouble, were able to bring the crowd under control, with aid from the army.

stealing the sovereign on his way out by picking up his cap from the drum.]

MRS BAINES [*with swimming eyes*] You see how we take the anger and the bitterness against you out of their hearts, Mr Undershaft.

UNDERSHAFT It is certainly most convenient and gratifying to all large employers of labor, Mrs Baines.

MRS BAINES Barbara: Jenny: I have good news: most wonderful news. [JENNY *runs to her.*] My prayers have been answered. I told you they would, Jenny, didnt I?

JENNY Yes, yes.

BARBARA [*moving nearer to the drum*] Have we got money enough to keep the shelter open?

MRS BAINES I hope we shall have enough to keep all the shelters open. Lord Saxmundham has promised us five thousand pounds—

BARBARA Hooray!

JENNY Glory!

MRS BAINES —if—

BARBARA "If!" If what?

MRS BAINES —if five other gentlemen will give a thousand each to make it up to ten thousand.

BARBARA Who is Lord Saxmundham? I never heard of him.

UNDERSHAFT [*who has pricked up his ears at the peer's name, and is now watching* BARBARA *curiously*] A new creation, my dear. You have heard of Sir Horace Bodger?

BARBARA Bodger! Do you mean the distiller? Bodger's whisky!

UNDERSHAFT That is the man. He is one of the greatest of our public benefactors. He restored the cathedral at Hakington. They made him a baronet for that. He gave half a million to the funds of his party: they made him a baron for that.

SHIRLEY What will they give him for the five thousand?

UNDERSHAFT There is nothing left to give him. So the five thousand, I should think, is to save his soul.

MRS BAINES Heaven grant it may! Oh Mr Undershaft, you have some very rich friends. Cant you help us towards the other five thousand? We are going to hold a great meeting this afternoon at the Assembly Hall in the Mile End Road. If I could only announce that one gentleman had come forward to support Lord Saxmundham, others would follow. Dont you know somebody? couldnt you? wouldnt you? [*Her eyes fill with tears.*] Oh, think of those poor people, Mr Undershaft: think of how much it means to them, and how little to a great man like you.

UNDERSHAFT [*sardonically gallant*] Mrs Baines: you are irresistible. I cant disappoint you; and I cant deny myself the satisfaction of making Bodger pay up. You shall have your five thousand pounds.

MRS BAINES Thank God!

UNDERSHAFT You dont thank m e?

MRS BAINES Oh sir, dont try to be cynical: dont be ashamed of being a good man. The Lord will bless you abundantly; and our prayers will be like a strong fortification round you all the days of your life. [*With a touch of caution.*] You will let me have the cheque to shew at the meeting, wont you? Jenny: go in and fetch a pen and ink. [JENNY *runs to the shelter door.*]

UNDERSHAFT Do not disturb Miss Hill: I have a fountain pen. [JENNY *halts. He sits at the table and writes the cheque.* CUSINS *rises to make room for him. They all watch him silently.*]

BILL [*cynically, aside to* BARBARA, *his voice and accent horribly debased*] Wot prawce selvytion nah?

BARBARA Stop. [UNDERSHAFT *stops writing: they all turn to her in surprise.*] Mrs Baines: are you really going to take this money?

MRS BAINES [*astonished*] Why not, dear?

BARBARA Why not! Do you know what my father is? Have you forgotten that Lord Saxmundham is Bodger the whisky man? Do you remember how we implored the County Council to stop him from writing Bodger's Whisky in letters of fire against the sky; so that the poor drink-ruined creatures on the Embankment could not wake up from their snatches of sleep without being reminded of their deadly thirst by that wicked sky sign? Do you know that the worst thing I have had to fight here is not the devil, but Bodger, Bodger, Bodger, with his whisky, his distilleries, and his tied houses?[6] Are you going to make our shelter another tied house for him, and ask me to keep it?

BILL Rotten dranken whisky it is too.

MRS BAINES Dear Barbara: Lord Saxmundham has a soul to be saved like any of us. If heaven has found the way to make a good use of his money, are we to set ourselves up against the answer to our prayers?

BARBARA I know he has a soul to be saved. Let him come down here; and I'll do my best to help him to his salvation. But he wants to send his cheque down to buy us, and go on being as wicked as ever.

UNDERSHAFT [*with a reasonableness which* CUSINS *alone perceives to be ironical*] My dear Barbara: alcohol is a very necessary article. It heals the sick—

BARBARA It does nothing of the sort.

UNDERSHAFT Well, it assists the doctor: that is perhaps a less questionable way of putting it. It makes life bearable to millions of people who could not endure their existence if they were quite sober. It enables Parliament to do things at eleven at night that no sane person would do at eleven in the morning. Is it Bodger's fault that this inestimable gift is deplorably abused by less than one per cent of the poor? [*He turns again to the table; signs the cheque; and crosses it.*]

MRS BAINES Barbara: will there be less drinking or more if all those poor souls we are saving come tomorrow and find the doors of our shelters shut in their faces? Lord Saxmundham gives us the money to stop drinking—to take his own business from him.

CUSINS [*impishly*] Pure self-sacrifice on Bodger's part, clearly! Bless dear Bodger! [BARBARA *almost breaks down as* ADOLPHUS, *too, fails her.*]

UNDERSHAFT [*tearing out the cheque and pocketing the book as he rises and goes past* CUSINS *to* MRS BAINES] I also, Mrs Baines, may claim a little disinterestedness. Think of my business! think of the widows and orphans! the men and lads torn to pieces with shrapnel and poisoned with lyddite![7] [MRS BAINES *shrinks; but he goes on remorselessly*] the oceans of blood, not one drop of which is shed in a

---

6. Inns or public houses whose operators are required to buy their potables from a particular brewery, which often owns the "tied house."

7. A high explosive, made up mainly of picric acid.

really just cause! the ravaged crops! the peaceful peasant forced, women and men, to till their fields, under the fire of opposing armies on pain of starvation! the bad blood of the fierce little cowards at home who egg on others to fight for the gratification of their national vanity! All this makes money for me: I am never richer, never busier than when the papers are full of it. Well, it is your work to preach peace on earth and goodwill to men. [MRS BAINES's *face lights up again.*] Every convert you make is a vote against war. [*Her lips move in prayer.*] Yet I give you this money to help you to hasten my own commercial ruin. [*He gives her the cheque.*]

CUSINS [*mounting the form in an ecstasy of mischief*]   The millennium will be inaugurated by the unselfishness of Undershaft and Bodger.[8] Oh be joyful! [*He takes the drum-sticks from his pocket and flourishes them.*]

MRS BAINES [*taking the cheque*]   The longer I live the more proof I see that there is an Infinite Goodness that turns everything to the work of salvation sooner or later. Who would have thought that any good could have come out of war and drink? And yet their profits are brought today to the feet of salvation to do its blessed work. [*She is affected to tears.*]

JENNY [*running to* MRS BAINES *and throwing her arms around her*]   Oh dear! how blessed, how glorious it all is!

CUSINS [*in a convulsion of irony*]   Let us seize this unspeakable moment. Let us march to the great meeting at once. Excuse me just an instant. [*He rushes into the shelter.* JENNY *takes her tambourine from the drum head.*]

MRS BAINES   Mr Undershaft: have you ever seen a thousand people fall on their knees with one impulse and pray? Come with us to the meeting. Barbara shall tell them that the Army is saved, and saved through you.

CUSINS [*returning impetuously from the shelter with a flag and a trombone, and coming between* MRS BAINES *and* UNDERSHAFT]   You shall carry the flag down the first street, Mrs Baines. [*He gives her the flag.*] Mr Undershaft is a gifted trombonist: he shall intone an Olympian diapason to the West Ham Salvation March.[9] [*Aside to* UNDERSHAFT, *as he forces the trombone on him.*] Blow, Machiavelli, blow.

UNDERSHAFT [*aside to him, as he takes the trombone*]   The trumpet in Zion! [CUSINS *rushes to the drum which he takes up and puts on.* UNDERSHAFT *continues, aloud.*] I will do my best. I could vamp a bass if I knew the tune.

CUSINS   It is a wedding chorus from one of Donizetti's operas; but we have converted it. We convert everything to good here, including Bodger. You remember the chorus. "For thee immense rejoicing— immenso giubilo—immenso giubilo."[1] [*With drum obbligato.*] Rum tum ti tum, tum tum ti ta—

BARBARA   Dolly: you are breaking my heart.

CUSINS   What is a broken heart more or less here? Dionysos Undershaft has descended. I am possessed.

---

8. A "millennium" is a period of universal harmony and prosperity like that described in *Revelation* 20.
9. "Diapason" is a musical term, used here to imply that Undershaft's trombone will provide a sublime accompaniment to the music of the band.
1. A reference to the wedding chorus in *Lucia di Lammermoor*, Act 2, which begins "Per te d'immenso giubilo."

MRS BAINES   Come, Barbara: I must have my dear Major to carry the flag with me.

JENNY   Yes, yes, Major darling.

CUSINS *snatches the tambourine out of* JENNY's *hand and mutely offers it to* BARBARA.

BARBARA [*coming forward a little as she puts the offer behind her with a shudder, whilst* CUSINS *recklessly tosses the tambourine back to* JENNY *and goes to the gate*]   I cant come.

JENNY   Not come!

MRS BAINES [*with tears in her eyes*]   Barbara: do you think I am wrong to take the money?

BARBARA [*impulsively going to her and kissing her*]   No, no: God help you, dear, you must: you are saving the Army. Go; and may you have a great meeting!

JENNY   But arnt you coming?

BARBARA . . No. [*She begins taking off the silver S brooch from her collar.*]

MRS BAINES   Barbara: what are you doing?

JENNY   Why are you taking your badge off? You cant be going to leave us, Major.

BARBARA [*quietly*]   Father: come here.

UNDERSHAFT [*coming to her*]   My dear! [*Seeing that she is going to pin the badge on his collar, he retreats to the penthouse in some alarm.*]

BARBARA [*following him*]   Dont be frightened. [*She pins the badge on and steps back towards the table, shewing him to the others.*] There! It's not much for £ 5000, is it?

MRS BAINES   Barbara: if you wont come and pray w i t h us, promise me you will pray f o r us.

BARBARA   I cant pray now. Perhaps I shall never pray again.

MRS BAINES   Barbara!

JENNY   Major!

BARBARA [*almost delirious*]   I cant bear any more. Quick march!

CUSINS [*calling to the procession in the street outside*]   Off we go. Play up, there! I m m e n s o g i u b i l o. [*He gives the time with his drum; and the band strikes up the march, which rapidly becomes more distant as the procession moves briskly away.*]

MRS BAINES   I must go, dear. Youre overworked: you will be all right tomorrow. We'll never lose you. Now Jenny: step out with the old flag. Blood and Fire! [*She marches out through the gate with her flag.*]

JENNY   Glory Hallelujah! [*Flourishing her tambourine and marching.*]

UNDERSHAFT [*to* CUSINS, *as he marches out past him easing the slide of his trombone*]   "My ducats and my daughter"![2]

CUSINS [*following him out*]   Money and gunpowder!

BARBARA   Drunkenness and Murder! My God: why hast thou forsaken me?

She sinks on the form with her face buried in her hands. The march passes away into silence. BILL WALKER *steals across to her.*

2. In Act 2, scene 8 of Shakespeare's *The Merchant of Venice*, Salanio tells Salarino of Shylock's discovery of Jessica's elopement and of the loss of the money she carried with her. Shylock is there reported to have cried, among other things, "My ducats and my daughter!"

BILL [*taunting*]   Wot prawce selvytion nah?

SHIRLEY   Dont you hit her when she's down.

BILL   She itt me wen aw wiz dahn. Waw shouldnt Aw git a bit o me aown beck?

BARBARA [*raising her head*]   I didnt take y o u r money, Bill. [*She crosses the yard to the gate and turns her back on the two men to hide her face from them.*]

BILL [*sneering after her*]   Naow, it warnt enaff for you. [*Turning to the drum, he misses the money.*] Ellow! If you aint took it sammun else ez. Weres it gorn? Bly me if Jenny Ill didnt tike it arter all!

RUMMY [*screaming at him from the loft*]   You lie, you dirty black-guard! Snobby Price pinched it off the drum when he took up his cap. I was up here all the time an see im do it.

BILL   Wot! Stowl maw manney! Waw didnt you call thief on him, you silly aold macker you?

RUMMY   To serve you aht for ittin me acrost the fice. It's cost y'pahnd, that az. [*Raising a paean of squalid triumph.*] I done you. I'm even with you. Ive ad it aht o y— [BILL *snatches up* SHIRLEY's *mug and hurls it at her. She slams the loft door and vanishes. The mug smashes against the door and falls in fragments.*]

BILL [*beginning to chuckle*]   Tell us, aol menn, wot o'clock this mawnin was it wen im as they call Snobby Prawce was sived?

BARBARA [*turning to him more composedly, and with unspoiled sweetness*]   About half past twelve, Bill. And he pinched your pound at a quarter to two. *I* know. Well, you cant afford to lose it. I'll send it to you.

BILL [*his voice and accent suddenly improving*]   Not if Aw wiz to stawve for it. Aw aint to be bought.

SHIRLEY   Aint you? Youd sell yourself to the devil for a pint o beer; ony there aint no devil to make the offer.

BILL [*unshamed*]   Sao Aw would, mite, and often ev, cheerful. But she cawnt baw me. [*Approaching* BARBARA.] You wanted maw saoul, did you? Well, you aint got it.

BARBARA   I nearly got it, Bill. But weve sold it back to you for ten thousand pounds.

SHIRLEY   And dear at the money!

BARBARA   No, Peter: it was worth more than money.

BILL [*salvationproof*]   It's nao good: you cawnt get rahnd me nah. Aw downt blieve in it; and Awve seen tody that Aw was rawt. [*Going.*] Sao long, aol soupkitchener! Ta, ta, Mijor Earl's Grendorter! [*Turning at the gate.*] Wot prawce selvytion nah? Snobby Prawce! Ha! ha!

BARBARA [*offering her hand*]   Goodbye, Bill.

BILL [*taken aback, half plucks his cap off; then shoves it on again defiantly*]   Git aht. [BARBARA *drops her hand, discouraged. He has a twinge of remorse.*] But thets aw rawt, you knaow. Nathink pasnl. Naow mellice. Sao long, Judy. [*He goes.*]

BARBARA   No malice. So long, Bill.

SHIRLEY [*shaking his head*]   You make too much of him, miss, in your innocence.

BARBARA [*going to him*]   Peter: I'm like you now. Cleaned out, and lost my job.

SHIRLEY   Youve youth an hope. Thats two better than me.

BARBARA   I'll get you a job, Peter. Thats hope for you: the youth will have to be enough for me. [*She counts her money.*] I have just enough left for two teas at Lockharts, a Rowton doss[3] for you, and my tram and bus home. [*He frowns and rises with offended pride. She takes his arm.*] Dont be proud, Peter: it's sharing between friends. And promise me youll talk to me and not let me cry. [*She draws him towards the gate.*]

SHIRLEY   Well, I'm not accustomed to talk to the like of you—

BARBARA [*urgently*]   Yes, yes: you must talk to me. Tell me about Tom Paine's books and Bradlaugh's lectures.[4] Come along.

SHIRLEY   Ah, if you would only read Tom Paine in the proper spirit, miss! [*They go out through the gate together.*]

Act 3

Next day after lunch LADY BRITOMART *is writing in the library in Wilton Crescent.* SARAH *is reading in the armchair near the window.* BARBARA, *in ordinary fashionable dress, pale and brooding, is on the settee.* CHARLES LOMAX *enters. He starts on seeing* BARBARA *fashionably attired and in low spirits.*

LOMAX   Youve left off your uniform!

BARBARA *says nothing; but an expression of pain passes over her face.*

LADY BRITOMART [*warning him in low tones to be careful*]   Charles!

LOMAX [*much concerned, coming behind the settee and bending sympathetically over* BARBARA]   I'm awfully sorry, Barbara. You know I helped you all I could with the concertina and so forth. [*Momentously.*] Still, I have never shut my eyes to the fact that there is a certain amout of tosh about the Salvation Army. Now the claims of the Church of England—

LADY BRITOMART   Thats enough, Charles. Speak of something suited to your mental capacity.

LOMAX   But surely the Church of England is suited to all our capacities.

BARBARA [*pressing his hand*]   Thank you for your sympathy, Cholly. Now go and spoon with Sarah.

LOMAX [*dragging a chair from the writing table and seating himself affectionately by* SARAH'*s side*]   How is my ownest today?

SARAH   I wish you wouldnt tell Cholly to do things, Barbara. He always comes straight and does them. Cholly: we're going to the works this afternoon.

LOMAX   What works?

SARAH   The cannon works.

LOMAX   What? your governor's shop!

SARAH   Yes.

3. A Rowton House was a subsidized institution providing inexpensive lodging for indigents. A "doss house" or "doss" is a slang term for a cheap or low-class rooming house.

4. Tom Paine (1737–1809) was the free-thinking author of *Common Sense* and *The Rights of Man*, who figured in both the French and American Revolutions. Charles Bradlaugh (1833–1891) was a notable English Freethinker and leader in the Secularist movement.

LOMAX   Oh I say!

> CUSINS *enters in poor condition. He also starts visibly when he sees* BARBARA *without her uniform.*

BARBARA   I expected you this morning, Dolly. Didnt you guess that?

CUSINS [*sitting down beside her*]   I'm sorry. I have only just breakfasted.

SARAH   But weve just finished lunch.

BARBARA   Have you had one of your bad nights?

CUSINS   No: I had rather a good night: in fact, one of the most remarkable nights I have ever passed.

BARBARA   The meeting?

CUSINS   No: after the meeting.

LADY BRITOMART   You should have gone to bed after the meeting. What were you doing?

CUSINS   Drinking.

LADY BRITOMART	Adolphus!
SARAH	Dolly!
BARBARA	Dolly!
LOMAX	Oh I say!

LADY BRITOMART   What were you drinking, may I ask?

CUSINS   A most devilish kind of Spanish burgundy, warranted free from added alcohol: a Temperance burgundy in fact. Its richness in natural alcohol made any addition superfluous.

BARBARA   Are you joking, Dolly?

CUSINS [*patiently*]   No. I have been making a night of it with the nominal head of this household: that is all.

LADY BRITOMART   Andrew made you drunk!

CUSINS   No: he only provided the wine. I think it was Dionysos who made me drunk. [*To* BARBARA.] I told you I was possessed.

LADY BRITOMART   Youre not sober yet. Go home to bed at once.

CUSINS   I have never before ventured to reproach you, Lady Brit; but how could you marry the Prince of Darkness?

LADY BRITOMART   It was much more excusable to marry him than to get drunk with him. That is a new accomplishment of Andrew's, by the way. He usent to drink.

CUSINS   He doesnt now. He only sat there and completed the wreck of my moral basis, the rout of my convictions, the purchase of my soul. He cares for you, Barbara. That is what makes him so dangerous to me.

BARBARA   That has nothing to do with it, Dolly. There are larger loves and diviner dreams than the fireside ones. You know that, dont you?

CUSINS   Yes: that is our understanding. I know it. I hold to it. Unless he can win me on that holier ground he may amuse me for a while; but he can get no deeper hold, strong as he is.

BARBARA   Keep to that; and the end will be right. Now tell me what happened at the meeting?

CUSINS   It was an amazing meeting. Mrs Baines almost died of emotion. Jenny Hill simply gibbered with hysteria. The Prince of Darkness played his trombone like a madman: its brazen roarings were like the laughter of the damned. 117 conversions took place then and there. They prayed with the most touching sincerity and gratitude for Bodger, and for the anonymous donor of the £ 5000. Your father would not let his name be given.

LOMAX   That was rather fine of the old man, you know. Most chaps would have wanted the advertisement.

CUSINS   He said all the charitable institutions would be down on him like kites on a battle-field if he gave his name.

LADY BRITOMART   Thats Andrew all over. He never does a proper thing without giving an improper reason for it.

CUSINS   He convinced me that I have all my life been doing improper things for proper reasons.

LADY BRITOMART   Adolphus: now that Barbara has left the Salvation Army, you had better leave it too. I will not have you playing that drum in the streets.

CUSINS   Your orders are already obeyed, Lady Brit.

BARBARA   Dolly: were you ever really in earnest about it? Would you have joined if you had never seen me?

CUSINS [*disingenuously*]   Well—er—well, possibly, as a collector of religions—

LOMAX [*cunningly*]   Not as a drummer, though, you know. You are a very clearheaded brainy chap, Dolly; and it must have been apparent to you that there is a certain amount of tosh about—

LADY BRITOMART   Charles: if you must drivel, drivel like a grown-up man and not like a schoolboy.

LOMAX [*out of countenance*]   Well, drivel is drivel, dont you know, whatever a man's age.

LADY BRITOMART   In good society in England, Charles, men drivel at all ages by repeating silly formulas with an air of wisdom. Schoolboys make their own formulas out of slang, like you. When they reach your age, and get political private secretaryships and things of that sort, they drop slang and get their formulas out of The Spectator or The Times. Y o u had better confine yourself to The Times. You will find that there is a certain amount of tosh about The Times; but at least its language is reputable.

LOMAX [*overwhelmed*]   You are so awfully strong-minded, Lady Brit—

LADY BRITOMART   Rubbish! [MORRISON *comes in.*] What is it?

MORRISON   If you please, my lady, Mr Undershaft has just drove up to the door.

LADY BRITOMART   Well, let him in. [MORRISON *hesitates.*] Whats the matter with you?

MORRISON   Shall I announce him, my lady; or is he at home here, so to speak, my lady?

LADY BRITOMART   Announce him.

MORRISON   Thank you, my lady. You wont mind my asking, I hope. The occasion is in a manner of speaking new to me.

LADY BRITOMART   Quite right. Go and let him in.

MORRISON   Thank you, my lady. [*He withdraws.*]

LADY BRITOMART   Children: go and get ready. [SARAH *and* BARBARA *go upstairs for their out-of-door wraps.*] Charles: go and tell Stephen to come down here in five minutes: you will find him in the drawing room. [CHARLES *goes.*] Adolphus: tell them to send round the carriage in about fifteen minutes. [ADOLPHUS *goes.*]

MORRISON [*at the door*]   Mr Undershaft.

UNDERSHAFT *comes in.* MORRISON *goes out.*

UNDERSHAFT   Alone! How fortunate!

LADY BRITOMART [*rising*]   Dont be sentimental, Andrew. Sit down. [*She sits on the settee: he sits beside her, on her left. She comes to the point before he has time to breathe.*] Sarah must have £ 800 a year until Charles Lomax comes into his property. Barbara will need more, and need it permanently, because Adolphus hasnt any property.

UNDERSHAFT [*resignedly*]   Yes, my dear: I will see to it. Anything else? for yourself, for instance?

LADY BRITOMART   I want to talk to you about Stephen.

UNDERSHAFT [*rather wearily*]   Dont, my dear. Stephen doesnt interest me.

LADY BRITOMART   He does interest me. He is our son.

UNDERSHAFT   Do you really think so? He has induced us to bring him into the world; but he chose his parents very incongruously, I think. I see nothing of myself in him, and less of you.

LADY BRITOMART   Andrew: Stephen is an excellent son, and a most steady, capable, highminded young man. You are simply trying to find an excuse for disinheriting him.

UNDERSHAFT   My dear Biddy: the Undershaft tradition disinherits him. It would be dishonest of me to leave the cannon foundry to my son.

LADY BRITOMART   It would be most unnatural and improper of you to leave it to anyone else, Andrew. Do you suppose this wicked and immoral tradition can be kept up for ever? Do you pretend that Stephen could not carry on the foundry just as well as all the other sons of the big business houses?

UNDERSHAFT   Yes: he could learn the office routine without understanding the business, like all the other sons; and the firm would go on by its own momentum until the real Undershaft—probably an Italian or a German—would invent a new method and cut him out.

LADY BRITOMART   There is nothing that any Italian or German could do that Stephen could not do. And Stephen at least has breeding.

UNDERSHAFT   The son of a foundling! Nonsense!

LADY BRITOMART   My son, Andrew! And even you may have good blood in your veins for all you know.

UNDERSHAFT   True. Probably I have. That is another argument in favor of a foundling.

LADY BRITOMART   Andrew: dont be aggravating. And dont be wicked. At present you are both.

UNDERSHAFT   This conversation is part of the Undershaft tradition, Biddy. Every Undershaft's wife has treated him to it ever since the house was founded. It is mere waste of breath. If the tradition be ever broken it will be for an abler man than Stephen.

LADY BRITOMART [*pouting*]   Then go away.

UNDERSHAFT [*deprecatory*]   Go away!

LADY BRITOMART   Yes: go away. If you will do nothing for Stephen, you are not wanted here. Go to your foundling, whoever he is; and look after h i m.

UNDERSHAFT   The fact is, Biddy—

LADY BRITOMART   Dont call me Biddy. I dont call you Andy.

UNDERSHAFT   I will not call my wife Britomart: it is not good sense. Seriously, my love, the Undershaft tradition has landed me in a difficulty. I am getting on in years; and my partner Lazarus has at last made a stand and insisted that the succession must be settled one way or the other; and of course he is quite right. You see, I havnt found a fit successor yet.

LADY BRITOMART [*obstinately*]   There is Stephen.

UNDERSHAFT   Thats just it: all the foundlings I can find are exactly like Stephen.

LADY BRITOMART   Andrew!!

UNDERSHAFT   I want a man with no relations and no schooling: that is, a man who would be out of the running altogether if he were not a strong man. And I cant find him. Every blessed foundling nowadays is snapped up in his infancy by Barnardo homes, or School Board officers, or Boards of Guardians;[5] and if he shews the least ability he is fastened on by schoolmasters; trained to win scholarships like a race-horse; crammed with secondhand ideas; drilled and disciplined in docility and what they call good taste; and lamed for life so that he is fit for nothing but teaching. If you want to keep the foundry in the family, you had better find an eligible foundling and marry him to Barbara.

LADY BRITOMART   Ah! Barbara! Your pet! You would sacrifice Stephen to Barbara.

UNDERSHAFT   Cheerfully. And you, my dear, would boil Barbara to make soup for Stephen.

LADY BRITOMART   Andrew: this is not a question of our likings and dislikings: it is a question of duty. It is your duty to make Stephen your successor.

UNDERSHAFT   Just as much as it is your duty to submit to your husband. Come, Biddy! these tricks of the governing class are of no use with me. I am one of the governing class myself; and it is a waste of time giving tracts to a missionary. I have the power in this matter; and I am not to be humbugged into using it for your purposes.

LADY BRITOMART   Andrew: you can talk my head off; but you cant change wrong into right. And your tie is all on one side. Put it straight.

UNDERSHAFT [*disconcerted*]   It wont stay unless it's pinned— [*He fumbles at it with childish grimaces.*]

STEPHEN *comes in.*

STEPHEN [*at the door*]   I beg your pardon. [*About to retire.*]

LADY BRITOMART   No: come in, Stephen. [STEPHEN *comes forward to his mother's writing table.*]

UNDERSHAFT [*not very cordially*]   Good afternoon.

STEPHEN [*coldly*]   Good afternoon.

UNDERSHAFT [*to* LADY BRITOMART]   He knows all about the tradition, I suppose?

LADY BRITOMART   Yes. [*To* STEPHEN.]   It is what I told you last night, Stephen.

UNDERSHAFT [*sulkily*]   I understand you want to come into the cannon business.

STEPHEN   *I* go into trade! Certainly not.

5. The Barnardo Homes (founded 1866–67) are private institutions for the care of orphans. Public responsibility for orphans in Great Britain centered on the Boards of Guardians for the various parish workhouses or poorhouses. In larger parishes or groups of parishes orphans were separated from other paupers. In some cases separate schools were maintained; in others they attended the local schools.

UNDERSHAFT [*opening his eyes, greatly eased in mind and manner*]
Oh! in that case—

LADY BRITOMART   Cannons are not trade, Stephen. They are enterprise.

STEPHEN   I have no intention of becoming a man of business in any
sense. I have no capacity for business and no taste for it. I intend to
devote myself to politics.

UNDERSHAFT [*rising*]   My dear boy: this is an immense relief to me.
And I trust it may prove an equally good thing for the country. I
was afraid you would consider yourself disparaged and slighted. [*He
moves towards* STEPHEN *as if to shake hands with him.*]

LADY BRITOMART [*rising and interposing*]   Stephen: I cannot allow
you to throw away an enormous property like this.

STEPHEN [*stiffly*]   Mother: there must be an end of treating me as a
child, if you please. [LADY BRITOMART *recoils, deeply wounded by his
tone.*] Until last night I did not take your attitude seriously, because
I did not think you meant it seriously. But I find now that you left
me in the dark as to matters which you should have explained to me
years ago. I am extremely hurt and offended. Any further discussion
of my intentions had better take place with my father, as between
one man and another.

LADY BRITOMART   Stephen! [*She sits down again, her eyes filling with
tears.*]

UNDERSHAFT [*with grave compassion*]   You see, my dear, it is only the
big men who can be treated as children.

STEPHEN   I am sorry, mother, that you have forced me—

UNDERSHAFT [*stopping him*]   Yes, yes, yes, yes: thats all right, Stephen. She wont interfere with you any more: your independence is
achieved: you have won your latchkey. Dont rub it in; and above all,
dont apologize. [*He resumes his seat.*] Now what about your future,
as between one man and another—I beg your pardon, Biddy: as between two men and a woman.

LADY BRITOMART [*who has pulled herself together strongly*]   I quite
understand, Stephen. By all means go your own way if you feel
strong enough. [STEPHEN *sits down magisterially in the chair at the
writing table with an air of affirming his majority.*]

UNDERSHAFT   It is settled that you do not ask for the succession to the
cannon business.

STEPHEN   I hope it is settled that I repudiate the cannon business.

UNDERSHAFT   Come, come! dont be so devilishly sulky: it's boyish.
Freedom should be generous. Besides, I owe you a fair start in life in
exchange for disinheriting you. You cant become prime minister all
at once. Havnt you a turn for something? What about literature, art,
and so forth?

STEPHEN   I have nothing of the artist about me, either in faculty or
character, thank Heaven!

UNDERSHAFT   A philosopher, perhaps? Eh?

STEPHEN   I make no such ridiculous pretension.

UNDERSHAFT   Just so. Well, there is the army, the navy, the Church,
the Bar. The Bar requires some ability. What about the Bar?

STEPHEN   I have not studied law. And I am afraid I have not the necessary push—I believe that is the name barristers give to their vulgarity—for success in pleading.

UNDERSHAFT   Rather a difficult case, Stephen. Hardly anything left but the stage, is there? [STEPHEN *makes an impatient movement.*] Well, come! is there a n y t h i n g you know or care for?

STEPHEN [*rising and looking at him steadily*]   I know the difference between right and wrong.

UNDERSHAFT [*hugely tickled*]   You dont say so! What! no capacity for business, no knowledge of law, no sympathy with art, no pretension to philosophy; only a simple knowledge of the secret that has puzzled all the philosophers, baffled all the lawyers, muddled all the men of business, and ruined most of the artists: the secret of right and wrong. Why, man, youre a genius, a master of masters, a god! At twentyfour, too!

STEPHEN [*keeping his temper with difficulty*]   You are pleased to be facetious. I pretend to nothing more than any honorable English gentleman claims as his birthright. [*He sits down angrily.*]

UNDERSHAFT   Oh, thats everybody's birthright. Look at poor little Jenny Hill, the Salvation lassie! she would think you were laughing at her if you asked her to stand up in the street and teach grammar or geography or mathematics or even drawing room dancing; but it never occurs to her to doubt that she can teach morals and religion. You are all alike, you respectable people. You cant tell me the bursting strain of a ten-inch gun, which is a very simple matter; but you all think you can tell me the bursting strain of a man under temptation. You darent handle high explosives; but youre all ready to handle honesty and truth and justice and the whole duty of man, and kill one another at that game. What a country! What a world!

LADY BRITOMART [*uneasily*]   What do you think he had better do, Andrew?

UNDERSHAFT   Oh, just what he wants to do. He knows nothing and he thinks he knows everything. That points clearly to a political career. Get him a private secretaryship to someone who can get him an Under Secretaryship; and then leave him alone. He will find his natural and proper place in the end on the Treasury Bench.

STEPHEN [*springing up again*]   I am sorry, sir, that you force me to forget the respect due to you as my father. I am an Englishman and I will not hear the Government of my country insulted. [*He thrusts his hands in his pockets, and walks angrily across to the window.*]

UNDERSHAFT [*with a touch of brutality*]   The government of your country! *I* am the government of your country: I, and Lazarus. Do you suppose that you and half a dozen amateurs like you, sitting in a row in that foolish gabble shop, can govern Undershaft and Lazarus? No, my friend: you will do what pays u s. You will make war when it suits us, and keep peace when it doesnt. You will find out that trade requires certain measures when we have decided on those measures. When I want anything to keep my dividends up, you will discover that my want is a national need. When other people want something to keep my dividends down, you will call out the police and military. And in return you shall have the support and applause of my newspapers, and the delight of imagining that you are a great statesman. Government of your country! Be off with you, my boy, and play with your caucuses and leading articles and historic parties and great leaders and burning questions and the rest of your toys. *I* am going back to my counting-house to pay the piper and call the tune.

STEPHEN [*actually smiling, and putting his hand on his father's shoulder with indulgent patronage*]   Really, my dear father, it is impossible to be angry with you. You dont know how absurd all this sounds to m e. You are very properly proud of having been industrious enough to make money; and it is greatly to your credit that you have made so much of it. But it has kept you in circles where you are valued for your money and deferred to for it, instead of in the doubtless very old-fashioned and behind-the-times public school and university where I formed my habits of mind. It is natural for you to think that money governs England; but you must allow me to think I know better.

UNDERSHAFT   And what d o e s govern England, pray?

STEPHEN   Character, father, character.

UNDERSHAFT   Whose character? Yours or mine?

STEPHEN   Neither yours nor mine, father, but the best elements in the English national character.

UNDERSHAFT   Stephen: Ive found your profession for you. Youre a born journalist. I'll start you with a high-toned weekly review. There!

Before STEPHEN *can reply* SARAH, BARBARA, LOMAX, *and* CUSINS *come in ready for walking.* BARBARA *crosses the room to the window and looks out.* CUSINS *drifts amiably to the armchair.* LOMAX *remains near the door, whilst* SARAH *comes to her mother.*
STEPHEN goes to the smaller writing table and busies himself with his letters.

SARAH   Go and get ready, mama: the carriage is waiting. [LADY BRITOMART *leaves the room.*]

UNDERSHAFT [*to* SARAH]   Good day, my dear. Good afternoon, Mr Lomax.

LOMAX [*vaguely*]   Ahdedoo.

UNDERSHAFT [*to* CUSINS]   Quite well after last night, Euripides, eh?

CUSINS   As well as can be expected.

UNDERSHAFT   Thats right. [*To* BARBARA.] So you are coming to see my death and devastation factory, Barbara?

BARBARA [*at the window*]   You came yesterday to see my salvation factory. I promised you a return visit.

LOMAX [*coming forward between* SARAH *and* UNDERSHAFT]   Youll find it awfully interesting. Ive been through the Woolwich Arsenal; and it gives you a ripping feeling of security, you know, to think of the lot of beggars we could kill if it came to fighting. [*To* UNDERSHAFT, *with sudden solemnity.*] Still, it must be rather an awful reflection for you, from the religious point of view as it were. Youre getting on, you know, and all that.

SARAH   You dont mind Cholly's imbecility, papa, do you?

LOMAX [*much taken aback*]   Oh I say!

UNDERSHAFT   Mr Lomax looks at the matter in a very proper spirit, my dear.

LOMAX   Just so. Thats all I meant, I assure you.

SARAH   Are you coming, Stephen?

STEPHEN   Well, I am rather busy—er— [*Magnanimously.*] Oh well, yes: I'll come. That is, if there is room for me.

UNDERSHAFT   I can take two with me in a little motor I am experimenting with for field use. You wont mind its being rather unfashionable. It's not painted yet; but it's bullet proof.

LOMAX [*appalled at the prospect of confronting Wilton Crescent in an unpainted motor*]   Oh I s a y!

SARAH   The carriage for me, thank you. Barbara doesnt mind what she's seen in.

LOMAX   I say, Dolly, old chap: do you really mind the car being a guy?[6] Because of course if you do I'll go in it. Still—

CUSINS   I prefer it.

LOMAX   Thanks awfully, old man. Come, my ownest. [*He hurries out to secure his seat in the carriage.* SARAH *follows him.*]

CUSINS [*moodily walking across to* LADY BRITOMART's *writing table*]   Why are we two coming to this Works Department of Hell? that is what I ask myself.

BARBARA   I have always thought of it as a sort of pit where lost creatures with blackened faces stirred up smoky fires and were driven and tormented by my father? Is it like that, dad?

UNDERSHAFT [*scandalized*]   My dear! It is a spotlessly clean and beautiful hillside town.

CUSINS   With a Methodist chapel? Oh d o say theres a Methodist chapel.

UNDERSHAFT   There are two: a Primitive one and a sophisticated one. There is even an Ethical Society; but it is not much patronized, as my men are all strongly religious.[7] In the High Explosives Sheds they object to the presence of Agnostics as unsafe.

CUSINS   And yet they dont object to you!

BARBARA   Do they obey all your orders?

UNDERSHAFT   I never give them any orders. When I speak to one of them it is "Well, Jones, is the baby doing well? and has Mrs Jones made a good recovery?" "Nicely, thank you, sir." And thats all.

CUSINS   But Jones has to be kept in order. How do you maintain discipline among your men?

UNDERSHAFT   I dont. They do. You see, the one thing Jones wont stand is any rebellion from the man under him, or any assertion of social equality between the wife of the man with 4 shillings a week less than himself, and Mrs Jones! Of course they all rebel against me, theoretically. Practically, every man of them keeps the man just below him in his place. I never meddle with them. I never bully them. I dont even bully Lazarus. I say that certain things are to be done; but I dont order anybody to do them. I dont say, mind you, that there is no ordering about and snubbing and even bullying. The men snub the boys and order them about; the carmen snub the sweepers; the artisans snub the unskilled laborers; the foremen drive and bully both the laborers and artisans; the assistant engineers find fault with the foremen; the chief engineers drop on the assistants; the departmental managers worry the chiefs; and the clerks have tall hats and hymnbooks and keep up the social tone by refusing to associate on equal terms with anybody. The result is a colossal profit, which comes to me.

CUSINS [*revolted*]   You really are a—well, what I was saying yesterday.

BARBARA   What was he saying yesterday?

6. An object of ridicule.
7. The Primitive Methodists (founded 1811) were an offshoot of Methodism which broke away originally because of their practice, under the leadership of Hugh Bourne, of "camp-meetings," services which lasted all day. They were not reunited with the parent group until the 1930s. A Society for Ethical Culture was founded in the United States in 1876. It taught that morality is the fundamental element in religion. It reached Great Britain in 1887.

UNDERSHAFT   Never mind, my dear. He thinks I have made you unhappy. Have I?

BARBARA   Do you think I can be happy in this vulgar silly dress? I! who have worn the uniform. Do you understand what you have done to me? Yesterday I had a man's soul in my hand. I set him in the way of life with his face to salvation. But when we took your money he turned back to drunkenness and derision. [*With intense conviction.*]   I will never forgive you that. If I had a child, and you destroyed its body with your explosives—if you murdered Dolly with your horrible guns—I could forgive you if my forgiveness would open the gates of heaven to you. But to take a human soul from me, and turn it into the soul of a wolf! that is worse than any murder.

UNDERSHAFT   Does my daughter despair so easily? Can you strike a man to the heart and leave no mark on him?

BARBARA   [*her face lighting up*]   Oh, you are right: he can never be lost now: where was my faith?

CUSINS   Oh, clever clever devil!

BARBARA   You may be a devil; but God speaks through you sometimes. [*She takes her father's hands and kisses them.*] You have given me back my happiness: I feel it deep down now, though my spirit is troubled.

UNDERSHAFT   You have learnt something. That always feels at first as if you had lost something.

BARBARA   Well, take me to the factory of death; and let me learn something more. There must be some truth or other behind all this frightful irony. Come, Dolly. [*She goes out.*]

CUSINS   My guardian angel! [*To* UNDERSHAFT.] Avaunt! [*He follows* BARBARA.]

STEPHEN   [*quietly, at the writing table*]   You must not mind Cusins, father. He is a very amiable good fellow; but he is a Greek scholar and naturally a little eccentric.

UNDERSHAFT   Ah, quite so. Thank you, Stephen. Thank you. [*He goes out.*]

STEPHEN *smiles patronizingly; buttons his coat responsibly; and crosses the room to the door.* LADY BRITOMART, *dressed for out-of-doors, opens it before he reaches it. She looks round for the others; looks at* STEPHEN; *and turns to go without a word.*

STEPHEN [*embarrassed*]   Mother—

LADY BRITOMART   Dont be apologetic, Stephen. And dont forget that you have outgrown your mother. [*She goes out.*]

Perivale St Andrews lies between two Middlesex hills, half climbing the northern one. It is an almost smokeless town of white walls, roofs of narrow green slates or red tiles, tall trees, domes, campaniles, and slender chimney shafts, beautifully situated and beautiful in itself. The best view of it is obtained from the crest of a slope about half a mile to the east, where the high explosives are dealt with. The foundry lies hidden in the depths between, the tops of its chimneys sprouting like huge skittles into the middle distance. Across the crest runs an emplacement of concrete, with a firestep, and a parapet which suggests a fortification, because there is a huge cannon of the obsolete Woolwich Infant pattern peering across it at the town.

The cannon is mounted on an experimental gun carriage: possibly the original model of the Undershaft disappearing rampart gun alluded to by STEPHEN. *The firestep, being a convenient place to sit, is furnished here and there with straw disc cushions; and at one place there is the additional luxury of a fur rug.*

BARBARA *is standing on the firestep, looking over the parapet towards the town. On her right is the cannon; on her left the end of a shed raised on piles, with a ladder of three or four steps up to the door, which opens outwards and has a little wooden landing at the threshold, with a fire bucket in the corner of the landing. Several dummy soldiers more or less mutilated, with straw protruding from their gashes, have been shoved out of the way under the landing. A few others are nearly upright against the shed; and one has fallen forward and lies, like a grotesque corpse, on the emplacement. The parapet stops short of the shed, leaving a gap which is the beginning of the path down the hill through the foundry to the town. The rug is on the firestep near this gap. Down on the emplacement behind the cannon is a trolley carrying a huge conical bombshell with a red band painted on it. Further to the right is the door of an office, which, like the sheds, is of the lightest possible construction.*

CUSINS *arrives by the path from the town.*

BARBARA   Well?

CUSINS   Not a ray of hope. Everything perfect! wonderful! real! It only needs a cathedral to be a heavenly city instead of a hellish one.

BARBARA   Have you found out whether they have done anything for old Peter Shirley?

CUSINS   They have found him a job as gatekeeper and timekeeper. He's frightfully miserable. He calls the time-keeping brainwork, and says he isnt used to it; and his gate lodge is so splendid that he's ashamed to use the rooms, and skulks in the scullery.

BARBARA   Poor Peter!

STEPHEN *arrives from the town. He carries a fieldglass.*

STEPHEN [*enthusiastically*]   Have you two seen the place? Why did you leave us?

CUSINS   I wanted to see everything I was not intended to see; and Barbara wanted to make the men talk.

STEPHEN   Have you found anything discreditable?

CUSINS   No. They call him Dandy Andy and are proud of his being a cunning old rascal; but it's all horribly, frightfully, immorally, unanswerably perfect.

SARAH *arrives.*

SARAH   Heavens! what a place! [*She crosses to the trolley.*]   Did you see the nursing home!? [*She sits down on the shell.*]

STEPHEN   Did you see the libraries and schools!?

SARAH   Did you see the ball room and the banqueting chamber in the Town Hall!?

STEPHEN   Have you gone into the insurance fund, the pension fund, the building society, the various applications of cooperation!?

UNDERSHAFT *comes from the office, with a sheaf of telegrams in his hand.*

UNDERSHAFT   Well, have you seen everything? I'm sorry I was called away. [*Indicating the telegrams.*] Good news from Manchuria.

STEPHEN   Another Japanese victory?

UNDERSHAFT   Oh, I dont know. Which side wins does not concern us here. No: the good news is that the aerial battleship is a tremendous success. At the first trial it has wiped out a fort with three hundred soldiers in it.

CUSINS [*from the platform*]   Dummy soldiers?

UNDERSHAFT [*striding across to* STEPHEN *and kicking the prostrate dummy brutally out of his way*]   No: the real thing.

> CUSINS *and* BARBARA *exchange glances. Then* CUSINS *sits on the step and buries his face in his hands.* BARBARA *gravely lays her hand on his shoulder. He looks up at her in whimsical desperation.*

UNDERSHAFT   Well, Stephen, what do you think of the place?

STEPHEN   Oh, magnificent. A perfect triumph of modern industry. Frankly, my dear father, I have been a fool: I had no idea of what it all meant: of the wonderful forethought, the power of organization, the administrative capacity, the financial genius, the colossal capital it represents. I have been repeating to myself as I came through your streets "Peace hath her victories no less renowned than War."[8] I have only one misgiving about it all.

UNDERSHAFT   Out with it.

STEPHEN   Well, I cannot help thinking that all this provision for every want of your workmen may sap their independence and weaken their sense of responsibility. And greatly as we enjoyed our tea at that splendid restaurant—how they gave us all that luxury and cake and jam and cream for threepence I really cannot imagine!—still you must remember that restaurants break up home life. Look at the continent, for instance! Are you sure so much pampering is really good for the men's characters?

UNDERSHAFT   Well you see, my dear boy, when you are organizing civilization you have to make up your mind whether trouble and anxiety are good things or not. If you decide that they are, then, I take it, you simply dont organize civilization; and there you are, with trouble and anxiety enough to make us all angels! But if you decide the other way, you may as well go through with it. However, Stephen, our characters are safe here. A sufficient dose of anxiety is always provided by the fact that we may be blown to smithereens at any moment.

SARAH   By the way, papa, where do you make the explosives?

UNDERSHAFT   In separate little sheds, like that one. When one of them blows up, it costs very little; and only the people quite close to it are killed.

> STEPHEN, *who is quite close to it, looks at it rather scaredly, and moves away quickly to the cannon. At the same moment the door of the shed is thrown abruptly open; and a foreman in*

8. Stephen is quoting John Milton's sonnet, "To the Lord General Cromwell, May 1652."

overalls and list slippers[9] *comes out on the little landing and holds the door for* LOMAX, *who appears in the doorway.*

LOMAX [*with studied coolness*]   My good fellow: you neednt get into a state of nerves. Nothing's going to happen to you; and I suppose it wouldnt be the end of the world if anything did. A little bit of British pluck is what y o u want, old chap. [*He descends and strolls across to* SARAH.]

UNDERSHAFT [*to the foreman*]   Anything wrong, Bilton?

BILTON [*with ironic calm*]   Gentleman walked into the high explosives shed and lit a cigaret, sir: thats all.

UNDERSHAFT   Ah, quite so. [*Going over to* LOMAX.] Do you happen to remember what you did with the match?

LOMAX   Oh come! I'm not a fool. I took jolly good care to blow it out before I chucked it away.

BILTON   The top of it was red hot inside, sir.

LOMAX   Well, suppose it was! I didn't chuck it into any of y o u r messes.

UNDERSHAFT   Think no more of it, Mr Lomax. By the way, would you mind lending me your matches.

LOMAX [*offering his box*]   Certainly.

UNDERSHAFT   Thanks. [*He pockets the matches.*]

LOMAX [*lecturing to the company generally*]   You know, these high explosives dont go off like gunpowder, except when theyre in a gun. When theyre spread loose, you can put a match to them without the least risk: they just burn quietly like a bit of paper. [*Warming to the scientific interest of the subject.*] Did you know that, Undershaft? Have you ever tried?

UNDERSHAFT   Not on a large scale, Mr Lomax. Bilton will give you a sample of gun cotton when you are leaving if you ask him. You can experiment with it at home. [BILTON *looks puzzled.*]

SARAH   Bilton will do nothing of the sort, papa. I suppose it's your business to blow up the Russians and Japs; but you might really stop short of blowing up poor Cholly. [BILTON *gives it up and retires into the shed.*]

LOMAX   My ownest, there is no danger. [*He sits beside her on the shell.*]

LADY BRITOMART *arrives from the town with a bouquet.*

LADY BRITOMART [*impetuously*]   Andrew: you shouldnt have let me see this place.

UNDERSHAFT   Why, my dear?

LADY BRITOMART   Never mind why: you shouldnt have: thats all. To think of all that [*indicating the town*] being yours! and that you have kept it to yourself all these years!

UNDERSHAFT   It does not belong to me. I belong to it. It is the Undershaft inheritance.

LADY BRITOMART   It is not. Your ridiculous cannons and that noisy banging foundry may be the Undershaft inheritance; but all that plate and linen, all that furniture and those houses and orchards and gardens belong to us. They belong to m e: they are not a man's business. I wont give them up. You must be out of your senses to throw them all away; and if you persist in such folly, I will call in a doctor.

---

9. Cloth coverings for the feet worn for safety in the munitions works.

UNDERSHAFT [*stooping to smell the bouquet*]   Where did you get the flowers, my dear?

LADY BRITOMART   Your men presented them to me in your William Morris Labor Church.[1]

CUSINS   Oh! It needed only that. A Labor Church! [*He mounts the firestep distractedly, and leans with his elbows on the parapet, turning his back to them.*]

LADY BRITOMART   Yes, with Morris's words in mosaic letters ten feet high round the dome. No MAN IS GOOD ENOUGH TO BE ANOTHER MAN'S MASTER. The cynicism of it!

UNDERSHAFT   It shocked the men at first, I am afraid. But now they take no more notice of it than of the ten commandments in church.

LADY BRITOMART   Andrew: you are trying to put me off the subject of the inheritance by profane jokes. Well, you shant. I dont ask it any longer for Stephen: he has inherited far too much of your perversity to be fit for it. But Barbara has rights as well as Stephen. Why should not Adolphus succeed to the inheritance? I could manage the town for him; and he can look after the cannons, if they are really necessary.

UNDERSHAFT   I should ask nothing better if Adolphus were a foundling. He is exactly the sort of new blood that is wanted in English business. But he's not a foundling; and theres an end of it. [*He makes for the office door.*]

CUSINS [*turning to them*]   Not quite. [*They all turn and stare at him.*] I think—Mind! I am not committing myself in any way as to my future course—but I t h i n k the foundling difficulty can be got over. [*He jumps down to the emplacement.*]

UNDERSHAFT [*coming back to him*]   What do you mean?

CUSINS   Well, I have something to say which is in the nature of a confession.

SARAH
LADY BRITOMART
BARBARA
STEPHEN
} Confession!

LOMAX   Oh I s a y!

CUSINS   Yes, a confession. Listen, all. Until I met Barbara I thought myself in the main an honorable, truthful man, because I wanted the approval of my conscience more than I wanted anything else. But the moment I saw Barbara, I wanted her far more than the approval of my conscience.

LADY BRITOMART   Adolphus!

CUSINS   It is true. You accused me yourself, Lady Brit, of joining the Army to worship Barbara; and so I did. She bought my soul like a flower at a street corner; but she bought it for herself.

UNDERSHAFT   What! Not for Dionysos or another?

CUSINS   Dionysos and all the others are in herself. I adored what was divine in her, and was therefore a true worshipper. But I was romantic about her too. I thought she was a woman of the people, and that a marriage with a professor of Greek would be far beyond the wildest social ambitions of her rank.

---

1. The first Labor Church was founded by John Trevor, a Unitarian minister and a socialist, to provide a religious movement for the working classes without the social practices and teachings of other churches. The movement was never large and was nearly dead at the time of the play. William Morris (1834–1896), the English author and artist, was a leader in the Socialist League.

LADY BRITOMART   Adolphus!!

LOMAX   Oh I say!!!

CUSINS   When I learnt the horrible truth—

LADY BRITOMART   What do you mean by the horrible truth, pray?

CUSINS   That she was enormously rich; that her grandfather was an earl; that her father was the Prince of Darkness—

UNDERSHAFT   Chut!

CUSINS   —and that I was only an adventurer trying to catch a rich wife, then I stooped to deceive her about my birth.

BARBARA [*rising*]   Dolly!

LADY BRITOMART   Your birth! Now Adolphus, dont dare to make up a wicked story for the sake of these wretched cannons. Remember: I have seen photographs of your parents; and the Agent General for South Western Australia knows them personally and has assured me that they are most respectable married people.

CUSINS   So they are in Australia; but here they are outcasts. Their marriage is legal in Australia, but not in England. My mother is my father's deceased wife's sister; and in this island I am consequently a foundling. [*Sensation.*][2]

BARBARA   Silly! [*She climbs to the cannon, and leans, listening, in the angle it makes with the parapet.*]

CUSINS   Is the subterfuge good enough, Machiavelli?

UNDERSHAFT [*thoughtfully*]   Biddy: this may be a way out of the difficulty.

LADY BRITOMART   Stuff! A man cant make cannons any the better for being his own cousin instead of his proper self. [*She sits down on the rug with a bounce that expresses her downright contempt for their casuistry.*]

UNDERSHAFT [*to CUSINS*]   You are an educated man. That is against the tradition.

CUSINS   Once in ten thousand times it happens that the schoolboy is a born master of what they try to teach him. Greek has not destroyed my mind: it has nourished it. Besides, I did not learn it at an English public school.

UNDERSHAFT   Hm! Well, I cannot afford to be too particular: you have cornered the foundling market. Let it pass. You are eligible, Euripides: you are eligible.

BARBARA   Dolly: yesterday morning, when Stephen told us all about the tradition, you became very silent; and you have been strange and excited ever since. Were you thinking of your birth then?

CUSINS   When the finger of Destiny suddenly points at a man in the middle of his breakfast, it makes him thoughtful.

UNDERSHAFT   Aha! You have had your eye on the business, my young friend, have you?

CUSINS   Take care! There is an abyss of moral horror between me and your accursed aerial battleships.

UNDERSHAFT   Never mind the abyss for the present. Let us settle the practical details and leave your final decision open. You know that you will have to change your name. Do you object to that?

---

2. Marriage between a man and the sister of his deceased wife was illegal in Great Britain until 1907. The issue is mentioned in Matthew Arnold's *Culture and Anarchy* (1869) and in W. S. Gilbert's *Iolanthe* (1882). In the latter the Queen of the Fairies distresses some members of the House of Lords by her threat to send her protégé Strephon into Parliament, where with her aid he will do various dreadful things. Along with making dukedoms open to competitive examination, "He shall prick that annual blister / Marriage with deceased wife's sister."

CUSINS Would any man named Adolphus—any man called Dolly!—
object to be called something else?

UNDERSHAFT Good. Now, as to money! I propose to treat you handsomely from the beginning. You shall start at a thousand a year.

CUSINS [*with sudden heat, his spectacles twinkling with mischief*] A
thousand! You dare offer a miserable thousand to the son-in-law of a
millionaire! No, by Heavens, Machiavelli! you shall not cheat m e.
You cannot do without m e; and I can do without you. I must
have two thousand five hundred a year for two years. At the end
of that time, if I am a failure, I go. But if I am a success, and stay
on, you must give me the other five thousand.

UNDERSHAFT What other five thousand?

CUSINS To make the two years up to five thousand a year. The two
thousand five hundred is only half pay in case I should turn out a
failure. The third year I must have ten per cent on the profits.

UNDERSHAFT [*taken aback*] Ten per cent! Why, man, do you know
what my profits are?

CUSINS Enormous, I hope: otherwise I shall require twentyfive per
cent.

UNDERSHAFT But, Mr Cusins, this is a serious matter of business. You
are not bringing any capital into the concern.

CUSINS What! no capital! Is my mastery of Greek no capital? Is my
access to the subtlest thought, the loftiest poetry yet attained by
humanity, no capital? My character! my intellect! my life! my career!
what Barbara calls my soul! are these no capital? Say another word;
and I double my salary.

UNDERSHAFT Be reasonable—

CUSINS [*peremptorily*] Mr Undershaft: you have my terms. Take
them or leave them.

UNDERSHAFT [*recovering himself*] Very well. I note your terms; and
I offer you half.

CUSINS [*disgusted*] Half!

UNDERSHAFT [*firmly*] Half.

CUSINS You call yourself a gentleman; and you offer me half!!

UNDERSHAFT I do not call myself a gentleman; but I offer you half.

CUSINS This to your future partner! your successor! your son-in-law!

BARBARA You are selling your own soul, Dolly, not mine. Leave me
out of the bargain, please.

UNDERSHAFT Come! I will go a step further for Barbara's sake. I will
give you three fifths; but that is my last word.

CUSINS Done!

LOMAX Done in the eye! Why, *I* get only eight hundred, you know.

CUSINS By the way, Mac, I am a classical scholar, not an arithmetical
one. Is three fifths more than half or less?

UNDERSHAFT More, of course.

CUSINS I would have taken two hundred and fifty. How you can
succeed in business when you are willing to pay all that money to a
University don who is obviously not worth a junior clerk's wages!—
well! What will Lazarus say?

UNDERSHAFT Lazarus is a gentle romantic Jew who cares for nothing
but string quartets and stalls at fashionable theatres. He will be
blamed for your rapacity in money matters, poor fellow! as he has
hitherto been blamed for mine. You are a shark of the first order,
Euripides. So much the better for the firm!

BARBARA   Is the bargain closed, Dolly? Does your soul belong to him now?

CUSINS   No: the price is settled: that is all. The real tug of war is still to come. What about the moral question?

LADY BRITOMART   There is no moral question in the matter at all, Adolphus. You must simply sell cannons and weapons to people whose cause is right and just, and refuse them to foreigners and criminals.

UNDERSHAFT [determinedly]   No: none of that. You must keep the true faith of an Armorer, or you dont come in here.

CUSINS   What on earth is the true faith of an Armorer?

UNDERSHAFT   To give arms to all men who offer an honest price for them, without respect of persons or principles: to aristocrat and republican, to Nihilist and Tsar, to Capitalist and Socialist, to Protestant and Catholic, to burglar and policeman, to black man, white man and yellow man, to all sorts and conditions, all nationalities, all faiths, all follies, all causes and all crimes. The first Undershaft wrote up in his shop IF GOD GAVE THE HAND, LET NOT MAN WITHHOLD THE SWORD. The second wrote up ALL HAVE THE RIGHT TO FIGHT: NONE HAVE THE RIGHT TO JUDGE. The third wrote up TO MAN THE WEAPON: TO HEAVEN THE VICTORY. The fourth had no literary turn; so he did not write up anything; but he sold cannons to Napoleon under the nose of George the Third. The fifth wrote up PEACE SHALL NOT PREVAIL SAVE WITH A SWORD IN HER HAND. The sixth, my master, was the best of all. He wrote up NOTHING IS EVER DONE IN THIS WORLD UNTIL MEN ARE PREPARED TO KILL ONE ANOTHER IF IT IS NOT DONE. After that, there was nothing left for the seventh to say. So he wrote up, simply, UNASHAMED.

CUSINS   My good Machiavelli, I shall certainly write something up on the wall; only, as I shall write it in Greek, you wont be able to read it. But as to your Armorer's faith, if I take my neck out of the noose of my own morality I am not going to put it into the noose of yours. I shall sell cannons to whom I please and refuse them to whom I please. So there!

UNDERSHAFT   From the moment when you become Andrew Undershaft, you will never do as you please again. Dont come here lusting for power, young man.

CUSINS   If power were my aim I should not come here for it. Y o u have no power.

UNDERSHAFT   None of my own, certainly.

CUSINS   I have more power than you, more will. You do not drive this place: it drives you. And what drives the place?

UNDERSHAFT [enigmatically]   A will of which I am a part.

BARBARA [startled]   Father! Do you know what you are saying; or are you laying a snare for my soul?

CUSINS   Dont listen to his metaphysics, Barbara. The place is driven by the most rascally part of society, the money hunters, the pleasure hunters, the military promotion hunters; and he is their slave.

UNDERSHAFT   Not necessarily. Remember the Armorer's Faith. I will take an order from a good man as cheerfully as from a bad one. If you good people prefer preaching and shirking to buying my weapons and fighting the rascals, dont blame me. I can make cannons: I cannot make courage and conviction. Bah! you tire me, Euripides, with your morality mongering. Ask Barbara: s h e understands.

[*He suddenly reaches up and takes* BARBARA's *hands, looking power-fully into her eyes.*] Tell him, my love, what power really means.

BARBARA [*hypnotized*]   Before I joined the Salvation Army, I was in my own power; and the consequence was that I never knew what to do with myself. When I joined it, I had not time enough for all the things I had to do.

UNDERSHAFT [*approvingly*]   Just so. And why was that, do you suppose?

BARBARA   Yesterday I should have said, because I was in the power of God. [*She resumes her self-possession, withdrawing her hands from his with a power equal to his own.*] But you came and shewed me that I was in the power of Bodger and Undershaft. Today I feel —oh! how can I put it into words? Sarah: do you remember the earthquake at Cannes, when we were little children?[3]—how little the surprise of the first shock mattered compared to the dread and horror of waiting for the second? That is how I feel in this place today. I stood on the rock I thought eternal; and without a word of warning it reeled and crumbled under me. I was safe with an infinite wisdom watching me, an army marching to Salvation with me; and in a moment, at a stroke of your pen in a cheque book, I stood alone; and the heavens were empty. That was the first shock of the earthquake: I am waiting for the second.

UNDERSHAFT   Come, come, my daughter! dont make too much of your little tinpot tragedy. What do we do here when we spend years of work and thought and thousands of pounds of solid cash on a new gun or an aerial battleship that turns out just a hairsbreadth wrong after all? Scrap it. Scrap it without wasting another hour or another pound on it. Well, you have made for yourself something that you call a morality or a religion or what not. It doesnt fit the facts. Well, scrap it. Scrap it and get one that does fit. That is what is wrong with the world at present. It scraps its obsolete steam engines and dynamos; but it wont scrap its old prejudices and its old moralities and its old religions and its old political constitutions. Whats the result? In machinery it does very well; but in morals and religion and politics it is working at a loss that brings it nearer bankruptcy every year. Dont persist in that folly. If your old religion broke down yesterday, get a newer and a better one for tomorrow.

BARBARA   Oh how gladly I would take a better one to my soul! But you offer me a worse one. [*Turning on him with sudden vehemence.*] Justify yourself: shew me some light through the darkness of this dreadful place, with its beautifully clean workshops, and respectable workmen, and model homes.

UNDERSHAFT   Cleanliness and respectability do not need justification, Barbara: they justify themselves. I see no darkness here, no dreadfulness. In your Salvation shelter I saw poverty, misery, cold and hunger. You gave them bread and treacle and dreams of heaven. I give from thirty shillings a week to twelve thousand a year. They find their own dreams; but I look after the drainage.

BARBARA   And their souls?

UNDERSHAFT   I save their souls just as I saved yours.

BARBARA [*revolted*]   Y o u saved my soul! What do you mean?

---

3. Cannes is a resort town on the Riviera, an area where earthquakes are common. If Barbara is referring to a specific one, there was a major one on Ash Wednesday, February, 23, 1887.

UNDERSHAFT   I fed you and clothed you and housed you. I took care that you should have money enough to live handsomely—more than enough; so that you could be wasteful, careless, generous. That saved your soul from the seven deadly sins.

BARBARA [*bewildered*]   The seven deadly sins!

UNDERSHAFT   Yes, the deadly seven. [*Counting on his fingers.*] Food, clothing, firing, rent, taxes, respectability and children.[4] Nothing can lift those seven millstones from Man's neck but money; and the spirit cannot soar until the millstones are lifted. I lifted them from your spirit. I enabled Barbara to become Major Barbara; and I saved her from the crime of poverty.

CUSINS   Do you call poverty a crime?

UNDERSHAFT   The worst of crimes. All the other crimes are virtues beside it: all the other dishonors are chivalry itself by comparison. Poverty blights whole cities; spreads horible pestilences; strikes dead the very souls of all who come within sight, sound, or smell of it. What you call crime is nothing: a murder here and a theft there, a blow now and a curse then: what do they matter? they are only the accidents and illnesses of life: there are not fifty genuine professional criminals in London. But there are millions of poor people, abject people, dirty people, ill fed, ill clothed people. They poison us morally and physically: they kill the happiness of society: they force us to do away with our own liberties and to organize unnatural cruelties for fear they should rise against us and drag us down into their abyss. Only fools fear crime: we all fear poverty. Pah! [*turning on* BARBARA] you talk of your half-saved ruffian in West Ham: you accuse me of dragging his soul back to perdition. Well, bring him to me here; and I will drag his soul back again to salvation for you. Not by words and dreams; but by thirtyeight shillings a week, a sound house in a handsome street, and a permanent job. In three weeks he will have a fancy waistcoat; in three months a tall hat and a chapel sitting; before the end of the year he will shake hands with a duchess at a Primrose League meeting, and join the Conservative Party.[5]

BARBARA   And will he be the better for that?

UNDERSHAFT   You know he will. Dont be a hypocrite, Barbara. He will be better fed, better housed, better clothed, better behaved; and his children will be pounds heavier and bigger. That will be better than an American cloth mattress in a shelter, chopping firewood, eating bread and treacle, and being forced to kneel down from time to time to thank heaven for it: knee drill, I think you call it. It is cheap work converting starving men with a Bible in one hand and a slice of bread in the other. I will undertake to convert West Ham to Mahometanism[6] on the same terms. Try your hand on m y men: their souls are hungry because their bodies are full.

BARBARA   And leave the east end to starve?

UNDERSHAFT [*his energetic tone dropping into one of bitter and brooding remembrance*] *I* was an east ender. I moralized and starved until one day I swore that I would be a full-fed free man at all costs; that nothing should stop me except a bullet, neither reason nor morals

---

4. "Firing" means heat. More traditional lists of the seven deadly sins include pride, envy, anger, covetousness, sloth, lechery, and gluttony.

5. The Primrose League, founded in 1883, was an organization composed of members of the Conservative Party. The name came from the custom at the time of wearing a primrose on the anniversary of Disraeli's death as a commemorative gesture.

6. Another name for Islam.

nor the lives of other men. I said "Thou shalt starve ere I starve"; and with that word I became free and great. I was a dangerous man until I had my will: now I am a useful, beneficent, kindly person. That is the history of most self-made millionaires, I fancy. When it is the history of every Englishman we shall have an England worth living in.

LADY BRITOMART   Stop making speeches, Andrew. This is not the place for them.

UNDERSHAFT [*punctured*]   My dear: I have no other means of conveying my ideas.

LADY BRITOMART   Your ideas are nonsense. You got on because you were selfish and unscrupulous.

UNDERSHAFT   Not at all. I had the strongest scruples about poverty and starvation. Your moralists are quite unscrupulous about both: they make virtues of them. I had rather be a thief than a pauper. I had rather be a murderer than a slave. I dont want to be either; but if you force the alternative on me, then, by Heaven, I'll choose the braver and more moral one. I hate poverty and slavery worse than any other crimes whatsoever. And let me tell you this. Poverty and slavery have stood up for centuries to your sermons and leading articles: they will not stand up to my machine guns. Dont preach at them: dont reason with them. Kill them.

BARBARA   Killing. Is that your remedy for everything?

UNDERSHAFT   It is the final test of conviction, the only lever strong enough to overturn a social system, the only way of saying Must. Let six hundred and seventy fools loose in the streets; and three policemen can scatter them. But huddle them together in a certain house in Westminister; and let them go through certain ceremonies and call themselves certain names until at last they get the courage to kill; and your six hundred and seventy fools become a government. Your pious mob fills up ballot papers and imagines it is governing its masters; but the ballot paper that really governs is the paper that has a bullet wrapped up in it.

CUSINS   That is perhaps why, like most intelligent people, I never vote.

UNDERSHAFT   Vote! Bah! When you vote, you only change the names of the cabinet. When you shoot, you pull down governments, inaugurate new epochs, abolish old orders and set up new. Is that historically true, Mr Learned Man, or is it not?

CUSINS   It is historically true. I loathe having to admit it. I repudiate your sentiments. I abhor your nature. I defy you in every possible way. Still, it is true. But it ought not to be true.

UNDERSHAFT   Ought! ought! ought! ought! ought! Are you going to spend your life saying ought, like the rest of our moralists? Turn your oughts into shalls, man. Come and make explosives with me. Whatever can blow men up can blow society up. The history of the world is the history of those who had courage enough to embrace this truth. Have you the courage to embrace it, Barbara?

LADY BRITOMART   Barbara: I positively forbid you to listen to your father's abominable wickedness. And you, Adolphus, ought to know better than to go about saying that wrong things are true. What does it matter whether they are true if they are wrong?

UNDERSHAFT   What does it matter whether they are wrong if they are true?

LADY BRITOMART [*rising*]   Children: come home instantly. Andrew:

I am exceedingly sorry I allowed you to call on us. You are wickeder than ever. Come at once.

BARBARA [*shaking her head*]   It's no use running away from wicked people, mamma.

LADY BRITOMART   It is every use. It shews your disapprobation of them.

BARBARA   It does not save them.

LADY BRITOMART   I can see that you are going to disobey me. Sarah: are you coming home or are you not?

SARAH   I daresay it's very wicked of papa to make cannons; but I dont think I shall cut him on that account.

LOMAX [*pouring oil on the troubled waters*]   The fact is, you know, there is a certain amount of tosh about this notion of wickedness. It doesnt work. You must look at facts. Not that I would say a word in favor of anything wrong; but then, you see, all sorts of chaps are always doing all sorts of things; and we have to fit them in somehow, dont you know. What I mean is that you cant go cutting everybody; and thats about what it comes to. [*Their rapt attention to his eloquence makes him nervous.*] Perhaps I dont make myself clear.

LADY BRITOMART   You are lucidity itself, Charles. Because Andrew is successful and has plenty of money to give to Sarah, you will flatter him and encourage him in his wickedness.

LOMAX [*unruffled*]   Well, where the carcase is, there will the eagles be gathered, dont you know. [*To* UNDERSHAFT.] Eh? What?

UNDERSHAFT   Precisely. By the way, m a y I call you Charles?

LOMAX   Delighted. Cholly is the usual ticket.

UNDERSHAFT [*to* LADY BRITOMART]   Biddy—

LADY BRITOMART [*violently*]   Dont dare call me Biddy. Charles Lomax: you are a fool. Adolphus Cusins: you are a Jesuit. Stephen: you are a prig. Barbara: you are a lunatic. Andrew: you are a vulgar tradesman. Now you all know my opinion; and m y conscience is clear, at all events. [*She sits down with a vehemence that the rug fortunately softens.*]

UNDERSHAFT   My dear: you are the incarnation of morality. [*She snorts.*] Your conscience is clear and your duty done when you have called everybody names. Come, Euripides! it is getting late; and we all want to go home. Make up your mind.

CUSINS   Understand this, you old demon—

LADY BRITOMART   Adolphus!

UNDERSHAFT   Let him alone, Biddy. Proceed, Euripides.

CUSINS   You have me in a horrible dilemma. I want Barbara.

UNDERSHAFT   Like all young men, you greatly exaggerate the difference between one young woman and another.

BARBARA   Quite true, Dolly.

CUSINS   I also want to avoid being a rascal.

UNDERSHAFT [*with biting contempt*]   You lust for personal righteousness, for self-approval, for what you call a good conscience, for what Barbara calls salvation, for what I call patronizing people who are not so lucky as yourself.

CUSINS   I do not: all the poet in me recoils from being a good man. But there are things in me that I must reckon with. Pity—

UNDERSHAFT   Pity! The scavenger of misery.

CUSINS   Well, love.

UNDERSHAFT   I know. You love the needy and the outcast: you love the oppressed races, the negro, the Indian ryot,[7] the underdog everywhere. Do you love the Japanese? Do you love the French? Do you love the English?

CUSINS   No. Every true Englishman detests the English. We are the wickedest nation on earth; and our success is a moral horror.

UNDERSHAFT   That is what comes of your gospel of love, is it?

CUSINS   May I not love even my father-in-law?

UNDERSHAFT   Who wants your love, man? By what right do you take the liberty of offering it to me? I will have your due heed and respect, or I will kill you. But your love! Damn your impertinence!

CUSINS [*grinning*]   I may not be able to control my affections, Mac.

UNDERSHAFT   You are fencing, Euripides. You are weakening: your grip is slipping. Come! try your last weapon. Pity and love have broken in your hand: forgiveness is still left.

CUSINS   No: forgiveness is a beggar's refuge. I am with you there: we must pay our debts.

UNDERSHAFT   Well said. Come! you will suit me. Remember the words of Plato.

CUSINS [*starting*]   Plato! Y o u dare quote Plato to m e!

UNDERSHAFT   Plato says, my friend, that society cannot be saved until either the Professors of Greek take to making gunpowder, or else the makers of gunpowder become Professors of Greek.[8]

CUSINS   Oh, tempter, cunning tempter!

UNDERSHAFT   Come! choose, man, choose.

CUSINS   But perhaps Barbara will not marry me if I make the wrong choice.

BARBARA   Perhaps not.

CUSINS [*desperately perplexed*]   You hear!

BARBARA   Father: do you love nobody?

UNDERSHAFT   I love my best friend.

LADY BRITOMART   And who is that, pray?

UNDERSHAFT   My bravest enemy. That is the man who keeps me up to the mark.

CUSINS   You know, the creature is really a sort of poet in his way. Suppose he is a great man, after all!

UNDERSHAFT   Suppose you stop talking and make up your mind, my young friend.

CUSINS   But you are driving me against my nature. I hate war.

UNDERSHAFT   Hatred is the coward's revenge for being intimidated. Dare you make war on war? Here are the means: my friend Mr Lomax is sitting on them.

LOMAX [*springing up*]   Oh I say! You dont mean that this thing is loaded, do you? My ownest: come off it.

SARAH [*sitting placidly on the shell*]   If I am to be blown up, the more thoroughly it is done the better. Dont fuss, Cholly.

LOMAX [*to* UNDERSHAFT, *strongly remonstrant*]   Your own daughter, you know!

UNDERSHAFT   So I see. [*To* CUSINS.] Well, my friend, may we expect you here at six tomorrow morning?

CUSINS [*firmly*]   Not on any account. I will see the whole establish-

7. An Indian word for peasant.   8. Plato actually spoke of philosophers and kings.

ment blown up with its own dynamite before I will get up at five.
My hours are healthy, rational hours: eleven to five.

UNDERSHAFT   Come when you please: before a week you will come
at six and stay until I turn you out for the sake of your health.
[*Calling.*] Bilton! [*He turns to* LADY BRITOMART, *who rises.*] My dear:
let us leave these two young people to themselves for a moment.
[BILTON *comes from the shed.*] I am going to take you through the
gun cotton shed.

BILTON   [*barring the way*]   You cant take anything explosive in here,
sir.

LADY BRITOMART   What do you mean? Are you alluding to me?

BILTON   [*unmoved*]   No, maam. Mr Undershaft has the other gentleman's matches in his pocket.

LADY BRITOMART   [*abruptly*]   Oh! I beg your pardon. [*She goes into
the shed.*]

UNDERSHAFT   Quite right, Bilton, quite right: here you are. [*He gives*
BILTON *the box of matches.*] Come, Stephen. Come, Charles. Bring
Sarah. [*He passes into the shed.*]

> BILTON *opens the box and deliberately drops the matches into
> the fire-bucket.*

LOMAX   Oh! I say. [BILTON *stolidly hands him the empty box.*] Infernal
nonsense! Pure scientific ignorance! [*He goes in.*]

SARAH   Am I all right, Bilton?

BILTON   Youll have to put on list slippers, miss: thats all. Weve got
em inside [*She goes in.*]

STEPHEN   [*very seriously to* CUSINS]   Dolly, old fellow, think. Think
before you decide. Do you feel that you are a sufficiently practical
man? It is a huge undertaking, an enormous responsibility. All this
mass of business will be Greek to you.

CUSINS   Oh, I think it will be much less difficult than Greek.

STEPHEN   Well, I just want to say this before I leave you to yourselves. Dont let anything I have said about right and wrong prejudice you against this great chance in life. I have satisfied myself
that the business is one of the highest character and a credit to our
country. [*Emotionally.*] I am very proud of my father. I—[*Unable
to proceed, he presses* CUSINS' *hand and goes hastily into the shed,
followed by* BILTON.]

> BARBARA *and* CUSINS, *left alone together, look at one another
> silently.*

CUSINS   Barbara: I am going to accept this offer.

BARBARA   I thought you would.

CUSINS   You understand, dont you, that I had to decide without con-
sulting you. If I had thrown the burden of the choice on you, you
would sooner or later have despised me for it.

BARBARA   Yes: I did not want you to sell your soul for me any more
than for this inheritance.

CUSINS   It is not the sale of my soul that troubles me: I have sold it
too often to care about that. I have sold it for a professorship. I have
sold it for an income. I have sold it to escape being imprisoned for
refusing to pay taxes for hangmen's ropes and unjust wars and things
that I abhor. What is all human conduct but the daily and hourly

sale of our souls for trifles? What I am now selling it for is neither
money nor position nor comfort, but for reality and for power.

BARBARA   You know that you will have no power, and that he has
none.

CUSINS   I know. It is not for myself alone. I want to make power for
the world.

BARBARA   I want to make power for the world too; but it must be
spiritual power.

CUSINS   I think all power is spiritual: these cannons will not go off by
themselves. I have tried to make spiritual power by teaching Greek.
But the world can never be really touched by a dead language and
a dead civilization. The people must have power; and the people
cannot have Greek. Now the power that is made here can be wielded
by all men.

BARBARA   Power to burn women's houses down and kill their sons and
tear their husbands to pieces.

CUSINS   You cannot have power for good without having power for
evil too. Even mother's milk nourishes murderers as well as heroes.
This power which only tears men's bodies to pieces has never been
so horribly abused as the intellectual power, the imaginative power,
the poetic, religious power that can enslave men's souls. As a teacher
of Greek I gave the intellectual man weapons against the common
man. I now want to give the common man weapons against the intellectual man. I love the common people. I want to arm them
against the lawyers, the doctors, the priests, the literary men, the
professors, the artists, and the politicians, who, once in authority,
are more disastrous and tyrannical than all the fools, rascals, and
impostors. I want a power simple enough for common men to use,
yet strong enough to force the intellectual oligarchy to use its
genius for the general good.

BARBARA   Is there no higher power than that? [*Pointing to the shell.*]

CUSINS   Yes; but that power can destroy the higher powers just as a
tiger can destroy a man: therefore Man must master that power first.
I admitted this when the Turks and Greeks were last at war. My
best pupil went out to fight for Hellas. My parting gift to him was
not a copy of Plato's Republic, but a revolver and a hundred Undershaft cartridges. The blood of every Turk he shot—if he shot any—is
on my head as well as on Undershaft's. That act committed me to this
place for ever. Your father's challenge has beaten me. Dare I make
war on war? I dare. I must. I will. And now, is it all over between us?

BARBARA   [*touched by his evident dread of her answer*]   Silly baby
Dolly! How could it be!

CUSINS   [*overjoyed*]   Then you—you—you— Oh for my drum! [*He
flourishes imaginary drumsticks.*]

BARBARA   [*angered by his levity*]   Take care, Dolly, take care. Oh, if
only I could get away from you and from father and from it all!
if I could have the wings of a dove and fly away to heaven!

CUSINS   And leave m e!

BARBARA   Yes, you, and all the other naughty mischievous children of
men. But I cant. I was happy in the Salvation Army for a moment.
I escaped from the world into a paradise of enthusiasm and prayer
and soul saving; but the moment our money ran short, it all came
back to Bodger: it was he who saved our people: he, and the Prince

of Darkness, my papa. Undershaft and Bodger: their hands stretch everywhere: when we feed a starving fellow creature, it is with their bread, because there is no other bread; when we tend the sick, it is in the hospitals they endow; if we turn from the churches they build, we must kneel on the stones of the streets they pave. As long as that lasts, there is no getting away from them. Turning our backs on Bodger and Undershaft is turning our backs on life.

CUSINS   I thought you were determined to turn your back on the wicked side of life.

BARBARA   There is no wicked side: life is all one. And I never wanted to shirk my share in whatever evil must be endured, whether it be sin or suffering. I wish I could cure you of middle-class ideas, Dolly.

CUSINS [*gasping*]   Middle cl—! A snub! A social snub to m e! from the daughter of a foundling!

BARBARA   That is why I have no class, Dolly: I come straight out of the heart of the whole people. If I were middle-class I should turn my back on my father's business; and we should both live in an artistic drawing room, with you reading the reviews in one corner, and I in the other at the piano, playing Schumann:[9] both very superior persons, and neither of us a bit of use. Sooner than that, I would sweep out the guncotton shed, or be one of Bodger's barmaids. Do you know what would have happened if you had refused papa's offer?

CUSINS   I wonder!

BARBARA   I should have given you up and married the man who accepted it. After all, my dear old mother has more sense than any of you. I felt like her when I saw this place—felt that I must have it—that never, never, never could I let it go; only she thought it was the houses and the kitchen ranges and the linen and china, when it was really all the human souls to be saved: not weak souls in starved bodies, sobbing with gratitude for a scrap of bread and treacle, but fullfed, quarrelsome, snobbish, uppish creatures, all standing on their little rights and dignities, and thinking that my father ought to be greatly obliged to them for making so much money for him—and so he ought. That is where salvation is really wanted. My father shall never throw it in my teeth again that my converts were bribed with bread. [*She is transfigured.*] I have got rid of the bribe of bread. I have got rid of the bribe of heaven. Let God's work be done for its own sake: the work he had to create us to do because it cannot be done except by living men and women. When I die, let him be in my debt, not I in his; and let me forgive him as becomes a woman of my rank.

CUSINS   Then the way of life lies through the factory of death?

BARBARA   Yes, through the raising of hell to heaven and of man to God, through the unveiling of an eternal light in the Valley of The Shadow. [*Seizing him with both hands.*] Oh, did you think my courage would never come back? did you believe that I was a deserter? that I, who have stood in the streets, and taken my people to my heart, and talked of the holiest and greatest things with them, could ever turn back and chatter foolishly to fashionable people about nothing in a drawing room? Never, never, never, never: Major Barbara will die with the colors. Oh! and I have my dear little Dolly

---

9. Robert Schumann (1810–1856) was a German composer; many of his early works were written for the piano.

boy still; and he has found me my place and my work. Glory Hallelujah! [*She kisses him.*]

CUSINS My dearest: consider my delicate health. I cannot stand as much happiness as you can.

BARBARA Yes: it is not easy work being in love with me, is it? But it's good for you. [*She runs to the shed, and calls, childlike.*] Mamma! Mamma! [BILTON *comes out of the shed, followed by* UNDERSHAFT.] I want Mamma.

UNDERSHAFT She is taking off her list slippers, dear. [*He passes on to* CUSINS.] Well? What does she say?

CUSINS She has gone right up into the skies.

LADY BRITOMART [*coming from the shed and stopping on the steps, obstructing* SARAH, *who follows with* LOMAX. BARBARA *clutches like a baby at her mother's skirt.*] Barbara: when will you learn to be independent and to act and think for yourself? I know as well as possible what that cry of "Mamma, Mamma," means. Always running to me!

SARAH [*touching* LADY BRITOMART's *ribs with her finger tips and imitating a bicycle horn*] Pip! pip!

LADY BRITOMART [*highly indignant*] How dare you say Pip! pip! to me, Sarah? You are both very naughty children. What do you want, Barbara?

BARBARA I want a house in the village to live in with Dolly. [*Dragging at the skirt.*] Come and tell me which one to take.

UNDERSHAFT [*to* CUSINS] Six o'clock tomorrow morning, Euripides.

THE END

Shaw's Spelling

Shaw has definite notions about the representation of language on the page, including an interest in spelling reform, a cause to which he left a substantial portion of his fortune. Three characteristic features of his own style are represented in *Major Barbara*, and to a lesser extent in *Caesar and Cleopatra*:

1. Certain contractions are printed without an apostrophe, as "cant," "didnt" and "isnt."
2. Certain abbreviations are printed without a period, as in "Who saved you, Mr Price?" and "Have you ever been in love with Poverty, like St Francis?"
3. A word or phrase may be printed with unusual spacing between the letters as a clue to way of speaking the line, as in: "Wot ev I dan to y o u? Aw aint smashed y o u r fice, ev Aw?"

In the last example Shaw uses unusual spelling to indicate, as closely as possible, the actual sounds made by speakers of lower class dialects. This kind of spelling is so common in Act 2 of *Major Barbara* that some help in reading it may be welcome. The four lower class speakers use the dialect in several ways. Peter Shirley, who prides himself on his education, uses relatively few forms. Rummy Mitchens and Snobby Price make some pretension to respectability but do not have Shirley's education. Therefore they use more such forms than he does. Bill Walker, who despises education and respectability, speaks a much more heavily dialectal language. There is more than a hint of defiance in his use of the language.

The following suggestions are offered to help students without training in linguistics follow the dialogue. They are empirical and pragmatic. Using them will not produce flawless speakers of the lower class speech of London's East End.

1. Reading the speech aloud, pronouncing the words with the sounds most commonly associated with the letters, will sometimes help. In some cases Shaw's spelling is more phonetic than the customary spelling of the word, as in *sez* for *says*, *(h)iz* for *his*, *enaff* for *enough*.

2. Initial *h* is frequently dropped from words like *av* for *have*, *appiness*, and *ands*. Less frequently an initial *h* is added to words beginning with a vowel, as in *hintroduced, hall hannerstenning* for *all understanding* and *hathers* for *others*. Rummy and Snobby particularly do this because they are trying to mimic people of higher class. They know that lower class speakers drop *h*'s, but they are not sure which words should have them.

3. Initial *wh* may be replaced by *w* as in *wot* for *what* and *wispering*.

4. A final consonant (or final pronounced consonant) may be dropped as in *an* for *and*, *ole* for *old*, *kep* for *kept*, *(h)a* for *(h)ave* and *lea* for *leave*. Less frequently a final consonant may be added, as in *acrost*, or one substituted for another, as in *wiv* for *with*.

5. The substitution of final *n* for final *ng*, common in other dialects, is frequent.

6. In certain words, *r* following a vowel is lost, as in *fust* for *first*, *stawt* for *start*, *aw* for *are*, and *dessay* for *dare say*. In others an *r* is added following a vowel as in *gorn* for *gone*, *lor* for *law*, and *jawr* for *jaw*. Two words add an *r* and drop another consonant, *arter* for *after* and *arf* for *half*.

7. A number of vowel sounds are different from those in Standard English, especially in Bill Walker's speeches. The most common are represented as follows:
   a. the *i* sound in *I* or *lie* as if *aw* or *loy* (two different sounds. He says *maw* and *moy* for *my*).
   b. the *a* sound in *mate* or *waiting* as if *mite* or *witin*.
   c. the *a* sound in *stand* or *am* as if *stend* or *em*.
   d. the *a* sound in *chance, cant,* or *ask* as if *chawnce, cawnt,* or *awsk*.
   e. the *o* sound in *know* or *go* as if *knaow* or *gow*.
   f. the *u* sound in *up* or *put* as if *ap* or *pat*.
   g. the *ou* sound in *pound* or *now* as if *pahnd* or *nah*.

SOPHOCLES

Oedipus Tyrannus*

CHARACTERS

OEDIPUS, *Ruler of Thebes*[1]
JOCASTA, *Wife of* OEDIPUS
CREON, *Brother of* JOCASTA
TEIRESIAS, *A Blind Prophet*
A PRIEST
MESSENGER 1
MESSENGER 2

A SHEPHERD
AN ATTENDANT
ANTIGONE
ISMENE } *Daughters of* OEDIPUS *and* JOCASTA
CHORUS OF THEBAN ELDERS

OEDIPUS   What is it, children, sons of the ancient house of Cadmus? Why do you sit as suppliants crowned with laurel branches? What is the meaning of the incense which fills the city? The pleas to end pain? The cries of sorrow? I chose not to hear it from my messengers, but came myself—I came, Oedipus, Oedipus, whose name is known to all. You, old one—age gives you the right to speak for all of them —you tell me why they sit before my altar. Has something frightened you? What brings you here? Some need? Some want? I'll help you all I can. I would be cruel did I not greet you with compassion when you are gathered here before me.

PRIEST   My Lord and King, we represent the young and old; some are priests and some the best of Theban youth. And I—I am a priest of Zeus. There are many more who carry laurel boughs like these— in the market-places, at the twin altars of Pallas, by the sacred ashes of Ismenus' oracle.[2] You see yourself how torn our city is, how she craves relief from the waves of death which now crash over her. Death is everywhere—in the harvests of the land, in the flocks that roam the pastures, in the unborn children of our mothers' wombs. A fiery plague is ravaging the city, festering, spreading its pestilence, wasting the house of Cadmus, filling the house of Hades with screams of pain and of fear. This is the reason why we come to you, these children and I. No, we do not think you a god. But we deem you a mortal set apart to face life's common issues and the trials which the gods dispense to men. It was you who once before came to Thebes and freed us from the spell that hypnotized our lives. You did this, and yet you knew no more than we—less even. You had no help from us. God aided you. Yes, you restored our life. And now a second time, great Oedipus, we turn to you for help. Find some relief for us, whether with god or man to guide your way. You helped us then. Yes. And we believe that you will help us now. O Lord, revive our city; restore her life. Think of your fame, your own repute. The people know you saved us from our past despair. Let no one say you raised us up to let us fall. Save us and keep us safe. You found good omens once to aid you and brought us fortune then. Find them

---

* Translated by Luci Berkowitz and Theodore F. Brunner.

1. See the note on Thebes and the House of Cadmus, p. 35.

2. Zeus was the king of the Greek gods. His daughter Pallas, or Athena, was spe- cifically a goddess of wisdom, but she had played an important part in the founding of Thebes. Apollo (or Phoebus), the sun god, had a shrine near Thebes, close to the river Ismenus.

again. If you will rule this land as king and lord, rule over men and not a wall encircling emptiness. No city wall, no ship can justify its claim to strength if it is stripped of men who give it life.

OEDIPUS   O my children, I know well the pain you suffer and understand what brings you here. You suffer—and yet not one among you suffers more than I. Each of you grieves for himself alone, while my heart must bear the strain of sorrow for all—myself and you and all our city's people. No, I am not blind to it. I have wept and in my weeping set my thoughts on countless paths, searching for an answer. I have sent my own wife's brother Creon, son of Menoeceus, to Apollo's Pythian shrine[3] to learn what I might say or do to ease our city's suffering. I am concerned that he is not yet here—he left many days ago. But this I promise: whenever he returns, whatever news he brings, whatever course the god reveals—*that* is the course that I shall take.

PRIEST   Well spoken. Look! They are giving signs that Creon is returning.

OEDIPUS   O God! If only he brings news as welcome as his smiling face.

PRIEST   I think he does. His head is crowned with laurel leaves.

OEDIPUS   We shall know soon enough. There. My Lord Creon, what word do you bring from the god?

Enter CREON.

CREON   Good news. I tell you this: if all goes well, our troubles will be past.

OEDIPUS   But what was the oracle? Right now I'm swaying between hope and fear.

CREON   If you want to hear it in the presence of these people, I shall tell you. If not, let's go inside.

OEDIPUS   Say it before all of us. I sorrow more for them than for myself.

CREON   Then I shall tell you exactly what the god Apollo answered. These are his words: Pollution. A hidden sore is festering in our land. We are to stop its growth before it is too late.

OEDIPUS   Pollution? How are we to save ourselves?

CREON   Blood for blood. To save ourselves we are to banish a man or pay for blood with blood. It is a murder which has led to this despair.

OEDIPUS   Murder? Whose? Did the god say whose . . . ?

CREON   My Lord, before you came to rule our city, we had a king. His name was Laius . . .

OEDIPUS   I know, although I never saw him.

CREON   He was murdered. And the god's command is clear: we must find the assassin and destroy him.

OEDIPUS   But where? Where is he to be found? How can we find the traces of a crime committed long ago?

CREON   He lives among us. If we seek, we will find; what we do not seek cannot be found.

OEDIPUS   Where was it that Laius met his death? At home? The country? In some foreign land?

CREON   One day he left and told us he would go to Delphi. That was the last we saw of him.

3. The oracle at Delphi was the principal shrine of Apollo and was called "Pythian" because it celebrated his victory over the monster Python.

OEDIPUS And there was no one who could tell what happened? No one who traveled with him? Did no one see? Is there no evidence?

CREON All perished. All—except one who ran in panic from the scene and could not tell us anything for certain, except . . .

OEDIPUS Except? What? What was it? One clue might lead to many. We have to grasp the smallest shred of hope.

CREON He said that robbers—many of them—fell upon Laius and his men and murdered them.

OEDIPUS Robbers? Who committed *murder?* Why? Unless they were paid assassins?

CREON We considered that. But the king was dead and we were plagued with trouble. No one came forth as an avenger.

OEDIPUS Trouble? What could have kept you from investigating the death of your king?

CREON The Sphinx.[4] The Sphinx was confounding us with her riddles, forcing us to abandon our search for the unknown and to tend to what was then before us.

OEDIPUS Then I—I shall begin again. I shall not cease until I bring the truth to light. Apollo has shown, and you have shown, the duty which we owe the dead. You have my gratitude. You will find me a firm ally, and together we shall exact vengeance for our land and for the god. I shall not rest till I dispel this defilement—not just for another man's sake, but for my own as well. For whoever the assassin—he might turn his hand against me too. Yes, I shall be serving Laius and myself. Now go, my children. Leave the steps of my altar. Go. Take away your laurel branches. Go to the people of Cadmus. Summon them. Tell them that I, their king, will leave nothing untried. And with the help of God, we shall find success—or ruin.

Exit OEDIPUS.

PRIEST Come, children. We have learned what we came to learn. Come, Apollo, come yourself, who sent these oracles! Come as our savior! Come! Deliver us from this plague!

CHORUS
O prophecy of Zeus, sweet is the sound of your words
as they come to our glorious city of Thebes
from Apollo's glittering shrine.
Yet I quake and I dread and I tremble at those words.
Io, Delian Lord![5]

What will you bring to pass? Disaster unknown,
or familiar to us, as the ever recurring seasons?
Tell me, O oracle,
heavenly daughter of blessèd hope.

Foremost I call on you, daughter of Zeus,
Athena, goddess supreme;

4. The Sphinx was a winged monster with the head of a woman and the body of a lion who had terrorized Thebes, demanding the answer to her riddle, "What walks on four feet in the morning, two at noon, and three in the evening?" When the young Oedipus appeared at Thebes, he saved the city by answering her riddle, "Man," thus bringing about her death.

5. "Io" was a cry of generalized meaning used by worshippers in praise or supplication. Apollo was called "Delian Lord" because he had been born on the island of Delos.

and on Artemis[6] shielding the world,
shielding this land from her circular shrine
graced with renown.
And on you I call, Phoebus, Lord of the unerring bow.

Come to my aid, you averters of doom!
Come to my aid if ever you came!
Come to my aid as once you did, when you quenched
the fires of doom that fell on our soil!
Hear me, and come to my aid!

Boundless the pain, boundless the grief I bear;
sickness pervades this land,
affliction without reprieve.
Barren the soil, barren of fruit;
children are born no longer to light;
all of us flutter in agony
winging our way into darkness and death.

Countless the number of dead in the land;
corpses of children cover the plain,
children dying before they have lived,
no one to pity them,
reeking, and spreading diseases and death.

Moaning and wailing our wives,
moaning and wailing our mothers
stream to the altars this way and that,
scream to the air with helpless cries.
Hear us, golden daughter of Zeus,
hear us! Send us release!

Ares[7] now rages in our midst
brandishing in his hands
the firebrands of disease,
raving, consuming, rousing the screams of death.
Hear us, O goddess!
Help us, and still his rage!
Turn back his assault!
Help us! Banish him from our land!
Drive him into the angry sea,
to the wave-swept border of Thrace![8]

We who escape him tonight
will be struck down at dawn.
Help us, O father Zeus,
Lord of the thunderbolt,
crush him! Destroy him!
Burn him with fires of lightning!

---

6. Artemis (called Diana by the Romans) was the twin sister of Apollo. She was primarily a moon goddess.
7. Ares (Roman Mars) was the war god.

8. Thrace was a region to the east and north of Macedonia, a relatively uncivilized section and a favorite haunt of Ares.

Help us, Apollo, Lycean Lord!
Stand at our side with your golden bow!
Artemis, help us!
Come from the Lycian[9] hills!
Come with your torches aflame!
Dionysus,[1] protector, come to our aid,
come with your revelers' band!
Burn with your torch the god
hated among the gods!

Enter OEDIPUS.

OEDIPUS I have heard your prayers and answer with relief and help,
if you will heed my words and tend the sickness with the cure it
cries for. My words are uttered as a stranger to the act, a stranger to
its tale. I cannot trace its path alone, without a sign. As a citizen
newer to Thebes than you, I make this proclamation: If one among
you knows who murdered Laius, the son of Labdacus, let him tell us
now. If he fears for his life, let him confess and know a milder penalty. He will be banished from this land. Nothing more. Or if you
know the assassin to be an alien, do not protect him with your silence. You will be rewarded. But if in fear you protect yourself or
any other man and keep your silence, then hear what I say now:
Whoever he is, this assassin must be denied entrance to your homes.
Any man where I rule is forbidden to receive him or speak to him or
share with him his prayers and sacrifice or offer him the holy rites of
purification. I command you to drive this hideous curse out of your
homes; I command you to obey the will of Pythian Apollo. I will
serve the god and the dead. On the assassin or assassins, I call down
the most vile damnation—for this vicious act, may the brand of
shame be theirs to wear forever. And if I knowingly harbor their
guilt within my own walls, I shall not exempt myself from the curse
that I have called upon them. It is for me, for God, and for this city
that staggers toward ruin that you must fulfill these injunctions. Even
if Heaven gave you no sign, you had the sacred duty to insure that
this act did not go unexamined, unavenged! It was the assassination
of a noble man—your king! Now that I hold the powers that he
once held, his bed, his wife—had fate been unopposed, his children
would have bound us closer yet—and now on him has this disaster
fallen. I will avenge him as I would avenge my own father. I will
leave nothing untried to expose the murderer of Laius, the son of
Labdacus, heir to the house of Cadmus and Agenor. On those who
deny me obedience, I utter this curse: May the gods visit them with
barrenness in their harvests, barrenness in their women, barrenness
in their fate. Worse still—may they be haunted and tormented and
never know the peace that comes with death. But for you, my people,
in sympathy with me—I pray that Justice and all the gods attend
you forever.

CHORUS You have made me swear an oath, my Lord, and under oath
I speak. I did not kill the king and cannot name the man who did.

---

9. Apollo was called "Lycean" apparently because he was regarded as a protector against wolves. Lycia was a region
of Asia Minor associated with Apollo and
Artemis.
  1. Dionysus, the god of wine, was related to the royal house of Thebes.

The question was Apollo's. He could name the man you seek.

OEDIPUS   I know. And yet no mortal can compel a god to speak.

CHORUS   The next-best thing, it seems to me . . .

OEDIPUS   Tell me. Tell me all your thoughts. We must consider everything.

CHORUS   There is one man, second only to Apollo, who can see the truth, who can clearly help us in our search—Teiresias.

OEDIPUS   I thought of this. On Creon's advice, I sent for him. Twice. He should be here.

CHORUS   There were some rumors once, but no one hears them now.

OEDIPUS   What rumors? I want to look at every tale that is told.

CHORUS   They said that travelers murdered Laius.

OEDIPUS   I have heard that too. And yet there's no one to be found who saw the murderer in the act.

CHORUS   He will come forth himself, once he has heard your curse, if he knows what it means to be afraid.

OEDIPUS   Why? Why should a man now fear words if then he did not fear to kill?

CHORUS   But there is one man who can point him out—the man in whom the truth resides, the god-inspired prophet. And there—they are bringing him now.

Enter TEIRESIAS, *guided by a servant.*

OEDIPUS   Teiresias, all things are known to you—the secrets of heaven and earth, the sacred and profane. Though you are blind, you surely see the plague that rakes our city. My Lord Teiresias, we turn to you as our only hope. My messengers may have told you—we have sent to Apollo and he has answered us. We must find Laius' murderers and deal with them. Or drive them out. Then—only then will we find release from our suffering. I ask you not to spare your gifts of prophecy. Look to the voices of prophetic birds or the answers written in the flames. Spare nothing. Save all of us—yourself, your city, your king, and all that is touched by this deathly pollution. We turn to you. My Lord, it is man's most noble role to help his fellow man the best his talents will allow.

TEIRESIAS   O God! How horrible wisdom is! How horrible when it does not help the wise! How could I have forgotten? I should not have come.

OEDIPUS   Why? What's wrong?

TEIRESIAS   Let me go. It will be better if you bear your own distress and I bear mine. It will be better this way.

OEDIPUS   This city gave you life and yet you refuse her an answer! You speak as if you were her enemy.

TEIRESIAS   No! No! It is because I see the danger in your words. And mine would add still more.

OEDIPUS   For God's sake, if you know, don't turn away from us! We are pleading. We are begging you.

TEIRESIAS   Because you are blind! No! I shall not reveal my secrets. I shall not reveal yours.

OEDIPUS   What? You know, and yet you refuse to speak? Would you betray us and watch our city fall helplessly to her death?

TEIRESIAS   I will not cause you further grief. I will not grieve myself. Stop asking me to tell; I will tell you nothing.

OEDIPUS   You will not tell? You monster! You could stir the stones of
earth to a burning rage! You will never tell? What will it take?

TEIRESIAS   Know yourself, Oedipus. You denounce me, but you do
not yet know yourself.

OEDIPUS   Yes! You disgrace your city. And then you expect us to control our rage!

TEIRESIAS   It does not matter if I speak; the future has already been
determined.

OEDIPUS   And if it has, then it is for you to tell me, *prophet!*

TEIRESIAS   I shall say no more. Rage, if you wish.

OEDIPUS   I *am* enraged. And now I will tell you what *I* think. I think
this was *your* doing. *You* plotted the crime, *you* saw it carried out.
It was *your* doing. All but the actual killing. And had you not been
blind, you would have done *that*, too!

TEIRESIAS   Do you believe what you have said? Then accept your own
decree! From this day on, deny yourself the right to speak to anyone.
You, Oedipus, are the desecrator, the polluter of this land!

OEDIPUS   You traitor! Do you think that you can get away with this?

TEIRESIAS   The truth is my protection.

OEDIPUS   Who taught you this? It did not come from prophecy!

TEIRESIAS   *You* taught me. *You* drove me, *you* forced me to say it
against my will.

OEDIPUS   Say it again. I want to make sure that I understand you.

TEIRESIAS   Understand me? Or are you trying to provoke me?

OEDIPUS   No, I want to be sure, I want to know. Say it again.

TEIRESIAS   I say that you, Oedipus Tyrannus, are the murderer you
seek.

OEDIPUS   So! A second time! Now twice you will regret what you have
said!

TEIRESIAS   Shall I tell you more? Shall I fan your flames of anger?

OEDIPUS   Yes. Tell me more. Tell me more—whatever suits you. It will
be in vain.

TEIRESIAS   I say you live in shame with the woman you love, blind
to your own calamity.

OEDIPUS   Do you think you can speak like this forever?

TEIRESIAS   I do, if there is any strength in truth.

OEDIPUS   There is—for everyone but you. You—you cripple! Your ears
are deaf, your eyes are blind, your mind—your *mind* is crippled!

TEIRESIAS   You fool! You slander me when one day you will hear the
same . . .

OEDIPUS   You live in night, Teiresias, in night that never turns to day.
And so, you cannot hurt me—or any man who sees the light.

TEIRESIAS   No—it is not I who will cause your fall. That is Apollo's
office—and he will discharge it.

OEDIPUS   Was this *your* trick—or Creon's?

TEIRESIAS   No, not Creon's. No, Oedipus. You are destroying yourself!

OEDIPUS   Ah, wealth and sovereignty and skill surpassing skill in life's
contentions, why must envy always attend them? This city *gave* me
power; I did not ask for it. And Creon, my friend, my trusted friend,
would plot to overthrow me—with this charlatan, this impostor, who
auctions off his magic wares! His eyes see profit clearly, but they are
blind in prophecy. Tell me, Teiresias, what makes you a prophet?
Where were you when the monster was here weaving her spells and
taunts? What words of relief did Thebes hear from you? Her riddle

would stagger the simple mind; it demanded the mind of a seer. Yet, put to the test, all your birds and god-craft proved useless; you had no answer. Then *I* came—ignorant Oedipus—*I* came and smothered her, using only my wit. There were no birds to tell me what to do. I am the man you would overthrow so you can stand near Creon's throne. You will regret—you and your conspirator—you will regret your attempt to purify this land. If you were not an old man, I would make you suffer the pain which you deserve for your audacity.

CHORUS   Both of you, my Lord, have spoken in bitter rage. No more —not when we must direct our every thought to obey the god's command.

TEIRESIAS   Though you are king, the right to speak does not belong to you alone. It is *my* right as well and I shall claim it. I am not your servant and Creon is not my patron. I serve only Loxian Apollo.[2] And I tell you this, since you mock my blindness. You have eyes, Oedipus, and do not see your own destruction. You have eyes and do not see what lives with you. Do you know whose son you are? I say that you have sinned and do not know it; you have sinned against your own—the living and the dead. A double scourge, your mother's and your father's curse, will drive you from this land. Then darkness will shroud those eyes that now can see the light. Cithaeron—the whole earth will resound with your mournful cries when you discover the meaning of the wedding-song that brought you to this place you falsely thought a haven. More sorrow still awaits you—more than you can know—to show you what you are and what our children are. Damn Creon, if you will; damn the words I say. No man on earth will ever know the doom that waits for you.

OEDIPUS   How much of this am I to bear? Leave! Now! Leave my house!

TEIRESIAS   I would not be here had you not sent for me.

OEDIPUS   I never would have sent for you had I known the madness I would hear.

TEIRESIAS   To you, I am mad; but not to your parents . . .

OEDIPUS   Wait! My parents? Who are my parents?

TEIRESIAS   This day shall bring you birth *and* death.

OEDIPUS   Why must you persist with riddles?

TEIRESIAS   Are you not the best of men when it comes to riddles?

OEDIPUS   You mock the very skill that proves me great.

TEIRESIAS   A great misfortune—which will destroy you.

OEDIPUS   I don't care. If I have saved this land, I do not care.

TEIRESIAS   Then I shall go. [*To his servant.*] Come, take me home.

OEDIPUS   Yes, go home. You won't be missed.

TEIRESIAS   I will go when I've said all that I came to say. I am not afraid of you. You cannot hurt me. And I tell you this: The man you seek—the man whose death or banishment you ordered, the man who murdered Laius—that man is here, passing as an alien, living in our midst. Soon it will be known to all of you—he is a native Theban. And he will find no joy in that discovery. His eyes now see, but soon they will be blind: rich now, but soon a beggar. Holding a scepter now, but soon a cane, he will grope for the earth beneath him—in a foreign land. Both brother and father to the children that he loves. Both son and husband to the woman who bore him. Both

2. Apollo was called "Loxian" because the answer given by his oracles at Delphi and elsewhere were frequently ambiguous.

heir and spoiler of his father's bed and the one who took his life.
Go, think on this. And if you find the words I speak are lies, *then*
say that I am blind.

Exeunt OEDIPUS, TEIRESIAS.

CHORUS

Who is he? Who is the man?
Who is the man whom the voice of the Delphian shrine
denounced as the killer, the murderer,
the man who committed the terrible crime?
Where is he? Where is he now?
Let him run, let him flee!
Let him rush with the speed of the wind on his flight!
For with fire and lightning the god will attack,
and relentlessy fate will pursue him and haunt him
and drive him to doom.

Do you hear? Do you hear the command of the god?
From Parnassus[3] he orders the hunt.
In vain will the murderer hide,
in vain will he run,
in vain will he lurk in the forests and caves
like an animal roaming the desolate hills.
Let him flee to the edge of the world:
On his heels he will find
the command of the god!

Confusion and fear
have been spread by the prophet's words.
For I cannot affirm, yet I cannot refute
what he spoke. And I'm lost, I am lost—
What am I to believe?
Now foreboding is gripping my heart.
Was there ever a strife between Laius and Polybus' house?[4]
Can I test? Can I prove?
Can I ever believe that the name of my king
has been soiled by a murder unknown?

It is Zeus and Apollo who know,
who can see the affairs of men.
But the seer and I,
we are mortal, and blind.
Who is right? Who can judge?
We are mortal, our wisdom assigned in degrees.
Does the seer know? Do I?
No, I will not believe in the prophet's charge
till the charge has been proved to my mind.
For I saw how the king
in the test with the Sphinx
proved his wisdom and worth
when he saved this city from doom.

3. Parnassus was a mountain near Delphi, sacred to Apollo and the Muses, minor
goddesses associated with the arts.

4. Polybus, the King of Corinth, and his
wife Merope were the reputed parents of
Oedipus.

No! I can *never* condemn the king!

Enter CREON.

CREON   My fellow citizens, anger has impelled me to come because I have heard the accusation which Oedipus has brought against me —and I will not tolerate it. If he thinks that I—in the midst of this torment—*I* have thought to harm him in any way, I will not spend the rest of my life branded by his charge. Doesn't he see the implications of such slander? To you, to my friends, to my city—I would be a traitor!

CHORUS   He spoke in anger—without thinking.

CREON   Yes—and who was it who said that the prophet lied on my advice?

CHORUS   It was said, but I don't know how it was meant.

CREON   And was this a charge leveled by one whose eyes were clear? Whose head was clear?

CHORUS   I don't know. I do not judge my master's actions. But here he comes.

Enter OEDIPUS.

OEDIPUS   Why have you come, Creon? Do you have the audacity to show your face in my presence? Assassin! And now you would steal my throne! What drove you to this plot? Did you see cowardice in me? Stupidity? Did you imagine that I would not see your treachery? Did you expect that I wouldn't act to stop you? You fool! Your plot was mad! You go after a throne without money, without friends! How do you think thrones are won?

CREON   You listen to me! And when you have heard me out, when you have heard the truth, *then* judge for yourself.

OEDIPUS   Ah yes, your oratory! I can learn nothing from that. This is what I have learned—you are my enemy!

CREON   Just let me say . . .

OEDIPUS   Say one thing—say that you are not a traitor.

CREON   If you think that senseless stubbornness is a precious gift, you are a fool.

OEDIPUS   If you think that you can threaten the house of Cadmus— your own house—and not pay for it, you are mad.

CREON   I grant you that. But tell me: just what is this terrible thing you say I have done to you?

OEDIPUS   Did you or did you not tell me to send for that—that— prophet?

CREON   I did. And I would again.

OEDIPUS   Then, how long since Laius . . . ?

CREON   What? I do not follow . . .

OEDIPUS   . . . Disappeared?

CREON   A long time ago.

OEDIPUS   Your Teiresias—was he—was he a prophet then?

CREON   Yes—and just as honored and just as wise.

OEDIPUS   Did he ever mention me—then?

CREON   Not in my presence.

OEDIPUS   But didn't you investigate the murder?

CREON   Of course we did—

OEDIPUS   And why didn't the prophet say anything *then?*

CREON   I do not know. It's not for me to try to understand.

OEDIPUS   You know this much which you will try to tell me . . .

CREON   What is it? I will tell you if I can.

OEDIPUS   Just this: Had he not acted under your instructions, he would not have named *me* killer of Laius.

CREON   If this is what he said, you ought to know. You heard him. But now I claim the right to question you, as you have me.

OEDIPUS   Ask what you wish. I am not the murderer.

CREON   Then answer me. Did you marry my sister?

OEDIPUS   Of course I did.

CREON   And do you rule on equal terms with her?

OEDIPUS   She has all that she wants from me.

CREON   And am I not the third and equal partner?

OEDIPUS   You are—and that is where you have proved yourself a traitor.

CREON   Not true. Consider rationally, as I have done. First ask yourself—would any man prefer a life of fear to one in which the selfsame rank, the self-same rights are guaranteed untroubled peace? I have no wish to be a king when I can act as one without a throne. And any man would feel the same, if he were wise. I share with you a king's prerogatives, yet you alone must face the danger lurking around the throne. If *I* were king, I would have to act in many ways against my pleasure. What added benefit could kingship hold when I have rank and rule without the threat of pain? I am not deluded —no, I would not look for honors beyond the ones which profit me. I have the favor of every man; each greets me first when he would hope to have *your* favor. Why should I exchange this for a throne? Only a fool would. No, I am not a traitor nor would I aid an act of treason. You want proof? Go to Delphi; ask if I have brought you the truth. Then, if you find me guilty of conspiracy with the prophet, command my death. I will face that. But do not condemn me without proof. You are wrong to judge the guilty innocent, the innocent guilty —without proof. Casting off a true friend is like casting off your greatest prize—your life. You will know in time that this is true. Time alone reveals the just; a single day condemns the guilty.

CHORUS   He is right, my Lord. Respect his words. A man who plans in haste will gamble the result.

OEDIPUS   This is a plot conceived in rashness. It must be met with quick response. I cannot sit and wait until the plot succeeds.

CREON   What will you do then? Do you intend to banish me?

OEDIPUS   No. No, not banish you. I want to see you *dead*—to make you an example for all aspiring to my throne.

CREON   Then you won't do as I suggest? You won't believe me?

OEDIPUS   You have not shown that you deserve belief.

CREON   No, because I see that you are mad.

OEDIPUS   In my own eyes, I am sane.

CREON   You should be sane in mine as well.

OEDIPUS   No. You are a traitor!

CREON   And what if you are wrong?

OEDIPUS   Still—*I* will rule.

CREON   Not when you rule treacherously.

OEDIPUS   O Thebes! My city! Listen to him!

CREON   *My* city too!

CHORUS   My Lords, no more. Here comes Jocasta. Perhaps the queen can end this bitter clash.

Enter JOCASTA.

JOCASTA   Why do you behave like senseless fools and quarrel without reason? Are you not ashamed to add trouble of your own when your city is sick and dying? Go, Creon. Go and leave us alone. Forget those petty grievances which you exaggerate. How important can they be?

CREON   This important, sister: Oedipus, your husband, in his insanity, has threatened me with banishment or death.

OEDIPUS   Yes, for I have realized his plot—a plot against my person.

CREON   May the gods haunt me forever, if that is true—if I am guilty of that charge.

JOCASTA   In the name of God, believe him, Oedipus! Believe him for the sake of his oath, for my own sake, and for theirs!

CHORUS   Listen to her, my Lord. I beg you to consider and comply.

OEDIPUS   What would you have me do?

CHORUS   Respect the oath that Creon gave you. Respect his past integrity.

OEDIPUS   Do you know what you are asking?

CHORUS   Yes, I know.

OEDIPUS   Then, tell me what you mean.

CHORUS   I mean that you are wrong to charge a friend who has invoked a curse upon his head. You are wrong to slander without proof and be the cause for his dishonor.

OEDIPUS   Then you must know that when you ask for this, you ask for banishment or doom—for *me*.

CHORUS

O God, no!
O Helios,[5] no!
May Heaven and Earth exact my doom
if that is what I thought!
When our city is torn by sickness
and my heart is torn with pain—
do not compound the troubles
that beset us!

OEDIPUS   Then, let him go, although it surely means my death—or banishment with dishonor. *Your* words—not his—have touched my heart. But Creon—wherever he may be—I will hate him.

CREON   You are hard when you should yield, cruel when you should pity. Such natures deserve the pain they bear.

OEDIPUS   Just go—and leave me in peace.

CREON   I will go—my guilt pronounced by you alone. Behold my judge and jury—Oedipus Tyrannus!

Exit CREON.

CHORUS   My queen, persuade your husband to rest awhile.

JOCASTA   I will—when I have learned the truth.

CHORUS   Blind suspicion has consumed the king. And Creon's passions flared beneath the sting of unjust accusations.

JOCASTA   Are *both* at fault?

CHORUS   Yes, both of them.

JOCASTA   But what is the reason for their rage?

---

5. Helios was the name of a sun god, hence Apollo.

CHORUS   Don't ask again. Our city is weary enough from suffering. Enough. Let the matter rest where it now stands.

OEDIPUS   Do you see what you have done? Do you see where you have come—with your good intentions, your noble efforts to dull the sharpness of my anger?

CHORUS
My Lord, I have said before
and now I say again:
I would be mad,
a reckless fool
to turn away my king,
who saved us from a sea of troubles
and set us on a fairer course,
and who will lead us once again
to peace, a haven from our pain.

JOCASTA   In the name of Heaven, my Lord, tell me the reason for your bitterness.

OEDIPUS   I will—because you mean more to me than anyone. The reason is Creon and his plot against my throne.

JOCASTA   But can you *prove* a plot?

OEDIPUS   He says that I—Oedipus—bear the guilt of Laius' death.

JOCASTA   How does he justify this charge?

OEDIPUS   He does not stain his own lips by saying it. No. He uses that false prophet to speak for him.

JOCASTA   Then, you can exonerate yourself because no mortal has the power of divination. And I can prove it. An oracle came to Laius once from the Pythian priests—I'll not say from Apollo himself— that he would die at the hands of his own child, his child and mine. Yet the story, which *we* heard was that robbers murdered Laius in a place where three roads meet. As for the child—when he was three days old, Laius drove pins into his ankles and handed him to someone to cast upon a deserted mountain path—to die. And so, Apollo's prophecy was unfulfilled—the child did not kill his father. And Laius' fears were unfulfilled—he did not die by the hand of his child. Yet, these had been the prophecies. You need not give them any credence. For the god will reveal what he wants.

OEDIPUS   Jocasta—my heart is troubled at your words. Suddenly, my thoughts are wandering, disturbed . . .

JOCASTA   What is it? What makes you so frightened?

OEDIPUS   Your statement—that Laius was murdered in a place where three roads meet. Isn't that what you said?

JOCASTA   Yes. That was the story then; that is the story now.

OEDIPUS   Where is this place where three roads meet?

JOCASTA   In the land called Phocis where the roads from Delphi and from Daulia converge.[6]

OEDIPUS   How long a time has passed since then?

JOCASTA   We heard it shortly before you came.

OEDIPUS   O God, what have you planned for me?

JOCASTA   What is it, Oedipus? What frightens you?

OEDIPUS   Do not ask me. Do not ask. Just tell me—what was Laius like? How old was he?

6. The Oracle at Delphi was located in the region of central Greece called Phocis. Daulia was a city to the east of Delphi.

JOCASTA   He was tall and his hair was lightly cast with silver tones, the contour of his body much like yours.

OEDIPUS   O God! Am I cursed and cannot see it?

JOCASTA   What is it, Oedipus? You frighten me.

OEDIPUS   It cannot be—that the prophet sees! Tell me one more thing.

JOCASTA   You frighten me, my Lord, but I will try to tell you what I know.

OEDIPUS   Who traveled with the king? Was he alone? Was there a guide? An escort? A few? Many?

JOCASTA   There were five—one of them a herald—and a carriage in which Laius rode.

OEDIPUS   O God! O God! I see it all now! Jocasta, who told you this?

JOCASTA   A servant—the only one who returned alive.

OEDIPUS   Is he here now? In our house?

JOCASTA   No. When he came back and saw you ruling where once his master was, he pleaded with me—begged me—to send him to the fields to tend the flocks, far from the city. And so I did. He was a good servant and I would have granted him more than that, if he had asked.

OEDIPUS   Could we arrange to have him here—now?

JOCASTA   Yes, but what do you want with him?

OEDIPUS   I am afraid, Jocasta. I have said too much and now I have to see him.

JOCASTA   Then he shall be brought. But I, too, must know the cause of your distress. I have the right to know.

OEDIPUS   Yes, you have that right. And I must tell you—now. You, more than anyone, will have to know what I am going through. My father was Polybus of Corinth, my mother a Dorian—Merope. I was held in high regard in Corinth until—until something strange occurred—something uncanny and strange, although I might have given it too much concern. There was a man dining with us one day who had had far too much wine and shouted at me—half-drunk and shouting that I was not rightly called my father's son. I could barely endure the rest of that day and on the next I went to my parents and questioned them. They were enraged at the remark. I felt relieved at their response. But still, this—this thing—kept gnawing at my heart. And it was spread about in vulgar whispers. And then, without my parents' knowledge, I went to Delphi, but Apollo did not say what I had gone to hear. Instead, he answered questions I had not asked and told of horror and misery beyond belief—how I would know my mother's bed and bring to the world a race of children too terrible for men to see and cause the death of my own father. I trembled at those words and fled from Corinth—as far as I could—to where no star could ever guide me back, where I could never see that infamous prophecy fulfilled. And as I traveled, I came to that place where you say the king was murdered. This is the truth, Jocasta—I was in that place where the three roads meet. There was a herald leading a carriage drawn by horses and a man riding in the carriage—just as you described. The man in front, and the old one, ordered me out of the path. I refused. The driver pushed. In anger, I struck him. The old man saw it, reached for his lash and waited till I had passed. Then he struck me on the head. But he paid—oh yes, he paid. He lost his balance and fell from the carriage and as he lay there helpless—on his back—I killed him. I

killed them all. But if this stranger had any tie with Laius—O God
—who could be more hated in the eyes of Heaven and Earth? *I* am
the one whom strangers and citizens are forbidden to receive! *I* am
the one to whom all are forbidden to speak! *I* am the one who must
be driven out! *I* am the one for whom my curse was meant! I have
touched his bed with the very hands that killed him! O God! The
sin! The horror! *I* am to be banished, never to see my people, never
to walk in my fatherland. Or else I must take my mother for a bride
and kill my father Polybus, who gave me life and cared for me.
What cruel god has sent this torture? Hear me, you gods, you holy
gods—I will never see that day! I will die before I ever see the stain
of this abominable act!

CHORUS   Your words frighten us, my Lord. But you must have hope
until you hear the story from the man who saw.

OEDIPUS   Yes—hope. My only hope is waiting for this shepherd.

JOCASTA   Why? What do you hope to find with him?

OEDIPUS   This—if his story agrees with what you say, then I am safe.

JOCASTA   What did I say that makes you sure of this?

OEDIPUS   You said he told of *robbers*—that *robbers* killed the king.
If he still *says robbers*, then I am not the guilty one—because no
man can talk of many when he means a single one. But if he
names a *single* traveler, there will be no doubt—the guilt is mine.

JOCASTA   You can be sure that this was what he said—and he cannot
deny it. The whole city heard him—not I alone. But even if he alters
what he said before, he cannot prove that Laius met his death as it
was prophesied. For Apollo said that he would die at the hand of
a child—of mine. And as it happens, the child is dead. So prophecy
is worthless. I wouldn't dignify it with a moment's thought.

OEDIPUS   You are right. But still—send someone for the shepherd.
Now.

JOCASTA   I shall—immediately. I shall do what you ask. But now—
let us go inside.

Exeunt OEDIPUS, JOCASTA.

CHORUS
   I pray, may destiny permit
   that honestly I live my life
   in word and deed.
   That I obey the laws
   the heavens have begotten
   and prescribed.
   Those laws created by Olympus,[7]
   laws pure, immortal,
   forever lasting, essence of the god
   who lives in them.
   On arrogance and pride
   a tyrant feeds.
   The goad of insolence,
   of senseless overbearing, blind conceit,
   of seeking things unseasonable,
   unreasonable,
   will prick a man to climb to heights

7. The highest mountain of the Greek peninsula and the reputed home of the gods.

where he must lose his footing
and tumble to his doom.
Ambition must be used
to benefit the state;
else it is wrong, and God
must strike it from this earth.
Forever, God, I pray,
may you stand at my side!

A man who goes through life
with insolence in word and deed,
who lacks respect for law and right,
and scorns the shrines and temples of the gods,
may he find evil fate and doom
as his reward for wantonness,
for seeking ill-begotten gains
and reaching after sacred things
with sacrilegious hands.
No! Surely no such man
escapes the wrath, the vengeance of the god!
For if he did, if he could find reward
in actions which are wrong,
why should I trouble to acclaim,
to honor you, God, in my song?

No longer shall my feet
take me to Delphi's sacred shrine;
no longer shall they Abae or Olympia's altars[8] seek
unless the oracles are shown to tell the truth
to mortals without fail!
Where are you, Zeus, all-powerful, all-ruling?
You must be told,
you must know in your all-pervading power:
Apollo's oracles now fall into dishonor,
and what the god has spoken about Laius
finds disregard.
Could God be dead?

    Enter JOCASTA.

JOCASTA My Lords, I want to lay these laurel wreaths and incense offerings at the shrines of Thebes—for Oedipus is torturing himself, tearing his heart with grief. His vision to weigh the present against the past is blurred by fear and terror. He devours every word of dread, drinks in every thought of pain, destruction, death. And I no longer have the power to ease his suffering. Now I turn to you, Apollo, since you are nearest, with prayer and suppliant offerings. Find some way to free us, end our agony! O God of Light, release us! You see the fear that grips us—like sailors who watch their captain paralyzed by some unknown terror on the seas.

    Enter MESSENGER 1.

---

8. Important oracles were located at Abae and Olympia in ancient times.

MESSENGER 1   Strangers, would you direct me to the house of Oedipus? Or if you know where I might find the king himself, please tell me.

CHORUS   This is his house, stranger. He is inside. But this is the queen —his wife, and mother of his children.

MESSENGER 1   Then, blessings on the house of Oedipus—his house, his children, and his wife.

JOCASTA   Blessings on you as well, stranger. Your words are kind. But why have you come? What is it?

MESSENGER 1   Good news, my lady—for your husband and your house.

JOCASTA   What news? Where do you come from?

MESSENGER 1   From Corinth, my lady. My news will surely bring you joy—but sorrow, too.

JOCASTA   What? How can that be?

MESSENGER 1   Your husband now is ruler of the Isthmus!

JOCASTA   Do you mean that Polybus of Corinth has been deposed?

MESSENGER 1   Deposed by death, my lady. He has passed away.

JOCASTA   What! Polybus dead?

MESSENGER 1   I swear on my life that this is true.

JOCASTA   [*to a servant*]   Go! Quickly! Tell your master. [*To the heavens.*] You prophecies—you divinely-uttered prophecies! Where do you stand now? The man that Oedipus feared, the man he dared not face lest he should be his killer—that man is dead! Time claimed his life—not Oedipus!

Enter OEDIPUS.

OEDIPUS   Why, Jocasta? Why have you sent for me again?

JOCASTA   I want you to listen to this man. Listen to him and judge for yourself the worth of those holy prophecies.

OEDIPUS   Who is he? What news could he have for me?

JOCASTA   He comes from Corinth with the news that—that Polybus— is dead.

OEDIPUS   What! Tell me.

MESSENGER 1   If you must know this first, then I shall tell you— plainly. Polybus has died.

OEDIPUS   How? An act of treason? Sickness? How?

MESSENGER 1   My Lord, only a slight shift in the scales is required to bring the agèd to their rest.

OEDIPUS   Then it was sickness. Poor old man.

MESSENGER 1   Sickness—yes. And the weight of years.

OEDIPUS   Oh, Jocasta! Why? Why should we even look to oracles, the prophetic words delivered at their shrines or the birds that scream above us? They led me to believe that I would kill my father. But he is dead and in his grave, while I stand here—never having touched a weapon. Unless he died of longing for his son. If that is so, then I *was* the instrument of his death. And those oracles! Where are they now? Polybus has taken them to his grave. What worth have they now?

JOCASTA   Have I not been saying this all along?

OEDIPUS   Yes, you have. But I was misled by fear.

JOCASTA   Now you will no longer have to think of it.

OEDIPUS   But—my mother's bed. I still have *that* to fear.

JOCASTA   No. No, mortals have no need to fear when chance reigns supreme. The knowledge of the future is denied to us. It is better to live as you will, live as you can. You need not fear a union with your mother. Men often, in their dreams, approach their mothers' beds, lie with them, possess them. But the man who sees that this is meaningless can live without the threat of fear.

OEDIPUS   You would be right, Jocasta, if my mother were not alive. But she *is* alive. And no matter what you say, I have reason to fear.

JOCASTA   At least your father's death has brought some comfort.

OEDIPUS   Yes—some comfort. But my fear is of *her* as long as she lives.

MESSENGER 1   Who is *she?* The woman you fear?

OEDIPUS   Queen Merope, old man, the wife of Polybus.

MESSENGER 1   But why does *she* instill fear in you?

OEDIPUS   There was an oracle—a dreadful oracle sent by the gods.

MESSENGER 1   Can you tell me—a stranger—what it is?

OEDIPUS   Yes, it is all right to tell. Once Loxian Apollo said that I would take my mother for my bride and murder my father with my own hands. This is the reason that I left Corinth long ago. Fortunately. And yet, I have often longed to see my parents.

MESSENGER 1   Is this the fear that drove you away from Corinth?

OEDIPUS   Yes. I did not want to kill my father.

MESSENGER 1   But I can free you from this fear, my Lord. My purpose for coming was a good one.

OEDIPUS   And I shall see that you receive a fitting reward.

MESSENGER 1   Yes—that's why I came. To fare well myself by your returning home.

OEDIPUS   Home? To Corinth? To my parents? Never.

MESSENGER 1   My son, you do not realize what you are doing.

OEDIPUS   What do you mean, old man? For God's sake, tell me what you mean.

MESSENGER 1   I mean—the reasons why you dread returning home.

OEDIPUS   I dread Apollo's prophecy—and its fulfillment.

MESSENGER 1   You mean the curse—the stain they say lies with your parents?

OEDIPUS   Yes, old man. That is the fear that lives with me.

MESSENGER 1   Then you must realize that this fear is groundless.

OEDIPUS   How can that be—if I am their son?

MESSENGER 1   Because Polybus was no relative of yours.

OEDIPUS   What are you saying! Polybus was *not* my father?

MESSENGER 1   No more than I.

OEDIPUS   No more than you? But you are nothing to me.

MESSENGER 1   He was not your father any more than I.

OEDIPUS   Then why did he call me his son?

MESSENGER 1   You were a gift to him—from me.

OEDIPUS   A gift? From you? And yet he loved me as his son?

MESSENGER 1   Yes, my Lord. He had been childless.

OEDIPUS   And when you gave me to him—had you bought me? Or found me?

MESSENGER 1   I found you—in the hills of Cithaeron.

OEDIPUS   What were you doing there?

MESSENGER 1   Tending sheep along the mountain side.

OEDIPUS   Then you were a—hired shepherd?

MESSENGER 1   Yes, my son—a hired shepherd who saved you at that time.

OEDIPUS   Saved me? Was I in pain when you found me? Was I in trouble?

MESSENGER 1   Yes, your ankles are the proof of that.

OEDIPUS   Ah, you mean this old trouble. What has that to do with it?

MESSENGER 1   When I found you, your ankles were pierced with rivets. And I freed you.

OEDIPUS   Yes, I have had this horrible stigma since infancy.

MESSENGER 1   And so it was the swelling in your ankles that caused your name: Oedipus—"Clubfoot."

OEDIPUS   Oh! Who did this to me? My father? Or my mother?

MESSENGER 1   I don't know. You will have to ask the man who handed you to me.

OEDIPUS   You mean—you did not find me? It was someone else?

MESSENGER 1   Another shepherd.

OEDIPUS   Who? Do you remember who he was?

MESSENGER 1   I think—he was of the house of Laius.

OEDIPUS   The king who ruled this city?

MESSENGER 1   Yes. He was a shepherd in the service of the king.

OEDIPUS   Is he still alive? Can I see him?

MESSENGER 1   [*addressing the* CHORUS]   You—you people here—could answer that.

OEDIPUS   Do any of you know this shepherd? Have you seen him in the fields? Here in Thebes? Tell me now! Now is the time to unravel this mystery—once and for all.

CHORUS   I think it is the shepherd you asked to see before. But the queen will know.

OEDIPUS   Jocasta, is that the man he means? Is it the shepherd we have sent for? Is *he* the one?

JOCASTA   Why? What difference does it make? Don't think about it. Pay no attention to what he said. It makes no difference.

OEDIPUS   No difference? When I must have every clue to untangle the line of mystery surrounding my birth?

JOCASTA   In the name of God, if you care at all for your own life, you must not go on with this. I cannot bear it any longer.

OEDIPUS   Do not worry, Jocasta. Even if I am a slave—a third-generation slave, it is no stain on your nobility.

JOCASTA   Oedipus! I beg you—don't do this!

OEDIPUS   I can't grant you that. I cannot leave the truth unknown.

JOCASTA   It is for *your* sake that I beg you to stop. For your own good.

OEDIPUS   My own good has brought me pain too long.

JOCASTA   God help you! May you never know what you are!

OEDIPUS   Go, someone, and bring the shepherd to me. Leave the queen to exult in her noble birth.

JOCASTA   God help you! This is all that I can say to you—now or ever.

Exit JOCASTA.

CHORUS   Why has the queen left like this—grief-stricken and tortured with pain? My Lord, I fear—I fear that from her silence some horror will burst forth.

OEDIPUS   Let it explode! I will still want to uncover the secret of my birth—no matter how horrible. She—she is a woman with a woman's pride—and she feels shame for my humble birth. But I am the child of Fortune—beneficent Fortune—and I shall not be shamed! She is my mother. My sisters are the months and they have seen me rise and fall. This is my family. I will never deny my birth—and I will learn its secret!

Exit OEDIPUS.

CHORUS
    Ah Cithaeron,
    if in my judgment I am right,
    if I interpret what I hear correctly,
    then—by Olympus' boundless majesty!—
    tomorrow's full moon will not pass
    before, Cithaeron, you will find
    that Oedipus will honor you
    as mother and as nurse!
    That we will praise you in our song,
    benevolent and friendly to our king.
    Apollo, our Lord, may you find joy in this!

    Who bore you, Oedipus? A nymph?
    Did Pan beget you in the hills?
    Were you begotten by Apollo?
    Perhaps so, for he likes the mountain glens.
    Could Hermes be your father?[9]
    Or Dionysus? Could it be
    that he received you as a gift
    high in the mountains from a nymph
    with whom he lay?

    Enter OEDIPUS.

OEDIPUS   My Lords, I have never met him, but could that be the
shepherd we have been waiting for? He seems to be of the same
age as the stranger from Corinth. And I can see now—those are
my servants who are bringing him here. But, perhaps you know—
if you have seen him before. Is he the shepherd?

    Enter SHEPHERD.

CHORUS   Yes. I recognize him. He was a shepherd in the service of
Laius—as loyal as any man could be.
OEDIPUS   Corinthian, I ask you—is this the man you mean?
MESSENGER 1   Yes, my Lord. This is the man.
OEDIPUS   And you, old man, look at me and answer what I ask. Were
you in the service of Laius?
SHEPHERD   I was. But not bought. I was reared in his house.
OEDIPUS   What occupation? What way of life?
SHEPHERD   Tending flocks—for most of my life.
OEDIPUS   And where did you tend those flocks?
SHEPHERD   Sometimes Cithaeron, sometimes the neighboring places.
OEDIPUS   Have you ever seen this man before?
SHEPHERD   What man do you mean? Doing what?
OEDIPUS   This man. Have you ever met him before?
SHEPHERD   Not that I recall, my Lord.
MESSENGER 1   No wonder, my Lord. But I shall help him to recall.
I am sure that he'll remember the time we spent on Cithaeron—
he with his two flocks and I with one. Six months—spring to autumn

---

9. Pan was a woodland god and a protector of herds. Hermes (Roman Mercury) was
the messenger of the gods.

—every year—for three years. In the winter I would drive my flocks to my fold in Corinth, and he to the fold of Laius. Isn't that right, sir?

SHEPHERD   That is what happened. But it was a long time ago.

MESSENGER 1   Then tell me this. Do you remember a child you gave me to bring up as my own?

SHEPHERD   What are you saying? Why are you asking me this?

MESSENGER 1   This, my friend, this—is that child.

SHEPHERD   Damn you! Will you keep your mouth shut!

OEDIPUS   Save your reproaches, old man. It is you who deserve them— your words deserve them.

SHEPHERD   But master—how have I offended?

OEDIPUS   By refusing to answer his question about the child.

SHEPHERD   He doesn't know what he's saying. He's crazy.

OEDIPUS   If you don't answer of your own accord, we'll make you talk.

SHEPHERD   No! My Lord, please! Don't hurt an old man.

OEDIPUS [*to the* CHORUS]   One of you—twist his hands behind his back!

SHEPHERD   Why? Why? What do you want to know?

OEDIPUS   Did you or did you not give him that child?

SHEPHERD   I did. I gave it to him—and I wish that I had died that day.

OEDIPUS   You tell the truth, or you'll have your wish now.

SHEPHERD   If I tell, it will be worse.

OEDIPUS   Still he puts it off!

SHEPHERD   I said that I gave him the child!

OEDIPUS   Where did you get it? Your house? Someone else's? Where?

SHEPHERD   Not mine. Someone else's.

OEDIPUS   Whose? One of the citizens'? Whose house?

SHEPHERD   O God, master! Don't ask me any more.

OEDIPUS   This is the last time that I ask you.

SHEPHERD   It was a child—of the house of Laius.

OEDIPUS   A slave? Or of his own line?

SHEPHERD   Ah master, do I *have* to speak?

OEDIPUS   You have to. And I *have* to hear.

SHEPHERD   They said—it was his child. But the queen could tell you best.

OEDIPUS   Why? Did *she* give you the child?

SHEPHERD   Yes, my Lord.

OEDIPUS   Why?

SHEPHERD   To—kill!

OEDIPUS   Her own child!

SHEPHERD   Yes. Because she was terrified of some dreadful prophecy.

OEDIPUS   What prophecy?

SHEPHERD   The child would kill his father.

OEDIPUS   Then why did you give him to this man?

SHEPHERD   I felt sorry for him, master. And I thought that he would take him to his own home. But he saved him from his suffering— for worse suffering yet. My Lord, if you are the man he says you are —O God—you were born to suffering!

OEDIPUS   O God! O no! I see it all now! All clear! O Light! I will never look on you again! Sin! Sin in my birth! Sin in my marriage! Sin in blood!

Exit OEDIPUS.

CHORUS

O generations of men, you are nothing!
You are nothing!
And I count you as not having lived at all!
Was there ever a man,
was there ever a man on this earth
who could say he was happy,
who knew happiness, true happiness,
not an image, a dream,
an illusion, a vision, which would disappear?
Your example, Oedipus,
your example, your fate, your disaster,
show that none of us mortals
ever knew, ever felt what happiness truly is.

Here is Oedipus,
fortune and fame and bliss
leading him by the hand,
prodding him on to heights
mortals had never attained.
Zeus, it was he who removed
the scourge of the riddling maid,
of the sharp-clawed, murderous Sphinx!
He restored me to life from the brink
of disaster, of doom and of death.
It was he who was honored and hailed,
who was crowned and acclaimed as our king.

Here is Oedipus:
Who on this earth has been
struck by a harder blow
or stung by a fate more perverse?
Wretched Oedipus!
Father and son alike,
pleasures you took from where
once you were given life.
Furrows your father ploughed
bore you in silence. How, how, oh how could it be?

Time found you out,
all-seeing, irrepressible time.
Time sits in judgment on
the union that never could be;
judges you, father and son,
begot and begetter alike.
Would that I never had
laid eyes on Laius' child!
Now I wail and I weep,
and my lips are drenched in lament.
It was you, who offered me life;
it is you, who now bring me death.

Enter MESSENGER 2.

MESSENGER 2   O you most honored citizens of Thebes, you will mourn for the things you will hear, you will mourn for the things you will see, and you will ache from the burden of sorrow—if you are true sons of the house of Labdacus, if you care, if you feel. The waters of Ister and Phasis[1] can never cleanse this house of the horrors hidden within it and soon to be revealed—horrors willfully done! Worst of the sorrows we know are those that are willfully done!

CHORUS   We have mourned enough for sorrows we have known. What more is there that you can add?

MESSENGER 2   One more and only one—Jocasta, the queen, is dead.

CHORUS   O God—no! How!

MESSENGER 2   By her own hand. But the most dreadful pain you have not seen. You have not seen the worst. I have seen it and I shall tell you what I can of her terrible suffering. She ran in frenzied despair through the palace halls and rushed straight to her bridal bed—her fingers clutching and tearing at her hair. Then, inside the bedroom, she flung the doors closed and cried out to Laius, long since dead. She cried out to him, remembering the son that she had borne long ago, the son who killed his father, the son who left her to bear a dread curse—the children of her own son! She wept pitifully for that bridal bed which she had twice defiled—husband born of husband, child born of child. I didn't see what happened then. I didn't see her die. At that moment the king rushed in and shrieked in horror. All eyes turned to him as he paced in frantic passion and confusion. He sprang at each of us and begged to have a sword. He begged to know where he could find the wife that was no wife to him, the woman who had been mother to him and to his children. Some power beyond the scope of man held him in its sway and guided him to her. It was none of us. Then—as if somebody had beckoned to him and bade him follow—he screamed in terror and threw himself against the doors that she had locked. His body's weight and force shattered the bolts and thrust them from their sockets and he rushed into the room. There we saw the queen hanging from a noose of twisted cords. And when the king saw her, he cried out and moaned in deep, sorrowful misery. Then he untied the rope that hung about her neck and laid her body on the ground. But what happened then was even worse. Her gold brooches, her pins—he tore them from her gown and plunged them into his eyes again and again and again and screamed, "No longer shall you see the suffering you have known and caused! You saw what was forbidden to be seen, yet failed to recognize those whom you longed to see! Now you shall see only darkness!" And as he cried out in such desperate misery, he struck his eyes over and over—until a shower of blood and tears splattered down his beard, like a torrent of crimson rain and hail. And now suffering is mingled with pain for man and wife for the sins that both have done. Not one alone. Once—long ago—this house was happy—and rightly so. But now—today—sorrow, destruction, death, shame—all torments that have a name—all, all are theirs to endure.

CHORUS   But the king—does he have any relief from his suffering now?

MESSENGER 2   He calls for someone to unlock the gates and reveal to

---

1. The Ister was a name for the lower Danube. The Phasis flowed from the Caucasus to the Black Sea. They are invoked here together as examples of large rivers.

Thebes his father's killer, his mother's—I can't say it. I cannot say this unholy word. He cries out that he will banish himself from the land to free this house of the curse that he has uttered. But he is weak, drained. There is no one to guide his way. The pain is more than he can bear. You will see for yourselves. The palace gates are opening. You will see a sight so hideous that even his most bitter enemy would pity him.

Enter OEDIPUS.

CHORUS
Ah!
Dread horror for men to see!
Most dreadful of all that I have seen!
Ah!
Wretched one,
what madness has possessed you?
What demon has descended upon you
and bound you to this dire fate?
Ah!
Wretched one,
I cannot bear to look at you.
I want to ask you more
and learn still more
and understand—
but I shudder at the sight of you!

OEDIPUS   Ah! Ah! Where has this misery brought me? Is this my own voice I hear—carried on the wings of the air? O Fate! What have you done to me?

CHORUS   Terrible! Too terrible to hear! Too terrible to see!

OEDIPUS   O cloud of darkness! Cruel! Driven by the winds of fate! Assaulting me! With no defense to hold you back! O God! The pain! The pain! My flesh aches from its wounds! My soul aches from the memory of its horrors!

CHORUS   Body and soul—each suffers and mourns.

OEDIPUS   Ah! You still remain with me—a constant friend. You still remain to care for me—a blind man now. Now there is darkness and I cannot see your face. But I can hear your voice and I know that you are near.

CHORUS   O my Lord, how could you have done this? How could you blind yourself? What demon drove you?

OEDIPUS   Apollo! It was Apollo! *He* brought this pain, this suffering to me. But it was my own hand that struck the blow. Not his. O God! Why should I have sight when all that I would see is ugliness?

CHORUS   It is as you say.

OEDIPUS   What is there for me to see and love? What sight would give me joy? What sound? Take me away! Take me out of this land! I am cursed! Doomed! I am the man most hated by the gods!

CHORUS   You have suffered equally for your fortune and for your disaster. I wish that you had never come to Thebes.

OEDIPUS   Damn the man who set me free! Who loosed the fetters from my feet and let me live! I never will forgive him. If he had let me die, I would never have become the cause—the grief . . .

CHORUS   I wish that it had been this way.

OEDIPUS   If it had been, I would not have come to this—killer of my father, bridegroom of the woman who gave me birth, despised by the gods, child of shame, father and brother to my children. Is there any horror worse than these—any horror that has not fallen upon Oedipus.

CHORUS My Lord, I cannot condone what you have done. You would have been better dead than alive and blind.

OEDIPUS I did what I had to. You know I did. No more advice. Could these eyes have looked upon my father in the house of Hades? Could these eyes have faced my mother in her agony? I sinned against them both—a sin no suicide could purge. Could I have joy at the sight of my children—born as they were born? With these eyes? Never! Could I look upon the city of Thebes? The turrets that grace her walls? The sacred statues of her gods? Never! Damned! I—the noblest of the sons of Thebes—I have damned myself. It was I who commanded that Thebes must cast out the one who is guilty, unholy, cursed by the heavenly gods. *I* was the curse of Thebes! Could these eyes look upon the people? Never! And if I could raise a wall to channel the fountain of my hearing, I would spare nothing to build a prison for this defiled body where sight and sound would never penetrate. Then only would I have peace—where grief could not reach my mind. O Cithaeron! Why did you receive me? Why did you not let me die then? Why did you let me live to show the world how I was born? O Polybus! O Corinth! My home that was no home! You raised me, thinking I was fair and never knowing the evil that festered beneath. Now—now see the evil from which I was born, the evil I have become. O God! The three roads! The hidden glen! The thickets! The pathway where three roads meet! The blood you drank from my hands—do you not know—it was the blood of my father! Do you remember? Do you remember what I did then and what I did for Thebes? Wedding-rites! You gave me birth and gave my children birth! Born of the same womb that bore my children! Father! Brother! Child! Incestuous sin! Bride! Wife! Mother! All of one union! All the most heinous sins that man can know! The most horrible shame—I can no longer speak of it. For the love of God, hide me somewhere. Hide me away from this land! Kill me! Cast me into the sea where you will never have to look at me again! I beg you—touch me—in my misery. Touch me. Do not be afraid. My sins are mine alone to bear and touch no other man.

Enter CREON.

CHORUS My Lord, Creon is here to act or counsel in what you ask. In your stead—he is now our sole protector.

OEDIPUS What can I say to him? How can I ask for his trust? I have wronged him. I know that now.

CREON I have not come to mock you, Oedipus, nor to reproach you for the past. But you—if you have no respect for men, at least respect the lord of the sun whose fires give life to men. Hide your naked guilt from his sight. No earth or sacred rain or light can endure its presence. [*To a servant.*] Take him inside. It is impious for any but his own family to see and hear his suffering.

OEDIPUS I ask you in the name of God to grant me one favor. You have been kinder to me than I deserved. But one favor. I ask it for you—not for myself.

CREON What do you ask of me?

OEDIPUS   Cast me out of this land. Cast me out to where no man can see me. Cast me out now.

CREON   I would have done so, you can be sure. But I must wait and do the will of the god.

OEDIPUS   He has signified his will—with clarity. Destroy the parricide! Destroy the unholy one! Destroy Oedipus!

CREON   That was the god's command, I know. But now—with what has happened—I think it better to wait and learn what we must do.

OEDIPUS   You mean that you would ask for guidance for a man so sorrowful as I?

CREON   Surely, you are ready to put your trust in the god—now.

OEDIPUS   Yes, I am ready now. But I ask this of you. Inside—she is lying inside—give her whatever funeral rites you wish. You will do the right thing for her. She is your sister. But for me—do not condemn this city—my father's city—to suffer any longer from my presence as long as I live. Let me go and live upon Cithaeron—O Cithaeron, your name is ever linked with mine! Where my parents chose a grave for me. Where they would have had me die. Where I shall die in answer to their wish. And yet, I know, neither sickness nor anything else will ever bring me death. For I would not have been saved from death that once. No—I was saved for a more dreadful fate. Let it be. Creon, do not worry about my sons. They are boys and will have all they need, no matter where they go. But my daughters—poor creatures! They never ate a single meal without their father. We shared everything together. Creon, take care of them. Creon, let me touch them one last time. And let me weep— one last time. Please, my Lord, please, allow it—you're generous, you're kind. If I could only touch them and feel that they are with me—as I used to—when I could see them. [*Enter* ANTIGONE *and* ISMENE.] What is that crying? Is it my daughters? Has Creon taken pity on me? Has he sent my daughters to me? Are they here?

CREON   Yes, Oedipus, they are here. I had them brought to you. I know how much you love them, how much you have always loved them.

OEDIPUS   Bless you for this, Creon. Heaven bless you and grant you greater kindness than it has granted me. Ah, children, where are you? Come—come, touch my hands, the hands of your father, the hands of your brother, the hands that blinded these eyes which once were bright—these eyes—your father's eyes which neither saw nor knew what he had done when he became your father. I weep for you, my children. I cannot see you now. But when I think of the bitterness that waits for you in life, what you will have to suffer— the festivals, the holidays—the sadness you will know when you should share in gaiety! And when you are old enough to marry— who will there be, who will be the man strong enough to bear the slander that will haunt you—because you are *my* children? What disgrace will you not know? Your father killed his father. And lay with the woman that bore him and his children. These are the taunts that will follow you. And what man will marry you? No man, my children. You will spend your lives unwed—without children of your own—barren and wasted. Ah, Creon, you are the only father left to them. We—their parents—are lost. We gave them life. And we are lost to them. Take care of them. See that they do not wander poor and lonely. Do not let them suffer for what I have done. Pity them. They are so young. So lost. They have no one but you. Take my hand and promise me. And oh, my children, if you were older, I could make you understand. But now, make this your prayer—to find some place where you can live and have a better life than what your father knew.

CREON   Enough, my Lord. Go inside now.

OEDIPUS   Yes. I do not want to, but I will go.

CREON   All things have their time and their place.

OEDIPUS   I shall go—on this condition.

CREON   What condition? I am listening.

OEDIPUS   That you will send me away.

CREON   That is the god's decision, not mine.

OEDIPUS   The gods will not care where I go.

CREON   Then you shall have your wish.

OEDIPUS   Then—you consent?

CREON   It has nothing to do with my consent.

OEDIPUS   Let me go away from here.

CREON   Go then—but leave the children.

OEDIPUS   No! Do not take them away from me!

CREON   Do not presume that you are still in power. Your power has not survived with you.

CHORUS

There goes Oedipus—
he was the man who was able
to answer the riddle proposed by the Sphinx.
Mighty Oedipus—
he was an object of envy
to all for his fortune and fame.
There goes Oedipus—
now he is drowning in waves of dread and despair.
Look at Oedipus—
proof that none of us mortals
can truly be thought of as happy
until he is granted deliverance from life,
until he is dead
and must suffer no more.

ANTON CHEKHOV

Three Sisters*

CHARACTERS

ANDREY SERGEYEVITCH PROZOROV[1]

NATALYA IVANOVNA (*also called NATASHA*), *his fiancée, afterwards his wife*

OLGA ⎫
MASHA ⎬ *his sisters*
IRINA ⎭

FYODOR ILYITCH KULIGIN, *a high-school teacher, husband of Masha*

LIEUTENANT COLONEL ALEXANDR IGNATYEVITCH VERSHININ, *Battery Commander*

BARON NIKOLAY LVOVITCH TUSENBACH, *Lieutenant*

VASSILY VASSILYEVITCH SOLYONY, *Captain*

IVAN ROMANITCH TCHEBUTYKIN, *army doctor*

ALEXEY PETROVITCH FEDOTIK, *Second Lieutenant*

VLADIMIR KARLOVITCH RODDEY, *Second Lieutenant*

FERAPONT, *an old porter from the Rural Board[2]*

ANFISA, *the nurse, an old woman of eighty*

The action takes place in a provincial town.

Act 1

In the house of the PROZOROVS. *A drawing room with columns beyond which a large room is visible. Midday; it is bright and sunny. The table in the farther room is being laid for lunch.*

OLGA, *in the dark-blue uniform of a high-school teacher, is correcting exercise books, at times standing still and then walking up and down;* MASHA, *in a black dress, with her hat on her knee, is reading a book;* IRINA, *in a white dress, is standing plunged in thought.*

OLGA   Father died just a year ago, on this very day—the fifth of May, your name-day, Irina.[3] It was very cold, snow was falling. I felt as though I should not live through it; you lay fainting as though you were dead. But now a year has passed and we can think of it calmly; you are already in a white dress, your face is radiant. [*The clock strikes twelve.*] The clock was striking then too. [*A pause.*] I remember the band playing and the firing at the cemetery as they carried the coffin. Though he was a general in command of a brigade, yet there weren't many people there. It was raining, though. Heavy rain and snow.

IRINA   Why recall it!

° Translated by Constance Garnett.

1. See the note on Russian names, p. 534.

2. The Rural Board was the local arm of the Imperial government. It was somewhat more powerful than the locally elected *zemstvo*, which is mentioned later in the play.

3. Like many Europeans, Irina observes not her birthday but the feast of the saint whose name she bears. Several Saint Irenes share May 5 as feast day, including a Byzantine martyr of the first century, beheaded during the reign of Domitian or Trajan and a Greek martyr burned to death in Thessalonica in 304 A.D.

BARON TUSENBACH, TCHEBUTYKIN, *and* SOLYONY *appear near the table in the dining room, beyond the columns.*

OLGA   It is warm today, we can have the windows open, but the birches are not in leaf yet. Father was given his brigade and came here with us from Moscow eleven years ago and I remember distinctly that in Moscow at this time, at the beginning of May, everything was already in flower; it was warm, and everything was bathed in sunshine. It's eleven years ago, and yet I remember it all as though we had left it yesterday. Oh, dear! I woke up this morning, I saw a blaze of sunshine. I saw the spring, and joy stirred in my heart. I had a passionate longing to be back at home again!

TCHEBUTYKIN   The devil it is!

TUSENBACH   Of course, it's nonsense.

MASHA, *brooding over a book, softly whistles a song.*

OLGA   Don't whistle, Masha. How can you! [*A pause.*] Being all day in school and then at my lessons till the evening gives me a perpetual headache and thoughts as gloomy as though I were old. And really these four years that I have been at the high-school I have felt my strength and my youth oozing away from me every day. And only one yearning grows stronger and stronger. . . .

IRINA   To go back to Moscow. To sell the house, to make an end of everything here, and off to Moscow. . . .

OLGA   Yes! To Moscow, and quickly.

TCHEBUTYKIN *and* TUSENBACH *laugh.*

IRINA   Andrey will probably be a professor, he will not live here anyhow. The only difficulty is poor Masha.

OLGA   Masha will come and spend the whole summer in Moscow every year.

MASHA *softly whistles a tune.*

IRINA   Please God it will all be managed. [*Looking out of window.*] How fine it is today. I don't know why I feel so lighthearted! I remembered this morning that it was my name-day and at once I felt joyful and thought of my childhood when mother was living. And I was thrilled by such wonderful thoughts, such thoughts!

OLGA   You are radiant today and looking lovelier than usual. And Masha is lovely too. Andrey would be nice-looking, but he has grown too fat and that does not suit him. And I have grown older and ever so much thinner. I suppose it's because I get so cross with the girls at school. Today now I am free, I am at home, and my head doesn't ache, and I feel younger than yesterday. I am only twenty-eight. . . . It's all quite right, it's all from God, but it seems to me that if I were married and sitting at home all day, it would be better. [*A pause.*] I should be fond of my husband.

TUSENBACH [*to* SOLYONY]   You talk such nonsense, I am tired of listening to you. [*Coming into the drawing room.*] I forgot to tell you, you will receive a visit today from Vershinin, the new commander of our battery. [*Sits down to the piano.*]

OLGA   Well, I shall be delighted.

IRINA   Is he old?

TUSENBACH   No, nothing to speak of. Forty or forty-five at the most.

[*Softly plays the piano.*] He seems to be a nice fellow. He is not stupid, that's certain. Only he talks a lot.

IRINA   Is he interesting?

TUSENBACH   Yes, he is all right, only he has a wife, a mother-in-law and two little girls. And it's his second wife too. He is paying calls and telling everyone that he has a wife and two little girls. He'll tell you so too. His wife seems a bit crazy, with her hair in a long plait like a girl's, always talks in a high-flown style, makes philosophical reflections and frequently attempts to commit suicide, evidently to annoy her husband. I should have left a woman like that years ago, but he puts up with her and merely complains.

SOLYONY   [*coming into the drawing room with* TCHEBUTYKIN] With one hand I can only lift up half a hundredweight, but with both hands I can lift up a hundredweight and a half or even a hundredweight and three-quarters.[4] From that I conclude that two men are not only twice but three times as strong as one man, or even more. . . .

TCHEBUTYKIN   [*reading the newspaper as he comes in*]   For hair falling out . . . two ounces of naphthaline in half a bottle of spirit . . . to be dissolved and used daily. . . . [*Puts it down in his notebook.*] Let's make a note of it! No, I don't want it. . . . [*Scratches it out.*] It doesn't matter.

IRINA   Ivan Romanitch, dear Ivan Romanitch!

TCHEBUTYKIN   What is it, my child, my joy?

IRINA   Tell me, why is it I am so happy today? As though I were sailing with the great blue sky above me and big white birds flying over it. Why is it? Why?

TCHEBUTYKIN   [*kissing both her hands, tenderly*]   My white bird. . . .

IRINA   When I woke up this morning, got up and washed, it suddenly seemed to me as though everything in the world was clear to me and that I knew how one ought to live. Dear Ivan Romanitch, I know all about it. A man ought to work, to toil in the sweat of his brow, whoever he may be, and all the purpose and meaning of his life, his happiness, his ecstasies lie in that alone. How delightful to be a workman who gets up before dawn and breaks stones on the road, or a shepherd, or a schoolmaster teaching children, or an engine-driver. . . . Oh, dear! to say nothing of human beings, it would be better to be an ox, better to be a humble horse and work, than a young woman who wakes at twelve o'clock, then has coffee in bed, then spends two hours dressing. . . . Oh, how awful that is! Just as one has a craving for water in hot weather I have a craving for work. And if I don't get up early and work, give me up as a friend, Ivan Romanitch.

TCHEBUTYKIN   [*tenderly*]   I'll give you up, I'll give you up. . . .

OLGA   Father trained us to get up at seven o'clock. Now Irina wakes at seven and lies in bed at least till nine thinking. And she looks so serious! [*Laughs.*]

IRINA   You are used to thinking of me as a child and are surprised when I look serious. I am twenty!

TUSENBACH   The yearning for work, oh dear, how well I understand it! I have never worked in my life. I was born in cold, idle Petersburg, in a family that had known nothing of work or cares of any kind. I

---

4. I.e., 150 to 175 pounds.

remember, when I came home from the school of cadets, a footman used to pull off my boots. I used to be troublesome, but my mother looked at me with reverential awe, and was surprised when other people did not do the same. I was guarded from work. But I doubt if they have succeeded in guarding me completely, I doubt it! The time is at hand, an avalanche is moving down upon us, a mighty clearing storm which is coming, is already near and will soon blow the laziness, the indifference, the distaste for work, the rotten boredom out of our society. I shall work, and in another twenty-five or thirty years everyone will have to work. Everyone!

TCHEBUTYKIN   I am not going to work.

TUSENBACH   You don't count.

SOLYONY   In another twenty-five years you won't be here, thank God. In two or three years you will kick the bucket, or I shall lose my temper and put a bullet through your head, my angel.

> *Pulls a scent-bottle out of his pocket and sprinkles his chest and hands.*

TCHEBUTYKIN [*laughs*]   And I really have never done anything at all. I haven't done a stroke of work since I left the University, I have never read a book, I read nothing but newspapers. . . . [*Takes another newspaper out of his pocket.*] Here . . . I know, for instance, from the newspapers that there was such a person as Dobrolyubov, but what he wrote, I can't say.[5] . . . Goodness only knows. . . .

> *A knock is heard on the floor from the story below.*

There . . . they are calling me downstairs, someone has come for me. I'll be back directly. . . . Wait a minute. . . . [*Goes out hurriedly, combing his beard.*]

IRINA   He's got something up his sleeve.

TUSENBACH   Yes, he went out with a solemn face; evidently he is just going to bring you a present.

IRINA   What a nuisance!

OLGA   Yes, it's awful. He is always doing something silly.

MASHA   By the sea-strand an oak tree green . . . upon that oak a chain of gold . . . upon that oak a chain of gold.[6] [*Gets up, humming softly.*]

OLGA   You are not very cheerful today, Masha.

> MASHA, *humming, puts on her hat.*

OLGA   Where are you going?

MASHA   Home.

IRINA   How queer! . . .

TUSENBACH   To go away from a name-day party!

MASHA   Never mind. . . . I'll come in the evening. Good-bye, my darling. . . . [*Kisses* IRINA.] Once again I wish you, be well and happy. In old days, when father was alive, we always had thirty or forty officers here on name-days; it was noisy, but today there is only a man and a half, and it is as still as the desert. . . . I'll go. . . .

---

5. Nicholas A. Dobrolyubov (1836–1861) was a distinguished literary critic and advanced social thinker, a forerunner of populism.
6. Masha is quoting from the opening of *Ruslan and Ludmila*, a long narrative poem by Alexander S. Pushkin (1799–1837), the most famous Russian poet of the nineteenth century. Several of the literary quotations in the play, including this one, appear more than once.

I am in the blues today, I am feeling glum, so don't you mind what I say. [*Laughing through her tears.*] We'll talk some other time, and so for now good-bye, darling, I am going. . . .

IRINA [*discontentedly*]   Oh, how tiresome you are. . . .

OLGA [*with tears*]   I understand you, Masha.

SOLYONY   If a man philosophizes, there will be philosophy or sophistry, anyway, but if a woman philosophizes, or two do it, then you may just snap your fingers!

MASHA   What do you mean to say by that, you terrible person?

SOLYONY   Nothing. He had not time to say "alack," before the bear was on his back.[7] [*A pause.*]

MASHA [*to* OLGA, *angrily*]   Don't blubber!

> *Enter* ANFISA *and* FERAPONT *carrying a cake.*

ANFISA   This way, my good man. Come in, your boots are clean. [*To* IRINA.] From the Rural Board, from Mihail Ivanitch Protopopov. . . . A cake.

IRINA   Thanks. Thank him. [*Takes the cake.*]

FERAPONT   What?

IRINA [*more loudly*]   Thank him from me!

OLGA   Nurse dear, give him some pie. Ferapont, go along, they will give you some pie.

FERAPONT   Eh?

ANFISA   Come along, Ferapont Spiridonitch, my good soul, come along . . .

> *Goes out with* FERAPONT.

MASHA   I don't like that Protopopov, that Mihail Potapitch or Ivanitch. He ought not to be invited.

IRINA   I did not invite him.

MASHA   That's a good thing.

> *Enter* TCHEBUTYKIN, *followed by an orderly with a silver samovar; a hum of surprise and displeasure.*

OLGA [*putting her hands over her face*]   A samovar! How awful! [*Goes out to the table in the dining room.*]

IRINA   My dear Ivan Romanitch, what are you thinking about!

TUSENBACH [*laughs*]   I warned you!

MASHA   Ivan Romanitch, you really have no conscience!

TCHEBUTYKIN   My dear girls, my darlings, you are all that I have, you are the most precious treasures I have on earth. I shall soon be sixty, I am an old man, alone in the world, a useless old man. . . . There is nothing good in me, except my love for you, and if it were not for you, I should have been dead long ago. . . . [*To* IRINA.] My dear, my little girl, I've known you from a baby. . . . I've carried you in my arms. . . . I loved your dear mother. . . .

IRINA   But why such expensive presents?

TCHEBUTYKIN [*angry and tearful*]   Expensive presents. . . . Get along with you! [*To the orderly.*] Take the samovar in there. . . . [*Mimicking.*] Expensive presents. . . .

> *The orderly carries the samovar into the dinng room.*

7. A quotation from the fable "The Peasant and the Laborer" by Ivan A. Krylov (1769–1844).

ANFISA [*crossing the room*] My dears, a colonel is here, a stranger. . . .
He has taken off his greatcoat, children, he is coming in here.
Irinushka, you must be nice and polite, dear. . . . [*As she goes out.*]
And it's time for lunch already . . . mercy on us. . . .

TUSENBACH   Vershinin, I suppose.

Enter VERSHININ.

TUSENBACH   Colonel Vershinin.

VERSHININ [*to* MASHA *and* IRINA]   I have the honor to introduce myself, my name is Vershinin. I am very, very glad to be in your house
at last. How you have grown up! Aie-aie!

IRINA   Please sit down. We are delighted to see you.

VERSHININ [*with animation*]   How glad I am, how glad I am! But there
are three of you sisters. I remember—three little girls. I don't remember your faces, but that your father, Colonel Prozorov, had three
little girls I remember perfectly, and saw them with my own eyes.
How time passes! Hey-ho, how it passes!

TUSENBACH   Alexandr Ignatyevitch has come from Moscow.

IRINA   From Moscow? You have come from Moscow?

VERSHININ   Yes. Your father was in command of a battery there, and
I was an officer in the same brigade. [*To* MASHA.] Your face, now, I
seem to remember.

MASHA   I don't remember you.

IRINA   Olya! Olya! [*Calls into the dining room.*] Olya, come!

OLGA *comes out of the dining room into the drawing room.*

IRINA   Colonel Vershinin is from Moscow, it appears.

VERSHININ   So you are Olga Sergeyevna, the eldest. . . . And you are
Marya. . . . And you are Irina, the youngest. . . .

OLGA   You come from Moscow?

VERSHININ   Yes. I studied in Moscow. I began my service there, I
served there for years, and at last I have been given a battery here—
I have come here as you see. I don't remember you exactly, I only
remember you were three sisters. I remember your father. If I shut
my eyes, I can see him as though he were living. I used to visit you in
Moscow. . . .

OLGA   I thought I remembered everyone, and now all at once . . .

VERSHININ   My name is Alexandr Ignatyevitch.

IRINA   Alexandr Ignatyevitch, you have come from Moscow. . . . What
a surprise!

OLGA   We are going to move there, you know.

IRINA   We are hoping to be there by the autumn. It's our native town,
we were born there. . . . In Old Basmanny Street.[8] . . . [*Both laugh
with delight.*]

MASHA   To see someone from our own town unexpectedly! [*Eagerly.*]
Now I remember! Do you remember, Olya, they used to talk of the
"love-sick major"? You were a lieutenant at that time and were in
love, and for some reason everyone called you "major" to tease
you. . . .

VERSHININ [*laughs*]   Yes, yes. . . . The love-sick major, that was it.

---

8. Old Basmanny Street (now Karl Marx/Bakunin Street) and Nyemetsky Street (now
Bauman Street) were in the part of Moscow called Lefortov (now Baumanski), where
many foreigners lived along with army officers and technical and professional people.

MASHA   You only had a moustache then. . . . Oh, how much older you look! [*Through tears.*] How much older!

VERSHININ   Yes, when I was called the love-sick major I was young, I was in love. Now it's very different.

OLGA   But you haven't a single grey hair. You have grown older but you are not old.

VERSHININ   I am in my forty-third year, though. Is it long since you left Moscow?

IRINA   Eleven years. But why are you crying, Masha, you queer girl? . . . [*Through her tears.*] I shall cry too. . . .

MASHA   I am all right. And in which street did you live?

VERSHININ   In Old Basmanny.

OLGA   And that's where we lived too. . . .

VERSHININ   At one time I lived in Nyemetsky Street. I used to go from there to the Red Barracks. There is a gloomy-looking bridge on the way, where the water makes a noise. It makes a lonely man feel melancholy. [*A pause.*] And here what a broad, splendid river! A marvelous river!

OLGA   Yes, but it is cold. It's cold here and there are gnats. . . .

VERSHININ   How can you! You've such a splendid healthy Russian climate here. Forest, river . . . and birches here too. Charming, modest birches, I love them better than any other trees. It's nice to live here. The only strange thing is that the railway station is fifteen miles away. . . . And no one knows why it is so.

SOLYONY   I know why it is. [*They all look at him.*] Because if the station had been near it would not have been so far, and if it is far, it's because it is not near.

An awkward silence.

TUSENBACH   He is fond of his joke, Vassily Vassilyevitch.

OLGA   Now I recall you, too. I remember.

VERSHININ   I knew your mother.

TCHEBUTYKIN   She was a fine woman, the Kingdom of Heaven be hers.

IRINA   Mother is buried in Moscow.

OLGA   In the Novo-Dyevitchy.[9] . . .

MASHA   Would you believe it, I am already beginning to forget her face. So people will not remember us either . . . they will forget us.

VERSHININ   Yes. They will forget us. Such is our fate, there is no help for it. What seems to us serious, significant, very important, will one day be forgotten or will seem unimportant. [*A pause.*] And it's curious that we can't possibly tell what exactly will be considered great and important, and what will seem paltry and ridiculous. Did not the discoveries of Copernicus or Columbus, let us say, seem useless and ridiculous at first,[1] while the nonsensical writings of some wiseacre seemed true? And it may be that our present life, which we accept so readily, will in time seem queer, uncomfortable, not sensible, not clean enough, perhaps even sinful. . . .

TUSENBACH   Who knows? Perhaps our age will be called a great one

---

9. The most famous nunnery in Moscow, construction of which was begun in 1524 by Grand Duke Vassily III, father of Ivan the Terrible. Many distinguished people are buried there, including Chekhov himself.

1. The Polish astronomer Nicolaus Co-pernicus (1473–1543) and the Italian navigator Christopher Columbus (1451–1506) are popularly believed to have discovered, respectively, that the earth revolves around the sun rather than *vice versa* and that the earth is spherical rather than flat.

and remembered with respect. Now we have no torture-chamber, no executions, no invasions, but at the same time how much unhappiness there is!

SOLYONY [*in a high-pitched voice*] Chook, chook, chook. . . . It's bread and meat to the baron to talk about ideas.

TUSENBACH Vassily Vassilyevitch, I ask you to let me alone. . . . [*Moves to another seat.*] It gets boring, at last.

SOLYONY [*in a high-pitched voice*] Chook, chook, chook. . . .

TUSENBACH [*to* VERSHININ] The unhappiness which one observes now—there is so much of it—does indicate, however, that society has reached a certain moral level.

VERSHININ Yes, yes, of course.

TCHEBUTYKIN You said just now, baron, that our age will be called great; but people are small all the same. . . .[*Gets up.*] Look how small I am.

A violin is played behind the scenes.

MASHA That's Andrey playing, our brother.

IRINA He is the learned one of the family. We expect him to become a professor. Father was a military man, but his son has gone in for a learned career.

MASHA It was father's wish.

OLGA We have been teasing him today. We think he is a little in love.

IRINA With a young lady living here. She will come in today most likely.

MASHA Oh, how she dresses! It's not that her clothes are merely ugly or out of fashion, they are simply pitiful. A queer gaudy yellowish skirt with some sort of vulgar fringe and a red blouse. And her cheeks scrubbed till they shine! Andrey is not in love with her— I won't admit that, he has some taste anyway—it's simply for fun, he is teasing us, playing the fool. I heard yesterday that she is going to be married to Protopopov, the chairman of our Rural Board. And a very good thing too. . . . [*At the side door.*] Andrey, come here, dear, for a minute!

Enter ANDREY.

OLGA This is my brother, Andrey Sergeyevitch.

VERSHININ My name is Vershinin.

ANDREY And mine is Prozorov. [*Mops his perspiring face.*] You are our new battery commander?

OLGA Only fancy, Alexandr Ignatyevitch comes from Moscow.

ANDREY Really? Well, then, I congratulate you. My sisters will let you have no peace.

VERSHININ I have had time to bore your sisters already.

IRINA See what a pretty picture-frame Andrey has given me today! [*Shows the frame.*] He made it himself.

VERSHININ [*looking at the frame and not knowing what to say*] Yes . . . it is a thing. . . .

IRINA And that frame above the piano, he made that too!

ANDREY *waves his hand in despair and moves away.*

OLGA He is learned, and he plays the violin, and he makes all sorts of things with the fretsaw. In fact he is good all round. Andrey, don't go! That's a way he has—he always tries to make off! Come here!

MASHA *and* IRINA *take him by the arms and, laughing, lead him back.*

MASHA   Come, come!

ANDREY   Leave me alone, please!

MASHA   How absurd he is! Alexandr Ignatyevitch used to be called the love-sick major at one time, and he was not a bit offended.

VERSHININ   Not in the least!

MASHA   And I should like to call you the love-sick violinist!

IRINA   Or the love-sick professor!

OLGA   He is in love! Andryusha is in love!

IRINA [*claps her hands*]   Bravo, bravo! Encore! Andryusha is in love!

TCHEBUTYKIN [*comes up behind* ANDREY *and puts both arms round his waist*]   Nature our hearts for love created![2] [*Laughs, then sits down and reads the newspaper which he takes out of his pocket.*]

ANDREY   Come, that's enough, that's enough. . . . [*Mops his face.*] I haven't slept all night and this morning I don't feel quite myself, as they say. I read till four o'clock and then went to bed, but it was no use. I thought of one thing and another, and then it gets light so early; the sun simply pours into my bedroom. I want while I am here during the summer to translate a book from the English. . . .

VERSHININ   You read English then?

ANDREY   Yes. Our father, the Kingdom of Heaven be his, oppressed us with education. It's absurd and silly, but it must be confessed I began to get fatter after his death, and I have grown too fat in one year, as though a weight had been taken off my body. Thanks to our father we all know English, French, and German, and Irina knows Italian too. But what it cost us!

MASHA   In this town to know three languages is an unnecessary luxury! Not even a luxury, but an unnecessary encumbrance, like a sixth finger. We know a great deal that is unnecessary.

VERSHININ   What next! [*Laughs.*] You know a great deal that is unnecessary! I don't think there can be a town so dull and dismal that intelligent and educated people are unnecessary in it. Let us suppose that of the hundred thousand people living in this town, which is, of course, uncultured and behind the times, there are only three of your sort. It goes without saying that you cannot conquer the mass of darkness round you; little by little, as you go on living, you will be lost in the crowd. You will have to give in to it. Life will get the better of you, but still you will not disappear without a trace. After you there may appear perhaps six like you, then twelve and so on until such as you form a majority. In two or three hundred years life on earth will be unimaginably beautiful, marvelous. Man needs such a life and, though he hasn't it yet, he must have a presentiment of it, expect it, dream of it, prepare for it; for that he must see and know more than his father and grandfather. [*Laughs.*] And you complain of knowing a great deal that's unnecessary.

MASHA [*takes off her hat*]   I'll stay to lunch.

IRINA [*with a sigh*]   All that really ought to be written down. . . .

ANDREY *has slipped away unobserved.*

TUSENBACH   You say that after many years life on earth will be beauti-

2. A line from a Russian popular song of the 1890s.

ful and marvelous. That's true. But in order to have any share, however far off, in it now one must be preparing for it, one must be working. . . .

VERSHININ [*gets up*]   Yes. What a lot of flowers you have! [*Looking round.*] And delightful rooms. I envy you! I've been knocking about all my life from one wretched lodging to another, always with two chairs and a sofa and stoves which smoke. What I have been lacking all my life is just such flowers. . . . [*Rubs his hands.*] But there, it's no use thinking about it!

TUSENBACH   Yes, we must work. I'll be bound you think the German is getting sentimental.[3] But on my honor I am Russian and I can't even speak German. My father belonged to the Orthodox Church. . . . [*A pause.*]

VERSHININ [*walks about the stage*]   I often think, what if one were to begin life over again, knowing what one is about! If one life, which has been already lived, were only a rough sketch so to say, and the second were the fair copy! Then, I fancy, every one of us would try before everything not to repeat himself, anyway he would create a different setting for his life; would have a house like this with plenty of light and masses of flowers. . . . I have a wife and two little girls, my wife is in delicate health and so on and so on, but if I were to begin life over again I would not marry. . . . No, no!

Enter KULIGIN *in the uniform of a schoolmaster.*

KULIGIN [*goes up to* IRINA]   Dear sister, allow me to congratulate you on your name-day and with all my heart to wish you good health and everything else that one can desire for a girl of your age. And to offer you as a gift this little book. [*Gives her a book.*] The history of our high-school for fifty years, written by myself. An insignificant little book, written because I had nothing better to do, but still you can read it. Good morning, friends. [*To* VERSHININ.] My name is Kuligin, teacher in the high-school here. [*To* IRINA.] In that book you will find a list of all who have finished their studies in our high-school during the last fifty years. *Feci quod potui, faciant meliora potentes.*[4] [*Kisses* MASHA.]

IRINA   Why, but you gave me a copy of this book at Easter.

KULIGIN [*laughs*]   Impossible! If that's so, give it back, or better still, give it to the Colonel. Please accept it, Colonel. Some day when you are bored you can read it.

VERSHININ   Thank you. [*Is about to take leave.*] I am extremely glad to have made your acquaintance. . . .

OLGA   You are going? No, no!

IRINA   You must stay to lunch with us. Please do.

OLGA   Pray do!

VERSHININ [*bows*]   I believe I have chanced on a name-day. Forgive me, I did not know and have not congratulated you. . . . [*Walks away with* OLGA *into the dining room.*]

KULIGIN   Today, gentlemen, is Sunday, a day of rest. Let us all rest and enjoy ourselves each in accordance with our age and our posi-

---

3. Great numbers of foreigners (known generically as "Germans") immigrated to Russia, beginning early in the 17th century. At various times they were the subject of distrust and prejudice from conservative elements in Russia, particularly the Orthodox Church.

4. Latin for "I have done what I can; let those who are more capable do better things."

tion. The carpets should be taken up for the summer and put away till the winter . . . Persian powder or naphthaline.[5] . . . The Romans were healthy because they knew how to work and they knew how to rest, they had *mens sana in corpore sano.*[6] Their life was molded into a certain framework. Our headmaster says that the most important thing in every life is its framework. . . . What loses its framework, comes to an end—and it's the same in our everyday life. [*Puts his arm round* MASHA's *waist, laughing.*] Masha loves me. My wife loves me. And the window curtains, too, ought to be put away together with the carpets. . . . Today I feel cheerful and in the best of spirits. Masha, at four o'clock this afternoon we have to be at the headmaster's. An excursion has been arranged for the teachers and their families.

MASHA   I am not going.

KULIGIN [*grieved*]   Dear Masha, why not?

MASHA   We'll talk about it afterward. . . . [*Angrily.*] Very well, I will go, only let me alone, please. . . . [*Walks away.*]

KULIGIN   And then we shall spend the evening at the headmaster's. In spite of the delicate state of his health, that man tries before all things to be sociable. He is an excellent, noble personality. A splendid man. Yesterday, after the meeting, he said to me, "I am tired, Fyodor Ilyitch, I am tired." [*Looks at the clock, then at his watch.*] Your clock is seven minutes fast. "Yes," he said, "I am tired."

Sounds of a violin behind the scenes.

OLGA   Come to lunch, please. There's a pie!

KULIGIN   Ah, Olga, my dear Olga! Yesterday I was working from early morning till eleven o'clock at night and was tired out, and today I feel happy. [*Goes up to the table in the dining room.*] My dear. . . .

TCHEBUTYKIN [*puts the newspaper in his pocket and combs his beard*] Pie? Splendid!

MASHA [*to* TCHEBUTYKIN, *sternly*]   Only mind you don't drink today! Do you hear? It's bad for you to drink.

TCHEBUTYKIN   Oh, come, that's a thing of the past. It's two years since I got drunk. [*Impatiently.*] But there, my good girl, what does it matter!

MASHA   Anyway, don't you dare to drink. Don't dare. [*Angrily, but so as not to be heard by her husband.*] Again, damnation take it, I am to be bored a whole evening at the headmaster's!

TUSENBACH   I wouldn't go if I were you. . . . It's very simple.

TCHEBUTYKIN   Don't go, my love.

MASHA   Oh, yes, don't go! . . . It's a damnable life, insufferable. . . . [*Goes to the dining room.*]

TCHEBUTYKIN [*following her*]   Come, come. . . .

SOLYONY [*going to the dining room*]   Chook, chook, chook. . . .

TUSENBACH   Enough, Vassily Vassilyevitch! Leave off!

SOLYONY   Chook, chook, chook. . . .

KULIGIN [*gaily*]   Your health, Colonel! I am a schoolmaster and one of the family here, Masha's husband. . . . She is very kind, really, very kind. . . .

VERSHININ   I'll have some of this dark-colored vodka. . . . [*Drinks.*] To your health! [*To* OLGA.] I feel so happy with all of you!

5. Persian (insect) powder is a form of pyrethrum.   6. Latin for "a sound mind in a sound body."

No one is left in the drawing room but IRINA *and* TUSENBACH.

IRINA   Masha is in low spirits today. She was married at eighteen, when she thought him the cleverest of men. But now it's not the same. He is the kindest of men, but he is not the cleverest.

OLGA [*impatiently*]   Andrey, do come!

ANDREY [*behind the scenes*]   I am coming. [*Comes in and goes to the table.*]

TUSENBACH   What are you thinking about?

IRINA   Nothing. I don't like that Solyony of yours, I am afraid of him. He keeps on saying such stupid things. . . .

TUSENBACH   He is a queer man. I am sorry for him and annoyed by him, but more sorry. I think he is shy. . . . When one is alone with him he is very intelligent and friendly, but in company he is rude, a bully. Don't go yet, let them sit down to the table. Let me be by you. What are you thinking of? [*A pause.*] You are twenty, I am not yet thirty. How many years have we got before us, a long, long chain of days full of my love for you. . . .

IRINA   Nikolay Lvovitch, don't talk to me about love.

TUSENBACH [*not listening*]   I have a passionate craving for life, for struggle, for work, and that craving is mingled in my soul with my love for you, Irina, and just because you are beautiful it seems to me that life too is beautiful! What are you thinking of?

IRINA   You say life is beautiful. . . . Yes, but what if it only seems so! Life for us three sisters has not been beautiful yet, we have been stifled by it as plants are choked by weeds. . . . I am shedding tears. . . . I mustn't do that. [*Hurriedly wipes her eyes and smiles.*] I must work, I must work. The reason we are depressed and take such a gloomy view of life is that we know nothing of work. We come of people who despised work. . . .

Enter NATALYA IVANOVNA; *she is wearing a pink dress with a green sash.*

NATASHA   They are sitting down to lunch already. . . . I am late. . . . [*Steals a glance at herself in the glass and sets herself to rights.*] I think my hair is all right. [*Seeing* IRINA.] Dear Irina Sergeyevna, I congratulate you! [*Gives her a vigorous and prolonged kiss.*] You have a lot of visitors, I really feel shy. . . . Good day, Baron!

OLGA [*coming into the drawing room*]   Well, here is Natalya Ivanovna! How are you, my dear? [*Kisses her.*]

NATASHA   Congratulations on the name-day. You have such a big party and I feel awfully shy. . . .

OLGA   Nonsense, we have only our own people. [*In an undertone, in alarm.*] You've got on a green sash! My dear, that's not nice!

NATASHA   Why, is that a bad omen?

OLGA   No, it's only that it doesn't go with your dress . . . and it looks queer. . . .

NATASHA [*in a tearful voice*]   Really? But you know it's not green exactly, it's more a neutral color. [*Follows* OLGA *into the dining room.*]

In the dining room they are all sitting down to lunch; there is no one in the drawing room.

KULIGIN   I wish you a good husband, Irina. It's time for you to think of getting married.

TCHEBUTYKIN   Natalya Ivanovna, I hope we may hear of your engagement, too.

KULIGIN   Natalya Ivanovna has got a suitor already.

MASHA [strikes her plate with her fork]   Ladies and gentlemen, I want to make a speech!

KULIGIN   You deserve three bad marks for conduct.

VERSHININ   How nice this cordial is! What is it made of?

SOLYONY   Beetles.

IRINA [in a tearful voice]   Ugh, ugh! How disgusting.

OLGA   We are going to have roast turkey and apple pie for supper. Thank God I am at home all day and shall be at home in the evening. . . . Friends, won't you come this evening?

VERSHININ   Allow me to come too.

IRINA   Please do.

NATASHA   They don't stand on ceremony.

TCHEBUTYKIN   Nature our hearts for love created! [Laughs.]

ANDREY [angrily]   Do leave off, I wonder you are not tired of it!

FEDOTIK and RODDEY come in with a big basket of flowers.

FEDOTIK   I say, they are at lunch already.

RODDEY [speaking loudly, with a lisp]   At lunch? Yes, they are at lunch already. . . .

FEDOTIK   Wait a minute. [Takes a snapshot.] One! Wait another minute. . . . [Takes another snapshot.] Two! Now it's ready.

They take the basket and walk into the dining room, where they are greeted noisily.

RODDEY [loudly]   My congratulations! I wish you everything, everything! The weather is delightful, perfectly magnificent. I've been out all the morning for a walk with the high-school boys. I teach them gymnastics.

FEDOTIK   You may move, Irina Sergeyevna, you may move. [Taking a photograph.] You look charming today. [Taking a top out of his pocket.] Here is a top, by the way. . . . It has a wonderful note. . . .

IRINA   How lovely!

MASHA   By the seashore an oak tree green. . . . Upon that oak a chain of gold. . . . [Complainingly.] Why do I keep saying that? That phrase has been haunting me all day. . . .

KULIGIN   Thirteen at table!

RODDEY [loudly]   Surely you do not attach importance to such superstitions? [Laughter.]

KULIGIN   If there are thirteen at table, it means that someone present is in love. It's not you, Ivan Romanovitch, by any chance? [Laughter.]

TCHEBUTYKIN   I am an old sinner, but why Natalya Ivanovna is overcome, I can't imagine . . .

Loud laughter; NATASHA runs out from the dining room into the drawing room followed by ANDREY.

ANDREY   Come, don't take any notice! Wait a minute . . . stop, I entreat you. . . .

NATASHA   I am ashamed. . . . I don't know what's the matter with me and they make fun of me. I know it's improper for me to leave the table like this, but I can't help it. . . . I can't . . . [*Covers her face with her hands.*]

ANDREY My dear girl, I entreat you, I implore you, don't be upset. I assure you they are only joking, they do it in all kindness. My dear, my sweet, they are all kind, warmhearted people and they are fond of me and of you. Come here to the window, here they can't see us. . . . [*Looks round.*]

NATASHA I am so unaccustomed to society! . . .

ANDREY Oh youth, lovely, marvelous youth! My dear, my sweet, don't be so distressed! Believe me, believe me. . . . I feel so happy, my soul is full of love and rapture. . . . Oh, they can't see us, they can't see us! Why, why, I love you, when I first loved you—oh, I don't know. My dear, my sweet, pure one, be my wife! I love you, I love you . . . as I have never loved anyone . . . [*A kiss.*]

>*Two officers come in and, seeing the pair kissing, stop in amazement.*

Act 2

The same scene as in Act 1. Eight o'clock in the evening. Behind the scenes in the street there is the faintly audible sound of a concertina. There is no light. NATALYA IVANOVNA *enters in a dressing gown, carrying a candle; she comes in and stops at the door leading to* ANDREY'S *room.*

NATASHA What are you doing, Andryusha? Reading? Never mind, I only just asked. . . .

>*Goes and opens another door and, peeping into it, shuts it again.*

Is there a light?

ANDREY [*enters with a book in his hand*] What is it, Natasha?

NATASHA I was looking to see whether there was a light. . . . It's Carnival, the servants are not themselves; one has always to be on the lookout for fear something goes wrong. Last night at twelve o'clock I passed through the dining room, and there was a candle left burning. I couldn't find out who had lighted it. [*Puts down the candle.*] What's the time?

ANDREY [*looking at his watch*] A quarter past eight.

NATASHA And Olga and Irina aren't in yet. They haven't come in. Still at work, poor dears! Olga is at the teachers' council and Irina at the telegraph office. . . . [*Sighs.*] I was saying to your sister this morning, "Take care of yourself, Irina darling," said I. But she won't listen. A quarter past eight, you say? I am afraid our Bobik is not at all well. Why is he so cold? Yesterday he was feverish and today he is cold all over. . . . I am so anxious!

ANDREY It's all right, Natasha. The boy is quite well.

NATASHA We had better be careful about his food, anyway. I am anxious. And I am told that the mummers are going to be here for the Carnival at nine o'clock this evening. It would be better for them not to come, Andryusha.

ANDREY I really don't know. They've been invited, you know.

NATASHA Baby woke up this morning, looked at me, and all at once he gave a smile; so he knew me. "Good morning, Bobik!" said I. "Good morning, darling!" And he laughed. Children understand; they understand very well. So I shall tell them, Andryusha, not to let the carnival party come in.

ANDREY [*irresolutely*]   That's for my sisters to say. It's for them to give orders.

NATASHA   Yes, for them too; I will speak to them. They are so kind. . . . [*Is going.*] I've ordered junket for supper. The doctor says you must eat nothing but junket, or you will never get thinner. [*Stops.*] Bobik is cold. I am afraid his room is chilly, perhaps. We ought to put him in a different room till the warm weather comes, anyway. Irina's room, for instance, is just right for a nursery: it's dry and the sun shines there all day. I must tell her; she might share Olga's room for the time. . . . She is never at home, anyway, except for the night. . . . [*A pause.*] Andryushantchik, why don't you speak?

ANDREY   Nothing. I was thinking. . . . Besides, I have nothing to say.

NATASHA   Yes . . . what was it I meant to tell you? . . . Oh, yes; Ferapont has come from the Rural Board, and is asking for you.

ANDREY [*yawns*]   Send him in.

> NATASHA *goes out;* ANDREY, *bending down to the candle which she has left behind, reads. Enter* FERAPONT; *he wears an old shabby overcoat, with the collar turned up, and has a scarf over his ears.*

ANDREY   Good evening, my good man. What is it?

FERAPONT   The chairman has sent a book and a paper of some sort here. . . . [*Gives the book and an envelope.*]

ANDREY   Thanks. Very good. But why have you come so late? It is past eight.

FERAPONT   Eh?

ANDREY [*louder*]   I say, you have come late. It is eight o'clock.

FERAPONT   Just so. I came before it was dark, but they wouldn't let me see you. The master is busy, they told me. Well, of course, if you are busy, I am in no hurry. [*Thinking that* ANDREY *has asked him a question.*] Eh?

ANDREY   Nothing. [*Examines the book.*] Tomorrow is Friday. We haven't a sitting, but I'll come all the same . . . and do my work. It's dull at home. . . . [*A pause.*] Dear old man, how strangely life changes and deceives one! Today I was so bored and had nothing to do, so I picked up this book—old university lectures—and I laughed. . . . Good heavens! I am the secretary of the Rural Board of which Protopopov is the chairman. I am the secretary, and the most I can hope for is to become a member of the Board! Me, a member of the local Rural Board, while I dream every night I am professor of the University of Moscow—a distinguished man, of whom all Russia is proud!

FERAPONT   I can't say, sir. . . . I don't hear well. . . .

ANDREY   If you did hear well, perhaps I should not talk to you. I must talk to somebody, and my wife does not understand me. My sisters I am somehow afraid of—I'm afraid they will laugh at me and make me ashamed. . . . I don't drink, I am not fond of restaurants, but how I should enjoy sitting at Tyestov's in Moscow at this moment, dear old chap!

FERAPONT   A contractor was saying at the Board the other day that there were some merchants in Moscow eating pancakes; one who ate forty, it seems, died. It was either forty or fifty, I don't remember.

ANDREY   In Moscow you sit in a huge room at a restaurant; you know no one and no one knows you, and at the same time you don't feel a stranger. . . . But here you know everyone and everyone knows you, and yet you are a stranger—a stranger. . . . A stranger, and lonely. . . .

FERAPONT   Eh? [*A pause.*] And the same contractor says—maybe it's not true—that there's a rope stretched right across Moscow.

ANDREY   What for?

FERAPONT   I can't say, sir. The contractor said so.

ANDREY   Nonsense. [*Reads.*] Have you ever been in Moscow?

FERAPONT   [*after a pause*]   No, never. It was not God's will I should. [*A pause.*] Am I to go?

ANDREY   You can go. Good-bye. [FERAPONT *goes out.*] Good-bye. [*Reading.*] Come tomorrow morning and take some papers here. . . . Go. . . . [*A pause.*] He has gone. [*A ring.*] Yes, it is a business. . . . [*Stretches and goes slowly into his own room.*]

> *Behind the scenes a* NURSE *is singing, rocking a baby to sleep. Enter* MASHA *and* VERSHININ. *While they are talking a maid-servant is lighting a lamp and candles in the dining room.*

MASHA   I don't know. [*A pause.*] I don't know. Of course habit does a great deal. After father's death, for instance, it was a long time before we could get used to having no orderlies in the house. But apart from habit, I think it's a feeling of justice makes me say so. Perhaps it is not so in other places, but in our town the most decent, honorable, and well-bred people are all in the army.

VERSHININ   I am thirsty. I should like some tea.

MASHA   [*glancing at the clock*]   They will soon be bringing it. I was married when I was eighteen, and I was afraid of my husband be-cause he was a teacher, and I had only just left school. In those days I thought him an awfully learned, clever, and important person. And now it is not the same, unfortunately. . . .

VERSHININ   Yes. . . . I see. . . .

MASHA   I am not speaking of my husband—I am used to him; but among civilians generally there are so many rude, ill-mannered, badly brought-up people. Rudeness upsets and distresses me: I am unhappy when I see that a man is not refined, not gentle, not polite enough. When I have to be among the teachers, my husband's colleagues, it makes me quite miserable.

VERSHININ   Yes. . . . But, to my mind, it makes no difference whether they are civilians or military men—they are equally uninteresting, in this town anyway. It's all the same! If one listens to a man of the educated class here, civilian or military, he is worried to death by his wife, worried to death by his house, worried to death by his estate, worried to death by his horses. . . . A Russian is peculiarly given to exalted ideas, but why is it he always falls so short in life? Why?

MASHA   Why?

VERSHININ   Why is he worried to death by his children and by his wife? And why are his wife and children worried to death by him?

MASHA   You are rather depressed this evening.

VERSHININ   Perhaps. . . . I've had no dinner today, and had nothing to eat since the morning. My daughter is not quite well, and when my little girls are ill I am consumed by anxiety; my conscience reproaches me for having given them such a mother. Oh, if you had seen her today! She is a wretched creature! We began quarreling at seven o'clock in the morning, and at nine I slammed the door and went away. [*A pause.*] I never talk about it. Strange, it's only to you I complain. [*Kisses her hand.*] Don't be angry with me. . . . Except for you I have no one—no one. . . .

>   *A pause.*

MASHA   What a noise in the stove! Before father died there was howling in the chimney. There, just like that.

VERSHININ   Are you superstitious?

MASHA   Yes.

VERSHININ   That's strange. [*Kisses her hand.*] You are a splendid, wonderful woman. Splendid! Wonderful! It's dark, but I see the light in your eyes.

MASHA   [*moves to another chair*]   It's lighter here.

VERSHININ   I love you—love, love. . . . I love your eyes, your movements, I see them in my dreams. . . . Splendid, wonderful woman!

MASHA   [*laughing softly*]   When you talk to me like that, for some reason I laugh, though I am frightened. . . . Please don't do it again. . . . [*In an undertone.*] You may say it, though; I don't mind. . . . [*Covers her face with her hands.*] I don't mind. . . . Someone is coming. Talk of something else.

>   IRINA *and* TUSENBACH *come in through the dining room.*

TUSENBACH   I've got a three-barreled name. My name is Baron Tusenbach-Krone-Altschauer, but I belong to the Orthodox Church and am just as Russian as you. There is very little of the German left in me—nothing, perhaps, but the patience and perseverance with which I bore you. I see you home every evening.

IRINA   How tired I am!

TUSENBACH   And every day I will come to the telegraph office and see you home. I'll do it for ten years, for twenty years, till you drive me away. . . . [*Seeing* MASHA *and* VERSHININ, *delightedly.*] Oh, it's you! How are you?

IRINA   Well, I am home at last. [*To* MASHA.] A lady came just now to telegraph to her brother in Saratov that her son died today, and she could not think of the address. So she sent it without an address—simply to Saratov.[7] She was crying. And I was rude to her for no sort of reason. Told her I had no time to waste. It was so stupid. Are the Carnival people coming tonight?

MASHA   Yes.

IRINA   [*sits down in an armchair*]   I must rest. I am tired.

TUSENBACH   [*with a smile*]   When you come from the office you seem so young, so forlorn. . . . [*A pause.*]

IRINA   I am tired. No, I don't like telegraph work, I don't like it.

MASHA   You've grown thinner. . . . [*Whistles.*] And you look younger, rather like a boy in the face.

---

7. A town of some size, located on the Volga about 450 miles southeast of Moscow.

TUSENBACH   That's the way she does her hair.

IRINA   I must find some other job, this does not suit me. What I so longed for, what I dreamed of, is the very thing that it's lacking in. . . . It is work without poetry, without meaning. . . . [*A knock on the floor.*] There's the doctor knocking. . . . [*To* TUSENBACH.] Do knock, dear. . . . I can't. . . . I am tired.

   TUSENBACH *knocks on the floor.*

IRINA   He will come directly. We ought to do something about it. The doctor and our Andrey were at the Club yesterday and they lost again. I am told Andrey lost two hundred roubles.[8]

MASHA   [*indifferently*]   Well, it can't be helped now.

IRINA   A fortnight ago he lost money, in December he lost money. I wish he'd make haste and lose everything, then perhaps we should go away from this town. By God, every night I dream of Moscow, it's perfect madness. [*Laughs.*] We'll move there in June and there is still left February, March, April, May . . . almost half a year.

MASHA   The only thing is Natasha must not hear of his losses.

IRINA   I don't suppose she cares.

   TCHEBUTYKIN, *who has only just got off his bed—he has been resting after dinner—comes into the dining room combing his beard, then sits down to the table and takes a newspaper out of his pocket.*

MASHA   Here he is . . . has he paid his rent?

IRINA   [*laughs*]   No. Not a kopek[9] for eight months. Evidently he has forgotten.

MASHA   [*laughs*]   How gravely he sits. [*They all laugh; a pause.*]

IRINA   Why are you so quiet, Alexandr Ignatyevitch?

VERSHININ   I don't know. I am longing for tea. I'd give half my life for a glass of tea. I have had nothing to eat since the morning.

TCHEBUTYKIN   Irina Sergeyevna!

IRINA   What is it?

TCHEBUTYKIN   Come here. *Venez ici.*[1] [IRINA *goes and sits down at the table.*] I can't do without you. [IRINA *lays out the cards for patience.*]

VERSHININ   Well, if they won't bring tea, let us discuss something.

TUSENBACH   By all means. What?

VERSHININ   What? Let us dream . . . for instance of the life that will come after us, in two or three hundred years.

TUSENBACH   Well? When we are dead, men will fly in balloons, change the fashion of their coats, will discover a sixth sense, perhaps, and develop it, but life will remain just the same, difficult, full of mysteries and happiness. In a thousand years man will sigh just the same, "Ah, how hard life is," and yet just as now he will be afraid of death and not want it.

VERSHININ   [*after a moment's thought*]   Well, I don't know. . . . It seems to me that everything on earth is bound to change by degrees

---

8. At the time of the play, one rouble was worth approximately 50 cents in American money. In the States the New York *Times* sold for one cent daily (two cents outside the metropolitan area) and three cents on Sundays. Bedsheets cost from 28 to 45 cents apiece. Old Crow was $1.10 a fifth, and a used grand piano could be purchased for from $175 to $300.

9. There are 100 kopeks in one rouble.

1. French for "Come here." At this period all cultivated, upper-class Russians spoke French.

and is already changing before our eyes. In two or three hundred, perhaps in a thousand years—the time does not matter—a new, happy life will come. We shall have no share in that life, of course, but we are living for it, we are working, well, yes, and suffering for it, we are creating it—and that alone is the purpose of our existence, and is our happiness, if you like.

MASHA *laughs softly.*

TUSENBACH   What is it?

MASHA   I don't know. I've been laughing all day.

VERSHININ   I was at the same school as you were, I did not go to the Military Academy; I read a great deal, but I do not know how to choose my books, and very likely I read quite the wrong things, and yet the longer I live the more I want to know. My hair is turning gray, I am almost an old man, but I know so little, oh so little! But all the same I fancy that I do know and thoroughly grasp what is essential and matters most. And how I should like to make you see that there is no happiness for us, that there ought not to be and will not be. . . . We must work and work, and happiness is the portion of our remote descendants. [*A pause.*] If it is not for me, at least it is for the descendants of my descendants. . . . [FEDOTIK *and* RODDEY *appear in the dining room; they sit down and sing softly, playing the guitar.*]

TUSENBACH   You think it's no use even dreaming of happiness! But what if I am happy?

VERSHININ   No.

TUSENBACH   [*flinging up his hands and laughing*]   It is clear we don't understand each other. Well, how am I to convince you? [MASHA *laughs softly.* TUSENBACH *holds up a finger to her.*] Laugh! [*To* VERSHININ.] Not only in two or three hundred years but in a million years life will be just the same; it does not change, it remains stationary, following its own laws which we have nothing to do with or which, anyway, we shall never find out. Migratory birds, cranes for instance, fly backward and forward, and whatever ideas, great or small, stray through their minds, they will still go on flying just the same without knowing where or why. They fly and will continue to fly, however philosophic they may become; and it doesn't matter how philosophical they are so long as they go on flying. . . .

MASHA   But still there is a meaning?

TUSENBACH   Meaning. . . . Here it is snowing. What meaning is there in that? [*A pause.*]

MASHA   I think man ought to have faith or ought to seek a faith, or else his life is empty, empty. . . . To live and not to understand why cranes fly; why children are born; why there are stars in the sky. . . . One must know what one is living for or else it is all nonsense and waste. [*A pause.*]

VERSHININ   And yet one is sorry that youth is over. . . .

MASHA   Gogol says: it's dull living in this world, friends![2]

TUSENBACH   And I say: it is difficult to argue with you, my friends, God bless you. . . .

TCHEBUTYKIN   [*reading the newspaper*]   Balzac was married at Berdit-

2. The concluding line of the short story "How the Two Ivans Quarreled" by Nikolai V. Gogol (1809–1852), best known outside Russia for his novel *Dead Souls* and his play *The Inspector General.*

chev.[3] [IRINA *hums softly.*] I really must put that down in my book. [*Writes.*] Balzac was married at Berditchev. [*Reads the paper.*]

IRINA [*lays out the cards for patience, dreamily*]   Balzac was married at Berditchev.

TUSENBACH   The die is cast. You know, Marya Sergeyevna, I've resigned my commission.

MASHA   So I hear. And I see nothing good in that. I don't like civilians.

TUSENBACH   Never mind. . . . [*Gets up.*] I am not good-looking enough for a soldier. But that does not matter, though. . . . I am going to work. If only for one day in my life, to work so that I come home at night tired out and fall asleep as soon as I get into bed. . . . [*Going into the dining room.*] Workmen must sleep soundly!

FEDOTIK [*to* IRINA]   I bought these chalks for you just now as I passed the shop. . . . And this penknife. . . .

IRINA   You've got into the way of treating me as though I were little, but I am grown up, you know. . . . [*Takes the chalks and the penknife, joyfully.*] How lovely!

FEDOTIK   And I bought a knife for myself . . . look . . . one blade, and another blade, a third, and this is for the ears, and here are scissors, and that's for cleaning the nails. . . .

RODDEY [*loudly*]   Doctor, how old are you?

TCHEBUTYKIN   I? Thirty-two. [*Laughter.*]

FEDOTIK   I'll show you another patience. . . . [*Lays out the cards.*]

The samovar is brought in; ANFISA *is at the samovar; a little later* NATASHA *comes in and is also busy at the table;* SOLYONY *comes in and, after greeting the others, sits down at the table.*

VERSHININ   What a wind there is!

MASHA   Yes. I am sick of the winter. I've forgotten what summer is like.

IRINA   It's coming out right, I see. We shall go to Moscow.

FEDOTIK   No, it's not coming out. You see, the eight is over the two of spades. [*Laughs.*] So that means you won't go to Moscow.

TCHEBUTYKIN [*reads from the newspaper*]   Tsi-tsi-kar.[4] Smallpox is raging there.

ANFISA [*going up to* MASHA]   Masha, come to tea, my dear. [*To* VERSHININ.] Come, your honor . . . excuse me, sir, I have forgotten your name. . . .

MASHA   Bring it here, nurse, I am not going there.

IRINA   Nurse!

ANFISA   I am coming!

NATASHA [*to* SOLYONY]   Little babies understand very well. "Good morning, Bobik, good morning, darling," I said. He looked at me in quite a special way. You think I say that because I am a mother, but no, I assure you! He is an extraordinary child.

SOLYONY   If that child were mine, I'd fry him in a frying-pan and eat him.

Takes his glass, comes into the drawing room and sits down in a corner.

3. Honoré de Balzac (1799–1850), the famous French novelist, married Countess Eveline Hanska in the Ukrainian town of Berditchev on March 14, 1850. They had begun to correspond as early as 1832, although she was married to an older man. Her husband died in 1841, but financial and other considerations delayed their marriage.

4. A city in Manchuria, also called Tsitsihar.

NATASHA [*covers her face with her hands*]   Rude, ill-bred man!

MASHA   Happy people don't notice whether it is winter or summer. I fancy if I lived in Moscow I should not mind what the weather was like. . . .

VERSHININ   The other day I was reading the diary of a French minister written in prison. The minister was condemned for the Panama affair.[5] With what enthusiasm and delight he describes the birds he sees from the prison window, which he never noticed before when he was a minister. Now that he is released, of course, he notices birds no more than he did before. In the same way, you won't notice Moscow when you live in it. We have no happiness and never do have, we only long for it.

TUSENBACH [*takes a box from the table*]   What has become of the sweets?

IRINA   Solyony has eaten them.

TUSENBACH   All?

ANFISA [*handing tea*]   There's a letter for you, sir.

VERSHININ   For me? [*Takes the letter.*] From my daughter. [*Reads.*] Yes, of course. . . . Excuse me, Marya Sergeyevna, I'll slip away. I won't have tea. [*Gets up in agitation.*] Always these upsets. . . .

MASHA   What is it? Not a secret?

VERSHININ [*in a low voice*]   My wife has taken poison again. I must go. I'll slip off unnoticed. Horribly unpleasant it all is. [*Kisses* MASHA's *hand.*] My fine, dear, splendid woman. . . . I'll go this way without being seen. . . . [*Goes out.*]

ANFISA   Where is he off to? I've just given him his tea. . . . What a man.

MASHA [*getting angry*]   Leave off! Don't pester, you give one no peace. . . . [*Goes with her cup to the table.*] You bother me, old lady.

ANFISA   Why are you so huffy? Darling!

ANDREY's *voice:* "Anfisa!"

ANFISA [*mimicking*]   Anfisa! he sits there. . . . [*Goes out.*]

MASHA [*by the table in the dining room, angrily*]   Let me sit down! [*Mixes the cards on the table.*] You take up all the table with your cards. Drink your tea!

IRINA   How cross you are, Masha!

MASHA   If I'm cross, don't talk to me. Don't interfere with me.

TCHEBUTYKIN [*laughing*]   Don't touch her, don't touch her!

MASHA   You are sixty, but you talk rot like a schoolboy.

NATASHA [*sighs*]   Dear Masha, why make use of such expressions in conversation? With your attractive appearance, I tell you straight out, you would be simply fascinating in a well-bred social circle if it were not for the things you say. *Je vous prie, pardonnez-moi, Marie, mais vous avez des manières un peu grossières.*[6]

---

5. From 1880 to 1889 a French group headed by Ferdinand de Lesseps, the builder of the Suez Canal, attempted to dig a canal across the Isthmus of Panama. It was a disaster, both from an engineering standpoint and from a financial one. In 1892 charges of fraud and bribery were made against the principals of the company and a number of politicians; a spectacular scandal resulted. Several officers of the company and Charles Baïhaut (1843–1905), a former Minister of Public Works, were convicted in 1893. After his release from several years in prison, Baïhaut published a book about his experiences called *Impressions Cellulaires* (1898).

6. French for "I beg your pardon, Marie (i.e., Masha), but you have manners which are a bit gross."

TUSENBACH [*suppressing a laugh*]　Give me . . . give me . . . I think there is some brandy there.

NATASHA　*Il paraît que mon Bobik déjà ne dort pas,*[7] he is awake. He is not well today. I must go to him, excuse me. . . . [*Goes out.*]

IRINA　Where has Alexandr Ignatyevitch gone?

MASHA　Home. Something queer with his wife again.

TUSENBACH [*goes up to* SOLYONY *with a decanter of brandy in his hand*]　You always sit alone, thinking, and there's no making out what you think about. Come, let us make it up. Let us have a drink of brandy. [*They drink.*] I shall have to play the piano all night, I suppose, play all sorts of trash. . . . Here goes!

SOLYONY　Why make it up? I haven't quarreled with you.

TUSENBACH　You always make me feel as though something had gone wrong between us. You are a queer character, there's no denying that.

SOLYONY [*declaims*]　I am strange, who is not strange! Be not wroth, Aleko![8]

TUSENBACH　I don't see what Aleko has got to do with it. . . .

SOLYONY　When I am *tête-à-tête*[9] with somebody, I am all right, just like anyone else, but in company I am depressed, ill at ease and . . . say all sorts of idiotic things, but at the same time I am more conscientious and straightforward than many. And I can prove it. . . .

TUSENBACH　I often feel angry with you, you are always attacking me when we are in company, and yet I somehow like you. Here goes, I am going to drink a lot today. Let's drink!

SOLYONY　Let us. [*Drinks.*] I have never had anything against you, Baron. But I have the temperament of Lermontov.[1] [*In a low voice.*] In fact I am rather like Lermontov to look at . . . so I am told. [*Takes out scent-bottle and sprinkles scent on his hands.*]

TUSENBACH　I have sent in my papers. I've had enough of it! I have been thinking of it for five years and at last I have come up to the scratch. I am going to work.

SOLYONY [*declaims*]　Be not wroth, Aleko. . . . Forget, forget thy dreams. . . .

> *While they are talking* ANDREY *comes in quietly with a book and sits down by a candle.*

TUSENBACH　I am going to work.

TCHEBUTYKIN [*coming into the drawing room with* IRINA]　And the food too was real Caucasian stuff: onion soup and for the meat course *tchehartma.* . . .

SOLYONY　*Tcheremsha* is not meat at all, it's a plant rather like our onion.

TCHEBUTYKIN　No, my dear soul, it's not onion, but mutton roasted in a special way.

SOLYONY　But I tell you that *tcheremsha* is an onion.

7. French for "It seems that my Bobik is already no longer asleep." Natasha's unidiomatic French identifies her as coming from a lower social class than the Prozorovs and their friends.

8. The first part of the speech is a quotation from the play *Woe from Wit* or *The Trouble with Reason* by Alexander S. Griboyedov (1795–1829). The second part refers to Aleko, the hero of "The Gypsies," a narrative poem by Pushkin. In the poem, Aleko, a young Russian, joins a Gypsy tribe and lives happily for a while with a Gypsy girl. When she deserts him for another, he stabs both the girl and her new lover and is ostracized by the tribe.

9. French for face-to-face (literally, head to head).

1. Mikhail Yurievitch Lermontov (1814–1841) was the great Romantic poet of 19th-century Russia, known for his melancholy and his fondness for morbid self-examination.

TCHEBUTYKIN   And I tell you that *tchehartma* is mutton.

SOLYONY   And I tell you that *tcheremsha* is an onion.

TCHEBUTYKIN   What's the use of my arguing with you? You have never been to the Caucasus or eaten *tchehartma*.

SOLYONY   I haven't eaten it because I can't bear it. *Tcheremsha* smells like garlic.

ANDREY [*imploringly*]   That's enough! Please!

TUSENBACH   When are the Carnival party coming?

IRINA   They promised to come at nine, so they will be here directly.

TUSENBACH [*embraces* ANDREY *and sings*]   "Oh my porch, oh my new porch . . ."

ANDREY [*dances and sings*]   "With posts of maple wood. . . ."

TCHEBUTYKIN [*dances*] "And lattice work complete. . . ."[2] [*Laughter.*]

TUSENBACH [*kisses* ANDREY]   Hang it all, let us have a drink. Andryusha, let us drink to our everlasting friendship. I'll go to the University when you do, Andryusha.

SOLYONY   Which? There are two universities in Moscow.

ANDREY   There is only one university in Moscow.

SOLYONY   I tell you there are two.

ANDREY   There may be three for aught I care. So much the better.

SOLYONY   There are two universities in Moscow! [*A murmur and hisses.*] There are two universities in Moscow: the old one and the new one. And if you don't care to hear, if what I say irritates you, I can keep quiet. I can even go into another room. [*Goes out at one of the doors.*]

TUSENBACH   Bravo, bravo! [*Laughs.*] Friends, begin, I'll sit down and play! Funny fellow that Solyony. . . . [*Sits down to the piano and plays a waltz.*]

MASHA [*dances a waltz alone*]   The baron is drunk, the baron is drunk, the baron is drunk.

 Enter NATASHA.

NATASHA [*to* TCHEBUTYKIN]   Ivan Romanitch!

 Says something to TCHEBUTYKIN, *then goes out softly.* TCHEBUTYKIN *touches* TUSENBACH *on the shoulder and whispers something to him.*

IRINA   What is it?

TCHEBUTYKIN   It's time we were going. Good night.

TUSENBACH   Good night. It's time to be going.

IRINA   But I say . . . what about the Carnival party?

ANDREY [*with embarrassment*]   They won't be coming. You see, dear, Natasha says Bobik is not well, and so. . . . In fact I know nothing about it, and don't care either.

IRINA [*shrugs her shoulders*]   Bobik is not well!

MASHA   Well, it's not the first time we've had to lump it! If we are turned out, we must go. [*To* IRINA.] It's not Bobik that is ill, but she is a bit . . . [*Taps her forehead with her finger.*] Petty, vulgar creature!

 ANDREY *goes by door on right to his own room,* TCHEBUTYKIN *following him; they are saying good-bye in the dining room.*

---

2. A traditional Russian dance-song.

FEDOTIK   What a pity! I was meaning to spend the evening, but of course if the child is ill . . . I'll bring him a toy tomorrow.

RODDEY [*loudly*]   I had a nap today after dinner on purpose, I thought I would be dancing all night. . . . Why, it's only nine o'clock.

MASHA   Let us go into the street; there we can talk. We'll decide what to do.

> *Sounds of* "Good-bye! Good night!" *The good-humored laugh of* TUSENBACH *is heard. All go out.* ANFISA *and the maidservant clear the table and put out the light. There is the sound of the nurse singing.* ANDREY, *in his hat and coat, and* TCHEBUTYKIN *come in quietly.*

TCHEBUTYKIN   I never had time to get married, because life has flashed by like lightning and because I was passionately in love with your mother, who was married.

ANDREY   One shouldn't get married. One shouldn't, because it's boring.

TCHEBUTYKIN   That's all very well, but what about loneliness? Say what you like, it's a dreadful thing to be lonely, my dear boy. . . . But no matter, though!

ANDREY   Let's make haste and go.

TCHEBUTYKIN   What's the hurry? We have plenty of time.

ANDREY   I am afraid my wife may stop me.

TCHEBUTYKIN   Oh!

ANDREY   I am not going to play today, I shall just sit and look on. I don't feel well. . . . What am I to do, Ivan Romanitch, I am so short of breath?

TCHEBUTYKIN   It's no use asking me! I don't remember, dear boy. . . . I don't know. . . .

ANDREY   Let us go through the kitchen. [*They go out.*]

> *A ring, then another ring; there is a sound of voices and laughter.*

IRINA [*enters*]   What is it?

ANFISA [*in a whisper*]   The mummers, all dressed up. [*A ring.*]

IRINA   Nurse, dear, say there is no one at home. They must excuse us.

> ANFISA *goes out.* IRINA *walks about the room in hesitation; she is excited. Enter* SOLYONY.

SOLYONY [*in perplexity*]   No one here. . . . Where are they all?

IRINA   They have gone home.

SOLYONY   How queer. Are you alone here?

IRINA   Yes. [*A pause.*] Good night.

SOLYONY   I behaved tactlessly, without sufficient restraint just now. But you are not like other people, you are pure and lofty, you see the truth. You alone can understand me. I love you, I love you deeply, infinitely.

IRINA   Good night! You must go.

SOLYONY   I can't live without you. [*Following her.*] Oh, my bliss! [*Through his tears.*] Oh, happiness! Those glorious, exquisite, marvelous eyes such as I have never seen in any other woman.

IRINA [*coldly*]   Don't, Vassily Vassilyitch!

SOLYONY   For the first time I am speaking of love to you, and I feel as though I were not on earth but on another planet. [*Rubs his fore-*

head.] But there, it does not matter. There is no forcing kindness, of course. . . . But there must be no happy rivals. . . . There must not. . . . I swear by all that is sacred I will kill any rival. . . . O exquisite being!

NATASHA *passes with a candle.*

NATASHA [*peeps in at one door, then at another and passes by the door that leads to her husband's room*] Andrey is there. Let him read. Excuse me, Vassily Vassilyitch, I did not know you were here, and I am in my dressing gown. . . .

SOLYONY   I don't care. Good-bye! [*Goes out.*]

NATASHA   You are tired, my poor, dear little girl! [*Kisses* IRINA.] You ought to go to bed earlier. . . .

IRINA   Is Bobik asleep?

NATASHA   He is asleep, but not sleeping quietly. By the way, dear, I keep meaning to speak to you, but either you are out or else I haven't the time. . . . I think Bobik's nursery is cold and damp. And your room is so nice for a baby. My sweet, my dear, you might move for a time into Olya's room!

IRINA [*not understanding*]   Where?

The sound of a three-horse sledge with bells driving up to the door.

NATASHA   You would be in the same room with Olya, and Bobik in your room. He is such a poppet. I said to him today, "Bobik, you are mine, you are mine!" and he looked at me with his funny little eyes. [*A ring.*] That must be Olya. How late she is!

The maid comes up to NATASHA *and whispers in her ear.*

NATASHA   Protopopov? What a queer fellow he is! Protopopov has come, and asks me to go out with him in his sledge. [*Laughs.*] How strange men are! . . . [*A ring.*] Somebody has come. I might go for a quarter of an hour. . . . [*To the maid.*] Tell him I'll come directly. [*A ring.*] You hear . . . it must be Olya. [*Goes out.*]

The maid runs out; IRINA *sits lost in thought;* KULIGIN, OLGA *and* VERSHININ *come in.*

KULIGIN   Well, this is a surprise! They said they were going to have an evening party.

VERSHININ   Strange! And when I went away half an hour ago they were expecting the Carnival people. . . .

IRINA   They have all gone.

KULIGIN   Has Masha gone too? Where has she gone? And why is Protopopov waiting below with his sledge? Whom is he waiting for?

IRINA   Don't ask questions. . . . I am tired.

KULIGIN   Oh, you little cross-patch. . . .

OLGA   The meeting is only just over. I am tired out. Our headmistress is ill and I have to take her place. Oh, my head, my head does ache; oh, my head! [*Sits down.*] Andrey lost two hundred roubles yesterday at cards. . . . The whole town is talking about it. . . .

KULIGIN   Yes, I am tired out by the meeting too. [*Sits down.*]

VERSHININ   My wife took it into her head to give me a fright, she nearly poisoned herself. It's all right now, and I'm glad, it's a relief.

. . . So we are to go away? Very well, then, I will say good night. Fyodor Ilyitch, let us go somewhere together! I can't stay at home, I absolutely can't. . . . Come along!

KULIGIN   I am tired. I am not coming. [*Gets up.*] I am tired. Has my wife gone home?

IRINA   I expect so.

KULIGIN [*kisses* IRINA'*s hand*]   Good-bye! I have all day tomorrow and next day to rest. Good night! [*Going.*] I do want some tea. I was reckoning on spending the evening in pleasant company. . . . *O fallacem hominum spem!*[3] . . . Accusative of exclamation.

VERSHININ   Well, then, I must go alone. [*Goes out with* KULIGIN, *whistling.*]

OLGA   My head aches, oh, how my head aches. . . . Andrey has lost at cards. . . . The whole town is talking about it. . . . I'll go and lie down. [*Is going.*] Tomorrow I shall be free. . . . Oh, goodness, how nice that is! Tomorrow I am free, and the day after I am free. . . . My head does ache, oh, my head. . . . [*Goes out.*]

IRINA [*alone*]   They have all gone away. There is no one left.

A concertina plays in the street, the nurse sings.

NATASHA [*in a fur cap and coat crosses the dining room, followed by the maid*]   I shall be back in half an hour. I shall only go a little way. [*Goes out.*]

IRINA [*left alone, in dejection*]   Oh, to go to Moscow, to Moscow!

Act 3

The bedroom of OLGA *and* IRINA. *On left and right beds with screens round them. Past two o'clock in the night. Behind the scenes a bell is ringing on account of a fire in the town, which has been going on for some time. It can be seen that no one in the house has gone to bed yet. On the sofa* MASHA *is lying, dressed as usual in black. Enter* OLGA *and* ANFISA.

ANFISA   They are sitting below, under the stairs. . . . I said to them, "Come upstairs; why, you mustn't stay there"—they only cried. "We don't know where father is," they said. "What if he is burned!" What an idea! And the poor souls in the yard . . . They are all undressed too.

OLGA [*taking clothes out of the cupboard*]   Take this gray dress . . . and this one . . . and the blouse too . . . and that skirt, nurse. . . . Oh, dear, what a dreadful thing! Kirsanov Street is burned to the ground, it seems. . . . Take this . . . take this. . . . [*Throws clothes into her arms.*] The Vershinins have had a fright, poor things. . . . Their house was very nearly burned. Let them stay the night here . . . we can't let them go home. . . . Poor Fedotik has had everything burned, he has not a thing left. . . .

ANFISA   You had better call Ferapont, Olya darling, I can't carry it all.

OLGA [*rings*]   No one will answer the bell. [*At the door.*] Come here, whoever is there!

---

3. Latin for "Oh, deceitful hope of mankind!"

Through the open door can be seen a window red with fire; the fire brigade is heard passing the house.

How awful it is! And how sickening!

Enter FERAPONT.

OLGA   Here take these, carry them downstairs. . . . The Kolotilin young ladies are downstairs . . . give it to them . . . and give this too.

FERAPONT   Yes, miss. In 1812 Moscow was burned too. . . . Mercy on us! The French marveled.[4]

OLGA   You can go now.

FERAPONT   Yes, miss. [*Goes out.*]

OLGA   Nurse darling, give them everything. We don't want anything, give it all to them. . . . I am tired, I can hardly stand on my feet. . . . We mustn't let the Vershinins go home. . . . The little girls can sleep in the drawing room, and Alexandr Ignatyevitch down below at the baron's. . . . Fedotik can go to the baron's, too, or sleep in our dining room. . . . As ill-luck will have it, the doctor is drunk, frightfully drunk, and no one can be put in his room. And Vershinin's wife can be in the drawing room too.

ANFISA [*wearily*]   Olya darling, don't send me away; don't send me away!

OLGA   That's nonsense, nurse. No one is sending you away.

ANFISA [*lays her head on* OLGA's *shoulder*]   My own, my treasure, I work, I do my best. . . . I'm getting weak, everyone will say "Be off!" And where am I to go? Where? I am eighty. Eighty-one.

OLGA   Sit down, nurse darling. . . . You are tired, poor thing. . . . [*Makes her sit down.*] Rest, dear good nurse. . . . How pale you are!

Enter NATASHA.

NATASHA   They are saying we must form a committee at once for the assistance of those whose houses have been burned. Well, that's a good idea. Indeed, one ought always to be ready to help the poor, it's the duty of the rich. Bobik and baby Sophie are both asleep, sleeping as though nothing were happening. There are such a lot of people everywhere, wherever one goes, the house is full. There is influenza in the town now; I am so afraid the children may get it.

OLGA [*not listening*]   In this room one does not see the fire, it's quiet here.

NATASHA   Yes . . . my hair must be untidy. [*In front of the looking glass.*] They say I have grown fatter . . . but it's not true! Not a bit! Masha is asleep, she is tired out, poor dear. . . . [*To* ANFISA *coldly.*] Don't dare to sit down in my presence! Get up! Go out of the room! [ANFISA *goes out; a pause.*] Why you keep that old woman, I can't understand!

OLGA [*taken aback*]   Excuse me, I don't understand either. . . .

NATASHA   She is no use here. She is a peasant; she ought to be in the country. . . . You spoil people! I like order in the house! There ought to be no useless servants in the house. [*Strokes her cheek.*] You are tired, poor darling. Our headmistress is tired! When baby Sophie is a big girl and goes to the high-school, I shall be afraid of you.

4. In the summer of 1812 Napoleon invaded Russia. The Russians retreated before him, burning and destroying everything in his path. He reached Moscow to find it abandoned and in flames. His disastrous retreat followed.

OLGA I shan't be headmistress.

NATASHA You will be elected, Olya. That's a settled thing.

OLGA I shall refuse. I can't. . . . It's too much for me. . . . [*Drinks water.*] You were so rude to nurse just now. . . . Excuse me, I can't endure it. . . . It makes me feel faint.

NATASHA [*perturbed*]. Forgive me, Olya; forgive me. . . . I did not mean to hurt your feelings.

> MASHA *gets up, takes her pillow, and goes out in a rage.*

OLGA You must understand, my dear, it may be that we have been strangely brought up, but I can't endure it. . . . Such an attitude oppresses me, it makes me ill. . . . I feel simply unnerved by it. . . .

NATASHA Forgive me; forgive me. . . . [*Kisses her.*]

OLGA The very slightest rudeness, a tactless word, upsets me. . . .

NATASHA I often say too much, that's true, but you must admit, dear, that she might just as well be in the country.

OLGA She has been thirty years with us.

NATASHA But now she can't work! Either I don't understand, or you won't understand me. She is not fit for work. She does nothing but sleep or sit still.

OLGA Well, let her sit still.

NATASHA [*surprised*] How, sit still? Why, she is a servant. [*Through tears.*] I don't understand you, Olya. I have a nurse to look after the children as well as a wet nurse for baby, and we have a housemaid and a cook, what do we want that old woman for? What's the use of her?

> *The alarm bell rings behind the scenes.*

OLGA This night has made me ten years older.

NATASHA We must come to an understanding, Olya. You are at the high-school, I am at home; you are teaching while I look after the house, and if I say anything about the servants, I know what I'm talking about; I do know what I'm talking about. . . . And that old thief, that old hag . . . [*stamps*] that old witch shall clear out of the house tomorrow! . . . I won't have people annoy me! I won't have it! [*Feeling that she has gone too far.*] Really, if you don't move downstairs, we shall always be quarreling. It's awful.

> *Enter* KULIGIN.

KULIGIN Where is Masha? It's time to be going home. The fire is dying down, so they say. [*Stretches.*] Only one part of the town has been burned, and yet there was a wind; it seemed at first as though the whole town would be destroyed. [*Sits down.*] I am exhausted. Olya, my dear . . . I often think if it had not been for Masha I should have married you. You are so good. . . . I am tired out. [*Listens.*]

OLGA What is it?

KULIGIN It is unfortunate the doctor should have a drinking bout just now; he is helplessly drunk. Most unfortunate. [*Gets up.*] Here he comes, I do believe. . . . Do you hear? Yes, he is coming this way. . . . [*Laughs.*] What a man he is, really. . . . I shall hide. [*Goes to the cupboard and stands in the corner.*] Isn't he a ruffian!

OLGA He has not drunk for two years and now he has gone and done it. . . . [*Walks away with* NATASHA *to the back of the room.*]

TCHEBUTYKIN *comes in; walking as though sober without stag-
gering, he walks across the room, stops, looks round; then goes
up to the washing-stand and begins to wash his hands.*

TCHEBUTYKIN [*morosely*]   The devil take them all . . . damn them all.
They think I am a doctor, that I can treat all sorts of complaints, and
I really know nothing about it, I have forgotten all I did know, I
remember nothing, absolutely nothing.

OLGA *and* NATASHA *go out unnoticed by him.*

The devil take them. Last Wednesday I treated a woman at Zasyp—
she died, and it's my fault that she died. Yes . . . I did know something twenty-five years ago, but now I remember nothing, nothing.
Perhaps I am not a man at all but only pretend to have arms and
legs and head; perhaps I don't exist at all and only fancy that I walk
about, eat and sleep. [*Weeps.*] Oh, if only I did not exist! [*Leaves
off weeping, morosely.*] I don't care! I don't care a scrap! [*A pause.*]
Goodness knows. . . . The day before yesterday there was a conversation at the club: they talked about Shakespeare, Voltaire.[5] . . . I
have read nothing, nothing at all, but I looked as though I had read
them. And the others did the same as I did. The vulgarity! The
meanness! And that woman I killed on Wednesday came back to
my mind . . . and it all came back to my mind and everything
seemed nasty, disgusting and all awry in my soul. . . . I went and
got drunk. . . .

Enter IRINA, VERSHININ, *and* TUSENBACH; TUSENBACH *is wearing
a fashionable new civilian suit.*

IRINA   Let us sit here. No one will come here.
VERSHININ   If it had not been for the soldiers, the whole town would
have been burned down. Splendid fellows! [*Rubs his hands with
pleasure.*] They are first-rate men! Splendid fellows!
KULIGIN [*going up to them*]   What time is it?
TUSENBACH   It's past three. It's getting light already.
IRINA   They are all sitting in the dining-room. No one seems to think
of going. And that Solyony of yours is sitting there too. . . . [*To
TCHEBUTYKIN.*] You had better go to bed, doctor.
TCHEBUTYKIN   It's all right. . . . Thank you! [*Combs his beard.*]
KULIGIN [*laughs*]   You are a bit fuddled, Ivan Romanitch! [*Slaps him
on the shoulder.*] Bravo! *In vino veritas,*[6] the ancients used to say.
TUSENBACH   Everyone is asking me to get up a concert for the benefit
of the families whose houses have been burned down.
IRINA   Why, who is there? . . .
TUSENBACH   We could get it up, if we wanted to. Marya Sergeyevna
plays the piano splendidly, to my thinking.
KULIGIN   Yes, she plays splendidly.
IRINA   She has forgotten. She has not played for three . . . or four
years.
TUSENBACH   There is absolutely no one who understands music in this
town, not one soul, but I do understand and on my honor I assure
you that Marya Sergeyevna plays magnificently, almost with genius.

5. Shakespeare and François Marie
Arouet, called Voltaire (1694–1778), the
French philosopher and playwright, are
cited as examples of the culture of Western
Europe as opposed to that of Russia.
6. Latin for "In wine (there is) truth,"
i.e., that people who have been drinking
are likely to speak the truth.

KULIGIN   You are right, Baron. I am very fond of her; Masha, I mean.
She is a good sort.

TUSENBACH   To be able to play so gloriously and to know that no one
understands you!

KULIGIN [*sighs*]   Yes. . . . But would it be suitable for her to take part
in a concert? [*A pause.*] I know nothing about it, my friends. Perhaps
it would be all right. There is no denying that our director is a fine
man, indeed a very fine man, very intelligent, but he has such views.
. . . Of course it is not his business, still if you like I'll speak to him
about it.

TCHEBUTYKIN *takes up a china clock and examines it.*

VERSHININ   I got dirty all over at the fire. I am a sight. [*A pause.*]
I heard a word dropped yesterday about our brigade being transferred ever so far away. Some say to Poland, and others to Tchita.[7]

TUSENBACH   I've heard something about it too. Well! The town will
be a wilderness then.

IRINA   We shall go away too.

TCHEBUTYKIN [*drops the clock, which smashes*]   To smithereens!

KULIGIN [*picking up the pieces*]   To smash such a valuable thing—oh,
Ivan Romanitch, Ivan Romanitch! I should give you minus zero for
conduct!

IRINA   That was mother's clock.

TCHEBUTYKIN   Perhaps. . . . Well, if it was hers, it was. Perhaps I did
not smash it, but it only seems as though I had. Perhaps it only seems
to us that we exist, but really we are not here at all. I don't know
anything—nobody knows anything. [*By the door.*] What are you
staring at? Natasha has got a little affair with Protopopov, and you
don't see it. . . . You sit here and see nothing, while Natasha has a
little affair with Protopopov. . . . [*Sings.*] May I offer you this date?[8]
. . . [*Goes out.*]

VERSHININ   Yes. . . . [*Laughs.*] How very queer it all is, really! [*A
pause.*] When the fire began I ran home as fast as I could. I went up
and saw our house was safe and sound and out of danger, but my
little girls were standing in the doorway in their nightgowns; their
mother was nowhere to be seen, people were bustling about, horses
and dogs were running about, and my children's faces were full of
alarm, horror, entreaty, and I don't know what; it wrung my heart
to see their faces. My God, I thought, what more have these children
to go through in the long years to come! I took their hands and ran
along with them, and could think of nothing else but what more
they would have to go through in this world! [*A pause.*] When I
came to your house I found their mother here, screaming, angry.
[MASHA *comes in with the pillow and sits down on the sofa.*] And
while my little girls were standing in the doorway in their nightgowns and the street was red with the fire, and there was a fearful
noise, I thought that something like it used to happen years ago
when the enemy would suddenly make a raid and begin plundering
and burning. . . . And yet, in reality, what a difference there is between what is now and has been in the past! And when a little more
time has passed—another two or three hundred years—people will

---

7. A town in Siberia some 3000 miles
from Moscow; also Chita.
8. Chekhov identified this passage as a
line from an operetta which he had heard
and of which he had forgotten the name.

look at our present manner of life with horror and derision, and everything of today will seem awkward and heavy, and very strange and uncomfortable. Oh, what a wonderful life that will be—what a wonderful life! [*Laughs.*] Forgive me, here I am airing my theories again! Allow me to go on. I have such a desire to talk about the future. I am in the mood. [*A pause.*] It's as though everyone were asleep. And so, I say, what a wonderful life it will be! Can you only imagine? . . . There are only three of your sort in the town now, but in generations to come there will be more and more and more; and the time will come when everything will be changed and be as you would have it; they will live in your way, and later on you too will be out of date—people will be born who will be better than you. . . . [*Laughs.*] I am in such a strange state of mind today. I have a fiendish longing for life. . . . [*Sings.*] Young and old are bound by love, and precious are its pangs[9]. . . . [*Laughs.*]

MASHA   Tram-tam-tam!

VERSHININ   Tam-tam!

MASHA   Tra-ra-ra?

VERSHININ   Tra-ta-ta! [*Laughs.*]

Enter FEDOTIK.

FEDOTIK [*dances*]   Burned to ashes! Burned to ashes! Everything I had in the world. [*Laughter.*]

IRINA   A queer thing to joke about. Is everything burned?

FEDOTIK [*laughs*]   Everything I had in the world. Nothing is left. My guitar is burned, and the camera and all my letters. . . . And the notebook I meant to give you—that's burned too.

Enter SOLYONY.

IRINA   No; please go, Vassily Vassilyitch. You can't stay here.

SOLYONY   How is it the baron can be here and I can't?

VERSHININ   We must be going, really. How is the fire?

SOLYONY   They say it is dying down. No, I really can't understand why the baron may be here and not I. [*Takes out a bottle of scent and sprinkles himself.*]

VERSHININ   Tram-tam-tam!

MASHA   Tram-tam!

VERSHININ [*laughs, to* SOLYONY]   Let us go into the dining room.

SOLYONY   Very well; we'll make a note of it. I might explain my meaning further, but fear I may provoke the geese.[1] . . . [*Looking at* TUSENBACH.] Chook, chook, chook! . . . [*Goes out with* VERSHININ *and* FEDOTIK.]

IRINA   How that horrid Solyony has made the room smell of tobacco! . . . [*In surprise.*] The baron is asleep! Baron, Baron!

TUSENBACH [*waking up*]   I am tired, though. . . . The brickyard. I am not talking in my sleep. I really am going to the brickyard directly, to begin work. . . . It's nearly settled. [*To* IRINA, *tenderly.*] You are so pale and lovely and fascinating. . . . It seems to me as though your paleness sheds a light through the dark air. . . . You are mel-

9. The song is from the opera *Eugene Onegin* by Peter I. Tchaikovsky, based on a novel in verse of the same name by Pushkin. It is sung in the opera by Prince Gremin, the husband of the heroine.

1. A quotation from the fable "The Geese" by Krylov.

ancholy; you are dissatisfied with life. . . . Ah, come with me; let us go and work together!

MASHA   Nikolay Lvovitch, do go!

TUSENBACH [*laughing*]   Are you here? I didn't see you. . . . [*Kisses* IRINA's *hand.*] Good-bye, I am going. . . . I look at you now, and I remember as though it were long ago how on your name-day you talked of the joy of work, and were so gay and confident. . . . And what a happy life I was dreaming of then! What has become of it? [*Kisses her hand.*] There are tears in your eyes. Go to bed, it's getting light . . . it is nearly morning. . . . If it were granted to me to give my life for you!

MASHA   Nikolay Lvovitch, do go! Come, really. . . .

TUSENBACH   I am going. [*Goes out.*]

MASHA [*lying down*]   Are you asleep, Fyodor?

KULIGIN   Eh?

MASHA   You had better go home.

KULIGIN   My darling Masha, my precious girl! . . .

IRINA   She is tired out. Let her rest, Fedya.

KULIGIN   I'll go at once. . . . My dear, charming wife! . . . I love you, my only one! . . .

MASHA [*angrily*]   *Amo, amas, amat; amamus, amatis, amant.*[2]

KULIGIN [*laughs*]   Yes, really she is wonderful. You have been my wife for seven years, and it seems to me as though we were only married yesterday. Honor bright! Yes, really you are a wonderful woman! I am content, I am content, I am content!

MASHA   I am bored, I am bored, I am bored! . . . [*Gets up and speaks, sitting down.*] And there's something I can't get out of my head. . . . It's simply revolting. It sticks in my head like a nail; I must speak of it. I mean about Andrey. . . . He has mortgaged this house in the bank and his wife has grabbed all the money, and you know the house does not belong to him alone, but to us four! He ought to know that, if he is a decent man.

KULIGIN   Why do you want to bother about it, Masha? What is it to you? Andryusha is in debt all round, so there it is.

MASHA   It's revolting, anyway. [*Lies down.*]

KULIGIN   We are not poor. I work—I go to the high-school, and then I give private lessons. . . . I do my duty. . . . There's no nonsense about me. *Omnia mea mecum porto,*[3] as the saying is.

MASHA   I want nothing, but it's the injustice that revolts me. [*A pause.*] Go, Fyodor.

KULIGIN [*kisses her*]   You are tired, rest for half an hour, and I'll sit and wait for you. . . . Sleep. . . . [*Goes.*] I am content, I am content, I am content. [*Goes out.*]

IRINA   Yes, how petty our Andrey has grown, how dull and old he has become beside that woman! At one time he was working to get a professorship and yesterday he was boasting of having succeeded at last in becoming a member of the Rural Board. He is a member, and Protopopov is chairman. . . . The whole town is laughing and talking of it and he is the only one who sees and knows nothing. . . . And

---

2. Latin for "I love, you love, he loves, we love, you love, they love," the present tense of the verb *amo*, frequently used as a sample verb in grammar texts.

3. Latin for "I carry all my (belongings about) with me."

here everyone has been running to the fire while he sits still in his room and takes no notice. He does nothing but play his violin. . . . [*Nervously.*] Oh, it's awful, awful, awful! [*Weeps.*] I can't bear it anymore, I can't! I can't, I can't! [OLGA *comes in and begins tidying up her table.* IRINA *sobs loudly.*]   Turn me out, turn me out, I can't bear it any more!

OLGA [*alarmed*]   What is it? What is it, darling?

IRINA [*sobbing*]   Where? Where has it all gone? Where is it? Oh, my God, my God! I have forgotten everything, everything . . . everything is in a tangle in my mind. . . . I don't remember the Italian for window or ceiling . . . I am forgetting everything; every day I forget something more and life is slipping away and will never come back, we shall never, never go to Moscow. . . . I see that we shan't go. . . .

OLGA   Darling, darling. . . .

IRINA [*restraining herself*]   Oh, I am wretched. . . . I can't work, I am not going to work. I have had enough of it, enough of it! I have been a telegraph clerk and now I have a job in the town council and I hate and despise every bit of the work they give me. . . . I am nearly twenty-four, I have been working for years, my brains are drying up, I am getting thin and old and ugly and there is nothing, nothing, not the slightest satisfaction, and time is passing and one feels that one is moving away from a real, fine life, moving farther and farther away and being drawn into the depths. I am in despair and I don't know how it is I am alive and have not killed myself yet. . . .

OLGA   Don't cry, my child, don't cry. It makes me miserable.

IRINA   I am not crying, I am not crying. . . . It's over. . . . There, I am not crying now. I won't . . . I won't.

OLGA   Darling, I am speaking to you as a sister, as a friend, if you care for my advice, marry the baron! [IRINA *weeps.* OLGA *speaks softly.*]   You know you respect him, you think highly of him. . . . It's true he is ugly, but he is such a thoroughly nice man, so good. . . . One doesn't marry for love, but to do one's duty. . . . That's what I think, anyway, and I would marry without love. Whoever proposed to me I would marry him, if only he were a good man. . . . I would even marry an old man. . . .

IRINA   I kept expecting we should move to Moscow and there I should meet my real one. I've been dreaming of him, loving him. . . . But it seems that was all nonsense, nonsense. . . .

OLGA [*puts her arms round her sister*]   My darling, lovely sister, I understand it all; when the baron left the army and came to us in a plain coat, I thought he looked so ugly that it positively made me cry. . . . He asked me, "Why are you crying?" How could I tell him! But if God brought you together I should be happy. That's a different thing, you know, quite different.

NATASHA *with a candle in her hand walks across the stage from door on right to door on left without speaking.*

MASHA [*sits up*]   She walks about as though it were she had set fire to the town.

OLGA   Masha, you are silly. The very silliest of the family, that's you. Please forgive me. [*A pause.*]

MASHA   I want to confess my sins, dear sisters. My soul is yearning. I am going to confess to you and never again to anyone. . . . I'll tell you this minute. [*Softly.*] It's my secret, but you must know everything. . . . I can't be silent. . . . [*A pause.*] I am in love, I am in love. . . . I love that man. . . . You have just seen him. . . . Well, I may as well say it straight out. I love Vershinin.

OLGA [*going behind her screen*]   Leave off. I don't hear anyway.

MASHA   But what am I to do? [*Clutches her head.*] At first I thought him queer . . . then I was sorry for him . . . then I came to love him . . . to love him with his voice, his words, his misfortunes, his two little girls. . . .

OLGA [*behind the screen*]   I don't hear you anyway. Whatever silly things you say I shan't hear them.

MASHA   Oh, Olya, you are silly. I love him—so that's my fate. It means that that's my lot. . . . And he loves me. . . . It's all dreadful. Yes? Is it wrong? [*Takes* IRINA *by the hand and draws her to herself.*] Oh, my darling. . . . How are we going to live our lives, what will become of us? . . . When one reads a novel it all seems stale and easy to understand, but when you are in love yourself you see that no one knows anything and we all have to settle things for ourselves. . . . My darling, my sister. . . . I have confessed it to you, now I'll hold my tongue. . . . I'll be like Gogol's madman[4] . . . silence . . . silence. . . .

Enter ANDREY *and after him* FERAPONT.

ANDREY [*angrily*].   What do you want? I can't make it out.

FERAPONT [*in the doorway, impatiently*]   I've told you ten times already, Andrey Sergeyevitch.

ANDREY   In the first place I am not Andrey Sergeyevitch, but Your Honor, to you!

FERAPONT   The firemen ask leave, Your Honor, to go through the garden on their way to the river. Or else they have to go round and round, an awful nuisance for them.

ANDREY   Very good. Tell them, very good. [FERAPONT *goes out.*] I am sick of them. Where is Olga? [OLGA *comes from behind the screen.*] I've come to ask you for the key of the cupboard, I have lost mine. You've got one, it's a little key.

OLGA *gives him the key in silence;* IRINA *goes behind her screen; a pause.*

ANDREY   What a tremendous fire! Now it's begun to die down. Hang it all, that Ferapont made me so cross I said something silly to him. Your Honor. . . . [*A pause.*] Why don't you speak, Olya? [*A pause.*] It's time to drop this foolishness and sulking all about nothing. . . . You are here, Masha, and you too, Irina—very well, then, let us have things out thoroughly, once for all. What have you against me? What is it?

OLGA   Leave off, Andryusha. Let us talk tomorrow. [*Nervously.*] What an agonizing night!

ANDREY [*greatly confused*]   Don't excite yourself. I ask you quite coolly, what have you against me? Tell me straight out. [VERSHININ'S *voice:* "Tram-tam-tam!"]

MASHA [*standing up, loudly*]   Tra-ta-ta! [*To* OLGA.] Good night, Olya, God bless you. . . .

---

4. The hero of Gogol's story "Memoirs of a Madman."

Goes behind the screen and kisses IRINA.

Sleep well. . . . Good night, Andrey. You'd better leave them now, they are tired out . . . you can go into things tomorrow. [*Goes out.*]

OLGA   Yes, really, Andryusha, let us put it off until tomorrow. . . . [*Goes behind her screen.*] It's time we were in bed.

ANDREY   I'll say what I have to say and then go. Directly. . . . First, you have something against Natasha, my wife, and I've noticed that from the very day of my marriage. Natasha is a splendid woman, conscientious, straightforward, and honorable—that's my opinion! I love and respect my wife, do you understand? I respect her, and I insist on other people respecting her too. I repeat, she is a conscientious, honorable woman, and all your disagreements are simply caprice, or rather the whims of old maids. Old maids never like and never have liked their sisters-in-law—that's the rule. [*A pause.*] Secondly, you seem to be cross with me for not being a professor, not working at something learned. But I am in the service of the Zemstvo,[5] I am a member of the Rural Board, and I consider this service just as sacred and elevated as the service of learning. I am a member of the Rural Board and I am proud of it, if you care to know. . . . [*A pause.*] Thirdly . . . there's something else I have to say. . . . I have mortgaged the house without asking your permission. . . . For that I am to blame, yes, and I ask your pardon for it. I was driven to it by my debts . . . thirty-five thousand. . . . I am not gambling now—I gave up cards long ago; but the chief thing I can say in self-defense is that you are, so to say, of the privileged sex—you get a pension . . . while I had not . . . my wages, so to speak. . . . [*A pause.*]

KULIGIN [*at the door*]   Isn't Masha here? [*Perturbed.*] Where is she? It's strange. . . . [*Goes out.*]

ANDREY   They won't listen. Natasha is an excellent, conscientious woman. [*Paces up and down the stage in silence, then stops.*] When I married her, I thought we should be happy . . . happy, all of us. . . . But, my God! [*Weeps.*] Dear sisters, darling sisters, you must not believe what I say, you mustn't believe it. . . . [*Goes out.*]

KULIGIN [*at the door, uneasily*]   Where is Masha? Isn't Masha here? How strange! [*Goes out.*]

The firebell rings in the street. The stage is empty.

IRINA [*behind the screen*]   Olya! Who is that knocking on the floor?

OLGA   It's the doctor, Ivan Romanitch. He is drunk.

IRINA   What a troubled night! [*A pause.*] Olya! [*Peeps out from behind the screen.*] Have you heard? The brigade is going to be taken away; they are being transferred to some place very far off.

OLGA   That's only a rumor.

IRINA   Then we shall be alone. . . .Olya!

OLGA   Well?

IRINA   My dear, my darling, I respect the baron, I think highly of him, he is a fine man—I will marry him, I consent, only let us go to Moscow! I entreat you, do let us go! There's nothing in the world better than Moscow! Let us go, Olya! Let us go!

---

5. An elected assembly at the county or provincial level which dealt with local economic and social problems.

Act 4

Old garden of the PROZOROVS' *house. A long avenue of fir trees, at the end of which is a view of the river. On the farther side of the river there is a wood. On the right the veranda of the house; on the table in it are bottles and glasses; evidently they have just been drinking champagne. It is twelve o'clock noon. People pass occasionally from the street across the garden to the river; five soldiers pass rapidly.* TCHEBUTYKIN, *in an affable mood, which persists throughout the act, is sitting in an easy chair in the garden, waiting to be summoned; he is wearing a military cap and has a stick.* IRINA, KULIGIN *with a decoration on his breast and with no moustache, and* TUSENBACH, *standing on the veranda, are saying good-bye to* FEDOTIK *and* RODDEY, *who are going down the steps; both officers are in marching uniform.*

TUSENBACH [*kissing* FEDOTIK] You are a good fellow; we've got on so happily together. [*Kisses* RODDEY.] Once more. . . . Good-bye, my dear boy. . . .

IRINA Till we meet again!

FEDOTIK No, it's good-bye for good; we shall never meet again.

KULIGIN Who knows! [*Wipes his eyes, smiles.*] Here I am crying too.

IRINA We shall meet some day.

FEDOTIK In ten years, or fifteen perhaps? But then we shall scarcely recognize each other—we shall greet each other coldly. . . . [*Takes a snapshot.*] Stand still. . . . Once more, for the last time.

RODDEY [*embraces* TUSENBACH] We shall not see each other again. . . . [*Kisses* IRINA'S *hand.*] Thank you for everything, everything. . . .

FEDOTIK [*with vexation*] Oh, do wait!

TUSENBACH Please God we shall meet again. Write to us. Be sure to write to us.

RODDEY [*taking a long look at the garden*] Good-bye, trees! [*Shouts.*] Halloo! [*A pause.*] Good-bye, echo!

KULIGIN I shouldn't wonder if you get married in Poland. . . . Your Polish wife will clasp you in her arms and call you *kochany!*[6] [*Laughs.*]

FEDOTIK [*looking at his watch*] We have less than an hour. Of our battery only Solyony is going on the barge; we are going with the rank and file. Three divisions of the battery are going today and three more tomorrow—and peace and quiet will descend upon the town.

TUSENBACH And dreadful boredom too.

RODDEY And where is Marya Sergeyevna?

KULIGIN Masha is in the garden.

FEDOTIK We must say good-bye to her.

RODDEY Good-bye. We must go, or I shall begin to cry. . . .

Hurriedly embraces TUSENBACH *and* KULIGIN *and kisses* IRINA'S *hand.*

We've had a splendid time here.

6. A Polish term of endearment.

FEDOTIK [*to* KULIGIN]   This is a little souvenir for you . . . a notebook with a pencil. . . . We'll go down here to the river. . . . [*As they go away both look back.*]

RODDEY [*shouts*]   Halloo-oo!

KULIGIN [*shouts*]   Good-bye!

> RODDEY *and* FEDOTIK *meet* MASHA *in the background and say good-bye to her; she walks away with them.*

IRINA   They've gone. . . . [*Sits down on the bottom step of the veranda.*]

TCHEBUTYKIN   They have forgotten to say good-bye to me.

IRINA   And what were you thinking about?

TCHEBUTYKIN   Why, I somehow forget, too. But I shall see them again soon, I am setting off tomorrow. Yes . . . I have one day more. In a year I shall be on the retired list. Then I shall come here again and shall spend the rest of my life near you. . . . There is only one year now before I get my pension. [*Puts a newspaper into his pocket and takes out another.*] I shall come here to you and arrange my life quite differently. . . . I shall become such a quiet . . . God-fearing . . . well-behaved person.

IRINA   Well, you do need to arrange your life differently, dear Ivan Romanitch. You certainly ought to somehow.

TCHEBUTYKIN   Yes, I feel it. [*Softly hums.*] "Tarara-boom-dee-ay— Tarara-boom-dee-ay."[7]

KULIGIN   Ivan Romanitch is incorrigible! Incorrigible!

TCHEBUTYKIN   You ought to take me in hand. Then I should reform.

IRINA   Fyodor has shaved off his moustache. I can't bear to look at him!

KULIGIN   Why, what's wrong?

TCHEBUTYKIN   I might tell you what your countenance looks like now, but I really can't.

KULIGIN   Well! It's the thing now, *modus vivendi*.[8] Our headmaster is clean-shaven and now I am second to him I have taken to shaving too. Nobody likes it, but I don't care. I am content. With moustache or without moustache I am equally content. [*Sits down.*]

> In the background ANDREY *is wheeling a baby asleep in a perambulator.*

IRINA   Ivan Romanitch, darling, I am dreadfully uneasy. You were on the boulevard yesterday, tell me what was it that happened?

TCHEBUTYKIN   What happened? Nothing. Nothing much. [*Reads the newspaper.*] It doesn't matter!

KULIGIN   The story is that Solyony and the baron met yesterday on the boulevard near the theater. . . .

TUSENBACH   Oh, stop it! Really. . . . [*With a wave of his hand walks away into the house.*]

KULIGIN   Near the theater. . . . Solyony began pestering the baron and he couldn't keep his temper and said something offensive. . . .

TCHEBUTYKIN   I don't know. It's all nonsense.

KULIGIN   A teacher at a divinity school wrote "nonsense" at the bottom

---

7. A passage from a popular nonsense song of the 1890s, attributed to Henry J. Sayers, an American, which had its first notable success in England.
8. Latin for "manner of living."

of an essay and the pupil puzzled over it thinking it was a Latin word. . . . [*Laughs.*] It was fearfully funny. . . . They say Solyony is in love with Irina and hates the baron. . . . That's natural. Irina is a very nice girl.

From the background behind the scenes, "Aa-oo! Halloo!"

IRINA [*starts*]   Everything frightens me somehow today. [*A pause.*] All my things are ready, after dinner I shall send off my luggage. The baron and I are to be married tomorrow, tomorrow we go to the brickyard and the day after that I shall be in the school. A new life is beginning. God will help me! How will it fare with me? When I passed my exam as a teacher I felt so happy, so blissful, that I cried. . . . [*A pause.*] The cart will soon be coming for my things. . . .

KULIGIN   That's all very well, but it does not seem serious. It's all nothing but ideas and very little that is serious. However, I wish you success with all my heart.

TCHEBUTYKIN [*moved to tenderness*]   My good, delightful darling. . . . My heart of gold. . . .

KULIGIN   Well, today the officers will be gone and everything will go on in the old way. Whatever people may say, Masha is a true, good woman. I love her dearly and am thankful for my lot! . . . People have different lots in life. . . . There is a man called Kozyrev serving in the Excise here.[9] He was at school with me, but he was expelled from the fifth form because he could never understand *ut consecutivum*.[1] Now he is frightfully poor and ill, and when I meet him I say, "How are you, *ut consecutivum*?" "Yes," he says, "just so—*consecutivum*" . . . and then he coughs. . . . Now I have always been successful, I am fortunate, I have even got the order of the Stanislav of the second degree[2] and I am teaching others that *ut consecutivum*. Of course I am clever, cleverer than very many people, but happiness does not lie in that. . . . [*A pause.*]

In the house the "Maiden's Prayer" is played on the piano.[3]

IRINA   Tomorrow evening I shall not be hearing that "Maiden's Prayer," I shan't be meeting Protopopov. . . . [*A pause.*] Protopopov is sitting there in the drawing room; he has come again today. . . .

KULIGIN   The headmistress has not come yet?

IRINA   No. They have sent for her. If only you knew how hard it is for me to live here alone, without Olya. . . . Now that she is headmistress and lives at the high-school and is busy all day long. I am alone, I am bored, I have nothing to do, and I hate the room I live in. . . . I have made up my mind, since I am not fated to be in Moscow, that so it must be. It must be destiny. There is no help for it. . . . It's all in God's hands, that's the truth. When Nikolay Lvovitch made me an offer again . . . I thought it over and made up my mind. . . . He is a

---

9. The Excise is the local tax office.
1. A reference to the practice in Latin grammar of introducing clauses of result with the conjunction *ut* and of using the subjunctive mood for the verb in the result clauses.
2. The Order of St. Stanislav was originally created in 1765 by Stanislav II, the last king of Poland. It was reestablished in 1815 by Czar Alexander I and included

four classes. In 1831 it was made an Imperial and Royal Order (three classes, plus a special class for foreigners). It was an order of merit rather than a military decoration.
3. "The Maiden's Prayer" was a popular piano piece of the period, the best known work of the Polish pianist and composer Teckla Badarzewska (1838–1864).

good man, it's wonderful really how good he is. . . . And I suddenly felt as though my soul had grown wings, my heart felt so light and again I longed for work, work. . . . Only something happened yesterday, there is some mystery hanging over me.

TCHEBUTYKIN   Nonsense.

NATASHA [*at the window*]   Our headmistress!

KULIGIN   The headmistress has come. Let us go in. [*Goes into the house with* IRINA.]

TCHEBUTYKIN [*reads the newspaper, humming softly*]   "Tarara-boom-dee-ay."

MASHA *approaches; in the background* ANDREY *is pushing the perambulator.*

MASHA   Here he sits, snug and settled.

TCHEBUTYKIN   Well, what then?

MASHA [*sits down*]   Nothing. . . . [*A pause.*] Did you love my mother?

TCHEBUTYKIN   Very much.

MASHA   And did she love you?

TCHEBUTYKIN [*after a pause*]   That I don't remember.

MASHA   Is my man here? It's just like our cook Marfa used to say about her policeman: is my man here?

TCHEBUTYKIN   Not yet.

MASHA   When you get happiness by snatches, by little bits, and then lose it, as I am losing it, by degrees one grows coarse and spiteful. . . . [*Points to her bosom.*] I'm boiling here inside. . . . [*Looking at* ANDREY, *who is pushing the perambulator.*] Here is our Andrey. . . . All our hopes are shattered. Thousands of people raised the bell, a lot of money and of labor was spent on it, and it suddenly fell and smashed.[4] All at once, for no reason whatever. That's just how it is with Andrey. . . .

ANDREY   When will they be quiet in the house? There is such a noise.

TCHEBUTYKIN   Soon. [*Looks at his watch.*] My watch is an old-fashioned one with a repeater. . . . [*Winds his watch, it strikes.*] The first, the second, and the fifth batteries are going at one o'clock. [*A pause.*] And I am going tomorrow.

ANDREY   For good?

TCHEBUTYKIN   I don't know. Perhaps I shall come back in a year. Though goodness knows. . . . It doesn't matter one way or another.

There is the sound of a harp and violin being played far away in the street.

ANDREY   The town will be empty. It's as though one put an extinguisher over it. [*A pause.*] Something happened yesterday near the theater; everyone is talking of it, and I know nothing about it.

TCHEBUTYKIN   It was nothing. Foolishness. Solyony began annoying the baron and he lost his temper and insulted him, and it came in the end to Solyony's having to challenge him. [*Looks at his watch.*] It's time, I fancy. . . . It was to be at half-past twelve in the Crown forest that we can see from here beyond the river. . . . Piff-paff!

4. Masha is perhaps referring to the gigantic bell called the Tsar Kolokol (or "King of Bells") in the Kremlin. It was originally cast at the behest of Boris Godunov to hang in the Ivan Bell Tower of the Kremlin, but it proved too heavy. The platform on which it rested fell on several occasions as a result of fire weakening its supports. It weighs about 200 tons and is over 20 feet high and more than 20 feet in diameter.

[*Laughs.*] Solyony imagines he is a Lermontov and even writes verses. Joking apart, this is his third duel.

MASHA   Whose?

TCHEBUTYKIN   Solyony's.

MASHA   And the baron's?

TCHEBUTYKIN   What about the baron? [*A pause.*]

MASHA   My thoughts are in a muddle. . . . Anyway, I tell you, you ought not to let them do it. He may wound the baron or even kill him.

TCHEBUTYKIN   The baron is a very good fellow, but one baron more or less in the world, what does it matter? Let them! It doesn't matter. [*Beyond the garden a shout of* "Aa-oo! Halloo!"] You can wait. That is Skvortsov, the second, shouting. He is in a boat. [*A pause.*]

ANDREY   In my opinion to take part in a duel, or to be present at it even in the capacity of a doctor, is simply immoral.

TCHEBUTYKIN   That only seems so. . . . We are not real, nothing in the world is real, we don't exist, but only seem to exist. . . . Nothing matters!

MASHA   How they keep on talking, talking all day long. [*Goes.*] To live in such a climate, it may snow any minute, and then all this talk on the top of it. [*Stops.*] I am not going indoors, I can't go in there. . . . When Vershinin comes, tell me. . . . [*Goes down the avenue.*] And the birds are already flying south. . . . [*Looks up.*] Swans or geese. . . . Darlings, happy things. . . . [*Goes out.*]

ANDREY   Our house will be empty. The officers are going, you are going, Irina is getting married, and I shall be left in the house alone.

TCHEBUTYKIN   What about your wife?

Enter FERAPONT *with papers.*

ANDREY   A wife is a wife. She is a straightforward, upright woman, good-natured, perhaps, but for all that there is something in her which makes her no better than some petty, blind, hairy animal. Anyway she is not a human being. I speak to you as to a friend, the one man to whom I can open my soul. I love Natasha, that is so, but sometimes she seems to me wonderfully vulgar, and then I don't know what to think, I can't account for my loving her or, anyway, having loved her.

TCHEBUTYKIN [*gets up*]   I am going away tomorrow, my boy, perhaps we shall never meet again, so this is my advice to you. Put on your cap, you know, take your stick and walk off . . . walk off and just go, go without looking back. And the farther you go, the better. [*A pause.*] But do as you like! It doesn't matter. . . .

SOLYONY *crosses the stage in the background with two officers; seeing* TCHEBUTYKIN *he turns toward him; the officers walk on.*

SOLYONY   Doctor, it's time! It's half-past twelve. [*Greets* ANDREY.]

TCHEBUTYKIN   Directly. I am sick of you all. [*To* ANDREY.] If anyone asks for me, Andryusha, say I'll be back directly. . . . [*Sighs.*] Oho-ho-ho!

SOLYONY   He had not time to say alack before the bear was on his back. [*Walks away with the doctor.*] Why are you croaking, old chap?

TCHEBUTYKIN   Come!

SOLYONY   How do you feel?

TCHEBUTYKIN [*angrily*]   Like a pig in clover.[5]

SOLYONY   The old chap need not excite himself. I won't do anything much, I'll only shoot him like a snipe. [*Takes out scent and sprinkles his hands.*] I've used a whole bottle today, and still they smell. My hands smell like a corpse. [*A pause.*] Yes. . . . Do you remember the poem? "And, restless, seeks the stormy ocean, as though in tempest there were peace."[6] . . .

TCHEBUTYKIN   Yes. He had not time to say alack before the bear was on his back.

> *Goes out with* SOLYONY. *Shouts are heard:* "Halloo! Oo-oo!" AN-DREY *and* FERAPONT *come in.*

FERAPONT   Papers for you to sign. . . .

ANDREY [*nervously*]   Let me alone! Let me alone! I entreat you! [*Walks away with the perambulator.*]

FERAPONT   That's what the papers are for—to be signed. [*Retires into the background.*]

> *Enter* IRINA *and* TUSENBACH *wearing a straw hat;* KULIGIN *crosses the stage shouting* "Aa-oo, Masha, aa-oo!"

TUSENBACH   I believe that's the only man in the town who is glad that the officers are going away.

IRINA   That's very natural. [*A pause.*] Our town will be empty now.

TUSENBACH   Dear, I'll be back directly.

IRINA   Where are you going?

TUSENBACH   I must go into the town, and then . . . to see my comrades off.

IRINA   That's not true. . . . Nikolay, why are you so absentminded today? [*A pause.*] What happened yesterday near the theater?

TUSENBACH [*with a gesture of impatience*]   I'll be here in an hour and with you again. [*Kisses her hands.*] My beautiful one . . . [*Looks into her face.*] For five years now I have loved you and still I can't get used to it, and you seem to me more and more lovely. What wonderful, exquisite hair! What eyes! I shall carry you off tomorrow, we will work, we will be rich, my dreams will come true. You shall be happy. There is only one thing, one thing: you don't love me!

IRINA   That's not in my power! I'll be your wife and be faithful and obedient, but there is no love, I can't help it. [*Weeps.*] I've never been in love in my life! Oh, I have so dreamed of love, I've been dreaming of it for years, day and night, but my soul is like a wonderful piano of which the key has been lost. [*A pause.*] You look uneasy.

TUSENBACH   I have not slept all night. There has never been anything in my life so dreadful that it could frighten me, and only that lost key frets at my heart and won't let me sleep. . . . Say something to me. . . . [*A pause.*] Say something to me. . . .

IRINA   What? What am I to say to you? What?

TUSENBACH   Anything.

IRINA   There, there! [*A pause.*]

TUSENBACH   What trifles, what little things suddenly *à propos*[7] of nothing acquire importance in life! One laughs at them as before, thinks

---

5. "To turn the pigs into the grass" is a proverbial expression meaning to create a diversion. Tchebutykin means that he is distracted.

6. A quotation from "The Sail," a poem by Lermontov.

7. A French phrase meaning "relating to" or "having to do with."

them nonsense, but still one goes on and feels that one has not the power to stop. Don't let us talk about it! I am happy. I feel as though I were seeing these pines, these maples, these birch trees for the first time in my life, and they all seem to be looking at me with curiosity and waiting. What beautiful trees, and, really, how beautiful life ought to be under them! [*A shout of* "Halloo! Aa-oo!"] I must be off; it's time. . . . See, that tree is dead, but it waves in the wind with the others. And so it seems to me that if I die I shall still have part in life, one way or another. Good-bye, my darling. . . . [*Kisses her hands.*] Those papers of yours you gave me are lying under the calendar on my table.

IRINA   I am coming with you.

TUSENBACH [*in alarm*]   No, no! [*Goes off quickly, stops in the avenue.*] Irina!

IRINA   What is it?

TUSENBACH [*not knowing what to say*]   I didn't have any coffee this morning. Ask them to make me some. [*Goes out quickly.*]

> IRINA *stands lost in thought, then walks away into the background of the scene and sits down on the swing. Enter* ANDREY *with the perambulator, and* FERAPONT *comes into sight.*

FERAPONT   Andrey Sergeyevitch, the papers aren't mine; they are Government papers. I didn't invent them.

ANDREY   Oh, where is it all gone? What has become of my past, when I was young, gay, and clever, when my dreams and thoughts were exquisite, when my present and my past were lighted up by hope? Why on the very threshold of life do we become dull, grey, uninteresting, lazy, indifferent, useless, unhappy? . . . Our town has been going on for two hundred years—there are a hundred thousand people living in it; and there is not one who is not like the rest, not one saint in the past, or the present, not one man of learning, not one artist, not one man in the least remarkable who could inspire envy or a passionate desire to imitate him. . . . They only eat, drink, sleep, and then die . . . others are born, and they also eat and drink and sleep, and not to be bored to stupefaction they vary their lives by nasty gossip, vodka, cards, litigation; and the wives deceive their husbands, and the husbands tell lies and pretend that they see and hear nothing, and an overwhelmingly vulgar influence weighs upon the children, and the divine spark is quenched in them and they become the same sort of pitiful, dead creatures, all exactly alike, as their fathers and mothers. . . . [*To* FERAPONT, *angrily.*] What do you want?

FERAPONT   Eh? There are papers to sign.

ANDREY   You bother me!

FERAPONT [*handing him the papers*]   The porter from the local treasury was saying just now that there was as much as two hundred degrees of frost in Petersburg this winter.[8]

ANDREY   The present is hateful, but when I think of the future, it is so nice! I feel so lighthearted, so free. A light dawns in the distance,

---

8. Two hundred degrees of frost normally means 200 degrees below the freezing point of water, which is very cold even for the Russian winter. Joseph Nicholas Delisle, a French astronomer, was in St. Petersburg from 1725 to 1747 at the invitation of Peter the Great. With the assistance of Josias Weitbrecht, he devised a thermometer which read 0 at the boiling point of water, 150 at the freezing point of water, and was graduated farther down to 200 or 205. Ferapont's temperature reading may have been on his scale.

I see freedom. I see how I and my children will become free from sloth, from kvass,[9] from goose and cabbage, from sleeping after dinner, from mean, parasitic living. . . .

FERAPONT He says that two thousand people were frozen to death. The people were terrified. It was either in Petersburg or Moscow, I don't remember.

ANDREY [*in a rush of tender feeling*] My dear sisters, my wonderful sisters! [*Through tears.*] Masha, my sister!

NATASHA [*in the window*] Who is talking so loud out there? Is that you, Andryusha? You will wake baby Sophie. *Il ne faut pas faire de bruit, la Sophie est dormée déja. Vous êtes un ours.*[1] [*Getting angry.*] If you want to talk, give the perambulator with the baby to somebody else. Ferapont, take the perambulator from the master!

FERAPONT Yes, ma'am. [*Takes the pram.*]

ANDREY [*in confusion*] I am talking quietly.

NATASHA [*petting her child, inside the room*] Bobik! Naughty Bobik! Little rascal!

ANDREY [*looking through the papers*] Very well, I'll look through them and sign what wants signing, and then you can take them back to the Board. . . .

> Goes into the house reading the papers; FERAPONT *pushes the pram farther into the garden.*

NATASHA [*speaking indoors*] Bobik, what is mamma's name? Darling, darling! And who is this? This is Auntie Olya. Say to Auntie, "Good morning, Olya!"

> Two wandering musicians, a man and a girl, enter and play a violin and a harp; from the house enter VERSHININ *with* OLGA *and* ANFISA, *and stand for a minute listening in silence;* IRINA *comes up.*

OLGA Our garden is like a public passage; they walk and ride through. Nurse, give those people something.

ANFISA [*gives money to the musicians*] Go away, and God bless you, my dear souls! [*The musicians bow and go away.*] Poor things. People don't play if they have plenty to eat. [*To* IRINA.] Good morning, Irisha! [*Kisses her.*] Aye, aye, my little girl, I am having a time of it! Living in the high-school, in a government flat, with dear Olya— that's what the Lord has vouchsafed me in my old age! I have never lived so well in my life, sinful woman that I am. . . . It's a big flat, and I have a room to myself and a bedstead. All at the government expense. I wake up in the night and, O Lord, Mother of God, there is no one in the world happier than I!

VERSHININ [*looks at his watch*] We are just going, Olga Sergeyevna. It's time to be off. [*A pause.*] I wish you everything, everything. . . . Where is Marya Sergeyevna?

IRINA She is somewhere in the garden. . . . I'll go and look for her.

VERSHININ Please be so good. I am in a hurry.

ANFISA I'll go and look for her too. [*Shouts.*] Mashenka, aa-oo! [*Goes with* IRINA *into the farther part of the garden.*] Aa-oo! Aa-oo!

---

9. A form of beer.
1. Unidiomatic French for "You mustn't make so much noise. Sophie is already asleep. You are a bear."

VERSHININ Everything comes to an end. Here we are parting. [*Looks at his watch.*] The town has given us something like a lunch; we have been drinking champagne, the mayor made a speech. I ate and listened, but my heart was here, with you all. . . . [*Looks round the garden.*] I've grown used to you. . . .

OLGA Shall we ever see each other again?

VERSHININ Most likely not. [*A pause.*] My wife and two little girls will stay here for another two months; please, if anything happens, if they need anything . . .

OLGA Yes, yes, of course. Set your mind at rest. [*A pause.*] By to-morrow there won't be a soldier in the town—it will all turn into a memory, and of course for us it will be like beginning a new life. . . . [*A pause.*] Nothing turns out as we would have it. I did not want to be a headmistress, and yet I am. It seems we are not to live in Moscow. . . .

VERSHININ Well. . . . Thank you for everything. . . . Forgive me if anything was amiss. . . . I have talked a great deal: forgive me for that too— don't remember evil against me.

OLGA [*wipes her eyes*] Why doesn't Masha come?

VERSHININ What else am I to say to you at parting? What am I to theorize about? . . . [*Laughs.*] Life is hard. It seems to many of us blank and hopeless; but yet we must admit that it goes on getting clearer and easier, and it looks as though the time were not far off when it will be full of happiness. [*Looks at his watch.*] It's time for me to go! In old days men were absorbed in wars, filling all their existence with marches, raids, victories, but now all that is a thing of the past, leaving behind it a great void which there is so far nothing to fill: humanity is searching for it passionately, and of course will find it. Ah, if only it could be quickly! [*A pause.*] If, don't you know, industry were united with culture and culture with industry. . . . [*Looks at his watch.*] But, I say, it's time for me to go. . . .

OLGA Here she comes.

MASHA *comes in.*

VERSHININ I have come to say good-bye. . . .

OLGA *moves a little away to leave them free to say good-bye.*

MASHA [*looking into his face*] Good-bye. . . . [*A prolonged kiss.*]

OLGA Come, come. . . .

MASHA *sobs violently.*

VERSHININ Write to me. . . . Don't forget me! Let me go! . . . Time is up! . . . Olga Sergeyevna, take her, I must . . . go . . . I am late. . . . [*Much moved, kisses* OLGA's *hands; then again embraces* MASHA *and quickly goes off.*]

OLGA Come, Masha! Leave off, darling.

Enter KULIGIN.

KULIGIN [*embarrassed*] Never mind, let her cry—let her. . . . My good Masha, my dear Masha! . . . You are my wife, and I am happy, anyway. . . . I don't complain; I don't say a word of blame. . . . Here Olya is my witness. . . . We'll begin the old life again, and I won't say one word, not a hint. . . .

MASHA [*restraining her sobs*]   By the sea-strand an oak tree green. . . .
Upon that oak a chain of gold. . . . Upon that oak a chain of gold.
. . . I am going mad. . . . By the sea-strand . . . an oak tree green. . . .

OLGA   Calm yourself, Masha. . . . Calm yourself. . . . Give her some
water.

MASHA   I am not crying now. . . .

KULIGIN   She is not crying now . . . she is good. . . .

The dim sound of a faraway shot.

MASHA   By the sea-strand an oak tree green, upon that oak a chain of
gold. . . . The cat is green . . . the oak is green. . . . I am mixing it
up. . . . [*Drinks water.*] My life is a failure. . . . I want nothing now.
. . . I shall be calm directly. . . . It doesn't matter. . . . What does
"strand" mean? Why do these words haunt me? My thoughts are in
a tangle.

Enter IRINA

OLGA   Calm yourself, Masha. Come, that's a good girl. Let us go indoors.

MASHA [*angrily*]   I am not going in. Let me alone! [*Sobs, but at once
checks herself.*] I don't go into that house now and I won't.

IRINA   Let us sit together, even if we don't say anything. I am going
away tomorrow, you know. . . . [*A pause.*]

KULIGIN   I took a false beard and moustache from a boy in the third
grade yesterday, just look. . . . [*Puts on the beard and moustache.*]
I look like the German teacher. . . . [*Laughs.*] Don't I? Funny creatures, those boys.

MASHA   You really do look like the German teacher.

OLGA [*laughs*]   Yes.

MASHA *weeps.*

IRINA   There, Masha!

KULIGIN   Awfully like. . . .

Enter NATASHA.

NATASHA [*to the maid*]   What? Mr. Protopopov will sit with Sophie,
and let Andrey Sergeyitch wheel Bobik up and down. What a lot
there is to do with children. . . . [*To* IRINA.] Irina, you are going
away tomorrow, what a pity. Do stay just another week.

Seeing KULIGIN *utters a shriek; the latter laughs and takes off
the beard and moustache.*

Well, what next, you gave me such a fright! [*To* IRINA.] I am used
to you and do you suppose that I don't feel parting with you? I shall
put Andrey with his violin into your room—let him saw away there!
—and we will put baby Sophie in his room. Adorable, delightful
baby! Isn't she a child! Today she looked at me with such eyes and
said "Mamma"!

KULIGIN   A fine child, that's true.

NATASHA   So tomorrow I shall be all alone here. [*Sighs.*] First of all I
shall have this avenue of fir trees cut down, and then that maple. . . .
It looks so ugly in the evening. . . . [*To* IRINA.] My dear, that sash
does not suit you at all. . . . It's in bad taste. You want something

light. And then I shall have flowers, flowers planted everywhere, and
there will be such a scent. . . . [*Severely.*] Why is there a fork lying
about on that seat? [*Going into the house, to the maid.*] Why is there
a fork lying about on this seat, I ask you? [*Shouts.*] Hold your
tongue!

KULIGIN   She is at it!

Behind the scenes the band plays a march; they all listen.

OLGA   They are going.

Enter TCHEBUTYKIN.

MASHA   Our people are going. Well . . . a happy journey to them! [*To
her husband.*] We must go home. . . . Where are my hat and cape?

KULIGIN   I took them into the house. . . . I'll get them directly. . . .

OLGA   Yes, now we can go home, it's time.

TCHEBUTYKIN   Olga Sergeyevna!

OLGA   What is it? [*A pause.*] What?

TCHEBUTYKIN   Nothing. . . . I don't know how to tell you. [*Whispers
in her ear.*]

OLGA [*in alarm*]   It can't be!

TCHEBUTYKIN   Yes . . . such a business. . . . I am so worried and worn
out, I don't want to say another word. . . . [*With vexation.*] But
there, it doesn't matter!

MASHA   What has happened?

OLGA [*puts her arms round* IRINA]   This is a terrible day. . . . I don't
know how to tell you, my precious. . . .

IRINA   What is it? Tell me quickly, what is it? For God's sake! [*Cries.*]

TCHEBUTYKIN   The baron has just been killed in a duel.

IRINA [*weeping quietly*]   I knew, I knew. . . .

TCHEBUTYKIN [*in the background of the scene sits down on a garden
seat*]   I am worn out. . . . [*Takes a newspaper out of his pocket.*] Let
them cry. . . . [*Sings softly.*] "Tarara-boom-dee-ay." . . . It doesn't
matter.

The three sisters stand with their arms round one another.

MASHA   Oh, listen to that band! They are going away from us; one has
gone altogether, gone forever. We are left alone to begin our life
over again. . . . We've got to live . . . we've got to live. . . .

IRINA [*lays her head on* OLGA's *bosom*]   A time will come when everyone will know what all this is for, why there is this misery; there will
be no mysteries and, meanwhile, we have got to live . . . we have got
to work, only to work! Tomorrow I shall go alone; I shall teach in the
school, and I will give all my life to those to whom it may be of use.
Now it's autumn; soon winter will come and cover us with snow,
and I will work, I will work.

OLGA [*embraces both her sisters*]   The music is so gay, so confident,
and one longs for life! O my God! Time will pass, and we shall go
away for ever, and we shall be forgotten, our faces will be forgotten,
our voices, and how many there were of us; but our sufferings will
pass into joy for those who will live after us, happiness and peace will
be established upon earth, and they will remember kindly and bless
those who have lived before. Oh, dear sisters, our life is not ended
yet. We shall live! The music is so gay, so joyful, and it seems as

though a little more and we shall know what we are living for, why
we are suffering. . . . If we only knew—if we only knew!

The music grows more and more subdued; KULIGIN, *cheerful
and smiling, brings the hat and cape;* ANDREY *pushes the perambulator in which* BOBIK *is sitting.*

TCHEBUTYKIN [*humming softly*]   "Tarara-boom-dee-ay!" [*Reads his
paper.*] It doesn't matter, it doesn't matter.

OLGA   If we only knew, if we only knew!

RUSSIAN NAMES

The use of names in Russian literature will confuse American students unless they bear certain facts in mind. Russian names, generally,
consist of three parts: the given name; the patronymic (ending in *itch*
for men and *vna* for women) based on the given name of the character's father; and the family name. The name Ivan Romanitch Tchebutykin, for example, tells us that the character's given name is Ivan,
that his father's given name was Roman and that the family name is
Tchebutykin. In general, strangers, or relative strangers, would use
the family name or an appropriate title to refer to or speak to a character.

For example, Tusenbach at first calls Vershinin either "Vershinin"
or "Colonel," but later calls him Alexandr Ignatyevitch. Friends of
the same rank would use the given name plus patronymic, *e.g.* Ivan
Romanitch, as all of the Prozorovs do for Tchebutykin. More intimate
relations are indicated by the use of the given name only or by nick-
names of varying degrees of intimacy. Andrey, Irina, and Marya,
for example, would be called Andryusha, Irisha, and Masha or Andryushantchik, Irinushka, and Mashenka, as dictated by circumstance.
Natasha, for example, calls Irina "Irina Sergeyevna" before her marriage to Andrey and "Irina" afterward. In the same way, Irina calls
Kuligin either Fyodor, his given name, or Fedya, a nickname, as the
particular moment renders appropriate.

The nurse Anfisa shows that in dealing with characters of various
ranks, the usual rules may be modified. She calls the three sisters
"Olya," "Mashenka," and "Irisha" or "Irinushka" with impunity because
she knew them as children. A different view is shown when Andrey
takes umbrage at being called Andrey Sergeyevitch, instead of "Your
Honor," by Ferapont.

Another point to be noted is that speakers in general use a more
formal term in speaking of someone in the second person than they do
in the third. Irina, for example, refers to "Solyony" in the third person
but calls him "Vassily Vassilyevitch" in person.

JEAN-CLAUDE VAN ITALLIE

Interview

A Fugue for Eight Actors[1]

FIRST INTERVIEWER	FOURTH APPLICANT
FIRST APPLICANT	SECOND INTERVIEWER
SECOND APPLICANT	THIRD INTERVIEWER
THIRD APPLICANT	FOURTH INTERVIEWER

The set is white and impersonal. Two subway stairs are at the back of the stage. On the sides there is one entrance for APPLI-CANTS *and another entrance for* INTERVIEWERS. *The only furniture or props needed are eight grey blocks.*

The actors, four men and four women, are dressed in black-and-white street clothes. During the employment agency section only, INTERVIEWERS *wear translucent plastic masks.*

There is an intermittent harpsichord accompaniment: dance variations (minuet, Virginia reel, twist) on a familiar American tune. But much of the music (singing, whistling, humming) is provided by the actors on stage. It is suggested, moreover, that as a company of actors and a director approach the play they find their own variations in rhythmic expression. The successful transition from one setting to the next depends on the actors' ability to play together as a company and to drop character instantaneously and completely in order to assume another character, or for a group effect.

> *The* FIRST INTERVIEWER *for an employment agency, a young woman, sits on stage as the* FIRST APPLICANT, *a Housepainter, enters.*

FIRST INTERVIEWER [*standing*] How do you do?

FIRST APPLICANT [*sitting*] Thank you, I said, not knowing where to sit.

> *The characters will often include the audience in what they say, as if they were being interviewed by the audience.*

FIRST INTERVIEWER [*pointedly*] Won't you sit down?

FIRST APPLICANT [*standing again quickly, afraid to displease*] I'm sorry.

FIRST INTERVIEWER [*busy with imaginary papers, pointing to a particular seat*] There. Name, please?

FIRST APPLICANT Jack Smith.

FIRST INTERVIEWER Jack what Smith?

FIRST APPLICANT Beg pardon?

FIRST INTERVIEWER Fill in the blank space, please. Jack blank space Smith.

---

1. *Interview* is a revision of an earlier play by the author as modified by his work with Joseph Chaikin and the members of the Open Theatre, of which Chaikin is the head. It was presented and published with two other short plays under the general title *America Hurrah*. The author had written that "*Interview* would not exist in its present form, however, without the collaboration, in rehearsal, of Joseph Chaikin and the actors of *America Hurrah*."

FIRST APPLICANT   I don't have any.
FIRST INTERVIEWER   I asked you to sit down. [*Pointing.*] There.
FIRST APPLICANT [*sitting*]   I'm sorry.
FIRST INTERVIEWER   Name, please?
FIRST APPLICANT   Jack Smith.
FIRST INTERVIEWER   You haven't told me your *middle* name.
FIRST APPLICANT   I haven't got one.
FIRST INTERVIEWER [*suspicious but writing it down*]   No middle name.

SECOND APPLICANT, *a woman, a Floorwasher, enters.*

FIRST INTERVIEWER   How do you do?
SECOND APPLICANT [*sitting*]   Thank you, I said, not knowing what.
FIRST INTERVIEWER   Won't you sit down?
SECOND APPLICANT [*standing*]   I'm sorry.
FIRST APPLICANT   I am sitting.
FIRST INTERVIEWER [*pointing*]   There. Name, please?
SECOND APPLICANT [*sitting*]   Jane Smith.
FIRST APPLICANT   Jack Smith.
FIRST INTERVIEWER   What blank space Smith?
SECOND APPLICANT   Ellen.
FIRST APPLICANT   Haven't got one.
FIRST INTERVIEWER   What job are you applying for?
FIRST APPLICANT   Housepainter.
SECOND APPLICANT   Floorwasher.
FIRST INTERVIEWER   We haven't many vacancies in that. What experience have you had?
FIRST APPLICANT   A lot.
SECOND APPLICANT   Who needs experience for floorwashing?
FIRST INTERVIEWER   You will help me by making your answers clear.
FIRST APPLICANT   Eight years.
SECOND APPLICANT   Twenty years.

THIRD APPLICANT, *a Banker, enters.*

FIRST INTERVIEWER   How do you do?
SECOND APPLICANT   I'm good at it.
FIRST APPLICANT   Very well.
THIRD APPLICANT [*sitting*]   Thank you, I said, as casually as I could.
FIRST INTERVIEWER   Won't you sit down?
THIRD APPLICANT [*standing again*]   I'm sorry.
SECOND APPLICANT   I am sitting.
FIRST APPLICANT [*standing again*]   I'm sorry.
FIRST INTERVIEWER [*pointing to a particular seat*]   There. Name, please?
FIRST APPLICANT   Jack Smith.
SECOND APPLICANT   Jane Smith.
THIRD APPLICANT   Richard Smith.
FIRST INTERVIEWER   What *exactly* Smith, please?
THIRD APPLICANT   Richard F.
SECOND APPLICANT   Jane Ellen.
FIRST APPLICANT   Jack None.
FIRST INTERVIEWER   What are you applying for?
FIRST APPLICANT   Housepainter.
SECOND APPLICANT   I need money.

THIRD APPLICANT   Bank president.

FIRST INTERVIEWER   How many years have you been in your present job?

THIRD APPLICANT   Three.

SECOND APPLICANT   Twenty.

FIRST APPLICANT   Eight.

FOURTH APPLICANT, *a Lady's Maid, enters.*

FIRST INTERVIEWER   How do you do?

FOURTH APPLICANT   I said thank you, not knowing where to sit.

THIRD APPLICANT   I'm fine.

SECOND APPLICANT   Do I have to tell you?

FIRST APPLICANT   Very well.

FIRST INTERVIEWER   Won't you sit down?

FOURTH APPLICANT   I'm sorry.

THIRD APPLICANT [*sitting again*]   Thank you.

SECOND APPLICANT [*standing again*]   I'm sorry.

FIRST APPLICANT [*sitting*]   Thanks.

FIRST INTERVIEWER [*pointing to a particular seat*]   There. Name, please?

FOURTH APPLICANT *sits.*

ALL APPLICANTS   Smith.

FIRST INTERVIEWER   What Smith?

FOURTH APPLICANT   Mary Victoria.

THIRD APPLICANT   Richard F.

SECOND APPLICANT   Jane Ellen.

FIRST APPLICANT   Jack None.

FIRST INTERVIEWER   How many years' experience have you had?

FOURTH APPLICANT   Eight years.

SECOND APPLICANT   Twenty years.

FIRST APPLICANT   Eight years.

THIRD APPLICANT   Three years four months and nine days not counting vacations and sick leave and the time both my daughters and my wife had the whooping cough.

FIRST INTERVIEWER   Just answer the questions, please.

FOURTH APPLICANT   Yes, sir.

THIRD APPLICANT   Sure.

SECOND APPLICANT   I'm sorry.

FIRST APPLICANT   That's what I'm doing.

SECOND INTERVIEWER, *a young man, enters and goes to inspect* APPLICANTS. *With the entrance of each* INTERVIEWER, *the speed of the action accelerates.*

SECOND INTERVIEWER   How do you do?

FIRST APPLICANT [*standing*]   I'm sorry.

SECOND APPLICANT [*sitting*]   Thank you.

THIRD APPLICANT [*standing*]   I'm sorry.

FOURTH APPLICANT [*sitting*]   Thank you.

SECOND INTERVIEWER   What's your name?

FIRST INTERVIEWER   Your middle name, please.

FIRST APPLICANT   Smith.

SECOND APPLICANT   Ellen.

THIRD APPLICANT   Smith, Richard F.
FOURTH APPLICANT   Mary Victoria Smith.
FIRST INTERVIEWER   What is your exact age?
SECOND INTERVIEWER   Have you any children?
FIRST APPLICANT   I'm thirty-two years old.
SECOND APPLICANT   One son.
THIRD APPLICANT   I have two daughters.
FOURTH APPLICANT   Do I have to tell you that?
FIRST INTERVIEWER   Are you married, single, or other?
SECOND INTERVIEWER   Have you ever earned more than that?
FIRST APPLICANT   No.
SECOND APPLICANT   Never.
THIRD APPLICANT   Married.
FOURTH APPLICANT   Single, NOW.

> THIRD INTERVIEWER, *a woman, enters.*

THIRD INTERVIEWER   How do you do?
FIRST APPLICANT [*sitting*]   Thank you.
SECOND APPLICANT [*standing*]   I'm sorry.
THIRD APPLICANT [*sitting*]   Thank you.
FOURTH APPLICANT [*standing*]   I'm sorry.

> FOURTH INTERVIEWER, *a man, appears on the heels of* THIRD INTERVIEWER.

FOURTH INTERVIEWER   How do you do?
FIRST APPLICANT [*standing*]   I'm sorry.
SECOND APPLICANT [*sitting*]   Thank you.
THIRD APPLICANT [*standing*]   I'm sorry.
FOURTH APPLICANT [*sitting*]   Thank you.
ALL INTERVIEWERS   What is your Social Security Number, please?

> APPLICANTS *do the next four speeches simultaneously.*

FIRST APPLICANT   333 dash 6598 dash 5590765439 dash 003.
SECOND APPLICANT   999 dash 5733 dash 699075432 dash 11.
THIRD APPLICANT [*sitting*]   I'm sorry. I left it home. I can call if you let me use the phone.
FOURTH APPLICANT   I always get it confused with my Checking Account Number.

> INTERVIEWERS *do the next four speeches in a round.*

FIRST INTERVIEWER   Will you be so kind as to tell me a little about yourself?
SECOND INTERVIEWER   Can you fill me in on something about your background please?
THIRD INTERVIEWER   It'd be a help to our employers if you'd give me a little for our files.
FOURTH INTERVIEWER   Now what would you say, say, to a prospective employer about yourself?

> APPLICANTS *address parts of the following four speeches, in particular, directly to the audience.*

FIRST APPLICANT   I've been a Union member twenty years, I said to them, if that's the kind of thing you want to know. Good health, I said. Veteran of two wars. Three kids. Wife's dead. Wife's sister, she takes care of them. I don't know why I'm telling you this, I said smiling.

Sits.

SECOND APPLICANT [*standing*]   So what do you want to know, I told the guy. I've been washin' floors for twenty years. Nobody's ever complained. I don't loiter after hours, I said to him. Just because my boy's been in trouble is no reason, I said, no reason—I go right home, I said to him. Right home.

Sits.

THIRD APPLICANT [*standing*]   I said that I was a Republican and we could start right there. And then I said that I spend most of my free time watching television or playing in the garden of my four-bedroom house with our two lovely daughters, aged nine and eleven. I mentioned that my wife plays with us too, and that her name is Katherine, although, I said casually, her good friends call her Kitty. I wasn't at all nervous.

Sits.

FOURTH APPLICANT [*standing*]   Just because I'm here, sir, I told him, is no reason for you to patronize me. I've been a lady's maid, I said, in houses you would not be allowed into. My father was a gentleman of leisure, *and* what's more, I said, my references are unimpeachable.

FIRST INTERVIEWER   I see.

SECOND INTERVIEWER   All right.

THIRD INTERVIEWER   That's fine.

FOURTH INTERVIEWER   Of course.

APPLICANTS *do the following four speeches simultaneously.*

FIRST APPLICANT   Just you call anybody at the Union and ask them. They'll hand me a clean bill of health.

SECOND APPLICANT   I haven't been to jail if that's what you mean. Not me. I'm clean.

THIRD APPLICANT   My record is impeccable. There's not a stain on it.

FOURTH APPLICANT   My references would permit me to be a governess, that's what.

FIRST INTERVIEWER [*going to* FIRST APPLICANT *and inspecting under his arms*]   When did you last have a job housepainting?

SECOND INTERVIEWER [*going to* SECOND APPLICANT *and inspecting her teeth*]   Where was the last place you worked?

THIRD INTERVIEWER [*going to* THIRD APPLICANT *and inspecting him*]   What was your last position in a bank?

FOURTH INTERVIEWER [*going to* FOURTH APPLICANT *and inspecting her*]   Have you got your references with you?

APPLICANTS *do the following four speeches simultaneously, with music under.*

FIRST APPLICANT   I've already told you I worked right along till I quit.

SECOND APPLICANT   Howard Johnson's on Fifty-first Street all last month.

THIRD APPLICANT   First Greenfield International and Franklin Banking Corporation Banking and Stone Incorporated.

FOURTH APPLICANT   I've got a letter right here in my bag. Mrs. Muggintwat only let me go because she died.

INTERVIEWERS *do the next four speeches in a round.*

FIRST INTERVIEWER [*stepping around and speaking to* SECOND APPLICANT]   Nothing terminated your job at Howard Johnson's? No franks, say, missing at the end of the day, I suppose?

SECOND INTERVIEWER [*stepping around and speaking to* THIRD APPLICANT]   It goes without saying, I suppose, that you could stand an FBI Security Test?

THIRD INTERVIEWER [*stepping around and speaking to* FOURTH APPLICANT]   I suppose there are no records of minor thefts or, shall we say, borrowings from your late employer?

FOURTH INTERVIEWER [*stepping around and speaking to* FIRST APPLICANT]   Nothing political in your Union dealings? Nothing Leftist, I suppose? Nothing Rightist either, I hope.

APPLICANTS and INTERVIEWERS *line up for a square dance. Music under the following.*

FIRST APPLICANT [*bowing to* FIRST INTERVIEWER]   What's it to you, buddy?

SECOND APPLICANT [*bowing to* SECOND INTERVIEWER]   Eleanor Roosevelt wasn't more honest.[2]

THIRD APPLICANT [*bowing to* THIRD INTERVIEWER]   My record is lily-white, sir!

FOURTH APPLICANT [*bowing to* FOURTH INTERVIEWER]   Mrs. Thumble-twat used to take me to the bank and I'd watch her open her box!

Each INTERVIEWER, *during his next speech, goes upstage to form another line.*

FIRST INTERVIEWER   Good!
SECOND INTERVIEWER   Fine!
THIRD INTERVIEWER   Swell!
FOURTH INTERVIEWER   Fine!

APPLICANTS *come downstage together; they do the next four speeches simultaneously and directly to the audience.*

FIRST APPLICANT   I know my rights. As a veteran. *And* a citizen. I know my rights. *And* my cousin is very well-known in certain circles, if you get what I mean. In the back room of a certain candy store in the Italian district of this city my cousin is *very* well known, if you get what I mean. I know my rights. And I know my cousin.

SECOND APPLICANT [*putting on a pious act, looking up to heaven*]   Holy Mary Mother of God, must I endure all the sinners of this earth? Must I go on a poor washerwoman in this City of Sin? Help me, oh my God, to leave this earthly crust, and damn your silly impudence, young man, if you think you can treat an old woman like this. You've got another thought coming, you have.

THIRD APPLICANT   I have an excellent notion to report you to the Junior Chamber of Commerce of this city of which I am the Secre-

2. Eleanor Roosevelt (1884–1962), the wife of President Franklin D. Roosevelt, was a public figure in her own right. An indefatigable supporter of good causes, she wrote, lectured, and traveled. For many years she wrote a widely syndicated newspaper column, "My Day." After her husband's death, she represented the United States at the United Nations for several years.

tary and was in line to be elected Vice President and still will be if you are able to find me gainful and respectable employ!

FOURTH APPLICANT   Miss Thumblebottom married into the Twiths and if you start insulting me, young man, you'll have to start in insulting the Twiths as well. A Twith isn't a nobody, you know, as good as a Thumbletwat, *and* they all call me their loving Mary, you know.

ALL INTERVIEWERS [*in a loud raucous voice*]   Do you smoke?

Each APPLICANT, *during his next speech, turns upstage.*

FIRST APPLICANT   No thanks.
SECOND APPLICANT   Not now.
THIRD APPLICANT   No thanks.
FOURTH APPLICANT   Not now.
ALL INTERVIEWERS [*again in a harsh voice and bowing or curtsying*]   Do you mind if I do?
FIRST APPLICANT   I don't care.
SECOND APPLICANT   Who cares?
THIRD APPLICANT   Course not.
FOURTH APPLICANT   Go ahead.

INTERVIEWERS *form a little group off to themselves.*

FIRST INTERVIEWER   I tried to quit but couldn't manage.
SECOND INTERVIEWER   I'm a three-pack-a-day man, I guess.
THIRD INTERVIEWER   If I'm gonna go I'd rather go smoking.
FOURTH INTERVIEWER   I'm down to five a day.

APPLICANTS *all start to sneeze.*

FIRST APPLICANT   Excuse me, I'm gonna sneeze.
SECOND APPLICANT   Have you got a hanky?
THIRD APPLICANT   I have a cold coming on.
FOURTH APPLICANT   I thought I had some tissues in my bag.

APPLICANTS *all sneeze.*

FIRST INTERVIEWER   Gezundheit.
SECOND INTERVIEWER   God bless you.
THIRD INTERVIEWER   Gezundheit.
FOURTH INTERVIEWER   God bless you.

APPLICANTS *all sneeze simultaneously.*

FIRST INTERVIEWER   God bless you.
SECOND INTERVIEWER   Gezundheit.
THIRD INTERVIEWER   God bless you.
FOURTH INTERVIEWER   Gezundheit.

APPLICANTS *return to their seats.*

FIRST APPLICANT   Thanks, I said.
SECOND APPLICANT   I said thanks.
THIRD APPLICANT   Thank you, I said.
FOURTH APPLICANT   I said thank you.

INTERVIEWERS *stand on their seats and say the following as if one person were speaking.*

FIRST INTERVIEWER   Do you
SECOND INTERVIEWER   speak any

THIRD INTERVIEWER   foreign
FOURTH INTERVIEWER   languages?
FIRST INTERVIEWER   Have you
SECOND INTERVIEWER   got a
THIRD INTERVIEWER   college
FOURTH INTERVIEWER   education?
FIRST INTERVIEWER   Do you
SECOND INTERVIEWER   take
THIRD INTERVIEWER   shorthand?
FOURTH INTERVIEWER   Have you
FIRST INTERVIEWER   any
SECOND INTERVIEWER   special
THIRD INTERVIEWER   qualifications?
FIRST INTERVIEWER   Yes?

FIRST APPLICANT [*stepping up to* INTERVIEWERS]   Sure, I can speak Italian, I said. My whole family is Italian so I oughta be able to, and I can match colors, like green to green, so that even your own mother couldn't tell the difference, begging your pardon, I said, I went through the eighth grade.

> *Steps back.*

SECOND INTERVIEWER   Next.

SECOND APPLICANT [*stepping up to* INTERVIEWERS]   My grandmother taught me some Gaelic, I told the guy. And my old man could rattle off in Yiddish when he had a load on.[3] I never went to school at all excepting church school, but I can write my name good and clear. Also, I said, I can smell an Irishman or a Yid a hundred miles off.

> *Steps back.*

THIRD INTERVIEWER   Next.

THIRD APPLICANT [*stepping up to* INTERVIEWERS]   I've never had any need to take shorthand in my position, I said to him. I've a Z.A. in business administration from Philadelphia, and a Z.Z.A. from M.Y.U. night school.[4] I mentioned that I speak a little Spanish, of course, and that I'm a whiz at model frigates and warships.

> *Steps back.*

FOURTH INTERVIEWER   Next.

FOURTH APPLICANT [*stepping up to* INTERVIEWERS]   I can sew a straight seam, I said, hand or machine, and I have been exclusively a lady's maid although I *can* cook and will too if I have someone to assist me, I said. Unfortunately, aside from self-education, grammar school is as far as I have progressed.

> *Steps back.*
> Each INTERVIEWER, *during his next speech, bows or curtsies to the* APPLICANT *nearest him.*

FIRST INTERVIEWER   Good.
SECOND INTERVIEWER   Fine.
THIRD INTERVIEWER   Very helpful.

---

3. Gaelic is the native language of Ireland. Yiddish is a form of German used by Jews in Germany and elsewhere. "Yid" is a derogatory term for a Jew.
4. The abbreviations are made-up ones which suggest such abbreviations as B.A. for Bachelor of Arts, B.B.A. for Bachelor of Business Administration, and N.Y.U. for New York University.

FOURTH INTERVIEWER   Thank you.

Each APPLICANT, *during his next speech, jumps on the back of the* INTERVIEWER *nearest him.*

FOURTH APPLICANT   You're welcome, I'm sure.
THIRD APPLICANT   Anything you want to know.
SECOND APPLICANT   Just ask me.
FIRST APPLICANT   Fire away, fire away.

The next eight speeches are spoken simultaneously, with APPLICANTS *on* INTERVIEWERS' *backs.*

FIRST INTERVIEWER   Well unless there's anything special you want to tell me, I think—

SECOND INTERVIEWER   Is there anything more you think I should know about before you—

THIRD INTERVIEWER   I wonder if we've left anything out of this questionnaire or if you—

FOURTH INTERVIEWER   I suppose I've got all the information down here unless you can—

FIRST APPLICANT   I've got kids to support, you know, and I need a job real quick—

SECOND APPLICANT   Do you think you could try and get me something today because I—

THIRD APPLICANT   How soon do you suppose I can expect to hear from your agency? Do you—

FOURTH APPLICANT   I don't like to sound pressureful, but you know I'm currently on unemploy—

Each APPLICANT, *during his next speech, jumps off* INTERVIEWER'S *back.*

FIRST APPLICANT   Beggin' your pardon.
SECOND APPLICANT   So sorry.
THIRD APPLICANT   Excuse me.
FOURTH APPLICANT   Go ahead.

Each INTERVIEWER, *during his next speech, bows or curtsies and remains in that position.*

FIRST INTERVIEWER   That's quite all right.
SECOND INTERVIEWER   I'm sorry.
THIRD INTERVIEWER   I'm sorry.
FOURTH INTERVIEWER   My fault.

Each APPLICANT, *during his next speech, begins leap-frogging over* INTERVIEWERS' *backs.*

FIRST APPLICANT   My fault.
SECOND APPLICANT   My fault.
THIRD APPLICANT   I'm sorry.
FOURTH APPLICANT   My fault.

Each INTERVIEWER, *during his next speech, begins leap-frogging too.*

FIRST INTERVIEWER   That's all right.
SECOD INTERVIEWER   My fault.
THIRD INTERVIEWER   I'm sorry.

FOURTH INTERVIEWER Excuse me.

The leap-frogging continues as the preceding eight lines are repeated simultaneously. Then the INTERVIEWERS *confer in a huddle and come out of it.*

FIRST INTERVIEWER Do you enjoy your work?
FIRST APPLICANT Sure, I said, I'm proud. Why not? Sure I know I'm no Rembrandt, I said, but I'm proud of my work, I said to him.
SECOND APPLICANT I told him it stinks. But what am I supposed to do, sit home and rot?
THIRD APPLICANT Do I like my work, he asked me. Well, I said, to gain time, do I like my work? Well, I said, I don't know.
FOURTH APPLICANT I told him straight out: for a sensible person, a lady's maid is the *only possible* way of life.
SECOND INTERVIEWER Do you think you're irreplaceable?
ALL APPLICANTS Oh, yes indeed.
ALL INTERVIEWERS Irreplaceable?
ALL APPLICANTS Yes, yes indeed.
THIRD INTERVIEWER Do you like me?
FIRST APPLICANT You're a nice man.
SECOND APPLICANT Huh?
THIRD APPLICANT Why do you ask?
FOURTH APPLICANT It's not a question of *like.*
FIRST INTERVIEWER Well, we'll be in touch with you.

This is the beginning of leaving the agency. Soft music under. APPLICANTS *and* INTERVIEWERS *push their seats into two masses of four boxes, one on each side of the stage.* APPLICANTS *leave first, joining hands to form a revolving door. All are now leaving the agency, not in any orderly fashion.* INTERVIEWERS *start down one of the subway stairs at the back of the stage and* APPLICANTS *start down the other. The following speeches overlap and are heard indistinctly as crowd noise.*

FOURTH INTERVIEWER What sort of day will it be?
FIRST APPLICANT I bet we'll have rain.
SECOND APPLICANT Cloudy, clearing in the afternoon.
THIRD APPLICANT Mild, I think, with some snow.
FOURTH APPLICANT Precisely the same as yesterday.
SECOND APPLICANT Can you get me one?
FIRST INTERVIEWER See you tomorrow.
THIRD APPLICANT When will I hear from you?
SECOND INTERVIEWER We'll let you know.
FOURTH APPLICANT Where's my umbrella?
THIRD INTERVIEWER I'm going to a movie.
FIRST APPLICANT So how about it?
FOURTH INTERVIEWER Good night.
THIRD APPLICANT Can you help me, Doctor, I asked.

When all of the actors are offstage, the FOURTH INTERVIEWER *makes a siren sound and the following speeches continue from downstairs as a loud crowd noise for a few moments; they overlap so that the stage is empty only briefly.*

FIRST INTERVIEWER It'll take a lot of work on your part.
SECOND INTERVIEWER I'll do what I can for you.

THIRD INTERVIEWER   Of course I'll do my best.

FIRST INTERVIEWER   God helps those who help themselves.

FIRST APPLICANT   I have sinned deeply, Father, I said.

FIRST INTERVIEWER   You certainly have. I hope you truly repent.

SECOND INTERVIEWER   In the name of the Father, etcetera, and the Holy Ghost.

THIRD INTERVIEWER   Jesus saves.

FOURTH APPLICANT   I said can you direct me to Fourteenth Street, please?

FIRST INTERVIEWER   Just walk down that way a bit and then turn left.

SECOND INTERVIEWER   Just walk down that way a bit and then turn right.

THIRD INTERVIEWER   Take a cab!

FOURTH APPLICANT   Do you hear a siren?

ALL INTERVIEWERS   What time is it?

FIRST APPLICANT   Half-past three.

SECOND APPLICANT   It must be about four.

THIRD APPLICANT   Half-past five.

FOURTH APPLICANT   My watch has stopped.

FIRST INTERVIEWER   Do you enjoy your work?

SECOND INTERVIEWER   Do you think you're irreplaceable?

THIRD INTERVIEWER   Do you like me?

> *The actor who played the* FOURTH INTERVIEWER *comes on stage while continuing to make the loud siren noise. The actress who played the* FOURTH APPLICANT *comes on stage and speaks directly to the audience.*

FOURTH APPLICANT   Can you direct me to Fourteenth Street, please, I said. I seem to have lost my—I started to say, and then I was nearly run down.

> *The remaining actors return to the stage to play various people on Fourteenth Street: ladies shopping, a panhandler, a man in a sandwich board, a peddler of "franks and orange," a snooty German couple, a lecher, a pair of sighing lovers, and so on. The actors walk straight forward toward the audience and then walk backwards to the rear of the stage. Each time they approach the audience, they do so as a different character. The actor will need to find the essential vocal and physical mannerisms of each character, play them, and drop them immediately to assume another character. The* FOURTH APPLICANT *continues to address the audience directly, to involve them in her hysteria, going up the aisle and back.*

FOURTH APPLICANT   I haven't got my Social Security—I started to say, I saw someone right in front of me and I said, could you direct me to Fourteenth Street, I have to get to Fourteenth Street, please, to get a bargain, I explained, although I could hardly remember what it was I wanted to buy. I read about it in the paper today, I said, only they weren't listening and I said to myself, my purpose for today is to get to—and I couldn't remember, I've set myself the task of—I've got to have—it's that I can save, I remembered, I can save if I can get that bargain at—and I couldn't remember where it was so I started to look for my wallet which I seem to have mislaid in my purse, and a man—please watch where you're going, I shouted with my purse half-open, and I seemed to forget—Fourteenth Street, I remembered, and you'd think with all these numbered streets and avenues a person wouldn't get lost—you'd think a person would *help* a person, you'd think so. So I asked the most respectable looking man I could find, I asked him, please can you direct me to Fourteenth Street. He wouldn't answer. Just wouldn't. I'm lost, I said to myself. The paper said—the television said—they said, I couldn't remember what they said. I turned for help: "Jesus Saves" the sign said, and a man was carrying it, both sides of his body, staring straight ahead. "Jesus Saves" the sign said.

> *The passers-by jostle her more and more.*

FOURTH APPLICANT   I couldn't remember where I was going. "Come and be saved" it said, so I asked the man with the sign, please, sir, won't you tell me how to, dear Lord, I thought, anywhere, please, sir, won't you tell me how to—can you direct me to Fourteenth Street, *please!*

> *The passers-by have covered the* FOURTH APPLICANT. *All actors mill about until they reach designated positions on the stage where they face the audience, a line of women and a line of men, students in a gym class. The* SECOND INTERVIEWER *has stayed coolly out of the crowd during this last; now he is the* GYM INSTRUCTOR.

GYM INSTRUCTOR   I took my last puff and strode resolutely into the room. Ready men, I asked brightly. And one and two and three and four and one and two and keep it up.

> *The* GYM INSTRUCTOR *is trying to help his students mold themselves into the kind of people seen in advertisements and the movies. As he counts to four the students puff out their chests, smile, and look perfectly charming. As he counts to four again, the students relax and look ordinary.*

GYM INSTRUCTOR   You wanna look like the guys in the movies, don't you, I said to the fellahs. Keep it up then. You wanna radiate that kinda charm and confidence they have in the movies, don't you, I said to the girls. Keep it up then, stick 'em out, that's what you got 'em for. Don't be ashamed. All of you, tuck in your butts, I said loudly. That's the ticket, I said, wishing to hell I had a cigarette. You're selling, selling all the time, that right, miss? Keep on selling, I said. And one and two and three and four and ever see that guy on TV, I said. What's his name, I asked them. What's his name? Aw, you know his name, I said, forgetting his name. Never mind, it'll come to you, I said. He comes in here too. See that, I said, grabbing a guy out of line and showing 'em his muscle. See that line, I said, making the guy feel good, know what that is? It's boyishness, I said. You come here, I said, throwing him back into the line, and it'll renew your youthfulness, I said, taking a deep breath. And one and two and three and four and smile, I said, smiling. Not so big, I said, smiling less. You look like creeps, I said, when you smile that big. When you smile, hold something back. Make like you're holding back something big, I said, a secret, I said. That's the ticket. And one and two and three and four and . . .

Accelerating the rhythm to a double count.

Anybody got a cigarette, I said suddenly, without thinking. I was just kidding, I said then, sheepishly. One and two and three and four, I said, wishing I had a cigarette. And one and two and three and four . . .

The rapid movements of the gym class become the vibrations of passengers on a moving subway train. The actors rush to the boxes stage left, continuing to vibrate. Two of the actors stand on the boxes and smile like subway advertisements while the others, directly in front of them, are pushed against each other on the crowded train. They make an appropriate soft subway noise, a kind of rhythmic hiss and, as the subway passengers, form their faces into frozen masks of indifference.

SECOND APPLICANT [*squeezing her way to an uncomfortable front seat and speaking half to herself*] God forgive me . . . you no-good chump, I said to him, I used to love you . . . not now. Not now . . . God forgive me . . . God forgive me for being old. Not now, I said. I wouldn't wipe the smell off your uncle's bottom now, not for turnips, no. God forgive me . . . Remember how we used to ride the roller coaster out at Coney Island, you and me?[5] Remember? Holding hands in the cold and I'd get so scared and you'd get so scared and we'd hug each other and buy another ticket . . . Remember? . . . Look now, I said. Look at me now! God forgive you for leaving me with nothing . . . God forgive you for being dead . . . God forgive me for being alive . . .

The actress who played the THIRD INTERVIEWER *slips out of the subway as though it were her stop and sits on a box, stage right, as a* TELEPHONE OPERATOR. *The other actors form a telephone circuit by holding hands in two concentric circles around the boxes, stage left; they change the hissing sound of the subway into the whistling of telephone circuits.*

TELEPHONE OPERATOR   Just one moment and I will connect you with Information.

The TELEPHONE OPERATOR *alternates her official voice with her ordinary voice; she uses the latter when she talks to her friend Roberta, another operator whom she reaches by flipping a switch. When she is talking to Roberta, the whistling of the telephone circuit changes into a different rhythm and the arms of the actors, which are forming the circuit, move into a different position.*

TELEPHONE OPERATOR   Just one moment and I will connect you with Information. Ow! Listen, Roberta, I said, I've got this terrible cramp. Hang up and dial again, please; we find nothing wrong with that number at all. You know what I ate, I said to her, you were there. Baked macaroni, Wednesday special, maple-nut fudge, I said. I'm sorry but the number you have reached is not—I can feel it

---

5. Coney Island is a beach and amusement park in New York City. Among its claims to fame is the report that the hotdog was invented there in 1867 by German immigrant Charles Feltman.

gnawing at me at the bottom of my belly, I told her. Do you think it's serious, Roberta? Appendicitis? I asked. Thank you for giving us the area code but the number you have reached is not in this area. Roberta, I asked her, do you think I have cancer? One moment, please, I'm sorry the number you have reached—ow! Well, if it's lunch, Roberta, I said to her, you know what they can do with it to-morrow. Ow! One moment, please, I said. Ow, I said, Roberta, I said, it really hurts.

> The TELEPHONE OPERATOR *falls off her seat in pain. The whis-tling of the telephone circuit becomes a siren. Three actors carry the* TELEPHONE OPERATOR *over to the boxes, stage left, which now serve as an operating table. Three actors imitate the* TELE-PHONE OPERATOR's *breathing pattern while four actors behind her make stylized sounds and movements as surgeons and nurses in the midst of an operation. The* TELEPHONE OPERATOR's *breathing accelerates, then stops. After a moment the actors begin spreading over the stage and making the muted sounds of a cocktail party: music, laughter, talk. The actors find a position and remain there, playing various aspects of a party in slow motion and muted tones. They completely ignore the* FIRST INTERVIEWER *who, as a* GIRL AT THE PARTY, *goes from person to person as if she were in a garden of living statues.*

GIRL AT THE PARTY [*rapidly and excitedly*]   And then after the am-bulance took off I went up in the elevator and into the party. Did you see the accident, I asked, and they said they did, and what did he look like, and I said he wore a brown coat and had straight brown hair. He stepped off the curb right in front of me. We had been walking up the same block, he a few feet ahead of me, this block right here, I said, but she wasn't listening. Hi, my name is Jill, I said to somebody sitting down and they looked at me and smiled so I said his arm was torn out of its socket and his face was on the pavement gasping but I didn't touch him and she smiled and walked away and I said after her, you aren't supposed to touch someone before—I *wanted* to help, I said, but she wasn't listening. When a man came up and said was it someone you knew and I said yes, it was someone I knew slightly, someone I knew, yes, and he offered me a drink and I said no thanks, I didn't want one, and he said well how well did I know him, and I said I knew him well, yes, I knew him very well. You were coming together to the party, he said. Yes, I said, excuse me. Hi, my name is Jill, did you hear a siren, and they said oh you're the one who saw it, was he killed?

> *Becoming resigned to the fact that no one is listening.*

And I said yes I was, excuse me, and went back across the room but couldn't find another face to talk to until I deliberately bumped into somebody because I had to tell them one of us couldn't come because of the accident. It was Jill. Jill couldn't come. I'm awfully sorry, I said, because of the accident. She had straight brown hair, I said, and was wearing a brown coat, and two or three people looked at me strangely and moved off. I'm sorry, I said to a man, and I laughed, and moved off. I'm dead, I said to several people and started to push them over, I'm dead, thank you, I said, thank you, please, I said, I'm dead, until two or three of them got hold of my arms and hustled me out. I'm sorry, I said, I couldn't come because of the accident. I'm sorry. Excuse me.

The GIRL AT THE PARTY *is lowered to the floor by two of the men and then all fall down except the actor who played the* FOURTH INTERVIEWER. *He remains seated as a* PSYCHIATRIST. *The* THIRD APPLICANT, *on the floor, props his head up on his elbow and speaks to the audience.*

THIRD APPLICANT   Can you help me, Doctor, I asked him.

The PSYCHIATRIST *crosses his legs and assumes a professional expression.*

THIRD APPLICANT   Well, it started, well it started, I said, when I was sitting in front of the television set with my feet on the coffee table. Now I've sat there hundreds of times, thousands maybe, with a can of beer in my hand. I like to have a can of beer in my hand when I watch the beer ads. But now for no reason I can think of, the ad was making me sick. So I used the remote control to get to another channel, but each channel made me just as sick. The television was one thing and I was a person, and I was going to be sick. So I turned it off and had a panicky moment. I smelled the beer in my hand and as I vomited I looked around the living room for something to grab on to, something to look at, but there was just our new furniture. I tried to get a hold of myself. I tried to stare straight ahead above the television set, at a little spot on the wall I know. I've had little moments like that before, Doctor, I said, panicky little moments like that when the earth seems to slip out from under, and everything whirls around and you try to hold onto something, some object, some thought, but I couldn't think of anything. Later the panic went away, I told him, it went away, and I'm much better now. But I don't feel like doing anything anymore, except sit and stare at the wall. I've lost my job. Katherine thought I should come and see you. Can you help me, Doctor, I asked him.

PSYCHIATRIST
Blah, blah, blah, blah, blah, blah, HOSTILE.
Blah, blah, blah, blah, blah, blah, PENIS.
Blah, blah, blah, blah, blah, blah, MOTHER.

Holding out his hand.

Blah, blah, blah, blah, blah, blah, MONEY.

The THIRD APPLICANT *takes the* PSYCHIATRIST's *hand and gets up, extending his left hand to the next actor. This begins a grand right and left with all the actors all over the stage.*[6]

ALL [*chanting as they do the grand right and left*]
Blah, blah, blah, blah, blah, blah, HOSTILE.
Blah, blah, blah, blah, blah, blah, PENIS.
Blah, blah, blah, blah, blah, blah, MOTHER.

6. A "grand right and left" is a square dance movement for four couples in which the men move in a circle counterclockwise and the women clockwise. Each dancer passes the first person he meets right shoulder to right shoulder, touching right hands as they pass. He passes the second person left shoulder to left shoulder, touching left hands. This alternation of left and right continues until he meets the fifth person, who is the same as the first one, completing the movement.

Blah, blah, blah, blah, blah, blah, MONEY.
Blah, blah, blah, blah, blah, blah, HOSTILE.
Blah, blah, blah, blah, blah, blah, PENIS.
Blah, blah, blah, blah, blah, blah, MOTHER.
Blah, blah, blah, blah, blah, blah, MONEY.

Forming couples and locking hands with arms crossed, continuing to move, but in a smaller circle.

Blah, blah, blah, blah, blah, blah, blah.
Blah, blah, blah, blah, blah, blah, blah.

Now they slow down to the speed of a church procession. The women bow their heads, letting their hair fall forward over their faces. The "blah, blah, blah" continues, but much more slowly while some of the women accompany it with a descant of "Kyrie Eleison."[7] After they have gone around in a circle once this way, the actor who played the FOURTH INTERVIEWER *sits with his back to the audience as a* PRIEST. *The* FIRST APPLICANT *kneels next to him, facing the audience as if in a confessional booth. The other six actors are at the back of the stage in two lines, swaying slightly, heads down. The women are in front with their hair still down over their faces.*

FIRST APPLICANT [*crossing himself perfunctorily and starting to speak; his manner is not impassioned; it is clear that he comes regularly to repeat this always fruitless ritual*]   Can you help me, Father, I said, as I usually do, and he said, as usual, nothing. I'm your friend, the housepainter, I said, the good housepainter. Remember me, Father? He continued, as usual, to say nothing. Almost the only color you get to paint these days, Father, I said, is white. Only white, Father, I said, not expecting any more from him than usual, but going on anyway. The color I really like to paint, Father, is red, I said. Pure brick red. Now there's a confession, Father. He said nothing. I'd like to take a trip to the country, Father, I said, and paint a barn door red, thinking that would get a rise out of him, but it didn't. God, I said then, deliberately taking the Lord's name in vain, the result of taking a three-inch brush and lightly kissing a coat of red paint on a barn door is something stunning and beautiful to behold. He still said nothing. Father, I said, springing it on him, Father, I'd like to join a monastery. My wife's sister, she could take care of the kids. Still nothing. Father, I said again, I'd like to join a monastery. Can you help me, Father? Nothing. Father, I said, I've tried lots of things in my life, I've gone in a lot of different directions, Father, and none of them seems any better than any other, Father, I said. Can you help me, Father, I said. But he said nothing as usual, and then, as usual, I went away.

The FIRST APPLICANT *and the* FOURTH INTERVIEWER, *who haven't moved at all during the confession, move upstage to join the others as the music starts up violently in a rock beat. The actors do a rock version of the Virginia reel.*

7. The Greek words *kyrie eleison* (Lord, have mercy upon us) are used to designate a part of the Mass which begins with those words.

SECOND INTERVIEWER [*loudly*]   My

    All bow to partners.

FOURTH APPLICANT [*loudly*]   fault.

    All dos-à-dos.[8]

SECOND APPLICANT [*loudly*]   Excuse

    All circle around.

FOURTH INTERVIEWER [*loudly*]   me.

    All peel off.[9]

FIRST INTERVIEWER [*loudly*]   Can you
SECOND APPLICANT [*loudly*]   help
FIRST APPLICANT [*loudly*]   me?
FOURTH INTERVIEWER [*loudly*]   Next.

    All continue dancing, joining hands at the center to form a revolving door again. They repeat the preceding eight speeches. Then the SECOND INTERVIEWER *speaks rapidly, as a* SQUARE DANCE CALLER.

SQUARE DANCE CALLER   Step right up, ladies and gents, and shake the hand of the next governor of this state. Shake his hand and say hello. Tell your friends you shook the hand of the next governor of the state. Step right up and shake his hand. Ask him questions. Tell him problems. Say hello. Step right up, shake his hand, shake the hand, ladies and gents, of the next governor of the state. Tell your folks: I shook his hand. When he's famous you'll be proud. Step right up, ladies and gents, and shake his hand. Ask him questions. Tell him problems. Say hello. Step right up, ladies and gents. Don't be shy. Shake the hand of the next governor of this state.

    The actors have formed a crowd, downstage right, facing the audience. They give the impression of being but a few of a great number of people, all trying to squeeze to the front to see and speak to the political candidate. The FOURTH INTERVIEWER, *now playing a* POLITICIAN *stands on a box, stage left, facing the audience. The* SECOND INTERVIEWER *stands by the crowd and keeps it in order.*

POLITICIAN   Thank you very much, I said cheerfully, and good luck to you, I said, turning my smile to the next one.

    The FIRST INTERVIEWER, *panting as the* GIRL AT THE PARTY, *squeezes out of the crowd and rushes up to the* POLITICIAN, *who smiles at her benignly.*

POLITICIAN   Our children *are* our most important asset, I agreed earnestly. Yes they are, I said solemnly. Children, I said, with a long

---

8. *Dos-à-dos* (French for back-to-back) is a square dance movement in which a man and woman approach each other, right shoulder to right shoulder, and circle each other back-to-back.

9. "Peel off" is a square dance movement which begins with the eight dancers arranged in two parallel lines of four. The lines are side by side, and each dancer is facing away from the center of his line. After the movement is completed, the dancers are arranged in two parallel lines again, but now the dancers in each line are side by side and the two lines face each other.

pause, are our most important asset. I only wish I could, madame, I said earnestly, standing tall, but rats, I said regretfully, are a city matter.

> *The* FIRST INTERVIEWER *returns to the crowd while the* THIRD INTERVIEWER, *as the* TELEPHONE OPERATOR, *rushes up to the* POLITICIAN. *She appeals to him, making the same noise she made when her stomach hurt her.*

POLITICIAN   Nobody knows more about red tape than I do, I said knowingly, and I wish you luck, I said, turning my smile to the next one.

> *The* THIRD INTERVIEWER *returns to the crowd and the* FOURTH APPLICANT *goes up to the* POLITICIAN.

POLITICIAN   I certainly will, I said, with my eyes sparkling, taking a pencil out of my pocket. And what's your name, I said, looking at her sweetly and signing my name at the same time. That's a lovely name, I said.

> *The* FOURTH APPLICANT *returns to the crowd while the* THIRD APPLICANT, *as an* OLDER MAN *shakes the* POLITICIAN's *hand.*

POLITICIAN   Yes sir, I said, those were the days. And good luck to you, sir, I said respectfully but heartily, and look out for the curb, I said, turning my smile to the next one.

> *The* THIRD APPLICANT *returns to the crowd and the* SECOND APPLICANT *approaches the* POLITICIAN.

POLITICIAN   Indeed yes, the air we breathe *is* foul, I said indignantly. I agree with you entirely, I said wholeheartedly. And if my opponent wins it's going to get worse, I said with conviction. We'd all die within ten years, I said. And good luck to you, madame, I said politely, and turned my smile to the next one.

> *The* FIRST APPLICANT *approaches him, his cap in his hand.*

POLITICIAN   Well, I said confidingly, getting a bill through the legislature is easier said than done, and answering violence, I said warningly, with violence, I said earnestly, is not the answer, and how do you do, I said, turning my smile to the next one.

> *Next, two* SIGHING LOVERS—*we saw them on Fourteenth Street —played by the* FIRST *and* SECOND INTERVIEWERS, *approach the* POLITICIAN.

POLITICIAN   No, I said, I never said my opponent would kill us all. No, I said, I never said that. May the best man win, I said manfully.

> *Half-hearted cheers. The* FIRST *and* SECOND INTERVIEWERS *return to the crowd.*

POLITICIAN   I do feel, I said without false modesty, that I'm better qualified in the field of foreign affairs than my opponents are, yes, I said, *but,* I said, with a pause for emphasis, foreign policy is the business of the President, not the Governor, therefore I will say nothing about the war, I said with finality.

> *The crowd makes a restive sound, then freezes.*

POLITICIAN Do you want us shaking hands, I asked the photographer, turning my profile to the left. Goodbye, I said cheerfully, and good luck to you too.

The crowd makes a louder protest, then freezes.

POLITICIAN I'm sorry, I said seriously, but I'll have to study that question a good deal more before I can answer it.

The crowd makes an angry noise, then freezes.

POLITICIAN Of course, I said frowning, we must all support the President, I said as I turned concernedly to the next one.

The crowd makes a very angry sound, then freezes.

POLITICIAN I'm sorry about the war, I said. Nobody could be sorrier than I am, I said sorrowfully. But I'm afraid, I said gravely, that there are no easy answers.

Smiles, pleased with himself.

Good luck to you too, I said cheerfully, and turned my smile to the next one.

> *The POLITICIAN topples from his box, beginning his speech all over again. Simultaneously, all the other actors lurch about the stage, speaking again in character: the SHOPPER ON FOURTEENTH STREET, the GYM INSTRUCTOR, the SUBWAY RIDER, the TELEPHONE OPERATOR, the GIRL AT THE PARTY, the ANALYSAND, and the HOUSEPAINTER. Simultaneously, they all stop and freeze, continue again, freeze again, then continue with music under. The SECOND INTERVIEWER, acting as policeman, begins to line them up in a diagonal line, like marching dolls, one behind the other. As they are put into line they begin to move their mouths without sound, like fish in a tank. The music stops. When all are in line the SECOND INTERVIEWER joins them.*

SECOND INTERVIEWER My
FOURTH APPLICANT fault.
SECOND APPLICANT Excuse
FOURTH INTERVIEWER me.
FIRST INTERVIEWER Can you
SECOND APPLICANT help
FIRST APPLICANT me?
FOURTH INTERVIEWER Next.

> *All continue marching in place, moving their mouths, and shouting their lines as the lights come slowly down.*

SECOND INTERVIEWER My
FOURTH APPLICANT fault.
SECOND APPLICANT Excuse
FOURTH INTERVIEWER me.
FIRST INTERVIEWER Can you
SECOND APPLICANT help
FIRST APPLICANT me?
FOURTH INTERVIEWER Next.

ED BULLINS

A Son, Come Home

CHARACTERS

MOTHER, *early 50s*   THE GIRL
SON, *30 years old*   THE BOY

> The BOY *and the* GIRL *wear black tights and shirts. They move the
> action of the play and express the* MOTHER's *and the* SON's *moods
> and tensions. They become various embodiments recalled from
> memory and history: they enact a number of personalities and
> move from mood to mood. The players are Black.*

> *At rise: Scene: Bare stage but for two chairs positioned so as not
> to interfere with the actions of the* BOY *and the* GIRL. *The* MOTHER
> *enters, sits in chair and begins to use imaginary iron and board.
> She hums a spiritual as she works.*

MOTHER   You came three times . . . Michael? It took you three times
to find me at home?

> *The* GIRL *enters, turns and peers through the cracked, imaginary
> door.*

SON'S VOICE [*offstage*]   Is Mrs. Brown home?
GIRL [*an old woman*]   What?
MOTHER   It shouldn't have taken you three times. I told you that I
would be here by two and you should wait, Michael.

> *The* SON *enters, passes the* GIRL *and takes his seat upon the
> other chair. The* BOY *enters, stops on other side of the imaginary
> door and looks through at the* GIRL.

BOY   Is Mrs. Brown in?
GIRL   Miss Brown ain't come in yet. Come back later . . . She'll be in
before dark.
MOTHER   It shouldn't have taken you three times . . . You should lis-
ten to me, Michael. Standin' all that time in the cold.
SON   It wasn't cold, Mother.
MOTHER   I told you that I would be here by two and you should wait,
Michael.
BOY   Please tell Mrs. Brown that her son's in town to visit her.
GIRL   You little Miss Brown's son? Well, bless the Lord.

> *Calls over her shoulder.*

Hey, Mandy, do you hear that? Little Miss Brown upstairs got a son
. . . a great big boy . . . He's come to visit her.
BOY   You'll tell her, won't you?
GIRL   Sure, I'll tell her.

> *Grins and shows gums.*

I'll tell her soon as she gets in.
MOTHER   Did you get cold, Michael?
SON   No, Mother. I walked around some . . . sightseeing.

BOY   I walked up Twenty-third Street toward South. I had phoned that I was coming.

MOTHER   Sightseeing? But this is your home, Michael . . . always has been.

BOY   Just before I left New York I phoned that I was taking the bus. Two hours by bus, that's all. That's all it takes. Two hours.

SON   This town seems so strange. Different than how I remember it.

MOTHER   Yes, you have been away for a good while . . . How long has it been, Michael?

BOY   Two hours down the Jersey Turnpike, the trip beginning at the New York Port Authority Terminal . . .

SON   . . . and then straight down through New Jersey to Philadelphia . . .

GIRL   . . . and home . . . Just imagine . . . little Miss Brown's got a son who's come home.

SON   Yes, home . . . an anachronism.

MOTHER   What did you say, Michael?

BOY   He said . . .

GIRL   [*late teens*]   What's an anachronism, Mike?

SON   Anachronism: 1: an error in chronology; *esp:* a chronological misplacing of persons, events, objects, or customs in regard to each other; 2: a person or a thing that is chronologically out of place— anachronistic/ *also* anachronic/ *or* anachronous—anachronistically/ *also* anachronously.

MOTHER   I was so glad to hear you were going to school in California.

BOY   College.

GIRL   Yes, I understand.

MOTHER   How long have you been gone, Michael?

SON   Nine years.

BOY   Nine years it's been. I wonder if she'll know me . . .

MOTHER   You've put on so much weight, son. You know that's not healthy.

GIRL   [*20 years old*]   And that silly beard . . . how . . .

SON   Oh . . . I'll take it off. I'm going on a diet tomorrow.

BOY   I wonder if I'll know her.

SON   You've put on some yourself, Mother.

MOTHER   Yes, the years pass. Thank the Lord.

BOY   I wonder if we've changed much.

GIRL   Yes, thank the Lord.

SON   The streets here seem so small.

MOTHER   Yes, it seems like that when you spend a little time in Los Angeles.

GIRL   I spent eighteen months there with your aunt when she was sick. She had nobody else to help her . . . she was so lonely. And you were in the service . . . away. You've always been away.

BOY   In Los Angeles the boulevards, the avenues, the streets . . .

SON   . . . are wide. Yes, they have some wide ones out West. Here, they're so small and narrow. I wonder how cars get through on both sides.

MOTHER   Why, you know how . . . we lived on Derby Street for over ten years, didn't we?

SON   Yeah, that was almost an alley.

MOTHER   Did you see much of your aunt before you left Los Angeles?

SON   What?

GIRL [*middle-aged woman to* BOY]   Have you found a job yet, Michael?

MOTHER   Your aunt. My sister.

BOY   Nawh, not yet . . . Today I just walked downtown . . . quite a ways . . . this place is plenty big, ain't it?

SON   I don't see too much of Aunt Sophie.

MOTHER   But you're so much alike.

GIRL   Well, your bags are packed and are sitting outside the door.

BOY   My bags?

MOTHER   You shouldn't be that way, Michael. You shouldn't get too far away from your family.

SON   Yes, Mother.

BOY   But I don't have any money. I had to walk downtown today. That's how much money I have. I've only been here a week.

GIRL   I packed your bags, Michael.

MOTHER   You never can tell when you'll need or want your family, Michael.

SON   That's right, Mother.

MOTHER   You and she are so much alike.

BOY   Well, goodbye, Aunt Sophie.

GIRL   [*silence*]

MOTHER   All that time in California and you hardly saw your aunt. My baby sister.

BOY   Tsk tsk tsk.

SON   I'm sorry, Mother.

MOTHER   In the letters I'd get from both of you there'd be no mention of the other. All these years. Did you see her again?

SON   Yes.

GIRL   [*on telephone*]   Michael? Michael who? . . . Ohhh . . . Bernice's boy.

MOTHER   You didn't tell me about this, did you?

SON   No, I didn't.

BOY   Hello, Aunt Sophie. How are you?

GIRL   I'm fine, Michael. How are you? You're looking well.

BOY   I'm getting on okay.

MOTHER   I prayed for you.

SON   Thank you.

MOTHER   Thank the Lord, Michael.

BOY   Got me a job working for the city.

GIRL   You did now.

BOY   Yes, I've brought you something.

GIRL   What's this, Michael . . . ohhh . . . it's money.

BOY   It's for the week I stayed with you.

GIRL   Fifty dollars. But, Michael, you didn't have to.

MOTHER   Are you still writing that radical stuff, Michael?

SON   Radical?

MOTHER   Yes . . . that stuff you write and send me all the time in those little books.

SON   My poetry, Mother?

MOTHER   Yes, that's what I'm talking about.

SON   No.

MOTHER   Praise the Lord, son. Praise the Lord. Didn't seem like anything I had read in school.

BOY   [*on telephone*]   Aunt Sophie? . . . Aunt Sophie? . . . It's me, Michael . . .

GIRL   Michael?

BOY   Yes . . . Michael . . .

GIRL   Oh . . . Michael . . . yes . . .

BOY   I'm in jail, Aunt Sophie . . . I got picked up for drunk driving.

GIRL   You did . . . how awful . . .

MOTHER   When you going to get your hair cut, Michael?

BOY   Aunt Sophie . . . will you please come down and sign my bail. I've got the money . . . I just got paid yesterday . . . They're holding more than enough for me . . . but the law says that someone has to sign for it.

MOTHER   You look almost like a hoodlum, Michael.

BOY   All you need to do is come down and sign . . . and I can get out.

MOTHER   What you tryin' to be . . . a savage or something? Are you keeping out of trouble, Michael?

GIRL   Ohhh . . . Michael . . . I'm sorry but I can't do nothin' like that . . .

BOY   But all you have to do is sign . . . I've got the money and everything.

GIRL   I'm sorry . . . I can't stick my neck out.

BOY   But, Aunt Sophie . . . if I don't get back to work I'll lose my job and everything . . . please . . .

GIRL   I'm sorry, Michael . . . I can't stick my neck out . . . I have to go now . . . Is there anyone I can call?

BOY   No.

GIRL   I could call your mother. She wouldn't mind if I reversed the charges on her, would she? I don't like to run my bills up.

BOY   No, thanks.

MOTHER   You and your aunt are so much alike.

SON   Yes, Mother. Our birthdays are in the same month.

MOTHER   Yes, that year was so hot . . . so hot and I was carrying you . . .

> As the MOTHER speaks the BOY comes over and takes her by the hand and leads her from the chair, and they stroll around the stage, arm in arm. The GIRL accompanies them and she and the BOY enact scenes from the MOTHER's mind.

. . . carrying you, Michael . . . and you were such a big baby . . . kicked all the time. But I was happy. Happy that I was having a baby of my own . . . I worked as long as I could and bought you everything you might need . . . diapers . . . and bottles . . . and your own spoon . . . and even toys . . . and even books . . . And it was so hot in Philadelphia that year . . . Your Aunt Sophie used to come over and we'd go for walks . . . sometimes up on the avenue . . . I was living in West Philly then . . . in that old terrible section they called "The Bottom." That's where I met your father.

GIRL   You're such a fool, Bernice. No nigger . . . man or boy's . . . ever going to do a thing to me like that.

MOTHER   Everything's going to be all right, Sophia.

GIRL   But what is he going to do? How are you going to take care of a baby by yourself?

MOTHER   Everything's going to be all right, Sophia. I'll manage.

GIRL   You'll manage? How? Have you talked about marriage?

MOTHER   Oh, please, Sophia!

GIRL   What do you mean "please"? Have you?

MOTHER   I just can't. He might think . . .

GIRL   Think! That dirty nigger better think. He better think before he really messes up. And you better too. You got this baby comin' on. What are you going to do?

MOTHER   I don't know . . . I don't know what I can do.

GIRL   Is he still tellin' you those lies about . . .

MOTHER   They're not lies.

GIRL   Haaaa . . .

MOTHER   They're not.

GIRL   Some smooth-talkin' nigger comes up from Georgia and tell you he escaped from the chain gang and had to change his name so he can't get married 'cause they might find out . . . What kinda shit is that, Bernice?

MOTHER   Please, Sophia. Try and understand. He loves me. I can't hurt him.

GIRL   Loves you . . . and puts you through this?

MOTHER   Please . . . I'll talk to him . . . Give me a chance.

GIRL   It's just a good thing you got a family, Bernice. It's just a good thing. You know that, don't cha?

MOTHER   Yes . . . yes, I do . . . but please don't say anything to him.

SON   I've only seen my father about a half dozen times that I remember, Mother. What was he like?

MOTHER   Down in The Bottom . . . that's where I met your father. I was young and hinkty[1] then. Had big pretty brown legs and a small waist. Everybody used to call me Bernie . . . and me and my sister would go to Atlantic City on the weekends and work as waitresses in the evenings and sit all afternoon on the black part of the beach at Boardwalk and Atlantic . . . getting blacker . . . and having the times of our lives. Your father probably still lives down in The Bottom . . . perched over some bar down there . . . drunk to the world . . . I can see him now . . . He had good white teeth then . . . not how they turned later when he started in drinkin' that wine and wouldn't stop . . . he was so nice then.

BOY   Awwww, listen, kid. I got my problems too.

GIRL   But Andy . . . I'm six months gone . . . and you ain't done nothin'.

BOY   Well, what can I do?

GIRL   Don't talk like that . . . What can you do? . . . You know what you can do.

BOY   You mean marry you? Now lissen, sweetheart . . .

GIRL   But what about our baby?

BOY   Your baby.

GIRL   Don't talk like that! It took more than me to get him.

BOY   Well . . . look . . . I'll talk to you later, kid. I got to go to work now.

GIRL   That's what I got to talk to you about too, Andy. I need some money.

BOY   Money! Is somethin' wrong with your head, woman? I ain't got no money.

GIRL   But I can't work much longer, Andy. You got to give me some money. Andy . . . you just gotta.

BOY   Woman . . . all I got to *ever* do is die and go to hell.

---

1. A Black slang word which means that she was snobbish or aloof because of her certainty of her own good looks and general worth.

GIRL   Well, you gonna do that, Andy. You sho are . . . you know that, don't you? . . . You know that.

MOTHER   . . . Yes, you are, man. Praise the Lord. We all are . . . All of us . . . even though he ain't come for you yet to make you pay. Maybe he's waitin' for us to go together so I can be a witness to the retribution that's handed down. A witness to all that He'll bestow upon your sinner's head . . . A witness! . . . That's what I am, Andy! Do you hear me? . . . A witness!

SON   Mother . . . what's wrong? What's the matter?

MOTHER   Thank the Lord that I am not blinded and will see the fulfillment of divine . . .

SON   Mother!

MOTHER   Oh . . . is something wrong, Michael?

SON   You're shouting and walking around . . .

MOTHER   Oh . . . it's nothing, son. I'm just feeling the power of the Lord.

SON   Oh . . . is there anything I can get you, Mother?

MOTHER   No, nothing at all.

She sits again and irons.

SON   Where's your kitchen? . . . I'll get you some coffee . . . the way you like it. I bet I still remember how to fix it.

MOTHER   Michael . . . I don't drink anything like that no more.

SON   No?

MOTHER   Not since I joined the service of the Lord.

SON   Yeah? . . . Well, do you mind if I get myself a cup?

MOTHER   Why, I don't have a kitchen. All my meals are prepared for me.

SON   Oh . . . I thought I was having dinner with you.

MOTHER   No. There's nothing like that here.

SON   Well, could I take you out to a restaurant? . . . Remember how we used to go out all the time and eat? I've never lost my habit of liking to eat out. Remember . . . we used to come down to this part of town and go to restaurants. They used to call it home cooking then . . . now, at least where I been out West and up in Harlem . . . we call it soul food. I bet we could find a nice little restaurant not four blocks from here, Mother. Remember that old man's place we used to go to on Nineteenth and South? I bet he's dead now . . . but . . .

MOTHER   I don't even eat out no more, Michael.

SON   No?

MOTHER   Sometimes I take a piece of holy bread to work . . . or some fruit . . . if it's been blessed by my Spiritual Mother.

SON   I see.

MOTHER   Besides . . . we have a prayer meeting tonight.

SON   On Friday?

MOTHER   Every night. You'll have to be going soon.

SON   Oh.

MOTHER   You're looking well.

SON   Thank you.

MOTHER   But you look tired.

SON   Do I?

MOTHER   Yes, those rings around your eyes might never leave. Your father had them.

SON   Did he?

MOTHER   Yes . . . and cowlicks . . . deep cowlicks on each side of his head.

SON   Yes . . . I remember.

MOTHER   Do you?

The BOY *and the* GIRL *take crouching positions behind and in front of them. They are in a streetcar. The* BOY *behind the* MOTHER *and* SON, *the* GIRL *across the aisle, a passenger.*

MOTHER [*young woman to the* BOY]   Keep your damn hands off him, Andy!

BOY [*chuckles*]   Awww, c'mon . . . Bernie. I ain't seen him since he was in the crib.

MOTHER   And you wouldn't have seen neither of us . . . if I had anything to do with it . . . Ohhh . . . why did I get on this trolley?

BOY   C'mon . . . Bernie . . . don't be so stuckup.

MOTHER   Don't even talk to us . . . and stop reaching after him.

BOY   Awww . . . c'mon . . . Bernie. Let me look at him.

MOTHER   Leave us alone. Look . . . people are looking at us.

The GIRL *across the aisle has been peeking at the trio but looks toward front at the mention of herself.*

BOY   Hey, big boy . . . do you know who I am?

MOTHER   Stop it, Andy! Stop it, I say . . . Mikie . . . don't pay any attention to him . . . you hear?

BOY   Hey, big boy . . . know who I am? . . . I'm your daddy. Hey, there . . .

MOTHER   Shut up . . . shut up, Andy . . . you nothin' to us.

BOY   Where you livin' at . . . Bernie? Let me come on by and see the little guy, huh?

MOTHER   No! You're not comin' near us . . . ever . . . you hear?

BOY   But I'm his father . . . look . . . Bernie . . . I've been an ass the way I've acted but . . .

MOTHER   He ain't got no father.

BOY   Oh, come off that nonsense, woman.

MOTHER   Mikie ain't got no father . . . his father's dead . . . you hear?

BOY   Dead?

MOTHER   Yes, dead. My son's father's dead.

BOY   What you talkin' about? . . . He's the spittin' image of me.

MOTHER   Go away . . . leave us alone, Andrew.

BOY   See there . . . he's got the same name as me. His first name is Michael after your father . . . and Andrew after me.

MOTHER   No, stop that, you hear?

BOY   Michael Andrew . . .

MOTHER   You never gave him no name . . . his name is Brown . . . Brown. The same as mine . . . and my sister's . . . and my daddy . . . You never gave him nothin' . . . and you're dead . . . go away and get buried.

BOY   You know that trouble I'm in . . . I got a wife down there, Bernie. I don't care about her . . . what could I do?

MOTHER [*rises, pulling up the* SON]   We're leavin' . . . don't you try and follow us . . . you hear, Andy? C'mon . . . Mikie . . . watch your step now.

BOY   Well . . . bring him around my job . . . you know where I work. That's all . . . bring him around on payday.

MOTHER [*leaving*]   We don't need anything from you . . . I'm working . . . just leave us alone.

> The BOY *turns to the* GIRL.

BOY [*shrugs*]   That's the way it goes . . . I guess. Ships passing on the trolley car . . . Hey . . . don't I know you from up around 40th and Market?

> The GIRL *turns away.*

SON   Yeah . . . I remember him. He always had liquor on his breath.

MOTHER   Yes . . . he did. I'm glad that stuff ain't got me no more . . . Thank the Lord.

GIRL [*35 years old*]   You want to pour me another drink, Michael?

BOY [*15 years old*]   You drink too much, Mother.

GIRL   Not as much as some other people I know.

BOY   Well, me and the guys just get short snorts, Mother. But you really hide some port.

GIRL   Don't forget you talkin' to your mother. You gettin' more like your father every day.

BOY   Is that why you like me so much?

GIRL [*grins drunkenly*]   Oh, hush up now, boy . . . and pour me a drink.

BOY   There's enough here for me too.

GIRL   That's okay . . . when Will comes in he'll bring something.

SON   How is Will, Mother?

MOTHER   I don't know . . . haven't seen Will in years.

SON   Mother.

MOTHER   Yes, Michael.

SON   Why you and Will never got married? . . . You stayed together for over ten years.

MOTHER   Oh, don't ask me questions like that, Michael.

SON   But why not?

MOTHER   It's just none of your business.

SON   But you could be married now . . . not alone in this room . . .

MOTHER   Will had a wife and child in Chester[2] . . . you know that.

SON   He could have gotten a divorce, Mother . . . Why . . .

MOTHER   Because he just didn't . . . that's why.

SON   You never hear from him?

MOTHER   Last I heard . . . Will had cancer.

SON   Oh, he did.

MOTHER   Yes.

SON   Why didn't you tell me? . . . You could have written.

MOTHER   Why?

SON   So I could have known.

MOTHER   So you could have known? Why?

SON   Because Will was like a father to me . . . the only one I've really known.

MOTHER   A father? And you chased him away as soon as you got big enough.

SON   Don't say that, Mother.

---

2. A town in Delaware to the southwest of Philadelphia.

MOTHER   You made me choose between you and Will.

SON   Mother.

MOTHER   The quarrels you had with him . . . the mean tricks you used to play . . . the lies you told to your friends about Will . . . He wasn't much . . . when I thought I had a sense of humor I us'ta call him just plain Will.[3] But we was his family.

SON   Mother, listen.

MOTHER   And you drove him away . . . and he didn't lift a hand to stop you.

SON   Listen, Mother.

MOTHER   As soon as you were big enough you did all that you could to get me and Will separated.

SON   Listen.

MOTHER   All right, Michael . . . I'm listening.

Pause.

SON   Nothing.

Pause. Lifts an imaginary object.

Is this your tambourine?

MOTHER   Yes.

SON   Do you play it?

MOTHER   Yes.

SON   Well?

MOTHER   Everything I do in the service of the Lord I do as well as He allows.

SON   You play it at your meetings.

MOTHER   Yes, I do. We celebrate the life He has bestowed upon us.

SON   I guess that's where I get it from.

MOTHER   Did you say something, Michael?

SON   Yes. My musical ability.

MOTHER   Oh . . . you've begun taking your piano lessons again?

SON   No . . . I was never any good at that.

MOTHER   Yes, three different teachers and you never got past the tenth lesson.

SON   You have a good memory, Mother.

MOTHER   Sometimes, son. Sometimes.

SON   I play an electric guitar in a combo.

MOTHER   You do? That's nice.

SON   That's why I'm in New York. We got a good break and came East.

MOTHER   That's nice, Michael.

SON   I was thinking that Sunday I could rent a car and come down to get you and drive you up to see our show. You'll get back in plenty of time to rest for work Monday.

MOTHER   No, I'm sorry. I can't do that.

SON   But you would like it, Mother. We could have dinner up in Harlem, then go down and . . .

MOTHER   I don't do anything like that any more, Michael.

SON   You mean you wouldn't come to see me play even if I were appearing here in Philly?

MOTHER   That's right, Michael. I wouldn't come. I'm past all that.

---

3. The central character of a popular and long-running radio serial *Just Plain Bill* was presented as a man of good heart but without other characteristics to raise him above the average.

SON Oh, I see.

MOTHER Yes, thank the Lord.

SON But it's my life, Mother.

MOTHER Good . . . then you have something to live for.

SON Yes.

MOTHER Well, you're a man now, Michael . . . I can no longer live it for you. Do the best with what you have.

SON Yes . . . Yes, I will, Mother.

GIRL's VOICE [*offstage*] Sister Brown . . . Sister Brown . . . hello.

MOTHER [*uneasy; peers at watch*] Oh . . . it's Mother Ellen . . . I didn't know it was so late.

GIRL [*enters*] Sister Brown . . . how are you this evening?

MOTHER Oh, just fine, Mother.

GIRL Good. It's nearly time for dinner.

MOTHER Oh, yes, I know.

GIRL We don't want to keep the others waiting at meeting . . . do we?

MOTHER No, we don't.

GIRL [*self-assured*] Hello, son.

SON Hello.

MOTHER Oh, Mother . . . Mother . . .

GIRL Yes, Sister Brown, what is it?

MOTHER Mother . . . Mother . . . this is . . . this is . . .

> *Pause.*

. . . this is . . .

SON Hello, I'm Michael. How are you?

MOTHER [*relieved*] Yes, Mother . . . This is Michael . . . my son.

GIRL Why, hello, Michael. I've heard so much about you from your mother. She prays for you daily.

SON [*embarrassed*] Oh . . . good.

GIRL [*briskly*] Well . . . I have to be off to see about the others.

MOTHER Yes, Mother Ellen.

GIRL [*as she exits; chuckles*] Have to tell everyone that you won't be keeping us waiting, Bernice.

> *Silence.*

SON Well, I guess I better be going, Mother.

MOTHER Yes.

SON I'll write.

MOTHER Please do.

SON I will.

MOTHER You're looking well . . . Thank the Lord.

SON Thank you, so are you, Mother.

> *He moves toward her and hesitates.*

MOTHER You're so much like your aunt. Give her my best . . . won't you?

SON Yes, I will, Mother.

MOTHER Take care of yourself, son.

SON Yes, Mother. I will.

> *The* SON *exits. The* MOTHER *stands looking after him as the lights go slowly down to . . .*

BLACKNESS

MEGAN TERRY

The Gloaming, Oh My Darling

CHARACTERS

MRS. TWEED	*Patients in a*	SON *of* MRS. WATERMELLON
MRS. WATERMELLON	*nursing home*	*His* SON *and* DAUGHTER
MR. BIRDSONG		DAUGHTER *of* MRS. TWEED
A NURSE		*Her* SON *and* DAUGHTER

Two women sit on two chairs in a nursing home. There are two beds in the small sunny room. One of the beds is occupied, but the sheet and blanket are drawn up over the head of the occupant. The two old women speak in Irish accents.

MRS. TWEED   Ah yes, Mrs. Watermellon, and the days go by and the days go by and the days go by and the days go by, and by and by the days go by. My God, how the days go by!

MRS. WATERMELLON   From where I sit . . . I have to agree with you. But they don't go fast enough by, Mrs. Tweed, not by a half sight, not by a full sight. The world is waiting for the sunrise, and I'm the only one who knows where it begins.

MRS. TWEED   Why do you keep it a secret?

MRS. WATERMELLON   No secret. I've told everyone. I've told and told and told everyone.

MRS. TWEED   Where does it begin then?

MRS. WATERMELLON   [*slapping her breast*]   Here. Right here. Right here it starts! From the old ticker it starts and pumps around and thumps around, coagulates in my belly and once a month bursts out onto the ground . . . but all the color's gone . . . all but one . . . all but . . . one. . .

MRS. TWEED   So that's where the sunrise went.

MRS. WATERMELLON   You three-minute egg. You runny, puny twelve-week's old, three-minute egg. You're underdone and overripe. What do you know? You only learned to speak when you got mad enough . . . I'm going to sleep. I'd as soon live in the mud with the turtles as to have to converse with the likes of you.

MRS. TWEED   Don't talk like that. That hurts me.

MRS. WATERMELLON   Nothing can hurt you if your mind is on a high plain.

MRS. TWEED   If you go to sleep on me, then I'll let him go.

MRS. WATERMELLON   If you let him go, Mrs. Tweed, then I'll tell you where your daughter is.

MRS. TWEED   I won't listen.

MRS. WATERMELLON   Oh yes, you'll listen. You'll listen to me tell you where she is. It makes you cry and you hate to cry. But once you get started crying you wake up everyone, and then they'll give you an enema.

MRS. TWEED   I don't care if they do. There's nothing more to come out. They've tubed, and they've squirted, and they've radiated and they've intravened . . . There's nothing more to come out of me. I haven't had reason to pick my nose in two years.

MRS. WATERMELLON   Do you think he's awake yet?

MRS. TWEED   Mrs. Watermellon, what if someone comes to visit him?

MRS. WATERMELLON   I won't let them see him.

MRS. TWEED   You have to let them see him if they're his folks.

MRS. WATERMELLON   Nope, you dope, I don't.

MRS. TWEED   You do have to let folks see him. What else would folks be coming up here for, if not to see him.

MRS. WATERMELLON   Perhaps he's passed on—passed over. I'll say he's gone West. *Anyway,* Mrs. Tweed, he's mine now.

MRS. TWEED   Why, he's ours, Mrs. Watermellon. You can't have him all to yourself!

MRS. WATERMELLON   That's what I did in the night. I *didn't* want you to find out, but since I see what a busybody you finally are, after all these bygone days, I'll tell you once and for all. He's mine!

MRS. TWEED   But we got him together. I carried the bottom end. You weak old tub, you couldn't even have lifted him from his bed by yourself. You'd have dropped and broken him. They'd have put us in jail for stealing and murder. They'd have electrocuted and hung us . . . they'd have . . .

MRS. WATERMELLON   Hush your mouth! Hush up. I won't have him disturbed by your temper.

MRS. TWEED   I'm going to give him back. Tonight I'll carry him back to the men's ward and tuck him in his crib.

MRS. WATERMELLON   No, you won't. He's mine.

MRS. TWEED   Ours.

MRS. WATERMELLON   Mine.

MRS. TWEED   Ours . . .

MRS. WATERMELLON   All right. All right, you pukey squashed robins egg, all right! All right, all right, you leftover maggot mangy mop rag. All right! All right, you dried-up, old snot rag, I'm going to tell you, *I'm going to tell* you right here and now. Do you hear me? I'm going to tell you right here and now.

MRS. TWEED   I don't want to hear. Not here. Not now.

> *A recorded voice of a young woman sings.* WATERMELLON *and* TWEED *freeze in their places during the song:*

VOICE   "In the gloaming, oh my darling,
When the lights are soft and low,
Will you think of me and love me
As you did once long ago?"[1]

MRS. WATERMELLON   [*coming back to life*]   I'm hungry for canned rhubarb! Never did get enough. My greedy little sister used to get up in the night when we's all asleep and sneak down to the fruit cellar and eat two quarts of rhubarb, every single night.

MRS. TWEED   She must a had the cleanest bowels in the whole country.

MRS. WATERMELLON   My mother had the best dinner. For her last birthday two days before she died my brother asked her what she wanted. She knew it was her last supper.

MRS. TWEED   Chicken baked in cream in the oven?

MRS. WATERMELLON   Nope, you dope. Pheasant she wanted. Cherry-stone clams, six of them, roast pheasant and wild-blackberry pie. She

---

1. "In the Gloaming" is a famous song, written about 1875 with words by Meta Orred and music by Annie Fortescue Harrison.

ate every bit of it. We watched her. She ate it all up, every speck of it. Cherrystone clams, six of them, roast pheasant, and wild-blackberry pie. Licked her lips.

MRS. TWEED   That rings a bell. I had pheasant once. Pheasant under glass. Looked so pretty, I didn't eat it. Where was that?

MRS. WATERMELLON   You had it at the old Biltmore.[2] She licked her lips and closed her eyes. She never opened them again.

MRS. TWEED   That rings a bell. Who'd I have it with? Did I taste it? Under a lovely glass bell. Who was I with?

MRS. WATERMELLON   You were with your husband, Mrs. Tweed. Your second husband. You did that on your anniversary. On your wedding anniversary, you dope. You've told me every one of your anniversary stories five hundred times a year.

MRS. TWEED [*laughs*]   It's gone from me. All gone from me. Fancy that, but it does ring a bell.

MRS. WATERMELLON   You can eat mushrooms under glass too. Don't you know?

MRS. TWEED   Myrtle Classen used to serve them at her bridge luncheons. Mushrooms, under glass. I didn't eat any of those either.

MRS. WATERMELLON   What have you done with him, Mrs. Tweed?

MRS. TWEED   I made him even.

MRS. WATERMELLON   *What* have you done with him?

MRS. TWEED   What'll you give me if I tell, Mrs. Watermellon?

MRS. WATERMELLON   Tell.

MRS. TWEED   Give.

MRS. WATERMELLON   Tell.

MRS. TWEED   Give.

MRS. WATERMELLON   Tell, tell.

MRS. TWEED   Give, give.

MRS. WATERMELLON   Tell, tell, tell!

MRS. TWEED   Give, give, give!

MRS. WATERMELLON [*melting*]   I give.

MRS. TWEED   All up?

MRS. WATERMELLON   All.

MRS. TWEED   Say it. Say it all, Mrs. Watermellon.

MRS. WATERMELLON   I give it all up. I give it all up to my uncle. My uncle. Uncle.

MRS. TWEED   Who is he? Who is he, your uncle, uncle?

MRS. WATERMELLON [*exhausted*]   You are. You . . . are . . . Mrs. Tweed.

MRS. TWEED   Then you've got to tell me what you did to Mr. Bird-song in the night.

MRS. WATERMELLON   Now?

MRS. TWEED   Not a moment too late.

MRS. WATERMELLON   I . . . I married him. I married Mr. Birdsong.

MRS. TWEED   No.

MRS. WATERMELLON   In the night, I lifted the covers from his body and I married him. Mrs. Birdsong. Mrs.

MRS. TWEED   But he was ours. We brought him here together.

MRS. WATERMELLON   In the night . . .

MRS. TWEED   It isn't fair. You didn't do it fair. He was . . .

MRS. WATERMELLON   I didn't want to do it, because we've been such good, such only friends. But I didn't want to tell you 'cause I don't

2. A famous hotel in New York City.

want you to stop rubbing my back on rainy days. I didn't want to tell you because I didn't want you to stop cleaning my nails on Sunday mornings. I didn't want to tell you because you eat those hard-cooked carrots for me on Wednesday nights. I didn't want to tell you 'cause you rub a nipple and make me feel sweet sixteen when we play boy friends. I didn't want to tell you because you're all I've got . . . you're all I've been given in this last twenty years. You're all I've seen in this never-never. I didn't want to tell you because you're the only one who can see *me*. I didn't want to tell you because you were all I had. But now I've got Mr. Birdsong. Mr. and Mrs. Birdsong.

MRS. TWEED   Don't tell me that. You shouldn't have told me that.

MRS. WATERMELLON   And you don't even know any good lifetime stories. I've been shut up with a life that never moved at all. The only thing you can remember is how . . .

MRS. TWEED   . . . Is how I rode out in the Maine snow night with my *Doctor* Father and he held his fur-coat arms around me on his horse and I sat in front of him with his fur-coat arms around me and I held his scratched and leather smelly doctor's bag. Held it tight so's not to drop it in the Maine snow night.

MRS. WATERMELLON   That's what I mean, just one sentimental perversion after another.

MRS. TWEED   There's nothing perverted about father love.

MRS. WATERMELLON   There is if there's something perverted about Father.

MRS. TWEED   Who?

MRS. WATERMELLON   You. You. You. Mrs. Tweed.

MRS. TWEED [*trying to rise*]   That did it. That did it. That just about did it in, all right.

MRS. WATERMELLON   Sit down, you old windbag.

MRS. TWEED   That did it. That did it, Mrs. Watermellon. That just about did it in, all right.

MRS. WATERMELLON   Sit down, you old battle-ax.

MRS. TWEED [*on a rising scale*]   That did it. That did it. That just about did it. That did it all right.

MRS. WATERMELLON   Sit down, you old blister.

MRS. TWEED [*bursts*]   *That did it!* [*She explodes into a convulsive dance. She sings. As she sings her accent disappears.*]
That's done it, that's better.
That's done it,
What ease.
That's done it,
That's better.
What took you so long,
You tease?

MRS. WATERMELLON   Don't leave me. I forbid you to go. Don't leave me, Tweed. Come back. Don't leave me here alone with a man.

MRS. TWEED [*dances herself down to the age of sixteen*]   I'm so tired. I'm so tired and so done in. We drank and drank so much grape punch and then that gentle Keith Lewiston took me behind the schoolhouse and you know what he did?

MRS. WATERMELLON   He hitched you to his buggy and drove you round the yard.

MRS. TWEED [*embracing her*]   He soul kissed me. He kissed my soul. Like this.

MRS. WATERMELLON [*dodges*]   Don't start that mush again.

MRS. TWEED [*still sixteen*]   He kissed my soul. Like this. [*She plants a kiss finally on* MRS. WATERMELLON's *neck.*]

MRS. WATERMELLON [*starts to howl in pain, but the howl changes to a kind of gargle and then to a girlish laugh. Her accent leaves also*] Did it make a strawberry? Did you make me a strawberry on my neck? [*Now* MRS. WATERMELLON *is also sixteen.*] Do it again and make a big red strawberry mark. Then we'll have to wear long scarves around our necks, to school, but everyone will know why. They'll think the boys kissed us behind the schoolhouse. Is it red yet? Is it strawberry red yet?

MRS. TWEED [*coming back to old age, knots an imaginary scarf around* MRS. WATERMELLON's *neck and her Irish accent returns*]   No—not —yet.

MRS. WATERMELLON [*chokes and laughs as if strangling*]   Don't. We're friends. We're best friends. We're girl friends. [*Her Irish accent returns.*] Don't kill me. I'm your mother.

MRS. TWEED   Save all that for Doctor. I'm on to you. Your smart-assed psycho—hology won't work on me any more. Save it for Mr. Birdsong. *If* you can find him.

MRS. WATERMELLON   What have you done with him?

MRS. TWEED   Wouldn't you like to know.

MRS. WATERMELLON   What have you done with him? What have you done with my . . .

MRS. TWEED   *Your* what?

MR. BIRDSONG [*still in a coma, but speaks out in a voice like W. C. Fields*[3]]   Stuck with the cattle through the storm. Dust blowed so hard couldn't see yer hand in front of yer face. Twister blowed us five hundred miles. Caught us in Illinois and set us down in Nebraska. Dust blowed bad, but I never lost a head nor did I even stop to make water.

MRS. WATERMELLON   I'm tired of trying to keep alive.

MRS. TWEED   We'll get off the shelf.

MRS. WATERMELLON   Canned beside the hybrid corn.

MRS. TWEED   And the pickles.

MRS. WATERMELLON   And the piccalilli.

MRS. TWEED   And the bread and butters.

MRS. WATERMELLON   Apple butter.

MRS. TWEED   Watermelon relish.

MR. BIRDSONG   We kept right on putting our lives on the line because some fool gave the order.

MRS. WATERMELLON   Found a family. All I wanted was to found a great family.

MRS. TWEED   I worked hard. The wire factory gave me a good pension. I could still run up and down ladders as good as the men.

MR. BIRDSONG   The heathens want ours. They've infiltrated us in plain clothes. The heathen emissaries of Satan want to sabotage us. Scorch that earth, boys. That's the ticket. I want to get back to my bride.

MRS. TWEED   No one cares what we do now, Mrs. Watermellon, we can share him. We can both be Mrs. Birdsongs. The Mormons done it and God didn't get mad at them.

MRS. WATERMELLON   In the night I climbed into his bed and married him.

---

3. A comedian (1880–1946), known for his raspy voice and mordant wit. Many of his classic film performances are still widely shown.

MRS. TWEED [*begins to cry very quietly*] No. No. No. I can't believe it. You promised we'd share him. And to think I trusted you. And to think I loved you like a dear sister. And to think I gave you all my tender feelings for all these whitehouse years. *And to think . . .* and to . . .

MRS. WATERMELLON Stop that yipping. It's your own fault. You left me all alone in the night. You went to sleep. You didn't keep watch. You turned out the light and went to sleep. They'd have shot you for that in World War I. You stopped guarding. I had to marry some-one! I can't die childless. I refuse!

MRS. TWEED Impossible! You have eleven children living, forty-nine grandchildren living, twenty great grandchildren living and three on the way. There's a lot of biscuit in your oven, and your ovens' ovens.

MRS. WATERMELLON I just wanted to make it even with you. You had two husbands, you, you white and wizened shrimp. Two husbands! You knew two cocks of the walk in your time. Why should I take a back seat? Why should you know more than me?

MRS. TWEED Is that your fountain of knowledge? I'll never get over this. Never, never. After all the friends we've been through. I'm going to divorce you.

MRS. WATERMELLON I don't care. I'm a newlywed. I have security.

MRS. TWEED I'll say! There's nothing more secure than a coma. *He's been in that coma for eighty days.*

MRS. WATERMELLON It'll make our adjustment easier.

MRS. TWEED. Adjustment?

MRS. WATERMELLON [*inordinately satisfied*] To married life. Since only one of us has to change his ways, we should become com-patible twice as fast.

MRS. TWEED [*very formal*] Mrs. Watermellon, I'm going to ring for the nurse to change my room.

MRS. WATERMELLON [*equally formal*] Mrs. Tweed, you better ring for the nurse to change your pants. See there, you've messed again.

MRS. TWEED You're fooling me.

MRS. WATERMELLON Maybe I am fooling you, but Mother Nature isn't. Ring for the nurse. Ring, ring, ring, ring, ring, ring. Tick a lock, this is a magic spot.

MRS. TWEED Don't be mad to me any more.

MRS. WATERMELLON Tick a lock, this is a magic spot.

MRS. TWEED Don't be mad to me any more.

MR. BIRDSONG Everywhere you look there's busloads of foreigners. Rats are infiltrating our ranks.

MRS. TWEED I hear a man's voice. Listen. Did you hear it?

MRS. WATERMELLON It's your longing. Your longing rising up and talking to you.

MRS. TWEED Sounds like my granddad. Just like him when he come back from the war.

MRS. WATERMELLON I don't hear anything but your heart ticks getting fainter and fainter.

MRS. TWEED Don't be so nice to me. You know I'm going to die, that's why you're so nice to me.

MRS. WATERMELLON Nonsense. You're not leaving before me. You're not leaving me alone in this hotel.

MR. BIRDSONG [MRS. TWEED *and* MRS. WATERMELLON *don't react to* MR. BIRDSONG *when he rises from bed.* BIRDSONG *rises from his bed*

*and stalks around the room, mounts a box to harangue the crowd—
his voice now sounds like Teddy Roosevelt*[4]]   As U.S. veteran of
the Indian Wars, I've come here before you to alarm you. Sons of
Liberty unite. Smash the rats of the world. We must cut off their
bloody hands. They're bringing this land that I love to wreck and
ruin. Wreck and ruin to our God-given America. Murderers of
women and children, red rats making balcony speeches. Balcony
speeches by the feeble-minded mockers of God. That's the stink of
Satan, boys. The stink of the murderers of Americans. The stink
smelled is the stink from Satan. Satan who uses the body as a house
to live in. The stink of Satan once smelled coming from these bodies
is never forgotten. They want to make the United States and
Mexico and Canada and Alaska into a death trap. Declare war on
these stinking infiltrators. They've made it easy to burn up American
bodies in the fiery furnaces of every hospital and prison. American
Veterans of foreign wars, boys. Unite to fight. Unite to fight before
they drug every one of us with their poisoned needles. Every man
has been sexually destroyed by the needle while asleep. Fight the
needle, boys. Don't let them burn up our unborn children. Why was
Roosevelt murdered? Why was Kennedy murdered? Why was
Stevenson murdered?[5] The rat bonecrushers of the world are out to
get us, all us American Veterans captive in these hospital jails. Unite
to fight the rats, boys. Unite to fight the rats. [*He returns to his bed
and his coma.*]

  The woman's voice is heard again.

VOICE "In the gloaming, oh my darling,
     When the lights are soft and low,
     Will you think of me and love me
     As you did once long ago?"
MRS. WATERMELLON I love President Kennedy.
MRS. TWEED Makes you feel good just to look at him.

  NURSE *enters with a fixed smile.* MRS. TWEED *and* MRS. WATER-
  MELLON *rush to hide the man. They both get on the bed and
  spread their nightgowns over him. They lapse into their oldest
  age.*

NURSE All right, you two—smarten up and look alive. [*She man-
handles them—pushing and pulling them into some sort of erect
state. They fall back to position like rag dolls—half cackling and
half gurgling.*] I said look alive! You're going to have a visit. Your
families have come to pay their monthly respects. Look alive, I said,
or they'll think we're not taking good care of you.
MRS. WATERMELLON [*frightened of the* NURSE] This woman's molesting me.
NURSE Hold your head up so I can get some rouge on that pasty cheek.
MRS. WATERMELLON This woman is molesting me.
NURSE Hold still, you old hag. I got to get some life in your face.
MRS. WATERMELLON I'll tell Dr. Sam on you and Dr. Ben and Dr.
Jim, too, and God and everybody.

---

4. Theodore Roosevelt (1858–1919) first
attained fame as a big-game hunter and
cavalry leader of the Rough Riders at the
Battle of San Juan Hill in 1898. He was
elected Vice President of the United States
in 1900 and succeeded to the presidency
on the death of William McKinley in 1901.
 5. John F. Kennedy (1917–1963), 35th
President of the United States, was assassinated in 1963. The other two persons
mentioned are in the same liberal Democratic tradition as Kennedy: Franklin D.
Roosevelt (1882–1945), 32nd President of
the United States, and Adlai E. Stevenson
(1900–1965), Democratic candidate for
President in 1952 and 1956. Both Roosevelt and Stevenson died natural deaths.

NURSE [*to* MRS. TWEED]   Your turn now, you little old crab.

MRS. TWEED [*playfully*]   What'll you give me if I let ya?

NURSE   Dirty-minded old ladies. If your family could only hear you.

MR. BIRDSONG [*under the ladies, belches*]   I rode five hundred miles with my cattle in the dust storm and never stopped once to make water. [WATERMELLON *mouths the lines.*]

NURSE   Who said that?

MRS. TWEED   She did—she always brags about how strong she used to be.

NURSE   Show me a little strength now. Sit up and look out of your eyes.

    MRS. TWEED *bites the nurse; the* NURSE *slaps* TWEED.

NURSE   Now there's some real color in your cheeks.

MRS. WATERMELLON [*howls*]   This woman is molesting us! [*The family enters.*]

NURSE [*like an overly cheerful, demented Katherine Hepburn*]   We're feeling very well today. We're glad to see our family today. [*She exits.*] Our family is glad to see us today.

SON WATERMELLON [*accompanied by his* SON *and* DAUGHTER]   Mother! [*He goes to her, ultrabeaming.*] You look wonderful! Doesn't she look wonderful, kids?

SON *and* DAUGHTER [*flatly*]   You look wonderful. You look wonderful. Grandma, you look wonderful.

MRS. WATERMELLON   Who's there? Is there anyone there? Knock once for yes.

DAUGHTER TWEED [*accompanied by her* SON *and* DAUGHTER, *crosses to* MRS. TWEED]   Oh, Mother, you look wonderful. Doesn't she look just wonderful, kids? Tell Mother how wonderful she looks.

SON *and* DAUGHTER [*run at* TWEED]   You look wonderful, Grandma— you look just wonderful.

    They climb all over her.

MRS. TWEED [*nearly suffocating*]   My dear children—my pretty grand-children. Grandma loves you so much.

DAUGHTER TWEED [*as children swarm all over* TWEED, *kissing and pummeling her*]   They love you so much, Mother. Isn't it wonderful for them that you're still alive?

GRANDSON *and* GRANDDAUGHTER TWEED   You feel just wonderful, Grandmother—just wonderful. [*They kiss and hug* TWEED *while she chokes and gasps.*]

SON WATERMELLON   Just sign right here, Mother. Here. I'll hold your hand around the pen.

MRS. WATERMELLON   What is it? Who are you?

SON WATERMELLON   I'm so grateful you haven't lost your sense of humor. Mother, you look downright beautiful. Color in your cheeks and everything. This isn't such a bad place after all, is it?

MRS. WATERMELLON [*knocks once for yes*]   You look a bit familiar around the eyes. I kept company with a young man once had shifty eyes kinda like yours.

SON WATERMELLON [*laughs heartily*]   Did you hear that, kids?

KIDS [*flat and bored*]   Hear what, Father?

SON WATERMELLON   Same old doll. What a doll my dear old mother was and still is. Just like the gal that married dear old Dad.[6]

---

6. A phrase from a song, "I Want a Girl Just like the Girl that Married Dear Old Dad," written in 1911 with words by William Dillon and music by Harry von Tilzer.

KIDS [*flat*]   Dear old shifty-eyed Dad.

SON WATERMELLON   Thanks for signing, honey-love. Makes it a lot easier for me now. Now look, sweetheart—you won't be seeing us for three months or so. Marge and the kids and I are going to Europe, but we'll send you a present from every port. How's about that? Give us a big smile and a kiss goodbye.

MRS. WATERMELLON   Then will you go?

SON WATERMELLON [*hurt*]   Mother! I had to take a day off from work and the kids out of school to drive up here! Marge is stuck with booking the passage.

MRS. WATERMELLON [*turns off—sighs—lies back down*]   I'll be all right. Don't worry about me.

SON WATERMELLON   Mother, don't be like this.

MRS. WATERMELLON   Don't worry, son, I won't *be* for much longer.

SON WATERMELLON [*kisses her on cheek*]   Goodbye, old girl.

KIDS   Goodbye, old girl. [*They exit.*]

MRS. WATERMELLON   Is there anyone there?

MRS. TWEED [*to* DAUGHTER]   Dorothy, where's your sister, Laura?

DAUGHTER TWEED   She isn't well, Mother. She has a bad cold. She was afraid she'd give it to you—and with your condition you know it could develop into pneumonia and you know . . . [*She makes an explosive gesture.*]

MRS. TWEED   Well, tell her I thank her for her consideration but I'd like to see her face once in a while.

DAUGHTER TWEED   Well, Mother, we got to be getting back, I guess —got the dogs and cats to feed.

KIDS   They sure do get mad at us if they don't get their dinner on time.

DAUGHTER TWEED   It sure was just wonderful to see you and see how good you look and how happy you look. That old lady who shares the room with you looks quiet and nice, too.

MRS. TWEED   Dorothy—take me home.

DAUGHTER TWEED   You know I'd love to, but you know what I'm up against with Harry.

MRS. TWEED   Dorothy, your children tire me.

DAUGHTER TWEED [*freezing up*]   Goodbye, Mother. I'll see you next month. I thought you'd want to see your own grandchildren.

MRS. TWEED   I've seen enough.

DAUGHTER TWEED [*gathering her children and leaving in a hurt rage*]   The sun always rose and set on Laura's head and it still does. And she hasn't been to see you in fifty years.

MRS. WATERMELLON   Is there anyone here?

MRS. TWEED   No, thank God. They've gone.

MRS. WATERMELLON   They didn't take him?

MRS. TWEED   I stopped them from it. I told them he'd eloped with a local tramp.

MRS. WATERMELLON   Where is he now?

MRS. TWEED   Under you, you old tub. I hope you haven't smothered him to death.

MRS. WATERMELLON [*feeling* MR. BIRDSONG]   Here's his head. [*She puts her ear to his chest.*] I hear a beat. Far away—a sweet little beat. [*She lifts the sheet and counts his arms.*] One, two. [*Counts his legs*] One, two. [*Counts his sex.*] One, two, three. I'm glad it has a handle on it. My husband said he wouldn't accept the baby otherwise.

MRS. TWEED Let me see his tiny hands. Oh, oh, the fingernails! [*She kisses the fingernails of* MR. BIRDSONG.]

MRS. WATERMELLON Why are you crying? A new baby should fill you with joy. Joy!

MRS. TWEED These fingernails. Look how tiny, the size of a pin head! And sharp! Oh, oh, the fingernails.

MRS. WATERMELLON God love him. A new life. God love it, God love it, God love it! [*She cuddles* MR. BIRDSONG.]

MRS. TWEED God spelled backwards is dog.

MRS. WATERMELLON A son, a son, we have a son. A son from God. [MR. BIRDSONG *gurgles like an infant.*]

MRS. TWEED Watch out for the teeth. They grow fast. My left nipple still carries a scar.

MR. BIRDSONG It was scorch the earth . . . scorch the earth of every village we took. After Lieutenant Pike[7] found his brother scalped and his guts strewn across the plain for the wolves to munch, we were ordered to cut down every peach tree, fill every irrigation ditch —burn every lodge and kill every horse, woman, and child of the Navaho.

MRS. WATERMELLON He'll make his mother proud.

MRS. TWEED My turn. [*She takes hold of* MR. BIRDSONG. MRS. WATERMELLON *holds on and glares.*] You act as if you did it all yourself.

MRS. WATERMELLON I did. It was my idea.

MRS. TWEED Not even you and forty million prayers could have raised him.

MRS. WATERMELLON It was my idea. All you were was a pair of arms.

MRS. TWEED And a good strong back—which you lack.

MR. BIRDSONG [*a young officer returning to Illinois on leave*] Mother! [*To* MRS. WATERMELLON.] It's fine to be home.

MRS. WATERMELLON You're thin.

MR. BIRDSONG Not for long. [*To* TWEED.] And what have we here— grown up and pretty as a prairie flower.

MRS. TWEED [*shyly*] I can still whip you on a fair day, Elijah.

MR. BIRDSONG [*advancing confidently and taking her wrists*] 'Tis fair today, Susan.

MRS. TWEED [*wilts and nearly swoons*] Mrs. Watermellon, your son's forgot his manners!

MRS. WATERMELLON Lige! Leave go this gal or marry her.

MR. BIRDSONG [*to* TWEED] I stayed with our cattle from here to Nebraska. It was the mightiest dust storm with twisters any man could remember. I rode five hundred miles without stopping to make water. I didn't lose a head. Marry me.

MRS. TWEED Marry me. Marry me. [*She goes into a slow-motion waltz with* BIRDSONG—MRS. WATERMELLON *joins them—while the voice of a woman sings a verse of "In the Gloaming."*]

MR. BIRDSONG [*they are at a picnic on the grass*] I have my orders, gals—ship out tomorrow. I'll miss your pretty faces—let's have one last roll.

MRS. TWEED *and* MRS. WATERMELLON You can't go, Donny—you've only been with us a week.

7. Zebulon M. Pike (1779–1813) was an American army officer who led expeditions to discover the source of the Mississippi River and to the Southwest, which was then a part of Mexico. He is best remembered as the discover of the mountain in Colorado which bears his name, Pike's Peak.

MR. BIRDSONG   Case you didn't hear it, babes, there's a war on. I killed off more than my quota of Huns and now good Old Uncle's sending me against the slants. What a secret weapons to throw at the Japs.

MRS. TWEED *and* MRS. WATERMELLON [*leap on him and roll him around in the grass, kissing and stroking him*]   The lucky Japs. The lucky Japs. You come back to us, you big, big stud. You hear, you come back to us.

MR. BIRDSONG   I rode all night, couldn't see a thing but I heard 'em. The dust so thick I couldn't make out the body of a single cow—but I felt 'em—five hundred miles into the twister and I never lost a head nor did I even stop to make water.

MRS. TWEED   I go out of my mind over a man in uniform.

MRS. WATERMELLON   I go into my mind with a man in my bed. [*She gets* MR. BIRDSONG *back to bed.*]

MRS. TWEED   They'll catch you.

MRS. WATERMELLON   If they catch me—they'll have you too.

MR. BIRDSONG [*as he's being put to bed*]   The Navaho all got up in their peaked plumed leather caps, blankets draped and heads held high—looked like a battalion of Roman Legionnaires. I felt time had slipped and slided and folded over—there I am in New Mexico fighting Roman warriors.

MRS. WATERMELLON   I can see the sunset, can you?

MRS. TWEED   Filters through.

MRS. WATERMELLON   The older I get the hotter I like it.

MRS. TWEED   You'll love it down below.

MRS. WATERMELLON   I'll turn you in. I'll tell the doctor.

MRS. TWEED   What could you tell the doctor?

MRS. WATERMELLON   How you follow him through the hall. How you don't have any pain in your chest and neck. You just crybaby about it so that he'll lift your nightgown and listen to your heartbeat through your dried-up titties.

MRS. TWEED   Yes, it's true. I like that.

MRS. WATERMELLON   No decency.

MRS. TWEED   Nonsense.

MRS. WATERMELLON   Of all the billions of Chinese in the world I have to be incarcerated with you. I served my time in the family way, I earned my arms and legs, I could drive from one town to another and visit New York. You'd think I'd have the right to choose my own cellmate, but no, no, I was placed in a place, it was planned and weighed, and examined, and organized for me. It was arranged. You were arranged for my best interests. I'd kill myself if they'd give me a sharp instrument.

MRS. TWEED   Your tongue will do.

MRS. WATERMELLON   Living with me has done you some improvement.

MRS. TWEED   You could do worse. You could be with balmy Mary McLemon. She spends every day picking nits off her clothes and her roommates. How'd you like her monkey hands and eyes all over you twenty-four hours a day. Or whining Mary McOrange who complains if it's hot and complains if it's cold and complains if the sun comes up and complains if it don't and complains if she's dry and complains if she's wet and complains if she lives and complains if she dies.

MRS. WATERMELLON   Maybe I am fooling you, but old Mother isn't. Tick a lock, this is a magic spot.

MRS. TWEED   Don't be bad to me anymore.

MRS. WATERMELLON   Maybe I am fooling you.

MRS. TWEED   Don't be mean to me any more.

MRS. WATERMELLON   Maybe I am fooling you, but I'm not responsible. No, I'm not—not any—any more. I'm not.

MRS. TWEED   I'm going to call your mother. I'll fly her here on a plane and have you committed. I'm going to phone your son. I'm going to fly him here and have you committed. I am. I will. You'll be committed.

MRS. WATERMELLON   Dry up, you old fart. I already am.

NURSE [*entering with tray*]   Time for cream of wheat. [*She smiles as she says this, but her voice is flat and mechanical.* TWEED *and* WATERMELLON *dive for their beds to hide* BIRDSONG *again.*] Time for your creamy wheat. Time for your wheat. Your cream's all gone. Time for the heap, the wheat's all dry. Sit up like good wrinkled girls and dribble it down your chins. Time for your cream of wheat, the sugar's all gone.

MRS. WATERMELLON   I'm tired of being a middleman for that pap. Flush it down the nearest john!

NURSE   I'll eat it myself. I'll eat it all up.

MRS. TWEED   It's worms. Look at her eat the pail full of worms.

MRS. WATERMELLON   You got it all wrong, Tweed. That's the worm and she's eating herself.

MRS. TWEED   Herself. And so she is. And to think of that.

MRS. WATERMELLON [*laughing and slapping* MRS. TWEED *on a knee*]   It's rich and richer and so so rich. I'd not thought it possible, but she's beaten us to it.

MRS. TWEED   Beaten us to it.

MRS. WATERMELLON   Yes, she's beaten us to it. Who'd ever have thought that she'd be the first worm. And she's done it before us.

MRS. TWEED   And we're so much older.

MRS. WATERMELLON   Of course we are. Nobody here could dare to be as old as we are. And look at that. Will you just look at that white worm. She's had the audacity to be a worm before us.

MRS. TWEED   And we're so much older.

NURSE   Time for your heat, the salve's all spread. Time for your bed, the sheet's all red. Time for the heap, the wheat's all cooked. Time for the deep, the syringe is plunged.

MRS. WATERMELLON *and* MRS. TWEED   And we're so much older. Nobody would dare to be as old or older. And we're so much older. [*They hold on to one another.*]

MRS. WATERMELLON   And older.

MRS. TWEED   And older.

MRS. WATERMELLON   In order.

MRS. TWEED   And older.

MRS. WATERMELLON   Tonight we'll be older still.

MRS. TWEED   In order.

MRS. WATERMELLON   If you'll stay up with me all night, then I'll let you.

NURSE   Time for the . . .

MRS. WATERMELLON   Keep right on eating and don't interrupt me.

NURSE   Time for the deep, the syringe is plunged. [*She gives them each a shot.*]

MRS. TWEED [*taking* MRS. WATERMELLON'S *hand*]   I won't close an eye.

MRS. WATERMELLON   Swear?

MRS. TWEED   I swear by Almighty God and little Lord Jesus asleep in
the hay.

MRS. WATERMELLON   Then I'll take you back.

MRS. TWEED   Do you promise?

MRS. WATERMELLON   I promise.

MRS. TWEED   Is he ours?

MRS. WATERMELLON   Since we're older together in order, then I do believe that we can now share him.

MRS. TWEED   Then I'll take *you* back. The two Mrs. Birdsongs!

NURSE   Time for your milk, the white's at night. Time for the drink to
put you in the pink. Time for the chalk, you're in the drink.

MRS. WATERMELLON [*to the* NURSE]   Will you get out of here? Can't
you see you're interfering with a honeymoon?

NURSE [*smiling, leaves*]   Only a few more to pin, then back to my bin.
Time for a sleep, the light's turned out. Time for the deep, the
syringe is shoved. [*She's gone.*]

MRS. WATERMELLON *and* MRS. TWEED [*they turn to one another*]   How
do you do, Mrs. Birdsong? How do *you* do, Mrs. Birdsong? [*They
begin to laugh and burst out of their age. The Irish accents disappear also.*]
THAT DID IT. THAT DID IT. THANK GOD, THAT DID IT.

> *They jump like young women, leap, float, bump into each other
> with gaiety, sing and end in a tumble on the floor.*

THAT did it, that's better.
That's done it,
What ease.
That did it, that's done it,
That's better.
What took you so long,
What took you so long,
Whatever on earth took you so long?

> *Two women sing very slowly in harmony while* MRS. TWEED
> *and* MRS. WATERMELLON *freeze.*

VOICES   "In the gloaming, oh my darling,
When the lights are soft and low,
Will you think of me and love me
As you did once long ago?"

MRS. TWEED *and* MRS. WATERMELLON
YOU TEASE
YOU TEASE
YOU TEASE
WHAT TOOK YOU SO LONG?

> *They jump up fiercely on the last line, still laughing. But now
> they change to a blank stare and say the final line in a singsong
> —death has grabbed them by the back of the neck.*

WHAT TOOK YOU SO LONG? SO LONG! SO LONG! SO LONG?

> *Then happily, saying goodbye—their arms around each other—
> they look out at the audience and smile.*

SO LONG . . .

CURTAIN

The Elements of Drama

ACTION   The Greek philosopher Aristotle was the first writer on drama whose work has survived. When he began the definition of tragedy, in *The Poetics,* with the phrase "an imitation of an action," he was using terms so basic that they are difficult to define. The term **imitation** (or **mimesis**) can be applied to all art, for art has some relation to reality, no matter how autonomous it may appear as a creation or as an object of experience. The character of this relation, the nature of the imitation, will vary from art to art, for music imitates reality in a different way from painting or literature. Even within a given art form the mode of imitation varies with the individual artist; Ibsen does not imitate reality in the same way that Shakespeare does. Some ways in which the mode of imitation varies, such as treatment of space and use of speech, are discussed elsewhere in this volume.

The playwright imitates by using a series of simulated events which are arranged to make a meaningful whole. The term **action** can be used for one of the events or for the whole series. This action characteristically involves a **conflict** or struggle between two persons, groups of persons, or forces which seems to be moving toward resolution, gaining intensity and complication, until the turning point (**climax** or **peripety**; see STRUCTURE) when the direction of the action changes.

The term **plot** generally refers to the arrangement of the action, the selection and ordering of events which make up the play. When the arrangement involves two or more series of events, which may be more or less discrete, the principal series is referred to as the plot and the other (or others) as the **subplot**.

AUDIENCE   When writing, the playwright assumes that some audience will see his play; the character of that audience will be determined, of course, by the social conditions of its age and by the kind of play. In Shakespeare's time early theaters like the Globe, where his works were performed, were open-air structures on the south bank of the Thames, across from London proper. The afternoon performances there drew a more general audience, including poor and uneducated elements of the populace, than the later indoor theaters like the Blackfriars, where some of his later plays were performed and where a sophisticated and affluent audience attended. Some individuals were part of both groups, just as in our time. In the New York theater the audiences for Broadway, Off-Broadway, and Off-Off-Broadway theaters may be as diverse as the plays presented. In cities outside New York there are different, and overlapping, audiences for touring companies with "name" stars, for local repertory or little theater groups, and for avant-garde or university theater groups.

An equally important distinction in this century has to do with the theoretical notions about the relations between the play and the audience. Four of these are of some importance.

The oldest, and probably still the most widespread, is the attitude of the commercial or "Broadway" theater, where the emphasis is on entertaining the audience, without much consideration of the audience's engagement in the play. The audience sits in the dark and responds. If it is amused, it applauds; if not, there are other ways of indicating its feeling. Entertainment value is not necessarily diminished —it may even be increased—if the audience becomes emotionally involved with the action or the characters, but entertainment comes first.

In the "serious" theater, by contrast, major playwrights, directors, and actors have worked generally toward empathy between the audience and the play, the audience responding to what it sees and hears by experiencing sympathetic emotions toward what is represented on stage. A major influence here is the rise of "The Method," a technique of acting based on or derived from the work of the Russian director Constantin Stanislavsky. In his productions with the Moscow Art Theater around the turn of the century, and particularly in the plays of Chekhov, Stanislavsky taught his actors to feel the emotions of the character rather than to play them and to feel them so intensely that the audience must also feel them. Physical methods such as the theater-in-the round or the thrust stage (see STAGE) help increase the empathy.

A later development in the serious theater toward audience detachment is associated with Bertolt Brecht, who first came into prominence in the 1920s. Brecht was reacting against Stanislavsky, and recently many others have joined the reaction. In his analytical or **epic theater,** Brecht worked to achieve as much detachment of the audience from the stage action as was possible. Then the audience could apply its intellect to the analysis and criticism of what is presented, without the distorting effects of emotional response. Methods of staging and acting should be conducive to the desired **A-effect** or **alienation effect,** a distancing of the audience from the action which permits rational and objective response.

The most recent development in this area aims at mutual participation between the audience and the stage. Still largely limited to the "avant-garde," this style is associated with Antonin Artaud and Jerzy Grotowski. For their followers the stage and the auditorium are regarded as a single theatrical environment in which the actors are the priests and acolytes of a theatrical ritual in which the members of the audience are communicants. The actors may invade the seating areas, and in some cases the audience is invited to take part in the action. Ideally the separation between the stage and auditorium and between actor and audience should disappear.

CHARACTER   Most simply a **character** is one of the persons who appears in the play, one of the **dramatis personae** (literally, the persons of the play). In another sense of the term, the treatment of character is a basic part of the playwright's work. Conventions of the period and the author's personal vision will affect the treatment of character. Molière, for example, uses a single name, usually classical in sound, for his characters (such as Alceste or Arsinoé), rather than a given name preceding the family name as people of Alceste's station would have borne in real life. Both Gregers Werle in *The Wild Duck* and Pentheus in *The Bacchae* are partially defined by their relation to their mothers. In Ibsen the relation is described in psychological terms, which though pre-Freudian, express a view of character common in Ibsen's time and in our own. Euripides represents the relation through visual means, having Pentheus put on one of his mother's dresses and ask Dionysus if the resemblance is not striking.

Most plays contain major characters and minor characters. The delineation and development of major characters is essential to the play; the conflict between Hamlet and Claudius depends upon the character of each. A minor character like Marcellus serves a specific function, to inform Hamlet of the appearance of his father's ghost. Once that is done, he can depart in peace, for we need not know what sort of person he is or what happens to him. The distinction between major and minor characters is one of degree, as the character of Horatio might illustrate.

The distinction between heroes (or heroines) and villains, between good guys and bad guys, between virtue and vice is useful in dealing with certain types of plays, but in many modern plays (and some not so modern) it is difficult to make. Is Gregers Werle in *The Wild Duck*, for example, a hero or a villain?

Another common term in drama is **protagonist.** Etymologically it means the first contestant. In the Greek drama, where the term arose, all the parts were played by one, two, or three actors (the more actors, the later the play), and the best actor, who got the principal part(s), was the protagonist. The second best actor was called the **deuteragonist.** Ideally, the term "protagonist" should be used only for the principal character. Several other characters can be defined by their relation to the protagonist. The **antagonist** is his principal rival in the conflict set forth in the play. A **foil** is a character who defines certain characteristics in the protagonist by exhibiting opposite traits or the same traits in a greater or lesser degree. A **confidant(e)** provides a ready ear to which the protagonist can address certain remarks which should be heard by the audience but not by the other characters. In *Hamlet,* for example, Hamlet is the protagonist, Claudius the antagonist, Laertes and Fortinbras foils (observe the way in which each goes about avenging the death or loss of property of his father), and Horatio the confidant.

Certain writers—for example, Molière and Pirandello—use a character type called the **raisonneur,** whose comments express the voice of reason and also, presumably, of the author. Philinte and the Father are examples of the raisonneur.

Another type of character is the **stereotype** or stock character, a character who reappears in various forms in many plays. Comedy is a particularly fruitful source of such figures, including the *miles gloriosus* or boastful soldier (a man who claims great valor but proves to be a coward when tested), the irascible old man (the source of elements in the character of Polonius), the witty servant, the coquette, the prude, the fop, and others. A stock character from another genre is the **revenger** of Renaissance tragedy. The role of Hamlet demonstrates how such a stereotype is modified by an author to create a great role, combining the stock elements with individual ones.

Sometimes groups of actors work together over a long period in relatively stable companies. In such a situation individual members of the group develop expertise in roles of a certain type, such as **leading man** and **leading lady** (those who play the principal parts), **juveniles** or **ingénues** of both sexes (those who specialize as young people), **character actors** (those who perform mature or eccentric types), and **heavies** or villains.

The **commedia dell'arte**, a popular form of the late Middle Ages and early Renaissance, employed actors who had standard lines of business and improvised the particular action in terms of their established characters and a sketchy outline of a plot. Frequently, Pantalone, an older man, generally a physician, was married to a young woman named Columbine. Her lover, Harlequin, was not only younger and more handsome than her husband but also more vigorous sexually. Pantalone's servants, Brighella, Truffaldino, and others, were employed in frustrating or assisting either the lovers in their meetings or the husband in discovering them.

A group of actors who function as a unit, called a **chorus,** was a characteristic feature of the Greek tragedy. The members of the chorus shared a common identity, such as Asian Bacchantes or old men of Thebes. The **choragos** (leader of the chorus) sometimes spoke and acted separately. In some of the plays the chorus participated directly in the action; in others they were restricted to observing the action and commenting on it. The chorus also separated the individual scenes by singing and dancing choral odes, though just what the singing and dancing were like is uncertain. The odes were in strict metrical patterns; sometimes they were direct comments on the action and characters, and at other times they were more general statements and judgments. A chorus in the Greek fashion is not common in later plays, although there are instances such as T. S. Eliot's *Murder in the Cathedral,* in which the Women of Canterbury serve as a chorus.

On occasion a single actor may perform the function of a chorus, as do the aptly named Chorus in Shakespeare's *Henry V* and the Stage Manager in Thornton Wilder's *Our Town.* Alfieri in *A View from the Bridge* functions both as a chorus and as a minor character in the action of the play.

D<small>IALOGUE</small>   The formal principle of drama is **dialogue,** the imitation of speech, customarily involving two or more persons. Dialogue will have some relation to real speech, but the character of that relation will vary greatly. In his translation of *The Misanthrope* Richard Wilbur uses heroic couplets to reproduce the effect of Molière's language. Obviously, few real people even in 17th-century France spoke in such a way. The form allows for various rhetorical figures, including one particular to the drama, **stichomythia,** in which two characters exchange short lines of similar structure, as in this exchange:

ORONTE   If, weighing us, she leans in your direction . . .
ALCESTE   If she regards you with the least affection . . .
ORONTE   I swear I'll yield her to you there and then.
ALCESTE   I swear I'll never see her face again.

Similar kinds of poetic dialogue—that is, speech which has metrical patterns and which is therefore obviously not like real speech—can be seen in Shakespeare and Euripides. Dialogue which aims at reproducing with high accuracy the cadences and patterns of actual speech can be seen in *A View from the Bridge*. Writers like Pirandello and Ibsen also imitate actual speech more closely than the writers of poetic dialogue. Within the framework of his characteristic mode of writing dialogue, an author will also write dialogue for an individual character which will set him apart from the others. Examples can be seen in the speeches of Gina in *The Wild Duck* and the gravediggers in *Hamlet*.

Aside from dialogue in general, there are several special uses of stage speech. Occasionally, only one character will speak. A **monologue** is a stage piece written for one character, a relatively rare type of play. More important are the **soliloquy,** which was common in Shakespeare and his contemporaries, in which a single character is left on stage and speaks, and the **aside,** generally associated with 19th-century melodrama, in which a character speaks but cannot be heard by the other characters.

Another special form of dialogue, which is sometimes met in the modern drama, is that in which speech is addressed directly to the audience. In older plays this occurs most frequently in prologues or epilogues (see Division), where the actor may speak in his own person, as was frequent in Restoration drama, or in his dramatic role as Dionysus does in *The Bacchae*. Sometimes a character may turn during the action and speak directly to the audience, or he may drop his role and speak directly to the audience. Both of these tactics occur in Thornton Wilder's *The Skin of Our Teeth*, which also includes scenes in which several actors drop their roles and speak to each other as actors.

DIVISION   Most plays can be divided into parts. The basic division is the **act,** either a series of actions occurring in a single place within a consecutive time span or a series of actions separated from the remainder of the play by purely formal considerations. Because Horace in his *Ars Poetica* recommended five acts, most European plays from the 16th to 19th centuries were divided into five acts. For writers like Shakespeare, whose plays were performed without intervals and with changes of place and time within the presentation, the act divisions seem generally to have been inserted to bring the plays in line with Horace's mandate. Some of the plays, notably *Henry V,* however, do seem to have acts with an organic character.

Greek tragedies and medieval mysteries are examples of plays written in one part, but in each case the play was conceived as a part of a larger structure. The tragedies were performed in groups of three followed by a farcical piece or **satyr play.** The mysteries were presented in cycles, some of which included twenty or more plays, presented consecutively in one day. The Greek tragedies had a formal division into a series of episodes, separated by the choral odes. A mystery play might have more informal divisions, as the three parts of *The Second Shepherds' Play* with scenes on the heath, at Mak's house, and at the stable in Bethlehem.

Playwrights in recent centuries from Molière to Arthur Miller have written **one-act plays,** short plays intended to serve as part of an evening's entertainment. These plays may have formal divisions such as the three scenes of Shaw's *A Village Wooing,* or informal ones such as the two parts of Strindberg's *Miss Julie,* which are separated by a ballet.

A formal division within an act is usually called a **scene.** The term may indicate real differences in time and place, as in *Hamlet,* or may be used for merely formal divisions like those in *The Misanthrope.* There, as in other French plays, a new scene begins with any entrance or exit of a major character.

The term **part** is used instead of act in some contemporary plays. *The Glass Menagerie* of Tennessee Williams consists of a series of scenes which are more or less closely related episodes of varying length. The scenes are grouped into two parts to allow for an **intermission** or pause in the action. Eugene O'Neill divided *Desire Under the Elms* into three parts, rather than acts, apparently to indicate that each is more self-contained and less closely related to the others than is customary.

Just as some plays are shorter than the length of an average performance, others exceed that length. Such superplays may involve an unusual number of acts, like O'Neill's *Strange Interlude* or a series of smaller "plays," like the five which make up Shaw's *Back to Methuselah.* Such longer plays may be presented in a single day, usually with an extra-long intermission to allow the audience time for a meal, as O'Neill did with *Strange Interlude,* or over a period of several days, as is customary with Richard Wagner's *The Ring of the Nibelung.*

The terms **prologue** and **epilogue** were used by the Greeks to indicate respectively portions of the play before the entrance of the chorus and after their final speech. Later the terms were used for speeches before and after the action, usually addressed to the audience and frequently making some comment about the play itself. The terms may also be used for action widely separated in time from the rest of the play, as in the prologue to Williams' *Summer and Smoke* and the epilogue to Shaw's *Saint Joan.*

EFFECT   Certain events in the drama produce the kind of immediate effect in moving the audience strongly which is called **theatrical** or **histrionic.** Aristotle cited the **scene of suffering** and the **scene of recog-**

nition (anagnorisis). The recognition scene is particularly dramatic because the recognition or discovery of the person or fact will automatically change the situation; a recognition scene without its peripety (see STRUCTURE) is hard to imagine. The discovery or recognition may be of a person, as in the brothel scene in *Six Characters,* or of a piece of information, as in the scene between Oedipus and the shepherd in *Oedipus Tyrannus.* The scene of suffering, often communicated in heightened language, provides an opportunity for the audience to share the feelings of the characters. The appearance of Hjalmar and Gina with the dead body of their child at the end of *The Wild Duck* can hardly fail to move the audience. Many such scenes are related to violence, either offstage, as in *Oedipus* and *The Wild Duck,* or onstage, as in *Hamlet.* If tastefully and skillfully used, the scene of violence is also powerful theatrically. If there is too much strawberry jam posing as blood, or if it is too obviously strawberry jam, the effect will be dissipated.

Another kind of theatrical effect depends on surprise. The entrance of Madame Pace is an example of a skillfully constructed **coup de théâtre.** An example of a humorous use of the device is the first appearance of Cleopatra in *Caesar and Cleopatra.* The interruption of Caesar's windy rhetoric by her "Psst! Old Gentleman!" deflates the conqueror of the world and surprises and delights the audience. A different kind of stage effect is the **deus ex machina.** The name comes from the appearance in the Greek drama of a "god," lowered in a piece of stage machinery, who by his unexpected and often improbable actions straightens out the complications of the plot to provide a suitable conclusion. Examples which do not involve such spectacular devices can be seen in Cusins' announcement that he is a "foundling" in *Major Barbara* or the appearance of the king's messenger in Molière's *Tartuffe.*

Another kind of theatrical effect is based on actualizing some potentiality in the play. When they learn that both the elder Werle and Hedvig in *The Wild Duck* are losing their eyesight, for example, most playgoers will expect more or less consciously that Hjalmar will somehow get the news about Werle. When Mrs. Sørby tells him, the expectation is realized. The term **foreshadowing** is sometimes used for such an effect. **Dramatic irony** is a similar effect in which a character says something with one meaning or with reference to other persons which comes true in another sense or in his own case. When Eddie in *A View from the Bridge* warns Catherine of the fate of informers, he little realizes that he himself could ever be guilty of the crime or receive the punishment of his peers for doing so.

GENRE   The notion of **genre** recognizes that certain significant groupings of plays can be made. Aristotle in the *Poetics* attempted to define the kind of play which can be called **tragedy.** Much later dramatic criticism has returned to restate or redefine what Aristotle said. I cannot here even summarize the various positions, but I will excerpt what seem to me the elements of tragedy.

Basic to tragedy is an order of values which transcends man and which man should obey. Among the Greeks this order rested on the notion of fate, among the Elizabethans on the notion of a highly structured universe in which the individual's place is determined, and among the French classical writers on a concept of honor and duty. A great individual, usually one of high rank, transgresses this order out of **hubris** (or **hybris**), the tendency of the will or the passion of man to step outside the prescribed limits. From this transgression come the tragic events of the work, the result of the order reasserting itself to punish the individual. The proper end of tragedy is the hero's realization that he has transgressed and that his troubles are the result of his guilt. Oedipus achieves a tragic realization which gives dignity and serenity to his exit at the end of *Oedipus Tyrannus*. Two other important terms used by Aristotle are **catharsis** (or **katharsis**), the effect of tragedy on the audience of purging it of such emotions as pity and fear, and **hamartia,** a flaw in an otherwise noble nature—for example, Othello's jealousy.

The history of the drama has included three great tragic periods, the England of Shakespeare, the Athens of Sophocles, and the France of Corneille and Racine. In other periods literary persons have written imitations of these great tragedies or have tried to fit the works of their own time into the definition. Several major contemporary writers seem to have sought to achieve tragic form. The degree of their success is a matter of opinion, but several factors may contribute to the many apparent failures, including the lack of heroic individual figures and the absence of a widely held system of values which transcend man and which can punish transgressors on this earth.

Although it is usually regarded as the polar opposite of tragedy, **comedy** has proved more difficult to define. As a kind of play, comedy is concerned with a system of social, rather than metaphysical, values. A fairly typical plot concerns a young man who is prevented at first from making a suitable marriage but who after difficulty does marry the right girl and is thereby reconciled to his society and restored to his appropriate place in it.

As a mode of apprehending reality, the **comic** is different from, but not inimical to, tragedy. The comic is easy to recognize but difficult to define. Why is it funny for a pompous, middle-aged gentleman, preferably with a top hat, to slip on a banana peel but not funny for an 84-year-old woman walking with a cane to do the same thing? Perhaps the answer is that in first case we see the event in two perspectives. The man seems prosperous and immune to silly accident, but the banana peel exists to remind us that he is only human beneath the signs of prosperity and the air of invulnerability. Only his dignity is likely to be harmed. In the case of the elderly woman, however, her age and condition remind us of her fragility and the real dangers of the accident. We see the event in only one perspective.

The great ages of tragedy have generally been also great eras of comedy, perhaps because the assumption of established values which is necessary for tragedy is so important for comedy. The lack of such values in our century may explain our lack of true comedy as well as tragedy.

Both tragedy and comedy contain more particular kinds. *Hamlet,* for example, belongs to the specific group of **revenge tragedies,** in which the duty to avenge close relatives is a part of the universal order. *The Misanthrope* represents the **comedy of manners,** in which the society represented is composed of persons of wealth, rank, and lack of real occupation, along with occasional servants. These plays are posited on the values of the highly artificial group called high society, with emphasis on wit, the importance of reputation, and the need for secrecy in love affairs. Other common types of comedy are the **comedy of humors,** which is based on a character whose personality is dominated by a single trait, and the **comedy of intrigue,** in which complications of plot and situation are dominant. Another way of discussing comedies divides them into **low comedies,** which depend on vulgar or obscene language and on vigorous physical actions such as pie-throwings, and **high comedies,** which use more elegant language and refined gestures.

The terms **melodrama** and **farce** are used for two large groups of plays which are rather like, respectively, tragedy and comedy, but which are generally regarded as inferior to the other kinds. In both of these "lower" forms, the emphasis is on situation rather than character, events being brought about usually by outside forces rather than the necessities of the individual's personality, and the plot is more episodic.

Two other kinds which bear certain resemblances to comedy are **satire** and **romance.** In both cases, the term is more widely used outside the drama but is sometimes used in dramatic criticism. What the two groups share is their dependence on values other than those of the society which they represent. In satire, the values of the society are the object of attack, in contrast to comedy, where those values are endorsed. One feature of romance is a suggestion that at least one of the characters, like Prospero in *The Tempest,* is aware of and lives by another and higher system of values than that of the society.

A more important group of plays for students of recent drama has affinities with tragedy without being tragedy. They deal in general with life on earth, with metaphysical values either not considered or denied and without endorsing social values. The French term **drame** has been offered as a name for such serious but nontragic plays which do not fit other categories. Others refer to them as **tragicomedies,** though they are not a mixture of tragedy and comedy, but a third something which is neither. Within this area we can distinguish the **problem play,** which treats some social issue, as Ibsen's *A Doll's House* treats the legal position of women, and the **domestic tragedy** (or **bourgeois drama**), in which the central character lacks the insight or heroic stature expected of a tragic hero, as in Arthur Miller's *Death of a Salesman.*

Other generic terms used in the drama are **masque** and **chronicle play** or **history play.** The masque was generally allegorical in plot and character and relied heavily on elaborate pageantry, including rich costumes, music, dancing, and spectacular sets and stage effects. Many masques were written to commemorate historical events. The chronicle play attempts to imitate historical events and to examine their relation to one another in dramatic terms.

GESTURE   The play even on the page contains material for generating the nonverbal elements of the drama. Some of these are prepared and set up before the performance begins, such as make-up, costumes, and sets. Others are prepared beforehand but occur during the performance and are controlled from outside the acting area, such as background music, sound effects, and lighting. All of these might be classed under Aristotle's term **spectacle.**

The other kind of gestural elements occur only during the performance even though they are also set up beforehand. The way in which the actor speaks a given line is a kind of gesture which borders on the verbal. Inflection, loudness, and tempo of speech are on the page only implicitly, and the realization in sound of the speeches greatly influences the character of the performance and its effect on the audience. Generally, for example, in performances of *Hamlet,* Claudius screams for light and runs from the stage, but in at least one version he spoke quietly with a tone of command and moved off stage in a stately manner. Here both the sound of the speech and the accompanying movement contribute to a different understanding of the scene.

The example just noted shows how closely related stage movement is to the words and the way they are spoken. The positions of the actors on stage and their movement from place to place are as important an interpretive element as the spectacle and the interpretation of the speeches. Some of the positions and movements are implicit in the text, as Hamlet's physical isolation from the other members of the court when he first appears. At other times the positions and movements are chosen by the director and his colleagues at rehearsal. The pattern of positions and movements is called the **blocking.** In any single performance of a production there will be small departures from the pre-arranged pattern. However, the overall pattern is generally adhered to because of its significance to the understanding of the play. The term **business** is used for a movement or gesture which occurs at an appropriate point. For example, when Ophelia is set to entrap Hamlet, her business is to walk, to carry a book, and to pretend to be reading.

Action without words, as at the end of the first act of *A View from the Bridge,* is called **pantomime.** The term is also used for an entire play which is presented without words. Such a play may also be called a **mime show.** The term **mime** is used for an actor who specializes in acting without using words and for his art. A special kind of silent performance is the **dumb show,** as in *Hamlet* and other plays of the period. Usually this section of the play introduces the play or a part of it and previews the action to come.

LITERARY MOVEMENTS   The history of the drama is partly concerned with the rise and fall of literary movements, some based on dominant styles such as the highly artificial linguistic structures of Euphuism, others on dominant forms such as the comedy of manners of the Restoration period, and others on sets of esthetic principles such as Symbolism. Movements can be traced in every period, but because of the content of this collection, those of the modern period can be traced more easily.

Studies of the modern drama frequently begin with the middle period plays (1870–80) of Henrik Ibsen. The increasing importance of science in explaining man and his environment and the development of such art forms as photography contributed to the rise of **realism**, a literary mode which strives to render persons and things in a manner as lifelike as possible. The expression of this striving in such plays as *The Wild Duck* and *Three Sisters* is typical of this dominant mode of the last hundred years.

Among the reactions to realism, **expressionism** has had the greatest and most lasting influence. The expressionist takes men, events, and things and arranges them not as they exist in the real world but in new ways, distortions of reality which express the artist's individual vision. The movement began with Strindberg and continues to our own time in various forms. The German playwright Bertolt Brecht has been a particularly influential figure in the survival of this dramatic mode.

The major ideological forces in the theater have been the rise of Existentialism and the works of the Italian playwright Luigi Pirandello. Although he was not a systematic philosopher, Pirandello gave dramatic form to a number of important ideas, many of which are the same as or very close to Existentialism: (1) It is impossible to know absolute truth, even if it exists; (2) the personality is the sum of one's experience and therefore constantly changing because every new experience modifies it; (3) language is dangerous because when I use a word, the meaning I ascribe to it is determined by my experience, and when another person hears it, he interprets it in terms of his own different set of experiences; (4) in dealing with each other, men build up **masks** to hide their real selves and thus render real communication impossible. Such ideas have been important in movements like **surrealism** and **dadaism** during the 1920s and the **theater of the absurd** of the 1950s.

An important development in recent years stems from Artaud's **theater of cruelty** and Grotowski's **poor theater**. Plays like the last three is this book are written and performed in ways which stress the ritual and communal aspects of the drama.

MYTH   **Myth** originally meant a story of communal origin which provided an explanation or religious interpretation of man, nature, the universe, and the relation between them. Most frequently the term was applied to the stories of other peoples and therefore implied that the story was false. However, research in anthropology and comparative religion have revealed underlying identities in myths of diverse places and cultures. The term itself came to be applied to the shared pattern of these stories, whether the individual stories come from the communal experience of a primitive tribe or from the pen of a sophisticated writer. Myth-making is a basic human activity. Myths are not "true" or "false"; they are an expression of that activity. At some level the construction of a dramatic plot will involve elements of myth.

The term **archetype** is widely used to refer to common "mythical" elements in literature, in character, and in plot construction. The term is frequently associated with the Swiss psychologist Carl G. Jung, who used it for the expressions in conscious form of the contents of the "collective unconscious," a part of the unconscious which he posited as being inherited and being held in common by all men. Those who reject the idea of collective unconsciousness suggest that the appearance of archetypal material in diverse cultures may be due to its transmission from one culture to another or to the similarity of human experience in different parts of the world.

The terms **symbol** and **allegory** are related to myth in that they refer to ways of talking about some higher (nonrational, nonconcrete, abstract or religious) reality in concrete ways. Unlike myth, however, they are the products of an individual maker rather than a communal expression. The easiest distinction between symbol and allegory is that in the latter a simple equation can be set up between the object and that which it represents—for example, Spenser's Una = Truth, whereas that for which a symbol stands eludes precise definition. This distinction is unfair to Spenser, since many of his allegorical figures have more than one meaning. The allegorist would tend to regard the surface of the work as a pleasant veil which makes the hidden meaning more palatable, whereas the symbolist would tend to regard the surface as the best, perhaps the only, expression of the unique vision of the artist. Some recent critics seem to regard "symbol" as a term of praise and "allegory" as a term of opprobrium.

The terms **natural symbol** or **conventional symbol** are used for certain common symbolic patterns. The rose is frequently a symbol for beauty on the probable but unprovable assumption that everyone finds roses beautiful. In Western writing the horse is frequently a symbol of sexuality, an identification which Swift used ironically in *Gulliver's Travels*. A **personal symbol** is one set up by an individual author for his own use, as Blake or Yeats did.

The term **ritual**, like myth, refers to communal experience. The drama rose from the rituals of Dionysus and the medieval Christian church. A ritual is a ceremony in which an act or a series of acts are performed on repeated and significant occasions and which is performed with certain elements of exact repetition. Ceremonies in general involve such repetition.

RULES   Critics of certain periods have talked about the "correct" way to write a play—that is, a series of rules to which an author should adhere. Experience has never justified the need of rules. Great writers have written "correctly" as Racine did or "incorrectly" as Shakespeare did.

Among the most famous rules are the three unities of action, place, and time. **Unity of action** requires that the events of the play constitute a single whole, but the term has been understood to refer to a single chain of causes and effects as in *Oedipus Tyrannus,* several series of events involving the same character as in *The Misanthrope,* or a series of apparently diverse events which contribute to a central focus as in *Three Sisters.* **Unity of place** requires a single scene as in *The Bacchae* or several scenes closely related in place as in *The Misanthrope.* In modern staging conditions, a single setting is often an economic necessity rather than an artistic one. **Unity of time** requires that the elapsed time on stage should not exceed one day, or a little more. *Oedipus Tyrannus* and *The Wild Duck* have unity of time, whereas *Hamlet* and *Three Sisters* do not.

Three other terms used in talking about the drama may be considered under this heading. Aristotle recommended that tragedy have **probability,** that events follow one another in rational, cause-and-effect order, that unexpected or unprepared-for events be excluded. Characters should observe **decorum,** dressing, speaking, and behaving in a manner appropriate to their rank, age, sex, and previously established traits of character. A play itself should observe **verisimilitude,** for no matter how fantastic the events on stage, they should seem true to the audience.

STAGE   In performance a play takes place on a **stage** or acting area, whose design and significance varies in different times and places. In the Greek theater, the audience was seated on a raised semicircle of seats (**amphitheater**) halfway around a circular area (**orchestra**) used primarily for dancing by the chorus. At the back of orchestra was the **skene** or stage house which represented the palace or temple before which the action took place. Shakespeare's stage, in contrast, basically involved a rectangular area built up within a generally round enclosure, so that the audience was on three sides of the principal acting area. However, there were subsidiary acting areas on either side as well a recessed area at the back of the stage which could represent Gertrude's chamber in *Hamlet* or the cave in *The Tempest* and an upper acting area which could serve as Juliet's balcony.

Modern stages are of three types. The **proscenium** stage evolved during the nineteenth century and is still the most common. For such a stage, the proscenium or proscenium arch is an architectural element which separates the auditorium from the stage and which makes the action seem more real because the audience is viewing it through an invisible fourth wall. The proscenium stage lends itself to the use of a curtain which can be lowered and raised or closed and parted between acts or scenes. Sometimes a part of the acting area is on the auditorium side of the proscenium. Such an area is an **apron** or forestage. In an **arena stage,** however, the audience is seated around the acting area. Entrances and exits are made through the auditorium, and restrictions on the sets are required to insure visibility. The third type of modern stage is the **thrust stage,** in which the audience is seated around three-fourths of the major acting area. All of the action may take place on this projecting area, or some may occur in the extended area on the fourth side.

The proscenium stage has been so dominant in the last hundred years that most stage directions assume it. **Right** and **left** (or **stage right** and **stage left**) assume that the actor is facing the audience directly and mean those directions as perceived by the actor looking through an invisible fourth wall. **Downstage** means nearer the audience, and **upstage** means farther from the audience.

Mise-en-scène refers to the nonpersonal elements of the dramatic presentation, including lighting, costumes, setting, make-up, and properties. **Properties** (or **props**) differ from parts of the setting because they are required by the action. In Ibsen's *Hedda Gabler,* for example, the stage directions call for a picture of Hedda's father above the mantel and a set of pistols which had belonged to him. The picture is a part of the setting because no speech or action refers to it, and the play can be given without it. The pistols, however, are props because Hedda gives one of them to Eilert Lovborg in Act 3 and shoots herself with the other in the final act.

STRUCTURE   The action of a play generally falls into five parts, which may or may not coincide with the division into acts and scenes.

The first of these, the **exposition,** presents the situation as it exists at the opening of the play, introducing the characters and defining the relationships among them. The conversation between Alceste and Philinte at the beginning of *The Misanthrope* is an example of a tightly constructed exposition; by contrast, *The Wild Duck* uses a more diffuse one.

The second part of a play, the **rising action,** consists of a series of events which complicate the original situation and create conflicts among the characters. In *The Bacchae,* for example, the complications include the decision of Cadmus and Teiresias to join the Bacchic worship, the arrest of Dionysus, and the miracle which brings about his release.

During the rising action, the flow of the action is in a single direction, but at some crucial moment an event occurs which changes the direction of the action. This is the third part of the play, the **climax** or **turning point.**

The fourth part of a play is the **falling action,** the changes which characterize the unwinding or unknotting of the complications. Generally the falling action requires less time than the rising action.

The final part of the play is its **conclusion** or **catastrophe.** The conclusion reestablishes a stable situation to end the drama.

The term **denouement** is frequently used by writers about dramatic structure, but some of them use it for the falling action and others for the conclusion or catastrophe.

List of Terms Defined